MYTHIC ASTROLOGY

MYTHIC ASTROLOGY

—LIZ GREENE—
CO-AUTHOR OF THE MYTHIC TAROT

CARDS ILLUSTRATED BY
ANTHEA TOORCHEN

A Fireside Book
Published by SIMON & SCHUSTER INC.
New York London Toronto Sydney Tokyo Singapore

Acknowledgments
The author would like to thank Alois Treindl for his innovative work in creating the Planetary Ingress and Ascendant Tables, and most of all Brian Hobley for his encouragement and support.

FIRESIDE
Simon & Schuster Inc.
Rockefeller Center
1230 Avenue of the Americas
New York
New York 10020

Library of Congress Cataloging-in-Publication Data

Greene, Liz
Mythic astrology / by Liz Greene
p. cm.
"A Fireside book"
ISBN 0-671-50094-5
1. Astrology. 2. Mythology I. Title.
BF1729.M9G74 1994
133.5--dc20 94-12162
CIP

1 3 5 7 9 8 6 4 2

AN EDDISON•SADD EDITION
Edited, designed and produced by
Eddison Sadd Editions
St Chad's Court, 146B King's Cross Road
London WC1X 9DH

Editor Cecilia Walters
Proofreader Barbara Nash
Designer Sarah Howerd
Photographer Stephen Marwood
Production Hazel Kirkman
and Charles James

Phototypeset in Bauer Bodoni by Dorchester Typesetting, Dorset, UK
Origination by Columbia Offset, Singapore
Produced by Mandarin Offset with printing and binding in Hong Kong

CONTENTS

INTRODUCTION

I know that I am mortal, the creature of one day.
But when I explore the winding courses of the stars
I no longer touch the Earth with my feet; I am standing
near Zeus himself, drinking my fill of Ambrosia,
the food of the gods.
Ptolemy, *Anthologia Palatina*, 2nd century C.E.

My evenings are taken up very largely with astrology.
I make horoscope calculations in order to find a clue
to the core of psychological truth.
C. G. Jung, in a letter to Sigmund Freud,
20th century C.E.

Astrology's great antiquity, its capacity to adapt to changing world-views, and the extraordinary intellectual caliber of its adherents over the centuries, remain a mystery to those who assume it to be the mere superstitious belief that events can be predicted in the stars. In order to understand astrology's power, depth and relevance to the modern era, it is necessary to know something about it. We would not presume to claim we have grasped the principles of music by listening to a pop song or the theme tune from a television soap. Likewise, astrology will not yield its insights to those who simply read Sun sign columns in newspapers and then pronounce judgment on the validity of the subject as a whole. We must begin at the beginning, with a willingness to learn and experiment, and a capacity to recognize that the great minds of history for whom astrology was of primary importance—Hippocrates, Plato, Augustus, Hadrian, Ptolemy, Galen, Newton, Goethe and Jung, to name but a few—may have understood something that has eluded our present definitions of reality.

Astrology's roots lie in an ancient world-view which perceived the universe as a single living organism, animated by divine order and intelligence. This world-view is currently finding renewed credibility through the researches of quantum physics and depth psychology, which have found new terms to define ancient truths. The precision and geometry of celestial movements seemed, to the minds of antiquity, to reflect the hidden nature and intentions of deity. Prediction has represented the best known (though perhaps not the most important) dimension of astrology over the ages. But predictive astrology did not arise from the simplistic notion that the planets make us do things. It was an outgrowth of the profound idea that if the heavens reflect the intelligent processes of a unified cosmic life, our own lives—as part of that greater whole—will also participate in its rhythms and cycles. The study of astrology is the study of the qualities of time. Put another way, it describes archetypal principles and the ways in which these are expressed in everyday life. This extremely sophisticated world-view, first formulated by ancient philosophy, precedes all the varied uses and abuses to which astrology has been put in its long journey from Sumeria and Babylon to the present day.

Astrology and myth have been intertwined since the dawn of history, and their images are woven together throughout Babylonian, Egyptian, Greco-Roman, medieval and Renaissance literature, art and architecture. But these are not merely curious artefacts reflecting defunct belief-systems relevant only to the historian. In their different ways, both astrology and myth offer a symbolic portrayal of universal human patterns. Myth presents these patterns in the form of stories; astrology presents them in the form of an orderly mapping of heavenly cycles and relationships. By the time astrology had taken its place as the universal science of the ancient world, myths were understood as a means of penetrating to the heart of astrological symbolism, and astrology was understood as a means of penetrating to the heart of life. Myths are psychological portraits which describe fundamental human needs and drives. Astrology, expressed through mythic images, is a six-thousand-year-old system of psychology—the most ancient, yet still the most sophisticated that we possess.

This book and card system are intended as an imaginative introduction to astrology for those who wish to grasp the emotional and intuitive, as well as the intellectual, levels on which astrology needs to be approached. For this reason, the main astrological symbols—planets and signs—are interpreted in the context of the ancient myths with which they have always been connected. The planetary and zodiacal cards portray, through their colors and landscapes as well as their human and animal images, the patterns and qualities of energy which they represent in the human psyche. Many individuals with a finely developed imaginative faculty process information pictorially as well as conceptually, and may find it limiting to approach astrology's complex language through words alone. For those who are already familiar with astrological concepts, these images can convey new insights. Thus this book is aimed at any reader, astrologically educated or not, who wishes to penetrate more deeply into the underlying life patterns which astrology describes.

Part One introduces the Sun, Moon and planets as psychological factors within the individual. Those familiar with astrology may be surprised to see the Ascendant included here, as it is not a planet. But this eastern point of the horoscope, which marks a particular zodiac sign rising at the time of birth, is a major feature of the personality. As the gateway through which planetary energies must pass as they are expressed to the outer world, the Ascendant, like the planets, is best understood as a dynamic force in life, and hence has been included in this section.

Part Two introduces the twelve signs of the zodiac, grouped in the traditional way according to one of the four elements—fire, earth, air or water—to which they belong.

Part Three explains how to use the Planetary Ingress Tables and the Table of Ascendants, so that the reader can accurately determine in which sign the Sun, Moon, Ascendant and planets were placed at birth. These tables will not enable the reader to cast a complete horoscope: he or she is referred to the end of the book for further reading and information (page 204). But they provide the sound basis for any astrological understanding of the individual's essential nature.

Part Four describes the combinations of every planet in every sign. Although the reader will initially wish to focus on his or her own planetary placements, perusing other combinations can help to deepen understanding of how other people think, feel and behave.

Part Five explores the astrological dynamics of relationship through the combinations of planets between two people.

Part Six examines the meaning of three important planets, Jupiter, Saturn and Uranus, as they currently move across the individual's birth horoscope. These interpretations are psychological rather than predictive; they describe the meaning of the time, and how to use it best.

Astrology is a vast and fascinating subject. For those unfamiliar with its language, it is perhaps best approached as a tool through which deeper and more objective insight into self and others can be gained.

The thorny issue of determinism and choice has occupied philosophical and religious thinkers for many centuries, and astrology lies at the core of this debate. There is no easy answer to the question of whether we are fated or free, for this depends upon our definitions of both. But the 18th-century German poet, Novalis, pointed toward a profound mystery when he wrote that "Fate and soul are two names for the same principle." To the extent that we truly know ourselves, our choices will be wiser and take greater account of future consequences. The study of astrology offers remarkable insights into the ways in which we unconsciously create, in the outer world, what we are in the inner one. Although different religious, moral and social frameworks have colored astrological interpretation over the ages, it is itself nondenominational and nonjudgmental, and affirms the value and unique potential of the individual. Any system of thought which has managed to survive virtually intact through six millennia of changing cultures, religions and definitions of reality, as well as strenuous efforts, past and present, to ignore or denigrate it, has something profoundly important to teach us about ourselves and life.

☆

Planetary Symbols

Planets	Symbols	Planets	Symbols
Sun	☉	Saturn	♄
Moon	☽	Chiron	⚷
Mercury	☿	Uranus	♅
Venus	♀	Neptune	♆
Mars	♂	Pluto	♇
Jupiter	♃	The Ascendant	ASC

Planetary Rulers*

Signs	Symbols	Planetary rulers	Signs	Symbols	Planetary rulers
Aries	♈	Mars	Libra	♎	Venus
Taurus	♉	Venus	Scorpio	♏	Pluto and Mars
Gemini	♊	Mercury	Sagittarius	♐	Jupiter
Cancer	♋	Moon	Capricorn	♑	Saturn
Leo	♌	Sun	Aquarius	♒	Uranus and Saturn
Virgo	♍	Mercury	Pisces	♓	Neptune and Jupiter

**A planetary ruler is that planet which best epitomizes in a dynamic way the qualities of the sign.*

PART ONE

THE PLANETARY GODS

The Sun

☉

The Sun is portrayed in every ancient mythology as the giver of life. Because of its obvious connection with the changing seasons and the sowing and harvesting of crops, the mythic sun gods mated with the earth and fertilized it in a great annual cycle. In Egypt the solar deity was called Ra, who rose out of the primal chaos of the Nile flood and from his own phallic life-force generated all the other gods. In Babylon the great solar disc of the god Shamash mounted the sky in a chariot each morning, and each evening descended into the depths of the earth. Most complex of the sun gods is the shining and enigmatic figure of the Greco-Roman Apollo. This highly sophisticated deity can teach us a good deal about the psychological meaning of the Sun in astrological symbolism. Slayer of the earth-snake Python and breaker of family curses, Apollo symbolizes the power of consciousness to free us from our bondage to deep-rooted and destructive complexes from the past. Called Apollo Longsight because of his power to prophesy, the god also embodies the human gift of foresight, which enables us to see the future consequences of our own actions. As the giver of knowledge he is an image of the civilizing

An Etruscan figure of the Sun god is shown with a crown of rays, the prototype of the golden halo appearing in medieval religious art.

power of human understanding, and as patron of the arts he reflects our capacity to endow our creative efforts with light and life.

The Sun is the core of the birth horoscope, reflecting each person's need to become a unique individual with the power to express that individuality through creative effort. This need exists in everyone, although sadly not everyone is willing to recognize its profound importance. The life-giving light of the Sun is a symbol of our urge to know ourselves and remain loyal to our own hearts. This allows us to make choices with greater clarity, honesty and integrity. Over the door of Apollo's temple at Delphi were carved the words: "Know thyself." In this simple statement lies the essential meaning of the Sun in astrology. The experience of "I" as a separate, worthwhile being is vitally necessary to every person's sense of continuity, value and meaning in life. The Sun gives warmth and light not merely on the biological level, but on the subtler levels of heart and spirit. On the Sun depends our conviction that we are fulfilling a deeper purpose and living a meaningful life. For the person who does not experience this central sense of "I", independent of identification with family, job or national collective, life passes in a fog of unfulfilled dreams and unsatisfied longings. Our fear of death grows in direct proportion to the absence of a life fully lived. If we do not express the Sun we pass into the future looking back over our shoulder, regretting what we have not done and whom we have not been. Thus Apollo in myth is portrayed as having power even over the Fates themselves. Although the Sun cannot confer physical immortality, it can engender a sense of the immortality of the spirit and the worth of a life honorably and creatively lived.

On the psychological level, our need to feel unique and important reflects the Sun's urge toward self-actualization. Whenever we try to express creative ideas or images—whether through artistic channels such as painting or music or through contributing individual style and flair to the ordinary tasks of everyday living—we are expressing the Sun. In some individuals the solar need to find a purpose in life may take the form of a spiritual or religious quest. The highest values toward which we aspire also reflect the light of the Sun, for it is these deeply felt individual values which give us a true core of inner morality and integrity. Without such personal values we must borrow our morality from the collective consensus which, although often noble, can also err horribly (witness the collective consensus of Nazism in the 1930s). The Sun thus reflects our individual conscience—not the artificial niceness of the person who does good because he or she fears to do otherwise, but that deeper voice which affirms a sense of decency and generosity even in the face of external opposition or internal frustration. Apollo was the most civilized of the Greek gods, the "gentleman of Olympus". This mythic attribute was, until quite recently, projected upon kings as the vessels of solar light on earth. The solar attribute of nobility arises not from blood or class, nor from a desire to secure the affection of others through service to them, but from an inner love of truth which is the most profound expression of the symbol of the Sun.

Many individuals find it difficult to express the unique qualities described by the Sun in the birth horoscope. Pressure to conform to others' ideas of what one should be may partly or wholly block the Sun's light. The expression of individual values is, by its very nature, adverse to the instinctual collective identification which constitutes security for so many people. To dare to be oneself may pose a threat to one's family as well as to one's social and professional group. We may believe that failing to conform to collective expectations makes us selfish or bad. Fear of others' criticism or envy may also shroud the light of the Sun. Each person who strives to express his or her own inner nature and values will sooner or later meet opposition from those who resent individual excellence. The sun gods in myth must invariably do battle with a monster or dragon, as Apollo does with the earth-snake. This monster may be understood on many different levels, but one of its meanings is the individual's struggle with the loneliness and dark sense of isolation which inevitably accompany any real creative effort. If the monster wins, we descend into apathy and depression. If the sun god triumphs, we can face life's challenges with a feeling of strength and authenticity. The symbolism of the Sun in astrology is complex, for although it appears in every birth horoscope it will be expressed in a totally unique way by each individual. Whatever our aptitudes, talents and material circumstances, it is the Sun which gives each one of us the sense that there is a point in being alive.

Apollo's chariot traverses the twelve signs of the zodiac during the course of the year, as the Roman charioteers once pursued the course of the circus which was modeled upon this great cosmic cycle. Having conquered the earth-snake in mortal battle, the god can now honor it and avail himself of its instinctual wisdom through his gift of prophecy. Refined, eternally youthful and above ordinary passions, the "gentleman of Olympus" shines his light upon rich and poor, good and evil alike, as the sun gives its warmth and light generously to everything living upon the earth.

The Moon

The magic of the ever-changing Moon fascinates us now as much as it did those past civilizations who saw a great and mysterious deity in its fluctuating faces and its link with the cycles of organic life. In myth the Moon is usually portrayed as female, although certain ancient peoples such as the Babylonians saw in its luminous face a young and beautiful male spirit who symbolized the ebb and flow of nature. The lunar deities presided over the cycles of the animal and vegetable kingdoms, governed menstruation and childbirth, and embodied the instinctual forces at the heart of life. In Egypt the Moon was represented as Isis, goddess of mercy and wisdom, and the archetypal image of woman in both maternal and erotic guise. The compassion of Isis was understood to be a power as great as the might of the war-gods or the procreative force of the Sun, and those in need of help appealed to her as the mother of all life. In Greece, the Moon was worshiped as the wild huntress Artemis, mistress of beasts, untameable and eternally virgin, whose great temple at Ephesus was one of the wonders of the ancient world. In Rome, she was known as Diana, twin sister of the sun god Apollo and protectress of children and animals. Her more sinister face, called Hecate and symbolized by the dark of the Moon, reflected her powers of sorcery and her rulership over the underworld of souls waiting to be reborn. These goddesses were worshiped primarily by women. They personified the female mysteries of conception and birth, and the deeper workings of Fate through the weaving of the tissues of the body in the underworld of the womb.

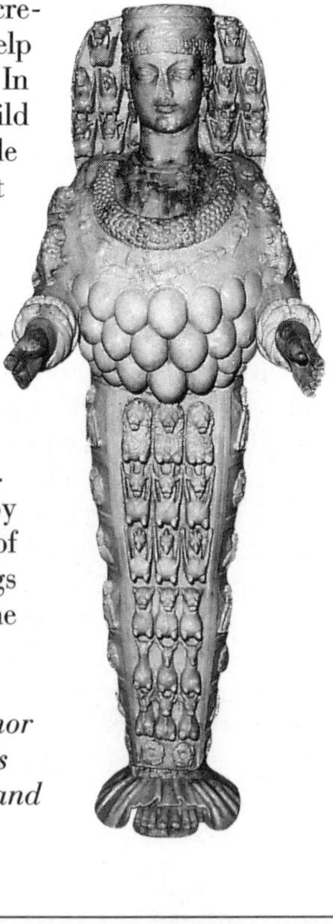

At Ephesus, a rich city on the coast of Asia Minor (now Turkey), the Greco-Roman Moon goddess was portrayed as many-breasted, the mother and protectress of all nature.

On the psychological level, the symbol of the Moon describes our most fundamental need for warmth, safety and nourishment, both physical and emotional. In infancy, these needs are paramount and direct. In adulthood they are also paramount, but are expressed both on subtle and on obvious levels, through our longing to share our feelings and our urge to feel protected and nurtured by family and community. We express the Moon through whatever makes us feel secure and sheltered from the storms of life. We can also offer comfort and nourishment to others just as we ourselves seek it, for the lunar deities reflect an instinctive compassion and responsiveness to helplessness and pain. The image of maternity portrayed in the mythic figures of the lunar goddesses is devoid of sentiment, and sometimes expresses the ferocity of an animal protecting its young. Lunar compassion is not flowery, but is a ruthless force of nature through which emerging life is protected and preserved. The cyclical nature of the Moon's phases, and its nearness to the earth, are in myth an image of the fluctuating life-force within the earth and within the human body. Our sense of unity with the human species and with all living things is reflected by the astrological symbol of the Moon. In order to feel contented and at peace, we need to experience our participation in a larger life, just as the very young child needs to feel connected to the life-giving mother.

Because of its monthly cycle, the Moon is also a symbol of time; it reflects our ability to feel connected with the past, responsive to the present, related to ordinary life and capable of interacting with others on an earthy and human level. The need to give and receive physical affection, the capacity to enjoy the scents and textures of beautiful things, and the pleasure we take in our gardens and our pets, are all expressions of the apparently ordinary—but immensely important—domain over which the Moon presides. The lunar need for safety and comfort is expressed by individuals in many different ways. For some, the longing to belong is amply satisfied by the feeling of empathy and containment provided by a loving family or close community. For others, work (particularly that which offers direct involvement with others) may offer an equally valid source of emotional and physical security. For many people, contact with the countryside or a relationship with animals and plants give a profound sense of connectedness. And for others, religious or spiritual fellowship, or a group with a shared ideology or philosophy, can provide the greater family which the Moon within all of us needs.

While the Sun in the birth horoscope reflects our quest for meaning and self-actualization, a life without the diffuse lunar light of relationship with the ordinary is barren and devoid of joy.

Our ability to express the Moon determines our capacity to feel contented. No amount of individual achievement can satisfy the Moon's longings if our strivings separate us too much from others. Many people find it hard to express such fundamental human needs openly, and seek surrogates without recognizing the depth of their emotional isolation. At the most basic level, the Moon reflects our ability to value and look after our ordinary physical and emotional well-being. Sometimes this innate gift for internal mothering is blocked by early experiences which foster the belief that one should not ask for anything from others. Because lunar needs make us vulnerable and dependent, we may deny them to avoid the risk of hurt and humiliation. We may also try to avoid pain by expressing our lunar needs indirectly and manipulatively, attempting to control others so that we will not feel at their mercy. The Moon is a great leveler, for it reminds us of our identity with all human beings in our capacity to experience loneliness, hunger, pain and fear. Under the soft and unifying light of the Moon, arrogance, and separativeness have no place. The Moon, portrayed in myth as the guardian of nature and young life, is not limited to the horoscopes of women. It appears in everyone's birth horoscope and symbolizes a universal human need. Although the physical level of the Moon's expression is enacted most vividly each time a woman bears a child, there are many kinds of children, not all of them corporeal, and many kinds of mothering, not all of them concrete. Called the "Lesser Light" in early astrology, the Moon was seen as lesser in size, not in importance. As the complement of the Sun, the Moon's light illuminates the feelings and needs of everyday life—but not with any ultimate goal since life itself is its own goal.

Artemis, the virgin goddess of the Moon, guards the mystery at the heart of nature, holding her knife up in warning to those who would intrude upon her sacred ground. Yet she is the protectress of all young helpless creatures. Her beasts gather around her—the panther who embodies her ferocity, the deer who symbolizes her gentleness, and the wolf who describes her solitude and fierce self-sufficiency. When the hunter Actaeon stumbled upon her bathing, she turned him into a stag so that he was torn to pieces by his own dogs. When Orion boasted in her sacred grove, she sent a giant scorpion to sting him to death. Nature thus possesses an unsuspected power to revenge herself upon those who do her dishonor.

THE MOON

Mercury

☿

The mysterious gift of human thought prompted the Greek poet, Menander, to write that the intellect in every human being was divine. In ancient myth, the powers of reflection, speech and communication are personified by a clever, quicksilver deity who taught human beings to write, build, navigate and calculate the course of the heavenly bodies. This enigmatic god symbolizes not only our capacity to think, but also the planning and organizing faculty which allows us to name and categorize the myriad components of the chaotic natural world. In Egypt, the god Thoth, portrayed sometimes as an ibis and sometimes as a baboon, was the patron of science and literature, wisdom and inventions, the spokesman of the gods and their keeper of records. Creator of the alphabet and endowed with total knowledge, Thoth invented arithmetic, surveying, geometry, astrology, medicine, music and writing. In Norse myth, this elusive and multifaceted god was called Loki, lord of fire, and an incorrigible manipulator. In Teutonic myth, he was known as Wotan, patron of magic and lord of the wild hunt, who sacrificed one of his eyes for the gift of wisdom. In Greece, he was personified as the tricky and unfathomable Hermes, lord of travelers and merchants, patron of thieves and liars, guide of the souls of the dead and messenger of the Olympian gods. The Romans knew him as Mercury, from which both the metal and the planet derive their name.

On the psychological level, the bewildering multiplicity of roles assigned to Mercury reflects the multileveled functions and capacities of the

The Egyptians imaged the mercurial and erudite god Thoth as a baboon because of the animal's cleverness, dexterity and gift for mimicry.

human mind. As patron of merchants and money, Mercury embodies the exchange of goods and services which forms the practical dimension of human interchange. As guide of souls, he symbolizes the mind's capacity to move inward in order to explore the hidden depths of the unconscious psyche. In both these roles, Mercury embodies the principle of communication—between human beings, and between the individual and the inner, invisible world. An amoral and cunning deity, Mercury could also play terrible tricks on humans, suggesting our remarkable ability to fool ourselves, and to follow what we believe to be "truth" into a morass of confusion and self-deception. The mythic images associated with the astrological symbol of Mercury also describe our fundamental urge to learn. Because we are obliged to go to school, and expected to acquire an education in order to progress in life, we are often unable to experience the simple delight of learning for its own sake. In childhood, our boundless curiosity about life is a reflection of Mercury. Why is the sky blue? How does a caterpillar become a butterfly? Our need to understand the names of things and how they are made is one of our most fundamental human impulses.

Just as Mercury has many mythological faces, human intelligence has many different forms, not all of them sufficiently valued by our academic establishments. The shrewd, worldly Mercury who invented coinage reflects a practical intelligence, which shows its best gifts when dealing with facts and concrete objects, yet may not be convinced by abstractions. Mercury as guide of souls portrays an intuitive intelligence, more at home in the imaginal world than in the domain of numbers and facts; it is often underrated, yet it reflects deep insight into human nature, and a gift for expressing inner truths through symbolic images. Mercury as messenger of the gods represents a fast-moving, comprehensive intelligence, which perceives connections between different spheres of knowledge and different levels of reality. This kind of intelligence may be indifferent to isolated facts, but builds mental bridges by translating disparate realities into a common language. And Mercury as inventor of science portrays the capacity for logic and the formulation of theoretical concepts. Whenever we pursue knowledge we are expressing Mercury. Also Mercurial is our urge to communicate, which is as fundamental a human requirement on the psychological level as breathing is to the body. Verbal language is only one dimension of communication. We also share our thoughts and feelings through body language, facial expression, inarticulate sounds and emotional atmosphere. We use clothes, cars, makeup and regional accents to tell others about ourselves. Our individual communicative gifts also vary. For some, the articulate use of words conveys a complex array of ideas. For others, artistic forms are the most natural medium of communication. Whenever art speaks to us Mercury is at work, translating the insight of the artist across space and time to the heart and mind of the reader, viewer or listener.

Many individuals find it difficult to express Mercury. The urge to learn may be dulled in childhood by teachers who have themselves lost all curiosity, or are envious of young minds more promising than their own. Families and social groups may scorn the pursuit of knowledge because they are mistakenly convinced that education is the hallmark of a particular social class, rather than the expression of a universal human need. Nothing is so destructive to Mercury as the refusal of others to listen; and nothing is so conducive to its flowering as a receptive and interested parent, teacher, partner, colleague or friend. But even if Mercury has had a slow start in our life, no planetary god can be permanently stifled or destroyed. No matter what our background, Mercury is alive and well within all of us; it can be expressed if we have the courage to follow our longing to learn and communicate. In myth, the god is portrayed as ever-youthful. The human mind is not bound by age or social position. One can go to university at sixty as well as at eighteen, and no lifetime is long enough to exhaust the fields of knowledge open to us. In ancient Greek cities a statue of the god was erected at every major crossroads, to help show the traveler on his or her way. At each crossroads of life, we too can seek the inner god of journeys, for he can be found in every spark of genuine curiosity about life. Through the eyes of Mercury, life itself is an endless road strewn with an infinite variety of fascinating things to discover and learn.

☿

Messenger of the Olympian deities and guide of souls to the underworld domain, the winged god Mercury holds aloft the caduceus entwined by two snakes. The serpents, one dark and one light, are the bearers of all instinctive wisdom and the secrets of life and death. Playful, coy and deceptively innocent, the god's smile can portend the sudden flash of inspired insight or the alluring vision of hopeless self-delusion.

☿

☿ MERCURY ☿

Venus

— ♀ —

As both the Morning and the Evening Star, the planet Venus has always been linked in myth with the goddess of beauty, joy and erotic love. Perhaps the magic of this heavenly body, rising just before dawn or gracing the sunset, evoked the image of an intimate deity tantalizingly close to the human heart, who was not ashamed to show herself naked to mortals. In Babylon, she was known as Ishtar, and she presided not over the sanctity of marriage and family, but over the pleasures of illicit erotic encounters. In Egypt, she was called Hathor, patroness of dance and orgiastic sexual rites, and was also portrayed as Bast, cat-headed mistress of magic and sexual arts. In Greece, she was called Aphrodite, a subtle and complex goddess, golden-skinned and golden-haired, vain and capricious but the undisputed bringer of all beauty and delight. In Greek art, unlike other more modest goddesses, she was portrayed nude, reflecting an unashamed appreciation of sexual love. Her sacred flowers—the rose and the lily—reflect her eroticism in their heavy perfume. Her bird, the dove, was seen as the gentlest and most affectionate of nature's creatures. Yet Aphrodite, whom the Romans called Venus, could also be terrible and threatening. In Sparta she was worshiped as a battle goddess, for the ancient Greeks understood that the ecstasy of bloodletting can, for some, be as sexually exciting as the act of sex itself—as the horrific overlap of war and mass rape have demonstrated throughout the centuries. Refined and primitive at the same time, she presided over artists, craftsmen and the arts of

Images such as this Babylonian figure of Ishtar are among the most ancient and sacred artefacts created by human beings to honor the power of erotic love.

cosmetic beautification. Yet she also embodied the forces of uncontrollable desire, for she afflicted unsuspecting mortals with the madness of obsessive lust, and could topple rulers and kingdoms into the golden net of her passions.

On the psychological level, Venus reflects our longing for beauty, pleasure and the powerful intoxication of being loved. This need to feel valuable and lovable impels us to form relationships in which the idealized passion of the other person reflects back to us our own innate beauty and worth. The need to be loved forms part of every passionate bond, for it is through others' appreciation of us that we discover and develop important aspects of our own natures. By adorning ourselves and creating beauty in the world around us, we also fulfill our Venusian longing to be part of a harmonious universe, where conflict and discord are seen as the prelude to greater unity—much as a lovers' quarrel can lead to greater affection and closeness. Just as those who love us reveal to us what we wish to become, those with whom we quarrel help us to define what truly matters to us. The astrological symbol of Venus is a reflection of our need to form personal values, since we express what we value most highly in the people and things we love. The Latin phrase *de gustibus non disputandum est*—one should never dispute other people's tastes—elegantly describes our instinctive understanding that, in matters of love, taste is a highly individual issue, where there is no established set of rules except the dictates of one's own heart, mind and eye. Our need to discover and express our own personal values is a profound reflection of who we really are as individuals. Even the apparently superficial details of life, such as choice of hairstyle and domestic decor, become surprisingly profound when we understand that it is through such simple human pursuits that we reveal our deepest sense of what is beautiful and worthwhile.

In myth, the goddess Venus was often inimical to marriage, since the passions which she engendered in human beings were frequently illicit, compulsive, and oblivious to moral codes. Yet this mischievous goddess was not perceived as innately evil or destructive. Her tendency to provoke crises invariably arose from an existing situation of stagnation, in which values had grown stale or twisted, or the individuals concerned had never properly formed their own identities. It is often through the suffering engendered by what we call the 'eternal triangle' that, with sufficient insight and self-honesty, we discover where we have grown stagnant and sold ourselves to a presiding collective value system in order to feel secure. Through such conflicts we also discover what we have not developed in ourselves, for it is in the mirror of the rival that we may glimpse our own unlived lives. Venus reflects a fundamental need within us to challenge those social and moral restrictions which we impose upon our hearts for the sake of safety and respectability, and draws us instead into relationships which connect us with an immediate, passionate and vivid sense of life. The Venusian urge within us is not always so troublesome, however, and we may succeed in discovering our own values within a framework which preserves stability and the continuity of long-standing relationships. But in those whom Venus has led into difficulty, there is often a profound—although unrecognized—need to make real choices and affirm real values, instead of relying on the facile borrowing of conventional morality as a shield against life.

Vanity and frivolity are both attributes of the mythic Venus, who was frequently portrayed in ancient art admiring herself in a mirror. They are also attributes of Venus within ourselves, seen by many to be undesirable and "selfish" qualities. A climate of political correctness and stern insistence on duty and self-sacrifice may make it difficult for many people, both men and women, to express the joyful, effervescent spirit of the goddess. Sadly, the impulse for self-beautification reflected by the planet has also been interpreted in some quarters as a "selling out", a ploy on the part of women too weak to live without the affirmation of men. But the great goddess of myth did not adorn herself for any reason other than her own pleasure. She chose her lovers according to what gave her satisfaction, not according to the security they could provide. Denying Venus within us leads the way to a soulless and dreary inner landscape of ugly buildings and eternally grey skies; and all the ideological correctness and social respectability in the world cannot compensate for what has been lost. The urge of Venus within us may sometimes lead us into terrible trouble. Yet this urge, like the goddess herself, is also life-enhancing and enormously creative, for it connects us with the joyful recognition that life is really a good place to be after all.

♀

The goddess of beauty and erotic love offers the apple to those who wish to taste the sweetness of life's pleasures and the bitterness of life's ungovernable sexual compulsions. The heady perfume of lilies enchants and confuses the senses, but this goddess is no mere frivolous conveyor of sensual delight. Through her artifice, the raw substance of nature is transformed into objects of beauty and grace, and through the suffering she inflicts on unsuspecting mortals, the greater design of life is unfolded.

♀

Mars

— ♂ —

In the myths of every ancient people, the gods of war have always occupied a prominent and honored place. War was personified by these fierce gods as the glorious expression of the human fighting spirit—not merely bloodthirsty and cruel, but also disciplined, courageous, honorable and directed toward a noble goal. The war gods of myth are almost always portrayed battling with a monster—an image not merely of the outer enemy, but also of the bestial dark force within human beings which must be conquered for the sake of humanity. Hercules, the quintessential Greco-Roman warrior hero, battled the Hydra and the Nemean Lion to free the people from destruction. The war gods symbolize not only the raw struggle for survival, but also the instinct to champion the weak, and defend the integrity of the soul as well as the life of the body. In Babylonian myth, the war god, Marduk, battled with his mother, the sea monster Tiamat, and carved heaven and earth out of her dismembered body. In Egypt, the fighting spirit was represented not by a god, but by a goddess—the lion-headed Sekhmet, daughter of the sun god Ra and dispenser of divine vengeance. In Norse myth, the ferocious Thor, personification of the Viking *berserker*, wielded his thunderbolts from the vault of heaven to smite the enemy. The Greek god of war was the flamboyant and virile Ares, who, according to Homer in *The Iliad*, was hairy, sweaty and

The Romans honored Mars as father and protector of their empire, and portrayed him as a mature and seasoned war lord in full battle dress.

three hundred feet tall. Known to the Romans as Mars, he fathered the twins Romulus and Remus who founded the city of Rome, and thus achieved his apogee in the classical world as the personification of Roman military might.

On the psychological level, Mars embodies our need to defend ourselves physically, emotionally, intellectually and spiritually, and define ourselves as separate individuals in a potentially hostile world. We fight not only individually but also through organized groups. We fight for our families, our countries, and for political or religious principles. Self-preservation in the human animal is also combined with the urge for self-definition, and psychological survival necessitates fighting for an individual identity. We fight to be more important than our fellows and better loved than our rivals. Sometimes our battles are disguised and called by other names, as in the domineering tactics of emotional blackmail or the inverted aggression of suicide—the ultimate act of war against life. Yet although aggression has many ugly and life-destroying forms, it needs containment and intelligent channeling, not forcible suppression. Anger is one of the most fundamental expressions of Mars, and although misdirected anger only causes suffering, we need to be able to feel angry when we are truly threatened by violation on any level. The capacity to say "No!" when we mean it is one of the most important and positive dimensions of Mars, for otherwise we become victims of life and of our own cowardice. Mars is the fighting arm of the Sun in the horoscope and enacts, on the worldly level, the need to express one's individuality and define one's own goals and values in an effective way. The phallic power of the war god describes our ability to know what we want, and do what is necessary to get it. This masculine capacity to take charge of one's life, equally relevant to men and women, is profoundly connected with feelings of potency and strength. Whatever we desire from life, Mars ensures that we stand some chance of getting it.

Many individuals experience conflict between their urge for self-assertion and their longing for emotional closeness. Consequently, they may find it hard to acknowledge or express perfectly healthy and justifiable anger, out of fear that others will reject them or find them unlovable. Early experiences may contribute to the conviction that defining one's own identity will antagonize one's family or social group. The experience of domestic violence—a Mars run amok—may also make it difficult for an individual to understand and express the positive and creative face of aggression, because the initial model has been so appalling. Yet we often fail to see the intimate connection between the expression of domestic violence—so commonly a reflection of deep feelings of impotence—and the apparent impotence of the victim, who ultimately wields the greater power because of his or her claim to the higher moral ground. No one could accuse the war gods of turning the other cheek, since, from their perspective, it will merely get punched as well. An inability to express Mars may lead to the deceptively noble—but ultimately unrewarding—stance of the martyr. Yet perennial martyrs, apparently unaggressive, so often provoke aggression in others.

The instinct to compete and win is also an expression of Mars, and we recognize its vitality and importance in such spheres as competitive sport. The war god will be satisfied by nothing less than first prize, because this is an affirmation of personal excellence and a reward for individual effort. Many people suffer deep inhibitions around the experience of competing—either because they are frightened of the humiliation of losing, or terrified of the inevitable envy of others if they win. Yet if we suppress our need to assert our individual capabilities because of fear, or in the name of political or spiritual ideology, we are left feeling frustrated, angry and envious ourselves. Mars expresses itself in different ways and on different levels according to the individual, and the competitive spirit may fulfill itself through intellectual or artistic effort, as well as through physical prowess. But somewhere within each of us is the need to be recognized as first and best in some sphere of life, however small, and we all require that sense of personal potency and worth which comes from achieving a hard-won goal. Every planet in the birth horoscope provides a balance to every other, and the naked fighting spirit of Mars is moderated and given meaning by our ideals, our sensitivity to others and our realistic acceptance of human limits. The mythic god of war is not innately vicious or evil. In his most creative form, he embodies a fundamental instinct which fights on the side of life.

The god of war fiercely guards his territory, warning away loudly those who would impose their will on him or intrude upon his rightful domain. He will strike if he must with the cutting edge of sword or word, but only if those who threaten him disregard his right to exist as he sees fit. Loud, forceful and aggressive, the lord of battle is unloved by the Olympian gods; yet he will fight their battles too, with the same honor and courage with which he fights his own.

Jupiter

♃

Jupiter is the largest planet, and in myth he is the biggest of the gods. In Babylon, this deity, king of heaven and dispenser of law and justice, was called Bel, Lord of the Air. He ruled over the hurricane and held the insignia of royalty which he bestowed upon the earthly kings of his choice. In Teutonic and Norse myth, he was known as Odin (Wotan), ruler of the gods, who granted heroism and victory and ordained the laws which governed human society. In Greece, he achieved his noblest and most humanized face as Zeus, father of gods and men. The name Zeus comes from a Sanskrit word which means light or lightning, and as bearer of the thunderbolt which illuminated heaven, Olympian Zeus was worshiped as the All-high throughout the ancient world. In many ways he resembles our Judeo-Christian image of the Almighty Father—omnipotent, omniscient and the source of all moral law. But Zeus was not solely a benevolent, fatherly deity. He was also restless, vain, bad-tempered and incurably promiscuous, and mated with innumerable mortal women to produce a race of heroes or demigods, who became the chief protagonists of Greek myth, poetry, drama and art. Son of the earth god Kronos, Zeus had to fight his father to claim his kingdom and establish the dominance of heaven over earth. To human beings, he was alternatively spiteful and generous—not unlike Yahveh of

Despite his childish tempers and tantrums, the Greco-Roman world imaged Jupiter as a regal and powerful figure in the prime of middle life.

the Old Testament—attempting to destroy the human race with a great flood, yet conferring immeasurable wealth, power and honor on those he favored. The Romans called him Jupiter, or Jove, and the joyful, energetic and dramatic nature of this god has found its way into the English language in the adjective "jovial".

On the psychological level, Jupiter, dispenser of law and giver of gifts, reflects our longing for a Father in Heaven—a need to experience some guiding spiritual principle at work in life. Although we might not recognize it by this name, our craving for the reassurance of moral absolutes reflects Jupiter at work within us. The mythic king of heaven personifies our deepest religious urge—not an inclination to orthodoxy, so much as a need to experience the universe as orderly, and in the wise and beneficent hand of a higher power who, even if occasionally temperamental, stands for ultimate justice. This instinctive religious urge may not always be clothed in the trappings of a recognized form of worship. It can also be expressed through the artist's quest for contact with the divine, and through our human efforts to create a social and legal system which dispenses an ideal of justice, as well as removing the criminal from the streets. We model our codes of right and wrong on the intuition of a higher set of laws, and this need for a world-view, or philosophy, which gives direction and moral authority to our lives, is reflected by the astrological Jupiter. The restlessness and promiscuity of Jupiter in myth represent our own restless longing for a future somehow bigger, better and brighter than the present. There is nothing quite so seductive as our dreams of the future, and no one quite so seductive as the king of heaven in myth (no mortal, male or female, ever refuses his amorous advances). The sometimes indiscriminate fashion in which we pursue new experiences may squander time, energy and resources; but such restless striving can also expand our awareness and give us a glimpse of immortality. Jupiter is the perennial adolescent of the divine pantheon, too big and brash to be stifled for long, and forever seeking new horizons. Through Jupiter, we discover our need to free ourselves from the bondage of time, age and circumstance in order to discover life all over again with the enthusiasm and optimism of youth.

Whenever we look around us and imagine possibilities bigger and better than the world in which we live, we are expressing Jupiter. When we say to ourselves, "Surely there is some lesson to be learned from this experience!"

it is the voice of Jupiter telling us there is an intelligent pattern hidden beneath seemingly chance events. Yet many people find it difficult to express the mythic giver of gifts in ordinary life. Fearful of the future, and lacking faith both in themselves and in life, some individuals cling too tightly to what they know rather than open doors to the possibilities of what might be. Early circumstances, such as chronic financial hardship, or a family atmosphere full of bitterness and fear, can make it hard for a person, later in life, to believe that anything will ever be better than it is. And if we believe that nothing better is possible, then we never take those few important steps toward a different future, but sink instead into the darkness of cynicism and hopelessness. Jupiter, in myth, was understood to be the bringer of good luck, dispensing his gifts like the lightning bolt from heaven. Yet to a great extent luck consists in our capacity to intuit opportunities, and to work toward making those opportunities manifest. In this sense we create our own luck, because we have enough faith in the future to take risks in the present.

In myth, Jupiter dealt with his children in a characteristic way. He left them some sign of their semi-divine destiny and then, having glimpsed a greener pasture of his own, vanished and let them get on with pursuing the future through their own resources. Only if they really got into trouble did he intervene, and then only indirectly. This sign from the god—we might call it an intuition of the "right" way to go—is a most important feature of the astrological Jupiter. It is through our hunches and intuitions that we sometimes discover the most profound clues to a future which is only possible if we have faith in our dreams, and the courage to journey into the unknown without guarantees. From the perspective of Jupiter, the greatest failure is aiming too low. A hopeful spirit depends, not on the concrete props of a reliable job or a solid bank account, but on a deep intuitive conviction that life is ultimately on our side. The urge to journey into the future, and the belief that we will somehow find the resources needed to get there, are both expressions of this bright planet which physically dominates the sky with its bigness, and equally dominates our dreams of the future with its message of enthusiasm and hope.

♃

The king of the gods contemplates with satisfaction the world he rules, envisaging an infinite number of possible futures which might add to its—and his—potency and glory. The throne on which he reclines is made not of wood or stone, but of living men and women whose adoration and earnest supplication fuel his strength, magnanimity and power, and give substance to his dreams.

♃

Saturn

♄

The Golden Age is an ancient and indestructible human dream. Not only the Bible, but the myths of the Sumerians, Babylonians, Greeks and Romans describe it, each with its own story of a Fall when divine law was transgressed by erring humans. And we conjure up the dream of the Golden Age now, whenever we turn to the past and glimpse the shining vision of a time of law and order, when human beings lived in harmony with the cycles of nature and had not yet degenerated into violence and corruption. In Hesiod's *Cosmogony*, this Golden Age was under the benign rule of the stern but just Greek deity, Kronos, whom the Romans called Saturn. He was a god of earth, not of heaven, and he governed the orderly cycles of the seasons, the irrevocable passage of time, and the laws by which men and women might live in accord with nature and their own mortality. As patron of agriculture and lord of the harvest, he symbolized the fertility of the tilled earth and conferred the rewards of honest effort. He was a working god and a wise king, who taught men and women how to press the olive and cultivate the vine. To those who obeyed his laws of discipline, time and mortality, he was a generous ruler who offered peace and abundance. To those who sought to impose their own will on the laws of life itself, he was a merciless and implacable judge. The Romans worshiped his friendly face at the year's end through the two-week carnival of the Saturnalia, which even Rio, in Brazil, has never succeeded

Although myth describes his youth, the god of time and earthly cycles was invariably portrayed in Greco-Roman art as a weary old man.

in surpassing. It has been suggested that the name Saturn comes from the Latin *sator*, meaning to sow; and on the most profound level this god symbolized the dictum that as we sow, so shall we reap.

On the psychological level, the earth god Saturn symbolizes our need to create solid and enduring structures, within which we can live peacefully and in accord with the limits of mortal life. The laws of Saturn are not the same as the idealized spiritual principles of Jupiter, but reflect a realistic acceptance of what is needed to keep individuals and societies safe and productive. Saturn's domain is not the afterlife, but the affairs of this world with all its failings and imperfections. Our profound need for order and security underpins our efforts to create social laws which curtail the excesses of human behavior, and preserve the tested and proven values of the past. Saturn is an unashamedly pragmatic deity, and impossible ideals of human perfection seem childish and irresponsible when challenged by the depth of his worldly wisdom. Unimpressed by polemics, the voice of Saturn within us tells us that we deserve to reap—and keep—the rewards of our efforts, and that self-sufficiency is more efficacious than demanding that others take responsibility for our welfare. We all need something of permanence in our lives, and the astrological Saturn symbolizes our urge to set boundaries for ourselves, internal and external, within which we can feel secure. We also need to embody our hopes and dreams in concrete form, and Saturn, as god of sowing and harvesting, reflects our urge to actualize our potentials and make some solid contribution to life.

Saturn is a conservative deity in the broadest sense, portraying our need to preserve what has proved its value and strength over time. He also represents our efforts to maintain the status quo in the face of threatening chaos and revolution. The fundamental human needs described by the astrological symbol of Saturn make us want to possess our own house, gain respect and remuneration for our efforts, and defend ourselves against those who try to take from us what we have worked so hard to achieve. Our pride in self-sufficiency, and the sense of self-respect we gain in having done something well, both reflect Saturn at work within us. The earthy nature of this deity describes our desire to see theories proven before we trust them and take risks with our intellectual, emotional or material resources. Time and experience are, for Saturn, the only true teachers. Any effort we make toward the establishing of a respectable place in society reflects our expression of Saturn, for the approval of the collective constitutes a very important dimension of what makes us feel safe. The intrinsically defensive nature of Saturn may also reveal a darker face, making us perceive as dangerous and subversive those who are foreign or different in race or lifestyle. This ancient earth god is not a trusting deity, and that which is unfamiliar must be tested—and perhaps even scapegoated—before it is allowed to pass through the guarded gate and enter the walls of the citadel.

Some people find it hard to express the needs of Saturn. Many individuals fear the limiting effects of their own security needs, convinced that their personal freedom and creativity will be curtailed by too many rules and responsibilities. They may avoid commitment on many levels because it demands the sacrifice of future possibilities. Yet those who fail to express Saturn overtly may find themselves seeking security covertly, hoping that some Saturnian surrogate—a reliable partner, an open-handed government or a supportive company hierarchy—will play the part of the earth god and provide what is needed without their having to work for it themselves. Although sometimes narrow and defensive, Saturn is the planetary symbol of the human capacity to provide for oneself in an unsympathetic world. Without this solid core we remain psychological infants, always crying for a surrogate parent who will feed and shelter us, and protect us from loneliness and extinction. In failing to honor Saturn, we give away our inner authenticity, authority and capacity to respect others' boundaries. Sometimes Saturn has hard lessons to teach about the necessity for separateness and self-reliance. Yet the myth of the Golden Age, over which this just and incorruptible god presided, is the potent symbol of a serenity which is available to all of us. It cannot be found in nostalgia for the past, nor through a surrogate parent in the present. But we may discover it by respecting those fundamental laws of life which require us to accept our expulsion from the Paradise Garden. In making peace with mortal limits, we discover the strength of Saturn within ourselves.

The Titan Saturn, his feet rooted in the stony earth over which he presides, faces us with the duality of his nature. In his right hand is the Cornucopia, the promised reward for adherence to nature's laws, and the image of the fecundity and peace of the Golden Age over which he rules. In his left hand is the scythe, symbol not only of the harvesting of the crops, but also of the harvesting of the mortal body which has fulfilled its earthly span. Life and death are thus knit together as part of the pattern of birth, maturation, decline and extinction, and those who can accept the laws and necessity of time can partake of the fruits of their labors in a spirit of serenity.

Chiron

⚷

The Greek myth of Chiron, the king of the centaurs whose incurable wound transformed him into a healer, is deeply relevant to our understanding of human suffering. The theme of the wounded healer-priest may be found in many cultures, and forms part of the training of the shaman in African and American Indian tribes. Yet nowhere is it so vividly portrayed as in the strange figure of Chiron. In myth, centaurs, half horse and half human, are images of the powerful forces of the instincts directed by human reason. Chiron, son of the earth god Saturn, was a denizen of forest and cave and a cunning hunter wise in plant and animal lore. He befriended the hero Hercules to his eventual misfortune, for Hercules accidently scratched him with the point of an arrow used to destroy the monster Hydra; this arrow was tainted with the monster's blood, a corrosive poison for which there was no antidote. Despite his wisdom, the centaur could not find a way to ease his agony and heal his wound. This injury, caused by carelessness rather than any deliberate act of violence, transformed Chiron. Unable to release himself from pain, yet unable to die because he was immortal, he found meaning in his suffering through healing others. He became the wise tutor to many young Greek princes, and led his untamed tribe of centaurs into civilized habits and greater friendship with human beings. The mythic theme of wisdom gleaned from suffering is symbolized in

Although he was a wise healer and teacher, Chiron's dark side was often portrayed in Greco-Roman art as a wild and savage hunter.

astrology by the planet Chiron, recently discovered and now demonstrated—through nearly twenty years of research—to be a profoundly important dimension of the birth horoscope.

The little planet itself, like the mythic centaur, is a maverick trapped within our solar system. An asteroid or dead comet caught in the gravitational pull of the Sun, it will one day leave as mysteriously as it entered. Its orbit is erratic and elliptical. On the psychological level, Chiron embodies urges and experiences which reflect this alien and alienated quality. When we are wounded by life's unfairness, we are trapped in our suffering, and experience the need to find meaning in our pain. It may not take the pain away, but it can help us cope creatively with feelings which otherwise would poison us with unending bitterness. Many of our hurts spring from our own attitudes, and even if we are reluctant to face this, we can, if pressed, recognize how we have brought misfortune upon ourselves through wrong choices or unconscious actions. We may also discover the roots of painful experiences in the unconscious ways in which we recreate our childhood hurts in adult life. Such wounds can be healed, because in recognizing our own contribution, we can alter our attitudes and create a better future. Even when we are injured by a person's malice, we have the comfort of moral, if not legal, judgment. But when life itself wounds us with its blind savagery—through the impact of wars, natural disasters, or an unfortunate genetic inheritance that is no single individual's fault—then we are bewildered and frightened because it seems that life has no justice after all, and we face the dark impersonal forces of chaos. Simple religious faith may help some people to make peace with such experiences. But many individuals need more than the promise that God's will is inscrutable and that the afterlife will be more pleasant.

Chiron reflects our need to stretch our understanding beyond collective social and religious precepts, for even Jupiter's faith in a benign cosmos may at some point fail to satisfy our demand to know why life is sometimes so dreadfully hard. Psychological insight of the Plutonian kind may also fail us, when we face tragedies that have no deeper purpose than that which we make for ourselves out of the ruins. In his efforts to alleviate his pain, the mythic Chiron became a skilled healer of others, for eventually there was nothing about pain which he did not know. Thus Chiron within us can lead us beyond self-pity and blame into an increasing understanding of the endemic nature of human unhappiness, and of the means available to help others cope with it. From this is born compassion—a frequently misused word which comes from a Greek root meaning "to feel with." We cannot experience compassion unless we have suffered. Avoiding the deeper challenges of life may allow us to feel a self-indulgent sentimentality in the face of human tragedy. But compassion as a living, healing force only springs from the experience of one's own incurable wound. When we face those areas within ourselves which have been irrevocably and pointlessly damaged by life—and we all have them—we realize how hard it is to be human, and how much nobility there is in human nature to prompt so many to respond to misfortune with integrity and generosity.

Chiron may be difficult to express, because the child in us is challenged to grow up and face life as it is, rather than as we wish it could be. Because this inner child always hopes for a happy ending to the story, we may stubbornly cling to our instinct to blame someone or something, rather than allow Chiron's hard-won wisdom to grow from stony ground. It is at the point where innocence is challenged by purposeless suffering that Chiron comes to meet us, for at such critical junctures our faith crumbles and we are at the mercy of life. Learning to carry our wounds without cynicism or self-pity can generate deep empathy and a profound capacity to share the loneliness of being human. Strangely, such silent sharing of a fundamental human dilemma may be more healing than the strenuous efforts of the professional do-gooder. Chiron's recent discovery may also reflect the timely nature of this quality of compassion without sentimentality, for as a collective we need it badly. We are at present faced with the collapse of many old values and the disintegration of a world-view which can no longer explain what is happening around us. In desperation, many people have retreated into the rigid moral and religious attitudes of the past in an effort to find someone or something to blame. Yet we may one day discover wiser and more mature ways of coping with the chaos in which we find ourselves. As we face the real nature of the wounds we carry, Chiron points toward the emerging compassion of childhood's end.

In anguish the wounded centaur seeks to pull the arrow from his thigh. But all his instinctive skill and knowledge cannot take away the pain he suffers, nor heal the wound of its corrosive poison. Yet despite the darkness which surrounds him, the light of the Sun—illuminating with merciless clarity that implacable unfairness of life which constitutes the true nature of his hurt—can draw forth wisdom and compassion to render bearable that which cannot be changed.

Uranus

— ♅ —

To ancient peoples, the beauty and vastness of the star-studded vault of heaven revealed the awesome power and intelligence of an invisible creator god. In Egypt, this ineffable deity was known as Atum, a formless spirit who bore within him the sum of all existence. The Egyptian sky goddess, Nut, was his feminine face, portrayed with her star-encrusted body bent to form the dome of heaven, touching the earth beneath with her fingertips and toes. In Babylon, the god of heaven was called Anu, whose name simply means "sky". He was the supreme creator god but, like the Egyptian Atum, he remained aloof and beyond the comprehension of mortal beings. So, too, did the ancient Greek god Ouranos or Uranus, whose name means "the sky crowned with stars" and who—true to his transcendent nature—was rarely portrayed in sculpture or painting. Unlike the colorful Zeus, that other great Greek divinity of the heights, Uranus was not endowed with lovable, fallible human traits. A much older power, his physical face was the sky itself, for he existed from the dawn of time, before the other gods came into being. The God of Genesis, whose spirit moved over the face of the primordial deep, is closely akin to the Greek portrayal of a vast, dimly sensed deity by whose power the design of creation is accomplished. Uranus, god of the starry heavens, is an ancient and awesome portrayal of the divine mind that conceived the idea of a universe before any universe was made.

The invisible heaven-god Uranus was represented in later Greco-Roman art by the muse Urania, patroness of astrology.

In order to grasp the astrological symbol of Uranus, we need to consider the process by which human beings make things happen in the world. Before we create any complex structure—a book, a house, a business, a musical composition, the constitution of a nation—we must have an idea of the finished product in our minds. This idea may be built up through logical thought or it may strike, fully formed, through a sudden flash of inspiration. We may be conscious of it or we may be guided unconsciously, unaware of the source of our actions. But without it, nothing coherent can be produced. The process of bringing an idea to birth in reality is evident, both in political leadership and in artistic fields such as architecture, interior design or theater direction, where the entire concept must be held in mind before any of the individual components can be fitted together. Some people are particularly gifted with this capacity to envisage the whole before it is manifest; such abilities are necessary in all managerial work, where different tasks and functions must be linked together by an overall concept. Some ancient systems of philosophy—such as Platonism and Stoicism, in which the cosmos is perceived as an interconnected, self-regulating system—bear the stamp of Uranian vision. So, too, does astrology. Today, most branches of science investigate the material components of the universe with great thoroughness, but without that far-seeing awareness of an interconnected whole of which Uranus is the astrological symbol.

On the psychological level, the creator god Uranus embodies our need to see beyond disparate events and objects, and glimpse the workings of the greater whole of which we are a part. Uranus also reflects our urge to transcend personal feelings in order to understand the overall pattern of our lives. The need for an objective perspective of life exists in all of us, although some people find it painful to achieve. Without it, we cannot discover how we fit into the bigger units of society and the world, but remain isolated and self-obsessed. With it, we can disengage from the emotional compulsions which occupy so much of our time and energy, and see with cool clarity our place in the overall scheme of things. Discovering such a perspective, especially at critical junctures in life, can be as nourishing to us as food. Without it we stumble through life blind and fearful, unable to understand the deeper thread of meaning that links our life experiences. Uranus may also be seen at work on a collective level, reflecting our universal human longing to know where we are going and why. The great turning points of human history occur, not because of the actions of any one individual, but through the power of ideas which break forth from the collective psyche and find an appropriate human mouthpiece. The Reformation, which swept northern Europe in the sixteenth century, began with an idea—that human beings were responsible directly to God and needed no papal intermediary—and found a mouthpiece in Martin Luther. The American and French revolutions of the eighteenth century likewise drew their power from an idea whose time had come—the right of everyone to contribute a voice to the future shape of the nation in which they live. Ideas can go badly wrong, as did the Bolshevik Revolution. Yet even when human nature distorts the purity of the vision, as it inevitably will, the idea itself reflects the Uranian need for progress and evolution.

Many people find it difficult to express Uranus, for they are required to detach themselves from their immediate emotional needs and look toward a bigger future design. Such detachment can feel cold and frightening, because it seems to belittle the value of the individual. We may know that a divorce, a change of career or a separation from family may ultimately be best for everyone, but that does not take away our very human pain and anger at such crisis points in life. We must pay a price for Uranian vision, for its clear light exposes all our petty propensities for manipulation, narcissism, spite and greed. Uranus also reflects our need for a code of ethics that lies beyond any individual sense of personal importance—a code which has no pity for our difficulties if they interfere with the efficient functioning of the whole. Many people are frightened of the disruption this strangely impersonal urge within them might unleash; they hope that by suppressing it they will not be called upon to stand on the mountaintop and look down, with honesty and clarity, at the road of their lives. Yet if we avoid expressing Uranus, its creative power will erupt into our personal world in spite of us—through change which we unconsciously need, and in some cases even provoke, but which we may experience as personally devastating when it arrives. The heavenly vision of Uranus may sometimes seem impersonal and cold, yet it offers us greater freedom through a new and broader perspective on our lives.

Lord of the starry heavens, Uranus, the architect of creation, designs the orderly patterns of the universe and envisages his creation imbued with symmetry and beauty. At this celestial drawing board no flaws appear, nor any disharmony arising from the imperfections of mortality. All is order and system, everything perfectly self-regulated and moving in its appointed path with elegant geometry—a vision of a cosmos, and of human potential, which forever inspires our hopes yet forever shames us as we struggle with our mortal limits.

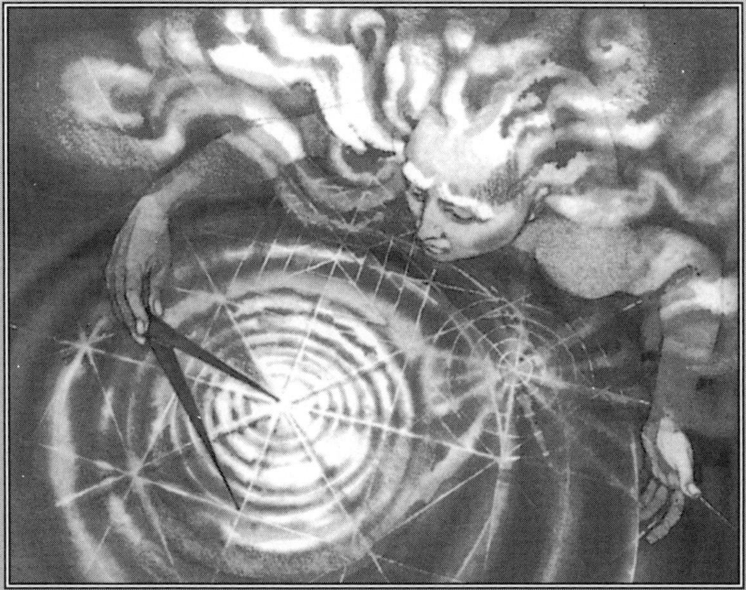

URANUS

Neptune

♆

Water is portrayed, in myth, as the womb of all living things and the source to which life returns to be reborn. In Sumer, the goddess of the sea was called Nammu, Mother of All. In Babylon, she was known as Tiamat and was depicted as a vast aquatic monster who gave birth to all the gods, then was eventually dismembered to make the heavens and the earth. In Hindu myth, the great goddess Maya personifies the boundless cosmic ocean out of which one universe after another emerges, only to dissolve into the primal waters again when its cycle has been fulfilled. In the archaic tales of Pelasgian Greece, the goddess Eurynome first created the ocean and danced upon its waves, coupling with a serpent to generate the cosmos. In later Greek myth, her image fragmented into many elusive deities of lake, river and spring, and every stream had its presiding nymph. The great god Okeanos also makes his appearance in Greek myth, encircling the globe of the earth with his ever-flowing and ever-fertile body. As the worship of the ancient mother goddesses was gradually superseded by the dynamic Olympian gods, the amorphous sea goddess Eurynome was pensioned off and blue-haired Poseidon, lord of earthquakes, bulls and horses, inherited the rulership of the sea. This powerful deity, capricious, temperamental and unfathomable as the waters over which he presided, was known to the Romans as Neptune, after whom the planet is named.

Fish-tailed Neptune and his consort Amphitrite, surrounded by fabulous sea-creatures, were a favorite theme in Roman bath mosaics.

The universality and mystery of the deities of the sea hint at our earliest experience of life in the waters of the womb, at one with the mother and possessing no independent identity or consciousness. Thus immersion in water is the mythic portrayal of union with the source of life, and this moving and potent motif has found its way into the Christian ritual of baptism as a symbol of purification and rebirth. The longing to reunite with the source of life, for cleansing and spiritual renewal, is also evident in the Hindu belief that bathing in the waters of Mother Ganges will release the weary soul from the endless wheel of karma. The sea goddesses of myth are vast and unknowable, amoral and unpredictable, gifted with prophecy and the power of self-fertilization. The image of water's limitless fertility also links it with the power of the imagination, which can give birth to an endless stream of images without need of an external source of fertilization. Water is the great mythic symbol of redemption, yet it is also the primary image of obliteration. In Babylonian, Greek, Hindu and Hebrew myth, the human race was nearly destroyed by a great heaven-sent flood, for the waters of oblivion are our end as well as our beginning. Yet despite our fear of extinction we long to feel connected with our source, nourished by its bounty and protected within its loving embrace. Our need for fusion with mother in infancy bears many similarities to our spiritual quest for fusion with the divine later in life. Neither negates the significance or truth of the other. Our craving for redemption belongs to both the infant and the adult, to both the body and the soul.

On the psychological level, Neptune reflects our need to lay down the lonely burden of material existence and experience the bliss of union with something greater. This is both an emotional and a spiritual imperative, although it expresses itself in different ways according to the individual's nature and personal beliefs. Some people seek Neptunian release through the comfort of an all-embracing ideology. Our belief in the State as a magical source of life and nourishment persists even in the face of the obvious human fallibility of any government or political system. Many people experience the ecstasy of transcendent union in the early stages of love, and feel bitterly disappointed when the beloved partner, parent or child turns out to be merely another human being, with feet of clay. Others seek the taste of oblivion through substances such as alcohol or heroin, for the illusory state of oneness which certain drugs produce may promise a sense of blessed renewal—until the body suffers the consequences. Our need for redemption, symbolized by Neptune, enacts itself through all our experiences of addiction, for it is through surrogates that we unconsciously seek to reunite with the oceanic source of life. It is through these same surrogates that we suffer our most bitter disillusionments. Religious and artistic involvement—especially the heightened emotional participation of shared music, drama or worship—can offer us a life-enhancing form of immersion in the mythic waters, for it is the inner world, rather than external surrogates, which provide the most authentic and transformative experiences of reunion with the source of life. The magic of the theater, cinema or concert hall, and the mysterious peace of synagogue, church, mosque or temple provide refuge from life's pain, where we can forget our loneliness and pool our deepest longings in a powerful flood of shared human aspiration.

Neptune does not reflect individualized tastes. The deity of the waters symbolizes a universal longing to transcend the pain of individual existence and return to the formless state of pre-birth. For this reason, Neptune is expressed through group trends and fashions, and reveals itself through collectives which share a common dream of redemption through some common ideal. When we long to look like everyone else, or submerge our individual values in a group identity, we are expressing Neptune. This abnegation of individuality, untempered by any critical faculty, can be as destructive as it is healing. The group can become a mob, unleashing a great flood of primal emotion which may destroy with appalling savagery. The purges of the Inquisition are only one example of the ways in which humanity has displayed terrifying cruelty over the centuries, in the name of spiritual redemption. Yet without Neptune we would feel isolated, bereft, and cut off from any spiritual or creative nourishment within. The need which Neptune symbolizes is a complex one, releasing the best and worst of human nature. Contained within a solid core of individual values and a capacity for honest reflection, Neptune embodies our finest aspirations, and our capacity to feel compassion for all other living things which spring from the same mysterious source.

Lord of dreams, visions and inchoate depths, the enigmatic god of sea and earthquake moves silently beneath the surface of life, concealing the gestating potentials of all that will one day emerge into the light of day. Prolonged immersion in his domain destroys us through addiction or madness, yet his waters also cleanse and renew us through the boundless riches of the imagination and the solace of compassion, washing away—for a time, at least—the suffering and loneliness of mortal existence.

Pluto

— ♇ —

Long before the concept of a Christian afterlife there existed the myth of an underworld, governed by a stern ruler of the dead, to which the souls of both good and evil journeyed. In the myths of Sumeria and Babylon, this impenetrable domain was the territory of a female deity called Ereshkigal, for our final abode was perceived as the same dark womb from which we emerged to take our place in earthly incarnation. In early Greek myth, the underworld was haunted by terrifying goddesses such as the Moirae or Fates, Hekate, the mistress of sorcery, and the Erinyes, goddesses of vengeance. But just as the sea eventually became the domain of the male deity, Poseidon, the underworld passed into the hands of the enigmatic god, Hades. The Romans knew him as Pluto, from the Greek meaning "giver of wealth." Invisible to the eyes of mortals, Pluto could be obsessive and violent. Yet he was inexorably just in his fashion. Guarded by a ferocious three-headed dog, his realm encompassed the calm restfulness of the Elysian Fields, abode of dead heroes, and the torture chambers of Tartaros, reserved for those who had in their lifetimes offended the gods. So immovable was the will of Pluto that, once a soul had passed into the underworld, no dictate from any other god could bring it back again, for the irrevocability of death has precedence over every other divine command. Yet Pluto could also be immensely seductive, and his charms are portrayed in myth by his tempting of Persephone with the sweetness of the pomegranate. Because

The jackal-headed Egyptian god Anubis presided over the ritual of embalming and guided the souls of the dead into the underworld.

death was understood to be an impenetrable mystery, few images of Pluto have survived from antiquity. Nor are there any temples to the Lord of the Dead, for his presence is everywhere: his altars exist in the mortal bodies of all living things.

On the psychological level, Pluto may be threatening to those who prefer to live solely on the surface of life. Our need to penetrate to the roots of things and seek insight into the underworld of the psyche is reflected by the astrological symbol of Pluto, but many people find such a need frightening and cling to a naive and childlike picture of life. Pluto also describes our urge to destroy what we have outgrown, for the Lord of the Dead is a profound symbol of the necessity for endings. No human life can progress without change, despite our efforts to halt the cycles of time. We express Pluto not only through death itself, but also each time we arrive at the end of a chapter of life, and are inexorably impelled to tear down what is old and stagnant so that we may be free to build anew. Our Plutonian urges, arising from some deep and mysterious place within, may conflict with well-established security needs which make us cling to the past, even when it has become lifeless and soul-destroying. The call of Pluto may therefore be suppressed, and only reveal itself in unconscious and compulsive ways. Then we may inadvertently set up situations where we ensure that the ending comes, despite our best efforts and apparently against our own will. Many relationship breakups reveal this secret Plutonian element. We may refuse to acknowledge that a partnership is destructive because we fear separation, loneliness or financial instability. Then we unconsciously provoke our partners into initiating an ending which we experience as forcibly imposed upon us. We can also exhibit Plutonian self-sabotage in work situations which are stifling and unhappy, but which provide material security. We may then subtly initiate conflict with employers or colleagues, yet express great anger and outrage when we are forced to seek a new direction in life.

Many people experience the workings of Pluto as a kind of fate, because they cannot acknowledge the underworld voice that heralds the time for change. Such individuals feel victimized when a crisis occurs which forces them into change against their will. Yet Pluto symbolizes a deeper will at work within us, which may not always accord with what we think we are. Pluto's needs are not wantonly destructive or malevolent.

They reveal that the flow of life is being blocked, and must be freed by the relinquishing of an old structure or attitude. Such endings always reflect the deeper requirements of the individual's life pattern, no matter how we might feel personally at the time. Pluto's mythic invisibility ensures that we only discover the true purpose of such changes afterward, and then only if we possess a willingness to explore our own depths. Many people choose to struggle against their own necessity, and then feel helpless, embittered and unforgiving when the battle is lost. Pluto is an aloof and inaccessible deity in myth, and his wisdom may seem to us cruel and implacable. Inner necessity is impervious to self-pity, just as Pluto in myth was impervious to human pleading. What has died is dead and cannot be resurrected in its old form. But life can flow freely again in new and more creative ways, provided we do not dam it up with bitterness and resentment.

From Pluto comes the priceless gift of recognizing when it is time to let go and move on. This is the real nature of the god's just law, for those who honor it possess an indestructible conviction of life's intelligent purposefulness. Failure to acknowledge Pluto can erode our trust and faith in life, because of the feeling that it has treated us unfairly. When we cling too possessively to people, situations or objects for the sake of power, security or emotional nourishment, we may experience Pluto's irrevocable law as a kind of violation. In myth, he is indeed a rapist, seizing the young virgin Persephone and dragging her down into his dark kingdom. Yet ultimately, having tasted the pomegranate, she chooses to stay. The feeling of being overwhelmed by life is experienced as savage and unfair only by the psychologically virgin who wish to remain childlike forever. The nature of Pluto's invasion of our daylight world is neither vicious nor evil, but reflects an inner necessity. In myth, Persephone passes from girl to woman and bears a child to her dark lord; and she is free to move between the upper and lower realms. This mythic image of a wisdom and creative fertility obtainable only by honest encounter with one's own depths, tells us why the Greeks and Romans called their underworld god by a name which means giver of riches. It is through Pluto that we learn how to survive in the face of crisis, and discover the real resources within ourselves.

Reclining languorously on a couch sparkling with gold and jewels, the lord of the underworld need not pursue us, but only sits and waits; for all things that live fulfill their appointed span and ultimately descend to his domain. Around him twines the serpent which embodies the secret of the forces of nature and the cycles of death and renewal. With his right hand he offers the pomegranate, symbol of fertility. For all endings are pregnant with the future, and release the life force, so that something new may be born from that which has passed away.

The Ascendant

ASC

The emergence of the Sun each morning seemed to ancient peoples a miraculous enactment of the rebirth of the Sun god, after his travails in the realms beneath the earth. The magical moment of sunrise is thus associated in myth with renewal and freedom from imprisoning darkness, and the earth's eastern horizon is the physical doorway to the future, where hope is born again. The symbol of the rising Sun promises the opportunity to remake the past, correct old mistakes, find fresh enthusiasm and believe in our dreams once more. "Hope," wrote Alexander Pope, "springs eternal in the human breast." This unquenchable faith in a future which we ourselves can make better is one of our greatest human resources, allowing us to shake off the pain and disappointment of the past. The Ascendant, in astrological symbolism, is that point on the earth's horizon which lies due east of the place of birth. This eastern point is the embodiment of the rising Sun. Because of the earth's daily rotation on its axis, the circle of the zodiac appears to revolve around us every twenty-four hours, and one of the twelve zodiacal signs will be rising on the eastern horizon according to the date and time of birth (see Table of Ascendants pages 156 to 163). This rising or Ascendant sign colors the doorway through which we, in the same way as the Sun, enter the world. It portrays our basic mode of self-expression each time we encounter any new situation, or whenever we need to assert our identity to the outer world. Where the Sun in the horoscope reflects our fundamental urge to express ourselves, the Ascendant, the solar doorway on the earthly plane, describes how we make that urge known to others and to our immediate environment.

Two-headed Roman Janus was the god of beginnings, presiding over daybreak and offering his protection to all new enterprises.

On the psychological level, the Ascendant is the boundary between our inner and outer worlds. Wherever the Sun, Moon and planets might be placed in an individual's horoscope, they can only display their energies and drives through the doorway of the Ascendant. In Roman myth, all gateways and doorways, visible and invisible, were under the rule of the enigmatic two-faced god Janus, who looked both forward and backward, and presided over all futures because they are mirrors of the past. Doorways are not just physical spaces through which we pass, but define separate territories and symbolize the link between one reality and another. The psychological boundary between self and others is invisible, yet as real and effective as a stone wall. We speak of being "walled in" when we cannot communicate, and we "open the door" to invite another into the private domain of our feelings and dreams. The Ascendant is the outer expression of the individual, the doorway through which all the planets—in their different zodiacal signs—pass from within us into the outer world. Through it, we view the world and act according to what we see. Others see us too, as we stand in this mysterious doorway, and respond according to what we reveal of ourselves. Although we may not always be conscious of how we tint life with our own subjective colors, nevertheless we carry certain assumptions and preconceptions, which affect how we express the various drives reflected by the planets within us. The Ascendant is the point of contact between us and the world, and the two-headed god Janus is a vivid image of the mysterious way in which our world-view is shaped, not by experience, as we like to think, but by our pre-existent images of what the world is like.

We are in fact selective, both in our recollection of the past and our receptivity to the future, according to the nature of this most personal of gateways. We unconsciously choose to attach importance to those experiences which will validate the world-view which we secretly carry within us. Through the Ascendant, we create our own reality according to how we perceive and respond to events and people in the outer world. In order to express the Ascendant most creatively, we need to recognize how our highly subjective view of reality makes us interpret and react to life in certain characteristic ways. Objective reality may exist but it is beyond our grasp, since everything we perceive is interpreted through individual eyes. We tend to assume that everyone sees the same things we do, yet no two people see even the simplest of objects in exactly the same way—as the old question about the glass of water demonstrates (is it half empty or half full?). Discovering the presence and power of our deep-rooted convictions about life may involve considerable self-honesty and courage, since it is easier and simpler to believe that life and other people are really the way we think they are. We not only interpret others' actions and motives according to our Ascendant, but over the course of life, we build up a picture of the world which determines how we communicate our beliefs, our morals and our ideals.

We cannot step out of our own doorway and become somebody else. But we can recognize and respect the differences of outlook between ourselves and those with different Ascendant signs. Comprehending the enormous power which our subjective attitudes wield over the kind of life we create for ourselves is one of the great secrets of inner peace. If we see life as a battleground in which only the strong survive, we will approach others with aggression, thereby provoking the same aggression in them, and having to cope with the consequences. If we then feel bitter and angry because people do not treat us kindly, who is ultimately responsible? But if we approach life in a spirit of optimism, believing that new opportunities lie around every corner, we will respond quickly and enthusiastically to any new possibility that might help us grow and expand our lives. Because we are prepared to act on our hunches and intuitions, we may seem more fortunate than our fellows. But is this really luck, or is it an attitude toward life which ultimately creates its own good fortune? There is a great mystery hidden in the Ascendant in the birth horoscope, because it holds the key to why we repeatedly meet with certain kinds of experiences. Janus, god of gateways, is a powerful mythic image which portrays the mysterious manner in which inner and outer realities mirror each other, pointing us toward a deeper understanding of the workings of what we call fate.

ASC

Janus, god of endings and beginnings, departures and returns, and guardian of all doors and gateways, looks inward to the secrets of the soul and outward to the rising sun which illuminates the external world and the potentials of the future. All experiences which enter an individual life from without must pass his watchful gaze and be judged, and all things emerging from within the individual must endure his scrutiny and obey his laws before venturing forth into the light of day

ASC

ASC THE ASCENDANT ASC

PART TWO

THE FOUR ELEMENTS AND THE SIGNS OF THE ZODIAC

The Element of Fire

In myth, the magical life-giving and life-destroying energies of fire portray the raw creative power of the godhead. Zeus and Thor hurled their fiery thunderbolts across the heavens as an emblem of their rulership, and the shining brilliance of the sun gods gave life and warmth to heaven and earth. The fire deities of myth could create a universe out of nothing—a potent image for the mysterious power within human beings to create outer reality from the magic of the imagination. The fire gods could be terrifying too. Thus when Zeus courted the mortal princess Semele, he appeared to her in his fiery essence and she was burnt to ashes. Fire also symbolizes the raw chaos before creation, and was understood by Greek philosophers such as Heraclitus to be the primal substance of which the cosmos was made. Fire was likewise worshiped in ancient Persia as the visible face of God and the source of all goodness. And fire was linked to artistic creativity in the figure of the Greek god Hephaestus, known to the Romans as Vulcan, who, as divine smith and artisan, built his forge over the fiery heart of a volcano and created objects of beauty and power for all the other gods.

On the psychological level, the element of fire symbolizes the power of the imagination—chaotic, unformed, but containing tremendous potency, offering to those prepared to work with it the power to generate reality from within. Imagination and vision are the most mysterious of human attributes, allowing us to move beyond material limits, and to create a future which contains possibilities greater than the present and the past. The imagination can also, like fire, become a destructive force, for it is through the grandiose fantasies of dictators that visions of global domination are formed and enacted. Our dreams of the future may be life-destroying as well as life-enhancing, leading not only to the creation of a better reality, but also to the ruin of what we have worked so many aeons to build. The power of imagination is a fundamental component in any human artistic effort. It is also deeply connected to what we call religious feeling, for all spiritual quests involve the imaginative recognition of a reality greater than the one which our senses perceive. Thus the fire gods are symbols of a higher creative power at work in the universe, and reflect our aspirations toward a spiritual state which transcends the limits of mortal existence.

The three fire signs of the zodiac, Aries, Leo and Sagittarius, all partake of the vitality and imaginative power of fire. But an individual's ability to express these dynamic signs productively depends largely upon a willingness to recognize the reality and importance of the imagination. Any planets placed in the fire signs in the birth horoscope will seek to express themselves with the color, drama and intensity of the mythic gods of fire. A person whose chart reveals many planets in fire, but who has circumscribed his or her life so that the playful and larger-than-life nature of fire is suppressed or numbed, may feel deeply frustrated and unhappy without realizing why. Such damming up of the vital creative force may lead to deep unconscious resentment and anger. Just as physical fire can be harnessed but not forced into rigid shapes, so, too, can creative inspiration be contained and directed but cannot be made to perform on cue through conscious coercion. The great sculptor Michelangelo once said that he did not make a statue—he released from the stone the thing of beauty and power which was inherent within it, struggling to be set free. Although the signs which belong to the element of fire may show a marked impatience with earthly limits, and may sometimes have to pay the consequences of their negligence, their strength lies in the power of the imagination to transform these limits, so that the outer world is filled with the magic of their fiery world within.

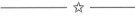

———— ☆ ————

Aries

— ♈ —

The sign of Aries begins the cycle of the zodiac at the vernal equinox, and its nature reflects the raw energy of spring when new shoots thrust above ground and the natural world begins to rouse from its winter sleep. In myth, the pioneering spirit of the first of the fire signs is reflected by the ram-headed Egyptian Ammon, self-engendered creator of all the other gods. The combative and heroic nature of Aries is portrayed in the tale of the Golden Fleece, the treasure sought by the Greek hero, Jason, and his Argonauts, on their long and difficult voyage. In Jason himself, a courageous and inspired but sometimes foolhardy figure, may be seen both the best and worst qualities of Aries. In fact much of the archetypal imagery of heroic tales—rivalry with the ruling king, the dragon fight, the rescuing of the damsel in distress—describes different facets of the figure of the crusader and champion who embodies Aries' fundamental approach to life. Ruled by the planet Mars and filled with the vigor of the god of war, Aries begins the sun's great yearly journey with a blare of trumpets and a passionate call to arms. Vision and enthusiasm are still untainted by worldly disillusionment, and energy is expressed in fierce bursts. No challenge is too great, no obstacle too daunting, no rival too powerful to frighten Aries away from battle.

The landscape of Aries is a turbulent one—a wild and stormy day in early spring, when new buds are ready to burst into blossom, and the

The ram-headed sphinxes at Luxor in Egypt symbolize the raw power of the creator-god Ammon, self-engendered and father of all the other gods.

changeable sky reflects the unsettled energy of seasonal transition. There is a quality of violence in this inner landscape, but it reflects the fierce urgency of nature and contains no malevolence or destructive intent. T. S. Eliot wrote in *The Waste Land* that April is "the cruellest month, breeding lilacs out of the dead land, stirring dull shoots with spring rain." The blind force necessary to bring life forth from stony winter ground may be glimpsed as spring gales tear trees from the earth, and the whole of the natural world seems torn by the convulsions of some gigantic birth. In the landscape of Aries, no new birth is possible without this cataclysm of nature, and it is inevitable that this sign will seek or generate conflict as a prelude to any new creative venture. The thrusting, phallic nature of Aries' energy, expressed on mental, emotional or physical levels, is not limited to men only, but is equally potent and vital in women. It is the irresistible challenge of the hard beginning and the invigorating struggle toward eventual conquest which enthuse Aries, and call forth its greatest courage and vision. The lone knight-errant, seeking new contests and new causes to be championed, is the embodiment of the questing spirit of Aries, which will inevitably seek to lead rather than follow, and would rather battle alone than compromise the power of the inner vision.

On the everyday level, the sign of Aries can express restlessness, vision, initiative, courage, impatience and explosive rage in the face of frustration. When this sign is emphasized in an individual birth chart, there is a profound need to pit oneself against life, and to experience one's own strength and potency through struggle, competition and the achievement of new goals. But sometimes a person whose horoscope reflects an emphasis in Aries may find it hard to express the restless and dynamic energy of the sign. This may be linked with early experiences which have undermined confidence and left fear and self-doubt in their wake. Yet even when it is denied outlets, the forceful nature of Aries' energy will not tolerate endless suppression. It may surface through bouts of explosive temper, periods of depression which mask great rage, or physical symptoms which translate emotional and creative frustration into repeating headaches, or other signs of deep inner distress. The fiery energy of Aries needs channels through which the individual can experience challenge and the opportunity to try out new and innovative ideas. Whether these channels are intellectual, emotional, physical or imaginative, it is important for those in whom the sign is strong to make plenty of room in their lives for the spirit of the pioneer. On the practical level, it might be wise for those in whom Aries is strongly emphasized to strive for independence in a field of work which gives them the freedom to make their own decisions and break new ground.

Planets placed in Aries will express their energies and drives with dash, drama and impulsiveness. The desire to be first and best is natural to Aries, and in order to express it, the individual needs to be able to face competition and tolerate others' criticism and envy. The more staid and structured the lifestyle, the more the Arien individual will feel stifled, bored, angry and frustrated. There is also a quality of naivety in this sign which is both noble and a liability, for life is seen with the freshness and unsullied idealism of youth. Aries' idealism—whether romantic, political or the reflection of a general world-view—infuses life with myth and magic, and is one of the great assets of the sign. Yet it may also prove difficult for the individual to cope with the meaner dimensions of human nature and the inevitably frustrating limits of the mundane world. The inexorable tyranny of time is Aries' greatest enemy, for its impulsiveness may lead the individual to assume that anything imagined or desired will be translated into reality now, rather than later. Waiting is hard for Aries, and performing all the dreary tasks necessary to make a vision concrete may severely test the person's already short supply of patience. Aries is neither lazy nor incapable of discipline. But impatience and a kind of sublime arrogance may cause the individual to abandon the goal before it is achieved, because of the inability to wait for things to ripen in their own time. The hot-blooded ram is an appropriate image for the combative instinct expressed by any planet placed in Aries. Rivalry and jealousy may cause many problems for Aries in personal life, and often the most desirable love-object is the one someone else has already claimed. Yet the fiery heart of this sign is transparently noble and there is neither malice nor spite to be found there—any more than one can attribute malice or spite to the turbulent life-force of early spring.

ARIES

In the landscape of Aries, two rams clash their horns in a ferocious contest of male supremacy against the backdrop of a fiery and turbulent early spring sky. Rams, like many Ariens, fight compulsively and will not tolerate any sharing of territory. In this stormy landscape the earth has not yet broken into life after its winter sleep, but the promise of growth may be glimpsed in the green shoots pushing forth above the ground. On a distant hill, a single standing stone rears its phallic silhouette against the sky, symbol of the power of heaven to quicken the receptive earth beneath.

Leo

– ♌ –

The lion has many faces in myth, traversing a spectrum from the most vengeful and savage to the kingliest and most noble. In Leo, the second of the fire signs, the creative power of fire is banked and concentrated, producing ferocious self-centeredness or the radiant and generous warmth of the Sun, which is Leo's planetary ruler. In Egypt, the lion-headed goddess, Sekhmet, known as the Eye of Ra, symbolized not only foresight but also the terrible anger of the sun god if his will was crossed. The rage of thwarted Leo is reflected in this ancient goddess, for in this sign the intuitive conviction of a unique destiny may produce not only great vision but also great pride and wilfulness. The Nemean lion, which Hercules conquered, is also a symbol of Leonine intensity which, unchecked by human reason, can trample over everything and everyone in its path. Yet after the battle, Hercules wore the lion's skin as his emblem, suggesting that Leo's powerful sense of personal destiny can be a source of immense strength and creativity. The great Anatolian earth goddess, Kybele, was invariably portrayed with a pair of lions, reflecting the creative potency of nature itself. Although savage, the lion in myth is always noble, never mean like the jackal or treacherous like the snake. Even at its most primitive, this sign possesses a magnanimity which raises it above the pettier dimensions of human nature. The creative vision of Leo is nothing less than the conviction of one's inner

The battle between Hercules and the Nemean lion reflects the struggle between consciousness and the destructive power of unbridled self-will.

divinity demanding expression through a life which is stamped with uniquely individual style.

The landscape of Leo is a glorious and dramatic stage set. No semi-detached houses lining dull suburban streets are to be found here, for only the noblest of palaces will suffice. The self-mythologizing tendencies of Leo are both childish and noble, contributing to intense self-centeredness as well as whole-hearted devotion to any person or thing that is deeply loved. The individual in whom this sign is emphasized needs above all to believe that he or she can offer life some individual gift which reflects a special destiny. Leo's creative potential is not limited to artistic work, for one can be creative simply by living one's life with zest, style and personal authenticity. Inner loyalties are deeply important to Leo, for it is these heartfelt values which provide the courage to express a sometimes lonely individual vision. Leo's need for an admiring audience may be a means of assuaging inner hurts, for when one lacks self-esteem one may constantly seek attention and approval in order to experience a sense of being lovable. The individual in whom Leo is emphasized in the birth horoscope may strive to be noticed in a variety of ways, which can seem demanding and imperious. Paradoxically, this most individualistic of signs often suffers from a deep lack of confidence, because any genuine affirmation of a special destiny implies separation from the security of the collective, and may result in feelings of being isolated and unloved.

On the everyday level, the fiery intensity of Leo may be expressed through deep devotion and commitment to loved ones, and to a creative ideal. Like the Sun, the strongly Leonine individual may unconsciously perceive others as planets orbiting around the shining center of his or her own life. Also like the Sun, Leo will give light and warmth unstintingly to these satellites, sparing nothing in order to make them happy. Yet it may be difficult for the person in whom Leo is strongly emphasized to fully accept others as truly separate entities, with their own values and dreams. For this reason, Leo may often experience feelings of deep betrayal and rage when a partner, sibling, friend, parent or child asserts the right to an independent life. This is not simple possessiveness, but reflects Leo's tendency to interpret love in highly idealized ways. It springs not from a mean heart but from a longing to make life, and other people, conform to an inner image of what life could be. For

Leo life must imitate art, and if the imitation is faulty then it must be improved upon—even if this means attempting to change others so that they conform to the glorious inner vision. Leo's difficulties in relationship spring not from insensitivity or lack of love, but from the dream of a grander, more beautiful world. If this dream is translated into creative effort, rather than being imposed wholesale upon others, Leo's contribution to life can be enormous and lasting.

Planets placed in Leo will express their energies and drives with dignity, drama, intensity and some of the heightened emotionality of a theater performance. Banality and meanness are Leo's greatest enemies, and the individual whose birth chart reflects an emphasis in this sign needs a large stage on which to perform. However circumscribed life might be, time must be found for discovering and developing individual talents and interests. Denied such outlets, Leo may descend into depression—and sometimes outrageously manipulative behavior—because the attention of others is so desperately required. Leo's need for the dramatic may be expressed through big new ideas, creative projects, dress or an exciting personal style. It may also be evident in a flair and originality which shine through even if work is repetitive and boring. Because the heart and soul of Leo are essentially childlike, those in whom the sign is prominent are often wonderful with children. They can encourage young potentials with generosity, and enter into a child's fantasy world without condescension or criticism. If Leo's inner world is crushed by self-doubt, this wonderfully childlike spirit may become childish as well, and the incessant quest for the adoring audience begins. Then the wounded lion will seek from others the validation which, in fact, is only sustaining if found within oneself. Whether the audience is one's family, one's work colleagues, one's friends or the whole world, it becomes vitally necessary to receive regular transfusions of love. But if this potent creative energy can be freed through the healing power of self-love, Leo has the magical gift of transforming a humble cottage into the palace of Kublai Kahn, and an ordinary human existence into a tale full of beauty, nobility and joy.

The lion stands in ceremonial posture, announcing to the world that the domain he guards is noble and magical and that due respect must be shown by those who wish to enter. The hot summer sun shines unceasingly on the towers of a fairytale palace, whose golden domes mirror the golden dome of heaven, and in whose richly appointed chambers might be housed a poet, a king, a princess or a divine child. The landscape of Leo reflects no vegetation, for this world is not subject to the earthly cycles of the seasons. It springs from the imagination, and is built from the elusive driftings of romantic fantasy and the aspirations of the human heart.

Sagittarius

♐

Sagittarius, the last of the fire signs, coincides with the increasing darkness of early winter. As the landscape becomes starker and the year moves toward its end, external activity is curtailed and the world of the imagination comes alive. The sign of Sagittarius is linked with the mythic centaur, whose origins go back to Babylon, and who is found in the figure of Chiron among the pantheon of the planetary gods. The centaur's duality is reflected in the contradictory nature of the sign, for it possesses both the raw vigor and power of the horse and the aspiring vision of the human spirit. The name Sagittarius comes from the Latin word for arrow, *sagitta*. The centaur's arrow, flying toward some distant goal, is an image of his quest for greater understanding, not only of his own mythic wound, but also of a universe in which the gods are just, though suffering and death are still part of the condition of all living things. Half beast and half divine, the centaur embodies the paradox of the human animal whose powerful and potentially destructive instincts are guided by hopes, ideals and a world-view which recognizes the sanctity of life. In myth, centaurs could be rowdy and uncontrollable, especially when drunk. Yet the arrow of Sagittarius in the heavens is aimed directly at the heart of Scorpio, thus suggesting that the centaur's enlightened vision can illuminate those darker human passions that lead us into blind destructiveness.

The mythic battle between the centaurs and the Lapiths describes the eternal conflict between raw instinct and the ideals of civilized society.

The landscape of Sagittarius is an endless road, along which the slow journey of understanding takes us from the narrow domain of home, family and neighborhood to the larger world, where we discover the similarities between disparate peoples and the uniting principles which secretly underly the surface diversity of life. Restless and forever on the move, the centaur is an eternal traveler for whom the journey is far more interesting than the reaching of the goal. The spirit of Sagittarius is adventurous and eternally hopeful, moving swiftly in pursuit of any future possibility which seems bigger and better than the present. The centaur's arrow also suggests those flashes of intuitive understanding which strike us out of the blue and then vanish, leaving us to gallop after them in the hope of capturing some of their elusive truth. Once a goal is reached—whether material, emotional, intellectual or spiritual—the excitement wanes, and only a new and even more fascinating possibility can again fan the flames of inspiration. Impatient with time and mundane limits, the expansive nature of Sagittarius is at its best if at least one door to the future is always left open. Nothing is so destructive to Sagittarius' enthusiasm for life as a narrow existence with no opportunity for growth and exploration of new ideas. A broad education—even if self-acquired—is therefore vital to those in whom the sign is emphasized. The dead weight of too much practical responsibility will sooner or later drive the centaur into flight—emotionally and intellectually if not physically. Equally important to Sagittarius is the need to communicate ideas and inspire others. The figure of Chiron, the wise teacher of myth, tells us that Sagittarius finds meaning and joy in the sharing of knowledge and vision.

On an everyday level, Sagittarius has much of the vitality and hopeful expectancy of youth. Those in whom this sign is strong tend to approach life as though every experience were provisional—a sort of trial run before the real thing comes along. With incorrigible optimism, they perceive the world as a huge adventure playground in which to try out new things, for Sagittarius holds the deep conviction that there will always be time to correct mistakes and create a better future. Thus Sagittarius has the gift of extracting important lessons from painful experiences without suffering the poison of personal bitterness, for such unhappy events become part of a past which is like a story told before the fire—transformed in the telling, so that the experience yields up its meaning while the memory of the pain drops away. Sagittarius is traditionally associated with luck, but the good fortune of the centaur really springs from a capacity to intuit opportunities, and take advantage of them in an optimistic spirit which sooner or later vindicates itself. This capacity to exploit promising situations others might overlook is one of the fundamental characteristics of the sign. Yet opportunistic though Sagittarius may be, it is neither cold nor calculating. Material ambition is rarely a goal in itself, but is a means to buy the freedom to pursue greater wisdom and more glorious dreams.

Planets placed in Sagittarius will express their energies and drives in a restless, enthusiastic and dramatic way. The planetary ruler of the sign is Jupiter, and in keeping with this volatile king of the gods, the Sagittarian spirit requires plenty of space in which to move and progress. This most fluid of the fire signs will not tolerate confinement in a cage, even if the cage is cleverly disguised as a nice house and a secure nine-to-five job. Social and moral conventions of the more specious kind may also propel the centaur into rebellion, for although Sagittarius has a profound sense of life's hidden purpose, this sign's deep moral searchings are highly individual and intolerant of common or garden variety human hypocrisy. Like the centaurs of myth, Sagittarius, too, may go on the rampage if the pressure of everyday life becomes too great, and the magic of the distant hills beckons. Because fire is the element of the creative imagination, those with the sign strongly emphasized in the birth chart are best suited to a life which provides constant new opportunities for variety and the exploration of new ideas. This does not necessitate a rootless and unstable existence, although there is a touch of the gypsy in every Sagittarian soul. But frequent travel—mental and spiritual if not physical—is a vital ingredient in the centaur's diet. The endless journeying of Sagittarius may follow an inner road, especially later in life, and the sign is associated with philosophy, and the quest for an inclusive world-view that can weld the often confusing fragments of life into a meaningful whole. Whether its fiery energy is expressed on inner or outer levels, for Sagittarius it is always better to travel hopefully than to arrive.

The centaur, carrying only his bow and arrow, pauses on the road to view the next stopping place on his journey, while the rising sun illuminates the winter landscape and promises new hopes and possibilities with the coming of a new day. Only the skeletal shapes of trees can be seen in this landscape, for it is the underlying laws of life which Sagittarius seeks, rather than the seductive diversity of its surface. Although a creature of forest and cave, the centaur nevertheless moves toward the centers of human habitation, for the sharing of his knowledge with others is a necessary dimension of his endless journeying.

The Element of Earth

The earth and all that lives and grows on it were imaged in myth as the living body of a great goddess. The Greeks called her Gaia, and this ancient name has recently become relevant again as a description of the planet's intricately woven ecological system. The earth goddess personified the life-force of nature, and offered peace and abundance to those who recognized and respected the interdependency of living things, and the laws by which they grow, mature and die. Earth is the densest of the astrological elements, requiring human intervention to achieve its maximum productivity, yet ultimately obeying only the eternal laws of the lunar month and the solar year. The sprouting of the seed, the maturing of the crops, the dead wasteland of winter harboring secret new life, were all portrayed in myth as miraculous processes within the body of the goddess. But this chthonic deity could also be dangerous, displaying her rage through earthquakes and volcanoes, and yielding nothing but arid sand and stone if angered by the impropriety of human beings. The animal kingdom was also her domain, depicting in its myriad forms the astonishing creative ingenuity and intelligence of the life-force hidden in matter. So too was the human body, which is born, grows, matures and dies according to the same natural laws that govern all other living things.

The landscape of Taurus, Virgo and Capricorn, the three earthy signs, is rich, fertile and full of abundant and complex life. Yet its subtle colors may be overlooked and underestimated by those with more flamboyant tastes. The colors of earth contain no artificial tints, but only those which we can see in sky, grass, tree, lake or stone. Earth is the element of the five senses, and the world of the earth signs is tactile and sensually potent, impinging on our eyes, ears, tongue, nose and skin. The earth signs resist aspects of life which might tempt them away from the solidity of their physical world, and may avoid experiences which require them to move out of step with the cyclical rhythms of their lives. The imaginative chaos of fire is not merely disturbing to the earth signs, but sometimes downright terrifying. Movement in the earthy world is slow and measured, gentle, and governed by the cycles of the seasons. Earth does not like to be hurried, for everything has its natural time of ripening and urgency can destroy delicate young growth. The volcanic eruptions of earth are infrequent, slow in coming, released under enormous pressure, and unstoppable until they have exhausted themselves. Planets placed in the earthy signs express themselves in sensual ways, seeking concrete outlets, and anchoring the human drives they represent in the structures of the material world.

On the psychological level, the element of earth reflects the perception of the senses and the hard-won wisdom of direct experience. Those in whom the element of earth is strong need to know that their desires can be translated into concrete form, for they will not pin their hopes, hearts or hard-won resources on fantasies and wisps of dreams. To be earthy means to be strong enough to face life as it is, without sentiment or self-deception. To be earthbound means to be imprisoned in a vision of life which is circumscribed by physical limits, and allows no vision or spark of immortality. The earth signs can be either or both. The earthy individual needs to make some concrete mark on the world, and self-confidence only grows from the conviction of a life usefully lived. Realistic about personal limits, earth will only strive for what is achievable. Through earth we are linked to the beauty of the physical world and the pleasure of our own bodies. We also discover the value of discipline, order, self-reliance and the conservation of our resources, for nature recycles everything and wastes nothing. The element of earth, symbolized by those ancient deities who governed the passage of the seasons and the immovable boundaries of natural law, confers the priceless gifts of patience and the capacity to fully savor life as it is, here and now.

———— ☆ ————

Taurus

♉

The bull is one of the most ancient symbols of the strength and fertilizing power of nature. All over the Mediterranean and the Middle East, the bull was worshiped as the consort of the earth goddess, and a vivid portrayal of these rites comes down to us in the frescoes of the bull dance, so beautifully portrayed at Knossos, in Crete. The animal's blend of slow, patient movement, and terrifying power when angered, epitomized the benign and destructive faces of the forces of nature. The Greek god, Poseidon, ruler of earthquakes, was worshiped in the form of a giant black bull who lived in the depths of the earth and shook the ground when he stamped in anger. Bulls also figure as the hero's bane in many myths, and none is more disturbing than the bull-headed, human-bodied Minotaur who lived at the heart of the Labyrinth and fed on human flesh. Here, the raw forces of nature are perceived as inimical to the heroic will, for instinctual compulsions erode self-reliance and undermine the capacity to direct one's life. In the Mithraic mysteries of the late Roman Empire, the bull became the clear symbol of primitive human passions, which had to be sacrificed to open the door to a higher level of consciousness. The Buddha, according to

The Roman god Mithras sacrificed the primal earth-bull so that its power could be transformed and channeled to enhance human life.

legend, was born under Taurus, and the image of the taming of the bull figures in many Buddhist tales. Taurus in myth is thus both an embodiment of earth's creative potency, and the eternal challenge of the instincts to the human will and spirit.

The landscape of Taurus is bursting with the lush beauty of late spring, when the whole of nature is occupied with procreation. In Western Europe and America, we still unconsciously honor the ancient fertility rites that were once performed before the great standing stones. We erect an innocently pretty Maypole—a thinly disguised symbol of the phallic potency of the earth. We even choose a May Queen, who in prehistoric times was sacrificed to the earth deities each year to ensure the fertility of the crops. In the Taurean landscape, the fields are verdant, the fruit trees are in blossom and humming with the sound of pollinating bees, and birds and animals display their extraordinary variety of mating rituals. In Taurus' world, nothing happens quickly; the seed is sown but must mature in its own time. One cannot stand over a plant and order it to grow, and equally one cannot stand over an individual with Taurus emphasized in the birth chart and demand that he or she hurry. The bull will not be pushed, but will eat, sleep and mate according to his own natural cycle, rather than that of the farmer who may wish for a little more action. The Taurean world is sensuous and indolent, yet beneath its slow surface flows the enormous power of the earth itself, moving according to an ancient and eternal rhythm, never rushing and never ceasing. For many gardeners this late spring landscape is the most beautiful of all, for its peace is redolent of hidden power, and the sense of future promise glows in every transient blossom.

On an everyday level, the peaceable, gentle energy of Taurus is expressed through qualities of patience and the ability to wait for things to ripen. Although the bull is an animal of great power, one might not recognize this if one sees it quietly grazing in a field. The strongly Taurean individual may often be underestimated by more volatile temperaments, because he or she will not advertise talents or skills until there is a sense that they can be effectively utilized. Many young people with a strong emphasis in Taurus may take a long time to choose a path in life, for this sign prefers to accrue practical experience and build something permanent, rather than making premature decisions which have to be undone later. Material security and stability are deeply important to

Taurus, and so too is the need to preserve the worthwhile things in life, even in the face of chaos and change. Taurus does not let go easily, and those with a strong emphasis in the sign may refuse to abandon a secure job, or stable relationship, even if they are deeply unhappy, unless they know that a better alternative can be more or less guaranteed. Taurus may become so attached to habitual routines and objects, that the individual may fight against positive changes simply because they are new. Traditional values matter to Taurus, although this conservative outlook toward life may not emerge until time and experience have tempered youthful ideals. The quiet, sometimes immovable surface of this earthy sign is deceptively simple. Enormous energy and tenacity lie beneath, as well as the capacity—like nature itself—to create forms of great beauty in the outer world.

Planets placed in Taurus will express their energies and drives in a slow, determined, tenacious and sometimes inflexible manner. Thus the sign may not reveal its most creative qualities until youth has passed. Strongly Taurean people may seem to be late developers on one level or another, waiting until values have crystallized and sufficient security is available before they gamble on an unknown future. Excitement for its own sake does not interest the bull—it is results that matter. Because Taurus possesses that often undervalued attribute of common sense, the creative efforts of the sign usually make a great impact on others because they are backed by experience rather than fantasy. Taurean rage may be infrequent and slow in coming, but once unleashed it can be devastating because there is usually a very good reason for it. Happily, the softer, kinder face of the bull is most often in evidence, and planets placed here—even forceful Mars—will be slowed and gentled in their expression. Aesthetic feeling runs deep in Taurus, and there is often great sensitivity to music, color and form. The development of personal taste is profoundly important for those with an emphasis in this sign, for it is through such practical expressions of individuality that they discover something truly stable and permanent within. Taurus may also be expressed through unsurpassed craftsmanship, particularly in the creation of objects which are useful as well as beautiful. But most importantly, the first of the earth signs possesses the wisdom to value ordinary life, finding experiences of beauty and harmony which require no heavenly validation. For Taurus, the divine can be discovered every day, on earth rather than in heaven.

♉ TAURUS ♉

Amidst the rolling hills and green fields of the Taurean landscape, cattle move in the unhurried steps of their mating dance. The trees are decked with blossom and spring flowers bloom in the grass, for the frosts of winter are passing and even fragile creatures can safely emerge in the warm spring sun. Against a benign sky rears the silhouette of an ancient stone circle, erected in prehistory to celebrate the fertile powers of earth and heaven and ensure the fecundity of the land. As long as the bull is not disturbed in the gratification of his desires, this serene landscape holds nothing that might threaten the peace and continuity of life.

Virgo

— ♍ —

The virgin goddesses of myth were not virgins in the sexual sense. In fact they were often portrayed as sensual and promiscuous. In Latin, the word *virgo* means 'unmarried' or 'self-possessed', and connotes not sexual purity but a self-sufficiency which made these deities eschew wifely roles. As mistress of herself, the virgin goddess belonged to no one, and therefore acted solely from her own will, rather than as the mouthpiece or consort of a male deity. The goddess Astraea, whose symbolism was exploited by Queen Elizabeth I as "cosmic" propaganda during her long reign, was known to the Greeks and Romans as the patron of justice and natural law, and presided over the orderly cycles of nature. Offended by the cruelty and boorishness of the human race, she abandoned the earth and withdrew into the heavens. Earlier "virgin" goddesses, such as the Syrio-Phoenician Atargatis, were not so refined. They presided over orgiastic rites, dispensed their favors through temple prostitutes, and personified the fertile abandonment of nature. Yet they too were virgins and gave themselves to those men or gods who pleased them, rather than to those to whom they owed a wifely duty. The virgin goddess of nature is an ancient symbol of the inviolable integrity of the earth itself. Despite our endless rape and wastage of her natural resources, the earth preserves its mystery, power and capacity for self-renewal.

The landscape of Virgo is intricate, orderly and subtle, and everything that grows and flowers within it can be used to benefit human life. Here are no garish dahlias or gladioli, but

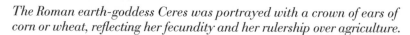

The Roman earth-goddess Ceres was portrayed with a crown of ears of corn or wheat, reflecting her fecundity and her rulership over agriculture.

only grey-leaved herbs and plants whose roots and flowers can be distilled into remedies for illness and pain. Although the virgin goddesses of myth personify the untamed heart of nature, the earth, like them, is willing to be wooed and cultivated—provided respect is shown for its laws. Knowledge of how to utilize and work in harmony with the powers of the earth and the cycles of time is an important dimension of Virgo, and reflects the sign's profound sympathy with nature rather than an attitude of conquest or ownership. The intricate tapestry of nature, expressed through the individual characteristics of each species, is reflected in the gentle rhythmic energy of Virgo—subtle, versatile and always in movement. If one spends quiet time communing with the natural world, one discovers that even in the stillness of winter there is tremendous activity everywhere. Worms tunnel into the earth, birds forage, insects of every variety propagate, eat and die, sap rises in bare trees and winter flowers burst into life. Nature is never still, and neither is Virgo. Nature is also, like Virgo, eminently efficient. If a species proves unviable it simply dies out, as the dinosaur did, and a newer, better adapted species emerges to take its place. The complexity of the life chain, whose extraordinary interconnectedess we are only now beginning to comprehend, is also portrayed in the landscape of Virgo, where every species relies upon another for its cycle of life.

On the everyday level, the ceaseless activity of nature is reflected in Virgo's need to utilize time in the most efficient way. Those in whom the sign is emphasized must be active, and their energies and efforts are directed toward the ordering of their world. The eager acquisition of knowledge and skills ensures that time is not wasted, and that results are useful and, if possible, helpful to others. So focused is Virgo on the rhythms of everyday life that it is sometimes difficult, for people in whom the sign is prominent, to lift their eyes above the rituals and routines of the immediate present to view, and be inspired by, the broader shape of the future. The ingenuity and creative versatility of Virgo are very great, and are often expressed through a variety of skills and talents. But this sign belongs to the element of earth, and Virgo may feel vaguely uneasy creating art for its own sake. The fruits of Virgo's fine craftsmanship are more likely to be both functional and beautiful, and the first takes priority over the second. The ancient meaning of *virgo* is evident in a deep dislike of feeling obligated to others, and despite Virgo's gentle and often self-deprecating manner those in whom the sign is emphasized have an intense need for privacy, and resent thoughtless invasion of their personal boundaries. Like the goddess Astraea, who withdrew from earth because she found the boorishness of human beings intolerable, Virgo's refinement creates a sometimes excessive sensitivity to anything coarse or brutish—including the individual's own strong emotions. Thus an emphasis in Virgo in the birth chart can be reflected in rigorous self-control, and a fear of feelings which threaten to disrupt the orderly patterns of life.

Planets placed in Virgo will express their energies and drives in a subtle and self-contained manner. Even unruly planets such as Mars and Jupiter become more orderly and well behaved. Virgo possesses cleverness, curiosity and adaptability, as well as a profound need to experience and understand life's intrinsic order. If a strongly Virgoan individual is threatened by chaos—internal or external—he or she may attempt to reestablish control through logical analysis and a preoccupation with detail. This has led to the sign being considered overly critical. Yet a critical attitude presupposes an ideal against which flawed reality is measured, and as an earth sign Virgo is too realistic to impose such ideals upon life. Discrimination, however, is Virgo's habitual defence against being overwhelmed by life, and the need to sift what works efficiently from what is pointless or wasteful is a means of restoring order to the world. Some individuals in whom the sign is emphasized may find that their need for privacy and autonomy leads to painful feelings of isolation. Yet because it is difficult for this sign to express vulnerability, the need for others may be demonstrated only through some form of practical service. The mythic relationship between untamed nature and the human beings who till the earth is a delicate one, easily thrown out of balance. Virgo may create its own prison through fear of violation. Yet at its best this sign radiates the serenity, integrity and creative ingenuity of those ancient goddesses who stood as potent symbols of the order and wisdom of the earth itself.

Contained by the symmetry of boundary walls, the landscape of Virgo reveals a garden of great intricacy and quiet beauty beneath an early autumn sun. All that grows within it is immaculately pruned and cared for, and every plant contributes something to the well-being of human life. The white aconite's roots yield an ointment that eases pain in muscles and joints; herbs for cooking scent the air; ivy provides food and shelter for the bees which pollinate the flowers. Useful weeds like the nettle also have their place, and pests are held in check not by poison, but by other species which allow the chain of life to move unbroken in accord with nature's subtle laws.

Capricorn

♑

The goat is a deeply paradoxical image in myth. A goat called Amalthea suckled the infant Zeus, and when he became king of the gods he placed her horn—the Cornucopia—in the heavens as an image of the earth's abundance. Goats were also symbols of licentiousness, and the great goat god Pan, with his wild train of satyrs, personified the uncontrolled life-force expressed as human lust. As pagan appreciation of nature gave way to Christian devaluing of instinctual life, the lascivious goat of Pan became the scapegoat, the animal embodiment of human failure and imperfection. Saturn, planetary ruler of Capricorn, was, like Amalthea, a personification of the riches of the earth, and in Greco-Roman myth he presided over the Golden Age, when human beings lived in harmony with natural law. Yet Saturn was also the god of time who set the limits of mortal life, and thus embodied not only the abundance of nature but also its grim mortality. The sign of Capricorn begins at the winter solstice, when the nights are longest and the sense of hope is at its lowest ebb. At this time of darkness and despair the mythic Sun god was reborn each year. The profound symbolism of light reborn from the darkness may be seen not only in Christian imagery, but also in the figures of Mithras and Sol Invictus, who shared a birthday with Jesus and were, like him, dominant in the religious life of the late Roman Empire. Thus the mythic backdrop of Capricorn the Goat

The image of the Cornucopia was used by the Romans to reflect the peace and prosperity promised to those who lived in accord with the law.

expresses many levels of meaning, from the sensuous abundance of the earth to the inevitability of death, and the hope of redemption that is born when the sense of mortality is most acute. Capricorn is a sign of both darkness and light, structure and abandonment. It is not surprising that those in whom the sign is prominent often have such difficulty in understanding the apparently contradictory facets of their own nature.

The landscape of Capricorn is fertile but mountainous, and portrays not only life's rewards but also its hardships. In the mountains, verdant, watered pastures alternate with barren, stony slopes, and an avalanche of rock or snow can destroy in a few moments what generations have worked to build. The stones of Capricorn's landscape are full of history and the ghosts of the past; and the tough mountain goats and tenacious pines which eke out a precarious livelihood on the slopes have seen many civilizations rise and fall. Those individuals in whom the last of the earth signs is emphasized are well aware of the fragility of fame and the transience of material success, and although they may struggle to achieve prominence, their ambitions are tempered by the knowledge that they, too, are mortal. Thus a solid contribution to future generations is often the older Capricorn's ultimate goal. The god of time is also the god of history, and awareness of the importance of time produces a valuing of the past and its contribution to the present and the future. Capricorn reflects a deep respect for tradition and the preservation of what has proved its worth through struggle and testing. The wisdom which is found at the mountaintop is not mere abstract philosophizing, but expresses a profound understanding of life's laws. This indestructible sense of certainty—in the face of life's unpredictability—can emerge only through the slow accruing of experience, and the enduring of failure as well as success.

On an everyday level, Capricorn is astute and worldly. Even as children, those in whom the sign is strong are hard to fool. Beneath the goat's shrewd appraisal of how to make one's way in this wicked world, there is often a powerful longing to break free and explore more imaginative realms. Yet Capricorn's preoccupation with survival may create self-imposed limits, and a strenuous self-control which closes the door on simple fun because it seems too self-indulgent. A deep sense of responsibility toward family and the past usually takes precedence over the pursuit of pleasure, and this sign can be relied upon to keep promises and discharge duties with care and integrity. Sometimes Capricorn's deeply conservative spirit may devalue anything which seems to come too easily, and a certain rigidity of thinking may reveal itself. Yet the mythic figure of Pan hints at the joyous abandonment hidden beneath the goat's apparently impenetrable self-containment. Capricorn can cope with loneliness better than most, and possesses the strength and discipline to keep working toward a goal, no matter how immovable the obstacles seem. Yet once on the mountaintop, those in whom the sign is strong may find themselves wondering why others seem to get the contents of the Cornucopia free. Perhaps it is because, lacking Capricorn's fierce pride and self-reliant spirit, these others are not ashamed to ask for help.

Planets placed in Capricorn will express their energies and drives in an understated but powerfully tenacious way. The real strength of Capricorn may not be evident until the individual is older, and has experienced enough of life to formulate lasting values and goals. For this reason, young people in whom the sign is strong may pass through periods when they seem anything but disciplined and wise, for it is necessary to test life and challenge existing authority before any permanent commitment is made. Those with an emphasis in Capricorn need, sooner or later (but more likely later), to make their mark on the world through a useful contribution to society. The goat's innate shrewdness helps them to understand that it is wiser to change the world slowly from within, than to destroy its time-honored structures in the name of ideological principles. Morality as an expression of social awareness is also fundamental to Capricorn, and is reflected in the sign's sharply defined conscience and dependence on hierarchical structures. When the Goat fights against such structures, it is not through impulse, but through the pragmatic realization that the road is blocked and must be cleared before sensible progress can be made. In Capricorn lies the enormous strength and power of earth, harnessed by the human will, directed with respect for the laws by which time and the maturation process operate, and ultimately aimed at supporting the future with the best of the past so that the safety and continuity of life can be preserved.

♑ CAPRICORN ♑

♑

Perched on a rocky slope, the sure-footed mountain goat surveys a world where crumbling walls and the bones of ancient cities reveal the glories of a noble past. Beneath the heaviness of the winter sky, when the nights are longest and the sun gives only feeble warmth, the indestructible pines push their strong roots deep into the soil, and tough winter grasses thrive between the stones. All that lives in Capricorn's landscape has proved its strength in the face of every challenge, and will survive when more transient things have fulfilled their time and passed away.

♑

The Element of Air

In myth, air is the abode of the Olympian gods. To the Greeks and Romans, these bright, intelligent powers were far above the primordial and unreasoning forces of the natural world and freely involved themselves in human affairs. Although divine, the gods of the heights squabbled, loved, lied, boasted and competed just like human beings, for unlike their chthonic counterparts, they related to each other and to the world beneath. The element of air was understood to embody the elusive brilliance of the mind and spirit, capricious and eternally in flux, yet higher and more noble than the everyday concerns of earthly life. Airy deities like Athena, whose Parthenon at Athens towers on its hilltop high above the city, transcended mortals in wisdom as well as power, and could pass fair judgment because they saw more and further, and were uncontaminated by the murky waters of instinctual compulsion. Instructor gods, such as the Egyptian Thoth and the Greek Hermes, taught human beings the use of the mind to master natural forces, transforming tribes into societies and mud huts into cities. The winged deities of air reflect human concepts and ideals, embodying a vision of the godhead which is intelligent, articulate and aware of the future course of human evolution.

On the psychological level, the element of air reflects the human gift of understanding and the ability to conceptualize and plan. The mind is not confined by earthly or instinctual limits. It views life from above, connecting disparate experiences and forming them into meaningful patterns which dissolve the imprisoning emotional bondage of the past. The mind's capacity for objectivity is suggested by air's mobility, detached from the weight of immediate personal needs. Ideas have enormous power to move events, both in individual lives and in history, and concepts such as democracy and equality have literally changed the world. Before we can progress, we need an idea of where we are going and a plan of how to get there. Without these we stumble blindly into the future, repeating the same mistakes and reacting without understanding. The three airy signs, Gemini, Libra and Aquarius, express in their different ways air's function of distilling experience into ideas. All three signs form concepts of how the world ought to be, measuring reality against ideal to establish whether a person, object or action is good or bad, right or wrong. The air gods' preoccupation with justice reflects the mind's ability to place what is fair before what is easy or instinctively gratifying, and their mythic role as culture-bringers portrays our potential to transform raw nature so that it serves human life. The absence of animal symbolism among the air signs tells us how far removed they are from the blind compulsions which dominate the animal side of human nature.

When our civilized attitudes are outraged by collective or individual cruelty or unfairness, it is the element of air which reflects the ideals we strive for and believe to be right. Those with air strongly represented in the birth horoscope long for the world to be fair and harmonious, and seek a code of ethics which can provide clear definitions of right and wrong. The air signs are not only just but can also be judgmental, perceiving life as black or white, and sometimes lacking the emotional flexibility to accept those subtler shades which color every human heart. Not every person with a strong emphasis in air may find it easy to express thoughts and opinions. Education and a free flow of communication are deeply important to those in whom the element is strong, and some may experience loss of confidence through an environment which opposes intellectual development, or denies the need for breathing space which all these signs require. Gemini, Aquarius and Libra, in common with the airy gods of myth, share a love of intellectual clarity and a vision of human perfection. The air signs reflect our striving for understanding, and our ideal of a world in which raw instinct is contained and directed by ethics and an appreciation of the human family.

☆

Gemini

♊

Twins appear in the myths of every ancient culture. Even our modern understanding of the divided ovum does not lessen the feeling of mystery surrounding two human beings who look so alike. In Greek myth, the twins Castor and Pollux appear identical, but the latter was the divine son of Zeus, while the former was the mortal son of King Tyndareus of Sparta. When Castor was killed Pollux wept bitterly over his body, for being immortal he could not follow his brother's shade to the kingdom of the dead. Zeus, taking pity on them, allowed them to alternate so that each could experience the spiritual heights and the mortal depths; yet they could never be together in either realm. Castor and Pollux were thus divided by the gulf between the realm of earth and the realm of heaven. Other mythic twins, such as Romulus and Remus, were divided by the gulf between good and evil. In Roman myth, these twins, sons of the war god Mars, were suckled as infants by a wolf. When they grew up Remus plotted his brother's murder, but Romulus killed him in self-defence and was honored as the founder of the city of Rome. From Greek myth also come the twins Zethus and Amphion, divided by their sharply contrasting natures and abilities. Although both were benign, Zethus was a strong and energetic warrior while Amphion was an artist and an intellectual, skilled in mathematics and the use of the lyre.

In the landscape of Gemini, first of the air signs, there are always two roads, which cannot be traveled at once. This dividing of the ways, reflected in the mythic image of the twins,

The twins Romulus and Remus reflect the duality of Roman values, which honored violence and aggression as well as dignity and self-discipline.

portrays an inner tension deeply challenging to those in whom the sign is strong. All human beings have contradictions, but no sign is as multi-faceted as Gemini. Living with the contradictions of one's nature is not easy, and often the solution seems to be to eschew one path in favor of the other. But both roads have value and are worthy of exploration, and, as with Castor and Pollux, any repudiation of half of oneself creates a sense of deep loss, and a feeling of discontent and incompleteness. Those with Gemini emphasized in the birth chart need to make peace with themselves through consciousness of the quest for inclusive knowledge underpinning their diversity. Often the two roads of Gemini's nature are reflected in a gift for abstract thought or spiritual awareness (Pollux, the divine twin), contrasted with a pragmatic mind comfortably ensconced in worldly affairs (Castor, the mortal twin). The dividing of the ways may also reflect a moral contradiction, where high ideals conflict with an impersonal amorality, as disturbing to the individual as it is to others who glimpse the dichotomy. Gemini is a fascinating sign because it presents a profound insight into life's diversity. In Gemini's world no truth is the whole truth, and nothing exists without its opposite. Communication is also fundamental to the sign, for it is necessary to find a common language through which all the different dimensions of life can be linked together.

On an everyday level, Gemini is restless, inquisitive and reluctant to be identified exclusively with any one direction or viewpoint. Eager for new stimuli and fascinated by human variety, Gemini resents being trapped by obligations which curtail the freedom to explore and exchange ideas. For this reason, many people in whom the sign is strong are happiest working in fields such as research, teaching or the media which offer the challenge of translating one dimension of life into another. Gemini's observant eye and versatile intellect crave a range of experiences—something which more single-minded people might deem superficial. But the world is too large for the Twins to limit the pursuit of knowledge to merely one subject. No single path, however noble, is likely to fulfill Gemini, for in keeping with its planetary ruler, Mercury, this sign wears many hats and plays many parts. For those with a strongly Geminian nature, there is often a sense of being several different people. Walt Whitman, the 19th-century American poet, was born with the Sun in Gemini, and wrote that he contained "multitudes". Gemini is sometimes described as fickle, but this term—as any Geminian knows—depends wholly upon one's frame of reference. Those with the sign emphasized in the birth chart are as capable of deep love and devotion as any other person. But love, for this elusive air sign, involves a relationship of minds as much as of hearts and bodies, and loyalty at the cost of frustration, depression and endless boredom may prove too high a price.

Planets placed in Gemini will express their energies and drives in a restless, sparkling and quicksilver manner. Feelings, ideas and physical energy may ebb and flow unpredictably, and it can sometimes be difficult to take a definite stand because so many points of view seem interesting and valid. Yet the key to that which unites the Twins lies in the myth of Castor and Pollux, for it is Olympian Zeus, giver of enlightenment, who directs their lives and fates. The unifying perspective of a philosophical or spiritual approach can give Gemini the sense that the diverse manifestations of life are linked on deeper levels by pattern and meaning. For this reason, higher education is important for those in whom the sign is prominent, and if this has not been possible in youth it may still be pursued in maturity. The broader the base of knowledge of life and the world, the easier it will be for Gemini to find creative connections and, in weaving together the disparate threads of knowledge, feel centered and whole. Although the present emphasis in education is on specialized learning, Gemini's breadth of vision requires more room in which to maneuver. Science and the arts, business and spiritual concerns, often sit side by side in those with the sign emphasized, and multiple talents are not unusual. Gemini symbolizes the gateway to a profound understanding of the many levels on which life operates. The mythic Twins are embodiments of the life-force at work through a wonderful variety of experiences and viewpoints, all of which comprise part of a great web of potential human understanding. Greatest of Gemini's many gifts is the ability to discover an individual language which unites this richly varied spectrum of life.

♊

Beyond the portal of birth Gemini's road divides. The level path takes the traveler through an everyday landscape of cottages, farms and all the paraphernalia of earthly life. The ascending path climbs the hills to the halls of higher learning, far above the concerns of ordinary life. In the landscape of Gemini, those who live above must descend to speak to those who live below, and those on the level ground must learn a language more complex than common speech to understand the lives of those above. Yet the road is really one road, and the apparent diversity of languages and spheres of training conceals the underlying unity of the world. All knowledge is part of one Knowledge.

♊

Libra

— ♎ —

The image of the scales or balance can be found in the myths of ancient Egypt, where the goddess Ma'at, guardian of justice, weighed the souls of the dead against a feather to determine how free they were of the burden of transgression. The balance is also associated with Athena, the Greek goddess of wisdom, who has passed into modern iconography as the blindfolded female figure of justice presiding over so many courtroom proceedings. Libra, second of the airy signs, is relatively "new", since it only made its appearance during the Hellenistic period, in the 3rd or 2nd century B.C.E. Before this, the claws of Scorpio, which in Babylon were portrayed holding the Lamp of Illumination, encompassed this segment of the heavens. Scorpio is a sign of great passion and also of vengeance, reflecting that instinctive sense of justice which demands an eye for an eye. Libra, evolving from its claws, reflects a willingness to use the faculty of reason to achieve a fair and objective judgment. The profound change in human values, reflected by Libra's emergence, is also portrayed in the myth of Orestes, who killed his mother at Apollo's command and was then hunted by the Furies, the ancient goddesses of vengeance. Athena, opposing the savagery of their blind retaliation, put Orestes' case before the first human jury. Through lengthy discussion and a majority vote, the jury deemed Orestes blameless and set him free. Thus for the first time in myth, it is a group of human beings, not a king or a god, who determines the nature of right and wrong. Libra, the

Ma'at, the Egyptian goddess of justice, is shown wearing the feather against which she weighed the human soul to measure its weight of sin.

only inanimate object in the imagery of the zodiac, symbolizes the detached perspective and the cooperative thinking which allow us to achieve a balanced and objective understanding of each other and of life.

The landscape of Libra is clean and precise, for raw nature is not welcome here. Ancient instinctual claims give way to a reasoned outlook, where experiences are measured against general principles rather than interpreted according to emotional need. The concept of fairness is a creation of the human mind; cheetahs do not meet in committee to discuss whether a particular antelope deserves to be eaten. Libra sets itself against the necessity of natural law, striving to create an ideal world in which reason takes precedence over simple survival. Those with the sign prominent in the birth chart also set high ideals for themselves, and although they may suffer for their principles, they wish to be—and be seen as—civilized human beings. Since this invariably means the denial of basic instincts and emotions, Libra may be overly critical of ordinary human failings. Yet so great is the power of the ideal, that the search for individual and social perfection creates perennial dissatisfaction with life. In keeping with Libra's planetary ruler, Venus, harmony and refinement matter greatly to those with the sign strong in the birth chart, and beauty—in ideas, people, objects, dress or small acts of courtesy and social grace—may be a more powerful motivation than worldly success. The great Roman emperor Augustus, born with the Sun in Libra, was—for a Roman emperor—exceptionally tasteful and restrained in his personal life and habits. His characteristically Libran vision of a united empire, in which different races and religions lived together in harmony, produced a forty-year peace unsurpassed in all the thousand years of the Roman state.

On an everyday level, Libra's highly civilized spirit may be expressed through working with others, for this sign is unmatched in creating an atmosphere of cooperation, where individuals with opposing viewpoints can achieve a balanced and mutually satisfying accord. Libra is often a gifted diplomat and peacemaker in both personal and professional life. The willingness to harmonize rather than antagonize has earned Libra the reputation of being indecisive. But those in whom the sign is strong are not incapable of knowing their own minds, and their views are often deeply felt and sharply defined. The continuing good will of others may, however, be more important than winning the battle only to lose the war. The goddess Athena was a strategist, and the capacity to make small compromises for the sake of a long-term plan is characteristic of Libra's subtle diplomatic skills. Spontaneous emotional reactions are sifted through a fine screen of ideals and principles, "oughts" and "shoulds", and if Libra cannot find others with whom to weigh and measure ideas, then the necessary committee will be found within. The courtesy and tact which are so often evident in Libran social interchange are expressed, not because the individual is incapable of nastiness or aggression, but because he or she is deeply convinced that such behavior is fair and right.

Planets placed in Libra will express their energies and drives in a cool, courteous and refined manner. Even the powerful instinctual forces of Mars and the Moon will be well behaved in public—often to the great frustration of both the planet and the individual. This youngest of the zodiac signs reflects a magnificent, but sometimes impossibly idealistic, longing for a perfect world. Such dreams are doomed to frequent disappointment by the inconsistencies of human nature. Nevertheless, those in whom Libra is emphasized are prepared to fight with great tenacity and commitment—not for their personal needs, but for the ideal to which they owe allegiance. For this reason, the calm equilibrium of Libra may sometimes break apart to reveal a dominant and aggressive face, for battle is often necessary to uphold justice. The Greeks understood this, and portrayed their goddess Athena not only as a wise judge, but also as a warrior. In personal life, Libra's idealism may provoke many battles, for the sign holds high ideals in love as well as in other spheres of life. As no relationship is capable of sustaining uninterrupted harmony, those with an emphasis in Libra may experience much disillusionment in matters of the heart. The Balance is the great astrological symbol of our belief that we can be better and more decent than we are. Through the power of reason, we rise above our greed and self-centeredness, and are able to give to life at least some of the beauty and harmony of Libra's indestructible ideals.

In the landscape of Libra, everything is mirrored and balanced by its opposite, for symmetry forms the basis of all harmony. No plants or animals mar the perfection of this hall of judgment, for the irrational, the instinctual and the disproportionate have no place here. The figure of justice is blind because no personal perspective is permitted to interfere with the careful weighing of life experience. The floor beneath her feet is made not of earth, but of the stark delineation of values—good and evil, beautiful and ugly, right and wrong. Created by the human mind and spirit, the landscape of Libra embodies the highest ideals of order and civilized interchange.

Aquarius

In Egyptian myth, the benign god Hapi carried on his shoulders a vast jug from which he poured out the waters of the Nile, thus initiating the great annual inundation on which the crops depended. The Greeks envisaged him as the beautiful Ganymede, beloved of Zeus and cup-bearer of the gods. But the mythic figure who best epitomizes Aquarius, last of the air signs, is a bearer of fire rather than water. The Greeks called him Prometheus, which means "he who has foresight"; he stole Zeus' divine flame and gave it to human beings so that they could learn to live as civilized creatures. The magical substance which the water-bearer carries, whether fire, water or the elixir of life, is not easy to define. But the myth of Prometheus suggests that it is the power of inspired knowledge which Aquarius pours forth—knowledge of harnessing the forces of nature to create an efficiently functioning world, in which everyone and everything has its role and contributes to the good of the whole. Prometheus was looked upon as the teacher of all civilizing arts. In a very early version of the myth, Prometheus actually made human beings out of clay. He invented architecture, astrology and astronomy, mathematics, geometry and the alphabet, and his gift of fire brought human beings out of their caves into the astonishing technology of the modern era. The fire of foresight inspires Aquarius to strive toward the creation of an orderly system—social, political, cosmic —in which every human being has a value and a part to play. The deeply inquiring mind of Aquarius is focused almost exclusively on human potential, for this sign embodies the power of the human mind to transform nature and change the world.

Ganymede was associated in Roman astrology with the sign of Aquarius because he carried the vessel containing the elixir of immortality.

In the landscape of Aquarius, human ingenuity dominates nature. The great inventions of the ancient world, from pottery and the wheel to the aqueduct, the making of concrete and the theorems of geometry, are reflections of our remarkable capacity to investigate the laws of nature and harness them for the benefit of society. Because the landscape of Aquarius is vast and full of new horizons, nearby things are often not seen in proper focus, and the questionable moral nature of some of our inventions may escape immediate recognition. Atomic power and genetic engineering might herald a glorious or a terrifying future. Even when an individual receives credit for one of these great leaps in knowledge, it is the human family as a whole which generates the spirit of exploration in which such discoveries take place. For Aquarius, knowledge is its own objective and does not require emotional validation or personal reward. The quest for truth which motivates this sign so deeply may thus be a truth divorced from personal feeling, and there is sometimes a painful gap between Aquarian ethics and ideals—invariably weighted on the side of the collective—and the individual's own equally valid needs. Sometimes those in whom Aquarius is emphasized idealize humanity, but are highly critical of individuals, including themselves. Yet the nobility and clarity of Aquarian vision, reflecting the planetary ruler Uranus, god of the starry heavens, has indeed brought fire from heaven and created the world anew.

On an everyday level, the truth-loving nature of Aquarius may be expressed through work which enhances the consciousness or well-being of others, particularly in spheres such as psychology, scientific research and political and social concerns. Those in whom the sign is strong will usually make the effort to be tolerant of differing viewpoints, lifestyles and personal beliefs, for Aquarius is opposed to the blindness of prejudice and the narrowness of a xenophobic spirit. The desire for truth creates a detached perspective and a gift for self-honesty, while the recognition of others' equality prompts a way of interrelating which is fair, decent and civilized. Sometimes the Aquarian emphasis on the importance of the collective can lead those in whom the sign is prominent to deny emotions and needs in themselves, and in others, because such needs are deemed "selfish". It may be difficult for Aquarius to think in terms of "me" because the rights and claims of the group—family, neighborhood, professional body, State—may seem of greater value. This most disciplined and steady of the air signs possesses a deep-rooted sense of responsibility to others, which springs from ethical precepts rather than practical or emotional necessity. Perennially optimistic about human potential and always willing to assume others are innocent until proven guilty, Aquarius is truly a citizen of the world.

Planets placed in Aquarius will express their energies and drives in a calm, detached and civilized manner. This sign is inclined to emotional distancing, and it may be hard for vulnerable feelings to be demonstrated or even acknowledged. Softer planets, such as Venus and the Moon, may express their needs in an impersonal way which is strikingly devoid of sentimentality. It is often those closest to the Aquarian individual who experience the sign's detachment, while more distant acquaintances and colleagues receive the full force of the Waterbearer's kindness, equanimity and concern. Aquarius is capable of immense loyalty and dedication, both to loved ones and to those larger causes so dear to the Aquarian heart. Yet those in whom the sign is emphasized may find their commitment underestimated, because they do not readily give voice to what they feel, only to what they think and believe. Complex and often misunderstood, Aquarius may rebel against traditional values—not from personal grievance but because a greater truth claims allegiance. Although often perceived as intensely individual, individualism for its own sake does not appeal to Aquarius' sober rationality. The strongly Aquarian nature may find it hard to fight for personal concerns and needs. Yet faced with a collective in need of help or encouragement, this sign can draw on enormous resources of tenacity, courage and genuine altruism. The far-seeing spirit of Prometheus is concerned, not with one person, nor even with the immediate future, but with the whole poignant, fallible, tough, vulnerable human family struggling toward some distant evolutionary goal, where the highest potentials of the mind and spirit are at last fulfilled.

AQUARIUS

In the cool landscape of Aquarius, the ingenuity of the human mind dominates the forces of nature, bringing water to the needy population of the city through the aqueduct's monumental arches of concrete, brick and stone. No single individual can claim credit for this invention, nor can any single person build it. Only the energy and commitment of the group, working in cooperation as each person contributes his or her individual skill and effort, can bring to birth such creations of the mind and spirit to transform the natural world, and improve the quality of human life.

The Element of Water

Water is the primal element out of which life emerged at the dawn of time. In myth, the earliest water deities were vast ocean-wombs in which the the universe was conceived. Water conceals the unfathomable mystery of life itself, and in its chaotic depths all things are merged and all life returns to be reborn. Mythic water goddesses, such as the Sumerian Nammu, portray not only our earliest experience of the waters of the womb, but also our dim sense of a life-source to which we will return after death. As compassionate mother of life, the sea was also perceived as a place of rebirth, and immersion in water led not only to literal death by drowning, but also to the cleansing of sin. At the bottom of the ocean lay the Norse cauldron of immortality, and the Babylonian tree of eternal life. To the Hindu, the rivers of India are still sacred, and the person who bathes in the waters of Mother Ganges will be freed from the wheel of rebirth. Water is also the element of fecundity, for without it the earth becomes a desert. The Greeks pictured the physical world as surrounded and fertilized by the great body of Okeanos, the eternal stream of life. The Old Testament tells us that the spirit of God moved over the face of the waters and divided them to accomplish the Creation, while the Koran tells us that out of water all life comes.

The landscape of water is perpetually shifting, benign and terrifying, repellent and enticing. The rhythms of the sea reflect the rhythms of our bodies and the cycles of the Moon, and the depths conceal not only monsters and the bones of the dead, but also lost treasure and the secrets of immortality. The magical and boundless realm of water is a landscape of the human heart, an image of those depths that lie within us all, and conceal both our secret darkness and our secret light. Water as the origin of life embodies the collective psyche from which every individual emerges, while water as the abode of savage monsters reflects the primal emotions, which we try so hard to tame through the efforts of the rational mind. Cancer, Scorpio and Pisces, the three water signs, are personified by cold-blooded creatures. The crab, the scorpion and the fishes, so alien to us, existed long before human beings, and reflect the monstrous sea deities of ancient myth. Yet in the womb we begin life like fishes, inhabitants of the waters with gills instead of lungs. The landscape of water is both frighteningly alien and intensely familiar.

Although we cannot survive in its depths, it encircles and enriches us like Okeanos. We enter it each night in sleep, in the oblivion of death, and in every experience of union in the arms of those we love.

On the psychological level, the three water signs reflect the shifting world of human feeling, defying explanation yet offering us tantalizing glimpses of our secret selves through dreams, mystical longings and our experience of unity with the rest of life. Those people with an emphasis in the water signs feel instinctively connected to others, and fear those experiences which require a sense of separateness and self-definition. The yearning to lose oneself in the stream of life may be expressed in creative ways, through imagination, vision, spiritual aspiration and the mystery of human love. It may also be expressed in destructive ways through the disintegrating effects of alcohol, drugs, madness, and the loss of individual integrity amidst the chaos of the mob. The water signs reflect the entire spectrum of human emotion, from our homeliest need for family and roots, through our most passionate desires, to our deepest longings to be one with what we call God. Water is the element of binding. Unresisting, it shapes itself to its channel, yet it dissolves or circumvents all obstacles in its path. In the same way, our emotional needs and longings are given shape by our outer lives, yet ultimately they flow through and over everything in their path, as we move toward that unity which is our beginning and our end. Water is the most human of the elements, linking us all in common suffering and aspiration. Yet it is also the most alien, revealing depths of which, even today, we know so little.

☆

Cancer

♋

The Crab has a curious mythic heritage. The Greeks perceived it as the creature of the goddess Hera, guardian of the family and the hearth. This sophisticated goddess protected those who honored the bonds of marriage, but was the jealous and implacable enemy of the illegitimate children her husband Zeus fathered on mortal women. When the hero Hercules, one of Zeus' illicit progeny, was battling the monster Hydra, she sent her crab to bite the hero's foot, to distract him during the fight. The crab caught hold of Hercules' heel with its powerful pincers and could not be shaken off. Although Hercules managed to conquer the Hydra, Hera placed her valiant crustacean in the heavens in gratitude for its loyalty. The crab's association with Hera reflects one of Cancer's best-known meanings, for Hera was the primary Greek symbol of domestic stability and continuity through the preservation of family bonds. In Egyptian myth, however, the zodiacal sign of Cancer took a subtler form. Instead of a crab, a scarab or dung beetle was associated with this segment of the zodiac which begins at the summer solstice, when the Sun is at the zenith of its power. The scarab is a more mysterious image than the crab, and gives us deeper insight into Cancer's complex nature. Because this beetle lays its eggs in a ball of dung which it rolls about until the larvae hatch, the Egyptians perceived it as a solar symbol from which new life mysteriously emerged, and understood the sign of Cancer to reflect the incarnation of the spirit into mortal form. Thus the first of the water signs is associated with the mystery of the spiritual source of life and with emotional loyalty to the values of the past.

The Egyptian scarab symbolized the midnight sun, emerging from the dark waters of the underworld to be reborn each morning.

The landscape of Cancer is the periphery of the sea, not its boundless depths. Because the crab is a creature which depends upon two elements for its survival, its habitat is the rocky or sandy interface between sea and land, open to the tides yet sheltered enough to provide protection. The crab is thus able to bridge two disparate worlds. This paradox is reflected in Cancer's need for material and emotional security to provide a base, from which forays into the depths can be accomplished with the knowledge that there is a safe place waiting. Often moody and subject to profound fluctuations of feeling, Cancer's inner world moves to the cyclical rhythms of its planetary ruler, the Moon. The ambiguous nature of the crab itself—hard and impenetrable on the outside, vulnerable and unformed within—also describes the characteristic Cancerian defence against hurt and disappointment. Cancer is realistic about the vagaries of life and can protect itself with surprising toughness and shrewdness. Those in whom the sign is emphasized are true survivors. Yet beneath the outer shell, this sign is enormously vulnerable and deeply fearful of loneliness and rejection. The crab's claws convey a powerful image of Cancer's tenacity and strength, for once this sign grips it will not let go. Yet like the crab, Cancer's movement toward a goal is oblique and subtle. The crab's moonlit watery world may not be displayed to every passer-by, yet it is full of rhythm, mystery and imaginative life.

On an everyday level, the crab's need for an earthy base is reflected in cautiousness and a preoccupation with security. Whether this security is provided by a close family, a reliable job or an indispensable role in a social or professional group, those with the sign prominent are extremely reluctant to leave the safety of what they know—even if their lives are deeply unhappy. Profound respect for the past may be expressed through a fascination for history, for Cancer's sense of imaginative empathy with what has gone before makes history a living reality. Often shy and reluctant to reveal thoughts and emotions which could incur criticism or rejection, Cancer may display a polished and sophisticated face to the world. The crab's tough carapace is vitally necessary, for Cancer's feelings are too intense to be offered lightly. Often highly romantic and far more passionate than they often dare show, those in whom the sign is strong may nevertheless be deeply mistrustful of new contacts and experiences. There is often a great gap between Cancer's outer life and the secret fantasy-world of the watery depths. This can sometimes lead to a clannish and defensive outlook, where everything foreign is seen as threatening. Yet the exotic and the esoteric are often irresistible to Cancer's mystical soul, and the boundlessness of the open sea forever beckons. Changeful, complex and often misunderstood, the Cancerian nature will always elude simple definition.

Planets placed in Cancer will express their energies and drives in a subtle, fluid, sensitive way. More forceful planets, such as Mars and the Sun, will be camouflaged and rendered highly sensitive to the emotional undercurrents in the environment. Cancer is highly intuitive and most at home with nonverbal forms of communication, and empathy with others' feelings may be so great as to be virtually psychic. This extreme sensitivity to atmosphere reflects an openness to the unconscious level of life, where individuals are not as separate as they might seem. People with an emphasis in Cancer are not merely attuned to this collective level of emotional experience; they depend upon it, for it provides them with a feeling of belonging, and a sense of emotional unity with the larger human family. Loneliness is abhorrent to Cancer, and many people with the sign prominent will do almost anything—including betrayal of their own deepest selves—to ensure that they are not left isolated. Cancer's psychic receptivity may sometimes be a double-edged gift, for it can create a dependency on others which undermines self-confidence and self-sufficiency, and opens the way to emotional victimization. Yet such openness is also a rare and precious thing. Tenderness and compassion are gifts of the Cancerian heart, and an intuitive understanding of others, a gift of the Cancerian mind. This mysterious and multifaceted sign, weak and strong at the same time, embodies our most protective feelings toward others, and our sense of rootedness in a history comprised not of sterile facts, but of living people who have loved, suffered and offered their most poignant dreams to all the generations which follow.

♋ CANCER ♋

♋

In the moonlit landscape of Cancer, the Crab seeks shelter among the protective rocks of a tidepool. Around it flows the teeming life of the sea, moving rhythmically with the tides and the phases of the Moon. The pearl held in the creature's claw is formed with patient effort, layer by layer over time, as a protection against life's pain. In this landscape buffeted by the sea of human feeling, suffering and beauty are inextricably linked together, and unlike those who journey blind across the seas, the Crab uses knowledge and experience of the past to ensure the continuity of life.

♋

Scorpio

♏

The Scorpion of Greek myth is a menacing creature, sent by the lunar goddess Artemis to kill the hunter Orion as a punishment for his pride. It also caused the disastrous bolting of the steeds of Apollo, as they galloped wildly across the heavens when his inexperienced son Phaëthon tried to commandeer the solar chariot: the earth was scorched and Phaëthon was hurled to his death. In early Mesopotamia, the Scorpion was known as the Stinger, the symbol of darkness which heralded the decline of the Sun's power in the autumn. It is thus connected with the chthonic powers of nature, which will rise up in anger if abused by the arrogant will of human beings. Both Orion and Phaëthon were guilty of what the Greeks called *hubris*—the pride which afflicts heroic souls, and makes them push beyond their appropriate limits to challenge the will and power of the gods. Although portrayed in myth as a dangerous creature, the Scorpion is not evil. The symbolism of the second water sign reflects the vengeance of outraged nature, and the stern justice which awaits those who lack humility in the face of the instinctual forces of life. As harbinger of the Sun's decline, Scorpio embodies the law of nature which decrees that even the strongest will must ultimately bow to the body's mortality. The image of the Scorpion was also adopted by the Roman Praetorian Guard as their emblem, in part because one of its planetary rulers is the war god Mars (the other being the underworld god Pluto), and in part because the cunning,

The monstrous Hydra which Hercules fought reflects the battle between consciousness and the compulsions of the dark side of human nature.

speed and lethal sting of the scorpion reflected the image these crack troops of the Empire wished their enemies to bear in mind.

The landscape of Scorpio, coinciding with the advent of winter and the slow death of the earth's vegetation, is mysterious and impenetrable. Like the heart of a jungle or a rain forest, Scorpio's landscape conveys depth, subtlety and a teeming, hidden, life, which can seem threatening to those who view the world more simplistically. The stillness of the deep pool, the slow smouldering of the sleeping volcano, are both Scorpionic images which convey the quiet power of this sign. The scorpion is unique among the creatures of nature in that, when cornered, it will sting itself to death. In folklore, this act of self-destruction is attributed to a preference for death rather than submission. While it may in actuality reflect confusion rather than deliberate suicide, the scorpion is thus linked with courage and the necessity for self-determination. The pride of Scorpio is one of its most fundamental characteristics, and the poet Milton, who had Scorpio on the Ascendant, put this sentiment beautifully in the mouth of Lucifer: " It is better to reign in Hell than serve in Heaven". In nature, scorpions are in fact remarkably tough; they can survive fire, nuclear tests, and the heat and aridity of a desert climate where little else will live. So, too, does the tenacity of the sign give those in whom it is prominent, endurance, and an indestructibility of the spirit which can survive great sorrow and hardship.

On the everyday level, Scorpio is endowed with great intensity of feeling. This includes all feelings—love, passion, need, hatred and anger. It is as though every human urge symbolized by the planets is magnified a hundredfold when it is expressed through the coloration of this sign. One does not simply dislike; one loathes. One does not find someone mildly congenial; one is passionately and irrevocably attached. One is not simply hurt by rejection; one is lacerated and vows revenge. The sting of the scorpion reflects the sign's inclination toward retaliation, because where human beings feel so intensely they do not easily forgive. Scorpio's need for intense emotional involvement is evenly matched by a deep fear of being controlled by others, and this creates an inner tension which gives the sign much of its smouldering quality. Those in whom the sign is strong have a taste for the dramatic, and need to infuse their experiences with richer and deeper colors—even if this means provoking crises and storms. Sometimes capable of extreme possessiveness, Scorpio, like its fellow water signs, needs a great degree of emotional closeness with loved ones. An acute sensitivity to others' unspoken motives makes the sign highly selective, and unresponsive to people who are in any way false or manipulative. Yet those with an emphasis in Scorpio tend to attach themselves passionately to those they love and are capable of extraordinary devotion and self-sacrifice. Such love, although not given lightly, will survive conflicts and disappointments which might shatter more superficial bonds. Beneath the Scorpion's tough carapace lies profound compassion for human suffering, and a penetrating insight into the ambiguities of the human soul.

Planets placed in Scorpio will express their energies and drives with great intensity and determination. Even gentler planets, like Venus and the Moon, will make their emotional needs known with a power which may disturb cooler natures—although such feelings, if rebuffed even slightly, will afterward be carefully concealed beneath a tough and indifferent veneer. Because Scorpio is a sign of such great sensitivity and feeling, caution and even suspicion may be the inevitable products of early emotional disappointments, and many people with this sign prominent habitually disguise their intensity, in order to protect themselves from hurt and humiliation. Like the crab, the scorpion possesses a hard outer shell and a soft, vulnerable inside. And like Cancer, Scorpio may also present to the outer world a sophisticated and apparently cynical surface which fools everyone, including the individual himself or herself. The insightfulness of Scorpio's perception of life often draws those in whom the sign is strong into a committed exploration of human nature—partly to come to terms with their own depths, and partly because the invisible dimensions of reality exercise such a profound fascination. Those with an emphasis in Scorpio may be defensive, enigmatic, proud, touchy and difficult to know. This sign, feared by the ancients yet recognized as the embodiment of life's most profound mysteries, symbolizes those deeper levels of existence which underpin the world of the senses and the unexplored regions of the human soul.

♏ SCORPIO ♏

♏

Scorpio's landscape is rich and complex, filled with exotic forms of life and imbued with heavy fragrance. The Scorpion sits beside a deep still pool where hidden life is concealed by the smooth mirror of the water's surface, and the depths can only be surmised—never known. Carnivorous plants and vines grow in profusion in this jungle landscape, while orchids, the most sexually provocative of flowers, perfume the air. The landscape of Scorpio is difficult to penetrate, dangerous as well as beautiful, for everything here is larger than life and deceptive in its outer form.

♏

Pisces

— ♓ —

In Syrian myth, the larger fish of Pisces was associated with the great fertility goddess, Derke or Atargatis, portrayed with a woman's head upon a huge fish's body. The Greeks identified this deity with their own Aphrodite, and believed the smaller fish to be her beautiful young lover, Adonis, who was killed by a boar. These two figures, bound together in the heavens, symbolized the great yearly cycle, in which the youthful spirit of newly emerging vegetative life emerged from the fertile womb of nature in the spring and died in the autumn, only to be reborn in the following spring. This eternal cycle of birth, death and rebirth, expressed through the rhythms of the natural world, also portrayed a profound truth about the nature of human beings. The larger fish became a symbol of the mortal body, with its insatiable appetites and blind instinctual needs. The smaller fish, associated with the goddess' ill-fated lover, became an image of the redemptive power of the immortal spirit which, although trapped in the cycle of mortality, is eternally reborn. The spiritual symbolism of the smaller fish was also reflected in the semi-divine figure of Orpheus the Fisher, in Greco-Roman myth, around whose tragic life a redeemer-cult was formed. The image of the fish as sacrificial savior or spiritual redeemer found its way into the iconography of early Christianity, where Jesus was himself the Fish and Peter the Fisher of Men. The mythic imagery of Pisces

Eros, the Greco-Roman god of love, rides on the back of a dolphin, reflecting the taming and redemptive power of love over raw instinct.

portrays to us the mystery of an immortal spirit which, although imprisoned in the darkness of the physical world, is forever redeemed and reborn.

The underwater landscape of Pisces is the magical kingdom at the bottom of the sea, where shapes both monstrous and beautiful swim through the waters, and the secret of immortality is hidden in the depths. The many myths of a magic cauldron, or tree, of eternal life, buried beneath the waves, tell us that Pisces embodies the human spirit's longing for eternity, doomed to conflict with the compulsions of the instincts yet triumphant even in the face of death. In the darkness at the bottom of the sea lurk life-threatening creatures which, rising up from the depths of the unconcious, terrify us with their blind hunger and savagery. These images reflect the flood of primitive emotion which lies beneath the civilized surface of human society. Throughout history, these unconscious forces have risen up to generate the collective madness of wars, purges and inquisitions. The exquisite and fragile creatures which also inhabit the depths of the sea express the ineffable beauty of life and of the human soul, communicable only through music, poetry, painting and mystical vision. Those in whom Pisces is strong do not have darker or lighter souls than other people; but they are more attuned than the other zodiacal signs to the deep currents of the collective psyche, for the sense of individual identity in Pisces is often blurred, and open to a more universal perception of life. The underwater world of Pisces belongs to all of us, generating not only our most appalling destructiveness but also our noblest and most exquisite creations. Those in whom the sign is emphasized are the witnesses and portrait artists of these denizens of the depths.

On an everyday level, Pisces' receptivity to the hidden world of the collective unconscious can lead to creative versatility and power, and a sense of profound compassion for all life. There is often deep religious feeling in Pisces, which reflects the visionary qualities of the sign's planetary rulers, Jupiter and Neptune. Such awareness of a larger, more inclusive universe can also cause problems, for there is no human dilemma which Pisces does not recognize or find familiar. Those in whom the sign is strong identify readily with every shade of the human emotional spectrum, and may find it difficult to defend their own ground or protect themselves from exploitation. The mythic image of the redeemer—who is also a victim—may express itself through sacrificial acts which confer subtle power as well as pain. Pisces is deeply in touch with the poignancy of mortal existence, for its place at the end of the zodiacal cycle reflects a gentle disengagement from the imperative self-expression which dominates the earlier signs. The longing to go home may express itself as a quest for oblivion, through compulsions such as alcoholism and drug addiction. Equally, it may be demonstrated compassionately through the need to heal this particular form of despair in others. Pisces can be mercurial and changeable as the currents of the sea, filled with a melancholy awareness of the transience of life. Yet, lacking the prickly pride of self-importance, Pisces also possesses a great capacity for laughter and sensual delight, for those in whom the sign is strong know the secret of how to let go.

Planets placed in Pisces will express their energies and drives in a fluid, sensitive and indirect way. In the strongly Piscean nature there is often a sense that life is a stage play with a painted backdrop and a limited run, and planets placed in Pisces perform their roles with subtle theatricality. This sense of unreality, combined with the sign's rich imagination, may produce wonderful creative gifts, particularly in drama, music and film. Extraordinary intuitive leaps may also occur in the fields of physics and mathematics, which may provide superb playgrounds for the far-ranging Piscean mind. Life viewed through the eyes of the Fishes is like a dream, and everyday happenings are infused with strange and subtle meanings. Flowing with the current is preferable to pointless struggle, and there is often deep trust in a higher intelligence wiser than any human being. Pisces' gentleness can sometimes lead to self-destructive passivity, and powerful primal emotions can flood consciousness, just as the great tides inundate the land. At such moments, it may seem as though chaos threatens the stability of ordinary life. Yet if the strongly Piscean individual is prepared to give shape to such feelings through creative forms, and can learn to live in peace with the duality of flesh and spirit, Pisces, last of the water signs and the completion of the zodiacal cycle, embodies all that is most compassionate, most universal and most deeply connected with that deeper reality which underpins the whole of existence.

♓ PISCES ♓

♓

In the underwater landscape of Pisces, the fishes, elusive and mercurial, share the depths with the octopus that guards the buried treasure. Those eager to reach the gold at the bottom of the sea and drink from the cauldron of immortality must fight their way through clinging, strangling tentacles and black clouds of ink, for the guardian will allow no greedy mortal to claim what belongs to the spirit alone. Yet the magical light of the ancient treasure is a beacon and a promise to those who have lost their way in life and can trust the currents of the waters to bring them safely home again.

♓

PART THREE
WORKING WITH THE CARDS

Every individual personality contains basic psychological drives—symbolized by the Sun, Moon, planets and Ascendant—which are expressed in particular ways, described by the zodiac signs in which they were placed at birth. To discover the unique astrological portrait of your own personality, lay the cards on the cloth in their appropriate places and explore the combinations of planets and signs given in Part Four. First, follow the steps given below that describe how to use the Planetary Ingress and Ascendants Tables (see page 124 *et seq.*).

Step 1: Convert your birth time to Greenwich Mean Time

The world is divided into standard time meridians (see map pages 116-7), which run east and west from the meridian of Greenwich, England (longitude 0W00). One degree of longitude equals four minutes of time. The greater the longitude one's birthplace is—i.e. the further away—east or west of Greenwich, the greater the number of hours between clock time at your birthplace and Greenwich Mean Time (GMT).

Determine the time meridian in which you were born from the Standard Time Meridians Table shown opposite. If you were born in the first half of the 20th century, it is possible that official time meridians in your area were not firmly established, and it may be necessary to consult local authorities, or an atlas of latitudes, longitudes and time changes such as *The International Atlas* or *The American Atlas*, to determine the correct time meridian.

Summer Time, Daylight Saving Time or War Time must be subtracted from the birth time before conversion into GMT. Many countries use the device of Summer Time or Daylight Saving Time to maximize daylight hours during the summer months. This involves putting the clocks forward one hour. The dates when such changes occur vary from country to country, and other factors can result in further changes during winter months. For example, in Great Britain, the combination of Summer Time and War Time between 1939 and 1945 resulted in the clocks being put forward two hours at certain times of year. If there is any doubt about what clock changes might have been in effect on the date of your birth, consult your local authority or one of the atlases mentioned above.

Standard Time Meridians Table

Find your time meridian below, then add or subtract—as indicated—the number of hours shown to or from the time of birth, to obtain the GMT at birth.

Great Britain: Standard Time Meridian = 0W00 (Greenwich Mean Time)

USA:
Eastern USA Standard Time Meridian 75W00 (Eastern Standard Time) = +5 hours
Central USA Standard Time Meridian 90W00 (Central Standard Time) = +6 hours
Midwestern USA Standard Time Meridian 105W00 (Rocky Mountain Standard Time)= +7 hours
Western USA Standard Time Meridian 120W00 (Pacific Standard Time) = +8 hours

Canada:
Standard Time Meridian 60W00 = +4 hours (New Brunswick, Nova Scotia, Prince Edward Island, part of Northwest Territories)
Standard Time Meridian 75W00 = +5 hours (Ontario, Quebec, part of Northwest Territories)
Standard Time Meridian 90W00 = +6 hours (Manitoba, part of Northwest Territories)
Standard Time Meridian 105W00 = +7 hours (Alberta, Saskatchewan, part of Northwest Territories)
Standard Time Meridian 120W00 = +8 hours (British Columbia, Yukon)

Australia:
Standard Time Meridian 120E00 = −8 hours (Western Australia)
Standard Time Meridian 142E30 = −9.30 hours (South Australia, Northern Territory)
Standard Time Meridian 150E00 = −10 hours (Victoria, Tasmania, New South Wales, Queensland, Canberra)

New Zealand: Standard Time Meridian 180E00 = −12 hours

South Africa: Standard Time Meridian 30E00 = −2 hours

Western Europe: Standard Time Meridian 15E00 (Central European Time)= −1 hour

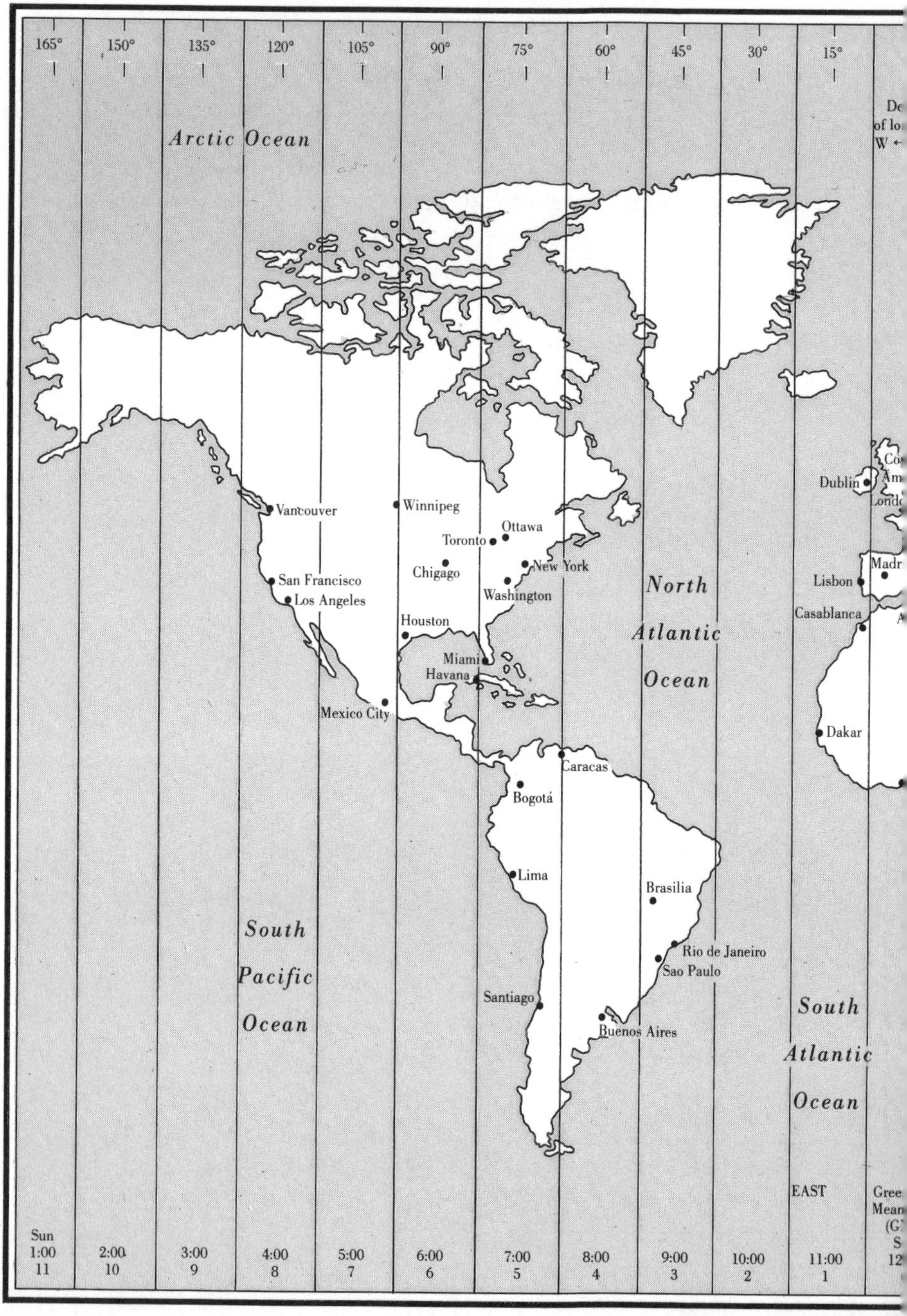
165°
150°
135°
120°
105°
90°
75°
60°
45°
30°
15°
Arctic Ocean
Vancouver
Winnipeg
Ottawa
Toronto
Chigago
New York
Washington
San Francisco
Los Angeles
Houston
Miami
Havana
Mexico City
North Atlantic Ocean
Dublin
Lisbon
Casablanca
Dakar
Caracas
Bogotá
Lima
Brasilia
Rio de Janeiro
Sao Paulo
Santiago
Buenos Aires
South Pacific Ocean
South Atlantic Ocean
EAST
Sun
1:00
11
2:00
10
3:00
9
4:00
8
5:00
7
6:00
6
7:00
5
8:00
4
9:00
3
10:00
2
11:00
1

30°
45°
60°
75°
90°
105°
120°
135°
150°
165°
180°
Arctic Ocean
North Pacific Ocean
Indian Ocean
St Petersburg
Moscow
Novosibirsk
Istanbul
Tehran
Baghdad
Damascus
Tel Aviv
Kuwait
Riyadh
Tashkent
Delhi
Karachi
Bombay
Dhaka
Calcutta
Rangoon
Bangkok
Beijing
Seoul
Tokyo
Shangai
Hong Kong
Manila
Singapore
Jakarta
Addis Ababa
Nairobi
Harare
Perth
Sydney
Melbourne
Wellington
International Date Line
W to E
subtract 24 hours
E to W
add 24 hours
International Date Line
Standard Time Meridians of the World
14:00 2
15:00 3
16:00 4
17:00 5
18:00 6
19:00 7
20:00 8
21:00 9
22:00 10
23:00 11
Sun 24:00 12
Sat 24:00 11
Sun 1:00 1

Step 2: Use the Table of Planetary Ingresses

Having obtained the GMT at your birth, you are now ready to look up the placements of your Sun, Moon and planets in the Table of Planetary Ingresses, to be found on pages 124 to 155. (For determining your Ascendant sign, see Step 3.) An ingress means an entry, and this table lists the exact times and dates of the entry of the Sun, Moon and nine planets into each new sign during the years between 1910 and 2010. The planets follow in order, with their symbols and names, from the Sun through Pluto, with the exception of the Moon whose positions are listed at the end.

As an example, we will determine the sign placements of just two planets, Saturn and the Moon, in the birth horoscope of Marilyn Monroe who was born at 9:30 A.M. on 1 June 1926 in Los Angeles, USA.

☆

Find the GMT for Marilyn's birth time. Los Angeles is in the Pacific Standard Time zone (Meridian 120W00) = +8 hours. There was no Daylight Saving Time in effect when Marilyn was born. 09:30 + 8 = 17:30 GMT.

☆

Find the page in the Table of Planetary Ingresses for the position of Saturn ♄ in June 1926 (page 133). Saturn entered Scorpio ♏ on 13 September 1924 at 22:01 GMT, and remained there until 2 December 1926 when it entered Sagittarius ♐ at 22:35 GMT. 1 June 1926, 17:30 GMT, falls between these two dates, and therefore Saturn was in Scorpio, the first of the two signs given.

☆

Find the page for the position of the Moon ☽ in June 1926 (page 137). On 31 May 1926 it entered Aquarius ♒ at 09:18 GMT, and remained there until 2 June 1926 when it entered Pisces ♓ at 11:53 GMT. 1 June 1926, 17:30 GMT, falls between these two dates, and therefore the Moon was in Aquarius, the first of the two signs given.

☆

Proceed in the same way with your own birth horoscope. As you determine the sign placements of your Sun, Moon and nine planets, list them in order on the notepad.

Step 3: Use the Table of Ascendants

The Ascendant is the east point of the horoscope where a particular sign will be rising at the time of your birth. If you have no idea of your birth time, you will be able to determine your planetary positions but not that of the Ascendant. Use the Table of Ascendants (see pages 156-163) to determine your own Ascendant sign.

The Tables of Ascendants gives a 24-hour time scale down the left-hand column and a 12-month calendar along the bottom. The point at which time and date intersect will indicate the Ascendant sign. There are four Tables, which cover the USA (Table A), Canada (Table B), Great Britain and Western Europe (Table C), Australia, New Zealand and South Africa (Table D). Choose the correct one according to your place of birth.

Because larger countries contain more than one Standard Time Meridian, we must adjust the GMT at the time of your birth. Add to—or subtract from—the GMT at your birth the number of hours indicated below. Find this adjusted time in the left-hand column of the correct Table of Ascendants.

If you were born in the USA (Table A):
Eastern Standard Time Meridian 75W00 = use GMT
Central Standard Time Meridian 90W00 = subtract 1 hour from GMT
Midwestern Standard Time Meridian 105W00 = subtract 2 hours from GMT
Western Standard Time Meridian 120W00 = subtract 3 hours from GMT

If you were born in Canada (Table B):
Standard Time Meridian 60W00 = add 1 hour to GMT
Standard Time Meridian 75W00 = use GMT
Standard Time Meridian 90W00 = subtract 1 hour from GMT
Standard Time Meridian 105W00 = subtract 2 hours from GMT
Standard Time Meridian 120W00 = subtract 3 hours from GMT

If you were born in Great Britain (Table C):
Standard Time Meridian 0W00 = use GMT

If you were born in Western Europe (Table C):
Standard Time Meridian 15E00 = add 1 hour to GMT

If you were born in Australia (Table D):
Standard Time Meridian 120E00 = subtract 2 hours from GMT
Standard Time Meridian 142E30 = subtract 30 minutes from GMT
Standard Time Meridian 150E00 = use GMT

If you were born in New Zealand (Table D):
Standard Time Meridian 180E00 = add 2 hours to GMT

If you were born in South Africa (Table D):
Standard Time Meridian 30E00 = subtract 9 hours from GMT

Then, using a ruler for accuracy, find the intersection point where your adjusted time of birth coincides with your date of birth. The diagonal sector of the graph in which this point occurs indicates your Ascendant sign. When you have found it, write it down on the notepad.

We will once again use the birth data of Marilyn Monroe as an example. We have already obtained her GMT at birth: 17:30 hours. To use the correct Table of Ascendants (USA = Table A), we must subtract 3 hours from the GMT because she was born in the Western Standard Time Meridian. This gives 14:30 hours. Look up this adjusted time in the left-hand column. The intersection point of 14:30 hours with Marilyn's birth date of 1 June indicates Leo on the Ascendant.

On page 202 can be found a description of the character qualities symbolized by Marilyn Monroe's Ascendant.

☆

Please note: Some slight inaccuracy in the the Ascendant may occur if the place of birth is a few degrees longitude east or west of the Standard Time Meridian. This may cause confusion to the reader if his or her Ascendant appears to fall between two different signs. In such cases an exact calculation is recommended, as follows. In any atlas, find the precise longitude for the place of birth. Convert this into the true local time by multiplying ×4 (1 degree of longitude = 4 minutes of time). Determine the difference between this true local time and the Standard Time Meridian. If the birth place is west of the Standard Time Meridian, subtract this difference from the newly calculated adjusted time. If the birth place is east of the Standard Time Meridian, add it. For example, Los Angeles is 118W15, and the true local time (×4) = 7 hours 53 minutes. The Western Standard Time Meridian—for Los Angeles—is 120W00 = 8 hours. This gives a difference of 7 minutes. As Los Angeles is slightly east of the Western Standard Time Meridian, this difference should be added to Marilyn's adjusted time of 14:30 hours, giving 14:37 hours for precisely determining the Ascendant.

☆

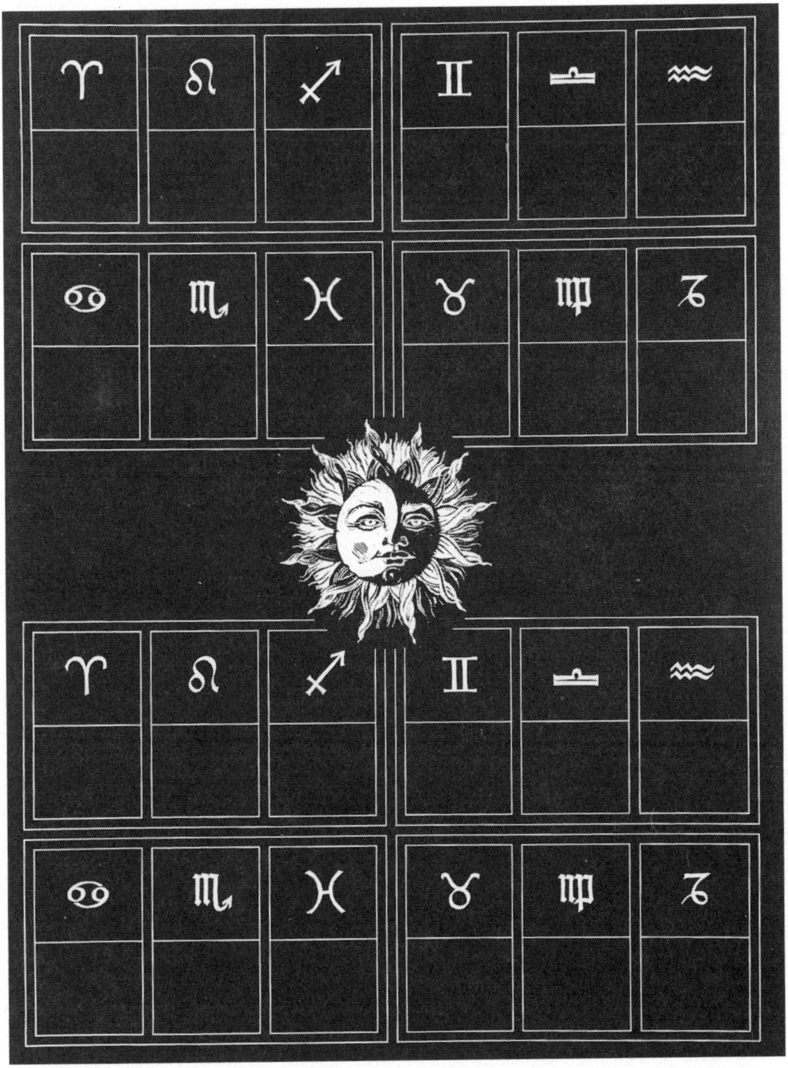

The cloth allows you to work visually with your own and another person's birth horoscope. Each zodiac sign has two spaces in which to place the appropriate sign card (above) and planet cards (below).

Step 4: Lay out the cards

Having noted the positions of your Sun, Moon, planets and Ascendant on the notepad, you are now ready to lay out the cards in their appropriate positions on the cloth.

The cards tell us a number of things about personality. In the list of combinations which follows in the next chapter, each planet is described in every sign. But the cards also reveal other qualities by their emphasis in particular elements.

To continue with our example, we have worked out the positions of the Sun, Moon, planets and Ascendant in Marilyn Monroe's birth horoscope. They are shown in the diagram opposite in their appropriate positions on the cloth.

In Marilyn's horoscope, the Sun and Mercury were in the air sign of Gemini, and Jupiter and the Moon were in Aquarius, another air sign. Mars and Uranus were in the water sign of Pisces, while Saturn was in Scorpio and Pluto in Cancer—both water signs. Venus was in the fire sign of Aries, while Neptune and the Ascendant were in Leo, also a fire sign. Of all twelve horoscope factors, only the newly discovered Chiron was in the element of earth, in the sign of Taurus.

A strong presence in any element (four or more placements) reflects an exaggeration of the attributes of that element. A weak presence in any element (one or no placements) reflects difficulties in dealing with the sphere of life symbolized by that element. We are all made differently, and the element balance simply makes an important statement about the personality, not a judgment on psychological stability or talent. Marilyn Monroe's idealism, charm and need to communicate (four planets in air), rich imagination and tendency toward self-mythologizing (two planets and Ascendant in fire) and emotional warmth and sensitivity (four planets in water) combined to produce a vibrant and charismatic personality. However, having only one planet in the element of earth, she found it difficult throughout her life to come to terms with the limits of material reality. The balance of elements tells us that Marilyn needed to shine, and longed to be loved and acknowledged by as many people as possible. She was well suited to the excitement and glamour of a film career. But she found it painful to cope with issues such as self-discipline, health, management of time and money and the inevitable limitations and disappointments of personal relationships.

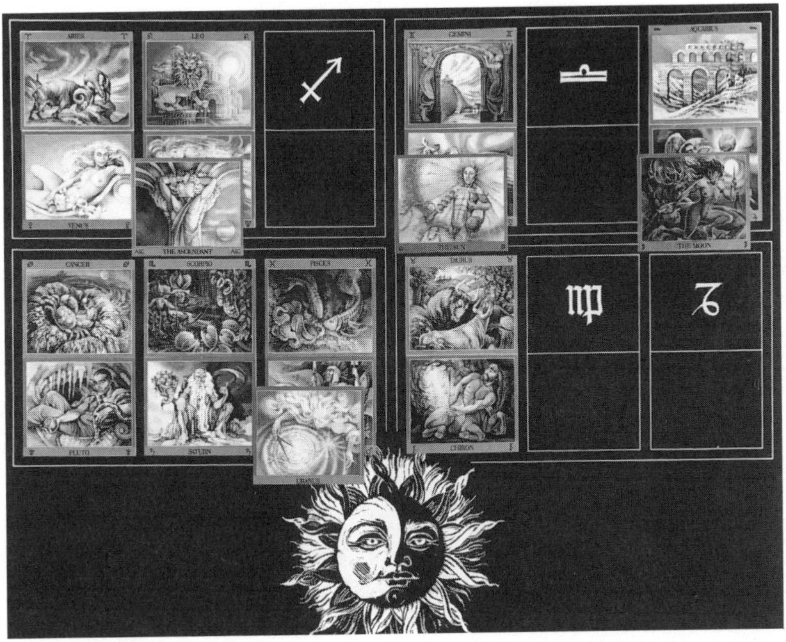

☉	Sun in Gemini	♊	♄	Saturn in Scorpio	♏
☽	Moon in Aquarius	♒	⚷	Chiron in Taurus	♉
☿	Mercury in Gemini	♊	♅	Uranus in Pisces	♓
♀	Venus in Aries	♈	♆	Neptune in Leo	♌
♂	Mars in Pisces	♓	♇	Pluto in Cancer	♋
♃	Jupiter in Aquarius	♒	ASC	Ascendant in Leo	♌

The sign and planet cards for Marilyn Monroe's birth horoscope are placed in their proper positions on the cloth. The water signs, Cancer, Scorpio and Pisces, are clearly emphasized, for Cancer and Scorpio each contains a planet, and Pisces in fact contains two. Fire is strong, with two placements in Leo and one in Aries. Air is also highlighted, with two planets in Gemini and two in Aquarius. Earth is the weakest element, with only one of the earth signs, Taurus, containing a planet. For a description of Marilyn's birth placements, see Part Four.

Table of Planetary Ingresses

☉ Sun	☉ Sun	☉ Sun	☉ Sun	☉ Sun	☉ Sun	☉ Sun
♒ 20 Jan 10 21:59	♈ 21 Mar 15 16:51	♊ 21 May 20 09:21	♌ 23 Jul 25 09:44	♎ 23 Sep 30 18:36	♐ 23 Nov 35 05:35	♒ 20 Jan 41 10:3
♓ 19 Feb 10 12:28	♉ 21 Apr 15 04:28	♋ 21 Jun 20 17:39	♍ 23 Aug 25 16:33	♏ 24 Oct 30 03:26	♑ 22 Dec 35 18:37	♓ 19 Feb 41 00:5
♈ 21 Mar 10 12:02	♊ 22 May 15 04:10	♌ 23 Jul 20 04:34	♎ 23 Sep 25 13:43	♐ 23 Nov 30 00:34	♒ 21 Jan 36 05:12	♈ 21 Mar 41 00:2
♉ 20 Apr 10 23:45	♋ 22 Jun 15 12:29	♍ 23 Aug 20 11:21	♏ 23 Oct 25 22:31	♑ 22 Dec 30 13:39	♓ 19 Feb 36 19:33	♉ 20 Apr 41 11:5
♊ 21 May 10 23:30	♌ 23 Jul 15 23:26	♎ 23 Sep 20 08:28	♐ 22 Nov 25 19:35	♒ 21 Jan 31 00:17	♈ 20 Mar 36 18:57	♊ 21 May 41 11:2
♋ 22 Jun 10 07:48	♍ 24 Aug 15 06:15	♏ 23 Oct 20 17:12	♑ 22 Dec 25 08:36	♓ 19 Feb 31 14:40	♉ 20 Apr 36 06:30	♋ 21 Jun 41 19:3
♌ 23 Jul 10 18:42	♎ 24 Sep 15 03:23	♐ 22 Nov 20 14:15	♒ 20 Jan 26 19:12	♈ 21 Mar 31 14:06	♊ 21 May 36 06:07	♌ 23 Jul 41 06:2
♍ 24 Aug 10 01:27	♏ 24 Oct 15 12:09	♑ 22 Dec 20 03:17	♓ 19 Feb 26 09:34	♉ 21 Apr 31 01:39	♋ 21 Jun 36 14:21	♍ 23 Aug 41 13:1
♎ 23 Sep 10 22:30	♐ 23 Nov 15 09:13	♒ 20 Jan 21 13:54	♈ 21 Mar 26 09:01	♊ 22 May 31 01:15	♌ 23 Jul 36 01:17	♎ 23 Sep 41 10:3
♏ 24 Oct 10 07:11	♑ 22 Dec 15 22:15	♓ 19 Feb 21 04:19	♉ 20 Apr 26 20:36	♋ 22 Jun 31 09:27	♍ 23 Aug 36 08:10	♏ 23 Oct 41 19:2
♐ 23 Nov 10 04:10	♒ 21 Jan 16 08:53	♈ 21 Mar 21 03:50	♊ 21 May 26 20:14	♌ 23 Jul 31 20:21	♎ 23 Sep 36 05:26	♐ 22 Nov 41 16:3
♑ 22 Dec 10 17:11	♓ 19 Feb 16 23:17	♉ 20 Apr 21 15:32	♋ 22 Jun 26 04:29	♍ 24 Aug 31 03:10	♏ 23 Oct 36 14:18	♑ 22 Dec 41 05:4
♒ 21 Jan 11 03:51	♈ 20 Mar 16 22:46	♊ 21 May 21 15:16	♌ 23 Jul 26 15:24	♎ 24 Sep 31 00:23	♐ 22 Nov 36 11:25	♒ 20 Jan 42 16:2
♓ 19 Feb 11 18:20	♉ 20 Apr 16 10:24	♋ 21 Jun 21 23:35	♍ 23 Aug 26 22:14	♏ 24 Oct 31 09:15	♑ 22 Dec 36 00:26	♓ 19 Feb 42 06:4
♈ 21 Mar 11 17:54	♊ 21 May 16 10:05	♌ 23 Jul 21 10:30	♎ 23 Sep 26 19:26	♐ 23 Nov 31 06:24	♒ 20 Jan 37 11:01	♈ 21 Mar 42 06:1
♉ 21 Apr 11 05:35	♋ 21 Jun 16 18:24	♍ 23 Aug 21 17:15	♏ 24 Oct 26 04:18	♑ 22 Dec 31 19:29	♓ 19 Feb 37 01:20	♉ 20 Apr 42 17:3
♊ 22 May 11 05:18	♌ 23 Jul 16 05:21	♎ 23 Sep 21 14:19	♐ 23 Nov 26 01:27	♒ 21 Jan 32 06:06	♈ 21 Mar 37 00:44	♊ 21 May 42 17:0
♋ 22 Jun 11 13:35	♍ 23 Aug 16 12:08	♏ 23 Oct 21 23:02	♑ 22 Dec 26 14:33	♓ 19 Feb 32 20:28	♉ 20 Apr 37 12:19	♋ 22 Jun 42 01:1
♌ 24 Jul 11 00:28	♎ 23 Sep 16 09:14	♐ 22 Nov 21 20:04	♒ 21 Jan 27 01:11	♈ 20 Mar 32 19:53	♊ 21 May 37 11:57	♌ 23 Jul 42 12:0
♍ 24 Aug 11 07:13	♏ 23 Oct 16 17:57	♑ 22 Dec 21 09:07	♓ 19 Feb 27 15:34	♉ 20 Apr 32 07:27	♋ 21 Jun 37 20:11	♍ 23 Aug 42 18:5
♎ 24 Sep 11 04:17	♐ 22 Nov 16 14:57	♒ 20 Jan 22 19:47	♈ 21 Mar 27 14:59	♊ 21 May 32 07:06	♌ 23 Jul 37 07:06	♎ 23 Sep 42 16:1
♏ 24 Oct 11 12:58	♑ 22 Dec 16 03:58	♓ 19 Feb 22 10:16	♉ 21 Apr 27 02:31	♋ 21 Jun 32 15:22	♍ 23 Aug 37 13:57	♏ 24 Oct 42 01:1
♐ 23 Nov 11 09:55	♒ 20 Jan 17 14:37	♈ 21 Mar 22 09:48	♊ 22 May 27 02:07	♌ 23 Jul 32 02:17	♎ 23 Sep 37 11:12	♐ 22 Nov 42 22:3
♑ 22 Dec 11 22:53	♓ 19 Feb 17 05:04	♉ 20 Apr 22 21:28	♋ 22 Jun 27 10:22	♍ 23 Aug 32 09:06	♏ 23 Oct 37 20:06	♑ 22 Dec 42 11:3
♒ 21 Jan 12 09:29	♈ 21 Mar 17 04:37	♊ 21 May 22 21:10	♌ 23 Jul 27 21:16	♎ 23 Sep 32 06:15	♐ 22 Nov 37 17:16	♒ 20 Jan 43 22:1
♓ 19 Feb 12 23:55	♉ 20 Apr 17 16:17	♋ 22 Jun 22 05:26	♍ 24 Aug 27 04:05	♏ 23 Oct 32 15:03	♑ 22 Dec 37 06:21	♓ 19 Feb 43 12:4
♈ 20 Mar 12 23:29	♊ 21 May 17 15:58	♌ 23 Jul 22 16:19	♎ 24 Sep 27 01:17	♐ 22 Nov 32 12:10	♒ 20 Jan 38 16:58	♈ 21 Mar 43 12:0
♉ 20 Apr 12 11:12	♋ 22 Jun 17 00:14	♍ 23 Aug 22 23:04	♏ 24 Oct 27 10:06	♑ 22 Dec 32 01:14	♓ 19 Feb 38 07:19	♉ 20 Apr 43 23:3
♊ 21 May 12 10:57	♌ 23 Jul 17 11:07	♎ 23 Sep 22 20:09	♐ 23 Nov 27 07:14	♒ 20 Jan 33 11:52	♈ 21 Mar 38 06:42	♊ 21 May 43 23:0
♋ 21 Jun 12 19:16	♍ 23 Aug 17 17:53	♏ 24 Oct 22 04:52	♑ 22 Dec 27 20:18	♓ 19 Feb 33 02:16	♉ 20 Apr 38 18:14	♋ 22 Jun 43 07:12
♌ 23 Jul 12 06:13	♎ 23 Sep 17 15:00	♐ 23 Nov 22 01:55	♒ 21 Jan 28 06:56	♈ 21 Mar 33 01:43	♊ 21 May 38 17:50	♌ 23 Jul 43 18:04
♍ 23 Aug 12 13:01	♏ 23 Oct 17 23:43	♑ 22 Dec 22 14:56	♓ 19 Feb 28 21:19	♉ 20 Apr 33 13:18	♋ 22 Jun 38 02:03	♍ 24 Aug 43 00:5
♎ 23 Sep 12 10:08	♐ 22 Nov 17 20:44	♒ 21 Jan 23 01:34	♈ 20 Mar 28 20:44	♊ 21 May 33 12:56	♌ 23 Jul 38 12:57	♎ 23 Sep 43 22:11
♏ 23 Oct 12 18:50	♑ 22 Dec 17 09:45	♓ 19 Feb 23 15:59	♉ 20 Apr 28 08:16	♋ 21 Jun 33 21:11	♍ 23 Aug 38 19:45	♏ 24 Oct 43 07:08
♐ 22 Nov 12 15:48	♒ 20 Jan 18 20:24	♈ 21 Mar 23 15:28	♊ 21 May 28 07:52	♌ 23 Jul 33 08:05	♎ 23 Sep 38 16:59	♐ 23 Nov 43 04:21
♑ 22 Dec 12 04:44	♓ 19 Feb 18 10:52	♉ 21 Apr 23 03:05	♋ 21 Jun 28 16:06	♍ 23 Aug 33 14:52	♏ 24 Oct 38 01:53	♑ 22 Dec 43 17:2
♒ 20 Jan 13 15:19	♈ 21 Mar 18 10:25	♊ 22 May 23 02:45	♌ 23 Jul 28 03:02	♎ 23 Sep 33 12:01	♐ 22 Nov 38 23:06	♒ 21 Jan 44 04:07
♓ 19 Feb 13 05:44	♉ 20 Apr 18 22:05	♋ 22 Jun 23 11:02	♍ 23 Aug 28 09:53	♏ 23 Oct 33 20:48	♑ 22 Dec 38 12:13	♓ 19 Feb 44 18:27
♈ 21 Mar 13 05:17	♊ 21 May 18 21:45	♌ 23 Jul 23 22:00	♎ 23 Sep 28 07:05	♐ 22 Nov 33 17:53	♒ 20 Jan 39 22:50	♈ 20 Mar 44 17:48
♉ 20 Apr 13 17:02	♋ 22 Jun 18 05:59	♍ 24 Aug 23 04:51	♏ 23 Oct 28 15:54	♑ 22 Dec 33 06:57	♓ 19 Feb 39 13:09	♉ 20 Apr 44 05:17
♊ 21 May 13 16:49	♌ 23 Jul 18 16:51	♎ 24 Sep 23 02:03	♐ 22 Nov 28 13:00	♒ 20 Jan 34 17:36	♈ 21 Mar 39 12:28	♊ 21 May 44 04:50
♋ 22 Jun 13 01:09	♍ 23 Aug 18 23:37	♏ 24 Oct 23 10:50	♑ 22 Dec 28 02:03	♓ 19 Feb 34 08:01	♉ 20 Apr 39 23:54	♋ 21 Jun 44 13:02
♌ 23 Jul 13 12:03	♎ 23 Sep 18 20:45	♐ 23 Nov 23 07:53	♒ 20 Jan 29 12:42	♈ 21 Mar 34 07:27	♊ 21 May 39 23:26	♌ 22 Jul 44 23:55
♍ 23 Aug 13 18:48	♏ 24 Oct 18 05:32	♑ 22 Dec 23 20:53	♓ 19 Feb 29 03:06	♉ 20 Apr 34 19:00	♋ 22 Jun 39 07:39	♍ 23 Aug 44 06:46
♎ 23 Sep 13 15:52	♐ 23 Nov 18 02:38	♒ 21 Jan 24 07:28	♈ 21 Mar 29 02:34	♊ 21 May 34 18:34	♌ 23 Jul 39 18:36	♎ 23 Sep 44 04:01
♏ 24 Oct 13 00:34	♑ 22 Dec 18 15:41	♓ 19 Feb 24 21:51	♉ 20 Apr 29 14:10	♋ 22 Jun 34 02:47	♍ 24 Aug 39 01:31	♏ 23 Oct 44 12:56
♐ 22 Nov 13 21:35	♒ 21 Jan 19 02:20	♈ 20 Mar 24 21:20	♊ 21 May 29 13:47	♌ 23 Jul 34 13:42	♎ 23 Sep 39 22:49	♐ 22 Nov 44 10:07
♑ 22 Dec 13 10:34	♓ 19 Feb 19 16:47	♉ 20 Apr 24 08:58	♋ 21 Jun 29 22:00	♍ 23 Aug 34 20:32	♏ 24 Oct 39 07:45	♑ 21 Dec 44 23:14
♒ 20 Jan 14 21:11	♈ 21 Mar 19 16:18	♊ 21 May 24 08:40	♌ 23 Jul 29 08:53	♎ 23 Sep 34 17:45	♐ 23 Nov 39 04:58	♒ 20 Jan 45 09:53
♓ 19 Feb 14 11:37	♉ 21 Apr 19 03:58	♋ 21 Jun 24 16:59	♍ 23 Aug 29 15:41	♏ 24 Oct 34 02:36	♑ 22 Dec 39 18:06	♓ 19 Feb 45 00:14
♈ 21 Mar 14 11:10	♊ 22 May 19 03:38	♌ 23 Jul 24 03:57	♎ 23 Sep 29 12:52	♐ 22 Nov 34 23:44	♒ 21 Jan 40 04:44	♈ 20 Mar 45 23:37
♉ 20 Apr 14 22:53	♋ 22 Jun 19 11:53	♍ 23 Aug 24 10:47	♏ 23 Oct 29 21:41	♑ 22 Dec 34 12:49	♓ 19 Feb 40 19:03	♉ 20 Apr 45 11:06
♊ 21 May 14 22:37	♌ 23 Jul 19 22:44	♎ 23 Sep 24 07:58	♐ 22 Nov 29 18:48	♒ 20 Jan 35 23:28	♈ 20 Mar 40 18:23	♊ 21 May 45 10:40
♋ 22 Jun 14 06:54	♍ 24 Aug 19 05:28	♏ 23 Oct 24 16:44	♑ 22 Dec 29 07:52	♓ 19 Feb 35 13:51	♉ 20 Apr 40 05:50	♋ 21 Jun 45 18:51
♌ 23 Jul 14 17:46	♎ 24 Sep 19 02:35	♐ 22 Nov 24 13:46	♒ 20 Jan 30 18:33	♈ 21 Mar 35 13:17	♊ 21 May 40 05:22	♌ 23 Jul 45 05:45
♍ 24 Aug 14 00:29	♏ 24 Oct 19 11:21	♑ 22 Dec 24 02:45	♓ 19 Feb 30 08:59	♉ 21 Apr 35 00:49	♋ 21 Jun 40 13:36	♍ 23 Aug 45 12:35
♎ 23 Sep 14 21:33	♐ 23 Nov 19 08:25	♒ 20 Jan 25 13:20	♈ 21 Mar 30 08:29	♊ 22 May 35 00:24	♌ 23 Jul 40 00:34	♎ 23 Sep 45 09:49
♏ 24 Oct 14 06:17	♑ 22 Dec 19 21:27	♓ 19 Feb 25 03:43	♉ 20 Apr 30 20:05	♋ 22 Jun 35 08:37	♍ 23 Aug 40 07:28	♏ 23 Oct 45 18:43
♐ 23 Nov 14 03:20	♒ 21 Jan 20 08:04	♈ 21 Mar 25 03:12	♊ 21 May 30 19:41	♌ 23 Jul 35 19:32	♎ 23 Sep 40 04:45	♐ 22 Nov 45 15:55
♑ 22 Dec 14 16:22	♓ 19 Feb 20 22:28	♉ 20 Apr 25 14:51	♋ 22 Jun 30 03:52	♍ 24 Aug 35 02:24	♏ 23 Oct 40 13:39	♑ 22 Dec 45 05:03
♒ 21 Jan 15 02:59	♈ 20 Mar 20 21:59	♊ 21 May 25 14:32	♌ 23 Jul 30 14:41	♎ 23 Sep 35 23:38	♐ 22 Nov 40 10:49	♒ 20 Jan 46 15:44
♓ 19 Feb 15 17:22	♉ 20 Apr 20 09:38	♋ 21 Jun 25 22:49	♍ 23 Aug 30 21:26	♏ 24 Oct 35 08:29	♑ 21 Dec 40 23:54	♓ 19 Feb 46 06:08

Sun	⊙ Sun	⊙ Sun	⊙ Sun	⊙ Sun	⊙ Sun	⊙ Sun
21 Mar 46 05:32	♊ 21 May 52 03:03	♌ 23 Jul 58 08:50	♎ 23 Sep 64 00:16	♐ 22 Nov 70 17:24	♒ 20 Jan 77 04:14	♈ 21 Mar 83 04:38
20 Apr 46 17:02	♋ 21 Jun 52 11:12	♍ 23 Aug 58 15:46	♏ 23 Oct 64 09:20	♑ 22 Dec 70 06:35	♓ 18 Feb 77 18:30	♉ 20 Apr 83 15:50
21 May 46 16:33	♌ 22 Jul 52 22:07	♎ 23 Sep 58 13:09	♐ 22 Nov 64 06:39	♒ 20 Jan 71 17:12	♈ 20 Mar 77 17:42	♊ 21 May 83 15:06
22 Jun 46 00:44	♍ 23 Aug 52 05:02	♏ 23 Oct 58 22:11	♑ 21 Dec 64 19:49	♓ 19 Feb 71 07:27	♉ 20 Apr 77 04:57	♋ 21 Jun 83 23:08
23 Jul 46 11:37	♎ 23 Sep 52 02:23	♐ 22 Nov 58 19:29	♒ 20 Jan 65 06:29	♈ 21 Mar 71 06:38	♊ 21 May 77 04:14	♌ 23 Jul 83 10:04
23 Aug 46 18:26	♏ 23 Oct 52 11:22	♑ 22 Dec 58 08:39	♓ 18 Feb 65 20:47	♉ 20 Apr 71 17:54	♋ 21 Jun 77 12:13	♍ 23 Aug 83 17:07
23 Sep 46 15:40	♐ 22 Nov 52 08:35	♒ 20 Jan 59 19:19	♈ 20 Mar 65 20:04	♊ 21 May 71 17:14	♌ 22 Jul 77 23:03	♎ 23 Sep 83 14:41
24 Oct 46 00:34	♑ 21 Dec 52 21:43	♓ 19 Feb 59 09:37	♉ 20 Apr 65 07:26	♋ 22 Jun 71 01:19	♍ 23 Aug 77 06:00	♏ 23 Oct 83 23:54
22 Nov 46 21:46	♒ 20 Jan 53 08:21	♈ 21 Mar 59 08:54	♊ 21 May 65 06:50	♌ 23 Jul 71 12:14	♎ 23 Sep 77 03:29	♐ 22 Nov 83 21:18
22 Dec 46 10:53	♓ 18 Feb 53 22:41	♉ 20 Apr 59 20:16	♋ 21 Jun 65 14:55	♍ 23 Aug 71 19:15	♏ 23 Oct 77 12:40	♑ 22 Dec 83 10:30
20 Jan 47 21:31	♈ 20 Mar 53 22:00	♊ 21 May 59 19:42	♌ 23 Jul 65 01:48	♎ 23 Sep 71 16:45	♐ 22 Nov 77 10:07	♒ 20 Jan 84 21:05
19 Feb 47 11:51	♉ 20 Apr 53 09:25	♋ 22 Jun 59 03:49	♍ 23 Aug 65 08:42	♏ 24 Oct 71 01:53	♑ 21 Dec 77 23:23	♓ 19 Feb 84 11:16
21 Mar 47 11:12	♊ 21 May 53 08:52	♌ 23 Jul 59 14:45	♎ 23 Sep 65 06:06	♐ 22 Nov 71 23:14	♒ 20 Jan 78 10:04	♈ 20 Mar 84 10:24
20 Apr 47 22:39	♋ 21 Jun 53 16:59	♍ 23 Aug 59 21:43	♏ 23 Oct 65 15:10	♑ 22 Dec 71 12:24	♓ 19 Feb 78 00:21	♉ 19 Apr 84 21:38
21 May 47 22:08	♌ 23 Jul 53 03:52	♎ 23 Sep 59 19:08	♐ 22 Nov 65 12:29	♒ 20 Jan 72 22:59	♈ 20 Mar 78 23:33	♊ 20 May 84 20:57
22 Jun 47 06:18	♍ 23 Aug 53 10:45	♏ 24 Oct 59 04:11	♑ 22 Dec 65 01:40	♓ 19 Feb 72 13:11	♉ 20 Apr 78 10:49	♋ 21 Jun 84 05:02
23 Jul 47 17:14	♎ 23 Sep 53 08:06	♐ 23 Nov 59 01:27	♒ 20 Jan 66 12:19	♈ 20 Mar 72 12:21	♊ 21 May 78 10:08	♌ 22 Jul 84 15:58
24 Aug 47 00:09	♏ 23 Oct 53 17:06	♑ 22 Dec 59 14:34	♓ 19 Feb 66 02:37	♉ 19 Apr 72 23:37	♋ 21 Jun 78 18:09	♍ 22 Aug 84 23:00
23 Sep 47 21:28	♐ 22 Nov 53 14:22	♒ 21 Jan 60 01:10	♈ 21 Mar 66 01:53	♊ 20 May 72 22:59	♌ 23 Jul 78 05:00	♎ 22 Sep 84 20:33
24 Oct 47 06:26	♑ 22 Dec 53 03:31	♓ 19 Feb 60 15:26	♉ 20 Apr 66 13:11	♋ 21 Jun 72 07:06	♍ 23 Aug 78 11:56	♏ 23 Oct 84 05:46
23 Nov 47 03:37	♒ 20 Jan 54 14:11	♈ 20 Mar 60 14:42	♊ 21 May 66 12:31	♌ 22 Jul 72 18:02	♎ 23 Sep 78 09:25	♐ 22 Nov 84 03:11
22 Dec 47 16:42	♓ 19 Feb 54 04:32	♉ 20 Apr 60 02:05	♋ 21 Jun 66 20:33	♍ 23 Aug 72 01:03	♏ 23 Oct 78 18:37	♑ 21 Dec 84 16:23
21 Jan 48 03:18	♈ 21 Mar 54 03:53	♊ 21 May 60 01:33	♌ 23 Jul 66 07:23	♎ 22 Sep 72 22:32	♐ 22 Nov 78 16:04	♒ 20 Jan 85 02:57
19 Feb 48 17:36	♉ 20 Apr 54 15:19	♋ 21 Jun 60 09:42	♍ 23 Aug 66 14:17	♏ 23 Oct 72 07:41	♑ 22 Dec 78 05:21	♓ 18 Feb 85 17:07
20 Mar 48 16:56	♊ 21 May 54 14:47	♌ 22 Jul 60 20:37	♎ 23 Sep 66 11:43	♐ 22 Nov 72 05:02	♒ 20 Jan 79 16:00	♈ 20 Mar 85 16:13
20 Apr 48 04:24	♋ 21 Jun 54 22:53	♍ 23 Aug 60 03:34	♏ 23 Oct 66 20:51	♑ 21 Dec 72 18:13	♓ 19 Feb 79 06:13	♉ 20 Apr 85 03:25
21 May 48 03:57	♌ 23 Jul 54 09:44	♎ 23 Sep 60 00:59	♐ 22 Nov 66 18:14	♒ 20 Jan 73 04:48	♈ 21 Mar 79 05:22	♊ 21 May 85 02:42
21 Jun 48 12:10	♍ 23 Aug 54 16:36	♏ 23 Oct 60 10:02	♑ 22 Dec 66 07:28	♓ 18 Feb 73 19:01	♉ 20 Apr 79 16:35	♋ 21 Jun 85 10:44
22 Jul 48 23:07	♎ 23 Sep 54 13:55	♐ 22 Nov 60 07:18	♒ 20 Jan 67 18:07	♈ 20 Mar 73 18:12	♊ 21 May 79 15:53	♌ 22 Jul 85 21:36
23 Aug 48 06:02	♏ 23 Oct 54 22:56	♑ 21 Dec 60 20:26	♓ 19 Feb 67 08:23	♉ 20 Apr 73 05:30	♋ 21 Jun 79 23:56	♍ 23 Aug 85 04:35
23 Sep 48 03:21	♐ 22 Nov 54 20:14	♒ 20 Jan 61 07:01	♈ 21 Mar 67 07:36	♊ 21 May 73 04:53	♌ 23 Jul 79 10:48	♎ 23 Sep 85 02:07
23 Oct 48 12:18	♑ 22 Dec 54 09:24	♓ 18 Feb 61 21:16	♉ 20 Apr 67 18:55	♋ 21 Jun 73 13:00	♍ 23 Aug 79 17:46	♏ 23 Oct 85 11:22
22 Nov 48 09:29	♒ 20 Jan 55 20:02	♈ 20 Mar 61 20:32	♊ 21 May 67 18:17	♌ 22 Jul 73 23:55	♎ 23 Sep 79 15:16	♐ 22 Nov 85 08:51
21 Dec 48 22:33	♓ 19 Feb 55 10:18	♉ 20 Apr 61 07:55	♋ 22 Jun 67 02:22	♍ 23 Aug 73 06:53	♏ 24 Oct 79 00:28	♑ 21 Dec 85 22:08
20 Jan 49 09:08	♈ 21 Mar 55 09:35	♊ 21 May 61 07:22	♌ 23 Jul 67 13:15	♎ 23 Sep 73 04:21	♐ 22 Nov 79 21:54	♒ 20 Jan 86 08:46
18 Feb 49 23:27	♉ 20 Apr 55 20:57	♋ 21 Jun 61 15:30	♍ 23 Aug 67 20:12	♏ 23 Oct 73 13:30	♑ 22 Dec 79 11:10	♓ 18 Feb 86 22:57
20 Mar 49 22:48	♊ 21 May 55 20:24	♌ 23 Jul 61 02:23	♎ 23 Sep 67 17:38	♐ 22 Nov 73 10:54	♒ 20 Jan 80 21:48	♈ 20 Mar 86 22:02
20 Apr 49 10:17	♋ 22 Jun 55 04:31	♍ 23 Aug 61 09:18	♏ 24 Oct 67 02:44	♑ 22 Dec 73 00:08	♓ 19 Feb 80 12:01	♉ 20 Apr 86 09:12
21 May 49 09:50	♌ 23 Jul 55 15:24	♎ 23 Sep 61 06:42	♐ 23 Nov 67 00:04	♒ 20 Jan 74 10:45	♈ 20 Mar 80 11:09	♊ 21 May 86 08:27
21 Jun 49 18:02	♍ 23 Aug 55 22:18	♏ 23 Oct 61 15:47	♑ 22 Dec 67 13:16	♓ 19 Feb 74 00:58	♉ 19 Apr 80 22:22	♋ 21 Jun 86 16:30
23 Jul 49 04:56	♎ 23 Sep 55 19:41	♐ 22 Nov 61 13:07	♒ 20 Jan 68 23:54	♈ 21 Mar 74 00:06	♊ 20 May 80 21:42	♌ 23 Jul 86 03:24
23 Aug 49 11:48	♏ 24 Oct 55 04:43	♑ 22 Dec 61 02:19	♓ 19 Feb 68 14:09	♉ 20 Apr 74 11:18	♋ 21 Jun 80 05:47	♍ 23 Aug 86 10:26
23 Sep 49 09:06	♐ 23 Nov 55 02:01	♒ 20 Jan 62 12:58	♈ 20 Mar 68 13:22	♊ 21 May 74 10:36	♌ 22 Jul 80 16:42	♎ 23 Sep 86 07:59
23 Oct 49 18:03	♑ 22 Dec 55 15:11	♓ 19 Feb 62 03:14	♉ 20 Apr 68 00:41	♋ 21 Jun 74 18:37	♍ 22 Aug 80 23:40	♏ 23 Oct 86 17:14
22 Nov 49 15:16	♒ 21 Jan 56 01:48	♈ 21 Mar 62 02:29	♊ 21 May 68 00:05	♌ 23 Jul 74 05:30	♎ 22 Sep 80 21:08	♐ 22 Nov 86 14:44
22 Dec 49 04:23	♓ 19 Feb 56 16:04	♉ 20 Apr 62 13:50	♋ 21 Jun 68 08:13	♍ 23 Aug 74 12:28	♏ 23 Oct 80 06:17	♑ 22 Dec 86 04:02
20 Jan 50 14:59	♈ 20 Mar 56 15:20	♊ 21 May 62 13:16	♌ 22 Jul 68 19:07	♎ 23 Sep 74 09:58	♐ 22 Nov 80 03:41	♒ 20 Jan 87 14:40
19 Feb 50 05:17	♉ 20 Apr 56 02:43	♋ 21 Jun 62 21:24	♍ 23 Aug 68 02:03	♏ 23 Oct 74 19:10	♑ 21 Dec 80 16:56	♓ 19 Feb 87 04:50
21 Mar 50 04:35	♊ 21 May 56 02:12	♌ 23 Jul 62 08:18	♎ 22 Sep 68 23:26	♐ 22 Nov 74 16:38	♒ 20 Jan 81 03:36	♈ 21 Mar 87 03:52
20 Apr 50 15:59	♋ 21 Jun 56 10:23	♍ 23 Aug 62 15:12	♏ 23 Oct 68 08:29	♑ 22 Dec 74 05:56	♓ 18 Feb 81 17:51	♉ 20 Apr 87 14:57
21 May 50 15:27	♌ 22 Jul 56 21:19	♎ 23 Sep 62 12:35	♐ 22 Nov 68 05:48	♒ 20 Jan 75 16:36	♈ 20 Mar 81 17:03	♊ 21 May 87 14:10
21 Jun 50 23:36	♍ 23 Aug 56 04:14	♏ 23 Oct 62 21:40	♑ 21 Dec 68 19:00	♓ 19 Feb 75 06:49	♉ 20 Apr 81 04:18	♋ 21 Jun 87 22:10
23 Jul 50 10:29	♎ 23 Sep 56 01:35	♐ 22 Nov 62 19:02	♒ 20 Jan 69 05:38	♈ 21 Mar 75 05:56	♊ 21 May 81 03:39	♌ 23 Jul 87 09:06
23 Aug 50 17:23	♏ 23 Oct 56 10:34	♑ 22 Dec 62 08:15	♓ 18 Feb 69 19:54	♉ 20 Apr 75 17:07	♋ 21 Jun 81 11:44	♍ 23 Aug 87 16:10
23 Sep 50 14:43	♐ 22 Nov 56 07:50	♒ 20 Jan 63 18:54	♈ 20 Mar 69 19:08	♊ 21 May 75 16:23	♌ 22 Jul 81 22:39	♎ 23 Sep 87 13:45
23 Oct 50 23:44	♑ 21 Dec 56 20:59	♓ 19 Feb 63 09:08	♉ 20 Apr 69 06:26	♋ 22 Jun 75 00:26	♍ 23 Aug 81 05:38	♏ 23 Oct 87 23:01
22 Nov 50 21:02	♒ 20 Jan 57 07:38	♈ 21 Mar 63 08:19	♊ 21 May 69 05:49	♌ 23 Jul 75 11:21	♎ 23 Sep 81 03:05	♐ 22 Nov 87 20:29
22 Dec 50 10:13	♓ 18 Feb 57 21:58	♉ 20 Apr 63 19:36	♋ 21 Jun 69 13:55	♍ 23 Aug 75 18:23	♏ 23 Oct 81 12:13	♑ 22 Dec 87 09:46
20 Jan 51 20:52	♈ 20 Mar 57 21:16	♊ 21 May 63 18:58	♌ 23 Jul 69 00:48	♎ 23 Sep 75 15:55	♐ 22 Nov 81 09:36	♒ 20 Jan 88 20:24
19 Feb 51 11:09	♉ 20 Apr 57 08:41	♋ 22 Jun 63 03:03	♍ 23 Aug 69 07:43	♏ 24 Oct 75 01:06	♑ 21 Dec 81 22:50	♓ 19 Feb 88 10:35
21 Mar 51 10:25	♊ 21 May 57 08:10	♌ 23 Jul 63 13:59	♎ 23 Sep 69 05:07	♐ 22 Nov 75 22:31	♒ 20 Jan 82 09:31	♈ 20 Mar 88 09:38
20 Apr 51 21:48	♋ 21 Jun 57 16:20	♍ 23 Aug 63 20:57	♏ 23 Oct 69 14:11	♑ 22 Dec 75 11:45	♓ 18 Feb 82 23:46	♉ 19 Apr 88 20:44
21 May 51 21:15	♌ 23 Jul 57 03:14	♎ 23 Sep 63 18:23	♐ 22 Nov 69 11:31	♒ 20 Jan 76 22:25	♈ 20 Mar 82 22:55	♊ 20 May 88 19:56
22 Jun 51 05:24	♍ 23 Aug 57 10:07	♏ 24 Oct 63 03:29	♑ 22 Dec 69 00:43	♓ 19 Feb 76 12:40	♉ 20 Apr 82 10:07	♋ 21 Jun 88 03:56
23 Jul 51 16:20	♎ 23 Sep 57 07:26	♐ 23 Nov 63 00:49	♒ 20 Jan 70 11:24	♈ 20 Mar 76 11:49	♊ 21 May 82 09:22	♌ 22 Jul 88 14:51
23 Aug 51 23:16	♏ 23 Oct 57 16:24	♑ 22 Dec 63 14:02	♓ 19 Feb 70 01:41	♉ 19 Apr 76 23:02	♋ 21 Jun 82 17:23	♍ 22 Aug 88 21:54
23 Sep 51 20:37	♐ 22 Nov 57 13:39	♒ 21 Jan 64 00:41	♈ 21 Mar 70 00:56	♊ 20 May 76 22:21	♌ 23 Jul 82 04:15	♎ 22 Sep 88 19:29
24 Oct 51 05:36	♑ 22 Dec 57 02:48	♓ 19 Feb 64 14:57	♉ 20 Apr 70 12:14	♋ 21 Jun 76 06:24	♍ 23 Aug 82 11:15	♏ 23 Oct 88 04:44
23 Nov 51 02:51	♒ 20 Jan 58 13:28	♈ 20 Mar 64 14:09	♊ 21 May 70 11:37	♌ 22 Jul 76 17:18	♎ 23 Sep 82 08:46	♐ 22 Nov 88 02:12
22 Dec 51 16:00	♓ 19 Feb 58 03:48	♉ 20 Apr 64 01:27	♋ 21 Jun 70 19:42	♍ 23 Aug 76 00:18	♏ 23 Oct 82 17:58	♑ 21 Dec 88 15:28
21 Jan 52 02:38	♈ 21 Mar 58 03:05	♊ 21 May 64 00:49	♌ 23 Jul 70 06:36	♎ 22 Sep 76 21:48	♐ 22 Nov 82 15:23	♒ 20 Jan 89 02:07
19 Feb 52 16:56	♉ 20 Apr 58 14:26	♋ 21 Jun 64 08:56	♍ 23 Aug 70 13:34	♏ 23 Oct 76 06:58	♑ 22 Dec 82 04:38	♓ 18 Feb 89 16:20
20 Mar 52 16:13	♊ 21 May 58 13:50	♌ 22 Jul 64 19:52	♎ 23 Sep 70 10:59	♐ 22 Nov 76 04:21	♒ 20 Jan 83 15:17	♈ 20 Mar 89 15:28
20 Apr 52 03:36	♋ 21 Jun 58 21:56	♍ 23 Aug 64 02:51	♏ 23 Oct 70 20:04	♑ 21 Dec 76 17:35	♓ 19 Feb 83 05:30	♉ 20 Apr 89 02:38

☉ Sun

♊ 21 May89 01:53
♋ 21 Jun 89 09:53
♌ 22 Jul 89 20:45
♍ 23 Aug89 03:46
♎ 23 Sep 89 01:19
♏ 23 Oct 89 10:35
♐ 22 Nov89 08:04
♑ 21 Dec89 21:22
♒ 20 Jan 90 08:01
♓ 18 Feb 90 22:14
♈ 20 Mar90 21:19
♉ 20 Apr90 08:26
♊ 21 May90 07:37
♋ 21 Jun 90 15:32
♌ 23 Jul 90 02:21
♍ 23 Aug90 09:21
♎ 23 Sep 90 06:55
♏ 23 Oct 90 16:14
♐ 22 Nov90 13:47
♑ 22 Dec 90 03:07
♒ 20 Jan 91 13:47
♓ 19 Feb 91 03:58
♈ 21 Mar91 03:02
♉ 20 Apr91 14:08
♊ 21 May91 13:20
♋ 21 Jun 91 21:18
♌ 23 Jul 91 08:11
♍ 23 Aug91 15:13
♎ 23 Sep 91 12:48
♏ 23 Oct 91 22:05
♐ 22 Nov91 19:36
♑ 22 Dec91 08:53
♒ 20 Jan 92 19:32
♓ 19 Feb 92 09:43
♈ 20 Mar92 08:48
♉ 19 Apr92 19:56
♊ 20 May92 19:12
♋ 21 Jun 92 03:14
♌ 22 Jul 92 14:08
♍ 22 Aug92 21:10
♎ 22 Sep 92 18:43
♏ 23 Oct 92 03:57
♐ 22 Nov92 01:26
♑ 21 Dec92 14:43
♒ 20 Jan 93 01:23
♓ 18 Feb 93 15:35
♈ 20 Mar93 14:40
♉ 20 Apr93 01:49
♊ 21 May93 01:01
♋ 21 Jun 93 08:59
♌ 22 Jul 93 19:50
♍ 23 Aug93 02:50
♎ 23 Sep 93 00:22
♏ 23 Oct 93 09:37
♐ 22 Nov93 07:07
♑ 21 Dec93 20:26
♒ 20 Jan 94 07:07
♓ 18 Feb 94 21:21
♈ 20 Mar94 20:28
♉ 20 Apr 94 07:36
♊ 21 May94 06:48
♋ 21 Jun 94 14:47
♌ 23 Jul 94 01:41
♍ 23 Aug94 08:43
♎ 23 Sep 94 06:19
♏ 23 Oct 94 15:36
♐ 22 Nov94 13:06
♑ 22 Dec94 02:23
♒ 20 Jan 95 13:00
♓ 19 Feb 95 03:10
♈ 21 Mar95 02:14
♉ 20 Apr95 13:21
♊ 21 May95 12:34
♋ 21 Jun 95 20:34

☉ Sun

♌ 23 Jul 95 07:29
♍ 23 Aug95 14:35
♎ 23 Sep 95 12:13
♏ 23 Oct 95 21:31
♐ 22 Nov95 19:01
♑ 22 Dec95 08:17
♒ 20 Jan 96 18:52
♓ 19 Feb 96 09:01
♈ 20 Mar96 08:03
♉ 19 Apr96 19:09
♊ 20 May96 18:23
♋ 21 Jun 96 02:23
♌ 22 Jul 96 13:18
♍ 22 Aug96 20:23
♎ 22 Sep 96 18:00
♏ 23 Oct 96 03:19
♐ 22 Nov96 00:49
♑ 21 Dec 96 14:06
♒ 20 Jan 97 00:42
♓ 18 Feb 97 14:51
♈ 20 Mar97 13:54
♉ 20 Apr97 01:02
♊ 21 May97 00:17
♋ 21 Jun 97 08:20
♌ 22 Jul 97 19:15
♍ 23 Aug97 02:19
♎ 22 Sep 97 23:56
♏ 23 Oct 97 09:15
♐ 22 Nov97 06:48
♑ 21 Dec97 20:07
♒ 20 Jan 98 06:46
♓ 18 Feb 98 20:55
♈ 20 Mar98 19:54
♉ 20 Apr98 06:56
♊ 21 May98 06:05
♋ 21 Jun 98 14:02
♌ 23 Jul 98 00:55
♍ 23 Aug98 07:59
♎ 23 Sep 98 05:37
♏ 23 Oct 98 14:59
♐ 22 Nov98 12:34
♑ 22 Dec98 01:56
♒ 20 Jan 99 12:37
♓ 19 Feb 99 02:47
♈ 21 Mar99 01:46
♉ 20 Apr99 12:46
♊ 21 May99 11:52
♋ 21 Jun 99 19:49
♌ 23 Jul 99 06:44
♍ 23 Aug99 13:51
♎ 23 Sep 99 11:31
♏ 23 Oct 99 20:52
♐ 22 Nov99 18:25
♑ 22 Dec99 07:44
♒ 20 Jan 00 18:23
♓ 19 Feb 00 08:33
♈ 20 Mar00 07:35
♉ 19 Apr00 18:39
♊ 20 May00 17:49
♋ 21 Jun 00 01:47
♌ 22 Jul 00 12:42
♍ 22 Aug00 19:48
♎ 22 Sep 00 17:27
♏ 23 Oct 00 02:47
♐ 22 Nov00 00:19
♑ 21 Dec00 13:37
♒ 20 Jan 01 00:16
♓ 18 Feb 01 14:27
♈ 20 Mar01 13:30
♉ 20 Apr01 00:36
♊ 20 May01 23:44
♋ 21 Jun 01 07:37
♌ 22 Jul 01 18:26
♍ 23 Aug01 01:27

☉ Sun

♎ 22 Sep 01 23:04
♏ 23 Oct 01 08:26
♐ 22 Nov01 06:00
♑ 21 Dec01 19:21
♒ 20 Jan 02 06:02
♓ 18 Feb 02 20:13
♈ 20 Mar02 19:16
♉ 20 Apr02 06:20
♊ 21 May02 05:29
♋ 21 Jun 02 13:24
♌ 23 Jul 02 00:15
♍ 23 Aug02 07:17
♎ 23 Sep 02 04:55
♏ 23 Oct 02 14:18
♐ 22 Nov02 11:54
♑ 22 Dec02 01:14
♒ 20 Jan 03 11:53
♓ 19 Feb 03 02:00
♈ 21 Mar03 00:59
♉ 20 Apr03 12:02
♊ 21 May03 11:12
♋ 21 Jun 03 19:10
♌ 23 Jul 03 06:04
♍ 23 Aug03 13:08
♎ 23 Sep 03 10:47
♏ 23 Oct 03 20:08
♐ 22 Nov03 17:43
♑ 22 Dec03 07:04
♒ 20 Jan 04 17:42
♓ 19 Feb 04 07:50
♈ 20 Mar04 06:48
♉ 19 Apr04 17:50
♊ 20 May04 16:59
♋ 21 Jun 04 00:56
♌ 22 Jul 04 11:50
♍ 22 Aug04 18:53
♎ 22 Sep 04 16:30
♏ 23 Oct 04 01:49
♐ 21 Nov04 23:22
♑ 21 Dec04 12:42
♒ 19 Jan 05 23:21
♓ 18 Feb 05 13:32
♈ 20 Mar05 12:33
♉ 19 Apr05 23:37
♊ 20 May05 22:47
♋ 21 Jun 05 06:46
♌ 22 Jul 05 17:40
♍ 23 Aug05 00:45
♎ 22 Sep 05 22:23
♏ 23 Oct 05 07:42
♐ 22 Nov05 05:15
♑ 21 Dec05 18:35
♒ 20 Jan 06 05:15
♓ 18 Feb 06 19:25
♈ 20 Mar06 18:25
♉ 20 Apr06 05:26
♊ 21 May06 04:31
♋ 21 Jun 06 12:25
♌ 22 Jul 06 23:17
♍ 23 Aug06 06:22
♎ 23 Sep 06 04:03
♏ 23 Oct 06 13:26
♐ 22 Nov06 11:02
♑ 22 Dec06 00:22
♒ 20 Jan 07 11:01
♓ 19 Feb 07 01:09
♈ 21 Mar07 00:07
♉ 20 Apr07 11:07
♊ 21 May07 10:11
♋ 21 Jun 07 18:06
♌ 23 Jul 07 05:00
♍ 23 Aug07 12:08
♎ 23 Sep 07 09:51
♏ 23 Oct 07 19:15

☉ Sun

♐ 22 Nov07 16:50
♑ 22 Dec07 06:08
♒ 20 Jan 08 16:43
♓ 19 Feb 08 06:49
♈ 20 Mar08 05:48
♉ 19 Apr08 16:51
♊ 20 May08 16:00
♋ 20 Jun 08 23:59
♌ 22 Jul 08 10:54
♍ 22 Aug08 18:02
♎ 22 Sep 08 15:44
♏ 23 Oct 08 01:08
♐ 21 Nov08 22:44
♑ 21 Dec08 12:04
♒ 19 Jan 09 22:40
♓ 18 Feb 09 12:46
♈ 20 Mar09 11:43
♉ 19 Apr09 22:44
♊ 20 May09 21:51
♋ 21 Jun 09 05:45
♌ 22 Jul 09 16:35
♍ 22 Aug09 23:38
♎ 22 Sep 09 21:18
♏ 23 Oct 09 06:43
♐ 22 Nov09 04:22
♑ 21 Dec09 17:47
♒ 20 Jan 10 04:28
♓ 18 Feb 10 18:35
♈ 20 Mar10 17:32
♉ 20 Apr10 04:29
♊ 21 May10 03:33
♋ 21 Jun 10 11:28
♌ 22 Jul 10 22:21
♍ 23 Aug10 05:27
♎ 23 Sep 10 03:09
♏ 23 Oct 10 12:35
♐ 22 Nov10 10:14
♑ 21 Dec 10 23:38

☿ Mercury

♒ 3 Jan 10 21:27
♑ 31 Jan 10 02:44
♒ 15 Feb 10 13:10
♓ 11 Mar10 21:34
♈ 29 Mar10 06:52
♉ 13 Apr10 00:27
♊ 30 Apr10 15:53
♉ 1 Jun 10 23:39
♊ 12 Jun 10 00:13
♋ 7 Jul 10 03:28
♌ 21 Jul 10 12:37
♍ 6 Aug10 04:37
♎ 27 Aug10 06:41
♍ 28 Sep 10 13:22
♎ 12 Oct 10 04:36
♏ 31 Oct 10 18:08
♐ 19 Nov10 08:12
♑ 8 Dec10 18:22
♒ 13 Feb 11 04:03
♓ 4 Mar11 21:13
♈ 21 Mar11 03:29
♉ 5 Apr11 09:03
♊ 13 Jun 11 01:26
♋ 28 Jun 11 23:59
♌ 13 Jul 11 03:19
♍ 30 Jul 11 13:40
♎ 6 Oct 11 20:49
♏ 24 Oct 11 06:33
♐ 12 Nov 11 04:56
♑ 3 Dec 11 01:43
♐ 27 Dec 11 16:37
♑ 15 Jan 12 07:15
♒ 7 Feb 12 02:24
♓ 25 Feb 12 06:31

☿ Mercury

♈ 12 Mar12 01:25
♉ 16 May12 19:53
♊ 5 Jun 12 05:10
♋ 19 Jun 12 08:59
♌ 4 Jul 12 08:59
♍ 26 Jul 12 08:13
♌ 21 Aug12 03:22
♍ 10 Sep 12 17:08
♎ 28 Sep 12 07:27
♏ 15 Oct 12 18:58
♐ 4 Nov12 14:46
♑ 10 Jan 13 05:20
♒ 30 Jan 13 01:43
♓ 16 Feb 13 10:43
♈ 4 Mar13 22:34
♓ 7 Apr13 15:02
♈ 14 Apr13 02:49
♉ 12 May13 06:14
♊ 28 May13 00:29
♋ 10 Jun 13 21:31
♌ 28 Jun 13 05:36
♍ 4 Sep 13 10:58
♎ 20 Sep 13 10:02
♏ 8 Oct 13 14:52
♐ 30 Oct 13 18:06
♏ 23 Nov13 12:29
♐ 13 Dec 13 08:51
♑ 3 Jan 14 19:19
♒ 22 Jan 14 15:50
♓ 8 Feb 14 19:10
♈ 16 Apr 14 16:05
♉ 5 May14 00:58
♊ 19 May14 10:03
♋ 3 Jun 14 05:52
♌ 11 Aug14 06:30
♍ 27 Aug14 10:45
♎ 12 Sep 14 15:46
♏ 2 Oct 14 05:53
♐ 8 Dec 14 04:53
♑ 27 Dec 14 17:40
♒ 15 Jan 15 04:27
♓ 2 Feb 15 10:33
♒ 23 Feb 15 15:06
♓ 19 Mar15 08:45
♈ 10 Apr15 19:21
♉ 26 Apr15 21:40
♊ 10 May15 23:46
♋ 29 May15 10:33
♌ 4 Aug15 08:59
♍ 19 Aug15 04:38
♎ 5 Sep 15 09:02
♏ 28 Sep 15 08:10
♎ 21 Oct 15 01:13
♏ 11 Nov15 14:08
♐ 1 Dec 15 09:17
♑ 20 Dec 15 11:14
♒ 8 Jan 16 01:21
♓ 15 Mar16 00:08
♈ 2 Apr16 10:59
♉ 17 Apr16 10:59
♊ 2 May16 16:13
♋ 10 Jul 16 18:17
♌ 26 Jul 16 01:42
♍ 10 Aug16 04:04
♎ 29 Aug16 04:52
♏ 4 Nov16 12:25
♐ 23 Nov16 03:39
♑ 12 Dec 16 07:13
♒ 1 Jan 17 17:07
♑ 18 Jan 17 04:30
♒ 15 Feb 17 03:20
♓ 8 Mar17 15:33
♈ 25 Mar17 11:34
♉ 9 Apr17 05:42

☿ Mercury

♊ 14 Jun 17 18:14
♋ 3 Jul 17 10:27
♌ 17 Jul 17 13:25
♍ 2 Aug17 19:30
♎ 26 Aug17 22:49
♍ 14 Sep 17 12:13
♎ 10 Oct 17 04:48
♏ 28 Oct 17 05:23
♐ 15 Nov17 21:28
♑ 5 Dec17 16:56
♒ 10 Feb 18 09:24
♓ 1 Mar18 07:52
♈ 17 Mar18 07:24
♉ 2 Apr18 13:14
♊ 10 Jun 18 01:21
♋ 24 Jun 18 23:49
♌ 9 Jul 18 08:38
♍ 28 Jul 18 01:27
♎ 3 Oct 18 08:59
♏ 20 Oct 18 16:47
♐ 8 Nov18 22:06
♑ 1 Dec18 16:19
♐ 15 Dec18 13:05
♑ 13 Jan 19 18:13
♒ 3 Feb 19 19:26
♓ 21 Feb 19 14:09
♈ 9 Mar19 10:42
♉ 16 May19 02:25
♊ 2 Jun 19 11:06
♋ 16 Jun 19 08:44
♌ 2 Jul 19 02:01
♍ 9 Sep 19 03:42
♎ 25 Sep 19 14:15
♏ 13 Oct 19 07:25
♐ 2 Nov19 19:06
♑ 8 Jan 20 05:55
♒ 27 Jan 20 13:49
♓ 13 Feb 20 18:41
♈ 2 Mar20 19:24
♓ 19 Mar20 16:27
♈ 17 Apr20 18:06
♉ 8 May20 23:55
♊ 24 May20 00:31
♋ 7 Jun 20 03:01
♌ 26 Jun 20 12:29
♋ 2 Aug20 22:10
♌ 10 Aug20 09:13
♍ 31 Aug20 18:29
♎ 16 Sep 20 17:13
♏ 5 Oct 20 09:26
♐ 30 Oct 20 12:40
♏ 10 Nov20 19:46
♐ 11 Dec 20 04:36
♑ 31 Dec 20 11:22
♒ 19 Jan 21 02:28
♓ 5 Feb 21 10:13
♈ 14 Apr21 02:12
♉ 1 May21 07:02
♊ 15 May21 10:09
♋ 31 May21 05:11
♌ 8 Aug21 07:41
♍ 23 Aug21 13:53
♎ 9 Sep 21 02:37
♏ 29 Sep 21 16:01
♐ 5 Dec21 00:27
♑ 24 Dec21 06:44
♒ 11 Jan 22 16:58
♓ 1 Feb 22 17:43
♒ 9 Feb 22 04:26
♓ 18 Mar22 06:31
♈ 7 Apr22 10:22
♉ 22 Apr22 23:18
♊ 7 May22 07:02
♋ 1 Jun 22 03:07

☿ Mercury

♊ 10 Jun 22 22
♋ 13 Jul 22 20
♌ 31 Jul 22 13
♍ 15 Aug22 08
♎ 2 Sep 22 04
♏ 1 Oct 22 09
♎ 5 Oct 22 01
♏ 8 Nov22 22
♐ 27 Nov22 23
♑ 17 Dec 22 00
♒ 4 Jan 23 23
♑ 6 Feb 23 15
♒ 13 Feb 23 23
♓ 13 Mar23 02
♈ 30 Mar23 18
♉ 14 Apr23 12
♊ 1 May23 05
♋ 8 Jul 23 12
♌ 23 Jul 23 02
♍ 7 Aug23 13
♎ 27 Aug23 22
♍ 4 Oct 23 11
♎ 11 Oct 23 22
♏ 2 Nov23 02
♐ 20 Nov23 16
♑ 10 Dec 23 00
♒ 14 Feb 24 03
♓ 5 Mar24 05
♈ 21 Mar24 15
♉ 5 Apr24 16
♊ 13 Jun 24 01
♋ 29 Jun 24 13
♌ 13 Jul 24 15
♍ 30 Jul 24 16
♎ 7 Oct 24 04
♏ 24 Oct 24 15
♐ 12 Nov24 12
♑ 2 Dec 24 23
♐ 31 Dec 24 15
♑ 14 Jan 25 07
♒ 7 Feb 25 08
♓ 25 Feb 25 16
♈ 13 Mar25 12
♉ 1 Apr25 15
♈ 15 Apr25 23
♉ 17 May25 01
♊ 6 Jun 25 15
♋ 20 Jun 25 23
♌ 5 Jul 25 17
♍ 26 Jul 25 11
♌ 27 Aug25 06
♍ 11 Sep 25 05
♎ 29 Sep 25 18
♏ 17 Oct 25 03
♐ 5 Nov25 18
♑ 11 Jan 26 07
♒ 31 Jan 26 10
♓ 17 Feb 26 21
♈ 6 Mar26 02
♉ 13 May26 10
♊ 29 May26 13
♋ 12 Jun 26 10
♌ 29 Jun 26 05
♍ 5 Sep 26 20
♎ 21 Sep 26 20
♏ 9 Oct 26 21
♐ 31 Oct 26 11
♏ 28 Nov26 05
♐ 13 Dec 26 20
♑ 5 Jan 27 01
♒ 24 Jan 27 01
♓ 10 Feb 27 04
♈ 17 Apr27 12
♉ 6 May27 11

Mercury	☿ Mercury	☿ Mercury	☿ Mercury	☿ Mercury	☿ Mercury	☿ Mercury
21 May 27 00:03	♊ 2 Jun 32 23:04	♊ 13 Jun 37 22:27	♈ 5 Apr 42 07:06	♈ 16 Apr 47 04:30	♈ 7 Mar 52 17:09	♊ 12 Jun 57 13:39
4 Jun 27 13:38	♋ 16 Jun 32 22:29	♋ 1 Jul 37 02:21	♉ 20 Apr 42 13:42	♉ 4 May 47 06:02	♉ 14 May 52 14:43	♋ 28 Jun 57 17:08
28 Jun 27 19:32	♌ 2 Jul 32 08:16	♌ 15 Jul 37 04:11	♊ 5 May 42 04:37	♊ 18 May 47 13:33	♊ 31 May 52 15:25	♌ 12 Jul 57 19:41
14 Jul 27 04:09	♍ 27 Jul 32 20:37	♍ 31 Jul 37 21:06	♋ 12 Jul 42 20:24	♋ 2 Jun 47 13:40	♋ 14 Jun 52 12:21	♍ 30 Jul 57 01:43
12 Aug 27 03:43	♌ 10 Aug 32 07:32	♎ 8 Oct 37 10:12	♌ 29 Jul 42 04:23	♌ 10 Aug 47 17:40	♌ 30 Jun 52 10:26	♎ 6 Oct 57 11:09
28 Aug 27 23:07	♍ 9 Sep 32 07:20	♏ 26 Oct 37 01:13	♍ 13 Aug 42 01:47	♍ 26 Aug 47 14:50	♍ 7 Sep 52 12:02	♏ 23 Oct 57 20:50
14 Sep 27 01:37	♎ 26 Sep 32 01:14	♐ 13 Nov 37 19:25	♎ 31 Aug 42 08:27	♎ 11 Sep 47 20:54	♎ 23 Sep 52 18:45	♐ 11 Nov 57 18:00
3 Oct 27 08:38	♏ 13 Oct 32 15:41	♑ 3 Dec 37 23:51	♏ 7 Nov 42 01:44	♏ 1 Oct 47 15:25	♏ 11 Oct 52 13:05	♑ 2 Dec 57 11:19
9 Dec 27 09:25	♐ 2 Nov 32 20:28	♐ 6 Jan 38 21:35	♐ 25 Nov 42 20:25	♐ 7 Dec 47 12:32	♐ 1 Nov 52 05:34	♐ 28 Dec 57 17:32
29 Dec 27 01:47	♑ 8 Jan 33 10:24	♑ 12 Jan 38 22:32	♑ 14 Dec 42 22:21	♑ 26 Dec 47 23:17	♑ 6 Jan 53 13:24	♑ 14 Jan 58 10:04
16 Jan 28 13:34	♒ 27 Jan 33 22:39	♒ 8 Feb 38 13:17	♒ 3 Jan 43 08:27	♒ 14 Jan 48 10:06	♒ 25 Jan 53 19:10	♒ 6 Feb 58 15:20
3 Feb 28 10:22	♓ 14 Feb 33 05:06	♓ 27 Feb 38 03:00	♑ 27 Jan 43 23:41	♓ 2 Feb 48 00:45	♓ 11 Feb 53 23:56	♓ 24 Feb 58 21:43
29 Feb 28 06:00	♈ 3 Mar 33 10:49	♈ 15 Mar 38 00:02	♒ 15 Feb 43 19:00	♒ 20 Feb 48 11:09	♈ 2 Mar 53 19:20	♈ 12 Mar 58 17:31
18 Mar 28 02:45	♓ 25 Mar 33 21:49	♉ 1 Apr 38 13:23	♓ 11 Mar 43 04:59	♓ 18 Mar 48 08:13	♓ 15 Mar 53 21:17	♉ 2 Apr 58 19:16
11 Apr 28 01:54	♈ 17 Apr 33 15:27	♈ 23 Apr 38 13:57	♈ 28 Mar 43 11:19	♈ 9 Apr 48 02:25	♈ 17 Apr 53 16:48	♈ 10 Apr 58 13:54
27 Apr 28 10:35	♉ 10 May 33 07:42	♉ 16 May 38 17:45	♉ 12 Apr 43 04:56	♉ 25 Apr 48 01:38	♉ 8 May 53 06:23	♉ 17 May 58 01:52
11 May 28 12:07	♊ 25 May 33 14:26	♊ 8 Jun 38 00:31	♊ 30 Apr 43 15:55	♊ 9 May 48 04:38	♊ 23 May 53 03:58	♊ 5 Jun 58 20:58
28 May 28 23:02	♋ 8 Jun 33 14:11	♋ 22 Jun 38 13:08	♉ 26 May 43 10:06	♋ 28 May 48 10:50	♋ 6 Jun 53 08:23	♋ 20 Jun 58 02:20
4 Aug 28 20:00	♌ 27 Jun 33 01:11	♌ 7 Jul 38 03:21	♊ 14 Jun 43 00:46	♊ 28 Jun 48 17:59	♌ 26 Jun 53 11:00	♌ 4 Jul 58 23:45
19 Aug 28 16:58	♍ 2 Sep 33 05:44	♍ 26 Jul 38 22:54	♋ 6 Jul 43 09:05	♋ 11 Jul 48 20:55	♋ 28 Jul 53 13:42	♍ 26 Jul 58 10:08
5 Sep 28 16:19	♎ 18 Sep 33 03:47	♌ 3 Sep 38 02:58	♌ 20 Jul 43 16:07	♌ 2 Aug 48 13:54	♌ 11 Aug 53 14:04	♌ 23 Aug 58 14:33
27 Sep 28 18:12	♏ 6 Oct 33 15:04	♍ 10 Sep 38 15:39	♍ 5 Aug 43 10:33	♍ 17 Aug 48 08:43	♍ 30 Aug 53 22:58	♍ 11 Sep 58 01:10
24 Oct 28 21:43	♐ 30 Oct 33 04:26	♎ 1 Oct 38 04:18	♎ 27 Aug 43 00:36	♎ 3 Sep 48 15:47	♎ 15 Sep 53 21:44	♎ 28 Sep 58 22:45
11 Nov 28 09:06	♏ 16 Nov 33 02:07	♏ 18 Oct 38 12:43	♍ 25 Sep 43 09:57	♏ 27 Sep 48 07:19	♏ 4 Oct 53 16:40	♏ 16 Oct 58 08:51
1 Dec 28 16:57	♐ 12 Dec 33 03:43	♐ 6 Nov 38 23:32	♎ 11 Oct 43 23:28	♎ 17 Oct 48 03:34	♐ 31 Oct 53 15:50	♐ 5 Nov 58 02:35
20 Dec 28 19:37	♑ 1 Jan 34 18:39	♑ 12 Jan 39 07:57	♏ 30 Oct 43 23:37	♏ 10 Nov 48 02:19	♏ 6 Nov 53 22:18	♑ 10 Jan 59 16:47
8 Jan 29 08:08	♒ 20 Jan 34 11:44	♒ 1 Feb 39 17:57	♐ 18 Nov 43 13:38	♐ 29 Nov 48 15:08	♐ 10 Dec 53 14:48	♒ 30 Jan 59 15:41
16 Mar 29 01:07	♓ 6 Feb 34 17:23	♓ 19 Feb 39 08:09	♑ 8 Dec 43 01:47	♑ 18 Dec 48 16:46	♑ 30 Dec 53 17:13	♓ 17 Feb 59 02:14
3 Apr 29 21:20	♈ 15 Apr 34 04:13	♈ 7 Mar 39 09:13	♒ 12 Feb 44 14:17	♒ 6 Jan 49 08:52	♒ 18 Jan 54 07:43	♈ 5 Mar 59 11:52
19 Apr 29 00:23	♉ 2 May 34 18:44	♉ 14 May 39 13:42	♓ 3 Mar 44 02:45	♓ 14 Mar 49 09:51	♓ 4 Feb 54 18:03	♉ 12 May 59 19:47
3 May 29 21:34	♊ 16 May 34 23:43	♊ 31 May 39 02:45	♈ 19 Mar 44 07:43	♈ 1 Apr 49 16:01	♈ 13 Apr 54 11:34	♊ 28 May 59 17:35
11 Jul 29 21:07	♋ 1 Jun 34 08:21	♋ 13 Jun 39 23:01	♉ 3 Apr 44 17:28	♉ 16 Apr 49 14:55	♉ 30 Apr 54 11:25	♋ 11 Jun 59 14:10
27 Jul 29 15:11	♌ 9 Aug 34 13:49	♌ 30 Jun 39 06:40	♊ 11 Jun 44 11:46	♊ 2 May 49 02:18	♊ 14 May 54 13:57	♌ 28 Jun 59 16:31
11 Aug 29 14:47	♍ 25 Aug 34 02:18	♍ 7 Sep 39 04:58	♋ 27 Jun 44 03:39	♋ 10 Jul 49 03:19	♋ 30 May 54 16:12	♍ 5 Sep 59 02:28
30 Aug 29 06:00	♎ 10 Sep 34 11:29	♎ 23 Sep 39 07:47	♌ 11 Jul 44 07:41	♌ 25 Jul 49 05:19	♌ 7 Aug 54 14:44	♎ 21 Sep 59 01:19
5 Nov 29 19:29	♏ 30 Sep 34 14:46	♏ 11 Oct 39 05:19	♍ 28 Jul 44 23:43	♍ 9 Aug 49 09:04	♍ 22 Aug 54 17:41	♏ 9 Oct 59 04:01
24 Nov 29 12:06	♐ 6 Dec 34 06:41	♐ 1 Nov 39 07:03	♎ 5 Oct 44 03:17	♎ 28 Aug 49 15:47	♎ 8 Sep 54 08:05	♐ 31 Oct 59 01:16
13 Dec 29 14:41	♑ 25 Dec 34 14:59	♏ 3 Dec 39 07:22	♏ 22 Oct 44 11:33	♏ 3 Nov 49 18:58	♏ 29 Sep 54 04:06	♏ 25 Nov 59 11:55
2 Jan 30 10:25	♒ 13 Jan 35 01:19	♐ 13 Dec 39 19:18	♐ 10 Nov 44 11:09	♐ 22 Nov 49 09:06	♎ 4 Nov 54 12:37	♐ 13 Dec 59 15:42
23 Jan 30 00:29	♓ 1 Feb 35 11:16	♑ 6 Jan 40 07:55	♑ 1 Dec 44 15:31	♑ 11 Dec 49 13:37	♏ 11 Nov 54 10:28	♑ 4 Jan 60 08:24
15 Feb 30 15:08	♒ 15 Feb 35 03:02	♒ 25 Jan 40 10:14	♐ 23 Dec 44 23:21	♒ 1 Jan 50 12:40	♐ 4 Dec 54 07:02	♒ 23 Jan 60 06:16
9 Mar 30 22:38	♓ 18 Mar 35 21:53	♓ 11 Feb 40 14:00	♑ 14 Jan 45 03:04	♑ 15 Jan 50 07:37	♑ 23 Dec 54 12:09	♓ 9 Feb 60 10:13
26 Mar 30 23:36	♈ 8 Apr 35 18:39	♈ 4 Mar 40 10:07	♒ 5 Feb 45 09:20	♒ 14 Feb 50 19:12	♒ 10 Jan 55 23:04	♈ 16 Apr 60 02:22
10 Apr 30 17:05	♉ 24 Apr 35 12:29	♓ 8 Mar 40 01:28	♓ 23 Feb 45 11:25	♓ 7 Mar 50 22:04	♓ 17 Mar 55 20:49	♉ 4 May 60 16:45
1 May 30 05:29	♊ 8 May 35 17:20	♈ 17 Apr 40 04:56	♈ 11 Mar 45 06:45	♈ 24 Mar 50 15:51	♈ 6 Apr 55 16:14	♊ 19 May 60 03:26
17 May 30 11:08	♋ 29 May 35 19:25	♉ 6 May 40 21:13	♉ 16 May 45 15:21	♉ 8 Apr 50 11:12	♉ 22 Apr 55 02:57	♋ 2 Jun 60 20:30
14 Jun 30 20:09	♊ 20 Jun 35 18:00	♊ 21 May 40 13:58	♊ 4 Jun 45 10:30	♊ 14 Jun 50 14:32	♊ 6 May 55 13:04	♌ 1 Jul 60 01:11
4 Jul 30 22:10	♋ 13 Jul 35 22:21	♋ 4 Jun 40 22:28	♋ 18 Jun 45 12:27	♋ 2 Jul 50 14:57	♋ 13 Jul 55 14:44	♋ 6 Jul 60 01:25
19 Jul 30 02:43	♌ 2 Aug 35 01:47	♌ 26 Jun 40 14:32	♌ 3 Jul 45 15:38	♌ 16 Jul 50 17:08	♌ 30 Jul 55 17:22	♌ 10 Aug 60 17:49
4 Aug 30 02:38	♍ 16 Aug 35 20:38	♋ 21 Jul 40 01:39	♍ 26 Jul 45 14:47	♍ 2 Aug 50 02:43	♍ 14 Aug 55 13:07	♍ 27 Aug 60 03:11
26 Aug 30 18:04	♎ 3 Sep 35 09:32	♌ 11 Aug 40 17:06	♌ 17 Aug 45 08:51	♎ 27 Aug 50 14:16	♎ 1 Sep 55 12:06	♎ 12 Sep 60 06:29
20 Sep 30 02:16	♏ 28 Sep 35 15:52	♍ 29 Aug 40 11:11	♍ 10 Sep 45 07:21	♍ 10 Sep 50 19:16	♏ 8 Nov 55 06:57	♏ 1 Oct 60 17:16
11 Oct 30 04:45	♎ 12 Oct 35 18:04	♎ 14 Sep 40 11:33	♎ 27 Sep 45 12:08	♎ 9 Oct 50 14:41	♐ 27 Nov 55 04:34	♐ 7 Dec 60 17:30
29 Oct 30 14:34	♏ 10 Nov 35 01:24	♏ 3 Oct 40 12:13	♏ 15 Oct 45 00:13	♏ 27 Oct 50 10:36	♑ 16 Dec 55 06:06	♑ 27 Dec 60 07:21
17 Nov 30 05:31	♐ 29 Nov 35 07:05	♐ 9 Dec 40 12:44	♐ 3 Nov 45 23:06	♐ 15 Nov 50 03:10	♒ 4 Jan 56 09:16	♒ 14 Jan 61 18:58
6 Dec 30 20:57	♑ 18 Dec 35 08:28	♑ 29 Dec 40 09:35	♑ 9 Jan 46 14:09	♑ 5 Dec 50 01:57	♑ 2 Feb 56 12:18	♓ 1 Feb 61 21:39
11 Feb 31 12:27	♒ 6 Jan 36 03:31	♒ 16 Jan 41 22:36	♒ 29 Jan 46 07:22	♒ 9 Feb 51 17:50	♒ 15 Feb 56 06:35	♒ 24 Feb 61 20:23
2 Mar 31 17:27	♓ 13 Mar 36 06:39	♓ 3 Feb 41 13:08	♓ 15 Feb 46 15:42	♓ 28 Feb 51 13:04	♓ 11 Mar 56 10:27	♓ 18 Mar 61 10:16
18 Mar 31 19:31	♈ 31 Mar 36 05:08	♒ 7 Mar 41 02:21	♈ 4 Mar 46 09:26	♈ 16 Mar 51 11:53	♈ 28 Mar 56 22:41	♈ 10 Apr 61 09:22
3 Apr 31 13:37	♉ 15 Apr 36 01:45	♓ 16 Mar 41 12:27	♓ 1 Apr 46 18:17	♉ 2 Apr 51 03:26	♉ 12 Apr 56 17:09	♉ 26 Apr 61 14:33
11 Jun 31 07:26	♊ 1 May 36 01:29	♈ 12 Apr 41 07:19	♈ 16 Apr 46 14:55	♈ 1 May 51 21:26	♊ 29 Apr 56 22:41	♊ 10 May 61 16:34
26 Jun 31 13:48	♋ 8 Jul 36 20:47	♉ 28 Apr 41 23:09	♉ 11 May 46 14:28	♉ 15 May 51 01:40	♋ 6 Jul 56 19:02	♋ 28 May 61 17:22
10 Jul 31 19:55	♌ 23 Jul 36 15:39	♊ 13 May 41 00:50	♊ 27 May 46 04:13	♊ 9 Jun 51 08:43	♌ 21 Jul 56 05:34	♌ 4 Aug 61 01:15
28 Jul 31 23:24	♍ 7 Aug 36 22:59	♋ 29 May 41 17:31	♋ 10 Jun 46 02:00	♋ 24 Jun 51 03:13	♍ 5 Aug 56 19:06	♍ 18 Aug 61 20:51
4 Oct 31 18:27	♎ 27 Aug 36 17:42	♌ 6 Aug 41 05:57	♌ 27 Jun 46 19:07	♌ 8 Jul 51 13:38	♎ 26 Aug 56 13:29	♎ 4 Sep 61 22:32
22 Oct 31 02:08	♏ 2 Nov 36 10:59	♍ 21 Aug 41 05:17	♍ 3 Sep 46 16:29	♍ 27 Jul 51 15:23	♍ 29 Sep 56 21:26	♏ 27 Sep 61 12:16
10 Nov 31 04:26	♐ 21 Nov 36 00:39	♎ 6 Sep 41 23:57	♎ 19 Sep 46 14:33	♎ 2 Oct 51 14:25	♎ 11 Oct 56 07:31	♎ 22 Oct 61 02:30
1 Dec 31 23:59	♑ 10 Dec 36 06:39	♏ 28 Sep 41 09:21	♏ 7 Oct 46 21:21	♏ 19 Oct 51 21:52	♏ 31 Oct 56 08:19	♏ 10 Nov 61 23:53
20 Dec 31 08:01	♒ 1 Jan 37 16:41	♎ 29 Oct 41 20:35	♐ 30 Oct 46 11:23	♐ 8 Nov 51 04:58	♐ 18 Nov 56 21:42	♐ 30 Nov 61 22:54
14 Jan 32 12:47	♑ 9 Jan 37 21:29	♏ 11 Nov 41 20:11	♏ 20 Nov 46 20:17	♑ 1 Dec 51 20:41	♑ 8 Dec 56 07:11	♑ 20 Dec 61 01:04
5 Feb 32 02:36	♒ 14 Feb 37 00:25	♐ 3 Dec 41 00:10	♐ 13 Dec 46 00:03	♐ 12 Dec 51 12:41	♒ 12 Feb 57 14:29	♒ 7 Jan 62 15:07
23 Feb 32 00:49	♓ 6 Mar 37 14:06	♑ 22 Dec 41 03:53	♑ 3 Jan 47 01:46	♑ 13 Jan 52 06:44	♓ 4 Mar 57 11:33	♓ 15 Mar 62 11:42
9 Mar 32 20:20	♈ 23 Mar 37 03:41	♒ 9 Jan 42 15:23	♒ 21 Jan 47 21:06	♒ 3 Feb 52 01:37	♈ 20 Mar 57 19:47	♈ 3 Apr 62 02:31
15 May 32 22:49	♉ 7 Apr 37 01:09	♓ 17 Mar 42 00:10	♓ 8 Feb 47 01:31	♓ 20 Feb 52 18:54	♉ 4 Apr 57 23:37	♉ 18 Apr 62 04:09

☿ Mercury	☿ Mercury	☿ Mercury	☿ Mercury	☿ Mercury	☿ Mercury	☿ Mercury
♊ 3May62 06:04	♊ 16May67 03:27	♈ 5Mar72 16:59	♈ 18Mar77 11:56	♈ 31Mar82 20:59	♒ 11Mar87 21:51	♈ 3Mar92 21
♋ 11 Jul 62 07:36	♋ 31May67 18:01	♉ 12May72 23:45	♉ 3Apr77 02:45	♉ 15Apr82 18:54	♓ 13Mar87 21:13	♓ 3Apr92 23
♌ 26 Jul 62 18:49	♌ 8Aug67 22:09	♊ 29May72 06:45	♊ 10 Jun 77 21:06	♊ 1May82 13:29	♈ 12Apr87 20:23	♈ 14Apr92 17
♍ 10Aug62 19:29	♍ 24Aug67 06:17	♋ 12 Jun 72 02:55	♋ 26 Jun 77 07:07	♋ 9 Jul 82 11:26	♉ 29Apr87 15:39	♉ 11May92 04
♎ 29Aug62 15:47	♎ 9 Sep 67 16:53	♌ 28 Jun 72 16:51	♌ 10 Jul 77 11:59	♌ 24 Jul 82 08:48	♊ 13May87 17:50	♊ 26May92 21
♏ 5Nov62 02:20	♏ 30 Sep 67 01:46	♍ 5 Sep 72 11:36	♍ 28 Jul 77 10:14	♍ 8Aug82 14:06	♋ 30May87 04:20	♋ 9 Jun 92 18
♐ 23Nov62 17:31	♐ 5Dec67 13:41	♎ 21 Sep 72 12:11	♎ 4 Oct 77 09:16	♎ 28Aug82 03:21	♌ 6Aug87 21:20	♌ 27 Jun 92 05
♑ 12Dec62 20:50	♑ 24Dec67 20:33	♏ 9 Oct 72 11:10	♏ 21 Oct 77 16:23	♏ 3Nov82 01:10	♍ 21Aug87 21:35	♍ 3 Sep 92 08
♒ 2 Jan 63 01:10	♒ 12 Jan 68 07:19	♐ 30 Oct 72 19:27	♐ 9Nov77 17:20	♐ 21Nov82 14:27	♎ 7 Sep 87 13:51	♎ 19 Sep 92 05
♑ 20 Jan 63 05:00	♓ 1 Feb 68 12:57	♏ 29Nov72 07:09	♑ 1Dec77 06:43	♑ 10Dec82 20:04	♏ 28 Sep 87 17:20	♏ 7 Oct 92 10
♒ 15 Feb 63 10:09	♒ 11 Feb 68 18:56	♐ 12Dec72 23:21	♐ 21Dec77 07:20	♒ 1 Jan 83 13:32	♎ 1Nov87 01:56	♐ 29 Oct 92 17
♓ 9Mar63 05:26	♓ 17Mar68 14:45	♑ 4 Jan 73 14:41	♑ 13 Jan 78 20:07	♑ 12 Jan 83 06:56	♏ 11Nov87 21:58	♏ 21Nov92 19
♈ 26Mar63 03:52	♈ 7Apr68 01:01	♒ 23 Jan 73 15:23	♒ 4 Feb 78 15:54	♒ 14 Feb 83 09:36	♐ 3Dec87 13:33	♐ 12Dec92 08
♉ 9Apr63 22:03	♉ 22Apr68 16:18	♓ 9 Feb 73 19:29	♓ 22 Feb 78 16:10	♓ 7Mar83 04:23	♑ 22Dec87 17:39	♑ 2 Jan 93 14
♊ 3May63 04:15	♊ 6May68 22:55	♈ 16Apr73 21:17	♈ 10Mar78 12:10	♈ 23Mar83 20:09	♒ 10 Jan 88 05:28	♒ 21 Jan 93 11
♉ 10May63 20:42	♋ 29May68 22:42	♉ 6May73 02:54	♉ 16May78 08:20	♉ 7Apr83 17:03	♓ 16Mar88 10:09	♓ 7 Feb 93 16
♊ 14 Jun 63 23:20	♊ 13 Jun 68 22:34	♊ 20May73 17:23	♊ 3 Jun 78 15:26	♊ 14 Jun 83 08:05	♈ 4Apr88 22:03	♈ 15Apr93 15
♋ 4 Jul 63 02:59	♋ 13 Jul 68 01:29	♋ 4 Jun 73 04:41	♋ 17 Jun 78 15:48	♋ 1 Jul 83 19:18	♉ 20Apr88 06:42	♉ 3May93 21
♌ 18 Jul 63 06:18	♌ 31 Jul 68 06:10	♌ 27 Jun 73 06:41	♌ 2 Jul 78 22:27	♌ 15 Jul 83 20:56	♊ 4May88 19:40	♊ 18May93 06
♍ 3Aug63 09:20	♍ 15Aug68 00:53	♋ 16 Jul 73 08:05	♍ 27 Jul 78 06:09	♍ 1Aug83 10:22	♋ 12 Jul 88 06:41	♋ 2 Jun 93 03
♎ 26Aug63 20:33	♎ 1 Sep 68 16:58	♌ 11Aug73 12:21	♌ 13Aug78 07:06	♎ 29Aug83 06:07	♌ 28 Jul 88 21:18	♌ 10Aug93 05
♍ 16 Sep 63 20:30	♏ 28 Sep 68 14:41	♍ 28Aug73 15:22	♍ 9 Sep 78 19:24	♍ 6 Sep 83 02:30	♍ 12Aug88 17:28	♍ 26Aug93 07
♎ 10 Oct 63 16:44	♎ 7 Oct 68 22:46	♎ 13 Sep 73 16:16	♎ 26 Sep 78 16:40	♎ 8 Oct 83 23:44	♎ 30Aug88 20:25	♎ 11 Sep 93 11
♏ 28 Oct 63 19:54	♏ 8Nov68 11:00	♏ 2 Oct 73 20:12	♏ 14 Oct 78 05:29	♏ 26 Oct 83 15:47	♏ 6Nov88 14:57	♏ 1 Oct 93 02
♐ 16Nov63 11:07	♐ 27Nov68 12:47	♐ 8Dec73 21:29	♐ 3Nov78 07:48	♐ 14Nov83 08:56	♐ 25Nov88 10:04	♐ 7Dec93 01
♑ 6Dec63 05:17	♑ 16Dec68 14:10	♑ 28Dec73 15:14	♑ 8 Jan 79 22:33	♑ 4Dec83 11:22	♑ 14Dec88 11:53	♑ 26Dec93 12
♒ 10 Feb 64 21:30	♒ 4 Jan 69 12:18	♒ 16 Jan 74 03:56	♒ 28 Jan 79 12:49	♒ 9 Feb 84 01:50	♒ 2 Jan 89 19:41	♒ 14 Jan 94 00
♓ 29 Feb 64 22:50	♓ 12Mar69 15:19	♓ 2 Feb 74 22:41	♓ 14 Feb 79 20:38	♓ 27 Feb 84 18:07	♑ 29 Jan 89 04:06	♓ 1 Feb 94 10
♈ 16Mar64 23:54	♈ 30Mar69 09:58	♒ 2Mar74 17:49	♈ 3Mar79 21:31	♈ 14Mar84 16:26	♒ 14 Feb 89 18:12	♒ 21 Feb 94 15
♉ 2Apr64 00:57	♉ 14Apr69 05:54	♓ 17Mar74 20:11	♓ 28Mar79 10:41	♉ 31Mar84 20:24	♓ 10Mar89 18:07	♓ 18Mar94 12
♊ 9 Jun 64 15:45	♊ 30Apr69 15:17	♈ 11Apr74 15:20	♈ 17Apr79 12:48	♈ 25Apr84 11:50	♈ 28Mar89 03:15	♈ 9Apr94 16
♋ 24 Jun 64 17:17	♋ 8 Jul 69 03:58	♉ 28Apr74 03:10	♉ 10May79 22:03	♉ 15May84 12:33	♉ 11Apr89 21:35	♉ 25Apr94 18
♌ 9 Jul 64 00:38	♌ 22 Jul 69 19:11	♊ 12May74 04:54	♊ 26May79 07:43	♊ 7 Jun 84 15:44	♊ 29Apr89 19:52	♊ 9May94 21
♍ 27 Jul 64 11:35	♍ 7Aug69 04:20	♋ 29May74 08:02	♋ 9 Jun 79 06:31	♋ 22 Jun 84 06:39	♉ 28May89 22:54	♋ 28May94 14
♎ 3 Oct 64 00:12	♎ 27Aug69 06:50	♌ 5Aug74 11:42	♌ 27 Jun 79 09:51	♌ 6 Jul 84 18:56	♊ 12 Jun 89 08:56	♊ 2 Jul 94 23
♏ 20 Oct 64 07:11	♍ 7 Oct 69 02:54	♍ 20Aug74 09:03	♍ 2 Sep 79 21:38	♍ 26 Jul 84 06:49	♋ 6 Jul 89 00:55	♋ 10 Jul 94 12
♐ 8Nov64 11:01	♎ 9 Oct 69 17:01	♎ 6 Sep 74 05:48	♎ 18 Sep 79 18:59	♎ 30 Sep 84 19:44	♌ 20 Jul 89 09:04	♌ 3Aug94 06
♑ 30Nov64 19:30	♏ 1Nov69 16:53	♏ 28 Sep 74 00:20	♏ 7 Oct 79 03:54	♏ 18 Oct 84 03:01	♍ 5Aug89 00:54	♍ 18Aug94 00
♐ 16Dec64 14:33	♐ 20Nov69 06:00	♎ 26 Oct 74 23:21	♐ 30 Oct 79 07:06	♐ 6Nov84 12:09	♎ 26Aug89 06:14	♎ 4 Sep 94 04
♑ 13 Jan 65 03:12	♑ 9Dec69 13:21	♏ 11Nov74 16:06	♏ 18Nov79 03:09	♑ 1Dec84 16:31	♍ 26 Sep 89 15:29	♏ 27 Sep 94 08
♒ 3 Feb 65 09:02	♒ 4 Jan 70 04:16	♐ 2Dec74 06:17	♐ 12Dec79 13:35	♐ 7Dec84 21:45	♎ 11 Oct 89 06:12	♎ 19 Oct 94 06
♓ 21 Feb 65 05:39	♑ 4 Jan 70 11:47	♑ 21Dec74 09:16	♑ 2 Jan 80 08:02	♑ 11 Jan 85 18:24	♏ 30 Oct 89 13:53	♏ 10Nov94 12
♈ 9Mar65 02:18	♒ 13 Feb 70 13:08	♒ 8 Jan 75 21:57	♒ 21 Jan 80 02:18	♒ 1 Feb 85 07:43	♐ 18Nov89 03:10	♐ 30Nov94 04
♉ 15May65 13:19	♓ 5Mar70 20:10	♓ 16Mar75 11:50	♓ 7 Feb 80 08:07	♓ 18 Feb 85 23:41	♑ 7Dec89 14:29	♑ 19Dec94 06
♊ 2 Jun 65 03:47	♈ 22Mar70 07:59	♈ 4Apr75 12:27	♈ 14Apr80 15:58	♈ 7Mar85 00:06	♒ 12 Feb 90 01:11	♒ 6 Jan 95 22
♋ 16 Jun 65 02:04	♉ 6Apr70 07:39	♉ 19Apr75 17:20	♉ 2May80 10:55	♉ 14May85 02:10	♓ 3Mar90 17:14	♓ 14Mar95 21
♌ 1 Jul 65 15:54	♊ 13 Jun 70 12:45	♊ 4May75 11:54	♊ 16May80 17:06	♊ 30May85 19:44	♈ 20Mar90 00:04	♈ 2Apr95 07
♍ 31 Jul 65 11:21	♋ 30 Jun 70 06:22	♋ 12 Jul 75 08:56	♋ 31May80 22:05	♋ 13 Jun 85 16:10	♉ 4Apr90 07:35	♉ 17Apr95 07
♌ 3Aug65 08:12	♌ 14 Jul 70 08:06	♌ 28 Jul 75 08:04	♌ 9Aug80 03:30	♌ 29 Jun 85 19:34	♊ 12 Jun 90 00:29	♊ 2May95 15
♍ 8 Sep 65 17:14	♍ 31 Jul 70 05:21	♍ 12Aug75 06:12	♍ 24Aug80 18:47	♍ 6 Sep 85 19:39	♋ 27 Jun 90 20:45	♋ 10 Jul 95 16
♎ 25 Sep 65 05:49	♎ 7 Oct 70 18:04	♎ 30Aug75 17:20	♎ 10 Sep 80 02:00	♎ 22 Sep 85 23:13	♌ 11 Jul 90 23:48	♌ 25 Jul 95 22
♏ 12 Oct 65 21:15	♏ 25 Oct 70 06:16	♏ 6Nov75 08:57	♏ 30 Sep 80 01:16	♏ 10 Oct 85 18:50	♍ 29 Jul 90 11:10	♍ 10Aug95 00
♐ 2Nov65 06:04	♐ 13Nov70 01:16	♐ 25Nov75 01:44	♐ 5Dec80 19:45	♐ 31 Oct 85 16:44	♎ 5 Oct 90 17:44	♎ 29Aug95 02
♑ 7 Jan 66 18:26	♑ 3Dec70 10:14	♑ 14Dec75 04:09	♑ 25Dec80 04:46	♏ 4Dec85 19:22	♏ 23 Oct 90 01:46	♏ 4Nov95 08
♒ 27 Jan 66 04:09	♐ 2 Jan 71 23:35	♒ 2 Jan 76 20:22	♒ 12 Jan 81 15:47	♐ 12Dec85 11:08	♐ 11Nov90 00:06	♐ 22Nov95 22
♓ 13 Feb 66 10:17	♑ 14 Jan 71 02:17	♑ 25 Jan 76 01:30	♓ 31 Jan 81 17:35	♑ 5 Jan 86 20:42	♑ 2Dec90 00:12	♑ 12Dec95 02
♈ 3Mar66 02:57	♒ 7 Feb 71 20:51	♒ 15 Feb 76 19:03	♒ 16 Feb 81 08:04	♒ 25 Jan 86 00:33	♐ 25Dec90 22:57	♒ 1 Jan 96 18
♓ 22Mar66 02:34	♓ 26 Feb 71 07:57	♓ 9Mar76 12:02	♓ 18Mar81 04:33	♓ 11 Feb 86 05:21	♑ 14 Jan 91 08:02	♑ 17 Jan 96 09
♈ 17Apr66 21:31	♈ 14Mar71 04:45	♈ 26Mar76 15:36	♈ 8Apr81 09:10	♈ 3Mar86 07:22	♒ 5 Feb 91 22:20	♒ 15 Feb 96 02
♉ 9May66 14:48	♉ 1Apr71 14:10	♉ 10Apr76 09:29	♉ 24Apr81 05:31	♓ 11Mar86 17:38	♓ 24 Feb 91 02:35	♓ 7Mar96 11
♊ 24May66 17:59	♈ 18Apr71 21:52	♊ 29Apr76 23:10	♊ 8May81 09:42	♈ 17Apr86 12:33	♈ 11Mar91 22:39	♈ 24Mar96 08
♋ 7 Jun 66 19:10	♉ 17May71 03:32	♉ 19May76 19:23	♋ 28May81 17:03	♉ 7May86 12:33	♉ 16May91 22:45	♉ 8Apr96 03
♌ 26 Jun 66 19:05	♊ 7 Jun 71 06:44	♊ 13 Jun 76 19:19	♊ 22 Jun 81 22:52	♊ 22May86 07:26	♊ 5 Jun 91 02:23	♊ 13 Jun 96 21
♍ 1 Sep 66 10:35	♋ 21 Jun 71 16:24	♋ 4 Jul 76 14:18	♋ 12 Jul 81 21:08	♋ 5 Jun 86 14:05	♋ 19 Jun 91 05:40	♋ 2 Jul 96 07
♎ 17 Sep 66 08:19	♌ 6 Jul 71 08:53	♌ 18 Jul 76 19:35	♌ 1Aug81 18:30	♌ 26 Jun 86 14:14	♌ 4 Jul 91 06:05	♌ 16 Jul 96 09
♏ 5 Oct 66 22:02	♍ 26 Jul 71 17:03	♍ 3Aug76 16:41	♍ 16Aug81 12:47	♋ 23 Jul 86 21:52	♍ 26 Jul 91 12:59	♍ 1Aug96 16
♐ 30 Oct 66 07:39	♌ 29Aug71 20:42	♎ 25Aug76 20:51	♎ 2 Sep 81 22:40	♌ 11Aug86 21:09	♌ 19Aug91 21:41	♎ 26Aug96 05
♏ 13Nov66 03:26	♍ 11 Sep 71 06:46	♍ 21 Sep 76 07:16	♏ 27 Sep 81 11:02	♍ 30Aug86 03:28	♍ 10 Sep 91 17:15	♍ 12 Sep 96 09
♐ 11Dec66 15:27	♎ 30 Sep 71 09:18	♎ 10 Oct 76 14:48	♎ 14 Oct 81 02:09	♎ 15 Sep 86 02:28	♎ 28 Sep 91 03:26	♎ 9 Oct 96 03
♑ 1 Jan 67 00:52	♏ 17 Oct 71 17:49	♏ 29 Oct 76 04:55	♏ 9Nov81 13:14	♏ 4 Oct 86 00:19	♏ 15 Oct 91 14:01	♏ 27 Oct 96 01
♒ 19 Jan 67 17:05	♐ 6Nov71 06:59	♐ 16Nov76 19:02	♐ 28Nov81 20:51	♐ 10Dec86 00:34	♐ 4Nov91 10:41	♐ 14Nov96 16
♓ 6 Feb 67 00:37	♑ 11 Jan 72 18:17	♑ 6Dec76 09:24	♑ 17Dec81 22:20	♑ 29Dec86 23:09	♑ 10 Jan 92 01:46	♑ 4Dec96 13
♈ 14Apr67 14:37	♒ 31 Jan 72 23:46	♒ 10 Feb 77 23:55	♒ 5 Jan 82 16:49	♒ 17 Jan 87 13:08	♒ 29 Jan 92 21:15	♒ 9 Feb 97 05
♉ 1May67 23:26	♓ 18 Feb 72 12:53	♓ 2Mar77 08:08	♓ 13Mar82 19:11	♓ 4 Feb 87 02:31	♓ 16 Feb 92 07:04	♓ 28 Feb 97 03

☿ Mercury

♈ 16 Mar 97 04:13
♉ 1 Apr 97 13:44
♈ 5 May 97 01:48
♉ 12 May 97 10:26
♊ 8 Jun 97 23:25
♋ 23 Jun 97 20:40
♌ 8 Jul 97 05:27
♍ 27 Jul 97 00:42
♎ 2 Oct 97 05:38
♏ 19 Oct 97 12:08
♐ 7 Nov 97 17:42
♑ 30 Nov 97 19:12
♐ 13 Dec 97 18:07
♑ 12 Jan 98 16:21
♒ 2 Feb 98 15:15
♓ 20 Feb 98 10:22
♈ 8 Mar 98 08:28
♉ 15 May 98 02:10
♊ 1 Jun 98 08:07
♋ 15 Jun 98 05:33
♌ 30 Jun 98 23:51
♍ 8 Sep 98 01:58
♎ 24 Sep 98 10:12
♏ 12 Oct 98 02:44
♐ 1 Nov 98 16:02
♑ 7 Jan 99 02:03
♒ 26 Jan 99 09:32
♓ 12 Feb 99 15:27
♈ 2 Mar 99 22:50
♓ 18 Mar 99 09:25
♈ 17 Apr 99 22:09
♉ 8 May 99 21:22
♊ 23 May 99 21:22
♋ 7 Jun 99 00:18
♌ 26 Jun 99 15:39
♋ 31 Jul 99 18:46
♌ 11 Aug 99 04:25
♍ 31 Aug 99 15:15
♎ 16 Sep 99 12:53
♏ 5 Oct 99 05:12
♐ 30 Oct 99 20:09
♏ 9 Nov 99 20:13
♐ 11 Dec 99 02:09
♑ 31 Dec 99 06:48
♒ 18 Jan 00 22:20
♓ 5 Feb 00 08:09
♈ 13 Apr 00 00:17
♉ 30 Apr 00 03:53
♊ 14 May 00 07:10
♋ 30 May 00 04:27
♌ 7 Aug 00 05:42
♍ 22 Aug 00 10:11
♎ 7 Sep 00 22:22
♏ 28 Sep 00 13:28
♎ 7 Nov 00 07:17
♏ 8 Nov 00 21:52
♐ 3 Dec 00 20:26
♑ 23 Dec 00 02:03
♒ 10 Jan 01 13:26
♓ 1 Feb 01 07:13
♒ 6 Feb 01 19:58
♓ 17 Mar 01 06:05
♈ 6 Apr 01 07:13
♉ 21 Apr 01 20:08
♊ 6 May 01 04:53
♋ 12 Jul 01 22:47
♌ 30 Jul 01 10:18
♍ 14 Aug 01 05:03
♎ 1 Sep 01 00:37
♏ 7 Nov 01 19:53
♐ 26 Nov 01 18:23
♑ 15 Dec 01 19:55
♒ 3 Jan 02 21:38
♑ 4 Feb 02 04:17

☿ Mercury

♒ 13 Feb 02 17:22
♓ 11 Mar 02 23:33
♈ 29 Mar 02 14:44
♉ 13 Apr 02 10:10
♊ 30 Apr 02 07:15
♋ 7 Jul 02 10:35
♌ 21 Jul 02 22:41
♍ 6 Aug 02 09:51
♎ 26 Aug 02 21:10
♍ 2 Oct 02 09:27
♎ 11 Oct 02 05:58
♏ 31 Oct 02 22:43
♐ 19 Nov 02 11:29
♑ 8 Dec 02 20:21
♒ 13 Feb 03 01:00
♓ 5 Mar 03 02:04
♈ 21 Mar 03 12:15
♉ 5 Apr 03 14:37
♊ 13 Jun 03 01:33
♋ 29 Jun 03 10:17
♌ 13 Jul 03 12:09
♍ 30 Jul 03 14:05
♎ 7 Oct 03 01:28
♏ 24 Oct 03 11:20
♐ 12 Nov 03 07:19
♑ 2 Dec 03 21:34
♐ 30 Dec 03 19:53
♑ 14 Jan 04 11:03
♒ 7 Feb 04 04:20
♓ 25 Feb 04 12:58
♈ 12 Mar 04 09:44
♉ 1 Apr 04 02:26
♈ 13 Apr 04 01:24
♉ 16 May 04 06:54
♊ 5 Jun 04 12:47
♋ 19 Jun 04 19:49
♌ 4 Jul 04 14:51
♍ 25 Jul 04 13:58
♌ 25 Aug 04 01:33
♍ 10 Sep 04 07:39
♎ 28 Sep 04 14:13
♏ 15 Oct 04 22:57
♐ 4 Nov 04 14:40
♑ 10 Jan 05 04:09
♒ 30 Jan 05 05:37
♓ 16 Feb 05 17:46
♈ 5 Mar 05 01:33
♉ 12 May 05 09:13
♊ 28 May 05 10:44
♋ 11 Jun 05 07:02
♌ 28 Jun 05 04:01
♍ 4 Sep 05 17:53
♎ 20 Sep 05 16:39
♏ 8 Oct 05 17:14
♐ 30 Oct 05 09:02
♏ 26 Nov 05 11:55
♐ 12 Dec 05 21:20
♑ 3 Jan 06 21:26
♒ 22 Jan 06 20:41
♓ 9 Feb 06 01:21
♈ 16 Apr 06 12:20
♉ 5 May 06 08:28
♊ 19 May 06 20:52
♋ 3 Jun 06 11:21
♌ 28 Jun 06 19:56
♋ 10 Jul 06 20:19
♌ 11 Aug 06 04:09
♍ 27 Aug 06 19:30
♎ 12 Sep 06 21:07
♏ 2 Oct 06 04:38
♐ 8 Dec 06 05:51
♑ 27 Dec 06 20:54
♒ 15 Jan 07 09:24
♓ 2 Feb 07 09:20

☿ Mercury

♒ 27 Feb 07 03:00
♓ 18 Mar 07 09:35
♈ 10 Apr 07 23:07
♉ 27 Apr 07 07:16
♊ 11 May 07 09:16
♋ 29 May 07 00:55
♌ 4 Aug 07 17:15
♍ 19 Aug 07 13:00
♎ 5 Sep 07 12:02
♏ 27 Sep 07 17:17
♎ 24 Oct 07 03:37
♏ 11 Nov 07 08:41
♐ 1 Dec 07 12:21
♑ 20 Dec 07 14:43
♒ 8 Jan 08 04:46
♓ 14 Mar 08 22:46
♈ 2 Apr 08 17:44
♉ 17 Apr 08 21:07
♊ 2 May 08 20:00
♋ 10 Jul 08 20:17
♌ 26 Jul 08 11:48
♍ 10 Aug 08 10:50
♎ 29 Aug 08 02:49
♏ 4 Nov 08 16:00
♐ 23 Nov 08 07:09
♑ 12 Dec 08 10:12
♒ 1 Jan 09 09:51
♑ 21 Jan 09 05:37
♒ 14 Feb 09 15:39
♓ 8 Mar 09 18:56
♈ 25 Mar 09 19:55
♉ 9 Apr 09 14:21
♊ 30 Apr 09 22:28
♉ 13 May 09 23:53
♊ 14 Jun 09 02:47
♋ 3 Jul 09 19:19
♌ 17 Jul 09 23:07
♍ 2 Aug 09 23:07
♎ 25 Aug 09 20:18
♍ 18 Sep 09 03:26
♎ 10 Oct 09 03:46
♏ 28 Oct 09 10:08
♐ 16 Nov 09 00:28
♑ 5 Dec 09 17:24
♒ 10 Feb 10 09:06
♓ 1 Mar 10 13:27
♈ 17 Mar 10 16:11
♉ 2 Apr 10 13:05
♊ 10 Jun 10 05:41
♋ 25 Jun 10 10:32
♌ 9 Jul 10 16:29
♍ 27 Jul 10 21:42
♎ 3 Oct 10 15:04
♏ 20 Oct 10 21:18
♐ 8 Nov 10 23:43
♑ 1 Dec 10 00:10
♐ 18 Dec 10 14:56

♀ Venus

♓ 15 Jan 10 20:55
♒ 29 Jan 10 09:12
♓ 5 Apr 10 09:53
♈ 7 May 10 02:26
♉ 3 Jun 10 14:57
♊ 29 Jun 10 19:31
♋ 25 Jul 10 07:01
♌ 19 Aug 10 05:56
♍ 12 Sep 10 18:29
♎ 6 Oct 10 23:10
♏ 30 Oct 10 22:53
♐ 23 Nov 10 20:08
♑ 17 Dec 10 16:37
♒ 10 Jan 11 13:28
♓ 3 Feb 11 12:02

♀ Venus

♈ 27 Feb 11 14:28
♉ 23 Mar 11 23:35
♊ 17 Apr 11 18:55
♋ 13 May 11 05:42
♌ 8 Jun 11 18:48
♍ 7 Jul 11 19:03
♎ 9 Nov 11 00:54
♏ 9 Dec 11 09:23
♐ 4 Jan 12 18:38
♑ 29 Jan 12 22:44
♒ 23 Feb 12 15:29
♓ 19 Mar 12 03:48
♈ 12 Apr 12 14:49
♉ 7 May 12 01:56
♊ 31 May 12 13:18
♋ 25 Jun 12 00:12
♌ 19 Jul 12 09:43
♍ 12 Aug 12 17:42
♎ 6 Sep 12 00:53
♏ 30 Sep 12 08:26
♐ 24 Oct 12 17:25
♑ 18 Nov 12 05:03
♒ 12 Dec 12 22:23
♓ 7 Jan 13 05:27
♈ 2 Feb 13 23:21
♉ 6 Mar 13 17:08
♈ 2 May 13 05:12
♉ 31 May 13 09:45
♊ 8 Jul 13 09:16
♋ 5 Aug 13 23:32
♌ 1 Sep 13 09:19
♍ 26 Sep 13 16:04
♎ 21 Oct 13 06:01
♏ 14 Nov 13 09:54
♐ 8 Dec 13 08:37
♑ 1 Jan 14 05:25
♒ 25 Jan 14 02:09
♓ 18 Feb 14 00:04
♈ 14 Mar 14 00:29
♉ 7 Apr 14 04:48
♊ 1 May 14 14:10
♋ 26 May 14 05:33
♌ 20 Jun 14 04:25
♍ 15 Jul 14 14:10
♎ 10 Aug 14 18:11
♏ 7 Sep 14 10:57
♐ 10 Oct 14 01:49
♏ 5 Dec 14 23:21
♐ 30 Dec 14 23:13
♑ 6 Feb 15 15:57
♒ 6 Mar 15 13:14
♓ 1 Apr 15 15:18
♈ 27 Apr 15 00:55
♉ 22 May 15 02:55
♊ 16 Jun 15 00:21
♋ 10 Jul 15 17:30
♌ 4 Aug 15 05:47
♍ 28 Aug 15 13:06
♎ 21 Sep 15 16:30
♏ 15 Oct 15 17:41
♐ 8 Nov 15 18:06
♑ 2 Dec 15 18:37
♒ 26 Dec 15 20:20
♓ 20 Jan 16 01:40
♈ 13 Feb 16 15:23
♉ 9 Mar 16 21:49
♊ 5 Apr 16 13:31
♋ 5 May 16 20:36
♌ 8 Sep 16 22:25
♍ 7 Oct 16 22:11
♎ 3 Nov 16 00:59
♏ 27 Nov 16 23:06
♐ 22 Dec 16 07:49
♑ 15 Jan 17 10:45

♀ Venus

♒ 8 Feb 17 11:50
♓ 4 Mar 17 13:09
♈ 28 Mar 17 16:01
♉ 21 Apr 17 21:16
♊ 16 May 17 05:08
♋ 9 Jun 17 15:15
♌ 4 Jul 17 03:20
♍ 28 Jul 17 17:51
♎ 22 Aug 17 12:19
♏ 16 Sep 17 12:59
♐ 11 Oct 17 23:33
♑ 7 Nov 17 05:00
♒ 5 Dec 17 13:13
♓ 5 Apr 18 20:11
♈ 6 May 18 20:57
♉ 3 Jun 18 05:26
♊ 29 Jun 18 08:12
♋ 24 Jul 18 18:43
♌ 18 Aug 18 17:05
♍ 12 Sep 18 05:23
♎ 6 Oct 18 09:59
♏ 30 Oct 18 09:43
♐ 23 Nov 18 07:01
♑ 17 Dec 18 03:33
♒ 10 Jan 19 00:28
♓ 2 Feb 19 23:08
♈ 27 Feb 19 01:43
♉ 23 Mar 19 11:07
♊ 17 Apr 19 07:02
♋ 12 May 19 18:58
♌ 8 Jun 19 10:34
♍ 7 Jul 19 18:16
♎ 9 Nov 19 08:04
♏ 9 Dec 19 03:28
♐ 4 Jan 20 09:19
♑ 29 Jan 20 11:54
♒ 23 Feb 20 03:47
♓ 18 Mar 20 15:31
♈ 12 Apr 20 02:06
♉ 6 May 20 12:54
♊ 31 May 20 00:05
♋ 24 Jun 20 10:53
♌ 18 Jul 20 20:25
♍ 12 Aug 20 04:30
♎ 5 Sep 20 11:52
♏ 29 Sep 20 19:44
♐ 24 Oct 20 05:11
♑ 17 Nov 20 17:28
♒ 12 Dec 20 11:45
♓ 6 Jan 21 20:32
♈ 2 Feb 21 18:34
♉ 7 Mar 21 09:18
♈ 25 Apr 21 23:46
♉ 2 Jun 21 04:21
♊ 8 Jul 21 05:57
♋ 5 Aug 21 14:41
♌ 31 Aug 21 22:23
♍ 26 Sep 21 04:08
♎ 20 Oct 21 17:34
♏ 13 Nov 21 21:10
♐ 7 Dec 21 19:46
♑ 31 Dec 21 16:31
♒ 24 Jan 22 13:13
♓ 17 Feb 22 11:06
♈ 13 Mar 22 11:29
♉ 6 Apr 22 15:50
♊ 1 May 22 01:21
♋ 25 May 22 17:03
♌ 19 Jun 22 16:32
♍ 15 Jul 22 03:22
♎ 10 Aug 22 09:29
♏ 7 Sep 22 07:15
♐ 10 Oct 22 22:33
♏ 28 Nov 22 21:48

♀ Venus

♐ 2 Jan 23 07:26
♑ 6 Feb 23 14:33
♒ 6 Mar 23 05:37
♓ 1 Apr 23 05:15
♈ 26 Apr 23 13:36
♉ 21 May 23 14:50
♊ 15 Jun 23 11:45
♋ 10 Jul 23 04:36
♌ 3 Aug 23 16:42
♍ 27 Aug 23 23:59
♎ 21 Sep 23 03:28
♏ 15 Oct 23 04:48
♐ 8 Nov 23 05:23
♑ 2 Dec 23 06:05
♒ 26 Dec 23 08:02
♓ 19 Jan 24 13:45
♈ 13 Feb 24 04:09
♉ 9 Mar 24 11:55
♊ 5 Apr 24 06:46
♋ 6 May 24 01:48
♌ 8 Sep 24 21:43
♍ 7 Oct 24 14:16
♎ 2 Nov 24 14:43
♏ 27 Nov 24 11:47
♐ 21 Dec 24 19:55
♑ 14 Jan 25 22:28
♒ 7 Feb 25 23:15
♓ 4 Mar 25 00:21
♈ 28 Mar 25 03:04
♉ 21 Apr 25 08:13
♊ 15 May 25 16:03
♋ 9 Jun 25 02:14
♌ 3 Jul 25 14:30
♍ 28 Jul 25 05:24
♎ 22 Aug 25 00:28
♏ 16 Sep 25 02:04
♐ 11 Oct 25 14:10
♑ 6 Nov 25 22:34
♒ 5 Dec 25 15:08
♓ 6 Apr 26 03:58
♈ 6 May 26 15:12
♉ 2 Jun 26 19:59
♊ 28 Jun 26 21:04
♋ 24 Jul 26 06:42
♌ 18 Aug 26 04:34
♍ 11 Sep 26 16:37
♎ 5 Oct 26 21:07
♏ 29 Oct 26 20:50
♐ 22 Nov 26 18:11
♑ 16 Dec 26 14:48
♒ 9 Jan 27 11:47
♓ 2 Feb 27 10:33
♈ 26 Feb 27 13:16
♉ 22 Mar 27 22:56
♊ 16 Apr 27 19:25
♋ 12 May 27 08:33
♌ 8 Jun 27 02:51
♍ 7 Jul 27 18:54
♎ 9 Nov 27 13:26
♏ 8 Dec 27 21:26
♐ 4 Jan 28 00:05
♑ 29 Jan 28 01:13
♒ 22 Feb 28 16:15
♓ 18 Mar 28 03:25
♈ 11 Apr 28 13:35
♉ 6 May 28 00:03
♊ 30 May 28 11:00
♋ 23 Jun 28 21:42
♌ 18 Jul 28 07:15
♍ 11 Aug 28 15:28
♎ 4 Sep 28 23:05
♏ 29 Sep 28 07:17
♐ 23 Oct 28 17:12
♑ 17 Nov 28 06:08

♀ Venus

♒ 12 Dec 28 01:25
♓ 6 Jan 29 12:01
♈ 2 Feb 29 14:33
♉ 8 Mar 29 07:29
♈ 20 Apr 29 02:05
♉ 3 Jun 29 09:47
♊ 8 Jul 29 01:59
♋ 5 Aug 29 05:39
♌ 31 Aug 29 11:23
♍ 25 Sep 29 16:13
♎ 20 Oct 29 05:12
♏ 13 Nov 29 08:34
♐ 7 Dec 29 07:03
♑ 31 Dec 29 03:43
♒ 24 Jan 30 00:21
♓ 16 Feb 30 22:11
♈ 12 Mar 30 22:33
♉ 6 Apr 30 02:57
♊ 30 Apr 30 12:36
♋ 25 May 30 04:36
♌ 19 Jun 30 04:38
♍ 14 Jul 30 16:34
♎ 10 Aug 30 00:53
♏ 7 Sep 30 04:05
♐ 12 Oct 30 02:44
♏ 22 Nov 30 07:44
♐ 3 Jan 31 20:02
♑ 6 Feb 31 12:24
♒ 5 Mar 31 21:45
♓ 31 Mar 31 19:03
♈ 26 Apr 31 02:09
♉ 21 May 31 02:38
♊ 14 Jun 31 23:04
♋ 9 Jul 31 15:34
♌ 3 Aug 31 03:29
♍ 27 Aug 31 10:42
♎ 20 Sep 31 14:15
♏ 14 Oct 31 15:44
♐ 7 Nov 31 16:32
♑ 1 Dec 31 17:29
♒ 25 Dec 31 19:43
♓ 19 Jan 32 01:51
♈ 12 Feb 32 16:58
♉ 9 Mar 32 02:06
♊ 5 Apr 32 00:18
♋ 6 May 32 09:03
♊ 13 Jul 32 10:34
♋ 28 Jul 32 12:35
♌ 8 Sep 32 19:44
♍ 7 Oct 32 05:45
♎ 2 Nov 32 04:01
♏ 27 Nov 32 00:06
♐ 21 Dec 32 07:42
♑ 14 Jan 33 09:56
♒ 7 Feb 33 10:29
♓ 3 Mar 33 11:24
♈ 27 Mar 33 13:57
♉ 20 Apr 33 19:00
♊ 15 May 33 02:46
♋ 8 Jun 33 13:01
♌ 3 Jul 33 01:29
♍ 27 Jul 33 16:45
♎ 21 Aug 33 12:23
♏ 15 Sep 33 14:54
♐ 11 Oct 33 04:31
♑ 6 Nov 33 16:02
♒ 5 Dec 33 18:00
♓ 6 Apr 34 09:22
♈ 6 May 34 08:53
♉ 2 Jun 34 10:10
♊ 28 Jun 34 09:37
♋ 23 Jul 34 18:21
♌ 17 Aug 34 15:44
♍ 11 Sep 34 03:32

♀ Venus	♀ Venus	♀ Venus	♀ Venus	♀ Venus	♀ Venus	♀ Venus
♎ 5 Oct 34 07:55	♊ 5 Jul 40 16:18	♊ 29 Apr 46 10:59	♈ 9 Apr 52 23:17	♐ 10 Oct 57 01:15	♐ 5 Nov 63 13:25	♌ 29 Aug 69 02:4
♏ 29 Oct 34 07:37	♋ 1 Aug 40 02:19	♋ 24 May 46 03:39	♉ 4 May 52 08:54	♑ 5 Nov 57 23:45	♑ 29 Nov 63 15:21	♍ 23 Sep 69 03:2
♐ 22 Nov 34 04:59	♌ 8 Sep 40 16:59	♌ 18 Jun 46 05:00	♊ 28 May 52 19:18	♒ 6 Dec 57 15:25	♒ 23 Dec 63 18:53	♎ 17 Oct 69 14:1
♑ 16 Dec 34 01:39	♍ 6 Oct 40 21:09	♍ 13 Jul 46 19:22	♋ 22 Jun 52 05:46	♓ 6 Apr 58 15:59	♓ 17 Jan 64 02:53	♏ 10 Nov 69 16:3
♒ 8 Jan 35 22:43	♎ 1 Nov 40 17:23	♎ 9 Aug 46 08:34	♌ 16 Jul 52 15:22	♈ 5 May 58 11:59	♈ 10 Feb 64 21:09	♐ 4 Dec 69 14:4
♓ 1 Feb 35 21:36	♏ 26 Nov 40 12:31	♏ 7 Sep 46 00:15	♍ 9 Aug 52 23:57	♉ 1 Jun 58 04:07	♉ 7 Mar 64 12:38	♑ 28 Dec 69 11:0
♈ 26 Feb 35 00:29	♐ 20 Dec 40 19:36	♐ 16 Oct 46 10:44	♎ 3 Sep 52 08:17	♊ 26 Jun 58 23:08	♊ 4 Apr 64 03:02	♒ 21 Jan 70 07:2
♉ 22 Mar 35 10:29	♑ 13 Jan 41 21:29	♏ 8 Nov 46 08:57	♏ 27 Sep 52 17:36	♋ 22 Jul 58 05:26	♋ 9 May 64 03:15	♓ 14 Feb 70 05:0
♊ 16 Apr 35 07:36	♒ 6 Feb 41 21:48	♐ 5 Jan 47 16:45	♐ 22 Oct 52 05:02	♌ 16 Aug 58 01:28	♊ 17 Jun 64 18:19	♈ 10 Mar 70 05:2
♋ 11 May 35 22:01	♓ 2 Mar 41 22:33	♑ 6 Feb 47 05:41	♑ 15 Nov 52 20:02	♍ 9 Sep 58 12:35	♋ 5 Aug 64 08:52	♉ 3 Apr 70 10:0
♌ 7 Jun 35 19:11	♈ 27 Mar 41 00:57	♒ 5 Mar 47 05:09	♒ 10 Dec 52 18:30	♎ 3 Oct 58 16:44	♌ 8 Sep 64 04:53	♊ 27 Apr 70 20:3
♍ 7 Jul 35 20:32	♉ 20 Apr 41 05:53	♓ 30 Mar 47 22:14	♓ 5 Jan 53 11:10	♏ 27 Oct 58 16:26	♍ 5 Oct 64 18:10	♋ 22 May 70 14:1
♎ 9 Nov 35 16:34	♊ 14 May 41 13:36	♈ 25 Apr 47 03:02	♈ 2 Feb 53 05:54	♐ 20 Nov 58 13:59	♎ 31 Oct 64 08:54	♌ 16 Jun 70 17:4
♏ 8 Dec 35 14:35	♋ 7 Jun 41 23:52	♉ 20 May 47 02:05	♉ 14 Mar 53 18:57	♑ 14 Dec 58 10:55	♏ 25 Nov 64 01:25	♍ 12 Jul 70 12:1
♐ 3 Jan 36 14:16	♌ 2 Jul 41 12:32	♊ 13 Jun 47 21:35	♈ 31 Mar 53 05:17	♒ 7 Jan 59 08:16	♐ 19 Dec 64 07:02	♎ 8 Aug 70 09:5
♑ 28 Jan 36 14:00	♍ 27 Jul 41 04:12	♋ 8 Jul 47 13:29	♉ 5 Jun 53 10:33	♓ 31 Jan 59 07:28	♑ 12 Jan 65 08:00	♏ 7 Sep 70 01:5
♒ 22 Feb 36 04:14	♎ 21 Aug 41 00:29	♌ 2 Aug 47 01:06	♊ 7 Jul 53 10:29	♈ 24 Feb 59 10:52	♒ 5 Feb 65 07:41	♐ 7 Jan 71 01:0
♓ 17 Mar 36 14:53	♏ 15 Sep 41 04:01	♍ 26 Aug 47 08:17	♋ 4 Aug 53 01:08	♉ 20 Mar 59 21:55	♓ 1 Mar 65 07:55	♑ 5 Feb 71 14:5
♈ 11 Apr 36 00:40	♐ 10 Oct 41 19:21	♎ 19 Sep 47 12:00	♌ 30 Aug 53 01:34	♊ 14 Apr 59 21:07	♈ 25 Mar 65 09:54	♒ 4 Mar 71 02:2
♉ 5 May 36 10:52	♑ 6 Nov 41 10:16	♏ 13 Oct 47 13:48	♍ 24 Sep 53 03:47	♋ 10 May 59 15:44	♉ 18 Apr 65 14:30	♓ 29 Mar 71 14:0
♊ 29 May 36 21:39	♒ 5 Dec 41 23:04	♐ 6 Nov 47 14:58	♎ 18 Oct 53 15:27	♌ 6 Jun 59 22:42	♊ 12 May 65 22:07	♈ 23 Apr 71 15:4
♋ 23 Jun 36 08:16	♓ 6 Apr 42 13:14	♑ 30 Nov 47 16:22	♏ 11 Nov 53 18:12	♍ 8 Jul 59 12:07	♋ 6 Jun 65 08:38	♉ 18 May 71 12:4
♌ 17 Jul 36 17:50	♈ 6 May 42 02:25	♒ 24 Dec 47 19:12	♐ 5 Dec 53 16:24	♌ 20 Sep 59 03:03	♌ 30 Jun 65 21:59	♊ 12 Jun 71 06:5
♍ 11 Aug 36 02:11	♉ 2 Jun 42 00:26	♓ 18 Jan 48 02:13	♑ 29 Dec 53 12:53	♍ 25 Sep 59 08:13	♍ 25 Jul 65 14:51	♋ 6 Jul 71 22:0
♎ 4 Sep 36 10:01	♊ 27 Jun 42 22:18	♈ 11 Feb 48 18:50	♒ 22 Jan 54 09:20	♎ 9 Nov 59 18:10	♎ 19 Aug 65 13:06	♌ 31 Jul 71 09:1
♏ 28 Sep 36 18:36	♋ 23 Jul 42 06:10	♉ 8 Mar 48 06:59	♓ 15 Feb 54 07:01	♏ 7 Dec 59 16:41	♏ 13 Sep 65 19:50	♍ 24 Aug 71 16:2
♐ 23 Oct 36 05:00	♌ 17 Aug 42 03:04	♊ 4 Apr 48 12:39	♈ 11 Mar 54 07:21	♐ 2 Jan 60 08:43	♐ 9 Oct 65 16:46	♎ 17 Sep 71 20:2
♑ 16 Nov 36 18:35	♍ 10 Sep 42 14:37	♋ 7 May 48 08:27	♉ 4 Apr 54 11:55	♑ 27 Jan 60 04:45	♑ 5 Nov 65 19:35	♏ 11 Oct 71 22:4
♒ 11 Dec 36 14:51	♎ 4 Oct 42 18:57	♊ 29 Jun 48 07:59	♊ 28 Apr 54 22:03	♒ 20 Feb 60 16:47	♒ 7 Dec 65 04:36	♐ 5 Nov 71 00:3
♓ 6 Jan 37 03:17	♏ 28 Oct 42 18:40	♋ 3 Aug 48 02:15	♋ 23 May 54 15:03	♓ 16 Mar 60 01:53	♑ 6 Feb 66 12:47	♑ 29 Nov 71 02:4
♈ 2 Feb 37 10:39	♐ 21 Nov 42 16:07	♌ 8 Sep 48 13:40	♌ 17 Jun 54 17:04	♈ 9 Apr 60 10:32	♒ 25 Feb 66 10:54	♒ 23 Dec 71 06:3
♉ 9 Mar 37 13:19	♑ 15 Dec 42 12:52	♍ 6 Oct 48 12:25	♍ 13 Jul 54 08:42	♉ 3 May 60 19:55	♓ 6 Apr 66 15:53	♓ 16 Jan 72 15:0
♈ 14 Apr 37 04:20	♒ 8 Jan 43 10:02	♎ 1 Nov 48 06:41	♎ 9 Aug 54 00:33	♊ 28 May 60 06:11	♈ 5 May 66 04:33	♈ 10 Feb 72 10:0
♉ 4 Jun 37 06:40	♓ 1 Feb 43 09:01	♏ 26 Nov 48 00:54	♏ 6 Sep 54 23:28	♋ 21 Jun 60 16:33	♉ 31 May 66 18:00	♉ 7 Mar 72 03:2
♊ 7 Jul 37 21:12	♈ 25 Feb 43 12:04	♐ 20 Dec 48 07:28	♐ 23 Oct 54 22:02	♌ 16 Jul 60 02:11	♊ 26 Jun 66 11:40	♊ 3 Apr 72 22:4
♋ 4 Aug 37 20:13	♉ 21 Mar 43 22:24	♑ 13 Jan 49 09:00	♏ 27 Oct 54 10:48	♍ 9 Aug 60 10:53	♋ 21 Jul 66 17:11	♋ 10 May 72 13:5
♌ 31 Aug 37 00:07	♊ 15 Apr 43 20:11	♒ 6 Feb 49 09:05	♐ 6 Jan 55 06:48	♎ 2 Sep 60 19:29	♌ 15 Aug 66 12:47	♊ 11 Jun 72 20:0
♍ 25 Sep 37 04:02	♋ 11 May 43 11:56	♓ 2 Mar 49 09:38	♑ 6 Feb 55 01:15	♏ 27 Sep 60 05:13	♍ 8 Sep 66 23:40	♋ 6 Aug 72 01:2
♎ 19 Oct 37 16:33	♌ 7 Jun 43 12:08	♈ 26 Mar 49 11:54	♒ 4 Mar 55 20:21	♐ 21 Oct 60 17:12	♎ 3 Oct 66 03:44	♌ 7 Sep 72 23:2
♏ 12 Nov 37 19:42	♍ 7 Jul 43 23:55	♉ 19 Apr 49 16:43	♓ 30 Mar 55 11:30	♑ 15 Nov 60 08:57	♏ 27 Oct 66 03:28	♍ 5 Oct 72 08:3
♐ 6 Dec 37 18:05	♎ 9 Nov 43 18:25	♊ 14 May 49 00:25	♈ 24 Apr 55 15:13	♒ 10 Dec 60 08:34	♐ 20 Nov 66 01:06	♎ 30 Oct 72 21:3
♑ 30 Dec 37 14:42	♏ 8 Dec 43 07:44	♋ 7 Jun 49 10:47	♉ 19 May 55 13:35	♓ 5 Jan 61 03:30	♑ 13 Dec 66 22:08	♏ 24 Nov 72 13:2
♒ 23 Jan 38 11:15	♐ 3 Jan 44 04:43	♌ 1 Jul 49 23:40	♊ 13 Jun 55 08:37	♈ 2 Feb 61 04:45	♒ 6 Jan 67 19:35	♐ 18 Dec 72 18:3
♓ 16 Feb 38 09:00	♑ 28 Jan 44 03:11	♍ 26 Jul 49 15:43	♋ 8 Jul 55 00:15	♉ 5 Jun 61 19:24	♓ 30 Jan 67 18:53	♑ 11 Jan 73 19:1
♈ 12 Mar 38 09:20	♒ 21 Feb 44 16:39	♎ 20 Aug 49 12:38	♌ 1 Aug 55 11:42	♊ 7 Jul 61 04:32	♈ 23 Feb 67 22:29	♒ 4 Feb 73 18:4
♉ 5 Apr 38 13:46	♓ 17 Mar 44 02:46	♏ 14 Sep 49 17:12	♍ 25 Aug 55 18:52	♋ 3 Aug 61 15:28	♉ 20 Mar 67 09:56	♓ 28 Feb 73 18:4
♊ 29 Apr 38 23:35	♈ 10 Apr 44 12:09	♐ 10 Oct 49 10:18	♎ 18 Sep 55 22:40	♌ 29 Aug 61 14:18	♊ 14 Apr 67 09:54	♈ 24 Mar 73 20:3
♋ 24 May 38 15:55	♉ 4 May 44 22:04	♑ 6 Nov 49 04:53	♏ 13 Oct 55 00:38	♍ 23 Sep 61 15:43	♋ 10 May 67 06:05	♉ 18 Apr 73 01:0
♌ 18 Jun 38 16:37	♊ 29 May 44 08:39	♒ 6 Dec 49 06:05	♐ 6 Nov 55 02:02	♎ 18 Oct 61 02:58	♌ 6 Jun 67 16:47	♊ 12 May 73 08:4
♍ 14 Jul 38 05:44	♋ 22 Jun 44 19:11	♓ 6 Apr 50 15:13	♑ 30 Nov 55 03:42	♏ 11 Nov 61 05:32	♍ 8 Jul 67 22:11	♋ 5 Jun 73 19:2
♎ 9 Aug 38 16:26	♌ 17 Jul 44 04:46	♈ 5 May 50 19:19	♒ 24 Dec 55 06:52	♐ 5 Dec 61 03:40	♌ 9 Sep 67 12:00	♌ 30 Jun 73 08:5
♏ 7 Sep 38 01:36	♍ 10 Aug 44 13:13	♉ 1 Jun 50 14:19	♓ 17 Jan 56 14:22	♑ 29 Dec 61 00:06	♍ 1 Oct 67 18:06	♍ 25 Jul 73 02:1
♐ 13 Oct 38 18:48	♎ 3 Sep 44 21:16	♊ 27 Jun 50 10:45	♈ 11 Feb 56 07:46	♒ 21 Jan 62 20:30	♎ 9 Nov 67 16:32	♎ 19 Aug 73 01:1
♏ 15 Nov 38 16:08	♏ 28 Sep 44 06:12	♋ 22 Jul 50 17:49	♉ 7 Mar 56 21:31	♓ 14 Feb 62 18:08	♏ 7 Dec 67 08:48	♏ 13 Sep 73 09:0
♐ 4 Jan 39 21:48	♐ 22 Oct 44 17:07	♌ 16 Aug 50 14:17	♊ 4 Apr 56 07:22	♈ 10 Mar 62 18:28	♐ 1 Jan 68 22:37	♐ 9 Oct 73 08:0
♑ 6 Feb 39 09:20	♑ 16 Nov 44 07:25	♍ 10 Sep 50 01:37	♋ 8 May 56 02:16	♉ 3 Apr 62 23:04	♑ 26 Jan 68 17:34	♑ 5 Nov 73 15:3
♒ 5 Mar 39 13:28	♒ 11 Dec 44 04:47	♎ 4 Oct 50 05:50	♊ 23 Jun 56 12:10	♊ 28 Apr 62 09:22	♒ 20 Feb 68 04:55	♒ 7 Dec 73 21:3
♓ 31 Mar 39 08:34	♓ 5 Jan 45 19:18	♏ 28 Oct 50 05:33	♋ 4 Aug 56 09:48	♋ 23 May 62 02:46	♓ 15 Mar 68 13:31	♑ 29 Jan 74 19:5
♈ 25 Apr 39 14:28	♈ 2 Feb 45 08:06	♐ 21 Nov 50 03:03	♌ 8 Sep 56 09:23	♌ 17 Jun 62 05:30	♈ 8 Apr 68 21:48	♒ 28 Feb 74 14:2
♉ 20 May 39 14:12	♉ 11 Mar 45 11:17	♑ 14 Dec 50 23:54	♍ 6 Oct 56 03:12	♍ 12 Jul 62 22:31	♉ 3 May 68 06:56	♓ 6 Apr 74 14:1
♊ 14 Jun 39 10:10	♈ 7 Apr 45 19:16	♒ 7 Jan 51 21:10	♎ 31 Oct 56 19:39	♎ 8 Aug 62 17:13	♊ 27 May 68 17:02	♈ 4 May 74 20:2
♋ 9 Jul 39 02:24	♉ 4 Jun 45 22:57	♓ 31 Jan 51 20:14	♏ 25 Nov 56 13:01	♏ 7 Sep 62 00:10	♋ 21 Jun 68 03:20	♉ 31 May 74 07:1
♌ 2 Aug 39 14:11	♊ 7 Jul 45 16:20	♈ 24 Feb 51 23:26	♐ 19 Dec 56 19:06	♐ 6 Jan 63 17:35	♌ 15 Jul 68 12:59	♊ 25 Jun 74 23:4
♍ 26 Aug 39 21:24	♋ 4 Aug 45 10:59	♉ 21 Mar 51 10:05	♑ 12 Jan 57 20:22	♑ 5 Feb 63 20:35	♍ 8 Aug 68 21:49	♋ 21 Jul 74 04:3
♎ 20 Sep 39 01:02	♌ 30 Aug 45 13:05	♊ 15 Apr 51 08:33	♒ 5 Feb 57 20:16	♒ 4 Mar 63 11:41	♎ 2 Sep 68 06:39	♌ 14 Aug 74 23:4
♏ 14 Oct 39 02:41	♍ 24 Sep 45 16:06	♋ 11 May 51 01:41	♓ 1 Mar 57 20:39	♓ 30 Mar 63 00:59	♏ 26 Sep 68 16:45	♍ 8 Sep 74 10:2
♐ 7 Nov 39 03:40	♎ 19 Oct 45 04:09	♌ 7 Jun 51 05:09	♈ 25 Mar 57 22:46	♈ 24 Apr 63 03:39	♐ 21 Oct 68 05:16	♎ 2 Oct 74 14:2
♑ 1 Dec 39 04:52	♏ 12 Nov 45 07:04	♍ 8 Jul 51 04:53	♉ 19 Apr 57 03:28	♉ 19 May 63 01:21	♑ 14 Nov 68 21:47	♏ 26 Oct 74 14:1
♒ 25 Dec 39 07:25	♐ 6 Dec 45 05:22	♎ 9 Nov 51 18:47	♊ 13 May 57 11:07	♊ 12 Jun 63 19:56	♒ 9 Dec 68 22:39	♐ 19 Nov 74 11:5
♓ 18 Jan 40 14:00	♑ 30 Dec 45 01:56	♏ 8 Dec 51 00:18	♋ 6 Jun 57 21:34	♋ 7 Jul 63 11:18	♓ 4 Jan 69 20:07	♑ 13 Dec 74 09:0
♈ 12 Feb 40 05:50	♒ 22 Jan 46 22:27	♐ 2 Jan 52 18:44	♌ 1 Jul 57 10:42	♌ 31 Jul 63 22:38	♈ 2 Feb 69 04:44	♒ 6 Jan 75 06:3
♉ 8 Mar 40 16:25	♓ 15 Feb 46 20:11	♑ 27 Jan 52 15:57	♍ 26 Jul 57 03:10	♍ 25 Aug 63 05:48	♉ 6 Jun 69 01:48	♓ 30 Jan 75 06:0
♊ 4 Apr 40 18:09	♈ 11 Mar 46 20:31	♒ 21 Feb 52 04:42	♎ 20 Aug 57 00:43	♎ 18 Sep 63 09:42	♊ 6 Jul 69 22:03	♈ 23 Feb 75 09:5
♋ 6 May 40 18:46	♉ 5 Apr 46 01:01	♓ 16 Mar 52 14:18	♏ 14 Sep 57 06:19	♏ 12 Oct 63 11:49	♋ 3 Aug 69 05:30	♉ 19 Mar 75 21:4

♀ Venus
♊ 13 Apr 75 22:25
♋ 9 May 75 20:11
♌ 6 Jun 75 10:54
♍ 9 Jul 75 11:06
♌ 2 Sep 75 15:36
♍ 4 Oct 75 05:19
♎ 9 Nov 75 13:52
♏ 7 Dec 75 00:28
♐ 1 Jan 76 12:14
♑ 26 Jan 76 06:08
♒ 19 Feb 76 16:50
♓ 15 Mar 76 00:59
♈ 8 Apr 76 08:56
♉ 2 May 76 17:48
♊ 27 May 76 03:43
♋ 20 Jun 76 13:56
♌ 14 Jul 76 23:36
♍ 8 Aug 76 08:35
♎ 1 Sep 76 17:44
♏ 26 Sep 76 04:17
♐ 20 Oct 76 17:22
♑ 14 Nov 76 10:42
♒ 9 Dec 76 12:53
♓ 4 Jan 77 13:01
♈ 2 Feb 77 05:54
♉ 6 Jun 77 06:10
♊ 6 Jul 77 15:09
♋ 2 Aug 77 19:18
♌ 28 Aug 77 15:09
♍ 22 Sep 77 15:05
♎ 17 Oct 77 01:37
♏ 10 Nov 77 03:51
♐ 4 Dec 77 01:48
♑ 27 Dec 77 22:09
♒ 20 Jan 78 18:29
♓ 13 Feb 78 16:06
♈ 9 Mar 78 16:29
♉ 2 Apr 78 21:13
♊ 27 Apr 78 07:53
♋ 22 May 78 02:03
♌ 16 Jun 78 06:18
♍ 12 Jul 78 02:14
♎ 8 Aug 78 03:08
♏ 7 Sep 78 05:07
♐ 7 Jan 79 06:38
♑ 5 Feb 79 09:15
♒ 3 Mar 79 17:18
♓ 29 Mar 79 03:17
♈ 23 Apr 79 04:02
♉ 18 May 79 00:29
♊ 11 Jun 79 18:13
♋ 6 Jul 79 09:02
♌ 30 Jul 79 20:07
♍ 24 Aug 79 03:16
♎ 17 Sep 79 07:21
♏ 11 Oct 79 09:48
♐ 4 Nov 79 11:50
♑ 28 Nov 79 14:19
♒ 22 Dec 79 18:34
♓ 16 Jan 80 03:36
♈ 9 Feb 80 23:39
♉ 6 Mar 80 18:54
♊ 3 Apr 80 19:46
♋ 12 May 80 20:52
♊ 5 Jun 80 05:45
♋ 6 Aug 80 14:25
♌ 7 Sep 80 17:57
♍ 4 Oct 80 23:06
♎ 30 Oct 80 10:38
♏ 24 Nov 80 01:35
♐ 18 Dec 80 06:21
♑ 11 Jan 81 06:48
♒ 4 Feb 81 06:07
♓ 28 Feb 81 06:01

♀ Venus
♈ 24 Mar 81 07:42
♉ 17 Apr 81 12:08
♊ 11 May 81 19:44
♋ 5 Jun 81 06:29
♌ 29 Jun 81 20:19
♍ 24 Jul 81 14:04
♎ 18 Aug 81 13:44
♏ 12 Sep 81 22:50
♐ 9 Oct 81 00:04
♑ 5 Nov 81 12:39
♒ 8 Dec 81 20:52
♑ 23 Jan 82 02:57
♒ 2 Mar 82 11:25
♓ 6 Apr 82 12:20
♈ 4 May 82 12:26
♉ 30 May 82 21:01
♊ 25 Jun 82 12:13
♋ 20 Jul 82 16:21
♌ 14 Aug 82 11:09
♍ 7 Sep 82 21:37
♎ 2 Oct 82 01:32
♏ 26 Oct 82 01:19
♐ 18 Nov 82 23:06
♑ 12 Dec 82 20:20
♒ 5 Jan 83 17:58
♓ 29 Jan 83 17:31
♈ 22 Feb 83 21:34
♉ 19 Mar 83 09:51
♊ 13 Apr 83 11:26
♋ 9 May 83 10:56
♌ 6 Jun 83 06:03
♍ 10 Jul 83 05:24
♌ 27 Aug 83 11:45
♍ 5 Oct 83 19:35
♎ 9 Nov 83 10:52
♏ 6 Dec 83 16:14
♐ 1 Jan 84 02:00
♑ 25 Jan 84 18:51
♒ 19 Feb 84 04:52
♓ 14 Mar 84 12:34
♈ 7 Apr 84 20:13
♉ 2 May 84 04:53
♊ 26 May 84 14:40
♋ 20 Jun 84 00:48
♌ 14 Jul 84 10:30
♍ 7 Aug 84 19:40
♎ 1 Sep 84 05:06
♏ 25 Sep 84 16:05
♐ 20 Oct 84 05:45
♑ 13 Nov 84 23:54
♒ 9 Dec 84 03:26
♓ 4 Jan 85 06:23
♈ 2 Feb 85 08:28
♉ 6 Jun 85 08:53
♊ 6 Jul 85 08:01
♋ 2 Aug 85 09:10
♌ 28 Aug 85 03:38
♍ 22 Sep 85 02:53
♎ 16 Oct 85 13:03
♏ 9 Nov 85 15:07
♐ 3 Dec 85 13:00
♑ 27 Dec 85 09:17
♒ 20 Jan 86 05:35
♓ 13 Feb 86 03:10
♈ 9 Mar 86 03:31
♉ 2 Apr 86 08:19
♊ 26 Apr 86 19:10
♋ 21 May 86 13:46
♌ 15 Jun 86 18:51
♍ 11 Jul 86 16:23
♎ 7 Aug 86 20:45
♏ 7 Sep 86 10:15
♐ 7 Jan 87 10:20
♑ 5 Feb 87 03:03

♀ Venus
♒ 3 Mar 87 07:55
♓ 28 Mar 87 16:20
♈ 22 Apr 87 16:07
♉ 17 May 87 11:55
♊ 11 Jun 87 05:15
♋ 5 Jul 87 19:49
♌ 30 Jul 87 06:49
♍ 23 Aug 87 14:00
♎ 16 Sep 87 18:12
♏ 10 Oct 87 20:48
♐ 3 Nov 87 23:04
♑ 28 Nov 87 01:51
♒ 22 Dec 87 06:29
♓ 15 Jan 88 16:03
♈ 9 Feb 88 13:03
♉ 6 Mar 88 10:21
♊ 3 Apr 88 17:07
♋ 17 May 88 16:25
♊ 27 May 88 07:37
♋ 6 Aug 88 23:23
♌ 7 Sep 88 11:37
♍ 4 Oct 88 13:14
♎ 29 Oct 88 23:19
♏ 23 Nov 88 13:34
♐ 17 Dec 88 17:55
♑ 10 Jan 89 18:07
♒ 3 Feb 89 17:15
♓ 27 Feb 89 16:59
♈ 23 Mar 89 18:32
♉ 16 Apr 89 22:52
♊ 11 May 89 06:28
♋ 4 Jun 89 17:17
♌ 29 Jun 89 07:21
♍ 24 Jul 89 01:31
♎ 18 Aug 89 01:58
♏ 12 Sep 89 12:22
♐ 8 Oct 89 15:59
♑ 5 Nov 89 10:13
♒ 10 Dec 89 04:53
♑ 16 Jan 90 15:25
♒ 3 Mar 90 17:51
♓ 6 Apr 90 09:13
♈ 4 May 90 03:52
♉ 30 May 90 10:13
♊ 25 Jun 90 00:14
♋ 20 Jul 90 03:41
♌ 13 Aug 90 22:05
♍ 7 Sep 90 08:21
♎ 1 Oct 90 12:12
♏ 25 Oct 90 12:03
♐ 18 Nov 90 09:58
♑ 12 Dec 90 07:18
♒ 5 Jan 91 05:03
♓ 29 Jan 91 04:44
♈ 22 Feb 91 09:02
♉ 18 Mar 91 21:45
♊ 13 Apr 91 00:10
♋ 9 May 91 01:28
♌ 6 Jun 91 01:16
♍ 11 Jul 91 05:05
♌ 21 Aug 91 15:08
♍ 6 Oct 91 21:15
♎ 9 Nov 91 06:36
♏ 6 Dec 91 07:21
♐ 31 Dec 91 15:19
♑ 25 Jan 92 07:14
♒ 18 Feb 92 16:40
♓ 13 Mar 92 23:56
♈ 7 Apr 92 07:15
♉ 1 May 92 15:41
♊ 26 May 92 01:18
♋ 19 Jun 92 11:22
♌ 13 Jul 92 21:06
♍ 7 Aug 92 06:25

♀ Venus
♎ 31 Aug 92 16:09
♏ 25 Sep 92 03:31
♐ 19 Oct 92 17:46
♑ 13 Nov 92 12:48
♒ 8 Dec 92 17:49
♓ 3 Jan 93 23:53
♈ 2 Feb 93 12:37
♉ 6 Jun 93 10:03
♊ 6 Jul 93 00:21
♋ 1 Aug 93 22:38
♌ 27 Aug 93 15:48
♍ 21 Sep 93 14:22
♎ 16 Oct 93 00:13
♏ 9 Nov 93 02:06
♐ 2 Dec 93 23:53
♑ 26 Dec 93 20:09
♒ 19 Jan 94 16:27
♓ 12 Feb 94 14:04
♈ 8 Mar 94 14:27
♉ 1 Apr 94 19:20
♊ 26 Apr 94 06:23
♋ 21 May 94 01:26
♌ 15 Jun 94 07:23
♍ 11 Jul 94 06:33
♎ 7 Aug 94 14:36
♏ 7 Sep 94 17:12
♐ 7 Jan 95 12:07
♑ 4 Feb 95 20:12
♒ 2 Mar 95 22:10
♓ 28 Mar 95 05:10
♈ 22 Apr 95 04:07
♉ 16 May 95 23:22
♊ 10 Jun 95 16:18
♋ 5 Jul 95 06:39
♌ 29 Jul 95 17:32
♍ 23 Aug 95 00:43
♎ 16 Sep 95 05:00
♏ 10 Oct 95 07:48
♐ 3 Nov 95 10:18
♑ 27 Nov 95 13:23
♒ 21 Dec 95 18:23
♓ 15 Jan 96 04:30
♈ 9 Feb 96 02:30
♉ 6 Mar 96 02:01
♊ 3 Apr 96 15:25
♋ 7 Aug 96 06:14
♌ 7 Sep 96 05:07
♍ 4 Oct 96 03:21
♎ 29 Oct 96 12:02
♏ 23 Nov 96 01:34
♐ 17 Dec 96 05:34
♑ 10 Jan 97 05:32
♒ 3 Feb 97 04:27
♓ 27 Feb 97 04:01
♈ 23 Mar 97 05:26
♉ 16 Apr 97 09:42
♊ 10 May 97 17:20
♋ 4 Jun 97 04:18
♌ 28 Jun 97 18:37
♍ 23 Jul 97 13:16
♎ 17 Aug 97 14:31
♏ 12 Sep 97 02:17
♐ 8 Oct 97 08:25
♑ 5 Nov 97 08:50
♒ 12 Dec 97 04:39
♑ 9 Jan 98 21:04
♒ 4 Mar 98 16:14
♓ 6 Apr 98 05:38
♈ 3 May 98 19:16
♉ 29 May 98 23:32
♊ 24 Jun 98 12:27
♋ 19 Jul 98 15:17
♌ 13 Aug 98 09:19
♍ 6 Sep 98 19:24

♀ Venus
♎ 30 Sep 98 23:13
♏ 24 Oct 98 23:06
♐ 17 Nov 98 21:06
♑ 11 Dec 98 18:33
♒ 4 Jan 99 16:25
♓ 28 Jan 99 16:17
♈ 21 Feb 99 20:49
♉ 18 Mar 99 09:59
♊ 12 Apr 99 13:17
♋ 8 May 99 16:28
♌ 5 Jun 99 21:25
♍ 12 Jul 99 15:17
♌ 15 Aug 99 14:14
♍ 7 Oct 99 16:51
♎ 9 Nov 99 02:19
♏ 5 Dec 99 22:41
♐ 31 Dec 99 04:54
♑ 24 Jan 00 19:52
♒ 18 Feb 00 04:43
♓ 13 Mar 00 11:36
♈ 6 Apr 00 18:37
♉ 1 May 00 02:49
♊ 25 May 00 12:15
♋ 18 Jun 00 22:15
♌ 13 Jul 00 08:02
♍ 6 Aug 00 17:32
♎ 31 Aug 00 03:35
♏ 24 Sep 00 15:26
♐ 19 Oct 00 06:18
♑ 13 Nov 00 02:14
♒ 8 Dec 00 08:48
♓ 3 Jan 01 18:14
♈ 2 Feb 01 19:14
♉ 6 Jun 01 10:25
♊ 5 Jul 01 16:44
♋ 1 Aug 01 12:18
♌ 27 Aug 01 04:12
♍ 21 Sep 01 02:09
♎ 15 Oct 01 11:42
♏ 8 Nov 01 13:28
♐ 2 Dec 01 11:11
♑ 26 Dec 01 07:25
♒ 19 Jan 02 03:42
♓ 12 Feb 02 01:18
♈ 8 Mar 02 01:42
♉ 1 Apr 02 06:39
♊ 25 Apr 02 17:56
♋ 20 May 02 13:27
♌ 14 Jun 02 20:16
♍ 10 Jul 02 21:08
♎ 7 Aug 02 09:08
♏ 8 Sep 02 03:04
♐ 7 Jan 03 13:07
♑ 4 Feb 03 13:27
♒ 2 Mar 03 12:40
♓ 27 Mar 03 18:14
♈ 21 Apr 03 16:18
♉ 16 May 03 10:58
♊ 10 Jun 03 03:32
♋ 4 Jul 03 17:38
♌ 29 Jul 03 04:25
♍ 22 Aug 03 11:35
♎ 15 Sep 03 15:58
♏ 9 Oct 03 18:56
♐ 2 Nov 03 21:42
♑ 27 Nov 03 01:07
♒ 21 Dec 03 06:32
♓ 14 Jan 04 17:16
♈ 8 Feb 04 16:20
♉ 5 Mar 04 18:12
♊ 3 Apr 04 14:57
♋ 7 Aug 04 11:02
♌ 6 Sep 04 22:15
♍ 3 Oct 04 17:20

♀ Venus
♎ 29 Oct 04 00:39
♏ 22 Nov 04 13:31
♐ 16 Dec 04 17:10
♑ 9 Jan 05 16:56
♒ 2 Feb 05 15:42
♓ 26 Feb 05 15:07
♈ 22 Mar 05 16:25
♉ 15 Apr 05 20:37
♊ 10 May 05 04:14
♋ 3 Jun 05 15:17
♌ 28 Jun 05 05:53
♍ 23 Jul 05 01:01
♎ 17 Aug 05 03:05
♏ 11 Sep 05 16:14
♐ 8 Oct 05 01:00
♑ 5 Nov 05 08:10
♒ 15 Dec 05 15:57
♑ 1 Jan 06 20:20
♒ 5 Mar 06 08:39
♓ 6 Apr 06 01:20
♈ 3 May 06 10:24
♉ 29 May 06 12:41
♊ 24 Jun 06 00:31
♋ 19 Jul 06 02:41
♌ 12 Aug 06 20:21
♍ 6 Sep 06 06:15
♎ 30 Sep 06 10:02
♏ 24 Oct 06 09:57
♐ 17 Nov 06 08:02
♑ 11 Dec 06 05:33
♒ 4 Jan 07 03:31
♓ 28 Jan 07 03:32
♈ 21 Feb 07 08:21
♉ 17 Mar 07 22:00
♊ 12 Apr 07 02:15
♋ 8 May 07 07:28
♌ 5 Jun 07 17:59
♍ 14 Jul 07 18:23
♌ 9 Aug 07 01:12
♍ 8 Oct 07 06:53
♎ 8 Nov 07 21:05
♏ 5 Dec 07 13:29
♐ 30 Dec 07 18:02
♑ 24 Jan 08 08:06
♒ 17 Feb 08 16:22
♓ 12 Mar 08 22:51
♈ 6 Apr 08 05:35
♉ 30 Apr 08 13:34
♊ 24 May 08 22:52
♋ 18 Jun 08 08:48
♌ 12 Jul 08 18:39
♍ 6 Aug 08 04:20
♎ 30 Aug 08 14:41
♏ 24 Sep 08 02:59
♐ 18 Oct 08 18:30
♑ 12 Nov 08 15:25
♒ 7 Dec 08 23:36
♓ 3 Jan 09 12:35
♈ 3 Feb 09 03:41
♓ 11 Apr 09 12:48
♈ 24 Apr 09 07:17
♉ 6 Jun 09 09:07
♊ 5 Jul 09 08:22
♋ 1 Aug 09 01:28
♌ 26 Aug 09 16:11
♍ 20 Sep 09 13:32
♎ 14 Oct 09 22:46
♏ 8 Nov 09 00:23
♐ 1 Dec 09 22:03
♑ 25 Dec 09 18:17
♒ 18 Jan 10 14:34
♓ 11 Feb 10 12:10
♈ 7 Mar 10 12:33
♉ 31 Mar 10 17:35

♀ Venus
♊ 25 Apr 10 05:05
♋ 20 May 10 01:05
♌ 14 Jun 10 08:50
♍ 10 Jul 10 11:31
♎ 7 Aug 10 03:47
♏ 8 Sep 10 15:44
♎ 8 Nov 10 03:08
♏ 30 Nov 10 00:32

♂ Mars
♉ 23 Jan 10 01:53
♊ 14 Mar 10 07:17
♋ 1 May 10 20:48
♌ 19 Jun 10 03:29
♍ 6 Aug 10 00:57
♎ 22 Sep 10 00:14
♏ 6 Nov 10 13:39
♐ 20 Dec 10 12:16
♑ 31 Jan 11 21:30
♒ 14 Mar 11 00:07
♓ 23 Apr 11 08:27
♈ 2 Jun 11 21:47
♉ 15 Jul 11 16:00
♊ 5 Sep 11 15:20
♉ 30 Nov 11 04:07
♊ 30 Jan 12 21:00
♋ 5 Apr 12 11:30
♌ 28 May 12 08:15
♍ 17 Jul 12 02:42
♎ 2 Sep 12 17:03
♏ 18 Oct 12 02:38
♐ 30 Nov 12 07:40
♑ 10 Jan 13 13:42
♒ 19 Feb 13 08:00
♓ 30 Mar 13 05:52
♈ 8 May 13 03:00
♉ 17 Jun 13 00:37
♊ 29 Jul 13 10:30
♋ 15 Sep 13 17:18
♌ 1 May 14 20:29
♍ 26 Jun 14 04:47
♎ 14 Aug 14 14:09
♏ 29 Sep 14 10:38
♐ 11 Nov 14 10:46
♑ 22 Dec 14 03:48
♒ 30 Jan 15 06:12
♓ 9 Mar 15 12:56
♈ 16 Apr 15 20:41
♉ 26 May 15 03:07
♊ 6 Jul 15 06:22
♋ 19 Aug 15 09:09
♌ 7 Oct 15 20:48
♍ 28 May 16 18:41
♎ 23 Jul 16 05:22
♏ 8 Sep 16 17:43
♐ 22 Oct 16 02:57
♑ 1 Dec 16 17:09
♒ 9 Jan 17 12:55
♓ 16 Feb 17 13:33
♈ 26 Mar 17 17:39
♉ 4 May 17 22:14
♊ 14 Jun 17 20:57
♋ 28 Jul 17 04:00
♌ 12 Sep 17 10:52
♍ 2 Nov 17 11:00
♎ 11 Jan 18 08:55
♍ 25 Feb 18 18:59
♎ 23 Jun 18 19:18
♏ 17 Aug 18 04:15
♐ 1 Oct 18 07:41
♑ 11 Nov 18 10:13
♒ 20 Dec 18 09:05
♓ 27 Jan 19 11:20
♈ 6 Mar 19 18:47

♂ Mars	♂ Mars	♂ Mars	♂ Mars	♂ Mars	♂ Mars	♂ Mars
♉ 15 Apr 19 05:00	♑ 29 Dec 29 10:44	♍ 19 Aug 40 15:58	♉ 10 Apr 51 09:36	♑ 24 Dec 61 17:49	♑ 12 Feb 73 05:50	♋ 29 Jun 83 06:53
♊ 26 May 19 09:37	♒ 6 Feb 30 18:20	♎ 5 Oct 40 14:21	♊ 21 May 51 15:32	♒ 1 Feb 62 23:06	♒ 26 Mar 73 20:58	♌ 13 Aug 83 16:54
♋ 8 Jul 19 17:13	♓ 17 Mar 30 05:54	♏ 20 Nov 40 17:15	♋ 3 Jul 51 23:41	♓ 12 Mar 62 07:58	♓ 8 May 73 04:08	♍ 30 Sep 83 00:12
♌ 23 Aug 19 06:17	♈ 24 Apr 30 17:26	♐ 4 Jan 41 19:42	♌ 18 Aug 51 10:55	♈ 19 Apr 62 16:58	♈ 20 Jun 73 20:53	♎ 18 Nov 83 10:26
♍ 10 Oct 19 03:52	♉ 3 Jun 30 03:15	♑ 17 Feb 41 23:32	♍ 5 Oct 51 00:20	♉ 28 May 62 23:47	♉ 12 Aug 73 14:56	♏ 11 Jan 84 03:20
♎ 30 Nov 19 12:10	♊ 14 Jul 30 12:54	♒ 2 Apr 41 11:45	♎ 24 Nov 51 06:11	♊ 9 Jul 62 03:49	♈ 29 Oct 73 22:57	♐ 17 Aug 84 19:51
♏ 31 Jan 20 23:18	♋ 28 Aug 30 11:27	♓ 16 May 41 05:04	♏ 20 Jan 52 01:33	♋ 22 Aug 62 11:37	♉ 24 Dec 73 08:08	♑ 5 Oct 84 06:02
♎ 23 Apr 20 20:28	♌ 20 Oct 30 14:43	♈ 2 Jul 41 05:17	♐ 27 Aug 52 18:53	♌ 11 Oct 62 23:54	♊ 27 Feb 74 10:10	♒ 15 Nov 84 18:08
♏ 10 Jul 20 18:14	♋ 16 Feb 31 14:27	♉ 11 Jan 42 22:20	♑ 12 Oct 52 04:45	♍ 3 Jun 63 06:29	♋ 20 Apr 74 08:17	♓ 25 Dec 84 06:37
♐ 4 Sep 20 20:27	♌ 30 Mar 31 03:46	♊ 7 Mar 42 08:04	♒ 21 Nov 52 19:39	♎ 27 Jul 63 04:14	♌ 9 Jun 74 00:53	♈ 2 Feb 85 17:19
♑ 18 Oct 20 13:21	♍ 10 Jun 31 14:57	♋ 26 Apr 42 06:17	♓ 30 Dec 52 21:35	♏ 12 Sep 63 09:11	♍ 27 Jul 74 14:04	♉ 15 Mar 85 05:06
♒ 27 Nov 20 13:37	♎ 1 Aug 31 16:37	♌ 14 Jun 42 03:55	♈ 8 Feb 53 01:06	♐ 25 Oct 63 17:31	♎ 12 Sep 74 19:08	♊ 26 Apr 85 09:13
♓ 5 Jan 21 07:39	♏ 17 Sep 31 08:43	♍ 1 Aug 42 08:27	♉ 20 Mar 53 06:53	♑ 5 Dec 63 09:03	♏ 28 Oct 74 07:04	♋ 9 Jun 85 10:40
♈ 13 Feb 21 05:20	♐ 30 Oct 31 12:46	♎ 17 Sep 42 10:10	♊ 1 May 53 06:07	♒ 13 Jan 64 06:13	♐ 10 Dec 74 22:05	♌ 25 Jul 85 04:03
♉ 25 Mar 21 06:25	♑ 10 Dec 31 03:10	♏ 1 Nov 42 22:36	♋ 14 Jun 53 03:48	♓ 20 Feb 64 07:32	♑ 21 Jan 75 18:49	♍ 10 Sep 85 01:31
♊ 6 May 21 01:44	♒ 18 Jan 32 00:34	♐ 15 Dec 42 16:51	♌ 29 Jul 53 19:25	♈ 29 Mar 64 11:24	♒ 3 Mar 75 05:31	♎ 27 Oct 85 15:16
♋ 18 Jun 21 20:34	♓ 25 Feb 32 02:36	♑ 26 Jan 43 19:09	♍ 14 Sep 53 17:59	♉ 7 May 64 14:40	♓ 11 Apr 75 19:15	♏ 14 Dec 85 19:00
♌ 3 Aug 21 11:00	♈ 3 Apr 32 07:01	♒ 8 Mar 43 12:41	♎ 1 Nov 53 14:18	♊ 17 Jun 64 11:42	♈ 21 May 75 08:13	♐ 2 Feb 86 06:27
♍ 19 Sep 21 11:39	♉ 12 May 32 10:52	♓ 17 Apr 43 10:25	♏ 20 Dec 53 11:22	♋ 30 Jul 64 18:22	♉ 1 Jul 75 03:52	♑ 28 Mar 86 03:47
♎ 6 Nov 21 16:12	♊ 22 Jun 32 09:19	♈ 27 May 43 09:24	♐ 9 Feb 54 19:17	♌ 15 Sep 64 05:22	♊ 14 Aug 75 20:46	♒ 9 Oct 86 01:01
♏ 26 Dec 21 11:48	♋ 4 Aug 32 19:52	♉ 7 Jul 43 23:04	♑ 12 Apr 54 16:27	♍ 6 Nov 64 03:20	♋ 17 Oct 75 08:42	♓ 26 Nov 86 02:35
♐ 18 Feb 22 16:15	♌ 20 Sep 32 19:43	♊ 23 Aug 43 23:57	♐ 3 Jul 54 07:25	♎ 29 Jun 65 01:11	♊ 25 Nov 75 18:32	♈ 8 Jan 87 12:20
♑ 13 Sep 22 13:02	♍ 13 Nov 32 21:26	♋ 28 Mar 44 09:53	♑ 24 Aug 54 13:20	♏ 20 Aug 65 12:16	♋ 18 Mar 76 13:14	♉ 20 Feb 87 14:44
♒ 30 Oct 22 18:54	♎ 6 Jul 33 22:02	♌ 22 May 44 14:15	♒ 21 Oct 54 12:02	♐ 4 Oct 65 06:46	♌ 16 May 76 11:10	♊ 5 Apr 87 16:37
♓ 11 Dec 22 13:09	♏ 26 Aug 33 06:34	♍ 12 Jul 44 02:54	♓ 4 Dec 54 07:41	♑ 14 Nov 65 07:19	♍ 6 Jul 76 23:26	♋ 21 May 87 03:01
♈ 21 Jan 23 10:06	♐ 9 Oct 33 11:34	♎ 29 Aug 44 00:23	♈ 15 Jan 55 04:33	♒ 23 Dec 65 05:36	♎ 24 Aug 76 05:54	♌ 6 Jul 87 16:46
♉ 4 Mar 23 00:41	♑ 19 Nov 33 07:18	♏ 13 Oct 44 12:09	♉ 26 Feb 55 10:22	♓ 30 Jan 66 07:01	♏ 8 Oct 76 20:23	♍ 22 Aug 87 19:51
♊ 16 Apr 23 02:53	♒ 28 Dec 33 03:42	♐ 25 Nov 44 16:11	♊ 10 Apr 55 23:08	♈ 9 Mar 66 12:55	♐ 20 Nov 76 23:53	♎ 8 Oct 87 19:27
♋ 30 May 23 21:18	♓ 4 Feb 34 04:13	♑ 5 Jan 45 19:31	♋ 26 May 55 00:49	♉ 17 Apr 66 20:34	♑ 1 Jan 77 00:41	♏ 24 Nov 87 03:19
♌ 16 Jul 23 01:25	♈ 14 Mar 34 09:08	♒ 14 Feb 45 09:57	♌ 11 Jul 55 09:22	♊ 28 May 66 22:07	♒ 9 Feb 77 11:56	♐ 8 Jan 88 15:24
♍ 1 Sep 23 00:57	♉ 22 Apr 34 15:39	♓ 25 Mar 45 03:43	♍ 27 Aug 55 10:13	♋ 11 Jul 66 03:14	♓ 20 Mar 77 02:19	♑ 22 Feb 88 10:15
♎ 18 Oct 23 04:17	♊ 2 Jun 34 16:20	♈ 2 May 45 20:28	♎ 13 Oct 55 11:19	♌ 25 Aug 66 15:52	♈ 27 Apr 77 15:45	♒ 6 Apr 88 21:44
♏ 4 Dec 23 02:10	♋ 15 Jul 34 21:32	♉ 11 Jun 45 11:52	♏ 29 Nov 55 01:33	♍ 12 Oct 66 18:37	♉ 6 Jun 77 02:59	♓ 22 May 88 07:42
♐ 19 Jan 24 19:05	♌ 30 Aug 34 13:43	♊ 23 Jul 45 08:59	♐ 14 Jan 56 02:27	♎ 4 Dec 66 00:55	♊ 17 Jul 77 15:12	♈ 13 Jul 88 20:00
♑ 6 Mar 24 19:02	♍ 18 Oct 34 04:59	♋ 7 Sep 45 20:55	♑ 28 Feb 56 20:04	♏ 12 Feb 67 12:21	♋ 1 Sep 77 00:20	♓ 23 Oct 88 22:21
♒ 24 Apr 24 15:58	♎ 11 Dec 34 09:32	♌ 11 Nov 45 21:05	♒ 14 Apr 56 23:39	♎ 31 Mar 67 06:08	♌ 26 Oct 77 18:56	♈ 1 Nov 88 12:38
♓ 24 Jun 24 16:29	♏ 29 Jul 35 17:32	♋ 26 Dec 45 15:03	♓ 3 Jun 56 07:51	♏ 19 Jul 67 22:56	♋ 26 Jan 78 01:58	♉ 19 Jan 89 08:10
♒ 24 Aug 24 15:38	♐ 16 Sep 35 12:58	♌ 22 Apr 46 19:30	♈ 6 Dec 56 11:22	♐ 10 Sep 67 01:44	♌ 10 Apr 78 18:49	♊ 11 Mar 89 08:51
♓ 19 Oct 24 18:40	♑ 28 Oct 35 18:21	♍ 20 Jun 46 08:31	♉ 28 Jan 57 14:18	♑ 23 Oct 67 02:14	♍ 14 Jun 78 02:37	♋ 29 Apr 89 04:37
♈ 19 Dec 24 11:09	♒ 7 Dec 35 04:33	♎ 9 Aug 46 13:16	♊ 17 Mar 57 21:33	♒ 1 Dec 67 20:11	♎ 4 Aug 78 09:07	♌ 16 Jun 89 14:10
♉ 5 Feb 25 10:17	♓ 14 Jan 36 13:59	♏ 24 Sep 46 16:34	♋ 4 May 57 15:21	♓ 9 Jan 68 09:49	♏ 19 Sep 78 20:56	♍ 3 Aug 89 13:35
♊ 24 Mar 25 00:41	♈ 22 Feb 36 04:09	♐ 6 Nov 46 18:22	♌ 21 Jun 57 12:17	♈ 17 Feb 68 03:17	♐ 2 Nov 78 01:20	♎ 19 Sep 89 14:37
♋ 9 May 25 22:43	♉ 1 Apr 36 21:29	♑ 17 Dec 46 10:55	♍ 8 Aug 57 05:27	♉ 27 Mar 68 23:43	♑ 12 Dec 78 17:38	♏ 4 Nov 89 05:29
♌ 26 Jun 25 09:07	♊ 13 May 36 09:16	♒ 25 Jan 47 11:44	♎ 24 Sep 57 04:31	♊ 8 May 68 14:14	♒ 20 Jan 79 17:07	♐ 18 Dec 89 04:57
♍ 12 Aug 25 21:11	♋ 25 Jun 36 21:53	♓ 4 Mar 47 16:46	♏ 8 Nov 57 21:03	♋ 21 Jun 68 05:03	♓ 27 Feb 79 20:25	♑ 29 Jan 90 14:10
♎ 28 Sep 25 19:00	♌ 10 Aug 36 09:42	♈ 11 Apr 47 23:02	♐ 23 Dec 57 01:29	♌ 5 Aug 68 17:07	♈ 7 Apr 79 01:08	♒ 11 Mar 90 15:54
♏ 13 Nov 25 14:01	♍ 26 Sep 36 14:51	♉ 21 May 47 03:39	♑ 3 Feb 58 18:56	♍ 21 Sep 68 18:39	♉ 16 May 79 04:25	♓ 20 Apr 90 22:09
♐ 28 Dec 25 00:35	♎ 14 Nov 36 14:52	♊ 1 Jul 47 03:34	♒ 17 Mar 58 07:11	♎ 9 Nov 68 06:10	♊ 26 Jun 79 01:54	♈ 31 May 90 07:10
♑ 9 Feb 26 03:34	♏ 5 Jan 37 20:39	♋ 13 Aug 47 21:25	♓ 27 Apr 58 02:30	♏ 29 Dec 68 22:08	♋ 8 Aug 79 13:28	♉ 12 Jul 90 14:43
♒ 23 Mar 26 04:39	♐ 13 Mar 37 03:17	♌ 1 Oct 47 02:30	♈ 7 Jun 58 06:20	♐ 25 Feb 69 06:21	♌ 24 Sep 79 21:21	♊ 31 Aug 90 11:39
♓ 3 May 26 17:03	♏ 14 May 37 22:50	♍ 1 Dec 47 11:44	♉ 21 Jul 58 07:02	♑ 21 Sep 69 06:35	♍ 19 Nov 79 21:36	♉ 14 Dec 90 07:48
♈ 15 Jun 26 00:49	♐ 8 Aug 37 22:13	♌ 12 Feb 48 10:27	♊ 21 Sep 58 05:26	♒ 4 Nov 69 18:50	♌ 11 Mar 80 20:46	♊ 21 Jan 91 01:13
♉ 1 Aug 26 09:13	♑ 30 Sep 37 09:08	♍ 18 May 48 20:52	♉ 29 Oct 58 00:01	♓ 15 Dec 69 14:22	♍ 4 May 80 02:26	♋ 3 Apr 91 00:48
♊ 22 Feb 27 00:42	♒ 11 Nov 37 18:30	♎ 17 Jul 48 05:25	♊ 10 Feb 59 13:56	♈ 24 Jan 70 21:29	♎ 10 Jul 80 17:58	♌ 26 May 91 12:18
♋ 17 Apr 27 01:28	♓ 21 Dec 37 17:45	♏ 3 Sep 48 13:58	♋ 10 Apr 59 09:46	♉ 7 Mar 70 01:28	♏ 29 Aug 80 05:50	♍ 15 Jul 91 12:36
♌ 6 Jun 27 11:35	♈ 30 Jan 38 12:43	♐ 17 Oct 48 05:43	♌ 1 Jun 59 02:25	♊ 18 Apr 70 18:58	♐ 12 Oct 80 06:26	♎ 1 Sep 91 06:38
♍ 25 Jul 27 07:47	♉ 12 Mar 38 07:47	♑ 26 Nov 48 21:58	♍ 20 Jul 59 11:03	♋ 2 Jun 70 06:50	♑ 22 Nov 80 01:42	♏ 16 Oct 91 19:04
♎ 10 Sep 27 14:18	♊ 23 Apr 38 18:39	♒ 4 Jan 49 17:49	♎ 5 Sep 59 22:46	♌ 18 Jul 70 06:43	♒ 30 Dec 80 22:30	♐ 29 Nov 91 02:18
♏ 26 Oct 27 00:20	♋ 7 Jun 38 01:28	♓ 11 Feb 49 18:05	♏ 21 Oct 59 09:40	♍ 3 Sep 70 04:57	♓ 6 Feb 81 22:48	♑ 9 Jan 92 09:46
♐ 8 Dec 27 11:00	♌ 22 Jul 38 22:26	♈ 21 Mar 49 22:02	♐ 3 Dec 59 18:08	♎ 20 Oct 70 10:57	♈ 17 Mar 81 02:39	♒ 18 Feb 92 04:37
♑ 19 Jan 28 02:02	♍ 7 Sep 38 20:22	♉ 30 Apr 49 02:32	♑ 14 Jan 60 04:59	♏ 6 Dec 70 16:34	♉ 25 Apr 81 07:16	♓ 28 Mar 92 02:04
♒ 28 Feb 28 06:29	♎ 25 Oct 38 06:20	♊ 10 Jun 49 00:56	♒ 23 Feb 60 04:11	♐ 23 Jan 71 01:34	♊ 5 Jun 81 05:26	♈ 5 May 92 21:35
♓ 7 Apr 28 14:26	♏ 11 Dec 38 23:25	♋ 23 Jul 49 05:54	♓ 2 Apr 60 06:24	♑ 12 Mar 71 10:11	♋ 18 Jul 81 08:54	♉ 14 Jun 92 15:55
♈ 16 May 28 21:34	♐ 29 Jan 39 09:49	♌ 7 Sep 49 04:51	♈ 11 May 60 07:19	♒ 3 May 71 20:58	♌ 2 Sep 81 01:52	♊ 26 Jul 92 18:58
♉ 26 Jun 28 09:03	♑ 21 Mar 39 07:25	♍ 27 Oct 49 00:58	♉ 20 Jun 60 09:04	♓ 6 Nov 71 12:30	♍ 21 Oct 81 01:56	♋ 12 Sep 92 06:05
♊ 9 Aug 28 04:09	♒ 25 May 39 00:21	♎ 26 Dec 49 05:24	♊ 2 Aug 60 04:31	♈ 26 Dec 71 18:04	♎ 16 Dec 81 00:14	♌ 27 Apr 93 23:39
♋ 3 Oct 28 03:46	♑ 21 Jul 39 19:27	♍ 28 Mar 50 11:04	♋ 21 Sep 60 04:06	♉ 10 Feb 72 14:03	♏ 3 Aug 82 11:45	♍ 23 Jun 93 07:42
♊ 20 Dec 28 05:23	♒ 24 Sep 39 01:13	♎ 11 Jun 50 20:26	♊ 5 Feb 61 00:34	♊ 27 Mar 72 04:29	♐ 20 Sep 82 01:20	♎ 12 Aug 93 01:10
♋ 10 Mar 29 23:17	♓ 19 Nov 39 15:56	♏ 10 Aug 50 16:47	♋ 7 Feb 61 05:14	♋ 12 May 72 13:14	♑ 31 Oct 82 23:04	♏ 27 Sep 93 02:15
♌ 13 May 29 02:32	♈ 4 Jan 40 00:05	♐ 25 Sep 50 19:48	♌ 6 May 61 01:12	♌ 28 Jun 72 16:08	♒ 10 Dec 82 06:16	♐ 9 Nov 93 05:29
♍ 4 Jul 29 10:02	♉ 17 Feb 40 01:53	♑ 6 Nov 50 06:40	♍ 28 Jun 61 23:47	♍ 15 Aug 72 00:58	♓ 17 Jan 83 13:10	♑ 20 Dec 93 00:34
♎ 21 Aug 29 21:51	♊ 1 Apr 40 18:40	♒ 15 Dec 50 08:58	♎ 17 Aug 61 00:41	♎ 30 Sep 72 23:23	♈ 25 Feb 83 00:19	♒ 28 Jan 94 04:05
♏ 6 Oct 29 12:26	♋ 17 May 40 14:45	♓ 22 Jan 51 13:05	♏ 1 Oct 61 20:02	♏ 15 Nov 72 22:17	♉ 5 Apr 83 14:03	♓ 7 Mar 94 11:01
♐ 18 Nov 29 13:29	♌ 3 Jul 40 10:31	♈ 1 Mar 51 22:03	♐ 13 Nov 61 21:50	♐ 30 Dec 72 16:12	♊ 16 May 83 21:43	♈ 14 Apr 94 18:01

♂ Mars
♉ 23 May 94 22:36
♊ 3 Jul 94 22:30
♋ 16 Aug 94 19:14
♌ 4 Oct 94 15:47
♍ 12 Dec 94 11:32
♌ 22 Jan 95 23:48
♍ 25 May 95 16:08
♎ 21 Jul 95 09:20
♏ 7 Sep 95 07:00
♐ 20 Oct 95 21:02
♑ 30 Nov 95 13:57
♒ 8 Jan 96 11:01
♓ 15 Feb 96 11:50
♈ 24 Mar 96 15:12
♉ 2 May 96 18:16
♊ 12 Jun 96 14:42
♋ 25 Jul 96 18:31
♌ 9 Sep 96 20:02
♍ 30 Oct 96 07:13
♎ 3 Jan 97 08:11
♍ 8 Mar 97 19:49
♎ 19 Jun 97 08:29
♏ 14 Aug 97 08:42
♐ 28 Sep 97 22:22
♑ 9 Nov 97 05:33
♒ 18 Dec 97 06:37
♓ 25 Jan 98 09:26
♈ 4 Mar 98 16:18
♉ 13 Apr 98 01:04
♊ 24 May 98 03:42
♋ 6 Jul 98 09:00
♌ 20 Aug 98 19:15
♍ 7 Oct 98 12:28
♎ 27 Nov 98 10:10
♏ 26 Jan 99 12:00
♎ 5 May 99 21:32
♏ 5 Jul 99 03:59
♐ 2 Sep 99 19:29
♑ 17 Oct 99 01:35
♒ 26 Nov 99 06:56
♓ 4 Jan 00 03:01
♈ 12 Feb 00 01:04
♉ 23 Mar 00 01:25
♊ 3 May 00 19:18
♋ 16 Jun 00 12:29
♌ 1 Aug 00 01:20
♍ 17 Sep 00 00:19
♎ 4 Nov 00 02:00
♏ 23 Dec 00 14:37
♐ 14 Feb 01 20:06
♑ 8 Sep 01 17:50
♒ 27 Oct 01 17:19
♓ 8 Dec 01 21:52
♈ 18 Jan 02 22:53
♉ 1 Mar 02 15:04
♊ 13 Apr 02 17:35
♋ 28 May 02 11:42
♌ 13 Jul 02 15:23
♍ 29 Aug 02 14:37
♎ 15 Oct 02 17:38
♏ 1 Dec 02 14:26
♐ 17 Jan 03 04:22
♑ 4 Mar 03 21:17
♒ 21 Apr 03 23:48
♓ 17 Jun 03 02:26
♈ 16 Dec 03 13:23
♉ 3 Feb 04 10:04
♊ 21 Mar 04 07:39
♋ 7 May 04 08:45
♌ 23 Jun 04 20:50
♍ 10 Aug 04 10:14
♎ 26 Sep 04 09:15
♏ 11 Nov 04 05:10
♐ 25 Dec 04 16:04

♂ Mars
♑ 6 Feb 05 18:32
♒ 20 Mar 05 18:02
♓ 1 May 05 02:57
♈ 12 Jun 05 02:29
♉ 28 Jul 05 05:11
♊ 17 Feb 06 22:43
♋ 14 Apr 06 00:59
♌ 3 Jun 06 18:42
♍ 22 Jul 06 18:52
♎ 8 Sep 06 04:18
♏ 23 Oct 06 16:38
♐ 6 Dec 06 04:58
♑ 16 Jan 07 20:54
♒ 26 Feb 07 01:32
♓ 6 Apr 07 08:49
♈ 15 May 07 14:06
♉ 24 Jun 07 21:26
♊ 7 Aug 07 06:01
♋ 28 Sep 07 23:54
♊ 31 Dec 07 16:01
♋ 4 Mar 08 10:01
♌ 9 May 08 20:19
♍ 1 Jul 08 16:21
♎ 19 Aug 08 10:03
♏ 4 Oct 08 04:34
♐ 16 Nov 08 08:26
♑ 27 Dec 08 07:30
♒ 4 Feb 09 15:55
♓ 15 Mar 09 03:20
♈ 22 Apr 09 13:44
♉ 31 May 09 21:18
♊ 12 Jul 09 02:56
♋ 25 Aug 09 17:15
♌ 16 Oct 09 15:32
♍ 7 Jun 10 06:11
♎ 29 Jul 10 23:46
♏ 14 Sep 10 22:37
♐ 28 Oct 10 06:47
♑ 7 Dec 10 23:49

♃ Jupiter
♏ 11 Nov 10 17:03
♐ 10 Dec 11 11:35
♑ 2 Jan 13 19:45
♒ 21 Jan 14 15:12
♓ 4 Feb 15 00:44
♈ 12 Feb 16 07:11
♉ 26 Jun 16 01:31
♈ 26 Oct 16 14:51
♉ 12 Feb 17 15:59
♊ 29 Jun 17 23:51
♋ 13 Jul 18 05:53
♌ 2 Aug 19 08:38
♍ 27 Aug 20 05:29
♎ 25 Sep 21 23:10
♏ 26 Oct 22 19:16
♐ 24 Nov 23 17:31
♑ 18 Dec 24 06:25
♒ 6 Jan 26 01:01
♓ 18 Jan 27 11:43
♈ 6 Jun 27 10:12
♓ 11 Sep 27 03:44
♈ 23 Jan 28 02:54
♉ 4 Jun 28 04:49
♊ 12 Jun 29 12:19
♋ 26 Jun 30 22:41
♌ 17 Jul 31 07:52
♍ 11 Aug 32 07:16
♎ 10 Sep 33 05:11
♏ 11 Oct 34 04:55
♐ 9 Nov 35 02:56
♑ 2 Dec 36 08:39
♒ 20 Dec 37 04:05
♓ 14 May 38 07:44

♃ Jupiter
♒ 30 Jul 38 03:02
♓ 29 Dec 38 18:34
♈ 11 May 39 14:07
♓ 30 Oct 39 00:45
♈ 20 Dec 39 17:03
♉ 16 May 40 07:53
♊ 26 May 41 12:47
♋ 10 Jun 42 10:36
♌ 30 Jun 43 21:46
♍ 26 Jul 44 01:04
♎ 25 Aug 45 06:06
♏ 25 Sep 46 10:19
♐ 24 Oct 47 03:00
♑ 15 Nov 48 10:38
♒ 12 Apr 49 19:17
♑ 27 Jun 49 18:29
♒ 30 Nov 49 20:08
♓ 15 Apr 50 08:57
♒ 15 Sep 50 02:21
♓ 1 Dec 50 19:58
♈ 21 Apr 51 14:57
♉ 28 Apr 52 20:50
♊ 9 May 53 15:33
♋ 24 May 54 04:44
♌ 13 Jun 55 00:07
♍ 17 Nov 55 03:59
♌ 18 Jan 56 02:02
♍ 7 Jul 56 19:02
♎ 13 Dec 56 02:17
♍ 19 Feb 57 15:35
♎ 7 Aug 57 02:12
♏ 13 Jan 58 12:52
♎ 20 Mar 58 19:12
♏ 7 Sep 58 08:52
♐ 10 Feb 59 13:46
♏ 24 Apr 59 14:09
♐ 5 Oct 59 14:40
♑ 1 Mar 60 13:10
♐ 10 Jun 60 01:51
♑ 26 Oct 60 03:02
♒ 15 Mar 61 08:01
♑ 12 Aug 61 08:51
♒ 4 Nov 61 02:51
♓ 25 Mar 62 22:08
♈ 4 Apr 63 03:20
♉ 12 Apr 64 06:53
♊ 22 Apr 65 14:33
♋ 21 Sep 65 04:40
♊ 17 Nov 65 03:06
♋ 5 May 66 14:53
♌ 27 Sep 66 13:19
♋ 16 Jan 67 03:48
♌ 23 May 67 08:22
♍ 19 Oct 67 10:51
♌ 27 Feb 68 03:30
♍ 15 Jun 68 14:45
♎ 15 Nov 68 22:44
♍ 30 Mar 69 21:34
♎ 15 Jul 69 13:31
♏ 16 Dec 69 15:56
♎ 30 Apr 70 06:41
♏ 15 Aug 70 18:00
♐ 14 Jan 71 08:49
♏ 5 Jun 71 02:09
♐ 11 Sep 71 15:35
♑ 6 Feb 72 19:37
♐ 24 Jul 72 16:37
♑ 25 Sep 72 18:23
♒ 23 Feb 73 09:28
♓ 8 Mar 74 11:12
♈ 18 Mar 75 16:48
♉ 26 Mar 76 10:25
♊ 23 Aug 76 10:25
♉ 16 Oct 76 20:23

♃ Jupiter
♊ 3 Apr 77 15:43
♋ 20 Aug 77 12:42
♊ 30 Dec 77 23:47
♋ 12 Apr 78 00:13
♌ 5 Sep 78 08:31
♋ 28 Feb 79 23:30
♌ 20 Apr 79 08:33
♍ 29 Sep 79 10:24
♎ 27 Oct 80 10:11
♏ 27 Nov 81 02:20
♐ 26 Dec 82 01:58
♑ 19 Jan 84 15:04
♒ 6 Feb 85 15:35
♓ 20 Feb 86 16:05
♈ 2 Mar 87 18:41
♉ 8 Mar 88 15:44
♊ 21 Jul 88 23:58
♉ 30 Nov 88 20:53
♊ 11 Mar 89 03:26
♋ 30 Jul 89 23:50
♌ 18 Aug 90 07:30
♍ 12 Sep 91 06:01
♎ 10 Oct 92 13:27
♏ 10 Nov 93 08:16
♐ 9 Dec 94 10:55
♑ 3 Jan 96 07:23
♒ 21 Jan 97 15:13
♓ 4 Feb 98 10:52
♈ 13 Feb 99 01:23
♉ 28 Jun 99 09:28
♈ 23 Oct 99 05:48
♉ 14 Feb 00 21:40
♊ 30 Jun 00 07:34
♋ 13 Jul 01 00:03
♌ 1 Aug 02 17:21
♍ 27 Aug 03 09:27
♎ 25 Sep 04 03:24
♏ 26 Oct 05 02:52
♐ 24 Nov 06 04:43
♑ 18 Dec 07 20:12
♒ 5 Jan 09 15:41
♓ 18 Jan 10 02:11
♈ 6 Jun 10 06:27
♓ 9 Sep 10 04:49

♄ Saturn
♉ 17 May 10 07:30
♈ 14 Dec 10 23:03
♉ 20 Jan 11 09:28
♊ 7 Jul 12 06:13
♉ 30 Nov 12 18:16
♊ 26 Mar 13 13:08
♋ 24 Aug 14 17:27
♊ 7 Dec 14 06:47
♋ 11 May 15 21:24
♌ 17 Oct 16 15:34
♋ 7 Dec 16 19:21
♌ 24 Jun 17 13:54
♍ 12 Aug 19 13:52
♎ 7 Oct 21 17:22
♏ 20 Dec 23 04:25
♎ 6 Apr 24 08:34
♏ 13 Sep 24 22:01
♐ 2 Dec 26 22:35
♑ 15 Mar 29 13:50
♐ 5 May 29 04:15
♑ 30 Nov 29 04:23
♒ 24 Feb 32 02:48
♑ 13 Aug 32 11:09
♒ 20 Nov 32 02:13
♓ 14 Feb 35 14:10
♈ 25 Apr 37 06:30
♓ 18 Oct 37 03:36
♈ 14 Jan 38 10:34

♄ Saturn
♉ 6 Jul 39 05:47
♈ 22 Sep 39 05:14
♉ 20 Mar 40 09:42
♊ 8 May 42 19:40
♋ 20 Jun 44 07:49
♌ 2 Aug 46 14:43
♍ 19 Sep 48 04:36
♌ 3 Apr 49 03:32
♍ 29 May 49 13:04
♎ 20 Nov 50 15:51
♍ 7 Mar 51 12:09
♎ 13 Aug 51 16:46
♏ 22 Oct 53 15:37
♐ 12 Jan 56 18:48
♏ 14 May 56 03:41
♐ 10 Oct 56 15:14
♑ 5 Jan 59 13:35
♒ 3 Jan 62 19:04
♓ 24 Mar 64 04:20
♒ 16 Sep 64 20:56
♓ 16 Dec 64 05:45
♈ 3 Mar 67 21:35
♉ 29 Apr 69 22:25
♊ 18 Jun 71 16:10
♉ 10 Jan 72 03:31
♊ 21 Feb 72 15:03
♋ 1 Aug 73 22:22
♊ 7 Jan 74 20:21
♋ 18 Apr 74 22:38
♌ 17 Sep 75 04:59
♋ 14 Jan 76 13:11
♌ 5 Jun 76 05:12
♍ 17 Nov 77 02:48
♌ 5 Jan 78 00:37
♍ 26 Jul 78 12:05
♎ 21 Sep 80 10:51
♏ 29 Nov 82 10:32
♎ 6 May 83 19:22
♏ 24 Aug 83 12:00
♐ 17 Nov 85 02:13
♑ 13 Feb 88 23:55
♐ 10 Jun 88 05:15
♑ 12 Nov 88 09:30
♒ 6 Feb 91 18:55
♓ 21 May 93 05:12
♒ 30 Jun 93 08:11
♓ 28 Jan 94 23:48
♈ 7 Apr 96 08:53
♉ 9 Jun 98 06:12
♈ 25 Oct 98 18:31
♉ 1 Mar 99 01:33
♊ 10 Aug 00 02:36
♉ 16 Oct 00 00:34
♊ 20 Apr 01 22:04
♋ 4 Jun 03 01:32
♌ 16 Jul 05 12:34
♍ 2 Sep 07 13:51
♎ 29 Oct 09 17:12
♍ 7 Apr 10 18:43
♎ 21 Jul 10 15:17

⚷ Chiron
♓ 20 Mar 10 10:20
♒ 29 Aug 10 07:41
♓ 15 Jan 11 11:22
♈ 31 Mar 18 11:56
♓ 22 Oct 18 14:40
♈ 28 Jan 19 19:31
♉ 25 May 26 02:47
♈ 20 Oct 26 06:47
♉ 25 Mar 27 12:07
♊ 7 Jun 33 02:54
♉ 22 Dec 33 06:41
♊ 23 Mar 34 14:55

⚷ Chiron
♋ 27 Aug 37 18:09
♊ 23 Nov 37 01:04
♋ 28 May 38 13:09
♌ 30 Sep 40 04:47
♋ 27 Dec 40 03:39
♌ 16 Jun 41 19:15
♍ 26 Jul 43 23:30
♎ 18 Nov 44 04:39
♍ 24 Mar 45 00:43
♎ 22 Jul 45 17:57
♏ 10 Nov 46 08:15
♐ 28 Nov 48 14:03
♑ 9 Feb 51 02:55
♐ 18 Jun 51 11:01
♑ 8 Nov 51 17:48
♒ 27 Jan 55 17:32
♓ 26 Mar 60 14:44
♒ 19 Aug 60 05:04
♓ 21 Jan 61 02:52
♈ 1 Apr 68 07:46
♓ 18 Oct 68 21:32
♈ 30 Jan 69 09:07
♉ 28 May 76 11:30
♈ 13 Oct 76 22:21
♉ 28 Mar 77 19:23
♊ 21 Jun 83 13:55
♉ 29 Nov 83 13:16
♊ 11 Apr 84 04:20
♋ 21 Jun 88 09:34
♌ 21 Jul 91 15:49
♍ 3 Sep 93 17:32
♎ 9 Sep 95 14:36
♏ 29 Dec 96 11:41
♎ 4 Apr 97 16:12
♏ 3 Sep 97 03:46
♐ 7 Jan 99 10:57
♏ 1 Jun 99 08:59
♐ 22 Sep 99 03:09
♑ 11 Dec 01 23:33
♒ 21 Feb 05 18:09
♑ 1 Aug 05 02:51
♒ 6 Dec 05 01:46
♓ 20 Apr 10 07:14
♒ 20 Jul 10 08:52

♅ Uranus
♒ 30 Jan 12 22:40
♑ 4 Sep 12 16:46
♒ 12 Nov 12 08:45
♓ 1 Apr 19 01:46
♒ 16 Aug 19 22:05
♓ 22 Jan 20 18:33
♈ 31 Mar 27 17:27
♓ 4 Nov 27 10:22
♈ 13 Jan 28 08:54
♉ 6 Jun 34 15:43
♈ 10 Oct 34 00:32
♉ 28 Mar 35 03:01
♊ 7 Aug 41 15:41
♉ 5 Oct 41 01:58
♊ 15 May 42 04:09
♋ 30 Aug 48 15:47
♊ 12 Nov 48 13:18
♋ 10 Jun 49 04:12
♌ 24 Aug 55 18:06
♋ 28 Jan 56 01:51
♌ 10 Jun 56 01:52
♍ 1 Nov 61 16:00
♌ 10 Jan 62 05:51
♍ 10 Aug 62 01:20
♎ 28 Sep 68 16:08
♍ 20 May 69 20:49
♎ 24 Jun 69 10:37
♏ 21 Nov 74 09:31

♅ Uranus
♎ 1 May 75 17:44
♏ 8 Sep 75 05:18
♐ 17 Feb 81 09:27
♏ 20 Mar 81 22:48
♐ 16 Nov 81 12:12
♑ 15 Feb 88 00:32
♐ 27 May 88 00:50
♑ 2 Dec 88 15:51
♒ 1 Apr 95 13:00
♑ 9 Jun 95 00:45
♒ 12 Jan 96 07:39
♓ 10 Mar 03 21:25
♒ 15 Sep 03 02:50
♓ 30 Dec 03 10:02
♈ 28 May 10 02:43
♓ 14 Aug 10 02:28

♆ Neptune
♌ 23 Sep 14 20:22
♋ 14 Dec 14 20:38
♌ 19 Jul 15 13:35
♋ 19 Mar 16 15:12
♌ 2 May 16 10:57
♍ 21 Sep 28 12:06
♌ 19 Feb 29 11:18
♍ 24 Jul 29 15:09
♎ 3 Oct 42 16:58
♍ 17 Apr 43 10:55
♎ 2 Aug 43 19:11
♏ 24 Dec 55 14:51
♎ 12 Mar 56 02:24
♏ 19 Oct 56 09:12
♎ 15 Jun 57 20:47
♏ 6 Aug 57 07:48
♐ 4 Jan 70 18:58
♏ 3 May 70 02:37
♐ 6 Nov 70 15:48
♑ 19 Jan 84 01:22
♐ 23 Jun 84 03:14
♑ 21 Nov 84 11:45
♒ 29 Jan 98 00:34
♑ 23 Aug 98 04:16
♒ 27 Nov 98 21:48

♇ Pluto
♋ 10 Sep 12 16:08
♊ 20 Oct 12 08:42
♋ 9 Jul 13 22:18
♊ 28 Dec 13 04:21
♋ 26 May 14 20:39
♌ 7 Oct 37 12:06
♋ 25 Nov 37 09:12
♌ 3 Aug 38 17:57
♋ 7 Feb 39 12:53
♌ 14 Jun 39 04:49
♍ 20 Oct 56 06:20
♌ 15 Jan 57 02:31
♍ 19 Aug 57 04:31
♌ 11 Apr 58 14:33
♍ 10 Jun 58 19:12
♎ 5 Oct 71 06:29
♍ 17 Apr 72 07:20
♎ 30 Jul 72 12:05
♏ 5 Nov 83 21:40
♎ 18 May 84 13:30
♏ 28 Aug 84 05:40
♐ 17 Jan 95 10:49
♏ 21 Apr 95 01:05
♐ 10 Nov 95 20:13
♑ 26 Jan 08 04:33
♐ 14 Jun 08 02:42
♑ 27 Nov 08 02:51

☽ Moon

Jan 1910
♎ 2 12:36
♏ 5 01:18
♐ 7 13:19
♑ 9 22:40
♒ 12 04:53
♓ 14 08:50
♈ 16 11:46
♉ 18 14:38
♊ 20 17:57
♋ 22 22:02
♌ 25 03:23
♍ 27 10:51
♎ 29 21:05

Feb 1910
♏ 1 09:32
♐ 3 22:04
♑ 6 08:03
♒ 8 14:13
♓ 10 17:13
♈ 12 18:41
♉ 14 20:19
♊ 16 23:19
♋ 19 04:02
♌ 21 10:28
♍ 23 18:40
♎ 26 04:58
♏ 28 17:15

Mar 1910
♐ 3 06:09
♑ 5 17:11
♒ 8 00:22
♓ 10 03:33
♈ 12 04:10
♉ 14 04:15
♊ 16 05:39
♋ 18 09:30
♌ 20 16:03
♍ 23 00:56
♎ 25 11:45
♏ 28 00:06
♐ 30 13:05

Apr 1910
♑ 2 00:55
♒ 4 09:31
♓ 6 14:00
♈ 8 15:05
♉ 10 14:33
♊ 12 14:27
♋ 14 16:33
♌ 16 21:55
♍ 19 06:34
♎ 21 17:43
♏ 24 06:18
♐ 26 19:13
♑ 29 07:11

May 1910
♒ 1 16:45
♓ 3 22:50
♈ 6 01:23
♉ 8 01:32
♊ 10 01:03
♋ 12 01:50
♌ 14 05:31
♍ 16 12:57
♎ 18 23:46
♏ 21 12:26
♐ 24 01:17
♑ 26 12:56
♒ 28 22:32
♓ 31 05:30

Jun 1910
♈ 2 09:37

☽ Moon

Jun 1910
♉ 4 11:19
♊ 6 11:41
♋ 8 12:16
♌ 10 14:51
♍ 12 20:52
♎ 15 06:41
♏ 17 19:07
♐ 20 07:56
♑ 22 19:14
♒ 25 04:14
♓ 27 10:58
♈ 29 15:44

Jul 1910
♉ 1 18:47
♊ 3 20:38
♋ 5 22:09
♌ 8 00:43
♍ 10 05:54
♎ 12 14:40
♏ 15 02:35
♐ 17 15:24
♑ 20 02:40
♒ 22 11:06
♓ 24 16:57
♈ 26 21:07
♉ 29 00:26
♊ 31 03:20

Aug 1910
♋ 2 06:10
♌ 4 09:40
♍ 6 14:58
♎ 8 23:12
♏ 11 10:33
♐ 13 23:26
♑ 16 11:04
♒ 18 19:31
♓ 21 00:40
♈ 23 03:41
♉ 25 06:02
♊ 27 08:43
♋ 29 12:13
♌ 31 16:48

Sep 1910
♍ 2 22:56
♎ 5 07:22
♏ 7 18:28
♐ 10 07:21
♑ 12 19:38
♒ 15 04:52
♓ 17 10:12
♈ 19 12:30
♉ 21 13:29
♊ 23 14:48
♋ 25 17:37
♌ 27 22:26
♍ 30 05:22

Oct 1910
♎ 2 14:28
♏ 5 01:44
♐ 7 14:36
♑ 10 03:25
♒ 12 13:50
♓ 14 20:22
♈ 16 23:06
♉ 18 23:26
♊ 20 23:17
♋ 23 00:25
♌ 25 04:07
♍ 27 10:53
♎ 29 20:29

Nov 1910
♏ 1 08:11

☽ Moon

Nov 1910
♐ 3 21:06
♑ 6 10:00
♒ 8 21:18
♓ 11 05:25
♈ 13 09:42
♉ 15 10:47
♊ 17 10:12
♋ 19 09:53
♌ 21 11:45
♍ 23 17:07
♎ 26 02:17
♏ 28 14:12

Dec 1910
♐ 1 03:14
♑ 3 15:56
♒ 6 03:16
♓ 8 12:19
♈ 10 18:21
♉ 12 21:13
♊ 14 21:39
♋ 16 21:11
♌ 18 21:48
♍ 21 01:24
♎ 23 09:09
♏ 25 20:35
♐ 28 09:40
♑ 30 22:13

Jan 1911
♒ 2 09:02
♓ 4 17:49
♈ 7 00:32
♉ 9 05:00
♊ 11 07:16
♋ 13 08:03
♌ 15 08:50
♍ 17 11:30
♎ 19 17:46
♏ 22 04:05
♐ 24 16:53
♑ 27 05:29
♒ 29 15:57
♓ 31 23:55

Feb 1911
♈ 3 05:57
♉ 5 10:36
♊ 7 14:02
♋ 9 16:28
♌ 11 18:33
♍ 13 21:39
♎ 16 03:21
♏ 18 12:38
♐ 21 00:52
♑ 23 13:36
♒ 26 00:17
♓ 28 07:50

Mar 1911
♈ 2 12:49
♉ 4 16:21
♊ 6 19:22
♋ 8 22:23
♌ 11 01:45
♍ 13 06:04
♎ 15 12:19
♏ 17 21:20
♐ 20 09:04
♑ 22 21:53
♒ 25 09:12
♓ 27 17:13
♈ 29 21:51

Apr 1911
♉ 1 00:13
♊ 3 01:49

☽ Moon

Apr 1911
♋ 5 03:52
♌ 7 07:14
♍ 9 12:22
♎ 11 19:35
♏ 14 05:06
♐ 16 16:45
♑ 19 05:33
♒ 21 17:32
♓ 24 02:40
♈ 26 08:02
♉ 28 10:13
♊ 30 10:39

May 1911
♋ 2 11:06
♌ 4 13:09
♍ 6 17:49
♎ 9 01:25
♏ 11 11:35
♐ 13 23:32
♑ 16 12:20
♒ 19 00:39
♓ 21 10:52
♈ 23 17:40
♉ 25 20:48
♊ 27 21:12
♋ 29 20:37
♌ 31 21:03

Jun 1911
♍ 3 00:13
♎ 5 07:06
♏ 7 17:20
♐ 10 05:36
♑ 12 18:27
♒ 15 06:43
♓ 17 17:26
♈ 20 01:31
♉ 22 06:14
♊ 24 07:46
♋ 26 07:20
♌ 28 06:54
♍ 30 08:34

Jul 1911
♎ 2 13:58
♏ 4 23:26
♐ 7 11:38
♑ 10 00:31
♒ 12 12:33
♓ 14 23:03
♈ 17 07:34
♉ 19 13:33
♊ 21 16:41
♋ 23 17:30
♌ 25 17:25
♍ 27 18:26
♎ 29 22:31

Aug 1911
♏ 1 06:43
♐ 3 18:20
♑ 6 07:09
♒ 8 19:01
♓ 11 05:00
♈ 13 13:02
♉ 15 19:11
♊ 17 23:23
♋ 20 01:42
♌ 22 02:54
♍ 24 04:26
♎ 26 08:05
♏ 28 15:15
♐ 31 02:00

Sep 1911
♑ 2 14:36

☽ Moon

Sep 1911
♒ 5 02:35
♓ 7 12:17
♈ 9 19:31
♉ 12 00:49
♊ 14 04:46
♋ 16 07:47
♌ 18 10:17
♍ 20 13:05
♎ 22 17:21
♏ 25 00:16
♐ 27 10:20
♑ 29 22:38

Oct 1911
♒ 2 10:55
♓ 4 20:59
♈ 7 03:55
♉ 9 08:12
♊ 11 10:55
♋ 13 13:12
♌ 15 15:54
♍ 17 19:41
♎ 20 01:04
♏ 22 08:36
♐ 24 18:34
♑ 27 06:36
♒ 29 19:13

Nov 1911
♓ 1 06:11
♈ 3 13:49
♉ 5 17:54
♊ 7 19:29
♋ 9 20:11
♌ 11 21:38
♍ 14 01:05
♎ 16 07:03
♏ 18 15:27
♐ 21 01:54
♑ 23 13:54
♒ 26 02:39
♓ 28 14:31
♈ 30 23:35

Dec 1911
♉ 3 04:43
♊ 5 06:18
♋ 7 05:55
♌ 9 05:38
♍ 11 07:26
♎ 13 12:35
♏ 15 21:08
♐ 18 08:07
♑ 20 20:24
♒ 23 09:05
♓ 25 21:17
♈ 28 07:35
♉ 30 14:30

Jan 1912
♊ 1 17:28
♋ 3 17:25
♌ 5 16:18
♍ 7 16:23
♎ 9 19:41
♏ 12 03:07
♐ 14 13:56
♑ 17 02:27
♒ 19 15:06
♓ 22 03:05
♈ 24 13:40
♉ 26 21:51
♊ 29 02:41
♋ 31 04:14

Feb 1912
♌ 2 03:47

☽ Moon

Feb 1912
♍ 4 03:22
♎ 6 05:12
♏ 8 10:52
♐ 10 20:34
♑ 13 08:51
♒ 15 21:33
♓ 18 09:12
♈ 20 19:16
♉ 23 03:25
♊ 25 09:14
♋ 27 12:29
♌ 29 13:43

Mar 1912
♍ 2 14:14
♎ 4 15:53
♏ 6 20:25
♐ 9 04:43
♑ 11 16:11
♒ 14 04:49
♓ 16 16:27
♈ 19 01:58
♉ 21 09:16
♊ 23 14:37
♋ 25 18:21
♌ 27 20:54
♍ 29 22:58

Apr 1912
♎ 1 01:39
♏ 3 06:15
♐ 5 13:47
♑ 8 00:23
♒ 10 12:46
♓ 13 00:42
♈ 15 10:14
♉ 17 16:50
♊ 19 21:02
♋ 21 23:53
♌ 24 02:22
♍ 26 05:17
♎ 28 09:14
♏ 30 14:47

May 1912
♐ 2 22:30
♑ 5 08:41
♒ 7 20:49
♓ 10 09:07
♈ 12 19:19
♉ 15 02:04
♊ 17 05:33
♋ 19 07:04
♌ 21 08:18
♍ 23 10:40
♎ 25 14:59
♏ 27 21:26
♐ 30 05:54

Jun 1912
♑ 1 16:16
♒ 4 04:18
♓ 6 16:54
♈ 9 04:02
♉ 11 11:46
♊ 13 15:32
♋ 15 16:24
♌ 17 16:16
♍ 19 17:09
♎ 21 20:32
♏ 24 02:57
♐ 26 11:57
♑ 28 22:49

Jul 1912
♒ 1 10:57
♓ 3 23:39

☽ Moon

Jul 1912
♈ 6 11:29
♉ 8 20:32
♊ 11 01:34
♋ 13 02:54
♌ 15 02:15
♍ 17 01:49
♎ 19 03:36
♏ 21 08:51
♐ 23 17:33
♑ 26 04:41
♒ 28 17:00
♓ 31 05:39

Aug 1912
♈ 2 17:39
♉ 5 03:36
♊ 7 10:09
♋ 9 12:57
♌ 11 13:00
♍ 13 12:14
♎ 15 12:48
♏ 17 16:27
♐ 19 23:58
♑ 22 10:42
♒ 24 23:06
♓ 27 11:39
♈ 29 23:21

Sep 1912
♉ 1 09:19
♊ 3 16:44
♋ 5 21:05
♌ 7 22:42
♍ 9 22:51
♎ 11 23:18
♏ 14 01:53
♐ 16 07:58
♑ 18 17:41
♒ 21 05:51
♓ 23 18:24
♈ 26 05:44
♉ 28 15:03
♊ 30 22:11

Oct 1912
♋ 3 03:09
♌ 5 06:11
♍ 7 07:55
♎ 9 09:24
♏ 11 12:04
♐ 13 17:18
♑ 16 01:55
♒ 18 13:29
♓ 21 02:07
♈ 23 13:28
♉ 25 22:14
♊ 28 04:22
♋ 30 08:35

Nov 1912
♌ 1 11:46
♍ 3 14:34
♎ 5 17:31
♏ 7 21:17
♐ 10 02:43
♑ 12 10:47
♒ 14 21:44
♓ 17 10:23
♈ 19 22:16
♉ 22 07:12
♊ 24 12:40
♋ 26 15:36
♌ 28 17:34
♍ 30 19:54

Dec 1912
♎ 2 23:26

☽ Moon

Dec 1912
♏ 5 04:21
♐ 7 10:48
♑ 9 19:09
♒ 12 05:50
♓ 14 18:25
♈ 17 06:59
♉ 19 16:56
♊ 21 22:50
♋ 24 01:11
♌ 26 01:43
♍ 28 02:27
♎ 30 04:55

Jan 1913
♏ 1 09:49
♐ 3 17:01
♑ 6 02:09
♒ 8 13:06
♓ 11 01:38
♈ 13 14:35
♉ 16 01:46
♊ 18 09:06
♋ 20 12:14
♌ 22 12:26
♍ 24 11:48
♎ 26 12:25
♏ 28 15:49
♐ 30 22:29

Feb 1913
♑ 2 07:58
♒ 4 19:24
♓ 7 08:02
♈ 9 20:59
♉ 12 08:46
♊ 14 17:37
♋ 16 22:28
♌ 18 23:46
♍ 20 23:08
♎ 22 22:37
♏ 25 00:10
♐ 27 05:10

Mar 1913
♑ 1 13:51
♒ 4 01:21
♓ 6 14:09
♈ 9 02:56
♉ 11 14:34
♊ 14 00:00
♋ 16 06:20
♌ 18 09:27
♍ 20 10:08
♎ 22 09:55
♏ 24 10:37
♐ 26 13:59
♑ 28 21:08
♒ 31 07:52

Apr 1913
♓ 2 20:38
♈ 5 09:21
♉ 7 20:31
♊ 10 05:30
♋ 12 12:09
♌ 14 16:30
♍ 16 18:53
♎ 18 20:02
♏ 20 21:14
♐ 23 00:02
♑ 25 05:56
♒ 27 15:32
♓ 30 03:53

May 1913
♈ 2 16:38
♉ 5 03:34

☽ Moon

May 1913
♊ 7 11:49
♋ 9 17:42
♌ 11 21:57
♍ 14 01:09
♎ 16 03:44
♏ 18 06:14
♐ 20 09:38
♑ 22 15:12
♒ 24 23:59
♓ 27 11:46
♈ 30 00:36

Jun 1913
♉ 1 11:44
♊ 3 19:42
♋ 6 00:40
♌ 8 03:51
♍ 10 06:31
♎ 12 09:27
♏ 14 13:00
♐ 16 17:31
♑ 18 23:40
♒ 21 08:20
♓ 23 19:44
♈ 26 08:37
♉ 28 20:21

Jul 1913
♊ 1 04:47
♋ 3 09:29
♌ 5 11:40
♍ 7 13:00
♎ 9 14:59
♏ 11 18:26
♐ 13 23:36
♑ 16 06:38
♒ 18 15:47
♓ 21 03:12
♈ 23 16:06
♉ 26 04:29
♊ 28 13:56
♋ 30 19:23

Aug 1913
♌ 1 21:24
♍ 3 21:43
♎ 5 22:12
♏ 8 00:22
♐ 10 05:03
♑ 12 12:24
♒ 14 22:09
♓ 17 09:51
♈ 19 22:47
♉ 22 11:29
♊ 24 22:02
♋ 27 04:53
♌ 29 07:55
♍ 31 08:16

Sep 1913
♎ 2 07:47
♏ 4 08:21
♐ 6 11:31
♑ 8 18:06
♒ 11 03:55
♓ 13 15:57
♈ 16 04:55
♉ 18 17:33
♊ 21 04:34
♋ 23 12:44
♌ 25 17:26
♍ 27 19:02
♎ 29 18:47

Oct 1913
♏ 1 18:31
♐ 3 20:07

☽ Moon

Oct 1913
♑ 6 01:10
♒ 8 10:08
♓ 10 22:06
♈ 13 11:08
♉ 15 23:30
♊ 18 10:12
♋ 20 18:45
♌ 23 00:45
♍ 25 04:06
♎ 27 05:17
♏ 29 05:30
♐ 31 06:29

Nov 1913
♑ 2 10:08
♒ 4 17:43
♓ 7 05:01
♈ 9 18:01
♉ 12 06:16
♊ 14 16:23
♋ 17 00:16
♌ 19 06:17
♍ 21 10:39
♎ 23 13:30
♏ 25 15:13
♐ 27 16:54
♑ 29 20:11

Dec 1913
♒ 2 02:42
♓ 4 12:59
♈ 7 01:45
♉ 9 14:11
♊ 12 00:08
♋ 14 07:12
♌ 16 12:09
♍ 18 16:00
♎ 20 19:19
♏ 22 22:20
♐ 25 01:28
♑ 27 05:35
♒ 29 12:00
♓ 31 21:37

Jan 1914
♈ 3 09:56
♉ 5 22:43
♊ 8 09:12
♋ 10 16:12
♌ 12 20:13
♍ 14 22:39
♎ 17 00:52
♏ 19 03:44
♐ 21 07:39
♑ 23 12:58
♒ 25 20:12
♓ 28 05:53
♈ 30 17:56

Feb 1914
♉ 2 06:53
♊ 4 18:19
♋ 7 02:15
♌ 9 06:26
♍ 11 08:00
♎ 13 08:37
♏ 15 09:55
♐ 17 13:03
♑ 19 18:37
♒ 22 02:41
♓ 24 13:00
♈ 27 01:08

Mar 1914
♉ 1 14:06
♊ 4 02:14
♋ 6 11:33

☽ Moo

Mar 191
♌ 8 17:
♍ 10 19:
♎ 12 18:
♏ 14 18:
♐ 16 20:
♑ 19 00:
♒ 21 08:
♓ 23 19:
♈ 26 07:
♉ 28 20:
♊ 31 08:

Apr 191
♋ 2 18:
♌ 5 02:
♍ 7 05:
♎ 9 06:
♏ 11 05:
♐ 13 05:
♑ 15 07:
♒ 17 14:
♓ 20 00:
♈ 22 13:
♉ 25 02:
♊ 27 14:
♋ 30 00:

May 191
♌ 2 08:
♍ 4 14:0
♎ 6 16:1
♏ 8 16:2
♐ 10 16:0
♑ 12 17:3
♒ 14 22:
♓ 17 07:3
♈ 19 19:
♉ 22 08:
♊ 24 20:3
♋ 27 06:2
♌ 29 14:2
♍ 31 20:1

Jun 1914
♎ 2 23:5
♏ 5 01:2
♐ 7 02:1
♑ 9 03:4
♒ 11 07:4
♓ 13 15:4
♈ 16 03:1
♉ 18 16:0
♊ 21 03:4
♋ 23 13:0
♌ 25 20:1
♍ 28 01:3
♎ 30 05:3

Jul 1914
♏ 2 08:1
♐ 4 10:2
♑ 6 12:5
♒ 8 17:1
♓ 11 00:3
♈ 13 11:1
♉ 15 23:4
♊ 18 11:4
♋ 20 21:1
♌ 23 03:4
♍ 25 08:0
♎ 27 11:0
♏ 29 13:4
♐ 31 16:3

Aug 1914
♑ 2 20:1
♒ 5 01:2

Moon

Aug 1914
♓ 7 09:03
♈ 9 19:24
♉ 12 07:45
♊ 14 20:05
♋ 17 06:10
♌ 19 12:52
♍ 21 16:30
♎ 23 18:18
♏ 25 19:43
♐ 27 21:59
♑ 30 01:57

Sep 1914
♒ 1 08:03
♓ 3 16:25
♈ 6 02:59
♉ 8 15:14
♊ 11 03:53
♋ 13 14:55
♌ 15 22:40
♍ 18 02:41
♎ 20 03:52
♏ 22 03:52
♐ 24 04:35
♑ 26 07:34
♒ 28 13:35
♓ 30 22:32

Oct 1914
♈ 3 09:37
♉ 5 21:58
♊ 8 10:39
♋ 10 22:25
♌ 13 07:35
♍ 15 13:01
♎ 17 14:49
♏ 19 14:22
♐ 21 13:41
♑ 23 14:55
♒ 25 19:39
♓ 28 04:13
♈ 30 15:34

Nov 1914
♉ 2 04:08
♊ 4 16:43
♋ 7 04:32
♌ 9 14:36
♍ 11 21:41
♎ 14 01:10
♏ 16 01:36
♐ 18 00:42
♑ 20 00:42
♒ 22 03:42
♓ 24 10:52
♈ 26 21:43
♉ 29 10:21

Dec 1914
♊ 1 22:53
♋ 4 10:18
♌ 6 20:12
♍ 9 04:02
♎ 11 09:08
♏ 13 11:23
♐ 15 11:40
♑ 17 11:47
♒ 19 13:47
♓ 21 19:24
♈ 24 05:02
♉ 26 17:18
♊ 29 05:52
♋ 31 17:01

Jan 1915
♌ 3 02:11
♍ 5 09:28

☽ Moon

Jan 1915
♎ 7 14:52
♏ 9 18:24
♐ 11 20:24
♑ 13 21:51
♒ 16 00:16
♓ 18 05:14
♈ 20 13:41
♉ 23 01:12
♊ 25 13:47
♋ 28 01:07
♌ 30 09:54

Feb 1915
♍ 1 16:10
♎ 3 20:32
♏ 5 23:47
♐ 8 02:33
♑ 10 05:25
♒ 12 09:09
♓ 14 14:39
♈ 16 22:45
♉ 19 09:36
♊ 21 22:04
♋ 24 09:56
♌ 26 19:10

Mar 1915
♍ 1 01:03
♎ 3 04:14
♏ 5 06:05
♐ 7 07:58
♑ 9 10:58
♒ 11 15:40
♓ 13 22:16
♈ 16 06:54
♉ 18 17:37
♊ 21 05:57
♋ 23 18:21
♌ 26 04:37
♍ 28 11:12
♎ 30 14:10

Apr 1915
♏ 1 14:49
♐ 3 15:05
♑ 5 16:46
♒ 7 21:03
♓ 10 04:07
♈ 12 13:31
♉ 15 00:37
♊ 17 12:56
♋ 20 01:36
♌ 22 12:52
♍ 24 20:52
♎ 27 00:46
♏ 29 01:23

May 1915
♐ 1 00:36
♑ 3 00:39
♒ 5 03:22
♓ 7 09:40
♈ 9 19:09
♉ 12 06:40
♊ 14 19:08
♋ 17 07:47
♌ 19 19:31
♍ 22 04:46
♎ 24 10:16
♏ 26 12:02
♐ 28 11:27
♑ 30 10:39

Jun 1915
♒ 1 11:49
♓ 3 16:31
♈ 6 01:06

☽ Moon

Jun 1915
♉ 8 12:30
♊ 11 01:06
♋ 13 13:37
♌ 16 01:12
♍ 18 10:52
♎ 20 17:38
♏ 22 21:03
♐ 24 21:45
♑ 26 21:22
♒ 28 21:54

Jul 1915
♓ 1 01:14
♈ 3 08:23
♉ 5 19:00
♊ 8 07:29
♋ 10 19:56
♌ 13 07:06
♍ 15 16:21
♎ 17 23:20
♏ 20 03:50
♐ 22 06:06
♑ 24 07:03
♒ 26 08:10
♓ 28 11:04
♈ 30 17:05

Aug 1915
♉ 2 02:39
♊ 4 14:42
♋ 7 03:10
♌ 9 14:07
♍ 11 22:41
♎ 14 04:55
♏ 16 09:16
♐ 18 12:18
♑ 20 14:38
♒ 22 17:03
♓ 24 20:35
♈ 27 02:21
♉ 29 11:07
♊ 31 22:38

Sep 1915
♋ 3 11:11
♌ 5 22:24
♍ 8 06:42
♎ 10 12:00
♏ 12 15:14
♐ 14 17:41
♑ 16 20:20
♒ 18 23:49
♓ 21 04:31
♈ 23 10:55
♉ 25 19:34
♊ 28 06:41
♋ 30 19:19

Oct 1915
♌ 3 07:12
♍ 5 16:04
♎ 7 21:08
♏ 9 23:19
♐ 12 00:20
♑ 14 01:56
♒ 16 05:14
♓ 18 10:37
♈ 20 17:57
♉ 23 03:08
♊ 25 14:14
♋ 28 02:52
♌ 30 15:25

Nov 1915
♍ 2 01:30
♎ 4 07:28
♏ 6 09:37

☽ Moon

Nov 1915
♐ 8 09:36
♑ 10 09:33
♒ 12 11:22
♓ 14 16:04
♈ 16 23:39
♉ 19 09:28
♊ 21 20:56
♋ 24 09:33
♌ 26 22:22
♍ 29 09:32

Dec 1915
♎ 1 17:08
♏ 3 20:33
♐ 5 20:47
♑ 7 19:53
♒ 9 20:00
♓ 11 22:57
♈ 14 05:29
♉ 16 15:13
♊ 19 03:02
♋ 21 15:44
♌ 24 04:23
♍ 26 15:50
♎ 29 00:41
♏ 31 05:55

Jan 1916
♐ 2 07:43
♑ 4 07:26
♒ 6 06:58
♓ 8 08:21
♈ 10 13:06
♉ 12 21:42
♊ 15 09:17
♋ 17 22:06
♌ 20 10:32
♍ 22 21:32
♎ 25 06:25
♏ 27 12:43
♐ 29 16:18
♑ 31 17:42

Feb 1916
♒ 2 18:09
♓ 4 19:16
♈ 6 22:45
♉ 9 05:49
♊ 11 16:29
♋ 14 05:12
♌ 16 17:38
♍ 19 04:08
♎ 21 12:13
♏ 23 18:08
♐ 25 22:20
♑ 28 01:12

Mar 1916
♒ 1 03:17
♓ 3 05:27
♈ 5 08:56
♉ 7 15:07
♊ 10 00:45
♋ 12 13:02
♌ 15 01:40
♍ 17 12:12
♎ 19 19:37
♏ 22 00:26
♐ 24 03:48
♑ 26 06:43
♒ 28 09:46
♓ 30 13:18

Apr 1916
♈ 1 17:48
♉ 4 00:10
♊ 6 09:19

☽ Moon

Apr 1916
♋ 8 21:10
♌ 11 10:00
♍ 13 21:06
♎ 16 04:40
♏ 18 08:48
♐ 20 10:52
♑ 22 12:34
♒ 24 15:07
♓ 26 19:04
♈ 29 00:35

May 1916
♉ 1 07:48
♊ 3 17:11
♋ 6 04:52
♌ 8 17:50
♍ 11 05:44
♎ 13 14:14
♏ 15 18:41
♐ 17 20:09
♑ 19 20:30
♒ 21 21:33
♓ 24 00:34
♈ 26 06:03
♉ 28 13:53
♊ 30 23:53

Jun 1916
♋ 2 11:45
♌ 5 00:46
♍ 7 13:14
♎ 9 22:58
♏ 12 04:40
♐ 14 06:40
♑ 16 06:33
♒ 18 06:16
♓ 20 07:39
♈ 22 11:54
♉ 24 19:25
♊ 27 05:43
♋ 29 17:54

Jul 1916
♌ 2 06:56
♍ 4 19:32
♎ 7 06:05
♏ 9 13:15
♐ 11 16:43
♑ 13 17:21
♒ 15 16:46
♓ 17 16:55
♈ 19 19:32
♉ 22 01:45
♊ 24 11:35
♋ 26 23:52
♌ 29 12:55

Aug 1916
♍ 1 01:17
♎ 3 11:53
♏ 5 19:55
♐ 8 00:56
♑ 10 03:08
♒ 12 03:28
♓ 14 03:29
♈ 16 05:02
♉ 18 09:45
♊ 20 18:26
♋ 23 06:20
♌ 25 19:23
♍ 28 07:29
♎ 30 17:33

Sep 1916
♏ 2 01:24
♐ 4 07:05
♑ 6 10:43

☽ Moon

Sep 1916
♒ 8 12:39
♓ 10 13:42
♈ 12 15:18
♉ 14 19:09
♊ 17 02:37
♋ 19 13:44
♌ 22 02:40
♍ 24 14:46
♎ 27 00:21
♏ 29 07:21

Oct 1916
♐ 1 12:27
♑ 3 16:23
♒ 5 19:28
♓ 7 21:59
♈ 10 00:40
♉ 12 04:44
♊ 14 11:37
♋ 16 21:57
♌ 19 10:38
♍ 21 23:03
♎ 24 08:45
♏ 26 15:08
♐ 28 19:07
♑ 30 22:00

Nov 1916
♒ 2 00:49
♓ 4 04:04
♈ 6 07:59
♉ 8 13:06
♊ 10 20:18
♋ 13 06:18
♌ 15 18:43
♍ 18 07:32
♎ 20 18:02
♏ 23 00:48
♐ 25 04:12
♑ 27 05:45
♒ 29 07:05

Dec 1916
♓ 1 09:29
♈ 3 13:34
♉ 5 19:35
♊ 8 03:40
♋ 10 13:59
♌ 13 02:17
♍ 15 15:18
♎ 18 02:49
♏ 20 10:52
♐ 22 14:57
♑ 24 16:07
♒ 26 16:05
♓ 28 16:41
♈ 30 19:25

Jan 1917
♉ 2 01:04
♊ 4 09:38
♋ 6 20:34
♌ 9 09:02
♍ 11 22:01
♎ 14 10:03
♏ 16 19:31
♐ 19 01:17
♑ 21 03:28
♒ 23 03:19
♓ 25 02:41
♈ 27 03:33
♉ 29 07:34
♊ 31 15:25

Feb 1917
♋ 3 02:30
♌ 5 15:15

☽ Moon

Feb 1917
♍ 8 04:08
♎ 10 16:03
♏ 13 02:06
♐ 15 09:22
♑ 17 13:23
♒ 19 14:32
♓ 21 14:06
♈ 23 14:00
♉ 25 16:19
♊ 27 22:34

Mar 1917
♋ 2 08:51
♌ 4 21:35
♍ 7 10:28
♎ 9 22:00
♏ 12 07:40
♐ 14 15:17
♑ 16 20:38
♒ 18 23:32
♓ 21 00:30
♈ 23 00:53
♉ 25 02:35
♊ 27 07:28
♋ 29 16:27

Apr 1917
♌ 1 04:38
♍ 3 17:31
♎ 6 04:53
♏ 8 13:54
♐ 10 20:50
♑ 13 02:07
♒ 15 05:56
♓ 17 08:24
♈ 19 10:10
♉ 21 12:31
♊ 23 17:04
♋ 26 01:07
♌ 28 12:30

May 1917
♍ 1 01:18
♎ 3 12:51
♏ 5 21:38
♐ 8 03:43
♑ 10 07:59
♒ 12 11:17
♓ 14 14:10
♈ 16 17:04
♉ 18 20:38
♊ 21 01:52
♋ 23 09:48
♌ 25 20:41
♍ 28 09:20
♎ 30 21:19

Jun 1917
♏ 2 06:34
♐ 4 12:27
♑ 6 15:45
♒ 8 17:45
♓ 10 19:42
♈ 12 22:30
♉ 15 02:48
♊ 17 09:01
♋ 19 17:33
♌ 22 04:26
♍ 24 16:58
♎ 27 05:25
♏ 29 15:36

Jul 1917
♐ 1 22:13
♑ 4 01:25
♒ 6 02:25
♓ 8 02:53

☽ Moon

Jul 1917
♈ 10 04:25
♉ 12 08:12
♊ 14 14:47
♋ 16 23:59
♌ 19 11:16
♍ 21 23:51
♎ 24 12:32
♏ 26 23:40
♐ 29 07:38
♑ 31 11:47

Aug 1917
♒ 2 12:50
♓ 4 12:20
♈ 6 12:19
♉ 8 14:36
♊ 10 20:23
♋ 13 05:39
♌ 15 17:18
♍ 18 06:01
♎ 20 18:41
♏ 23 06:15
♐ 25 15:27
♑ 27 21:14
♒ 29 23:27
♓ 31 23:11

Sep 1917
♈ 2 22:20
♉ 4 23:06
♊ 7 03:18
♋ 9 11:39
♌ 11 23:12
♍ 14 12:01
♎ 17 00:32
♏ 19 11:54
♐ 21 21:31
♑ 24 04:36
♒ 26 08:33
♓ 28 09:39
♈ 30 09:16

Oct 1917
♉ 2 09:25
♊ 4 12:13
♋ 6 19:05
♌ 9 05:49
♍ 11 18:31
♎ 14 06:58
♏ 16 17:53
♐ 19 03:00
♑ 21 10:13
♒ 23 15:16
♓ 25 18:02
♈ 27 19:08
♉ 29 19:59
♊ 31 22:25

Nov 1917
♋ 3 04:08
♌ 5 13:41
♍ 8 01:55
♎ 10 14:25
♏ 13 01:12
♐ 15 09:36
♑ 17 15:55
♒ 19 20:37
♓ 22 00:03
♈ 24 02:35
♉ 26 04:55
♊ 28 08:13
♋ 30 13:47

Dec 1917
♌ 2 22:31
♍ 5 10:06
♎ 7 22:41

☽ Moon

Dec 1917
♏ 10 09:51
♐ 12 18:10
♑ 14 23:34
♒ 17 02:59
♓ 19 05:31
♈ 21 08:06
♉ 23 11:26
♊ 25 16:02
♋ 27 22:28
♌ 30 07:14

Jan 1918
♍ 1 18:22
♎ 4 06:55
♏ 6 18:49
♐ 9 03:57
♑ 11 09:27
♒ 13 11:56
♓ 15 12:54
♈ 17 14:03
♉ 19 16:48
♊ 21 21:51
♋ 24 05:16
♌ 26 14:44
♍ 29 01:58
♎ 31 14:25

Feb 1918
♏ 3 02:51
♐ 5 13:14
♑ 7 19:56
♒ 9 22:46
♓ 11 22:57
♈ 13 22:30
♉ 15 23:31
♊ 18 03:29
♋ 20 10:49
♌ 22 20:52
♍ 25 08:32
♎ 27 21:00

Mar 1918
♏ 2 09:31
♐ 4 20:47
♑ 7 05:04
♒ 9 09:23
♓ 11 10:12
♈ 13 09:16
♉ 15 08:48
♊ 17 10:57
♋ 19 16:57
♌ 22 02:36
♍ 24 14:29
♎ 27 03:06
♏ 29 15:27

Apr 1918
♐ 1 02:46
♑ 3 11:58
♒ 5 17:55
♓ 7 20:22
♈ 9 20:19
♉ 11 19:40
♊ 13 20:37
♋ 16 00:57
♌ 18 09:18
♍ 20 20:45
♎ 23 09:24
♏ 25 21:37
♐ 28 08:30
♑ 30 17:32

May 1918
♒ 3 00:12
♓ 5 04:07
♈ 7 05:40
♉ 9 06:05

☽ Moon

May 1918
♊ 11 07:06
♋ 13 10:30
♌ 15 17:30
♍ 18 04:00
♎ 20 16:24
♏ 23 04:37
♐ 25 15:08
♑ 27 23:27
♒ 30 05:37

Jun 1918
♓ 1 09:53
♈ 3 12:37
♉ 5 14:30
♊ 7 16:36
♋ 9 20:13
♌ 12 02:35
♍ 14 12:09
♎ 17 00:09
♏ 19 12:29
♐ 21 23:04
♑ 24 06:50
♒ 26 12:01
♓ 28 15:26
♈ 30 18:04

Jul 1918
♉ 2 20:44
♊ 5 00:03
♋ 7 04:42
♌ 9 11:20
♍ 11 20:32
♎ 14 08:08
♏ 16 20:40
♐ 19 07:48
♑ 21 15:46
♒ 23 20:19
♓ 25 22:32
♈ 27 23:58
♉ 30 02:06

Aug 1918
♊ 1 05:47
♋ 3 11:21
♌ 5 18:48
♍ 8 04:16
♎ 10 15:45
♏ 13 04:26
♐ 15 16:21
♑ 18 01:16
♒ 20 06:11
♓ 22 07:48
♈ 24 07:56
♉ 26 08:35
♊ 28 11:19
♋ 30 16:49

Sep 1918
♌ 2 00:52
♍ 4 10:55
♎ 6 22:34
♏ 9 11:18
♐ 11 23:50
♑ 14 10:01
♒ 16 16:14
♓ 18 18:26
♈ 20 18:08
♉ 22 17:27
♊ 24 18:30
♋ 26 22:44
♌ 29 06:24

Oct 1918
♍ 1 16:45
♎ 4 04:43
♏ 6 17:27
♐ 9 06:04

☽ Moon

Oct 1918
♑ 11 17:05
♒ 14 00:53
♓ 16 04:41
♈ 18 05:14
♉ 20 04:20
♊ 22 04:10
♋ 24 06:39
♌ 26 12:53
♍ 28 22:41
♎ 31 10:44

Nov 1918
♏ 2 23:31
♐ 5 11:51
♑ 7 22:49
♒ 10 07:25
♓ 12 12:51
♈ 14 15:11
♉ 16 15:27
♊ 18 15:20
♋ 20 16:46
♌ 22 21:22
♍ 25 05:50
♎ 27 17:24
♏ 30 06:12

Dec 1918
♐ 2 18:20
♑ 5 04:41
♒ 7 12:51
♓ 9 18:47
♈ 11 22:33
♉ 14 00:35
♊ 16 01:48
♋ 18 03:34
♌ 20 07:24
♍ 22 14:32
♎ 25 01:09
♏ 27 13:47
♐ 30 02:03

Jan 1919
♑ 1 12:01
♒ 3 19:15
♓ 6 00:18
♈ 8 04:00
♉ 10 07:01
♊ 12 09:48
♋ 14 12:56
♌ 16 17:16
♍ 18 23:56
♎ 21 09:42
♏ 23 21:59
♐ 26 10:34
♑ 28 20:53
♒ 31 03:43

Feb 1919
♓ 2 07:38
♈ 4 10:02
♉ 6 12:22
♊ 8 15:30
♋ 10 19:45
♌ 13 01:17
♍ 15 08:31
♎ 17 18:06
♏ 20 06:03
♐ 22 18:56
♑ 25 06:07
♒ 27 13:36

Mar 1919
♓ 1 17:14
♈ 3 18:28
♉ 5 19:14
♊ 7 21:09
♋ 10 01:08

☽ Moon

Mar 1919
♌ 12 07:18
♍ 14 15:25
♎ 17 01:28
♏ 19 13:24
♐ 22 02:23
♑ 24 14:24
♒ 26 23:11
♓ 29 03:45
♈ 31 04:57

Apr 1919
♉ 2 04:40
♊ 4 04:56
♋ 6 07:22
♌ 8 12:47
♍ 10 21:06
♎ 13 07:42
♏ 15 19:53
♐ 18 08:51
♑ 20 21:13
♒ 23 07:08
♓ 25 13:16
♈ 27 15:40
♉ 29 15:36

May 1919
♊ 1 15:01
♋ 3 15:50
♌ 5 19:37
♍ 8 03:00
♎ 10 13:31
♏ 13 01:57
♐ 15 14:53
♑ 18 03:06
♒ 20 13:23
♓ 22 20:44
♈ 25 00:46
♉ 27 02:02
♊ 29 01:53
♋ 31 02:04

Jun 1919
♌ 2 04:26
♍ 4 10:18
♎ 6 19:57
♏ 9 08:14
♐ 11 21:11
♑ 14 09:04
♒ 16 18:58
♓ 19 02:31
♈ 21 07:38
♉ 23 10:28
♊ 25 11:42
♋ 27 12:28
♌ 29 14:24

Jul 1919
♍ 1 19:05
♎ 4 03:34
♏ 6 15:17
♐ 9 04:12
♑ 11 15:56
♒ 14 01:13
♓ 16 08:06
♈ 18 13:05
♉ 20 16:43
♊ 22 19:19
♋ 24 21:25
♌ 26 23:59
♍ 29 04:27
♎ 31 12:05

Aug 1919
♏ 2 23:07
♐ 5 11:56
♑ 7 23:52
♒ 10 08:56

☽ Moon

Aug 1919
♓ 12 14:59
♈ 14 18:59
♉ 16 22:04
♊ 19 01:02
♋ 21 04:13
♌ 23 07:59
♍ 25 13:08
♎ 27 20:41
♏ 30 07:14

Sep 1919
♐ 1 19:57
♑ 4 08:20
♒ 6 17:53
♓ 8 23:45
♈ 11 02:47
♉ 13 04:35
♊ 15 06:35
♋ 17 09:38
♌ 19 14:07
♍ 21 20:14
♎ 24 04:24
♏ 26 14:59
♐ 29 03:36

Oct 1919
♑ 1 16:27
♒ 4 03:02
♓ 6 09:44
♈ 8 12:44
♉ 10 13:33
♊ 12 13:59
♋ 14 15:39
♌ 16 19:31
♍ 19 01:58
♎ 21 10:50
♏ 23 21:52
♐ 26 10:30
♑ 28 23:34
♒ 31 11:07

Nov 1919
♓ 2 19:18
♈ 4 23:30
♉ 7 00:31
♊ 9 00:03
♋ 11 00:03
♌ 13 02:13
♍ 15 07:40
♎ 17 16:31
♏ 20 03:58
♐ 22 16:47
♑ 25 05:45
♒ 27 17:36
♓ 30 03:02

Dec 1919
♈ 2 09:02
♉ 4 11:33
♊ 6 11:36
♋ 8 10:55
♌ 10 11:28
♍ 12 15:06
♎ 14 22:47
♏ 17 10:00
♐ 19 22:58
♑ 22 11:48
♒ 24 23:19
♓ 27 08:55
♈ 29 16:05
♉ 31 20:28

Jan 1920
♊ 2 22:12
♋ 4 22:19
♌ 6 22:29
♍ 9 00:45

☽ Moon

Jan 1920
♎ 11 06:47
♏ 13 16:56
♐ 16 05:43
♑ 18 18:33
♒ 21 05:39
♓ 23 14:34
♈ 25 21:32
♉ 28 02:43
♊ 30 06:05

Feb 1920
♋ 1 07:54
♌ 3 09:06
♍ 5 11:18
♎ 7 16:19
♏ 10 01:13
♐ 12 13:19
♑ 15 02:13
♒ 17 13:19
♓ 19 21:38
♈ 22 03:36
♉ 24 08:05
♊ 26 11:41
♋ 28 14:40

Mar 1920
♌ 1 17:22
♍ 3 20:40
♎ 6 01:52
♏ 8 10:09
♐ 10 21:34
♑ 13 10:24
♒ 15 21:57
♓ 18 06:24
♈ 20 11:43
♉ 22 14:58
♊ 24 17:25
♋ 26 20:01
♌ 28 23:20
♍ 31 03:47

Apr 1920
♎ 2 09:59
♏ 4 18:33
♐ 7 05:41
♑ 9 18:24
♒ 12 06:31
♓ 14 15:49
♈ 16 21:29
♉ 19 00:07
♊ 21 01:14
♋ 23 02:22
♌ 25 04:48
♍ 27 09:21
♎ 29 16:18

May 1920
♏ 2 01:37
♐ 4 12:58
♑ 7 01:39
♒ 9 14:08
♓ 12 00:31
♈ 14 07:23
♉ 16 10:35
♊ 18 11:13
♋ 20 11:01
♌ 22 11:49
♍ 24 15:10
♎ 26 21:49
♏ 29 07:32
♐ 31 19:20

Jun 1920
♑ 3 08:04
♒ 5 20:37
♓ 8 07:42
♈ 10 15:56

☽ Moon

Jun 1920
♉ 12 20:35
♊ 14 21:57
♋ 16 21:26
♌ 18 21:01
♍ 20 22:44
♎ 23 04:05
♏ 25 13:18
♐ 28 01:14
♑ 30 14:05

Jul 1920
♒ 3 02:30
♓ 5 13:36
♈ 7 22:38
♉ 10 04:45
♊ 12 07:40
♋ 14 08:03
♌ 16 07:32
♍ 18 08:12
♎ 20 12:02
♏ 22 20:02
♐ 25 07:30
♑ 27 20:21
♒ 30 08:36

Aug 1920
♓ 1 19:17
♈ 4 04:09
♉ 6 10:55
♊ 8 15:14
♋ 10 17:11
♌ 12 17:41
♍ 14 18:27
♎ 16 21:27
♏ 19 04:11
♐ 21 14:44
♑ 24 03:21
♒ 26 15:35
♓ 29 01:54
♈ 31 10:02

Sep 1920
♉ 2 16:19
♊ 4 20:57
♋ 7 00:03
♌ 9 02:02
♍ 11 03:54
♎ 13 07:10
♏ 15 13:18
♐ 17 22:57
♑ 20 11:08
♒ 22 23:32
♓ 25 09:57
♈ 27 17:34
♉ 29 22:49

Oct 1920
♊ 2 02:32
♋ 4 05:28
♌ 6 08:13
♍ 8 11:23
♎ 10 15:44
♏ 12 22:13
♐ 15 07:29
♑ 17 19:15
♒ 20 07:51
♓ 22 18:56
♈ 25 02:52
♉ 27 07:33
♊ 29 09:59
♋ 31 11:34

Nov 1920
♌ 2 13:37
♍ 4 17:03
♎ 6 22:22
♏ 9 05:49

☽ Moon

Nov 1920
♐ 11 15:26
♑ 14 03:02
♒ 16 15:43
♓ 19 03:39
♈ 21 12:44
♉ 23 18:01
♊ 25 20:00
♋ 27 20:12
♌ 29 20:32

Dec 1920
♍ 1 22:44
♎ 4 03:49
♏ 6 11:50
♐ 8 22:09
♑ 11 09:58
♒ 13 22:38
♓ 16 11:02
♈ 18 21:29
♉ 21 04:21
♊ 23 07:15
♋ 25 07:13
♌ 27 06:16
♍ 29 06:37
♎ 31 10:05

Jan 1921
♏ 2 17:26
♐ 5 03:57
♑ 7 16:09
♒ 10 04:49
♓ 12 17:10
♈ 15 04:14
♉ 17 12:39
♊ 19 17:23
♋ 21 18:35
♌ 23 17:45
♍ 25 17:04
♎ 27 18:46
♏ 30 00:24

Feb 1921
♐ 1 10:02
♑ 3 22:13
♒ 6 10:58
♓ 8 23:03
♈ 11 09:50
♉ 13 18:44
♊ 16 00:54
♋ 18 03:57
♌ 20 04:34
♍ 22 04:20
♎ 24 05:20
♏ 26 09:27
♐ 28 17:35

Mar 1921
♑ 3 05:02
♒ 5 17:45
♓ 8 05:43
♈ 10 15:57
♉ 13 00:14
♊ 15 06:28
♋ 17 10:36
♌ 19 12:52
♍ 21 14:08
♎ 23 15:49
♏ 25 19:33
♐ 28 02:33
♑ 30 12:57

Apr 1921
♒ 2 01:21
♓ 4 13:27
♈ 6 23:30
♉ 9 06:59
♊ 11 12:15

☽ Moon

Apr 1921
♋ 13 15:58
♌ 15 18:47
♍ 17 21:21
♎ 20 00:24
♏ 22 04:53
♐ 24 11:44
♑ 26 21:27
♒ 29 09:25

May 1921
♓ 1 21:46
♈ 4 08:13
♉ 6 15:31
♊ 8 19:51
♋ 10 22:18
♌ 13 00:16
♍ 15 02:51
♎ 17 06:46
♏ 19 12:21
♐ 21 19:52
♑ 24 05:34
♒ 26 17:16
♓ 29 05:49
♈ 31 17:04

Jun 1921
♉ 3 01:03
♊ 5 05:17
♋ 7 06:47
♌ 9 07:18
♍ 11 08:40
♎ 13 12:09
♏ 15 18:10
♐ 18 02:27
♑ 20 12:38
♒ 23 00:23
♓ 25 13:03
♈ 28 01:02
♉ 30 10:13

Jul 1921
♊ 2 15:22
♋ 4 16:55
♌ 6 16:34
♍ 8 16:26
♎ 10 18:27
♏ 12 23:42
♐ 15 08:04
♑ 17 18:42
♒ 20 06:43
♓ 22 19:23
♈ 25 07:41
♉ 27 17:57
♊ 30 00:36

Aug 1921
♋ 1 03:18
♌ 3 03:11
♍ 5 02:18
♎ 7 02:51
♏ 9 06:32
♐ 11 13:58
♑ 14 00:29
♒ 16 12:41
♓ 19 01:20
♈ 21 13:29
♉ 24 00:06
♊ 26 07:57
♋ 28 12:17
♌ 30 13:31

Sep 1921
♍ 1 13:07
♎ 3 13:05
♏ 5 15:23
♐ 7 21:20
♑ 10 06:57

☽ Moon

Sep 1921
♒ 12 19:00
♓ 15 07:38
♈ 17 19:28
♉ 20 05:40
♊ 22 13:41
♋ 24 19:05
♌ 26 21:57
♍ 28 23:01
♎ 30 23:40

Oct 1921
♏ 3 01:36
♐ 5 06:21
♑ 7 14:44
♒ 10 02:12
♓ 12 14:50
♈ 15 02:33
♉ 17 12:07
♊ 19 19:20
♋ 22 00:31
♌ 24 04:08
♍ 26 06:40
♎ 28 08:48
♏ 30 11:33

Nov 1921
♐ 1 16:07
♑ 3 23:37
♒ 6 10:16
♓ 8 22:50
♈ 11 10:51
♉ 13 20:18
♊ 16 02:40
♋ 18 06:40
♌ 20 09:32
♍ 22 12:16
♎ 24 15:31
♏ 26 19:37
♐ 29 01:02

Dec 1921
♑ 1 08:32
♒ 3 18:40
♓ 6 07:02
♈ 8 19:36
♉ 11 05:45
♊ 13 12:07
♋ 15 15:12
♌ 17 16:34
♍ 19 18:02
♎ 21 20:51
♏ 24 01:32
♐ 26 08:01
♑ 28 16:16
♒ 31 02:31

Jan 1922
♓ 2 14:43
♈ 5 03:41
♉ 7 14:57
♊ 9 22:26
♋ 12 01:47
♌ 14 02:20
♍ 16 02:12
♎ 18 03:20
♏ 20 07:01
♐ 22 13:32
♑ 24 22:28
♒ 27 09:16
♓ 29 21:33

Feb 1922
♈ 1 10:34
♉ 3 22:40
♊ 6 07:41
♋ 8 12:29
♌ 10 13:40

☽ Moon

Feb 1922
♍ 12 12:59
♎ 14 12:34
♏ 16 14:22
♐ 18 19:31
♑ 21 04:04
♒ 23 15:11
♓ 26 03:44
♈ 28 16:40

Mar 1922
♉ 3 04:51
♊ 5 14:48
♋ 7 21:18
♌ 10 00:09
♍ 12 00:22
♎ 13 23:43
♏ 16 00:12
♐ 18 03:33
♑ 20 10:40
♒ 22 21:17
♓ 25 09:55
♈ 27 22:49
♉ 30 10:37

Apr 1922
♊ 1 20:28
♋ 4 03:46
♌ 6 08:12
♍ 8 10:09
♎ 10 10:36
♏ 12 11:07
♐ 14 13:25
♑ 16 19:01
♒ 19 04:27
♓ 21 16:42
♈ 24 05:37
♉ 26 17:07
♊ 29 02:19

May 1922
♋ 1 09:11
♌ 3 14:05
♍ 5 17:19
♎ 7 19:21
♏ 9 21:00
♐ 11 23:31
♑ 14 04:25
♒ 16 12:45
♓ 19 00:20
♈ 21 13:11
♉ 24 00:45
♊ 26 09:28
♋ 28 15:26
♌ 30 19:33

Jun 1922
♍ 1 22:47
♎ 4 01:43
♏ 6 04:42
♐ 8 08:17
♑ 10 13:30
♒ 12 21:25
♓ 15 08:24
♈ 17 21:11
♉ 20 09:08
♊ 22 18:01
♋ 24 23:27
♌ 27 02:28
♍ 29 04:36

Jul 1922
♎ 1 07:04
♏ 3 10:29
♐ 5 15:05
♑ 7 21:12
♒ 10 05:27
♓ 12 16:15

☽ Moon

Jul 1922
♈ 15 04:58
♉ 17 17:27
♊ 20 03:09
♋ 22 08:56
♌ 24 11:26
♍ 26 12:21
♎ 28 13:26
♏ 30 15:58

Aug 1922
♐ 1 20:34
♑ 4 03:21
♒ 6 12:18
♓ 8 23:22
♈ 11 12:04
♉ 14 00:56
♊ 16 11:41
♋ 18 18:39
♌ 20 21:45
♍ 22 22:15
♎ 24 22:05
♏ 26 23:01
♐ 29 02:26
♑ 31 08:53

Sep 1922
♒ 2 18:11
♓ 5 05:41
♈ 7 18:28
♉ 10 07:23
♊ 12 18:49
♋ 15 03:12
♌ 17 07:47
♍ 19 09:08
♎ 21 08:44
♏ 23 08:27
♐ 25 10:10
♑ 27 15:15
♒ 30 00:02

Oct 1922
♓ 2 11:40
♈ 5 00:35
♉ 7 13:19
♊ 10 00:44
♋ 12 09:51
♌ 14 16:01
♍ 16 19:04
♎ 18 19:43
♏ 20 19:26
♐ 22 20:05
♑ 24 23:33
♒ 27 06:59
♓ 29 18:06

Nov 1922
♈ 1 07:03
♉ 3 19:39
♊ 6 06:33
♋ 8 15:22
♌ 10 22:05
♍ 13 02:36
♎ 15 05:00
♏ 17 05:59
♐ 19 06:52
♑ 21 09:31
♒ 23 15:35
♓ 26 01:39
♈ 28 14:19

Dec 1922
♉ 1 02:59
♊ 3 13:33
♋ 5 21:33
♌ 8 03:32
♍ 10 08:08
♎ 12 11:39

☽ Moon

Dec 1922
♏ 14 14:14
♐ 16 16:28
♑ 18 19:34
♒ 21 01:08
♓ 23 10:13
♈ 25 22:22
♉ 28 11:12
♊ 30 22:02

Jan 1923
♋ 2 05:39
♌ 4 10:34
♍ 6 13:59
♎ 8 16:58
♏ 10 20:04
♐ 12 23:33
♑ 15 03:56
♒ 17 10:05
♓ 19 18:57
♈ 22 06:36
♉ 24 19:33
♊ 27 07:07
♋ 29 15:18
♌ 31 19:57

Feb 1923
♍ 2 22:11
♎ 4 23:38
♏ 7 01:37
♐ 9 04:58
♑ 11 10:07
♒ 13 17:18
♓ 16 02:43
♈ 18 14:19
♉ 21 03:14
♊ 23 15:30
♋ 26 00:57
♌ 28 06:30

Mar 1923
♍ 2 08:41
♎ 4 09:01
♏ 6 09:16
♐ 8 11:05
♑ 10 15:33
♒ 12 23:01
♓ 15 09:07
♈ 17 21:05
♉ 20 09:59
♊ 22 22:32
♋ 25 09:04
♌ 27 16:13
♍ 29 19:36
♎ 31 20:06

Apr 1923
♏ 2 19:26
♐ 4 19:33
♑ 6 22:19
♒ 9 04:47
♓ 11 14:50
♈ 14 03:08
♉ 16 16:06
♊ 19 04:32
♋ 21 15:27
♌ 23 23:57
♍ 26 04:56
♎ 28 06:48
♏ 30 06:33

May 1923
♐ 2 05:59
♑ 4 07:14
♒ 6 12:04
♓ 8 21:05
♈ 11 09:11
♉ 13 22:14

☽ Moo

May 192
♊ 16 10:
♋ 18 21:
♌ 21 05:
♍ 23 11:
♎ 25 15:
♏ 27 16:
♐ 29 16:
♑ 31 17:

Jun 1923
♒ 2 21:
♓ 5 04:
♈ 7 16:0
♉ 10 04:5
♊ 12 17:0
♋ 15 03:0
♌ 17 11:1
♍ 19 17:2
♎ 21 21:4
♏ 24 00:2
♐ 26 01:4
♑ 28 03:1
♒ 30 06:4

Jul 1923
♓ 2 13:2
♈ 4 23:5
♉ 7 12:2
♊ 10 00:3
♋ 12 10:3
♌ 14 17:5
♍ 16 23:0
♎ 19 03:0
♏ 21 06:0
♐ 23 08:4
♑ 25 11:3
♒ 27 15:4
♓ 29 22:2

Aug 1923
♈ 1 08:1
♉ 3 20:2
♊ 6 08:4
♋ 8 19:07
♌ 11 02:1
♍ 13 06:44
♎ 15 09:27
♏ 17 11:38
♐ 19 14:12
♑ 21 17:4
♒ 23 23:02
♓ 26 06:24
♈ 28 16:14
♉ 31 04:11

Sep 1923
♊ 2 16:49
♋ 5 03:58
♌ 7 11:53
♍ 9 16:1
♎ 11 18:03
♏ 13 18:47
♐ 15 20:05
♑ 17 23:13
♒ 20 04:52
♓ 22 13:02
♈ 24 23:23
♉ 27 11:22
♊ 30 00:05

Oct 1923
♋ 2 11:59
♌ 4 21:14
♍ 7 02:40
♎ 9 04:35
♏ 11 04:25
♐ 13 04:08

☽ Moon

Oct 1923
♑ 15 05:42
♒ 17 10:28
♓ 19 18:42
♈ 22 05:32
♉ 24 17:47
♊ 27 06:28
♋ 29 18:38

Nov 1923
♌ 1 04:59
♍ 3 12:06
♎ 5 15:23
♏ 7 15:38
♐ 9 14:38
♑ 11 14:37
♒ 13 17:39
♓ 16 00:46
♈ 18 11:24
♉ 20 23:52
♊ 23 12:31
♋ 26 00:27
♌ 28 11:01
♍ 30 19:18

Dec 1923
♎ 3 00:24
♏ 5 02:14
♐ 7 01:57
♑ 9 01:31
♒ 11 03:09
♓ 13 08:34
♈ 15 18:07
♉ 18 06:21
♊ 20 19:02
♋ 23 06:39
♌ 25 16:39
♍ 28 00:50
♎ 30 06:51

Jan 1924
♏ 1 10:22
♐ 3 11:48
♑ 5 12:22
♒ 7 13:54
♓ 9 18:13
♈ 12 02:21
♉ 14 13:47
♊ 17 02:27
♋ 19 14:05
♌ 21 23:33
♍ 24 06:48
♎ 26 12:14
♏ 28 16:08
♐ 30 18:52

Feb 1924
♑ 1 21:03
♒ 3 23:43
♓ 6 04:12
♈ 8 11:36
♉ 10 22:08
♊ 13 10:33
♋ 15 22:33
♌ 18 08:08
♍ 20 14:45
♎ 22 18:57
♏ 24 21:46
♐ 27 00:15
♑ 29 03:12

Mar 1924
♒ 2 07:11
♓ 4 12:44
♈ 6 20:25
♉ 9 06:35
♊ 11 18:43
♋ 14 07:07

☽ Moon

Mar 1924
♌ 16 17:30
♍ 19 00:26
♎ 21 04:00
♏ 23 05:27
♐ 25 06:29
♑ 27 08:36
♒ 29 12:46
♓ 31 19:12

Apr 1924
♈ 3 03:45
♉ 5 14:11
♊ 8 02:12
♋ 10 14:51
♌ 13 02:14
♍ 15 10:20
♎ 17 14:26
♏ 19 15:24
♐ 21 15:05
♑ 23 15:33
♒ 25 18:29
♓ 28 00:38
♈ 30 09:38

May 1924
♉ 2 20:36
♊ 5 08:47
♋ 7 21:30
♌ 10 09:29
♍ 12 18:56
♎ 15 00:28
♏ 17 02:10
♐ 19 01:33
♑ 21 00:48
♒ 23 02:04
♓ 25 06:49
♈ 27 15:15
♉ 30 02:22

Jun 1924
♊ 1 14:47
♋ 4 03:26
♌ 6 15:28
♍ 9 01:40
♎ 11 08:40
♏ 13 11:57
♐ 15 12:17
♑ 17 11:29
♒ 19 11:42
♓ 21 14:51
♈ 23 21:55
♉ 26 08:26
♊ 28 20:50

Jul 1924
♋ 1 09:27
♌ 3 21:10
♍ 6 07:15
♎ 8 14:54
♏ 10 19:36
♐ 12 21:31
♑ 14 21:48
♒ 16 22:11
♓ 19 00:30
♈ 21 06:11
♉ 23 15:35
♊ 26 03:36
♋ 28 16:11
♌ 31 03:37

Aug 1924
♍ 2 13:04
♎ 4 20:19
♏ 7 01:23
♐ 9 04:31
♑ 11 06:20
♒ 13 07:52

☽ Moon

Aug 1924
♓ 15 10:28
♈ 17 15:32
♉ 19 23:54
♊ 22 11:13
♋ 24 23:48
♌ 27 11:18
♍ 29 20:18

Sep 1924
♎ 1 02:37
♏ 3 06:54
♐ 5 10:00
♑ 7 12:40
♒ 9 15:32
♓ 11 19:16
♈ 14 00:41
♉ 16 08:38
♊ 18 19:23
♋ 21 07:53
♌ 23 19:51
♍ 26 05:06
♎ 28 10:53
♏ 30 14:00

Oct 1924
♐ 2 15:54
♑ 4 18:02
♒ 6 21:19
♓ 9 02:06
♈ 11 08:30
♉ 13 16:49
♊ 16 03:22
♋ 18 15:47
♌ 21 04:21
♍ 23 14:32
♎ 25 20:48
♏ 27 23:26
♐ 30 00:03

Nov 1924
♑ 1 00:38
♒ 3 02:52
♓ 5 07:34
♈ 7 14:39
♉ 9 23:43
♊ 12 10:34
♋ 14 22:56
♌ 17 11:50
♍ 19 23:10
♎ 22 06:51
♏ 24 10:17
♐ 26 10:38
♑ 28 09:58
♒ 30 10:25

Dec 1924
♓ 2 13:38
♈ 4 20:10
♉ 7 05:33
♊ 9 16:52
♋ 12 05:20
♌ 14 18:12
♍ 17 06:06
♎ 19 15:14
♏ 21 20:25
♐ 23 21:55
♑ 25 21:18
♒ 27 20:41
♓ 29 22:05

Jan 1925
♈ 1 02:56
♉ 3 11:30
♊ 5 22:52
♋ 8 11:32
♌ 11 00:13
♍ 13 11:54

☽ Moon

Jan 1925
♎ 15 21:32
♏ 18 04:11
♐ 20 07:33
♑ 22 08:23
♒ 24 08:09
♓ 26 08:45
♈ 28 11:59
♉ 30 18:57

Feb 1925
♊ 2 05:32
♋ 4 18:10
♌ 7 06:49
♍ 9 18:00
♎ 12 03:06
♏ 14 09:54
♐ 16 14:27
♑ 18 17:02
♒ 20 18:21
♓ 22 19:36
♈ 24 22:21
♉ 27 04:03

Mar 1925
♊ 1 13:25
♋ 4 01:37
♌ 6 14:21
♍ 9 01:24
♎ 11 09:43
♏ 13 15:37
♐ 15 19:51
♑ 17 23:06
♒ 20 01:50
♓ 22 04:33
♈ 24 08:04
♉ 26 13:34
♊ 28 22:07
♋ 31 09:41

Apr 1925
♌ 2 22:31
♍ 5 09:54
♎ 7 18:04
♏ 9 23:03
♐ 12 02:05
♑ 14 04:32
♒ 16 07:22
♓ 18 11:02
♈ 20 15:44
♉ 22 21:59
♊ 25 06:32
♋ 27 17:44
♌ 30 06:36

May 1925
♍ 2 18:37
♎ 5 03:25
♏ 7 08:21
♐ 9 10:28
♑ 11 11:30
♒ 13 13:08
♓ 15 16:23
♈ 17 21:34
♉ 20 04:41
♊ 22 13:50
♋ 25 01:07
♌ 27 13:58
♍ 30 02:34

Jun 1925
♎ 1 12:29
♏ 3 18:21
♐ 5 20:33
♑ 7 20:45
♒ 9 20:53
♓ 11 22:39
♈ 14 03:02

☽ Moon

Jun 1925
♉ 16 10:15
♊ 18 19:56
♋ 21 07:36
♌ 23 20:30
♍ 26 09:21
♎ 28 20:14

Jul 1925
♏ 1 03:32
♐ 3 06:54
♑ 5 07:24
♒ 7 06:49
♓ 9 07:06
♈ 11 09:52
♉ 13 16:04
♊ 16 01:37
♋ 18 13:32
♌ 21 02:31
♍ 23 15:16
♎ 26 02:29
♏ 28 10:55
♐ 30 15:55

Aug 1925
♑ 1 17:46
♒ 3 17:41
♓ 5 17:23
♈ 7 18:46
♉ 9 23:24
♊ 12 07:56
♋ 14 19:38
♌ 17 08:40
♍ 19 21:12
♎ 22 08:05
♏ 24 16:43
♐ 26 22:49
♑ 29 02:19
♒ 31 03:41

Sep 1925
♓ 2 04:02
♈ 4 05:02
♉ 6 08:27
♊ 8 15:38
♋ 11 02:34
♌ 13 15:29
♍ 16 03:56
♎ 18 14:17
♏ 20 22:17
♐ 23 04:17
♑ 25 08:36
♒ 27 11:29
♓ 29 13:19

Oct 1925
♈ 1 15:06
♉ 3 18:20
♊ 6 00:34
♋ 8 10:32
♌ 10 23:08
♍ 13 11:42
♎ 15 21:57
♏ 18 05:12
♐ 20 10:11
♑ 22 13:57
♒ 24 17:12
♓ 26 20:14
♈ 28 23:23
♉ 31 03:29

Nov 1925
♊ 2 09:43
♋ 4 19:05
♌ 7 07:15
♍ 9 20:06
♎ 12 06:51
♏ 14 14:05

☽ Moon

Nov 1925
♐ 16 18:12
♑ 18 20:38
♒ 20 22:47
♓ 23 01:37
♈ 25 05:31
♉ 27 10:46
♊ 29 17:50

Dec 1925
♋ 2 03:18
♌ 4 15:12
♍ 7 04:13
♎ 9 15:51
♏ 12 00:03
♐ 14 04:23
♑ 16 05:59
♒ 18 06:35
♓ 20 07:51
♈ 22 10:57
♉ 24 16:24
♊ 27 00:18
♋ 29 10:26
♌ 31 22:26

Jan 1926
♍ 3 11:25
♎ 5 23:43
♏ 8 09:18
♐ 10 15:01
♑ 12 17:09
♒ 14 17:07
♓ 16 16:48
♈ 18 18:03
♉ 20 22:15
♊ 23 05:54
♋ 25 16:29
♌ 28 04:51
♍ 30 17:48

Feb 1926
♎ 2 06:10
♏ 4 16:38
♐ 7 00:01
♑ 9 03:49
♒ 11 04:37
♓ 13 03:57
♈ 15 03:47
♉ 17 06:08
♊ 19 12:21
♋ 21 22:27
♌ 24 10:59
♍ 26 23:59

Mar 1926
♎ 1 12:03
♏ 3 22:27
♐ 6 06:39
♑ 8 12:06
♒ 10 14:40
♓ 12 15:04
♈ 14 14:52
♉ 16 16:06
♊ 18 20:41
♋ 21 05:29
♌ 23 17:34
♍ 26 06:36
♎ 28 18:26
♏ 31 04:16

Apr 1926
♐ 2 12:07
♑ 4 18:04
♒ 6 22:00
♓ 9 00:03
♈ 11 01:02
♉ 13 02:30
♊ 15 06:20

☽ Moon

Apr 1926
♋ 17 13:54
♌ 20 01:07
♍ 22 13:58
♎ 25 01:52
♏ 27 11:18
♐ 29 18:18

May 1926
♑ 1 23:32
♒ 4 03:31
♓ 6 06:31
♈ 8 08:55
♉ 10 11:33
♊ 12 15:46
♋ 14 22:52
♌ 17 09:19
♍ 19 21:53
♎ 22 10:03
♏ 24 19:41
♐ 27 02:13
♑ 29 06:24
♒ 31 09:18

Jun 1926
♓ 2 11:53
♈ 4 14:45
♉ 6 18:28
♊ 8 23:42
♋ 11 07:14
♌ 13 17:28
♍ 16 05:48
♎ 18 18:18
♏ 21 04:39
♐ 23 11:34
♑ 25 15:18
♒ 27 17:01
♓ 29 18:13

Jul 1926
♈ 1 20:14
♉ 3 23:58
♊ 6 05:56
♋ 8 14:16
♌ 11 00:50
♍ 13 13:07
♎ 16 01:51
♏ 18 13:07
♐ 20 21:10
♑ 23 01:28
♒ 25 02:48
♓ 27 02:46
♈ 29 03:13
♉ 31 05:46

Aug 1926
♊ 2 11:24
♋ 4 20:07
♌ 7 07:12
♍ 9 19:38
♎ 12 08:26
♏ 14 20:17
♐ 17 05:39
♑ 19 11:23
♒ 21 13:31
♓ 23 13:14
♈ 25 12:30
♉ 27 13:24
♊ 29 17:38

Sep 1926
♋ 1 01:48
♌ 3 13:00
♍ 6 01:40
♎ 8 14:22
♏ 11 02:15
♐ 13 12:21
♑ 15 19:36

☽ Moon

Sep 1926
♒ 17 23:22
♓ 20 00:06
♈ 21 23:20
♉ 23 23:12
♊ 26 01:50
♋ 28 08:34
♌ 30 19:09

Oct 1926
♍ 3 07:48
♎ 5 20:28
♏ 8 07:58
♐ 10 17:53
♑ 13 01:46
♒ 15 07:02
♓ 17 09:29
♈ 19 09:56
♉ 21 10:01
♊ 23 11:50
♋ 25 17:07
♌ 28 02:30
♍ 30 14:42

Nov 1926
♎ 2 03:22
♏ 4 14:37
♐ 6 23:51
♑ 9 07:10
♒ 11 12:41
♓ 13 16:22
♈ 15 18:28
♉ 17 19:54
♊ 19 22:10
♋ 22 02:54
♌ 24 11:09
♍ 26 22:35
♎ 29 11:13

Dec 1926
♏ 1 22:39
♐ 4 07:32
♑ 6 13:52
♒ 8 18:21
♓ 10 21:43
♈ 13 00:32
♉ 15 03:23
♊ 17 06:59
♋ 19 12:19
♌ 21 20:16
♍ 24 07:01
♎ 26 19:30
♏ 29 07:28
♐ 31 16:49

Jan 1927
♑ 2 22:51
♒ 5 02:10
♓ 7 04:05
♈ 9 05:59
♉ 11 08:55
♊ 13 13:30
♋ 15 19:59
♌ 18 04:31
♍ 20 15:09
♎ 23 03:26
♏ 25 15:53
♐ 28 02:20
♑ 30 09:11

Feb 1927
♒ 1 12:22
♓ 3 13:07
♈ 5 13:20
♉ 7 14:50
♊ 9 18:54
♋ 12 01:50
♌ 14 11:10

☽ Moon

Feb 1927
♍ 16 22:15
♎ 19 10:30
♏ 21 23:08
♐ 24 10:33
♑ 26 18:55
♒ 28 23:13

Mar 1927
♓ 3 00:05
♈ 4 23:18
♉ 6 23:07
♊ 9 01:28
♋ 11 07:29
♌ 13 16:51
♍ 16 04:21
♎ 18 16:48
♏ 21 05:20
♐ 23 17:05
♑ 26 02:38
♒ 28 08:38
♓ 30 10:53

Apr 1927
♈ 1 10:31
♉ 3 09:36
♊ 5 10:25
♋ 7 14:41
♌ 9 22:59
♍ 12 10:18
♎ 14 22:53
♏ 17 11:19
♐ 19 22:48
♑ 22 08:34
♒ 24 15:42
♓ 26 19:37
♈ 28 20:43
♉ 30 20:29

May 1927
♊ 2 20:52
♋ 4 23:51
♌ 7 06:38
♍ 9 17:02
♎ 12 05:26
♏ 14 17:51
♐ 17 04:57
♑ 19 14:10
♒ 21 21:15
♓ 24 02:01
♈ 26 04:37
♉ 28 05:50
♊ 30 07:02

Jun 1927
♋ 1 09:50
♌ 3 15:37
♍ 6 00:55
♎ 8 12:48
♏ 11 01:15
♐ 13 12:15
♑ 15 20:51
♒ 18 03:04
♓ 20 07:25
♈ 22 10:29
♉ 24 12:54
♊ 26 15:26
♋ 28 19:03

Jul 1927
♌ 1 00:48
♍ 3 09:26
♎ 5 20:47
♏ 8 09:16
♐ 10 20:36
♑ 13 05:06
♒ 15 10:31
♓ 17 13:43

☽ Moon

Jul 1927
♈ 19 15:58
♉ 21 18:23
♊ 23 21:46
♋ 26 02:30
♌ 28 09:00
♍ 30 17:41

Aug 1927
♎ 2 04:43
♏ 4 17:15
♐ 7 05:13
♑ 9 14:22
♒ 11 19:45
♓ 13 22:04
♈ 15 22:57
♉ 18 00:12
♊ 20 03:08
♋ 22 08:18
♌ 24 15:38
♍ 27 00:55
♎ 29 12:02

Sep 1927
♏ 1 00:35
♐ 3 13:09
♑ 5 23:28
♒ 8 05:49
♓ 10 08:16
♈ 12 08:18
♉ 14 08:03
♊ 16 09:28
♋ 18 13:48
♌ 20 21:12
♍ 23 07:01
♎ 25 18:29
♏ 28 07:05
♐ 30 19:53

Oct 1927
♑ 3 07:12
♒ 5 15:06
♓ 7 18:50
♈ 9 19:15
♉ 11 18:18
♊ 13 18:12
♋ 15 20:49
♌ 18 03:06
♍ 20 12:42
♎ 23 00:27
♏ 25 13:07
♐ 28 01:47
♑ 30 13:21

Nov 1927
♒ 1 22:26
♓ 4 03:55
♈ 6 05:53
♉ 8 05:37
♊ 10 05:03
♋ 12 06:15
♌ 14 10:47
♍ 16 19:13
♎ 19 06:40
♏ 21 19:25
♐ 24 07:53
♑ 26 19:00
♒ 29 04:06

Dec 1927
♓ 1 10:36
♈ 3 14:20
♉ 5 15:47
♊ 7 16:11
♋ 9 17:11
♌ 11 20:31
♍ 14 03:24
♎ 16 13:54

☽ Moon

Dec 1927
♏ 19 02:31
♐ 21 14:58
♑ 24 01:37
♒ 26 09:54
♓ 28 16:00
♈ 30 20:18

Jan 1928
♉ 1 23:14
♊ 4 01:20
♋ 6 03:27
♌ 8 06:52
♍ 10 12:53
♎ 12 22:17
♏ 15 10:25
♐ 17 23:06
♑ 20 09:48
♒ 22 17:27
♓ 24 22:24
♈ 27 01:47
♉ 29 04:42
♊ 31 07:46

Feb 1928
♋ 2 11:21
♌ 4 15:53
♍ 6 22:09
♎ 9 07:03
♏ 11 18:40
♐ 14 07:31
♑ 16 18:53
♒ 19 02:46
♓ 21 07:05
♈ 23 09:09
♉ 25 10:42
♊ 27 13:07
♋ 29 17:04

Mar 1928
♌ 2 22:38
♍ 5 05:51
♎ 7 15:04
♏ 10 02:30
♐ 12 15:23
♑ 15 03:33
♒ 17 12:30
♓ 19 17:20
♈ 21 18:54
♉ 23 19:06
♊ 25 19:53
♋ 27 22:41
♌ 30 04:04

Apr 1928
♍ 1 11:53
♎ 3 21:46
♏ 6 09:27
♐ 8 22:19
♑ 11 10:55
♒ 13 21:06
♓ 16 03:19
♈ 18 05:40
♉ 20 05:36
♊ 22 05:09
♋ 24 06:13
♌ 26 10:11
♍ 28 17:27

May 1928
♎ 1 03:35
♏ 3 15:37
♐ 6 04:32
♑ 8 17:08
♒ 11 03:57
♓ 13 11:34
♈ 15 15:30
♉ 17 16:26

☽ Moon

May 1928
♊ 19 15:57
♋ 21 15:57
♌ 23 18:16
♍ 26 00:06
♎ 28 09:35
♏ 30 21:39

Jun 1928
♐ 2 10:37
♑ 4 22:59
♒ 7 09:40
♓ 9 17:53
♈ 11 23:13
♉ 14 01:45
♊ 16 02:24
♋ 18 02:34
♌ 20 04:02
♍ 22 08:26
♎ 24 16:42
♏ 27 04:16
♐ 29 17:12

Jul 1928
♑ 2 05:23
♒ 4 15:32
♓ 6 23:22
♈ 9 05:03
♉ 11 08:49
♊ 13 10:59
♋ 15 12:20
♌ 17 14:06
♍ 19 17:52
♎ 22 01:01
♏ 24 11:46
♐ 27 00:34
♑ 29 12:46
♒ 31 22:33

Aug 1928
♓ 3 05:34
♈ 5 10:33
♉ 7 14:18
♊ 9 17:22
♋ 11 20:03
♌ 13 22:57
♍ 16 03:07
♎ 18 09:52
♏ 20 19:56
♐ 23 08:28
♑ 25 20:58
♒ 28 06:56
♓ 30 13:30

Sep 1928
♈ 1 17:26
♉ 3 20:07
♊ 5 22:42
♋ 8 01:51
♌ 10 05:49
♍ 12 11:01
♎ 14 18:12
♏ 17 04:04
♐ 19 16:22
♑ 22 05:15
♒ 24 16:00
♓ 26 23:01
♈ 29 02:31

Oct 1928
♉ 1 03:59
♊ 3 05:09
♋ 5 07:21
♌ 7 11:17
♍ 9 17:13
♎ 12 01:14
♏ 14 11:28
♐ 16 23:44

☽ Moon

Oct 1928
♑ 19 12:49
♒ 22 00:33
♓ 24 08:49
♈ 26 13:04
♉ 28 14:16
♊ 30 14:11

Nov 1928
♋ 1 14:40
♌ 3 17:14
♍ 5 22:41
♎ 8 07:04
♏ 10 17:52
♐ 13 06:20
♑ 15 19:24
♒ 18 07:39
♓ 20 17:18
♈ 22 23:14
♉ 25 01:30
♊ 27 01:23
♋ 29 00:43

Dec 1928
♌ 1 01:28
♍ 3 05:16
♎ 5 12:51
♏ 7 23:45
♐ 10 12:28
♑ 13 01:29
♒ 15 13:35
♓ 17 23:48
♈ 20 07:15
♉ 22 11:25
♊ 24 12:40
♋ 26 12:17
♌ 28 12:07
♍ 30 14:12

Jan 1929
♎ 1 20:07
♏ 4 06:09
♐ 6 18:49
♑ 9 07:50
♒ 11 19:32
♓ 14 05:21
♈ 16 13:06
♉ 18 18:36
♊ 20 21:43
♋ 22 22:52
♌ 24 23:16
♍ 27 00:47
♎ 29 05:18
♏ 31 13:56

Feb 1929
♐ 3 01:58
♑ 5 14:59
♒ 8 02:34
♓ 10 11:42
♈ 12 18:40
♉ 15 00:01
♊ 17 04:01
♋ 19 06:45
♌ 21 08:41
♍ 23 10:58
♎ 25 15:15
♏ 27 22:53

Mar 1929
♐ 2 10:02
♑ 4 22:54
♒ 7 10:43
♓ 9 19:43
♈ 12 01:51
♉ 14 06:04
♊ 16 09:23
♋ 18 12:23

☽ Moon

Mar 1929
♌ 20 15:27
♍ 22 19:05
♎ 25 00:11
♏ 27 07:49
♐ 29 18:25

Apr 1929
♑ 1 07:02
♒ 3 19:17
♓ 6 04:51
♈ 8 10:57
♉ 10 14:17
♊ 12 16:13
♋ 14 18:04
♌ 16 20:50
♍ 19 01:05
♎ 21 07:13
♏ 23 15:34
♐ 26 02:15
♑ 28 14:42

May 1929
♒ 1 03:18
♓ 3 13:50
♈ 5 20:50
♉ 8 00:17
♊ 10 01:22
♋ 12 01:44
♌ 14 03:02
♍ 16 06:33
♎ 18 12:52
♏ 20 21:53
♐ 23 09:03
♑ 25 21:34
♒ 28 10:16
♓ 30 21:37

Jun 1929
♈ 2 05:57
♉ 4 10:34
♊ 6 11:57
♋ 8 11:36
♌ 10 11:25
♍ 12 13:20
♎ 14 18:38
♏ 17 03:32
♐ 19 15:02
♑ 22 03:44
♒ 24 16:23
♓ 27 03:58
♈ 29 13:21

Jul 1929
♉ 1 19:31
♊ 3 22:13
♋ 5 22:20
♌ 7 21:37
♍ 9 22:09
♎ 12 01:53
♏ 14 09:43
♐ 16 20:59
♑ 19 09:47
♒ 21 22:19
♓ 24 09:38
♈ 26 19:12
♉ 29 02:24
♊ 31 06:42

Aug 1929
♋ 2 08:15
♌ 4 08:11
♍ 6 08:23
♎ 8 10:55
♏ 10 17:21
♐ 13 03:44
♑ 15 16:20
♒ 18 04:49

☽ Moon

Aug 1929
♓ 20 15:45
♈ 23 00:46
♉ 25 07:54
♊ 27 13:02
♋ 29 16:03
♌ 31 17:27

Sep 1929
♍ 2 18:27
♎ 4 20:51
♏ 7 02:20
♐ 9 11:37
♑ 11 23:44
♒ 14 12:16
♓ 16 23:06
♈ 19 07:30
♉ 21 13:45
♊ 23 18:24
♋ 25 21:52
♌ 28 00:27
♍ 30 02:51

Oct 1929
♎ 2 06:09
♏ 4 11:39
♐ 6 20:18
♑ 9 07:48
♒ 11 20:24
♓ 14 07:39
♈ 16 16:02
♉ 18 21:29
♊ 21 00:54
♋ 23 03:24
♌ 25 05:55
♍ 27 09:08
♎ 29 13:39
♏ 31 20:01

Nov 1929
♐ 3 04:46
♑ 5 15:56
♒ 8 04:32
♓ 10 16:29
♈ 13 01:42
♉ 15 07:18
♊ 17 09:53
♋ 19 10:53
♌ 21 11:58
♍ 23 14:31
♎ 25 19:22
♏ 28 02:39
♐ 30 12:07

Dec 1929
♑ 2 23:25
♒ 5 11:57
♓ 8 00:27
♈ 10 10:56
♉ 12 17:49
♊ 14 20:48
♋ 16 21:05
♌ 18 20:34
♍ 20 21:21
♎ 23 01:02
♏ 25 08:11
♐ 27 18:11
♑ 30 05:55

Jan 1930
♒ 1 18:29
♓ 4 07:04
♈ 6 18:26
♉ 9 02:58
♊ 11 07:34
♋ 13 08:35
♌ 15 07:37
♍ 17 06:57

☽ Moon

Jan 1930
♎ 19 08:44
♏ 21 14:24
♐ 23 23:56
♑ 26 11:52
♒ 29 00:34
♓ 31 12:58

Feb 1930
♈ 3 00:22
♉ 5 09:48
♊ 7 16:07
♋ 9 18:55
♌ 11 19:01
♍ 13 18:14
♎ 15 18:50
♏ 17 22:44
♐ 20 06:48
♑ 22 18:12
♒ 25 06:56
♓ 27 19:12

Mar 1930
♈ 2 06:08
♉ 4 15:18
♊ 6 22:15
♋ 9 02:34
♌ 11 04:25
♍ 13 04:54
♎ 15 05:43
♏ 17 08:46
♐ 19 15:23
♑ 22 01:39
♒ 24 14:04
♓ 27 02:23
♈ 29 12:59
♉ 31 21:23

Apr 1930
♊ 3 03:42
♋ 5 08:11
♌ 7 11:09
♍ 9 13:11
♎ 11 15:17
♏ 13 18:44
♐ 16 00:49
♑ 18 10:06
♒ 20 21:58
♓ 23 10:22
♈ 25 21:09
♉ 28 05:08
♊ 30 10:26

May 1930
♋ 2 13:54
♌ 4 16:32
♍ 6 19:10
♎ 8 22:30
♏ 11 03:06
♐ 13 09:38
♑ 15 18:39
♒ 18 06:03
♓ 20 18:33
♈ 23 05:55
♉ 25 14:15
♊ 27 19:07
♋ 29 21:25
♌ 31 22:45

Jun 1930
♍ 3 00:37
♎ 5 04:03
♏ 7 09:29
♐ 9 16:55
♑ 12 02:20
♒ 14 13:38
♓ 17 02:11
♈ 19 14:14

☽ Moon

Jun 1930
♉ 21 23:35
♊ 24 05:00
♋ 26 06:57
♌ 28 07:06
♍ 30 07:28

Jul 1930
♎ 2 09:47
♏ 4 14:55
♐ 6 22:49
♑ 9 08:49
♒ 11 20:22
♓ 14 08:56
♈ 16 21:25
♉ 19 07:53
♊ 21 14:38
♋ 23 17:22
♌ 25 17:19
♍ 27 16:35
♎ 29 17:18
♏ 31 21:04

Aug 1930
♐ 3 04:24
♑ 5 14:34
♒ 8 02:26
♓ 10 15:02
♈ 13 03:31
♉ 15 14:37
♊ 17 22:45
♋ 20 03:02
♌ 22 03:58
♍ 24 03:13
♎ 26 02:58
♏ 28 05:10
♐ 30 11:04

Sep 1930
♑ 1 20:34
♒ 4 08:27
♓ 6 21:06
♈ 9 09:20
♉ 11 20:17
♊ 14 05:00
♋ 16 10:42
♌ 18 13:18
♍ 20 13:46
♎ 22 13:44
♏ 24 15:07
♐ 26 19:34
♑ 29 03:48

Oct 1930
♒ 1 15:08
♓ 4 03:47
♈ 6 15:51
♉ 9 02:14
♊ 11 10:29
♋ 13 16:29
♌ 15 20:19
♍ 17 22:25
♎ 19 23:43
♏ 22 01:32
♐ 24 05:23
♑ 26 12:26
♒ 28 22:53
♓ 31 11:22

Nov 1930
♈ 2 23:34
♉ 5 09:37
♊ 7 16:58
♋ 9 22:04
♌ 12 01:45
♍ 14 04:41
♎ 16 07:27
♏ 18 10:36

☽ Moon

Nov 1930
♐ 20 15:00
♑ 22 21:41
♒ 25 07:22
♓ 27 19:32
♈ 30 08:05

Dec 1930
♉ 2 18:31
♊ 5 01:32
♋ 7 05:31
♌ 9 07:52
♍ 11 10:04
♎ 13 13:05
♏ 15 17:19
♐ 17 22:54
♑ 20 06:11
♒ 22 15:43
♓ 25 03:35
♈ 27 16:28
♉ 30 03:51

Jan 1931
♊ 1 11:34
♋ 3 15:21
♌ 5 16:32
♍ 7 17:06
♎ 9 18:48
♏ 11 22:40
♐ 14 04:50
♑ 16 13:01
♒ 18 23:03
♓ 21 10:54
♈ 23 23:54
♉ 26 12:09
♊ 28 21:18
♋ 31 02:09

Feb 1931
♌ 2 03:24
♍ 4 02:56
♎ 6 02:54
♏ 8 05:04
♐ 10 10:20
♑ 12 18:38
♒ 15 05:14
♓ 17 17:22
♈ 20 06:20
♉ 22 18:53
♊ 25 05:12
♋ 27 11:46

Mar 1931
♌ 1 14:25
♍ 3 14:21
♎ 5 13:33
♏ 7 14:03
♐ 9 17:29
♑ 12 00:38
♒ 14 11:02
♓ 16 23:26
♈ 19 12:23
♉ 22 00:44
♊ 24 11:18
♋ 26 19:04
♌ 28 23:28
♍ 31 00:57

Apr 1931
♎ 2 00:49
♏ 4 00:50
♐ 6 02:51
♑ 8 08:20
♒ 10 17:39
♓ 13 05:48
♈ 15 18:47
♉ 18 06:50
♊ 20 16:55

☽ Moon

Apr 1931
♋ 23 00:42
♌ 25 06:03
♍ 27 09:09
♎ 29 10:35

May 1931
♏ 1 11:26
♐ 3 13:14
♑ 5 17:35
♒ 8 01:36
♓ 10 13:01
♈ 13 01:56
♉ 15 13:53
♊ 17 23:26
♋ 20 06:25
♌ 22 11:27
♍ 24 15:07
♎ 26 17:51
♏ 28 20:07
♐ 30 22:47

Jun 1931
♑ 2 03:07
♒ 4 10:22
♓ 6 21:00
♈ 9 09:43
♉ 11 21:54
♊ 14 07:21
♋ 16 13:38
♌ 18 17:36
♍ 20 20:32
♎ 22 23:22
♏ 25 02:34
♐ 27 06:26
♑ 29 11:35

Jul 1931
♒ 1 18:56
♓ 4 05:09
♈ 6 17:39
♉ 9 06:13
♊ 11 16:13
♋ 13 22:30
♌ 16 01:41
♍ 18 03:21
♎ 20 05:06
♏ 22 07:56
♐ 24 12:18
♑ 26 18:22
♒ 29 02:24
♓ 31 12:45

Aug 1931
♈ 3 01:09
♉ 5 14:04
♊ 8 01:01
♋ 10 08:10
♌ 12 11:31
♍ 14 12:25
♎ 16 12:45
♏ 18 14:10
♐ 20 17:46
♑ 22 23:58
♒ 25 08:37
♓ 27 19:27
♈ 30 07:56

Sep 1931
♉ 1 20:58
♊ 4 08:42
♋ 6 17:14
♌ 8 21:47
♍ 10 23:03
♎ 12 22:43
♏ 14 22:40
♐ 17 00:39
♑ 19 05:47

☽ Moon

Sep 1931
♒ 21 14:17
♓ 24 01:28
♈ 26 14:08
♉ 29 03:06

Oct 1931
♊ 1 15:03
♋ 4 00:37
♌ 6 06:49
♍ 8 09:34
♎ 10 09:50
♏ 12 09:17
♐ 14 09:51
♑ 16 13:18
♒ 18 20:38
♓ 21 07:31
♈ 23 20:20
♉ 26 09:11
♊ 28 20:47
♋ 31 06:26

Nov 1931
♌ 2 13:39
♍ 4 18:07
♎ 6 20:03
♏ 8 20:21
♐ 10 20:39
♑ 12 22:51
♒ 15 04:39
♓ 17 14:31
♈ 20 03:08
♉ 22 15:59
♊ 25 03:11
♋ 27 12:09
♌ 29 19:05

Dec 1931
♍ 2 00:16
♎ 4 03:44
♏ 6 05:43
♐ 8 07:04
♑ 10 09:17
♒ 12 14:09
♓ 14 22:50
♈ 17 10:48
♉ 19 23:45
♊ 22 10:59
♋ 24 19:21
♌ 27 01:16
♍ 29 05:40
♎ 31 09:17

Jan 1932
♏ 2 12:23
♐ 4 15:15
♑ 6 18:37
♒ 8 23:43
♓ 11 07:48
♈ 13 19:06
♉ 16 08:01
♊ 18 19:46
♋ 21 04:22
♌ 23 09:39
♍ 25 12:47
♎ 27 15:07
♏ 29 17:43
♐ 31 21:06

Feb 1932
♑ 3 01:38
♒ 5 07:48
♓ 7 16:14
♈ 10 03:17
♉ 12 16:04
♊ 15 04:27
♋ 17 14:02
♌ 19 19:48

☽ Moon

Feb 1932
♍ 21 22:24
♎ 23 23:22
♏ 26 00:19
♐ 28 02:38

Mar 1932
♑ 1 07:06
♒ 3 13:59
♓ 5 23:15
♈ 8 10:34
♉ 10 23:19
♊ 13 12:02
♋ 15 22:45
♌ 18 05:55
♍ 20 09:18
♎ 22 09:57
♏ 24 09:35
♐ 26 10:07
♑ 28 13:07
♒ 30 19:29

Apr 1932
♓ 2 05:04
♈ 4 16:52
♉ 7 05:48
♊ 9 18:26
♋ 12 05:46
♌ 14 14:21
♍ 16 19:21
♎ 18 21:00
♏ 20 20:33
♐ 22 19:57
♑ 24 21:14
♒ 27 02:04
♓ 29 10:54

May 1932
♈ 1 22:46
♉ 4 11:45
♊ 7 00:19
♋ 9 11:34
♌ 11 20:46
♍ 14 03:13
♎ 16 06:32
♏ 18 07:15
♐ 20 06:48
♑ 22 07:12
♒ 24 10:30
♓ 26 17:56
♈ 29 05:08
♉ 31 18:04

Jun 1932
♊ 3 06:32
♋ 5 17:20
♌ 8 02:14
♍ 10 09:06
♎ 12 13:41
♏ 14 16:00
♐ 16 16:46
♑ 18 17:31
♒ 20 20:12
♓ 23 02:25
♈ 25 12:33
♉ 28 01:07
♊ 30 13:34

Jul 1932
♋ 3 00:06
♌ 5 08:18
♍ 7 14:32
♎ 9 19:12
♏ 11 22:27
♐ 14 00:37
♑ 16 02:35
♒ 18 05:44
♓ 20 11:34

☽ Moo…

Jul 1932
♈ 22 20:…
♉ 25 08:…
♊ 27 21:…
♋ 30 08:…

Aug 193…
♌ 1 15:…
♍ 3 21:…
♎ 6 00:…
♏ 8 03:…
♐ 10 06:3…
♑ 12 09:3…
♒ 14 13:…
♓ 16 20:1…
♈ 19 05:1…
♉ 21 16:…
♊ 24 05:3…
♋ 26 16:4…
♌ 29 01:0…
♍ 31 05:…

Sep 1932
♎ 2 08:3…
♏ 4 10:0…
♐ 6 11:5…
♑ 8 15:1…
♒ 10 20:1…
♓ 13 03:3…
♈ 15 13:0…
♉ 18 00:3…
♊ 20 13:1…
♋ 23 01:1…
♌ 25 10:3…
♍ 27 16:0…
♎ 29 18:2…

Oct 1932
♏ 1 18:4…
♐ 3 19:0…
♑ 5 21:0…
♒ 8 01:4…
♓ 10 09:2…
♈ 12 19:3…
♉ 15 07:2…
♊ 17 20:0…
♋ 20 08:2…
♌ 22 18:5…
♍ 25 02:0…
♎ 27 05:1…
♏ 29 05:3…
♐ 31 04:4…

Nov 1932
♑ 2 04:54
♒ 4 08:05
♓ 6 15:05
♈ 9 01:24
♉ 11 13:33
♊ 14 02:13
♋ 16 14:31
♌ 19 01:35
♍ 21 10:07
♎ 23 15:07
♏ 25 16:38
♐ 27 15:59
♑ 29 15:17

Dec 1932
♒ 1 16:46
♓ 3 22:07
♈ 6 07:34
♉ 8 19:40
♊ 11 08:25
♋ 13 20:27
♌ 16 07:12
♍ 18 16:08
♎ 20 22:31

☽ Moon

Dec 1932
♏ 23 01:52
♐ 25 02:42
♑ 27 02:31
♒ 29 03:22
♓ 31 07:15

Jan 1933
♈ 2 15:12
♉ 5 02:36
♊ 7 15:19
♋ 10 03:16
♌ 12 13:26
♍ 14 21:41
♎ 17 04:02
♏ 19 08:24
♐ 21 10:54
♑ 23 12:18
♒ 25 13:57
♓ 27 17:31
♈ 30 00:20

Feb 1933
♉ 1 10:39
♊ 3 23:04
♋ 6 11:12
♌ 8 21:16
♍ 11 04:43
♎ 13 09:59
♏ 15 13:46
♐ 17 16:42
♑ 19 19:22
♒ 21 22:28
♓ 24 02:56
♈ 26 09:42
♉ 28 19:19

Mar 1933
♊ 3 07:17
♋ 5 19:42
♌ 8 06:17
♍ 10 13:41
♎ 12 18:03
♏ 14 20:27
♐ 16 22:18
♑ 19 00:46
♒ 21 04:38
♓ 23 10:15
♈ 25 17:49
♉ 28 03:31
♊ 30 15:12

Apr 1933
♋ 2 03:49
♌ 4 15:15
♍ 6 23:32
♎ 9 04:00
♏ 11 05:32
♐ 13 05:52
♑ 15 06:53
♒ 17 10:02
♓ 19 15:53
♈ 22 00:14
♉ 24 10:30
♊ 26 22:17
♋ 29 10:57

May 1933
♌ 1 23:06
♍ 4 08:40
♎ 6 14:17
♏ 8 16:07
♐ 10 15:43
♑ 12 15:15
♒ 14 16:45
♓ 16 21:33
♈ 19 05:44
♉ 21 16:26

☽ Moon

May 1933
♊ 24 04:31
♋ 26 17:11
♌ 29 05:32
♍ 31 16:05

Jun 1933
♎ 2 23:14
♏ 5 02:24
♐ 7 02:32
♑ 9 01:32
♒ 11 01:41
♓ 13 04:49
♈ 15 11:49
♉ 17 22:11
♊ 20 10:25
♋ 22 23:06
♌ 25 11:16
♍ 27 22:00
♎ 30 06:10

Jul 1933
♏ 2 10:56
♐ 4 12:32
♑ 6 12:16
♒ 8 12:05
♓ 10 14:01
♈ 12 19:30
♉ 15 04:48
♊ 17 16:43
♋ 20 05:24
♌ 22 17:18
♍ 25 03:35
♎ 27 11:43
♏ 29 17:21
♐ 31 20:26

Aug 1933
♑ 2 21:40
♒ 4 22:21
♓ 7 00:10
♈ 9 04:40
♉ 11 12:44
♊ 13 23:57
♋ 16 12:31
♌ 19 00:22
♍ 21 10:07
♎ 23 17:29
♏ 25 22:44
♐ 28 02:21
♑ 30 04:51

Sep 1933
♒ 1 06:59
♓ 3 09:44
♈ 5 14:14
♉ 7 21:34
♊ 10 08:00
♋ 12 20:24
♌ 15 08:30
♍ 17 18:13
♎ 20 00:51
♏ 22 05:00
♐ 24 07:48
♑ 26 10:23
♒ 28 13:26
♓ 30 17:26

Oct 1933
♈ 2 22:50
♉ 5 06:17
♊ 7 16:17
♋ 10 04:28
♌ 12 17:01
♍ 15 03:24
♎ 17 10:07
♏ 19 13:28
♐ 21 14:54

☽ Moon

Oct 1933
♑ 23 16:13
♒ 25 18:48
♓ 27 23:17
♈ 30 05:40

Nov 1933
♉ 1 13:52
♊ 4 00:01
♋ 6 12:04
♌ 9 00:57
♍ 11 12:23
♎ 13 20:12
♏ 15 23:51
♐ 18 00:34
♑ 20 00:23
♒ 22 01:20
♓ 24 04:49
♈ 26 11:12
♉ 28 20:02

Dec 1933
♊ 1 06:44
♋ 3 18:52
♌ 6 07:48
♍ 8 19:59
♎ 11 05:18
♏ 13 10:26
♐ 15 11:49
♑ 17 11:09
♒ 19 10:37
♓ 21 12:15
♈ 23 17:15
♉ 26 01:42
♊ 28 12:42
♋ 31 01:06

Jan 1934
♌ 2 13:55
♍ 5 02:08
♎ 7 12:19
♏ 9 19:10
♐ 11 22:17
♑ 13 22:37
♒ 15 21:56
♓ 17 22:17
♈ 20 01:27
♉ 22 08:25
♊ 24 18:53
♋ 27 07:23
♌ 29 20:11

Feb 1934
♍ 1 08:00
♎ 3 17:59
♏ 6 01:31
♐ 8 06:14
♑ 10 08:23
♒ 12 08:57
♓ 14 09:27
♈ 16 11:39
♉ 18 17:03
♊ 21 02:16
♋ 23 14:21
♌ 26 03:13
♍ 28 14:45

Mar 1934
♎ 3 00:01
♏ 5 06:59
♐ 7 11:58
♑ 9 15:21
♒ 11 17:36
♓ 13 19:25
♈ 15 22:00
♉ 18 02:45
♊ 20 10:50
♋ 22 22:12

☽ Moon

Mar 1934
♌ 25 11:02
♍ 27 22:44
♎ 30 07:36

Apr 1934
♏ 1 13:35
♐ 3 17:37
♑ 5 20:45
♒ 7 23:42
♓ 10 02:52
♈ 12 06:40
♉ 14 11:55
♊ 16 19:41
♋ 19 06:26
♌ 21 19:09
♍ 24 07:19
♎ 26 16:31
♏ 28 22:06

May 1934
♐ 1 01:01
♑ 3 02:53
♒ 5 05:05
♓ 7 08:26
♈ 9 13:08
♉ 11 19:23
♊ 14 03:37
♋ 16 14:16
♌ 19 02:54
♍ 21 15:34
♎ 24 01:42
♏ 26 07:51
♐ 28 10:29
♑ 30 11:12

Jun 1934
♒ 1 11:55
♓ 3 14:06
♈ 5 18:31
♉ 8 01:16
♊ 10 10:13
♋ 12 21:13
♌ 15 09:52
♍ 17 22:51
♎ 20 09:58
♏ 22 17:24
♐ 24 20:49
♑ 26 21:24
♒ 28 21:02
♓ 30 21:37

Jul 1934
♈ 3 00:38
♉ 5 06:47
♊ 7 15:54
♋ 10 03:20
♌ 12 16:06
♍ 15 05:06
♎ 17 16:46
♏ 20 01:30
♐ 22 06:27
♑ 24 08:03
♒ 26 07:44
♓ 28 07:20
♈ 30 08:45

Aug 1934
♉ 1 13:24
♊ 3 21:48
♋ 6 09:12
♌ 8 22:07
♍ 11 10:58
♎ 13 22:32
♏ 16 07:50
♐ 18 14:11
♑ 20 17:27
♒ 22 18:18

☽ Moon

Aug 1934
♓ 24 18:08
♈ 26 18:44
♉ 28 21:54
♊ 31 04:54

Sep 1934
♋ 2 15:39
♌ 5 04:31
♍ 7 17:15
♎ 10 04:22
♏ 12 13:19
♐ 14 20:03
♑ 17 00:35
♒ 19 03:06
♓ 21 04:13
♈ 23 05:13
♉ 25 07:46
♊ 27 13:32
♋ 29 23:14

Oct 1934
♌ 2 11:43
♍ 5 00:30
♎ 7 11:20
♏ 9 19:31
♐ 12 01:32
♑ 14 06:04
♒ 16 09:32
♓ 18 12:09
♈ 20 14:28
♉ 22 17:34
♊ 24 22:57
♋ 27 07:45
♌ 29 19:41

Nov 1934
♍ 1 08:35
♎ 3 19:40
♏ 6 03:32
♐ 8 08:33
♑ 10 11:56
♒ 12 14:51
♓ 14 17:56
♈ 16 21:26
♉ 19 01:46
♊ 21 07:47
♋ 23 16:24
♌ 26 03:53
♍ 28 16:51

Dec 1934
♎ 1 04:38
♏ 3 13:05
♐ 5 17:52
♑ 7 20:09
♒ 9 21:33
♓ 11 23:30
♈ 14 02:51
♉ 16 07:56
♊ 18 14:58
♋ 21 00:10
♌ 23 11:37
♍ 26 00:31
♎ 28 12:58
♏ 30 22:41

Jan 1935
♐ 2 04:26
♑ 4 06:44
♒ 6 07:04
♓ 8 07:17
♈ 10 09:02
♉ 12 13:24
♊ 14 20:42
♋ 17 06:37
♌ 19 18:26
♍ 22 07:19

☽ Moon

Jan 1935
♎ 24 19:58
♏ 27 06:45
♐ 29 14:10
♑ 31 17:47

Feb 1935
♒ 2 18:26
♓ 4 17:47
♈ 6 17:49
♉ 8 20:22
♊ 11 02:35
♋ 13 12:23
♌ 16 00:35
♍ 18 13:32
♎ 21 02:02
♏ 23 13:03
♐ 25 21:39
♑ 28 03:04

Mar 1935
♒ 2 05:16
♓ 4 05:13
♈ 6 04:40
♉ 8 05:43
♊ 10 10:10
♋ 12 18:51
♌ 15 06:47
♍ 17 19:51
♎ 20 08:07
♏ 22 18:44
♐ 25 03:23
♑ 27 09:48
♒ 29 13:41
♓ 31 15:15

Apr 1935
♈ 2 15:32
♉ 4 16:18
♊ 6 19:35
♋ 9 02:48
♌ 11 13:51
♍ 14 02:46
♎ 16 15:00
♏ 19 01:09
♐ 21 09:06
♑ 23 15:13
♒ 25 19:43
♓ 27 22:39
♈ 30 00:26

May 1935
♉ 2 02:09
♊ 4 05:26
♋ 6 11:49
♌ 8 21:54
♍ 11 10:25
♎ 13 22:47
♏ 16 08:54
♐ 18 16:12
♑ 20 21:20
♒ 23 01:08
♓ 25 04:13
♈ 27 06:58
♉ 29 09:59
♊ 31 14:11

Jun 1935
♋ 2 20:43
♌ 5 06:18
♍ 7 18:25
♎ 10 06:59
♏ 12 17:34
♐ 15 00:56
♑ 17 05:21
♒ 19 07:56
♓ 21 09:55
♈ 23 12:21

☽ Moon

Jun 1935
♉ 25 15:54
♊ 27 21:06
♋ 30 04:26

Jul 1935
♌ 2 14:12
♍ 5 02:08
♎ 7 14:51
♏ 10 02:14
♐ 12 10:27
♑ 14 15:03
♒ 16 16:53
♓ 18 17:31
♈ 20 18:33
♉ 22 21:20
♊ 25 02:41
♋ 27 10:42
♌ 29 21:03

Aug 1935
♍ 1 09:06
♎ 3 21:54
♏ 6 09:56
♐ 8 19:24
♑ 11 01:09
♒ 13 03:21
♓ 15 03:18
♈ 17 02:55
♉ 19 04:07
♊ 21 08:25
♋ 23 16:16
♌ 26 03:00
♍ 28 15:20
♎ 31 04:07

Sep 1935
♏ 2 16:21
♐ 5 02:48
♑ 7 10:07
♒ 9 13:44
♓ 11 14:15
♈ 13 13:21
♉ 15 13:10
♊ 17 15:47
♋ 19 22:26
♌ 22 08:49
♍ 24 21:18
♎ 27 10:05
♏ 29 22:05

Oct 1935
♐ 2 08:40
♑ 4 17:02
♒ 6 22:20
♓ 9 00:26
♈ 11 00:20
♉ 12 23:53
♊ 15 01:17
♋ 17 06:20
♌ 19 15:34
♍ 22 03:43
♎ 24 16:31
♏ 27 04:14
♐ 29 14:17
♑ 31 22:30

Nov 1935
♒ 3 04:38
♓ 5 08:20
♈ 7 09:54
♉ 9 10:29
♊ 11 11:52
♋ 13 15:56
♌ 15 23:50
♍ 18 11:09
♎ 20 23:52
♏ 23 11:35

☽ Moon

Nov 1935
♐ 25 21:08
♑ 28 04:28
♒ 30 09:59

Dec 1935
♓ 2 14:02
♈ 4 16:52
♉ 6 19:03
♊ 8 21:36
♋ 11 01:53
♌ 13 09:06
♍ 15 19:32
♎ 18 07:57
♏ 20 20:02
♐ 23 05:44
♑ 25 12:27
♒ 27 16:46
♓ 29 19:42
♈ 31 22:15

Jan 1936
♉ 3 01:10
♊ 5 05:03
♋ 7 10:28
♌ 9 18:01
♍ 12 04:04
♎ 14 16:09
♏ 17 04:37
♐ 19 15:10
♑ 21 22:18
♒ 24 02:02
♓ 26 03:34
♈ 28 04:35
♉ 30 06:37

Feb 1936
♊ 1 10:38
♋ 3 16:57
♌ 6 01:25
♍ 8 11:47
♎ 10 23:45
♏ 13 12:23
♐ 15 23:56
♑ 18 08:20
♒ 20 12:46
♓ 22 13:56
♈ 24 13:35
♉ 26 13:51
♊ 28 16:29

Mar 1936
♋ 1 22:25
♌ 4 07:20
♍ 6 18:17
♎ 9 06:25
♏ 11 19:03
♐ 14 07:05
♑ 16 16:50
♒ 18 22:52
♓ 21 00:59
♈ 23 00:31
♉ 24 23:37
♊ 27 00:31
♋ 29 04:51
♌ 31 13:03

Apr 1936
♍ 3 00:07
♎ 5 12:30
♏ 8 01:05
♐ 10 13:02
♑ 12 23:22
♒ 15 06:48
♓ 17 10:37
♈ 19 11:21
♉ 21 10:38
♊ 23 10:37

☽ Moon

Apr 1936
♋ 25 13:22
♌ 27 20:02
♍ 30 06:21

May 1936
♎ 2 18:42
♏ 5 07:16
♐ 7 18:53
♑ 10 04:56
♒ 12 12:46
♓ 14 17:52
♈ 16 20:13
♉ 18 20:47
♊ 20 21:12
♋ 22 23:19
♌ 25 04:41
♍ 27 13:47
♎ 30 01:38

Jun 1936
♏ 1 14:10
♐ 4 01:37
♑ 6 11:02
♒ 8 18:17
♓ 10 23:27
♈ 13 02:46
♉ 15 04:48
♊ 17 06:29
♋ 19 09:08
♌ 21 14:05
♍ 23 22:15
♎ 26 09:22
♏ 28 21:52

Jul 1936
♐ 1 09:26
♑ 3 18:33
♒ 6 00:56
♓ 8 05:10
♈ 10 08:10
♉ 12 10:45
♊ 14 13:38
♋ 16 17:27
♌ 18 22:57
♍ 21 06:53
♎ 23 17:30
♏ 26 05:53
♐ 28 17:55
♑ 31 03:23

Aug 1936
♒ 2 09:25
♓ 4 12:36
♈ 6 14:21
♉ 8 16:11
♊ 10 19:11
♋ 12 23:51
♌ 15 06:19
♍ 17 14:44
♎ 20 01:16
♏ 22 13:35
♐ 25 02:09
♑ 27 12:34
♒ 29 19:12
♓ 31 22:05

Sep 1936
♈ 2 22:43
♉ 4 23:04
♊ 7 00:54
♋ 9 05:15
♌ 11 12:12
♍ 13 21:19
♎ 16 08:12
♏ 18 20:31
♐ 21 09:23
♑ 23 20:52

☽ Moon

Sep 1936
♒ 26 04:52
♓ 28 08:39
♈ 30 09:10

Oct 1936
♉ 2 08:25
♊ 4 08:37
♋ 6 11:28
♌ 8 17:44
♍ 11 03:01
♎ 13 14:18
♏ 16 02:46
♐ 18 15:37
♑ 21 03:37
♒ 23 12:59
♓ 25 18:27
♈ 27 20:09
♉ 29 19:34
♊ 31 18:49

Nov 1936
♋ 2 20:00
♌ 5 00:36
♍ 7 08:59
♎ 9 20:14
♏ 12 08:51
♐ 14 21:33
♑ 17 09:19
♒ 19 19:10
♓ 22 02:03
♈ 24 05:36
♉ 26 06:29
♊ 28 06:12
♋ 30 06:40

Dec 1936
♌ 2 09:43
♍ 4 16:30
♎ 7 02:55
♏ 9 15:27
♐ 12 04:06
♑ 14 15:25
♒ 17 00:42
♓ 19 07:43
♈ 21 12:26
♉ 23 15:05
♊ 25 16:24
♋ 27 17:36
♌ 29 20:14

Jan 1937
♍ 1 01:45
♎ 3 10:54
♏ 5 22:57
♐ 8 11:42
♑ 10 22:53
♒ 13 07:24
♓ 15 13:28
♈ 17 17:48
♉ 19 21:06
♊ 21 23:53
♋ 24 02:38
♌ 26 06:07
♍ 28 11:30
♎ 30 19:48

Feb 1937
♏ 2 07:09
♐ 4 19:58
♑ 7 07:33
♒ 9 16:00
♓ 11 21:09
♈ 14 00:11
♉ 16 02:34
♊ 18 05:22
♋ 20 09:03
♌ 22 13:50

☽ Moon

Feb 1937
♍ 24 20:04
♎ 27 04:26

Mar 1937
♏ 1 15:22
♐ 4 04:07
♑ 6 16:22
♒ 9 01:35
♓ 11 06:50
♈ 13 09:00
♉ 15 09:54
♊ 17 11:18
♋ 19 14:25
♌ 21 19:35
♍ 24 02:43
♎ 26 11:46
♏ 28 22:50
♐ 31 11:31

Apr 1937
♑ 3 00:16
♒ 5 10:38
♓ 7 16:59
♈ 9 19:28
♉ 11 19:39
♊ 13 19:34
♋ 15 21:02
♌ 18 01:11
♍ 20 08:15
♎ 22 17:50
♏ 25 05:20
♐ 27 18:04
♑ 30 06:55

May 1937
♒ 2 18:07
♓ 5 01:56
♈ 7 05:47
♉ 9 06:32
♊ 11 05:56
♋ 13 06:00
♌ 15 08:27
♍ 17 14:18
♎ 19 23:34
♏ 22 11:17
♐ 25 00:10
♑ 27 12:52
♒ 30 00:13

Jun 1937
♓ 1 08:57
♈ 3 14:21
♉ 5 16:36
♊ 7 16:46
♋ 9 16:32
♌ 11 17:44
♍ 13 22:00
♎ 16 06:07
♏ 18 17:30
♐ 21 06:25
♑ 23 18:57
♒ 26 05:53
♓ 28 14:36
♈ 30 20:50

Jul 1937
♉ 3 00:34
♊ 5 02:15
♋ 7 02:53
♌ 9 03:59
♍ 11 07:15
♎ 13 14:03
♏ 16 00:35
♐ 18 13:19
♑ 21 01:50
♒ 23 12:19
♓ 25 20:20

☽ Moon

Jul 1937
♈ 28 02:15
♉ 30 06:31

Aug 1937
♊ 1 09:29
♋ 3 11:34
♌ 5 13:35
♍ 7 16:54
♎ 9 22:58
♏ 12 08:36
♐ 14 20:58
♑ 17 09:36
♒ 19 20:04
♓ 22 03:28
♈ 24 08:23
♉ 26 11:56
♊ 28 15:01
♋ 30 18:03

Sep 1937
♌ 1 21:21
♍ 4 01:34
♎ 6 07:48
♏ 8 16:58
♐ 11 04:58
♑ 13 17:50
♒ 16 04:50
♓ 18 12:19
♈ 20 16:31
♉ 22 18:49
♊ 24 20:46
♋ 26 23:24
♌ 29 03:13

Oct 1937
♍ 1 08:28
♎ 3 15:31
♏ 6 00:54
♐ 8 12:43
♑ 11 01:46
♒ 13 13:36
♓ 15 22:03
♈ 18 02:32
♉ 20 04:09
♊ 22 04:40
♋ 24 05:46
♌ 26 08:42
♍ 28 14:01
♎ 30 21:46

Nov 1937
♏ 2 07:48
♐ 4 19:45
♑ 7 08:49
♒ 9 21:18
♓ 12 07:06
♈ 14 12:59
♉ 16 15:12
♊ 18 15:10
♋ 20 14:47
♌ 22 15:55
♍ 24 19:55
♎ 27 03:21
♏ 29 13:45

Dec 1937
♐ 2 02:05
♑ 4 15:07
♒ 7 03:39
♓ 9 14:20
♈ 11 21:54
♉ 14 01:49
♊ 16 02:42
♋ 18 02:02
♌ 20 01:48
♍ 22 03:56
♎ 24 09:52

☽ Moon

Dec 1937
♏ 26 19:44
♐ 29 08:11
♑ 31 21:16

Jan 1938
♒ 3 09:30
♓ 5 20:06
♈ 8 04:28
♉ 10 10:05
♊ 12 12:50
♋ 14 13:22
♌ 16 13:10
♍ 18 14:13
♎ 20 18:26
♏ 23 02:54
♐ 25 14:50
♑ 28 03:57
♒ 30 15:59

Feb 1938
♓ 2 01:58
♈ 4 09:54
♉ 6 15:58
♊ 8 20:07
♋ 10 22:25
♌ 12 23:33
♍ 15 00:57
♎ 17 04:27
♏ 19 11:36
♐ 21 22:33
♑ 24 11:27
♒ 26 23:35

Mar 1938
♓ 1 09:13
♈ 3 16:16
♉ 5 21:29
♊ 8 01:33
♋ 10 04:45
♌ 12 07:23
♍ 14 10:05
♎ 16 14:08
♏ 18 20:53
♐ 21 07:00
♑ 23 19:31
♒ 26 07:55
♓ 28 17:51
♈ 31 00:33

Apr 1938
♉ 2 04:42
♊ 4 07:33
♋ 6 10:07
♌ 8 13:04
♍ 10 16:51
♎ 12 22:01
♏ 15 05:21
♐ 17 15:18
♑ 20 03:30
♒ 22 16:09
♓ 25 02:53
♈ 27 10:08
♉ 29 14:01

May 1938
♊ 1 15:45
♋ 3 16:51
♌ 5 18:41
♍ 7 22:16
♎ 10 04:05
♏ 12 12:15
♐ 14 22:40
♑ 17 10:50
♒ 19 23:37
♓ 22 11:07
♈ 24 19:35
♉ 27 00:16

☽ Moon

May 1938
♊ 29 01:52
♋ 31 01:52

Jun 1938
♌ 2 02:08
♍ 4 04:21
♎ 6 09:35
♏ 8 18:00
♐ 11 04:56
♑ 13 17:20
♒ 16 06:07
♓ 18 18:02
♈ 21 03:39
♉ 23 09:49
♊ 25 12:25
♋ 27 12:28
♌ 29 11:46

Jul 1938
♍ 1 12:24
♎ 3 16:08
♏ 5 23:48
♐ 8 10:44
♑ 10 23:21
♒ 13 12:05
♓ 15 23:55
♈ 18 10:02
♉ 20 17:30
♊ 22 21:42
♋ 24 22:54
♌ 26 22:25
♍ 28 22:17
♎ 31 00:34

Aug 1938
♏ 2 06:49
♐ 4 17:01
♑ 7 05:32
♒ 9 18:14
♓ 12 05:44
♈ 14 15:34
♉ 16 23:25
♊ 19 04:50
♋ 21 07:39
♌ 23 08:27
♍ 25 08:43
♎ 27 10:26
♏ 29 15:25

Sep 1938
♐ 1 00:27
♑ 3 12:29
♒ 6 01:10
♓ 8 12:28
♈ 10 21:40
♉ 13 04:53
♊ 15 10:22
♋ 17 14:09
♌ 19 16:26
♍ 21 18:01
♎ 23 20:18
♏ 26 00:56
♐ 28 09:01
♑ 30 20:19

Oct 1938
♒ 3 08:57
♓ 5 20:26
♈ 8 05:22
♉ 10 11:42
♊ 12 16:10
♋ 14 19:30
♌ 16 22:19
♍ 19 01:08
♎ 21 04:42
♏ 23 09:59
♐ 25 17:53

☽ Moon

Oct 1938
♑ 28 04:38
♒ 30 17:07

Nov 1938
♓ 2 05:08
♈ 4 14:34
♉ 6 20:40
♊ 9 00:03
♋ 11 01:59
♌ 13 03:49
♍ 15 06:37
♎ 17 11:03
♏ 19 17:25
♐ 22 01:56
♑ 24 12:37
♒ 27 00:58
♓ 29 13:29

Dec 1938
♈ 2 00:02
♉ 4 07:00
♊ 6 10:18
♋ 8 11:08
♌ 10 11:18
♍ 12 12:37
♎ 14 16:26
♏ 16 23:12
♐ 19 08:30
♑ 21 19:38
♒ 24 07:58
♓ 26 20:40
♈ 29 08:13
♉ 31 16:47

Jan 1939
♊ 2 21:19
♋ 4 22:20
♌ 6 21:32
♍ 8 21:08
♎ 10 23:10
♏ 13 04:53
♐ 15 14:09
♑ 18 01:43
♒ 20 14:14
♓ 23 02:50
♈ 25 14:41
♉ 28 00:28
♊ 30 06:49

Feb 1939
♋ 1 09:22
♌ 3 09:06
♍ 5 08:03
♎ 7 08:29
♏ 9 12:21
♐ 11 20:23
♑ 14 07:40
♒ 16 20:21
♓ 19 08:51
♈ 21 20:22
♉ 24 06:18
♊ 26 13:46
♋ 28 18:06

Mar 1939
♌ 2 19:30
♍ 4 19:17
♎ 6 19:26
♏ 8 21:59
♐ 11 04:22
♑ 13 14:34
♒ 16 03:00
♓ 18 15:31
♈ 21 02:40
♉ 23 11:58
♊ 25 19:14
♋ 28 00:19

☽ Moon

Mar 1939
♌ 30 03:14

Apr 1939
♍ 1 04:39
♎ 3 05:48
♏ 5 08:21
♐ 7 13:47
♑ 9 22:46
♒ 12 10:32
♓ 14 23:04
♈ 17 10:12
♉ 19 18:56
♊ 22 01:16
♋ 24 05:43
♌ 26 08:54
♍ 28 11:26
♎ 30 14:02

May 1939
♏ 2 17:36
♐ 4 23:10
♑ 7 07:33
♒ 9 18:40
♓ 12 07:08
♈ 14 18:40
♉ 17 03:27
♊ 19 09:06
♋ 21 12:23
♌ 23 14:33
♍ 25 16:50
♎ 27 20:05
♏ 30 00:47

Jun 1939
♐ 1 07:15
♑ 3 15:49
♒ 6 02:40
♓ 8 15:03
♈ 11 03:09
♉ 13 12:42
♊ 15 18:32
♋ 17 21:06
♌ 19 21:58
♍ 21 22:56
♎ 24 01:30
♏ 26 06:24
♐ 28 13:38
♑ 30 22:53

Jul 1939
♒ 3 09:53
♓ 5 22:17
♈ 8 10:49
♉ 10 21:26
♊ 13 04:20
♋ 15 07:16
♌ 17 07:30
♍ 19 07:07
♎ 21 08:10
♏ 23 12:03
♐ 25 19:09
♑ 28 04:50
♒ 30 16:14

Aug 1939
♓ 2 04:41
♈ 4 17:21
♉ 7 04:46
♊ 9 13:05
♋ 11 17:21
♌ 13 18:09
♍ 15 17:20
♎ 17 17:04
♏ 19 19:19
♐ 22 01:13
♑ 24 10:32
♒ 26 22:08

☽ Moon

Aug 1939
♓ 29 10:42
♈ 31 23:14

Sep 1939
♉ 3 10:46
♊ 5 20:01
♋ 8 01:51
♌ 10 04:11
♍ 12 04:09
♎ 14 03:38
♏ 16 04:43
♐ 18 09:01
♑ 20 17:10
♒ 23 04:23
♓ 25 16:59
♈ 28 05:21
♉ 30 16:28

Oct 1939
♊ 3 01:37
♋ 5 08:16
♌ 7 12:10
♍ 9 13:46
♎ 11 14:16
♏ 13 15:18
♐ 15 18:36
♑ 18 01:21
♒ 20 11:39
♓ 23 00:05
♈ 25 12:27
♉ 27 23:08
♊ 30 07:30

Nov 1939
♋ 1 13:41
♌ 3 18:01
♍ 5 20:56
♎ 7 23:03
♏ 10 01:13
♐ 12 04:41
♑ 14 10:41
♒ 16 19:59
♓ 19 07:59
♈ 21 20:35
♉ 24 07:22
♊ 26 15:09
♋ 28 20:11
♌ 30 23:33

Dec 1939
♍ 3 02:22
♎ 5 05:22
♏ 7 08:57
♐ 9 13:32
♑ 11 19:51
♒ 14 04:42
♓ 16 16:13
♈ 19 05:02
♉ 21 16:31
♊ 24 00:37
♋ 26 05:03
♌ 28 07:05
♍ 30 08:29

Jan 1940
♎ 1 10:43
♏ 3 14:35
♐ 5 20:12
♑ 8 03:29
♒ 10 12:41
♓ 13 00:03
♈ 15 12:54
♉ 18 01:15
♊ 20 10:31
♋ 22 15:35
♌ 24 17:11
♍ 26 17:12

☽ Moon

Jan 1940
♎ 28 17:43
♏ 30 20:17

Feb 1940
♐ 2 01:35
♑ 4 09:26
♒ 6 19:21
♓ 9 06:58
♈ 11 19:48
♉ 14 08:35
♊ 16 19:09
♋ 19 01:46
♌ 21 04:19
♍ 23 04:11
♎ 25 03:29
♏ 27 04:13
♐ 29 07:54

Mar 1940
♑ 2 15:02
♒ 5 01:07
♓ 7 13:06
♈ 10 02:00
♉ 12 14:43
♊ 15 01:52
♋ 17 09:56
♌ 19 14:14
♍ 21 15:21
♎ 23 14:48
♏ 25 14:33
♐ 27 16:31
♑ 29 21:59

Apr 1940
♒ 1 07:12
♓ 3 19:10
♈ 6 08:09
♉ 8 20:38
♊ 11 07:31
♋ 13 16:03
♌ 15 21:43
♍ 18 00:34
♎ 20 01:22
♏ 22 01:32
♐ 24 02:48
♑ 26 06:49
♒ 28 14:38

May 1940
♓ 1 01:55
♈ 3 14:51
♉ 6 03:12
♊ 8 13:33
♋ 10 21:33
♌ 13 03:22
♍ 15 07:17
♎ 17 09:40
♏ 19 11:12
♐ 21 13:00
♑ 23 16:34
♒ 25 23:18
♓ 28 09:38
♈ 30 22:18

Jun 1940
♉ 2 10:43
♊ 4 20:49
♋ 7 04:02
♌ 9 09:00
♍ 11 12:40
♎ 13 15:43
♏ 15 18:31
♐ 17 21:33
♑ 20 01:44
♒ 22 08:14
♓ 24 17:55
♈ 27 06:12

☽ Moon

Jun 1940
♉ 29 18:51

Jul 1940
♊ 2 05:15
♋ 4 12:10
♌ 6 16:12
♍ 8 18:44
♎ 10 21:06
♏ 13 00:06
♐ 15 04:04
♑ 17 09:17
♒ 19 16:21
♓ 22 01:58
♈ 24 14:00
♉ 27 02:55
♊ 29 14:03
♋ 31 21:32

Aug 1940
♌ 3 01:20
♍ 5 02:50
♎ 7 03:49
♏ 9 05:45
♐ 11 09:28
♑ 13 15:14
♒ 15 23:07
♓ 18 09:09
♈ 20 21:13
♉ 23 10:16
♊ 25 22:12
♋ 28 06:53
♌ 30 11:31

Sep 1940
♍ 1 12:57
♎ 3 12:54
♏ 5 13:16
♐ 7 15:36
♑ 9 20:45
♒ 12 04:51
♓ 14 15:24
♈ 17 03:42
♉ 19 16:45
♊ 22 05:04
♋ 24 14:56
♌ 26 21:08
♍ 28 23:41
♎ 30 23:46

Oct 1940
♏ 2 23:12
♐ 4 23:53
♑ 7 03:28
♒ 9 10:43
♓ 11 21:17
♈ 14 09:49
♉ 16 22:49
♊ 19 10:59
♋ 21 21:17
♌ 24 04:50
♍ 26 09:09
♎ 28 10:37
♏ 30 10:25

Nov 1940
♐ 1 10:21
♑ 3 12:22
♒ 5 18:02
♓ 8 03:45
♈ 10 16:12
♉ 13 05:12
♊ 15 17:00
♋ 18 02:52
♌ 20 10:38
♍ 22 16:10
♎ 24 19:24
♏ 26 20:44

☽ Moon

Nov 1940
♐ 28 21:18
♑ 30 22:50

Dec 1940
♒ 3 03:12
♓ 5 11:34
♈ 7 23:26
♉ 10 12:26
♊ 13 00:07
♋ 15 09:19
♌ 17 16:16
♍ 19 21:34
♎ 22 01:36
♏ 24 04:29
♐ 26 06:36
♑ 28 08:58
♒ 30 13:08

Jan 1941
♓ 1 20:34
♈ 4 07:33
♉ 6 20:27
♊ 9 08:26
♋ 11 17:33
♌ 13 23:39
♍ 16 03:45
♎ 18 06:59
♏ 20 10:03
♐ 22 13:16
♑ 24 17:01
♒ 26 22:05
♓ 29 05:34
♈ 31 16:01

Feb 1941
♉ 3 04:40
♊ 5 17:08
♋ 8 02:57
♌ 10 09:07
♍ 12 12:21
♎ 14 14:07
♏ 16 15:52
♐ 18 18:36
♑ 20 22:53
♒ 23 05:01
♓ 25 13:18
♈ 27 23:54

Mar 1941
♉ 2 12:22
♊ 5 01:11
♋ 7 12:03
♌ 9 19:18
♍ 11 22:51
♎ 13 23:51
♏ 16 00:02
♐ 18 01:07
♑ 20 04:24
♒ 22 10:33
♓ 24 19:29
♈ 27 06:38
♉ 29 19:13

Apr 1941
♊ 1 08:06
♋ 3 19:43
♌ 6 04:25
♍ 8 09:21
♎ 10 10:55
♏ 12 10:32
♐ 14 10:08
♑ 16 11:38
♒ 18 16:30
♓ 21 01:06
♈ 23 12:33
♉ 26 01:22
♊ 28 14:10

☽ Moon

May 1941
♋ 1 01:55
♌ 3 11:33
♍ 5 18:05
♎ 7 21:11
♏ 9 21:33
♐ 11 20:50
♑ 13 21:03
♒ 16 00:14
♓ 18 07:32
♈ 20 18:33
♉ 23 07:25
♊ 25 20:09
♋ 28 07:36
♌ 30 17:14

Jun 1941
♍ 2 00:38
♎ 4 05:17
♏ 6 07:13
♐ 8 07:24
♑ 10 07:32
♒ 12 09:41
♓ 14 15:32
♈ 17 01:30
♉ 19 14:02
♊ 22 02:44
♋ 24 13:50
♌ 26 22:54
♍ 29 06:02

Jul 1941
♎ 1 11:16
♏ 3 14:33
♐ 5 16:13
♑ 7 17:21
♒ 9 19:36
♓ 12 00:41
♈ 14 09:33
♉ 16 21:29
♊ 19 10:09
♋ 21 21:14
♌ 24 05:47
♍ 26 12:03
♎ 28 16:40
♏ 30 20:08

Aug 1941
♐ 1 22:49
♑ 4 01:17
♒ 6 04:32
♓ 8 09:50
♈ 10 18:12
♉ 13 05:31
♊ 15 18:08
♋ 18 05:37
♌ 20 14:15
♍ 22 19:52
♎ 24 23:21
♏ 27 01:48
♐ 29 04:12
♑ 31 07:17

Sep 1941
♒ 2 11:38
♓ 4 17:51
♈ 7 02:28
♉ 9 13:31
♊ 12 02:05
♋ 14 14:08
♌ 16 23:35
♍ 19 05:28
♎ 21 08:17
♏ 23 09:24
♐ 25 10:24
♑ 27 12:44
♒ 29 17:16

☽ Moo

Oct 1941
♓ 2 00:1
♈ 4 09:3
♉ 6 20:5
♊ 9 09:2
♋ 11 21:5
♌ 14 08:2
♍ 16 15:3
♎ 18 18:5
♏ 20 19:2
♐ 22 19:0
♑ 24 19:4
♒ 26 23:0
♓ 29 05:5
♈ 31 15:3

Nov 1941
♉ 3 03:1
♊ 5 15:5
♋ 8 04:2
♌ 10 15:4
♍ 13 00:2
♎ 15 05:2
♏ 17 06:4
♐ 19 05:5
♑ 21 05:1
♒ 23 06:4
♓ 25 12:0
♈ 27 21:2
♉ 30 09:17

Dec 1941
♊ 2 21:59
♋ 5 10:21
♌ 7 21:42
♍ 10 07:11
♎ 12 13:45
♏ 14 16:51
♐ 16 17:10
♑ 18 16:27
♒ 20 16:53
♓ 22 20:32
♈ 25 04:23
♉ 27 15:42
♊ 30 04:26

Jan 1942
♋ 1 16:41
♌ 4 03:32
♍ 6 12:41
♎ 8 19:48
♏ 11 00:24
♐ 13 02:31
♑ 15 03:07
♒ 17 03:52
♓ 19 06:43
♈ 21 13:07
♉ 23 23:18
♊ 26 11:43
♋ 29 00:03
♌ 31 10:36

Feb 1942
♍ 2 18:57
♎ 5 01:17
♏ 7 05:55
♐ 9 09:06
♑ 11 11:19
♒ 13 13:27
♓ 15 16:50
♈ 17 22:46
♉ 20 07:57
♊ 22 19:46
♋ 25 08:14
♌ 27 19:05

Mar 1942
♍ 2 03:05

Moon

Mar 1942
♎ 4 08:23
♏ 6 11:50
♐ 8 14:28
♑ 10 17:08
♒ 12 20:30
♓ 15 01:08
♈ 17 07:40
♉ 19 16:38
♊ 22 03:59
♋ 24 16:32
♌ 27 04:03
♍ 29 12:36
♎ 31 17:36

Apr 1942
♏ 2 19:54
♐ 4 21:04
♑ 6 22:41
♒ 9 01:56
♓ 11 07:19
♈ 13 14:48
♉ 16 00:17
♊ 18 11:36
♋ 21 00:09
♌ 23 12:20
♍ 25 22:02
♎ 28 03:49
♏ 30 05:59

May 1942
♐ 2 06:03
♑ 4 06:04
♒ 6 07:55
♓ 8 12:43
♈ 10 20:31
♉ 13 06:36
♊ 15 18:14
♋ 18 06:48
♌ 20 19:20
♍ 23 06:06
♎ 25 13:21
♏ 27 16:32
♐ 29 16:39
♑ 31 15:44

Jun 1942
♒ 2 15:59
♓ 4 19:13
♈ 7 02:10
♉ 9 12:15
♊ 12 00:11
♋ 14 12:49
♌ 17 01:19
♍ 19 12:32
♎ 21 21:03
♏ 24 01:50
♐ 26 03:08
♑ 28 02:29
♒ 30 02:00

Jul 1942
♓ 2 03:45
♈ 4 09:10
♉ 6 18:22
♊ 9 06:09
♋ 11 18:51
♌ 14 07:07
♍ 16 18:08
♎ 19 03:01
♏ 21 09:01
♐ 23 11:58
♑ 25 12:38
♒ 27 12:37
♓ 29 13:49
♈ 31 17:55

☽ Moon

Aug 1942
♉ 3 01:47
♊ 5 12:53
♋ 8 01:30
♌ 10 13:39
♍ 13 00:08
♎ 15 08:30
♏ 17 14:37
♐ 19 18:34
♑ 21 20:46
♒ 23 22:07
♓ 25 23:55
♈ 28 03:38
♉ 30 10:28

Sep 1942
♊ 1 20:39
♋ 4 08:59
♌ 6 21:15
♍ 9 07:30
♎ 11 15:04
♏ 13 20:18
♐ 15 23:57
♑ 18 02:48
♒ 20 05:27
♓ 22 08:33
♈ 24 12:57
♉ 26 19:34
♊ 29 05:04

Oct 1942
♋ 1 17:02
♌ 4 05:34
♍ 6 16:12
♎ 8 23:32
♏ 11 03:46
♐ 13 06:10
♑ 15 08:13
♒ 17 11:01
♓ 19 15:05
♈ 21 20:36
♉ 24 03:52
♊ 26 13:18
♋ 29 00:59
♌ 31 13:47

Nov 1942
♍ 3 01:18
♎ 5 09:21
♏ 7 13:27
♐ 9 14:47
♑ 11 15:18
♒ 13 16:48
♓ 15 20:27
♈ 18 02:30
♉ 20 10:37
♊ 22 20:34
♋ 25 08:16
♌ 27 21:09
♍ 30 09:28

Dec 1942
♎ 2 18:54
♏ 5 00:06
♐ 7 01:34
♑ 9 01:06
♒ 11 00:56
♓ 13 02:55
♈ 15 08:03
♉ 17 16:16
♊ 20 02:45
♋ 22 14:45
♌ 25 03:35
♍ 27 16:09
♎ 30 02:44

Jan 1943
♏ 1 09:39

☽ Moon

Jan 1943
♐ 3 12:34
♑ 5 12:35
♒ 7 11:42
♓ 9 12:03
♈ 11 15:20
♉ 13 22:21
♊ 16 08:38
♋ 18 20:53
♌ 21 09:43
♍ 23 22:02
♎ 26 08:46
♏ 28 16:50
♐ 30 21:33

Feb 1943
♑ 1 23:15
♒ 3 23:10
♓ 5 23:07
♈ 8 01:00
♉ 10 06:16
♊ 12 15:24
♋ 15 03:24
♌ 17 16:18
♍ 20 04:19
♎ 22 14:29
♏ 24 22:24
♐ 27 03:59

Mar 1943
♑ 1 07:18
♒ 3 08:56
♓ 5 09:54
♈ 7 11:41
♉ 9 15:53
♊ 11 23:38
♋ 14 10:49
♌ 16 23:40
♍ 19 11:42
♎ 21 21:20
♏ 24 04:22
♐ 26 09:23
♑ 28 13:04
♒ 30 15:57

Apr 1943
♓ 1 18:27
♈ 3 21:17
♉ 6 01:37
♊ 8 08:41
♋ 10 19:02
♌ 13 07:38
♍ 15 19:58
♎ 18 05:40
♏ 20 12:03
♐ 22 15:56
♑ 24 18:39
♒ 26 21:21
♓ 29 00:35

May 1943
♈ 1 04:39
♉ 3 09:57
♊ 5 17:15
♋ 8 03:16
♌ 10 15:37
♍ 13 04:21
♎ 15 14:43
♏ 17 21:19
♐ 20 00:32
♑ 22 01:59
♒ 24 03:23
♓ 26 05:57
♈ 28 10:16
♉ 30 16:24

Jun 1943
♊ 2 00:29

☽ Moon

Jun 1943
♋ 4 10:45
♌ 6 23:02
♍ 9 12:02
♎ 11 23:21
♏ 14 06:58
♐ 16 10:36
♑ 18 11:30
♒ 20 11:34
♓ 22 12:36
♈ 24 15:52
♉ 26 21:51
♊ 29 06:26

Jul 1943
♋ 1 17:12
♌ 4 05:39
♍ 6 18:44
♎ 9 06:43
♏ 11 15:40
♐ 13 20:36
♑ 15 22:06
♒ 17 21:45
♓ 19 21:30
♈ 21 23:08
♉ 24 03:52
♊ 26 12:03
♋ 28 23:03
♌ 31 11:42

Aug 1943
♍ 3 00:45
♎ 5 12:50
♏ 7 22:39
♐ 10 05:08
♑ 12 08:09
♒ 14 08:37
♓ 16 08:07
♈ 18 08:32
♉ 20 11:39
♊ 22 18:33
♋ 25 05:06
♌ 27 17:48
♍ 30 06:46

Sep 1943
♎ 1 18:32
♏ 4 04:20
♐ 6 11:38
♑ 8 16:13
♒ 10 18:18
♓ 12 18:46
♈ 14 19:09
♉ 16 21:14
♊ 19 02:41
♋ 21 12:09
♌ 24 00:33
♍ 26 13:29
♎ 29 00:56

Oct 1943
♏ 1 10:04
♐ 3 17:02
♑ 5 22:10
♒ 8 01:39
♓ 10 03:44
♈ 12 05:12
♉ 14 07:26
♊ 16 12:06
♋ 18 20:27
♌ 21 08:11
♍ 23 21:09
♎ 26 08:37
♏ 28 17:14
♐ 30 23:14

Nov 1943
♑ 2 03:36

☽ Moon

Nov 1943
♒ 4 07:09
♓ 6 10:15
♈ 8 13:10
♉ 10 16:32
♊ 12 21:31
♋ 15 05:22
♌ 17 16:26
♍ 20 05:20
♎ 22 17:18
♏ 25 02:09
♐ 27 07:35
♑ 29 10:43

Dec 1943
♒ 1 13:01
♓ 3 15:35
♈ 5 18:59
♉ 7 23:30
♊ 10 05:32
♋ 12 13:46
♌ 15 00:36
♍ 17 13:21
♎ 20 01:55
♏ 22 11:45
♐ 24 17:43
♑ 26 20:24
♒ 28 21:21
♓ 30 22:17

Jan 1944
♈ 2 00:33
♉ 4 04:58
♊ 6 11:44
♋ 8 20:47
♌ 11 07:57
♍ 13 20:38
♎ 16 09:28
♏ 18 20:27
♐ 21 03:53
♑ 23 07:26
♒ 25 08:10
♓ 27 07:48
♈ 29 08:14
♉ 31 11:06

Feb 1944
♊ 2 17:16
♋ 5 02:39
♌ 7 14:19
♍ 10 03:07
♎ 12 15:54
♏ 15 03:23
♐ 17 12:14
♑ 19 17:32
♒ 21 19:27
♓ 23 19:09
♈ 25 18:31
♉ 27 19:36

Mar 1944
♊ 1 00:05
♋ 3 08:37
♌ 5 20:19
♍ 8 09:17
♎ 10 21:54
♏ 13 09:11
♐ 15 18:30
♑ 18 01:13
♒ 20 04:55
♓ 22 05:59
♈ 24 05:42
♉ 26 06:01
♊ 28 08:58
♋ 30 15:58

Apr 1944
♌ 2 02:53

☽ Moon

Apr 1944
♍ 4 15:48
♎ 7 04:21
♏ 9 15:11
♐ 12 00:02
♑ 14 06:55
♒ 16 11:45
♓ 18 14:28
♈ 20 15:36
♉ 22 16:29
♊ 24 18:58
♋ 27 00:48
♌ 29 10:35

May 1944
♍ 1 23:04
♎ 4 11:39
♏ 6 22:17
♐ 9 06:26
♑ 11 12:32
♒ 13 17:09
♓ 15 20:34
♈ 17 23:03
♉ 20 01:15
♊ 22 04:26
♋ 24 10:03
♌ 26 19:04
♍ 29 06:58
♎ 31 19:36

Jun 1944
♏ 3 06:31
♐ 5 14:27
♑ 7 19:41
♒ 9 23:12
♓ 12 01:58
♈ 14 04:40
♉ 16 07:51
♊ 18 12:11
♋ 20 18:28
♌ 23 03:25
♍ 25 14:57
♎ 28 03:39
♏ 30 15:09

Jul 1944
♐ 2 23:38
♑ 5 04:41
♒ 7 07:14
♓ 9 08:39
♈ 11 10:18
♉ 13 13:16
♊ 15 18:11
♋ 18 01:21
♌ 20 10:50
♍ 22 22:24
♎ 25 11:07
♏ 27 23:16
♐ 30 08:49

Aug 1944
♑ 1 14:42
♒ 3 17:10
♓ 5 17:35
♈ 7 17:43
♉ 9 19:19
♊ 11 23:38
♋ 14 07:03
♌ 16 17:07
♍ 19 05:00
♎ 21 17:44
♏ 24 06:12
♐ 26 16:51
♑ 29 00:12
♒ 31 03:44

Sep 1944
♓ 2 04:14

☽ Moon

Sep 1944
♈ 4 03:27
♉ 6 03:28
♊ 8 06:13
♋ 10 12:46
♌ 12 22:50
♍ 15 11:00
♎ 17 23:47
♏ 20 12:10
♐ 22 23:16
♑ 25 07:55
♒ 27 13:09
♓ 29 14:58

Oct 1944
♈ 1 14:30
♉ 3 13:46
♊ 5 14:59
♋ 7 19:55
♌ 10 05:02
♍ 12 17:03
♎ 15 05:54
♏ 17 18:03
♐ 20 04:49
♑ 22 13:48
♒ 24 20:18
♓ 26 23:53
♈ 29 00:53
♉ 31 00:45

Nov 1944
♊ 2 01:28
♋ 4 05:04
♌ 6 12:43
♍ 8 23:58
♎ 11 12:44
♏ 14 00:47
♐ 16 11:01
♑ 18 19:19
♒ 21 01:46
♓ 23 06:18
♈ 25 08:57
♉ 27 10:22
♊ 29 11:55

Dec 1944
♋ 1 15:16
♌ 3 21:52
♍ 6 08:03
♎ 8 20:28
♏ 11 08:41
♐ 13 18:49
♑ 16 02:21
♒ 18 07:44
♓ 20 11:39
♈ 22 14:42
♉ 24 17:24
♊ 26 20:26
♋ 29 00:43
♌ 31 07:19

Jan 1945
♍ 2 16:48
♎ 5 04:43
♏ 7 17:12
♐ 10 03:55
♑ 12 11:27
♒ 14 15:57
♓ 16 18:27
♈ 18 20:20
♉ 20 22:47
♊ 23 02:34
♋ 25 08:04
♌ 27 15:32
♍ 30 01:08

Feb 1945
♎ 1 12:45

☽ Moon

Feb 1945
♏ 4 01:22
♐ 6 12:56
♑ 8 21:29
♒ 11 02:12
♓ 13 03:52
♈ 15 04:12
♉ 17 05:04
♊ 19 08:00
♋ 21 13:42
♌ 23 21:58
♍ 26 08:13
♎ 28 19:56

Mar 1945
♏ 3 08:32
♐ 5 20:44
♑ 8 06:36
♒ 10 12:39
♓ 12 14:50
♈ 14 14:33
♉ 16 13:55
♊ 18 15:04
♋ 20 19:31
♌ 23 03:31
♍ 25 14:10
♎ 28 02:14
♏ 30 14:49

Apr 1945
♐ 2 03:07
♑ 4 13:50
♒ 6 21:27
♓ 9 01:10
♈ 11 01:37
♉ 13 00:39
♊ 15 00:31
♋ 17 03:13
♌ 19 09:51
♍ 21 20:02
♎ 24 08:14
♏ 26 20:52
♐ 29 08:55

May 1945
♑ 1 19:39
♒ 4 04:05
♓ 6 09:20
♈ 8 11:25
♉ 10 11:25
♊ 12 11:12
♋ 14 12:51
♌ 16 17:56
♍ 19 02:55
♎ 21 14:42
♏ 24 03:20
♐ 26 15:10
♑ 29 01:24
♒ 31 09:34

Jun 1945
♓ 2 15:25
♈ 4 18:50
♉ 6 20:23
♊ 8 21:15
♋ 10 23:01
♌ 13 03:19
♍ 15 11:06
♎ 17 22:06
♏ 20 10:35
♐ 22 22:26
♑ 25 08:14
♒ 27 15:36
♓ 29 20:51

Jul 1945
♈ 2 00:29
♉ 4 03:04

☽ Moon

Jul 1945
♊ 6 05:19
♋ 8 08:10
♌ 10 12:43
♍ 12 19:57
♎ 15 06:12
♏ 17 18:28
♐ 20 06:35
♑ 22 16:28
♒ 24 23:16
♓ 27 03:26
♈ 29 06:07
♉ 31 08:28

Aug 1945
♊ 2 11:23
♋ 4 15:22
♌ 6 20:52
♍ 9 04:23
♎ 11 14:20
♏ 14 02:24
♐ 16 14:55
♑ 19 01:30
♒ 21 08:32
♓ 23 12:05
♈ 25 13:30
♉ 27 14:34
♊ 29 16:46
♋ 31 20:59

Sep 1945
♌ 3 03:19
♍ 5 11:36
♎ 7 21:48
♏ 10 09:47
♐ 12 22:37
♑ 15 10:10
♒ 17 18:19
♓ 19 22:18
♈ 21 23:10
♉ 23 22:53
♊ 25 23:31
♋ 28 02:38
♌ 30 08:46

Oct 1945
♍ 2 17:33
♎ 5 04:16
♏ 7 16:23
♐ 10 05:17
♑ 12 17:32
♒ 15 03:06
♓ 17 08:33
♈ 19 10:09
♉ 21 09:31
♊ 23 08:49
♋ 25 10:10
♌ 27 14:54
♍ 29 23:11

Nov 1945
♎ 1 10:07
♏ 3 22:29
♐ 6 11:17
♑ 8 23:35
♒ 11 09:58
♓ 13 17:04
♈ 15 20:24
♉ 17 20:48
♊ 19 20:03
♋ 21 20:13
♌ 23 23:11
♍ 26 05:58
♎ 28 16:17

Dec 1945
♏ 1 04:42
♐ 3 17:29

☽ Moon

Dec 1945
♑ 6 05:23
♒ 8 15:33
♓ 10 23:20
♈ 13 04:15
♉ 15 06:29
♊ 17 07:03
♋ 19 07:27
♌ 21 09:30
♍ 23 14:43
♎ 25 23:44
♏ 28 11:42
♐ 31 00:32

Jan 1946
♑ 2 12:10
♒ 4 21:37
♓ 7 04:46
♈ 9 09:55
♉ 11 13:25
♊ 13 15:42
♋ 15 17:32
♌ 17 20:03
♍ 20 00:40
♎ 22 08:31
♏ 24 19:39
♐ 27 08:26
♑ 29 20:17

Feb 1946
♒ 1 05:23
♓ 3 11:32
♈ 5 15:38
♉ 7 18:46
♊ 9 21:45
♋ 12 00:58
♌ 14 04:50
♍ 16 10:03
♎ 18 17:36
♏ 21 04:04
♐ 23 16:40
♑ 26 05:01
♒ 28 14:34

Mar 1946
♓ 2 20:25
♈ 4 23:23
♉ 7 01:08
♊ 9 03:11
♋ 11 06:28
♌ 13 11:14
♍ 15 17:32
♎ 18 01:40
♏ 20 12:04
♐ 23 00:30
♑ 25 13:16
♒ 27 23:50
♓ 30 06:26

Apr 1946
♈ 1 09:16
♉ 3 09:57
♊ 5 10:25
♋ 7 12:20
♌ 9 16:37
♍ 11 23:20
♎ 14 08:13
♏ 16 19:03
♐ 19 07:29
♑ 21 20:27
♒ 24 07:55
♓ 26 15:53
♈ 28 19:45
♉ 30 20:31

May 1946
♊ 2 20:03
♋ 4 20:22

☽ Moon

May 1946
♌ 6 23:04
♍ 9 04:56
♎ 11 13:53
♏ 14 01:08
♐ 16 13:45
♑ 19 02:41
♒ 21 14:30
♓ 23 23:38
♈ 26 05:04
♉ 28 07:04
♊ 30 06:55

Jun 1946
♋ 1 06:29
♌ 3 07:39
♍ 5 11:56
♎ 7 19:56
♏ 10 07:04
♐ 12 19:50
♑ 15 08:39
♒ 17 20:15
♓ 20 05:42
♈ 22 12:19
♉ 24 15:55
♊ 26 17:07
♋ 28 17:11
♌ 30 17:48

Jul 1946
♍ 2 20:44
♎ 5 03:20
♏ 7 13:40
♐ 10 02:20
♑ 12 15:04
♒ 15 02:16
♓ 17 11:15
♈ 19 17:58
♉ 21 22:35
♊ 24 01:18
♋ 26 02:43
♌ 28 03:57
♍ 30 06:32

Aug 1946
♎ 1 12:04
♏ 3 21:22
♐ 6 09:35
♑ 8 22:23
♒ 11 09:23
♓ 13 17:40
♈ 15 23:37
♉ 18 03:59
♊ 20 07:22
♋ 22 10:06
♌ 24 12:38
♍ 26 15:54
♎ 28 21:15
♏ 31 05:49

Sep 1946
♐ 2 17:30
♑ 5 06:23
♒ 7 17:40
♓ 10 01:45
♈ 12 06:49
♉ 14 10:03
♊ 16 12:45
♋ 18 15:41
♌ 20 19:12
♍ 22 23:38
♎ 25 05:40
♏ 27 14:11
♐ 30 01:32

Oct 1946
♑ 2 14:28
♒ 5 02:26

☽ Moon

Oct 1946
♓ 7 11:08
♈ 9 16:05
♉ 11 18:20
♊ 13 19:36
♋ 15 21:23
♌ 18 00:35
♍ 20 05:35
♎ 22 12:33
♏ 24 21:40
♐ 27 09:02
♑ 29 21:59

Nov 1946
♒ 1 10:35
♓ 3 20:31
♈ 6 02:28
♉ 8 04:49
♊ 10 05:07
♋ 12 05:15
♌ 14 06:52
♍ 16 11:04
♎ 18 18:12
♏ 21 03:57
♐ 23 15:43
♑ 26 04:39
♒ 28 17:29

Dec 1946
♓ 1 04:29
♈ 3 12:04
♉ 5 15:48
♊ 7 16:30
♋ 9 15:50
♌ 11 15:47
♍ 13 18:08
♎ 16 00:07
♏ 18 09:42
♐ 20 21:48
♑ 23 10:49
♒ 25 23:29
♓ 28 10:43
♈ 30 19:30

Jan 1947
♉ 2 01:05
♊ 4 03:26
♋ 6 03:28
♌ 8 02:53
♍ 10 03:44
♎ 12 07:53
♏ 14 16:14
♐ 17 04:02
♑ 19 17:09
♒ 22 05:36
♓ 24 16:22
♈ 27 01:10
♉ 29 07:45
♊ 31 11:51

Feb 1947
♋ 2 13:38
♌ 4 14:02
♍ 6 14:42
♎ 8 17:39
♏ 11 00:28
♐ 13 11:14
♑ 16 00:11
♒ 18 12:38
♓ 20 22:57
♈ 23 06:57
♉ 25 13:07
♊ 27 17:46

Mar 1947
♋ 1 20:58
♌ 3 23:00
♍ 6 00:46

☽ Moon

Mar 1947
♎ 8 03:50
♏ 10 09:50
♐ 12 19:33
♑ 15 07:59
♒ 17 20:35
♓ 20 06:57
♈ 22 14:22
♉ 24 19:29
♊ 26 23:15
♋ 29 02:25
♌ 31 05:22

Apr 1947
♍ 2 08:30
♎ 4 12:39
♏ 6 18:56
♐ 9 04:12
♑ 11 16:07
♒ 14 04:50
♓ 16 15:46
♈ 18 23:25
♉ 21 03:55
♊ 23 06:27
♋ 25 08:22
♌ 27 10:44
♍ 29 14:15

May 1947
♎ 1 19:23
♏ 4 02:35
♐ 6 12:08
♑ 8 23:54
♒ 11 12:40
♓ 14 00:20
♈ 16 08:56
♉ 18 13:51
♊ 20 15:51
♋ 22 16:27
♌ 24 17:18
♍ 26 19:49
♎ 29 00:53
♏ 31 08:41

Jun 1947
♐ 2 18:53
♑ 5 06:51
♒ 7 19:37
♓ 10 07:46
♈ 12 17:33
♉ 14 23:45
♊ 17 02:21
♋ 19 02:32
♌ 21 02:06
♍ 23 03:01
♎ 25 06:50
♏ 27 14:16
♐ 30 00:45

Jul 1947
♑ 2 13:02
♒ 5 01:49
♓ 7 14:02
♈ 10 00:34
♉ 12 08:11
♊ 14 12:16
♋ 16 13:15
♌ 18 12:35
♍ 20 12:19
♎ 22 14:33
♏ 24 20:40
♐ 27 06:39
♑ 29 19:01

Aug 1947
♒ 1 07:49
♓ 3 19:48
♈ 6 06:19

☽ Moon

Aug 1947
♉ 8 14:42
♊ 10 20:17
♋ 12 22:49
♌ 14 23:06
♍ 16 22:48
♎ 19 00:03
♏ 21 04:44
♐ 23 13:33
♑ 26 01:30
♒ 28 14:17
♓ 31 02:03

Sep 1947
♈ 2 12:02
♉ 4 20:10
♊ 7 02:18
♋ 9 06:12
♌ 11 08:03
♍ 13 08:51
♎ 15 10:16
♏ 17 14:10
♐ 19 21:49
♑ 22 08:56
♒ 24 21:37
♓ 27 09:24
♈ 29 18:58

Oct 1947
♉ 2 02:15
♊ 4 07:43
♋ 6 11:46
♌ 8 14:41
♍ 10 16:57
♎ 12 19:31
♏ 14 23:45
♐ 17 06:52
♑ 19 17:13
♒ 22 05:38
♓ 24 17:45
♈ 27 03:30
♉ 29 10:16
♊ 31 14:36

Nov 1947
♋ 2 17:32
♌ 4 20:03
♍ 6 22:54
♎ 9 02:42
♏ 11 08:02
♐ 13 15:33
♑ 16 01:36
♒ 18 13:44
♓ 21 02:15
♈ 23 12:52
♉ 25 20:05
♊ 27 23:55
♋ 30 01:31

Dec 1947
♌ 2 02:30
♍ 4 04:23
♎ 6 08:13
♏ 8 14:24
♐ 10 22:49
♑ 13 09:13
♒ 15 21:15
♓ 18 09:58
♈ 20 21:36
♉ 23 06:10
♊ 25 10:47
♋ 27 12:03
♌ 29 11:42
♍ 31 11:47

Jan 1948
♎ 2 14:09
♏ 4 19:50

☽ Moon

Jan 1948
♐ 7 04:40
♑ 9 15:40
♒ 12 03:53
♓ 14 16:34
♈ 17 04:43
♉ 19 14:41
♊ 21 21:01
♋ 23 23:23
♌ 25 22:59
♍ 27 21:56
♎ 29 22:29

Feb 1948
♏ 1 02:27
♐ 3 10:25
♑ 5 21:29
♒ 8 09:58
♓ 10 22:36
♈ 13 10:37
♉ 15 21:07
♊ 18 04:55
♋ 20 09:08
♌ 22 10:07
♍ 24 09:23
♎ 26 09:05
♏ 28 11:23

Mar 1948
♐ 1 17:40
♑ 4 03:50
♒ 6 16:13
♓ 9 04:52
♈ 11 16:32
♉ 14 02:40
♊ 16 10:44
♋ 18 16:13
♌ 20 18:58
♍ 22 19:42
♎ 24 20:02
♏ 26 21:49
♐ 29 02:46
♑ 31 11:33

Apr 1948
♒ 2 23:18
♓ 5 11:55
♈ 7 23:28
♉ 10 08:58
♊ 12 16:19
♋ 14 21:41
♌ 17 01:16
♍ 19 03:30
♎ 21 05:16
♏ 23 07:49
♐ 25 12:31
♑ 27 20:21
♒ 30 07:15

May 1948
♓ 2 19:43
♈ 5 07:27
♉ 7 16:47
♊ 9 23:19
♋ 12 03:38
♌ 14 06:39
♍ 16 09:14
♎ 18 12:07
♏ 20 15:55
♐ 22 21:21
♑ 25 05:07
♒ 27 15:30
♓ 30 03:45

Jun 1948
♈ 1 15:54
♉ 4 01:43
♊ 6 08:06

☽ Moon

Jun 1948
♋ 8 11:28
♌ 10 13:12
♍ 12 14:48
♎ 14 17:33
♏ 16 22:03
♐ 19 04:28
♑ 21 12:50
♒ 23 23:15
♓ 26 11:22
♈ 28 23:55

Jul 1948
♉ 1 10:39
♊ 3 17:47
♋ 5 21:06
♌ 7 21:53
♍ 9 22:03
♎ 11 23:30
♏ 14 03:27
♐ 16 10:10
♑ 18 19:13
♒ 21 06:02
♓ 23 18:12
♈ 26 06:56
♉ 28 18:33
♊ 31 03:01

Aug 1948
♋ 2 07:20
♌ 4 08:13
♍ 6 07:33
♎ 8 07:29
♏ 10 09:56
♐ 12 15:48
♑ 15 00:51
♒ 17 12:02
♓ 20 00:22
♈ 22 13:04
♉ 25 01:03
♊ 27 10:39
♋ 29 16:33
♌ 31 18:41

Sep 1948
♍ 2 18:21
♎ 4 17:36
♏ 6 18:34
♐ 8 22:51
♑ 11 06:56
♒ 13 17:58
♓ 16 06:26
♈ 18 19:01
♉ 21 06:45
♊ 23 16:39
♋ 25 23:45
♌ 28 03:34
♍ 30 04:40

Oct 1948
♎ 2 04:30
♏ 4 04:58
♐ 6 07:54
♑ 8 14:30
♒ 11 00:42
♓ 13 13:02
♈ 16 01:36
♉ 18 12:53
♊ 20 22:14
♋ 23 05:21
♌ 25 10:09
♍ 27 12:53
♎ 29 14:16
♏ 31 15:31

Nov 1948
♐ 2 18:10
♑ 4 23:39

☽ Moon

Nov 1948
♒ 7 08:40
♓ 9 20:33
♈ 12 09:11
♉ 14 20:23
♊ 17 05:01
♋ 19 11:11
♌ 21 15:32
♍ 23 18:48
♎ 25 21:32
♏ 28 00:18
♐ 30 03:51

Dec 1948
♑ 2 09:16
♒ 4 17:31
♓ 7 04:45
♈ 9 17:29
♉ 12 05:08
♊ 14 13:43
♋ 16 19:01
♌ 18 22:03
♍ 21 00:18
♎ 23 02:59
♏ 25 06:38
♐ 27 11:28
♑ 29 17:46

Jan 1949
♒ 1 02:07
♓ 3 12:57
♈ 6 01:40
♉ 8 14:02
♊ 10 23:30
♋ 13 04:56
♌ 15 07:08
♍ 17 07:52
♎ 19 09:03
♏ 21 11:59
♐ 23 17:08
♑ 26 00:21
♒ 28 09:26
♓ 30 20:25

Feb 1949
♈ 2 09:03
♉ 4 21:56
♊ 7 08:39
♋ 9 15:22
♌ 11 18:00
♍ 13 18:06
♎ 15 17:44
♏ 17 18:53
♐ 19 22:49
♑ 22 05:49
♒ 24 15:25
♓ 27 02:53

Mar 1949
♈ 1 15:35
♉ 4 04:32
♊ 6 16:04
♋ 9 00:21
♌ 11 04:33
♍ 13 05:24
♎ 15 04:40
♏ 17 04:25
♐ 19 06:30
♑ 21 12:04
♒ 23 21:09
♓ 26 08:49
♈ 28 21:41
♉ 31 10:28

Apr 1949
♊ 2 22:02
♋ 5 07:09
♌ 7 12:59

☽ Moon

Apr 1949
♍ 9 15:31
♎ 11 15:48
♏ 13 15:28
♐ 15 16:23
♑ 17 20:15
♒ 20 03:58
♓ 22 15:07
♈ 25 04:00
♉ 27 16:40
♊ 30 03:47

May 1949
♋ 2 12:42
♌ 4 19:11
♍ 6 23:11
♎ 9 01:06
♏ 11 01:53
♐ 13 02:57
♑ 15 05:56
♒ 17 12:18
♓ 19 22:25
♈ 22 11:01
♉ 24 23:41
♊ 27 10:26
♋ 29 18:38

Jun 1949
♌ 1 00:35
♍ 3 04:53
♎ 5 07:57
♏ 7 10:13
♐ 9 12:24
♑ 11 15:40
♒ 13 21:26
♓ 16 06:38
♈ 18 18:44
♉ 21 07:29
♊ 23 18:19
♋ 26 02:01
♌ 28 07:00
♍ 30 10:26

Jul 1949
♎ 2 13:22
♏ 4 16:21
♐ 6 19:45
♑ 9 00:02
♒ 11 06:08
♓ 13 15:01
♈ 16 02:42
♉ 18 15:35
♊ 21 02:56
♋ 23 10:51
♌ 25 15:19
♍ 27 17:36
♎ 29 19:20
♏ 31 21:43

Aug 1949
♐ 3 01:24
♑ 5 06:36
♒ 7 13:33
♓ 9 22:45
♈ 12 10:19
♉ 14 23:17
♊ 17 11:21
♋ 19 20:14
♌ 22 01:07
♍ 24 02:55
♎ 26 03:24
♏ 28 04:19
♐ 30 07:00

Sep 1949
♑ 1 12:04
♒ 3 19:36
♓ 6 05:25

☽ Moon

Sep 1949
♈ 8 17:12
♉ 11 06:11
♊ 13 18:46
♋ 16 04:51
♌ 18 11:04
♍ 20 13:34
♎ 22 13:42
♏ 24 13:21
♐ 26 14:21
♑ 28 18:06

Oct 1949
♒ 1 01:13
♓ 3 11:19
♈ 5 23:27
♉ 8 12:25
♊ 11 01:02
♋ 13 11:50
♌ 15 19:34
♍ 17 23:42
♎ 20 00:47
♏ 22 00:18
♐ 24 00:07
♑ 26 02:10
♒ 28 07:49
♓ 30 17:20

Nov 1949
♈ 2 05:34
♉ 4 18:36
♊ 7 06:54
♋ 9 17:34
♌ 12 02:00
♍ 14 07:42
♎ 16 10:35
♏ 18 11:19
♐ 20 11:16
♑ 22 12:20
♒ 24 16:24
♓ 27 00:35
♈ 29 12:17

Dec 1949
♉ 2 01:21
♊ 4 13:28
♋ 6 23:31
♌ 9 07:27
♍ 11 13:31
♎ 13 17:44
♏ 15 20:13
♐ 17 21:32
♑ 19 22:59
♒ 22 02:24
♓ 24 09:19
♈ 26 20:04
♉ 29 08:57
♊ 31 21:12

Jan 1950
♋ 3 06:56
♌ 5 13:58
♍ 7 19:05
♎ 9 23:08
♏ 12 02:27
♐ 14 05:16
♑ 16 08:06
♒ 18 12:07
♓ 20 18:41
♈ 23 04:37
♉ 25 17:07
♊ 28 05:42
♋ 30 15:49

Feb 1950
♌ 1 22:33
♍ 4 02:36
♎ 6 05:19

☽ Moon

Feb 1950
♏ 8 07:50
♐ 10 10:51
♑ 12 14:44
♒ 14 19:57
♓ 17 03:10
♈ 19 13:00
♉ 22 01:11
♊ 24 14:02
♋ 27 01:02

Mar 1950
♌ 1 08:30
♍ 3 12:24
♎ 5 14:00
♏ 7 14:55
♐ 9 16:37
♑ 11 20:06
♒ 14 01:52
♓ 16 09:59
♈ 18 20:20
♉ 21 08:31
♊ 23 21:27
♋ 26 09:16
♌ 28 18:04
♍ 30 23:00

Apr 1950
♎ 2 00:40
♏ 4 00:35
♐ 6 00:36
♑ 8 02:29
♒ 10 07:24
♓ 12 15:37
♈ 15 02:31
♉ 17 14:59
♊ 20 03:53
♋ 22 16:01
♌ 25 01:57
♍ 27 08:29
♎ 29 11:25

May 1950
♏ 1 11:38
♐ 3 10:51
♑ 5 11:08
♒ 7 14:21
♓ 9 21:33
♈ 12 08:17
♉ 14 20:58
♊ 17 09:52
♋ 19 21:50
♌ 22 08:05
♍ 24 15:50
♎ 26 20:26
♏ 28 22:01
♐ 30 21:43

Jun 1950
♑ 1 21:27
♒ 3 23:17
♓ 6 04:56
♈ 8 14:43
♉ 11 03:11
♊ 13 16:04
♋ 16 03:44
♌ 18 13:37
♍ 20 21:31
♎ 23 03:09
♏ 25 06:18
♐ 27 07:26
♑ 29 07:48

Jul 1950
♒ 1 09:19
♓ 3 13:51
♈ 5 22:24
♉ 8 10:12

☽ Moon

Jul 1950
♊ 10 23:01
♋ 13 10:33
♌ 15 19:52
♍ 18 03:05
♎ 20 08:33
♏ 22 12:26
♐ 24 14:55
♑ 26 16:39
♒ 28 18:55
♓ 30 23:18

Aug 1950
♈ 2 07:02
♉ 4 18:05
♊ 7 06:43
♋ 9 18:26
♌ 12 03:36
♍ 14 10:03
♎ 16 14:31
♏ 18 17:49
♐ 20 20:35
♑ 22 23:22
♒ 25 02:52
♓ 27 08:01
♈ 29 15:44

Sep 1950
♉ 1 02:18
♊ 3 14:44
♋ 6 02:53
♌ 8 12:33
♍ 10 18:54
♎ 12 22:27
♏ 15 00:26
♐ 17 02:12
♑ 19 04:48
♒ 21 08:59
♓ 23 15:09
♈ 25 23:31
♉ 28 10:07
♊ 30 22:26

Oct 1950
♋ 3 10:58
♌ 5 21:39
♍ 8 04:53
♎ 10 08:29
♏ 12 09:31
♐ 14 09:44
♑ 16 10:55
♒ 18 14:26
♓ 20 20:52
♈ 23 05:58
♉ 25 17:02
♊ 28 05:22
♋ 30 18:02

Nov 1950
♌ 2 05:37
♍ 4 14:20
♎ 6 19:10
♏ 8 20:28
♐ 10 19:51
♑ 12 19:25
♒ 14 21:14
♓ 17 02:38
♈ 19 11:38
♉ 21 23:07
♊ 24 11:38
♋ 27 00:13
♌ 29 12:01

Dec 1950
♍ 1 21:53
♎ 4 04:28
♏ 6 07:19
♐ 8 07:17

☽ Moo

Dec 195
♑ 10 06:
♒ 12 06:
♓ 14 10:
♈ 16 17:
♉ 19 05:
♊ 21 17:
♋ 24 06:
♌ 26 17:
♍ 29 03:
♎ 31 11:

Jan 1951
♏ 2 15:
♐ 4 17:
♑ 6 17:
♒ 8 17:
♓ 10 19:
♈ 13 02:
♉ 15 12:
♊ 18 00:
♋ 20 13:
♌ 23 00:
♍ 25 09:2
♎ 27 16:4
♏ 29 22:0

Feb 195
♐ 1 01:
♑ 3 02:
♒ 5 04:
♓ 7 06:2
♈ 9 11:4
♉ 11 20:
♊ 14 08:1
♋ 16 20:5
♌ 19 08:0
♍ 21 16:4
♎ 23 23:0
♏ 26 03:
♐ 28 06:4

Mar 195
♑ 2 09:2
♒ 4 12:1
♓ 6 15:4
♈ 8 21:1
♉ 11 05:
♊ 13 16:
♋ 16 05:0
♌ 18 16:4
♍ 21 01:
♎ 23 07:2
♏ 25 10:
♐ 27 12:4
♑ 29 14:5
♒ 31 18:0

Apr 195
♓ 2 22:4
♈ 5 05:
♉ 7 13:5
♊ 10 00:4
♋ 12 13:0
♌ 15 01:1
♍ 17 11:0
♎ 19 17:1
♏ 21 19:5
♐ 23 20:4
♑ 25 21:1
♒ 27 23:3
♓ 30 04:1

May 195
♈ 2 11:2
♉ 4 20:4
♊ 7 07:5
♋ 9 20:1

☽ Moon

May 1951
♌ 12 08:48
♍ 14 19:43
♎ 17 03:04
♏ 19 06:23
♐ 21 06:44
♑ 23 06:07
♒ 25 06:41
♓ 27 10:04
♈ 29 16:52

Jun 1951
♉ 1 02:33
♊ 3 14:02
♋ 6 02:31
♌ 8 15:11
♍ 11 02:46
♎ 13 11:30
♏ 15 16:16
♐ 17 17:26
♑ 19 16:38
♒ 21 16:04
♓ 23 17:49
♈ 25 23:13
♉ 28 08:16
♊ 30 19:50

Jul 1951
♋ 3 08:27
♌ 5 21:00
♍ 8 08:35
♎ 10 18:03
♏ 13 00:18
♐ 15 03:03
♑ 17 03:14
♒ 19 02:41
♓ 21 03:28
♈ 23 07:21
♉ 25 15:06
♊ 28 02:07
♋ 30 14:41

Aug 1951
♌ 2 03:07
♍ 4 14:17
♎ 6 23:34
♏ 9 06:23
♐ 11 10:30
♑ 13 12:18
♒ 15 12:53
♓ 17 13:52
♈ 19 16:58
♉ 21 23:26
♊ 24 09:26
♋ 26 21:44
♌ 29 10:09
♍ 31 20:59

Sep 1951
♎ 3 05:31
♏ 5 11:48
♐ 7 16:11
♑ 9 19:06
♒ 11 21:11
♓ 13 23:21
♈ 16 02:47
♉ 18 08:41
♊ 20 17:46
♋ 23 05:33
♌ 25 18:07
♍ 28 05:05
♎ 30 13:08

Oct 1951
♏ 2 18:23
♐ 4 21:48
♑ 7 00:29
♒ 9 03:18

☽ Moon

Oct 1951
♓ 11 06:46
♈ 13 11:19
♉ 15 17:37
♊ 18 02:21
♋ 20 13:41
♌ 23 02:24
♍ 25 14:00
♎ 27 22:24
♏ 30 03:09

Nov 1951
♐ 1 05:20
♑ 3 06:40
♒ 5 08:42
♓ 7 12:22
♈ 9 17:52
♉ 12 01:07
♊ 14 10:15
♋ 16 21:27
♌ 19 10:11
♍ 21 22:35
♎ 24 08:08
♏ 26 13:32
♐ 28 15:20
♑ 30 15:23

Dec 1951
♒ 2 15:45
♓ 4 18:07
♈ 6 23:17
♉ 9 07:04
♊ 11 16:53
♋ 14 04:22
♌ 16 17:04
♍ 19 05:51
♎ 21 16:39
♏ 23 23:38
♐ 26 02:27
♑ 28 02:24
♒ 30 01:35

Jan 1952
♓ 1 02:10
♈ 3 05:41
♉ 5 12:42
♊ 7 22:42
♋ 10 10:33
♌ 12 23:19
♍ 15 11:59
♎ 17 23:19
♏ 20 07:43
♐ 22 12:22
♑ 24 13:39
♒ 26 13:07
♓ 28 12:46
♈ 30 14:32

Feb 1952
♉ 1 19:50
♊ 4 04:54
♋ 6 16:43
♌ 9 05:35
♍ 11 18:01
♎ 14 04:59
♏ 16 13:44
♐ 18 19:42
♑ 20 22:49
♒ 22 23:48
♓ 25 00:01
♈ 27 01:11
♉ 29 05:01

Mar 1952
♊ 2 12:35
♋ 4 23:40
♌ 7 12:29
♍ 10 00:51

☽ Moon

Mar 1952
♎ 12 11:16
♏ 14 19:20
♐ 17 01:15
♑ 19 05:19
♒ 21 07:54
♓ 23 09:39
♈ 25 11:34
♉ 27 15:05
♊ 29 21:35

Apr 1952
♋ 1 07:38
♌ 3 20:09
♍ 6 08:39
♎ 8 18:55
♏ 11 02:13
♐ 13 07:08
♑ 15 10:41
♒ 17 13:43
♓ 19 16:40
♈ 21 19:56
♉ 24 00:14
♊ 26 06:40
♋ 28 16:05

May 1952
♌ 1 04:11
♍ 3 16:56
♎ 6 03:38
♏ 8 10:48
♐ 10 14:50
♑ 12 17:09
♒ 14 19:14
♓ 16 22:05
♈ 19 02:06
♉ 21 07:29
♊ 23 14:37
♋ 26 00:05
♌ 28 11:58
♍ 31 00:56

Jun 1952
♎ 2 12:25
♏ 4 20:19
♐ 7 00:20
♑ 9 01:46
♒ 11 02:26
♓ 13 04:00
♈ 15 07:28
♉ 17 13:10
♊ 19 21:03
♋ 22 07:03
♌ 24 19:02
♍ 27 08:05
♎ 29 20:17

Jul 1952
♏ 2 05:25
♐ 4 10:26
♑ 6 12:03
♒ 8 11:55
♓ 10 11:59
♈ 12 13:56
♉ 14 18:44
♊ 17 02:37
♋ 19 13:04
♌ 22 01:20
♍ 24 14:24
♎ 27 02:53
♏ 29 13:03
♐ 31 19:37

Aug 1952
♑ 2 22:27
♒ 4 22:41
♓ 6 22:04
♈ 8 22:33

☽ Moon

Aug 1952
♉ 11 01:45
♊ 13 08:35
♋ 15 18:51
♌ 18 07:18
♍ 20 20:22
♎ 23 08:41
♏ 25 19:09
♐ 28 02:52
♑ 30 07:23

Sep 1952
♒ 1 09:03
♓ 3 09:00
♈ 5 08:57
♉ 7 10:47
♊ 9 16:05
♋ 12 01:23
♌ 14 13:37
♍ 17 02:41
♎ 19 14:41
♏ 22 00:43
♐ 24 08:32
♑ 26 14:05
♒ 28 17:24
♓ 30 18:52

Oct 1952
♈ 2 19:34
♉ 4 21:05
♊ 7 01:14
♋ 9 09:15
♌ 11 20:49
♍ 14 09:50
♎ 16 21:44
♏ 19 07:09
♐ 21 14:12
♑ 23 19:28
♒ 25 23:27
♓ 28 02:22
♈ 30 04:34

Nov 1952
♉ 1 06:58
♊ 3 11:02
♋ 5 18:12
♌ 8 04:55
♍ 10 17:46
♎ 13 05:56
♏ 15 15:18
♐ 17 21:33
♑ 20 01:40
♒ 22 04:51
♓ 24 07:54
♈ 26 11:09
♉ 28 14:54
♊ 30 19:53

Dec 1952
♋ 3 03:08
♌ 5 13:22
♍ 8 01:57
♎ 10 14:34
♏ 13 00:38
♐ 15 06:59
♑ 17 10:17
♒ 19 12:02
♓ 21 13:45
♈ 23 16:29
♉ 25 20:45
♊ 28 02:47
♋ 30 10:53

Jan 1953
♌ 1 21:16
♍ 4 09:40
♎ 6 22:36
♏ 9 09:43

☽ Moon

Jan 1953
♐ 11 17:13
♑ 13 20:55
♒ 15 21:57
♓ 17 22:07
♈ 19 23:08
♉ 22 02:20
♊ 24 08:20
♋ 26 17:06
♌ 29 04:05
♍ 31 16:34

Feb 1953
♎ 3 05:31
♏ 5 17:20
♐ 8 02:19
♑ 10 07:31
♒ 12 09:17
♓ 14 08:58
♈ 16 08:31
♉ 18 09:50
♊ 20 14:26
♋ 22 22:47
♌ 25 10:04
♍ 27 22:50

Mar 1953
♎ 2 11:40
♏ 4 23:30
♐ 7 09:19
♑ 9 16:09
♒ 11 19:37
♓ 13 20:17
♈ 15 19:39
♉ 17 19:44
♊ 19 22:34
♋ 22 05:28
♌ 24 16:13
♍ 27 05:03
♎ 29 17:51

Apr 1953
♏ 1 05:19
♐ 3 14:58
♑ 5 22:28
♒ 8 03:27
♓ 10 05:49
♈ 12 06:19
♉ 14 06:31
♊ 16 08:26
♋ 18 13:52
♌ 20 23:26
♍ 23 11:51
♎ 26 00:40
♏ 28 11:51
♐ 30 20:52

May 1953
♑ 3 03:54
♒ 5 09:12
♓ 7 12:46
♈ 9 14:49
♉ 11 16:12
♊ 13 18:27
♋ 15 23:16
♌ 18 07:46
♍ 20 19:30
♎ 23 08:15
♏ 25 19:31
♐ 28 04:08
♑ 30 10:16

Jun 1953
♒ 1 14:45
♓ 3 18:11
♈ 5 21:01
♉ 7 23:41
♊ 10 03:02

☽ Moon

Jun 1953
♋ 12 08:17
♌ 14 16:26
♍ 17 03:36
♎ 19 16:15
♏ 22 03:57
♐ 24 12:47
♑ 26 18:28
♒ 28 21:51

Jul 1953
♓ 1 00:08
♈ 3 02:23
♉ 5 05:23
♊ 7 09:42
♋ 9 15:54
♌ 12 00:27
♍ 14 11:27
♎ 17 00:03
♏ 19 12:16
♐ 21 21:58
♑ 24 04:06
♒ 26 07:03
♓ 28 08:07
♈ 30 08:56

Aug 1953
♉ 1 10:56
♊ 3 15:10
♋ 5 21:59
♌ 8 07:15
♍ 10 18:32
♎ 13 07:07
♏ 15 19:43
♐ 18 06:29
♑ 20 13:52
♒ 22 17:28
♓ 24 18:12
♈ 26 17:46
♉ 28 18:10
♊ 30 21:06

Sep 1953
♋ 2 03:29
♌ 4 13:04
♍ 7 00:47
♎ 9 13:27
♏ 12 02:05
♐ 14 13:31
♑ 16 22:20
♒ 19 03:29
♓ 21 05:06
♈ 23 04:30
♉ 25 03:45
♊ 27 05:00
♋ 29 09:55

Oct 1953
♌ 1 18:52
♍ 4 06:39
♎ 6 19:27
♏ 9 07:55
♐ 11 19:19
♑ 14 04:51
♒ 16 11:33
♓ 18 14:55
♈ 20 15:27
♉ 22 14:47
♊ 24 15:04
♋ 26 18:23
♌ 29 01:54
♍ 31 13:03

Nov 1953
♎ 3 01:50
♏ 5 14:11
♐ 8 01:06
♑ 10 10:18

☽ Moon

Nov 1953
♒ 12 17:30
♓ 14 22:17
♈ 17 00:35
♉ 19 01:15
♊ 21 01:54
♋ 23 04:31
♌ 25 10:40
♍ 27 20:40
♎ 30 09:05

Dec 1953
♏ 2 21:30
♐ 5 08:08
♑ 7 16:32
♒ 9 22:59
♓ 12 03:46
♈ 14 07:06
♉ 16 09:22
♊ 18 11:27
♋ 20 14:40
♌ 22 20:22
♍ 25 05:23
♎ 27 17:10
♏ 30 05:42

Jan 1954
♐ 1 16:39
♑ 4 00:45
♒ 6 06:09
♓ 8 09:43
♈ 10 12:27
♉ 12 15:09
♊ 14 18:29
♋ 16 23:00
♌ 19 05:24
♍ 21 14:13
♎ 24 01:29
♏ 26 14:02
♐ 29 01:42
♑ 31 10:26

Feb 1954
♒ 2 15:38
♓ 4 18:03
♈ 6 19:14
♉ 8 20:47
♊ 10 23:54
♋ 13 05:09
♌ 15 12:35
♍ 17 22:00
♎ 20 09:13
♏ 22 21:43
♐ 25 09:59
♑ 27 19:57

Mar 1954
♒ 2 02:06
♓ 4 04:32
♈ 6 04:40
♉ 8 04:32
♊ 10 06:06
♋ 12 10:37
♌ 14 18:16
♍ 17 04:20
♎ 19 15:57
♏ 22 04:25
♐ 24 16:55
♑ 27 03:54
♒ 29 11:36
♓ 31 15:16

Apr 1954
♈ 2 15:40
♉ 4 14:43
♊ 6 14:40
♋ 8 17:28
♌ 11 00:05

☽ Moon

Apr 1954
♍ 13 10:02
♎ 15 21:57
♏ 18 10:31
♐ 20 22:54
♑ 23 10:10
♒ 25 19:01
♓ 28 00:21
♈ 30 02:08

May 1954
♉ 2 01:42
♊ 4 01:06
♋ 6 02:30
♌ 8 07:28
♍ 10 16:21
♎ 13 04:03
♏ 15 16:41
♐ 18 04:53
♑ 20 15:48
♒ 23 00:48
♓ 25 07:08
♈ 27 10:31
♉ 29 11:34
♊ 31 11:41

Jun 1954
♋ 2 12:46
♌ 4 16:34
♍ 7 00:06
♎ 9 10:58
♏ 11 23:29
♐ 14 11:36
♑ 16 22:04
♒ 19 06:25
♓ 21 12:36
♈ 23 16:43
♉ 25 19:09
♊ 27 20:41
♋ 29 22:35

Jul 1954
♌ 2 02:16
♍ 4 08:55
♎ 6 18:52
♏ 9 07:03
♐ 11 19:18
♑ 14 05:39
♒ 16 13:19
♓ 18 18:32
♈ 20 22:07
♉ 23 00:52
♊ 25 03:30
♋ 27 06:41
♌ 29 11:10
♍ 31 17:49

Aug 1954
♎ 3 03:13
♏ 5 15:02
♐ 8 03:32
♑ 10 14:19
♒ 12 21:54
♓ 15 02:16
♈ 17 04:37
♉ 19 06:26
♊ 21 08:56
♋ 23 12:49
♌ 25 18:22
♍ 28 01:43
♎ 30 11:11

Sep 1954
♏ 1 22:48
♐ 4 11:31
♑ 6 23:09
♒ 9 07:30
♓ 11 11:55

☽ Moon

Sep 1954
♈ 13 13:22
♉ 15 13:44
♊ 17 14:54
♋ 19 18:12
♌ 22 00:03
♍ 24 08:10
♎ 26 18:10
♏ 29 05:51

Oct 1954
♐ 1 18:40
♑ 4 07:03
♒ 6 16:44
♓ 8 22:16
♈ 10 23:58
♉ 12 23:31
♊ 14 23:09
♋ 17 00:49
♌ 19 05:40
♍ 21 13:44
♎ 24 00:12
♏ 26 12:10
♐ 29 00:58
♑ 31 13:35

Nov 1954
♒ 3 00:21
♓ 5 07:34
♈ 7 10:42
♉ 9 10:49
♊ 11 09:51
♋ 13 09:59
♌ 15 13:02
♍ 17 19:51
♎ 20 06:01
♏ 22 18:12
♐ 25 07:01
♑ 27 19:23
♒ 30 06:18

Dec 1954
♓ 2 14:37
♈ 4 19:34
♉ 6 21:22
♊ 8 21:16
♋ 10 21:06
♌ 12 22:48
♍ 15 03:53
♎ 17 12:50
♏ 20 00:43
♐ 22 13:34
♑ 25 01:40
♒ 27 12:00
♓ 29 20:09

Jan 1955
♈ 1 01:55
♉ 3 05:24
♊ 5 07:04
♋ 7 08:00
♌ 9 09:41
♍ 11 13:42
♎ 13 21:14
♏ 16 08:14
♐ 18 21:00
♑ 21 09:08
♒ 23 18:58
♓ 26 02:10
♈ 28 07:19
♉ 30 11:06

Feb 1955
♊ 1 14:02
♋ 3 16:36
♌ 5 19:28
♍ 7 23:42
♎ 10 06:33

☽ Moon

Feb 1955
♏ 12 16:37
♐ 15 05:06
♑ 17 17:33
♒ 20 03:32
♓ 22 10:09
♈ 24 14:06
♉ 26 16:46
♊ 28 19:24

Mar 1955
♋ 2 22:39
♌ 5 02:48
♍ 7 08:08
♎ 9 15:19
♏ 12 01:04
♐ 14 13:12
♑ 17 02:01
♒ 19 12:46
♓ 21 19:44
♈ 23 23:09
♉ 26 00:31
♊ 28 01:41
♋ 30 04:05

Apr 1955
♌ 1 08:20
♍ 3 14:30
♎ 5 22:33
♏ 8 08:37
♐ 10 20:41
♑ 13 09:39
♒ 15 21:19
♓ 18 05:28
♈ 20 09:29
♉ 22 10:30
♊ 24 10:24
♋ 26 11:09
♌ 28 14:08
♍ 30 19:57

May 1955
♎ 3 04:25
♏ 5 15:03
♐ 8 03:18
♑ 10 16:18
♒ 13 04:28
♓ 15 13:52
♈ 17 19:20
♉ 19 21:11
♊ 21 20:56
♋ 23 20:33
♌ 25 21:52
♍ 28 02:15
♎ 30 10:07

Jun 1955
♏ 1 20:53
♐ 4 09:23
♑ 6 22:20
♒ 9 10:29
♓ 11 20:31
♈ 14 03:23
♉ 16 06:50
♊ 18 07:37
♋ 20 07:15
♌ 22 07:36
♍ 24 10:25
♎ 26 16:54
♏ 29 03:04

Jul 1955
♐ 1 15:33
♑ 4 04:29
♒ 6 16:18
♓ 9 02:08
♈ 11 09:32
♉ 13 14:20

☽ Moon

Jul 1955
♊ 15 16:43
♋ 17 17:30
♌ 19 18:03
♍ 21 20:06
♎ 24 01:15
♏ 26 10:18
♐ 28 22:23
♑ 31 11:18

Aug 1955
♒ 2 22:51
♓ 5 08:04
♈ 7 14:59
♉ 9 20:02
♊ 11 23:33
♋ 14 01:50
♌ 16 03:34
♍ 18 05:57
♎ 20 10:33
♏ 22 18:36
♐ 25 06:02
♑ 27 18:56
♒ 30 06:34

Sep 1955
♓ 1 15:22
♈ 3 21:23
♉ 6 01:36
♊ 8 04:58
♋ 10 08:00
♌ 12 11:02
♍ 14 14:33
♎ 16 19:35
♏ 19 03:18
♐ 21 14:10
♑ 24 03:00
♒ 26 15:06
♓ 29 00:12

Oct 1955
♈ 1 05:46
♉ 3 08:52
♊ 5 10:59
♋ 7 13:22
♌ 9 16:41
♍ 11 21:11
♎ 14 03:13
♏ 16 11:23
♐ 18 22:07
♑ 21 10:50
♒ 23 23:32
♓ 26 09:36
♈ 28 15:46
♉ 30 18:30

Nov 1955
♊ 1 19:23
♋ 3 20:11
♌ 5 22:19
♍ 8 02:36
♎ 10 09:15
♏ 12 18:11
♐ 15 05:16
♑ 17 17:58
♒ 20 06:58
♓ 22 18:09
♈ 25 01:47
♉ 27 05:27
♊ 29 06:11

Dec 1955
♋ 1 05:46
♌ 3 06:07
♍ 5 08:49
♎ 7 14:47
♏ 9 23:59
♐ 12 11:33

☽ Moon

Dec 1955
♑ 15 00:23
♒ 17 13:18
♓ 20 01:01
♈ 22 10:04
♉ 24 15:32
♊ 26 17:33
♋ 28 17:18
♌ 30 16:36

Jan 1956
♍ 1 17:31
♎ 3 21:43
♏ 6 05:59
♐ 8 17:32
♑ 11 06:33
♒ 13 19:19
♓ 16 06:47
♈ 18 16:16
♉ 20 23:10
♊ 23 03:05
♋ 25 04:20
♌ 27 04:06
♍ 29 04:17
♎ 31 06:55

Feb 1956
♏ 2 13:32
♐ 5 00:12
♑ 7 13:07
♒ 10 01:51
♓ 12 12:51
♈ 14 21:48
♉ 17 04:48
♊ 19 09:50
♋ 21 12:49
♌ 23 14:11
♍ 25 15:05
♎ 27 17:20
♏ 29 22:44

Mar 1956
♐ 3 08:08
♑ 5 20:31
♒ 8 09:18
♓ 10 20:11
♈ 13 04:26
♉ 15 10:32
♊ 17 15:11
♋ 19 18:47
♌ 21 21:30
♍ 23 23:52
♎ 26 02:59
♏ 28 08:18
♐ 30 16:55

Apr 1956
♑ 2 04:37
♒ 4 17:23
♓ 7 04:36
♈ 9 12:46
♉ 11 18:03
♊ 13 21:30
♋ 16 00:14
♌ 18 03:00
♍ 20 06:16
♎ 22 10:36
♏ 24 16:44
♐ 27 01:25
♑ 29 12:43

May 1956
♒ 2 01:27
♓ 4 13:14
♈ 6 22:05
♉ 9 03:24
♊ 11 06:00
♋ 13 07:21

☽ Moon

May 1956
♌ 15 08:52
♍ 17 11:39
♎ 19 16:25
♏ 21 23:26
♐ 24 08:46
♑ 26 20:10
♒ 29 08:51
♓ 31 21:09

Jun 1956
♈ 3 07:04
♉ 5 13:21
♊ 7 16:09
♋ 9 16:42
♌ 11 16:45
♍ 13 18:03
♎ 15 21:58
♏ 18 05:02
♐ 20 14:54
♑ 23 02:42
♒ 25 15:25
♓ 28 03:54
♈ 30 14:42

Jul 1956
♉ 2 22:25
♊ 5 02:25
♋ 7 03:20
♌ 9 02:42
♍ 11 02:34
♎ 13 04:54
♏ 15 10:55
♐ 17 20:37
♑ 20 08:40
♒ 22 21:28
♓ 25 09:49
♈ 27 20:53
♉ 30 05:39

Aug 1956
♊ 1 11:15
♋ 3 13:32
♌ 5 13:27
♍ 7 12:50
♎ 9 13:50
♏ 11 18:19
♐ 14 02:59
♑ 16 14:46
♒ 19 03:37
♓ 21 15:46
♈ 24 02:29
♉ 26 11:23
♊ 28 17:58
♋ 30 21:51

Sep 1956
♌ 1 23:14
♍ 3 23:20
♎ 6 00:04
♏ 8 03:26
♐ 10 10:45
♑ 12 21:45
♒ 15 10:27
♓ 17 22:33
♈ 20 08:47
♉ 22 17:00
♊ 24 23:24
♋ 27 03:59
♌ 29 06:48

Oct 1956
♍ 1 08:24
♎ 3 10:01
♏ 5 13:19
♐ 7 19:45
♑ 10 05:47
♒ 12 18:08

☽ Moon

Oct 1956
♓ 15 06:24
♈ 17 16:35
♉ 20 00:07
♊ 22 05:28
♋ 24 09:23
♌ 26 12:27
♍ 28 15:09
♎ 30 18:10

Nov 1956
♏ 1 22:24
♐ 4 04:56
♑ 6 14:23
♒ 9 02:19
♓ 11 14:50
♈ 14 01:36
♉ 16 09:12
♊ 18 13:45
♋ 20 16:18
♌ 22 18:10
♍ 24 20:31
♎ 27 00:10
♏ 29 05:34

Dec 1956
♐ 1 12:58
♑ 3 22:35
♒ 6 10:15
♓ 8 22:56
♈ 11 10:36
♉ 13 19:15
♊ 16 00:06
♋ 18 01:52
♌ 20 02:11
♍ 22 02:55
♎ 24 05:38
♏ 26 11:08
♐ 28 19:19
♑ 31 05:36

Jan 1957
♒ 2 17:24
♓ 5 06:04
♈ 7 18:22
♉ 10 04:26
♊ 12 10:43
♋ 14 13:06
♌ 16 12:51
♍ 18 12:04
♎ 20 12:55
♏ 22 17:02
♐ 25 00:51
♑ 27 11:31
♒ 29 23:41

Feb 1957
♓ 1 12:20
♈ 4 00:41
♉ 6 11:36
♊ 8 19:34
♋ 10 23:38
♌ 13 00:18
♍ 14 23:16
♎ 16 22:49
♏ 19 01:05
♐ 21 07:22
♑ 23 17:26
♒ 26 05:42
♓ 28 18:24

Mar 1957
♈ 3 06:30
♉ 5 17:20
♊ 8 02:03
♋ 10 07:44
♌ 12 10:12
♍ 14 10:20

☽ Moon

Mar 1957
♎ 16 09:59
♏ 18 11:14
♐ 20 15:53
♑ 23 00:33
♒ 25 12:16
♓ 28 00:59
♈ 30 12:54

Apr 1957
♉ 1 23:10
♊ 4 07:29
♋ 6 13:37
♌ 8 17:24
♍ 10 19:13
♎ 12 20:08
♏ 14 21:45
♐ 17 01:42
♑ 19 09:07
♒ 21 19:53
♓ 24 08:22
♈ 26 20:21
♉ 29 06:17

May 1957
♊ 1 13:46
♋ 3 19:08
♌ 5 22:53
♍ 8 01:36
♎ 10 03:57
♏ 12 06:48
♐ 14 11:13
♑ 16 18:13
♒ 19 04:11
♓ 21 16:19
♈ 24 04:33
♉ 26 14:42
♊ 28 21:46
♋ 31 02:05

Jun 1957
♌ 2 04:45
♍ 4 06:59
♎ 6 09:45
♏ 8 13:40
♐ 10 19:09
♑ 13 02:36
♒ 15 12:22
♓ 18 00:14
♈ 20 12:44
♉ 22 23:38
♊ 25 07:06
♋ 27 11:01
♌ 29 12:31

Jul 1957
♍ 1 13:24
♎ 3 15:16
♏ 5 19:09
♐ 8 01:20
♑ 10 09:34
♒ 12 19:42
♓ 15 07:31
♈ 17 20:13
♉ 20 07:57
♊ 22 16:33
♋ 24 21:05
♌ 26 22:16
♍ 28 21:59
♎ 30 22:20

Aug 1957
♏ 2 01:00
♐ 4 06:46
♑ 6 15:22
♒ 9 02:01
♓ 11 14:01
♈ 14 02:45

☽ Moon

Aug 1957
♉ 16 14:59
♊ 19 00:51
♋ 21 06:48
♌ 23 08:51
♍ 25 08:26
♎ 27 07:41
♏ 29 08:45
♐ 31 13:06

Sep 1957
♑ 2 21:05
♒ 5 07:49
♓ 7 20:03
♈ 10 08:44
♉ 12 20:56
♊ 15 07:25
♋ 17 14:49
♌ 19 18:30
♍ 21 19:11
♎ 23 18:33
♏ 25 18:40
♐ 27 21:27
♑ 30 03:58

Oct 1957
♒ 2 14:03
♓ 5 02:17
♈ 7 14:56
♉ 10 02:47
♊ 12 13:00
♋ 14 20:54
♌ 17 01:59
♍ 19 04:23
♎ 21 05:03
♏ 23 05:31
♐ 25 07:33
♑ 27 12:40
♒ 29 21:31

Nov 1957
♓ 1 09:17
♈ 3 21:59
♉ 6 09:37
♊ 8 19:08
♋ 11 02:23
♌ 13 07:36
♍ 15 11:07
♎ 17 13:25
♏ 19 15:17
♐ 21 17:51
♑ 23 22:29
♒ 26 06:15
♓ 28 17:15

Dec 1957
♈ 1 05:55
♉ 3 17:47
♊ 6 03:00
♋ 8 09:16
♌ 10 13:23
♍ 12 16:28
♎ 14 19:22
♏ 16 22:35
♐ 19 02:30
♑ 21 07:46
♒ 23 15:18
♓ 26 01:40
♈ 28 14:11
♉ 31 02:36

Jan 1958
♊ 2 12:20
♋ 4 18:21
♌ 6 21:21
♍ 8 22:58
♎ 11 00:51
♏ 13 04:02

☽ Moon

Jan 1958
♐ 15 08:49
♑ 17 15:12
♒ 19 23:22
♓ 22 09:41
♈ 24 22:02
♉ 27 10:55
♊ 29 21:46

Feb 1958
♋ 1 04:40
♌ 3 07:38
♍ 5 08:11
♎ 7 08:23
♏ 9 10:03
♐ 11 14:11
♑ 13 20:54
♒ 16 05:51
♓ 18 16:39
♈ 21 05:01
♉ 23 18:04
♊ 26 05:51
♋ 28 14:16

Mar 1958
♌ 2 18:26
♍ 4 19:15
♎ 6 18:36
♏ 8 18:34
♐ 10 20:56
♑ 13 02:36
♒ 15 11:27
♓ 17 22:41
♈ 20 11:16
♉ 23 00:15
♊ 25 12:19
♋ 27 21:52
♌ 30 03:45

Apr 1958
♍ 1 06:01
♎ 3 05:54
♏ 5 05:16
♐ 7 06:06
♑ 9 10:00
♒ 11 17:40
♓ 14 04:38
♈ 16 17:22
♉ 19 06:16
♊ 21 18:02
♋ 24 03:46
♌ 26 10:43
♍ 28 14:40
♎ 30 16:06

May 1958
♏ 2 16:14
♐ 4 16:43
♑ 6 19:20
♒ 9 01:29
♓ 11 11:26
♈ 13 23:57
♉ 16 12:49
♊ 19 00:13
♋ 21 09:22
♌ 23 16:14
♍ 25 20:59
♎ 27 23:55
♏ 30 01:33

Jun 1958
♐ 1 02:53
♑ 3 05:22
♒ 5 10:33
♓ 7 19:23
♈ 10 07:19
♉ 12 20:11
♊ 15 07:30

☽ Moon

Jun 1958
♋ 17 16:03
♌ 19 22:03
♍ 22 02:22
♎ 24 05:42
♏ 26 08:30
♐ 28 11:11
♑ 30 14:32

Jul 1958
♒ 2 19:44
♓ 5 03:56
♈ 7 15:17
♉ 10 04:08
♊ 12 15:46
♋ 15 00:15
♌ 17 05:31
♍ 19 08:42
♎ 21 11:11
♏ 23 13:57
♐ 25 17:25
♑ 27 21:52
♒ 30 03:52

Aug 1958
♓ 1 12:11
♈ 3 23:14
♉ 6 12:03
♊ 9 00:16
♋ 11 09:24
♌ 13 14:43
♍ 15 17:07
♎ 17 18:17
♏ 19 19:49
♐ 21 22:47
♑ 24 03:38
♒ 26 10:27
♓ 28 19:24
♈ 31 06:34

Sep 1958
♉ 2 19:23
♊ 5 08:06
♋ 7 18:21
♌ 10 00:41
♍ 12 03:19
♎ 14 03:44
♏ 16 03:49
♐ 18 05:16
♑ 20 09:12
♒ 22 16:02
♓ 25 01:33
♈ 27 13:07
♉ 30 01:57

Oct 1958
♊ 2 14:49
♋ 5 01:59
♌ 7 09:50
♍ 9 13:49
♎ 11 14:44
♏ 13 14:12
♐ 15 14:09
♑ 17 16:22
♒ 19 22:03
♓ 22 07:19
♈ 24 19:10
♉ 27 08:07
♊ 29 20:49

Nov 1958
♋ 1 08:08
♌ 3 17:02
♍ 5 22:45
♎ 8 01:16
♏ 10 01:29
♐ 12 01:03
♑ 14 01:54

☽ Moon

Nov 1958
♒ 16 05:52
♓ 18 13:55
♈ 21 01:28
♉ 23 14:29
♊ 26 03:00
♋ 28 13:50
♌ 30 22:40

Dec 1958
♍ 3 05:17
♎ 5 09:30
♏ 7 11:28
♐ 9 12:02
♑ 11 12:46
♒ 13 15:37
♓ 15 22:11
♈ 18 08:44
♉ 20 21:37
♊ 23 10:08
♋ 25 20:32
♌ 28 04:33
♍ 30 10:40

Jan 1959
♎ 1 15:20
♏ 3 18:41
♐ 5 20:55
♑ 7 22:49
♒ 10 01:51
♓ 12 07:39
♈ 14 17:09
♉ 17 05:32
♊ 19 18:15
♋ 22 04:46
♌ 24 12:13
♍ 26 17:13
♎ 28 20:54
♏ 31 00:05

Feb 1959
♐ 2 03:10
♑ 4 06:28
♒ 6 10:40
♓ 8 16:50
♈ 11 01:54
♉ 13 13:46
♊ 16 02:39
♋ 18 13:50
♌ 20 21:37
♍ 23 02:05
♎ 25 04:28
♏ 27 06:14

Mar 1959
♐ 1 08:32
♑ 3 12:05
♒ 5 17:16
♓ 8 00:25
♈ 10 09:53
♉ 12 21:36
♊ 15 10:29
♋ 17 22:27
♌ 20 07:22
♍ 22 12:27
♎ 24 14:27
♏ 26 14:54
♐ 28 15:31
♑ 30 17:48

Apr 1959
♒ 1 22:41
♓ 4 06:22
♈ 6 16:32
♉ 9 04:31
♊ 11 17:24
♋ 14 05:47
♌ 16 15:54

☽ Moon

Apr 1959
♍ 18 22:27
♎ 21 01:18
♏ 23 01:33
♐ 25 00:58
♑ 27 01:32
♒ 29 04:55

May 1959
♓ 1 11:57
♈ 3 22:18
♉ 6 10:38
♊ 8 23:34
♋ 11 11:56
♌ 13 22:40
♍ 16 06:37
♎ 18 11:06
♏ 20 12:24
♐ 22 11:51
♑ 24 11:24
♒ 26 13:09
♓ 28 18:41
♈ 31 04:17

Jun 1959
♉ 2 16:36
♊ 5 05:35
♋ 7 17:43
♌ 10 04:18
♍ 12 12:49
♎ 14 18:41
♏ 16 21:38
♐ 18 22:14
♑ 20 22:01
♒ 22 23:00
♓ 25 03:08
♈ 27 11:26
♉ 29 23:10

Jul 1959
♊ 2 12:04
♋ 5 00:03
♌ 7 10:07
♍ 9 18:15
♎ 12 00:26
♏ 14 04:33
♐ 16 06:42
♑ 18 07:42
♒ 20 09:05
♓ 22 12:40
♈ 24 19:53
♉ 27 06:42
♊ 29 19:23

Aug 1959
♋ 1 07:23
♌ 3 17:08
♍ 6 00:29
♎ 8 05:56
♏ 10 09:59
♐ 12 12:58
♑ 14 15:18
♒ 16 17:53
♓ 18 21:59
♈ 21 04:51
♉ 23 14:57
♊ 26 03:18
♋ 28 15:32
♌ 31 01:33

Sep 1959
♍ 2 08:30
♎ 4 12:56
♏ 6 15:53
♐ 8 18:20
♑ 10 21:04
♒ 13 00:43
♓ 15 05:53

☽ Moon

Sep 1959
♈ 17 13:15
♉ 19 23:12
♊ 22 11:15
♋ 24 23:49
♌ 27 10:35
♍ 29 18:03

Oct 1959
♎ 1 22:08
♏ 3 23:53
♐ 6 00:54
♑ 8 02:38
♒ 10 06:12
♓ 12 12:05
♈ 14 20:19
♉ 17 06:39
♊ 19 18:39
♋ 22 07:21
♌ 24 19:02
♍ 27 03:48
♎ 29 08:41
♏ 31 10:14

Nov 1959
♐ 2 10:02
♑ 4 10:05
♒ 6 12:13
♓ 8 17:35
♈ 11 02:09
♉ 13 13:03
♊ 16 01:16
♋ 18 13:56
♌ 21 02:03
♍ 23 12:07
♎ 25 18:40
♏ 27 21:21
♐ 29 21:12

Dec 1959
♑ 1 20:11
♒ 3 20:35
♓ 6 00:16
♈ 8 07:59
♉ 10 18:55
♊ 13 07:23
♋ 15 20:00
♌ 18 07:57
♍ 20 18:29
♎ 23 02:28
♏ 25 07:00
♐ 27 08:16
♑ 29 07:38
♒ 31 07:15

Jan 1960
♓ 2 09:18
♈ 4 15:20
♉ 7 01:22
♊ 9 13:44
♋ 12 02:23
♌ 14 13:58
♍ 17 00:03
♎ 19 08:13
♏ 21 13:58
♐ 23 17:02
♑ 25 18:00
♒ 27 18:19
♓ 29 19:56

Feb 1960
♈ 1 00:38
♉ 3 09:15
♊ 5 20:58
♋ 8 09:36
♌ 10 21:07
♍ 13 06:34
♎ 15 13:55

☽ Moon

Feb 1960
♏ 17 19:2[illegible]
♐ 19 23:1[illegible]
♑ 22 01:3[illegible]
♒ 24 03:3[illegible]
♓ 26 06:0[illegible]
♈ 28 10:3[illegible]

Mar 1960
♉ 1 18:18
♊ 4 05:07
♋ 6 17:36
♌ 9 05:24
♍ 11 14:47
♎ 13 21:19
♏ 16 01:37
♐ 18 04:37
♑ 20 07:14
♒ 22 10:10
♓ 24 14:02
♈ 26 19:29
♉ 29 03:13
♊ 31 13:31

Apr 1960
♋ 3 01:45
♌ 5 14:00
♍ 8 00:01
♎ 10 06:35
♏ 12 10:01
♐ 14 11:38
♑ 16 13:01
♒ 18 15:31
♓ 20 19:55
♈ 23 02:22
♉ 25 10:50
♊ 27 21:16
♋ 30 09:22

May 1960
♌ 2 21:58
♍ 5 08:58
♎ 7 16:29
♏ 9 20:06
♐ 11 20:55
♑ 13 20:50
♒ 15 21:51
♓ 18 01:23
♈ 20 07:54
♉ 22 16:59
♊ 25 03:54
♋ 27 16:06
♌ 30 04:50

Jun 1960
♍ 1 16:37
♎ 4 01:31
♏ 6 06:19
♐ 8 07:31
♑ 10 06:48
♒ 12 06:23
♓ 14 08:17
♈ 16 13:41
♉ 18 22:33
♊ 21 09:45
♋ 23 22:09
♌ 26 10:51
♍ 28 22:52

Jul 1960
♎ 1 08:45
♏ 3 15:08
♐ 5 17:42
♑ 7 17:35
♒ 9 16:43
♓ 11 17:19
♈ 13 21:06
♉ 16 04:47

☽ Moon

Jul 1960
- ♊ 18 15:39
- ♋ 21 04:08
- ♌ 23 16:45
- ♍ 26 04:31
- ♎ 28 14:32
- ♏ 30 21:54

Aug 1960
- ♐ 2 02:04
- ♑ 4 03:25
- ♒ 6 03:21
- ♓ 8 03:42
- ♈ 10 06:21
- ♉ 12 12:35
- ♊ 14 22:29
- ♋ 17 10:42
- ♌ 19 23:17
- ♍ 22 10:41
- ♎ 24 20:09
- ♏ 27 03:23
- ♐ 29 08:19
- ♑ 31 11:08

Sep 1960
- ♒ 2 12:35
- ♓ 4 13:51
- ♈ 6 16:26
- ♉ 8 21:44
- ♊ 11 06:30
- ♋ 13 18:09
- ♌ 16 06:46
- ♍ 18 18:06
- ♎ 21 02:58
- ♏ 23 09:17
- ♐ 25 13:41
- ♑ 27 16:54
- ♒ 29 19:32

Oct 1960
- ♓ 1 22:14
- ♈ 4 01:46
- ♉ 6 07:08
- ♊ 8 15:16
- ♋ 11 02:17
- ♌ 13 14:54
- ♍ 16 02:39
- ♎ 18 11:32
- ♏ 20 17:06
- ♐ 22 20:16
- ♑ 24 22:28
- ♒ 27 00:57
- ♓ 29 04:26
- ♈ 31 09:11

Nov 1960
- ♉ 2 15:27
- ♊ 4 23:44
- ♋ 7 10:25
- ♌ 9 22:59
- ♍ 12 11:23
- ♎ 14 21:07
- ♏ 17 02:53
- ♐ 19 05:17
- ♑ 21 06:02
- ♒ 23 07:04
- ♓ 25 09:49
- ♈ 27 14:50
- ♉ 29 21:59

Dec 1960
- ♊ 2 07:00
- ♋ 4 17:51
- ♌ 7 06:20
- ♍ 9 19:12
- ♎ 12 06:09
- ♏ 14 13:12
- ♐ 16 16:07

☽ Moon

Dec 1960
- ♑ 18 16:17
- ♒ 20 15:49
- ♓ 22 16:47
- ♈ 24 20:34
- ♉ 27 03:29
- ♊ 29 13:01

Jan 1961
- ♋ 1 00:21
- ♌ 3 12:53
- ♍ 6 01:47
- ♎ 8 13:30
- ♏ 10 22:08
- ♐ 13 02:40
- ♑ 15 03:41
- ♒ 17 02:55
- ♓ 19 02:31
- ♈ 21 04:26
- ♉ 23 09:50
- ♊ 25 18:49
- ♋ 28 06:21
- ♌ 30 19:04

Feb 1961
- ♍ 2 07:47
- ♎ 4 19:26
- ♏ 7 04:50
- ♐ 9 11:00
- ♑ 11 13:50
- ♒ 13 14:15
- ♓ 15 13:53
- ♈ 17 14:41
- ♉ 19 18:21
- ♊ 22 01:51
- ♋ 24 12:48
- ♌ 27 01:34

Mar 1961
- ♍ 1 14:11
- ♎ 4 01:20
- ♏ 6 10:23
- ♐ 8 17:03
- ♑ 10 21:18
- ♒ 12 23:28
- ♓ 15 00:26
- ♈ 17 01:32
- ♉ 19 04:25
- ♊ 21 10:31
- ♋ 23 20:21
- ♌ 26 08:47
- ♍ 28 21:29
- ♎ 31 08:20

Apr 1961
- ♏ 2 16:36
- ♐ 4 22:33
- ♑ 7 02:51
- ♒ 9 06:02
- ♓ 11 08:31
- ♈ 13 10:55
- ♉ 15 14:16
- ♊ 17 19:54
- ♋ 20 04:49
- ♌ 22 16:42
- ♍ 25 05:30
- ♎ 27 16:33
- ♏ 30 00:26

May 1961
- ♐ 2 05:24
- ♑ 4 08:39
- ♒ 6 11:24
- ♓ 8 14:22
- ♈ 10 17:55
- ♉ 12 22:25
- ♊ 15 04:34
- ♋ 17 13:16

☽ Moon

May 1961
- ♌ 20 00:44
- ♍ 22 13:37
- ♎ 25 01:17
- ♏ 27 09:34
- ♐ 29 14:11
- ♑ 31 16:20

Jun 1961
- ♒ 2 17:45
- ♓ 4 19:50
- ♈ 6 23:23
- ♉ 9 04:37
- ♊ 11 11:40
- ♋ 13 20:49
- ♌ 16 08:15
- ♍ 18 21:11
- ♎ 21 09:31
- ♏ 23 18:50
- ♐ 26 00:05
- ♑ 28 01:59
- ♒ 30 02:17

Jul 1961
- ♓ 2 02:52
- ♈ 4 05:11
- ♉ 6 10:01
- ♊ 8 17:26
- ♋ 11 03:12
- ♌ 13 14:56
- ♍ 16 03:54
- ♎ 18 16:38
- ♏ 21 03:04
- ♐ 23 09:41
- ♑ 25 12:29
- ♒ 27 12:42
- ♓ 29 12:13
- ♈ 31 12:55

Aug 1961
- ♉ 2 16:18
- ♊ 4 23:03
- ♋ 7 08:56
- ♌ 9 20:58
- ♍ 12 09:59
- ♎ 14 22:43
- ♏ 17 09:43
- ♐ 19 17:43
- ♑ 21 22:07
- ♒ 23 23:25
- ♓ 25 23:02
- ♈ 27 22:48
- ♉ 30 00:36

Sep 1961
- ♊ 1 05:52
- ♋ 3 14:59
- ♌ 6 03:00
- ♍ 8 16:04
- ♎ 11 04:33
- ♏ 13 15:22
- ♐ 15 23:54
- ♑ 18 05:41
- ♒ 20 08:43
- ♓ 22 09:36
- ♈ 24 09:40
- ♉ 26 10:42
- ♊ 28 14:31
- ♋ 30 22:18

Oct 1961
- ♌ 3 09:42
- ♍ 5 22:45
- ♎ 8 11:03
- ♏ 10 21:18
- ♐ 13 05:20
- ♑ 15 11:23
- ♒ 17 15:36

☽ Moon

Oct 1961
- ♓ 19 18:09
- ♈ 21 19:35
- ♉ 23 21:07
- ♊ 26 00:24
- ♋ 28 07:02
- ♌ 30 17:28

Nov 1961
- ♍ 2 06:16
- ♎ 4 18:41
- ♏ 7 04:40
- ♐ 9 11:50
- ♑ 11 16:59
- ♒ 13 20:59
- ♓ 16 00:18
- ♈ 18 03:10
- ♉ 20 06:03
- ♊ 22 09:59
- ♋ 24 16:20
- ♌ 27 02:01
- ♍ 29 14:24

Dec 1961
- ♎ 2 03:07
- ♏ 4 13:29
- ♐ 6 20:24
- ♑ 9 00:30
- ♒ 11 03:11
- ♓ 13 05:41
- ♈ 15 08:44
- ♉ 17 12:38
- ♊ 19 17:47
- ♋ 22 00:49
- ♌ 24 10:25
- ♍ 26 22:29
- ♎ 29 11:25
- ♏ 31 22:41

Jan 1962
- ♐ 3 06:23
- ♑ 5 10:24
- ♒ 7 12:00
- ♓ 9 12:53
- ♈ 11 14:34
- ♉ 13 18:01
- ♊ 15 23:41
- ♋ 18 07:39
- ♌ 20 17:49
- ♍ 23 05:53
- ♎ 25 18:51
- ♏ 28 06:53
- ♐ 30 15:58

Feb 1962
- ♑ 1 21:09
- ♒ 3 22:56
- ♓ 5 22:52
- ♈ 7 22:50
- ♉ 10 00:34
- ♊ 12 05:17
- ♋ 14 13:19
- ♌ 17 00:03
- ♍ 19 12:26
- ♎ 22 01:21
- ♏ 24 13:35
- ♐ 26 23:46

Mar 1962
- ♑ 1 06:37
- ♒ 3 09:51
- ♓ 5 10:17
- ♈ 7 09:32
- ♉ 9 09:40
- ♊ 11 12:34
- ♋ 13 19:25
- ♌ 16 05:55
- ♍ 18 18:32

☽ Moon

Mar 1962
- ♎ 21 07:28
- ♏ 23 19:28
- ♐ 26 05:48
- ♑ 28 13:45
- ♒ 30 18:42

Apr 1962
- ♓ 1 20:42
- ♈ 3 20:41
- ♉ 5 20:25
- ♊ 7 21:59
- ♋ 10 03:11
- ♌ 12 12:35
- ♍ 15 00:56
- ♎ 17 13:53
- ♏ 20 01:36
- ♐ 22 11:26
- ♑ 24 19:19
- ♒ 27 01:07
- ♓ 29 04:39

May 1962
- ♈ 1 06:12
- ♉ 3 06:49
- ♊ 5 08:16
- ♋ 7 12:27
- ♌ 9 20:35
- ♍ 12 08:10
- ♎ 14 21:02
- ♏ 17 08:42
- ♐ 19 18:02
- ♑ 22 01:07
- ♒ 24 06:30
- ♓ 26 10:29
- ♈ 28 13:15
- ♉ 30 15:17

Jun 1962
- ♊ 1 17:40
- ♋ 3 21:56
- ♌ 6 05:22
- ♍ 8 16:11
- ♎ 11 04:50
- ♏ 13 16:44
- ♐ 16 02:03
- ♑ 18 08:29
- ♒ 20 12:49
- ♓ 22 15:58
- ♈ 24 18:43
- ♉ 26 21:34
- ♊ 29 01:09

Jul 1962
- ♋ 1 06:18
- ♌ 3 13:55
- ♍ 6 00:21
- ♎ 8 12:47
- ♏ 11 01:05
- ♐ 13 10:59
- ♑ 15 17:32
- ♒ 17 21:07
- ♓ 19 23:00
- ♈ 22 00:33
- ♉ 24 02:56
- ♊ 26 06:56
- ♋ 28 13:00
- ♌ 30 21:20

Aug 1962
- ♍ 2 07:57
- ♎ 4 20:17
- ♏ 7 08:55
- ♐ 9 19:47
- ♑ 12 03:17
- ♒ 14 07:07
- ♓ 16 08:17
- ♈ 18 08:25

☽ Moon

Aug 1962
- ♉ 20 09:20
- ♊ 22 12:27
- ♋ 24 18:33
- ♌ 27 03:29
- ♍ 29 14:35

Sep 1962
- ♎ 1 03:00
- ♏ 3 15:45
- ♐ 6 03:25
- ♑ 8 12:19
- ♒ 10 17:26
- ♓ 12 19:02
- ♈ 14 18:33
- ♉ 16 18:01
- ♊ 18 19:28
- ♋ 21 00:25
- ♌ 23 09:06
- ♍ 25 20:30
- ♎ 28 09:07
- ♏ 30 21:48

Oct 1962
- ♐ 3 09:39
- ♑ 5 19:34
- ♒ 8 02:21
- ♓ 10 05:28
- ♈ 12 05:41
- ♉ 14 04:43
- ♊ 16 04:50
- ♋ 18 08:04
- ♌ 20 15:29
- ♍ 23 02:30
- ♎ 25 15:13
- ♏ 28 03:48
- ♐ 30 15:19

Nov 1962
- ♑ 2 01:17
- ♒ 4 09:01
- ♓ 6 13:52
- ♈ 8 15:45
- ♉ 10 15:45
- ♊ 12 15:44
- ♋ 14 17:48
- ♌ 16 23:39
- ♍ 19 09:32
- ♎ 21 21:57
- ♏ 24 10:32
- ♐ 26 21:43
- ♑ 29 07:00

Dec 1962
- ♒ 1 14:25
- ♓ 3 19:53
- ♈ 5 23:17
- ♉ 8 00:59
- ♊ 10 02:07
- ♋ 12 04:21
- ♌ 14 09:20
- ♍ 16 17:58
- ♎ 19 05:40
- ♏ 21 18:17
- ♐ 24 05:32
- ♑ 26 14:18
- ♒ 28 20:42
- ♓ 31 01:20

Jan 1963
- ♈ 2 04:47
- ♉ 4 07:33
- ♊ 6 10:14
- ♋ 8 13:41
- ♌ 10 19:00
- ♍ 13 03:06
- ♎ 15 14:04
- ♏ 18 02:35

☽ Moon

Jan 1963
- ♐ 20 14:20
- ♑ 22 23:23
- ♒ 25 05:13
- ♓ 27 08:35
- ♈ 29 10:44
- ♉ 31 12:54

Feb 1963
- ♊ 2 16:03
- ♋ 4 20:40
- ♌ 7 03:05
- ♍ 9 11:35
- ♎ 11 22:17
- ♏ 14 10:37
- ♐ 16 22:56
- ♑ 19 08:59
- ♒ 21 15:23
- ♓ 23 18:17
- ♈ 25 19:05
- ♉ 27 19:38

Mar 1963
- ♊ 1 21:38
- ♋ 4 02:07
- ♌ 6 09:14
- ♍ 8 18:33
- ♎ 11 05:34
- ♏ 13 17:51
- ♐ 16 06:26
- ♑ 18 17:33
- ♒ 21 01:21
- ♓ 23 05:04
- ♈ 25 05:38
- ♉ 27 04:57
- ♊ 29 05:13
- ♋ 31 08:13

Apr 1963
- ♌ 2 14:45
- ♍ 5 00:20
- ♎ 7 11:49
- ♏ 10 00:13
- ♐ 12 12:47
- ♑ 15 00:26
- ♒ 17 09:33
- ♓ 19 14:53
- ♈ 21 16:30
- ♉ 23 15:51
- ♊ 25 15:06
- ♋ 27 16:27
- ♌ 29 21:24

May 1963
- ♍ 2 06:12
- ♎ 4 17:41
- ♏ 7 06:15
- ♐ 9 18:42
- ♑ 12 06:13
- ♒ 14 15:50
- ♓ 16 22:31
- ♈ 19 01:47
- ♉ 21 02:21
- ♊ 23 01:53
- ♋ 25 02:28
- ♌ 27 05:58
- ♍ 29 13:21

Jun 1963
- ♎ 1 00:08
- ♏ 3 12:38
- ♐ 6 01:00
- ♑ 8 12:06
- ♒ 10 21:21
- ♓ 13 04:20
- ♈ 15 08:46
- ♉ 17 10:54
- ♊ 19 11:44

☽ Moon

Jun 1963
- ♋ 21 12:46
- ♌ 23 15:44
- ♍ 25 21:56
- ♎ 28 07:40
- ♏ 30 19:47

Jul 1963
- ♐ 3 08:10
- ♑ 5 19:02
- ♒ 8 03:36
- ♓ 10 09:52
- ♈ 12 14:16
- ♉ 14 17:15
- ♊ 16 19:27
- ♋ 18 21:44
- ♌ 21 01:14
- ♍ 23 07:06
- ♎ 25 16:01
- ♏ 28 03:38
- ♐ 30 16:07

Aug 1963
- ♑ 2 03:12
- ♒ 4 11:25
- ♓ 6 16:45
- ♈ 8 20:06
- ♉ 10 22:37
- ♊ 13 01:15
- ♋ 15 04:39
- ♌ 17 09:16
- ♍ 19 15:40
- ♎ 22 00:25
- ♏ 24 11:38
- ♐ 27 00:14
- ♑ 29 11:56
- ♒ 31 20:37

Sep 1963
- ♓ 3 01:37
- ♈ 5 03:52
- ♉ 7 05:02
- ♊ 9 06:45
- ♋ 11 10:07
- ♌ 13 15:29
- ♍ 15 22:47
- ♎ 18 07:59
- ♏ 20 19:10
- ♐ 23 07:49
- ♑ 25 20:14
- ♒ 28 06:02
- ♓ 30 11:46

Oct 1963
- ♈ 2 13:48
- ♉ 4 13:50
- ♊ 6 13:58
- ♋ 8 16:00
- ♌ 10 20:53
- ♍ 13 04:33
- ♎ 15 14:23
- ♏ 18 01:52
- ♐ 20 14:32
- ♑ 23 03:20
- ♒ 25 14:19
- ♓ 27 21:35
- ♈ 30 00:39

Nov 1963
- ♉ 1 00:42
- ♊ 2 23:48
- ♋ 5 00:08
- ♌ 7 03:23
- ♍ 9 10:13
- ♎ 11 20:07
- ♏ 14 07:56
- ♐ 16 20:39
- ♑ 19 09:22

☽ Moon

Nov 1963
- ♒ 21 20:51
- ♓ 24 05:31
- ♈ 26 10:25
- ♉ 28 11:49
- ♊ 30 11:15

Dec 1963
- ♋ 2 10:45
- ♌ 4 12:19
- ♍ 6 17:25
- ♎ 9 02:21
- ♏ 11 14:03
- ♐ 14 02:53
- ♑ 16 15:20
- ♒ 19 02:28
- ♓ 21 11:28
- ♈ 23 17:40
- ♉ 25 20:57
- ♊ 27 21:58
- ♋ 29 22:07
- ♌ 31 23:09

Jan 1964
- ♍ 3 02:47
- ♎ 5 10:09
- ♏ 7 21:03
- ♐ 10 09:48
- ♑ 12 22:13
- ♒ 15 08:47
- ♓ 17 17:03
- ♈ 19 23:10
- ♉ 22 03:23
- ♊ 24 06:04
- ♋ 26 07:51
- ♌ 28 09:45
- ♍ 30 13:09

Feb 1964
- ♎ 1 19:25
- ♏ 4 05:12
- ♐ 6 17:34
- ♑ 9 06:10
- ♒ 11 16:39
- ♓ 14 00:08
- ♈ 16 05:09
- ♉ 18 08:45
- ♊ 20 11:48
- ♋ 22 14:49
- ♌ 24 18:11
- ♍ 26 22:30
- ♎ 29 04:46

Mar 1964
- ♏ 2 13:53
- ♐ 5 01:46
- ♑ 7 14:34
- ♒ 10 01:35
- ♓ 12 09:05
- ♈ 14 13:15
- ♉ 16 15:30
- ♊ 18 17:26
- ♋ 20 20:11
- ♌ 23 00:14
- ♍ 25 05:41
- ♎ 27 12:47
- ♏ 29 22:03

Apr 1964
- ♐ 1 09:40
- ♑ 3 22:35
- ♒ 6 10:23
- ♓ 8 18:46
- ♈ 10 23:08
- ♉ 13 00:36
- ♊ 15 01:05
- ♋ 17 02:23
- ♌ 19 05:39

☽ Moon

Apr 1964
- ♍ 21 11:17
- ♎ 23 19:07
- ♏ 26 05:00
- ♐ 28 16:45

May 1964
- ♑ 1 05:42
- ♒ 3 18:05
- ♓ 6 03:42
- ♈ 8 09:15
- ♉ 10 11:09
- ♊ 12 11:02
- ♋ 14 10:53
- ♌ 16 12:31
- ♍ 18 17:02
- ♎ 21 00:41
- ♏ 23 10:57
- ♐ 25 23:02
- ♑ 28 11:59
- ♒ 31 00:32

Jun 1964
- ♓ 2 11:00
- ♈ 4 18:02
- ♉ 6 21:19
- ♊ 8 21:50
- ♋ 10 21:16
- ♌ 12 21:35
- ♍ 15 00:27
- ♎ 17 06:53
- ♏ 19 16:48
- ♐ 22 05:02
- ♑ 24 18:01
- ♒ 27 06:21
- ♓ 29 16:55

Jul 1964
- ♈ 2 00:52
- ♉ 4 05:42
- ♊ 6 07:43
- ♋ 8 07:57
- ♌ 10 08:01
- ♍ 12 09:44
- ♎ 14 14:40
- ♏ 16 23:32
- ♐ 19 11:27
- ♑ 22 00:26
- ♒ 24 12:30
- ♓ 26 22:35
- ♈ 29 06:25
- ♉ 31 12:00

Aug 1964
- ♊ 2 15:28
- ♋ 4 17:13
- ♌ 6 18:11
- ♍ 8 19:50
- ♎ 10 23:51
- ♏ 13 07:30
- ♐ 15 18:43
- ♑ 18 07:37
- ♒ 20 19:38
- ♓ 23 05:13
- ♈ 25 12:15
- ♉ 27 17:23
- ♊ 29 21:15

Sep 1964
- ♋ 1 00:13
- ♌ 3 02:36
- ♍ 5 05:12
- ♎ 7 09:19
- ♏ 9 16:19
- ♐ 12 02:47
- ♑ 14 15:29
- ♒ 17 03:47
- ♓ 19 13:22

☽ Moon

Sep 1964
- ♈ 21 19:43
- ♉ 23 23:46
- ♊ 26 02:46
- ♋ 28 05:39
- ♌ 30 08:52

Oct 1964
- ♍ 2 12:42
- ♎ 4 17:44
- ♏ 7 00:56
- ♐ 9 11:01
- ♑ 11 23:31
- ♒ 14 12:14
- ♓ 16 22:32
- ♈ 19 05:04
- ♉ 21 08:24
- ♊ 23 10:03
- ♋ 25 11:37
- ♌ 27 14:13
- ♍ 29 18:25

Nov 1964
- ♎ 1 00:24
- ♏ 3 08:24
- ♐ 5 18:43
- ♑ 8 07:05
- ♒ 10 20:07
- ♓ 13 07:27
- ♈ 15 15:10
- ♉ 17 18:57
- ♊ 19 19:59
- ♋ 21 20:04
- ♌ 23 20:58
- ♍ 26 00:02
- ♎ 28 05:53
- ♏ 30 14:30

Dec 1964
- ♐ 3 01:23
- ♑ 5 13:52
- ♒ 8 02:57
- ♓ 10 14:59
- ♈ 13 00:12
- ♉ 15 05:32
- ♊ 17 07:21
- ♋ 19 07:03
- ♌ 21 06:31
- ♍ 23 07:41
- ♎ 25 12:04
- ♏ 27 20:10
- ♐ 30 07:20

Jan 1965
- ♑ 1 20:06
- ♒ 4 09:03
- ♓ 6 21:05
- ♈ 9 07:07
- ♉ 11 14:10
- ♊ 13 17:48
- ♋ 15 18:35
- ♌ 17 17:58
- ♍ 19 17:55
- ♎ 21 20:27
- ♏ 24 03:00
- ♐ 26 13:31
- ♑ 29 02:21
- ♒ 31 15:17

Feb 1965
- ♓ 3 02:55
- ♈ 5 12:43
- ♉ 7 20:23
- ♊ 10 01:36
- ♋ 12 04:13
- ♌ 14 04:54
- ♍ 16 05:05
- ♎ 18 06:45

☽ Moon

Feb 1965
♏20 11:45
♐22 20:56
♑25 09:16
♒27 22:14

Mar 1965
♓ 2 09:38
♈ 4 18:44
♉ 7 01:49
♊ 9 07:13
♋11 11:02
♌13 13:23
♍15 14:56
♎17 17:04
♏19 21:32
♐22 05:36
♑24 17:06
♒27 05:58
♓29 17:31

Apr 1965
♈ 1 02:18
♉ 3 08:28
♊ 5 12:54
♋ 7 16:24
♌ 9 19:23
♍11 22:14
♎14 01:38
♏16 06:42
♐18 14:31
♑21 01:23
♒23 14:03
♓26 02:01
♈28 11:11
♉30 17:03

May 1965
♊ 2 20:26
♋ 4 22:38
♌ 7 00:49
♍ 9 03:47
♎11 08:04
♏13 14:09
♐15 22:31
♑18 09:19
♒20 21:50
♓23 10:13
♈25 20:18
♉28 02:48
♊30 05:58

Jun 1965
♋ 1 07:05
♌ 3 07:46
♍ 5 09:33
♎ 7 13:29
♏ 9 20:03
♐12 05:09
♑14 16:20
♒17 04:51
♓19 17:28
♈22 04:28
♉24 12:15
♊26 16:18
♋28 17:20
♌30 16:59

Jul 1965
♍ 2 17:11
♎ 4 19:42
♏ 7 01:37
♐ 9 10:52
♑11 22:28
♒14 11:07
♓16 23:44
♈19 11:12
♉21 20:13

☽ Moon

Jul 1965
♊24 01:47
♋26 03:53
♌28 03:37
♍30 02:54

Aug 1965
♎ 1 03:54
♏ 3 08:19
♐ 5 16:48
♑ 8 04:21
♒10 17:08
♓13 05:37
♈15 16:56
♉18 02:27
♊20 09:20
♋22 13:04
♌24 14:01
♍26 13:37
♎28 13:52
♏30 16:53

Sep 1965
♐ 1 23:59
♑ 4 10:50
♒ 6 23:33
♓ 9 11:56
♈11 22:49
♉14 07:55
♊16 15:05
♋18 20:00
♌20 22:35
♍22 23:29
♎25 00:15
♏27 02:46
♐29 08:41

Oct 1965
♑ 1 18:28
♒ 4 06:47
♓ 6 19:13
♈ 9 05:53
♉11 14:16
♊13 20:39
♋16 01:26
♌18 04:51
♍20 07:13
♎22 09:21
♏24 12:31
♐26 18:08
♑29 03:04
♒31 14:48

Nov 1965
♓ 3 03:22
♈ 5 14:21
♉ 7 22:29
♊10 03:54
♋12 07:29
♌14 10:13
♍16 12:54
♎18 16:10
♏20 20:36
♐23 02:56
♑25 11:45
♒27 23:03
♓30 11:39

Dec 1965
♈ 2 23:22
♉ 5 08:10
♊ 7 13:27
♋ 9 15:57
♌11 17:08
♍13 18:35
♎15 21:33
♏18 02:40
♐20 10:00

☽ Moon

Dec 1965
♑22 19:26
♒25 06:43
♓27 19:16
♈30 07:39

Jan 1966
♉ 1 17:45
♊ 4 00:06
♋ 6 02:40
♌ 8 02:49
♍10 02:34
♎12 03:52
♏14 08:08
♐16 15:39
♑19 01:44
♒21 13:25
♓24 01:58
♈26 14:32
♉29 01:42
♊31 09:43

Feb 1966
♋ 2 13:41
♌ 4 14:14
♍ 6 13:12
♎ 8 12:50
♏10 15:14
♐12 21:32
♑15 07:25
♒17 19:25
♓20 08:04
♈22 20:29
♉25 07:52
♊27 17:02

Mar 1966
♋ 1 22:47
♌ 4 00:56
♍ 6 00:36
♎ 7 23:48
♏10 00:46
♐12 05:17
♑14 13:54
♒17 01:34
♓19 14:18
♈22 02:33
♉24 13:31
♊26 22:41
♋29 05:23
♌31 09:12

Apr 1966
♍ 2 10:31
♎ 4 10:40
♏ 6 11:30
♐ 8 14:53
♑10 22:01
♒13 08:41
♓15 21:13
♈18 09:26
♉20 20:00
♊23 04:26
♋25 10:47
♌27 15:09
♍29 17:49

May 1966
♎ 1 19:31
♏ 3 21:23
♐ 6 00:52
♑ 8 07:12
♒10 16:51
♓13 04:54
♈15 17:14
♉18 03:48
♊20 11:39
♋22 17:00

☽ Moon

May 1966
♌24 20:37
♍26 23:21
♎29 01:59
♏31 05:11

Jun 1966
♐ 2 09:38
♑ 4 16:10
♒ 7 01:20
♓ 9 12:56
♈12 01:26
♉14 12:29
♊16 20:25
♋19 01:05
♌21 03:29
♍23 05:08
♎25 07:22
♏27 11:03
♐29 16:31

Jul 1966
♑ 1 23:51
♒ 4 09:14
♓ 6 20:39
♈ 9 09:15
♉11 21:03
♊14 05:51
♋16 10:44
♌18 12:28
♍20 12:47
♎22 13:38
♏24 16:31
♐26 22:04
♑29 06:04
♒31 16:01

Aug 1966
♓ 3 03:35
♈ 5 16:14
♉ 8 04:37
♊10 14:37
♋12 20:41
♌14 22:50
♍16 22:35
♎18 22:05
♏20 23:23
♐23 03:50
♑25 11:36
♒27 21:55
♓30 09:47

Sep 1966
♈ 1 22:27
♉ 4 10:58
♊ 6 21:51
♋ 9 05:26
♌11 09:01
♍13 09:26
♎15 08:33
♏17 08:34
♐19 11:21
♑21 17:52
♒24 03:47
♓26 15:48
♈29 04:29

Oct 1966
♉ 1 16:46
♊ 4 03:43
♋ 6 12:12
♌ 8 17:24
♍10 19:27
♎12 19:29
♏14 19:21
♐16 20:59
♑19 01:55
♒21 10:40

☽ Moon

Oct 1966
♓23 22:20
♈26 11:02
♉28 23:05
♊31 09:27

Nov 1966
♋ 2 17:42
♌ 4 23:35
♍ 7 03:09
♎ 9 04:54
♏11 05:53
♐13 07:36
♑15 11:36
♒17 19:02
♓20 05:52
♈22 18:30
♉25 06:36
♊27 16:30
♋29 23:49

Dec 1966
♌ 2 05:01
♍ 4 08:48
♎ 6 11:43
♏ 8 14:17
♐10 17:13
♑12 21:30
♒15 04:18
♓17 14:16
♈20 02:39
♉22 15:06
♊25 01:13
♋27 07:58
♌29 11:57
♍31 14:33

Jan 1967
♎ 2 17:03
♏ 4 20:16
♐ 7 00:27
♑ 9 05:53
♒11 13:05
♓13 22:44
♈16 10:47
♉18 23:39
♊21 10:37
♋23 17:50
♌25 21:20
♍27 22:36
♎29 23:32

Feb 1967
♏ 1 01:43
♐ 3 05:55
♑ 5 12:09
♒ 7 20:16
♓10 06:18
♈12 18:16
♉15 07:18
♊17 19:15
♋20 03:47
♌22 08:04
♍24 09:04
♎26 08:45
♏28 09:09

Mar 1967
♐ 2 11:52
♑ 4 17:34
♒ 7 02:03
♓ 9 12:40
♈12 00:52
♉14 13:53
♊17 02:18
♋19 12:09
♌21 18:03
♍23 20:08

☽ Moon

Mar 1967
♎25 19:50
♏27 19:11
♐29 20:08

Apr 1967
♑ 1 00:10
♒ 3 07:48
♓ 5 18:28
♈ 8 06:56
♉10 19:55
♊13 08:14
♋15 18:36
♌18 01:54
♍20 05:42
♎22 06:41
♏24 06:19
♐26 06:27
♑28 08:53
♒30 14:57

May 1967
♓ 3 00:46
♈ 5 13:09
♉ 8 02:09
♊10 14:07
♋13 00:10
♌15 07:48
♍17 12:51
♎19 15:31
♏21 16:30
♐23 17:06
♑25 18:58
♒27 23:43
♓30 08:17

Jun 1967
♈ 1 20:06
♉ 4 09:03
♊ 6 20:51
♋ 9 06:17
♌11 13:18
♍13 18:23
♎15 21:58
♏18 00:25
♐20 02:19
♑22 04:46
♒24 09:10
♓26 16:49
♈29 03:52

Jul 1967
♉ 1 16:42
♊ 4 04:38
♋ 6 13:47
♌ 8 19:58
♍11 00:07
♎13 03:19
♏15 06:17
♐17 09:22
♑19 12:59
♒21 17:59
♓24 01:27
♈26 11:59
♉29 00:40
♊31 12:59

Aug 1967
♋ 2 22:31
♌ 5 04:26
♍ 7 07:36
♎ 9 09:34
♏11 11:44
♐13 14:52
♑15 19:17
♒18 01:16
♓20 09:17
♈22 19:47

☽ Moon

Aug 1967
♉25 08:20
♊27 21:07
♋30 07:34

Sep 1967
♌ 1 14:08
♍ 3 17:07
♎ 5 18:03
♏ 7 18:44
♐ 9 20:39
♑12 00:42
♒14 07:08
♓16 15:52
♈19 02:46
♉21 15:19
♊24 04:20
♋26 15:44
♌28 23:41

Oct 1967
♍ 1 03:38
♎ 3 04:34
♏ 5 04:14
♐ 7 04:32
♑ 9 07:03
♒11 12:44
♓13 21:37
♈16 08:57
♉18 21:40
♊21 10:37
♋23 22:26
♌26 07:39
♍28 13:19
♎30 15:31

Nov 1967
♏ 1 15:26
♐ 3 14:51
♑ 5 15:44
♒ 7 19:45
♓10 03:42
♈12 14:57
♉15 03:52
♊17 16:39
♋20 04:12
♌22 13:46
♍24 20:45
♎27 00:48
♏29 02:13

Dec 1967
♐ 1 02:10
♑ 3 02:24
♒ 5 04:56
♓ 7 11:18
♈ 9 21:42
♉12 10:31
♊14 23:17
♋17 10:22
♌19 19:20
♍22 02:20
♎24 07:26
♏26 10:36
♐28 12:09
♑30 13:11

Jan 1968
♒ 1 15:24
♓ 3 20:35
♈ 6 05:44
♉ 8 18:01
♊11 06:53
♋13 17:53
♌16 02:09
♍18 08:11
♎20 12:47
♏22 16:27

☽ Moon

Jan 1968
♐24 19:23
♑26 21:57
♒29 01:05
♓31 06:15

Feb 1968
♈ 2 14:39
♉ 5 02:14
♊ 7 15:08
♋10 02:34
♌12 10:49
♍14 16:02
♎16 19:21
♏18 21:59
♐21 00:47
♑23 04:11
♒25 08:36
♓27 14:42
♈29 23:14

Mar 1968
♉ 3 10:27
♊ 5 23:16
♋ 8 11:20
♌10 20:26
♍13 01:51
♎15 04:23
♏17 05:33
♐19 06:53
♑21 09:34
♒23 14:16
♓25 21:14
♈28 06:31
♉30 17:54

Apr 1968
♊ 2 06:39
♋ 4 19:12
♌ 7 05:28
♍ 9 12:03
♎11 15:01
♏13 15:32
♐15 15:23
♑17 16:23
♒19 19:56
♓22 02:45
♈24 12:31
♉27 00:21
♊29 13:10

May 1968
♋ 2 01:49
♌ 4 12:53
♍ 6 20:57
♎ 9 01:20
♏11 02:29
♐13 01:53
♑15 01:30
♒17 03:21
♓19 08:52
♈21 18:13
♉24 06:15
♊26 19:11
♋29 07:42
♌31 18:53

Jun 1968
♍ 3 03:51
♎ 5 09:49
♏ 7 12:30
♐ 9 12:43
♑11 12:06
♒13 12:46
♓15 16:41
♈18 00:49
♉20 12:24
♊23 01:21

☽ Moon

Jun 1968
♋25 13:42
♌28 00:30
♍30 09:25

Jul 1968
♎ 2 16:09
♏ 4 20:20
♐ 6 22:04
♑ 8 22:24
♒10 23:03
♓13 02:02
♈15 08:51
♉17 19:29
♊20 08:12
♋22 20:30
♌25 06:54
♍27 15:09
♎29 21:32

Aug 1968
♏ 1 02:11
♐ 3 05:10
♑ 5 06:57
♒ 7 08:37
♓ 9 11:45
♈11 17:52
♉14 03:35
♊16 15:50
♋19 04:15
♌21 14:39
♍23 22:20
♎26 03:44
♏28 07:38
♐30 10:40

Sep 1968
♑ 1 13:21
♒ 3 16:19
♓ 5 20:27
♈ 8 02:48
♉10 12:05
♊12 23:54
♋15 12:27
♌17 23:25
♍20 07:15
♎22 12:00
♏24 14:39
♐26 16:30
♑28 18:44
♒30 22:10

Oct 1968
♓ 3 03:20
♈ 5 10:35
♉ 7 20:06
♊10 07:43
♋12 20:22
♌15 08:07
♍17 16:58
♎19 22:05
♏22 00:05
♐24 00:32
♑26 01:13
♒28 03:42
♓30 08:53

Nov 1968
♈ 1 16:50
♉ 4 03:01
♊ 6 14:47
♋ 9 03:26
♌11 15:44
♍14 01:54
♎16 08:26
♏18 11:06
♐20 11:04
♑22 10:20

☽ Moon

Nov 1968
♒24 11:02
♓26 14:52
♈28 22:25

Dec 1968
♉ 1 08:57
♊ 3 21:05
♋ 6 09:43
♌ 8 22:02
♍11 08:59
♎13 17:08
♏15 21:31
♐17 22:27
♑19 21:32
♒21 20:59
♓23 23:00
♈26 05:01
♉28 14:56
♊31 03:10

Jan 1969
♋ 2 15:52
♌ 5 03:54
♍ 7 14:41
♎ 9 23:32
♏12 05:31
♐14 08:19
♑16 08:39
♒18 08:17
♓20 09:20
♈22 13:43
♉24 22:12
♊27 09:52
♋29 22:36

Feb 1969
♌ 1 10:28
♍ 3 20:40
♎ 6 05:00
♏ 8 11:18
♐10 15:23
♑12 17:28
♒14 18:31
♓16 20:03
♈18 23:48
♉21 07:01
♊23 17:40
♋26 06:10
♌28 18:11

Mar 1969
♍ 3 04:06
♎ 5 11:33
♏ 7 16:56
♐ 9 20:47
♑11 23:40
♒14 02:09
♓16 05:03
♈18 09:27
♉20 16:20
♊23 02:12
♋25 14:17
♌28 02:36
♍30 12:53

Apr 1969
♎ 1 20:03
♏ 4 00:22
♐ 6 02:57
♑ 8 05:04
♒10 07:46
♓12 11:40
♈14 17:13
♉17 00:42
♊19 10:28
♋21 22:16
♌24 10:50

☽ Moon

Apr 196
♍26 21:5
♎29 05:4

May 196
♏ 1 09:4
♐ 3 11:1
♑ 5 11:5
♒ 7 13:2
♓ 9 17:0
♈11 23:0
♉14 07:2
♊16 17:4
♋19 05:3
♌21 18:1
♍24 06:0
♎26 15:0
♏28 20:0
♐30 21:3

Jun 1969
♑ 1 21:0
♒ 3 21:0
♓ 5 23:1
♈ 8 04:3
♉10 13:0
♊12 23:4
♋15 11:5
♌18 00:3
♍20 12:5
♎22 23:0
♏25 05:3
♐27 08:0
♑29 07:4

Jul 1969
♒ 1 06:4
♓ 3 07:2
♈ 5 11:1
♉ 7 18:5
♊10 05:3
♋12 17:4
♌15 06:2
♍17 18:4
♎20 05:1
♏22 13:0
♐24 17:1
♑26 18:0
♒28 17:3
♓30 17:31

Aug 1969
♈ 1 19:54
♉ 4 02:01
♊ 6 11:48
♋ 8 23:57
♌11 12:37
♍14 00:32
♎16 10:50
♏18 18:53
♐21 00:11
♑23 02:48
♒25 03:35
♓27 04:03
♈29 05:57
♉31 10:49

Sep 1969
♊ 2 19:23
♋ 5 06:56
♌ 7 19:35
♍10 07:20
♎12 17:01
♏15 00:24
♐17 05:42
♑19 09:13
♒21 11:31
♓23 13:22

☽ Moon

Sep 1969
- ♈ 25 15:55
- ♉ 27 20:28
- ♊ 30 04:05

Oct 1969
- ♋ 2 14:51
- ♌ 5 03:24
- ♍ 7 15:20
- ♎ 10 00:48
- ♏ 12 07:18
- ♐ 14 11:33
- ♑ 16 14:35
- ♒ 18 17:21
- ♓ 20 20:25
- ♈ 23 00:17
- ♉ 25 05:32
- ♊ 27 13:00
- ♋ 29 23:12

Nov 1969
- ♌ 1 11:33
- ♍ 4 00:00
- ♎ 6 09:58
- ♏ 8 16:17
- ♐ 10 19:30
- ♑ 12 21:08
- ♒ 14 22:52
- ♓ 17 01:51
- ♈ 19 06:31
- ♉ 21 12:52
- ♊ 23 20:58
- ♋ 26 07:10
- ♌ 28 19:21

Dec 1969
- ♍ 1 08:13
- ♎ 3 19:16
- ♏ 6 02:30
- ♐ 8 05:42
- ♑ 10 06:20
- ♒ 12 06:27
- ♓ 14 07:56
- ♈ 16 11:55
- ♉ 18 18:34
- ♊ 21 03:27
- ♋ 23 14:08
- ♌ 26 02:20
- ♍ 28 15:19
- ♎ 31 03:17

Jan 1970
- ♏ 2 12:02
- ♐ 4 16:32
- ♑ 6 17:30
- ♒ 8 16:48
- ♓ 10 16:37
- ♈ 12 18:47
- ♉ 15 00:20
- ♊ 17 09:06
- ♋ 19 20:13
- ♌ 22 08:39
- ♍ 24 21:32
- ♎ 27 09:41
- ♏ 29 19:33

Feb 1970
- ♐ 1 01:49
- ♑ 3 04:21
- ♒ 5 04:19
- ♓ 7 03:37
- ♈ 9 04:17
- ♉ 11 07:58
- ♊ 13 15:28
- ♋ 16 02:16
- ♌ 18 14:52
- ♍ 21 03:41
- ♎ 23 15:29

☽ Moon

Feb 1970
- ♏ 26 01:23
- ♐ 28 08:38

Mar 1970
- ♑ 2 12:54
- ♒ 4 14:34
- ♓ 6 14:49
- ♈ 8 15:16
- ♉ 10 17:43
- ♊ 12 23:36
- ♋ 15 09:17
- ♌ 17 21:39
- ♍ 20 10:29
- ♎ 22 21:56
- ♏ 25 07:09
- ♐ 27 14:06
- ♑ 29 19:00
- ♒ 31 22:08

Apr 1970
- ♓ 3 00:00
- ♈ 5 01:31
- ♉ 7 04:02
- ♊ 9 09:01
- ♋ 11 17:32
- ♌ 14 05:15
- ♍ 16 18:06
- ♎ 19 05:34
- ♏ 21 14:15
- ♐ 23 20:14
- ♑ 26 00:26
- ♒ 28 03:43
- ♓ 30 06:37

May 1970
- ♈ 2 09:32
- ♉ 4 13:05
- ♊ 6 18:17
- ♋ 9 02:16
- ♌ 11 13:21
- ♍ 14 02:10
- ♎ 16 14:01
- ♏ 18 22:49
- ♐ 21 04:11
- ♑ 23 07:13
- ♒ 25 09:25
- ♓ 27 11:58
- ♈ 29 15:26
- ♉ 31 20:03

Jun 1970
- ♊ 3 02:09
- ♋ 5 10:25
- ♌ 7 21:16
- ♍ 10 10:01
- ♎ 12 22:27
- ♏ 15 08:01
- ♐ 17 13:39
- ♑ 19 16:05
- ♒ 21 17:01
- ♓ 23 18:11
- ♈ 25 20:51
- ♉ 28 01:34
- ♊ 30 08:23

Jul 1970
- ♋ 2 17:20
- ♌ 5 04:25
- ♍ 7 17:10
- ♎ 10 06:02
- ♏ 12 16:40
- ♐ 14 23:25
- ♑ 17 02:19
- ♒ 19 02:44
- ♓ 21 02:36
- ♈ 23 03:42
- ♉ 25 07:17

☽ Moon

Jul 1970
- ♊ 27 13:52
- ♋ 29 23:13

Aug 1970
- ♌ 1 10:43
- ♍ 3 23:34
- ♎ 6 12:32
- ♏ 8 23:56
- ♐ 11 08:06
- ♑ 13 12:24
- ♒ 15 13:31
- ♓ 17 13:01
- ♈ 19 12:50
- ♉ 21 14:45
- ♊ 23 20:03
- ♋ 26 04:57
- ♌ 28 16:37
- ♍ 31 05:35

Sep 1970
- ♎ 2 18:25
- ♏ 5 05:54
- ♐ 7 14:57
- ♑ 9 20:51
- ♒ 11 23:33
- ♓ 13 23:56
- ♈ 15 23:34
- ♉ 18 00:20
- ♊ 20 04:01
- ♋ 22 11:40
- ♌ 24 22:54
- ♍ 27 11:52
- ♎ 30 00:33

Oct 1970
- ♏ 2 11:35
- ♐ 4 20:31
- ♑ 7 03:10
- ♒ 9 07:25
- ♓ 11 09:30
- ♈ 13 10:12
- ♉ 15 11:00
- ♊ 17 13:43
- ♋ 19 19:58
- ♌ 22 06:11
- ♍ 24 18:56
- ♎ 27 07:36
- ♏ 29 18:14

Nov 1970
- ♐ 1 02:24
- ♑ 3 08:32
- ♒ 5 13:10
- ♓ 7 16:32
- ♈ 9 18:51
- ♉ 11 20:50
- ♊ 13 23:48
- ♋ 16 05:22
- ♌ 18 14:35
- ♍ 21 02:49
- ♎ 23 15:38
- ♏ 26 02:24
- ♐ 28 10:02
- ♑ 30 15:05

Dec 1970
- ♒ 2 18:44
- ♓ 4 21:55
- ♈ 7 01:03
- ♉ 9 04:24
- ♊ 11 08:33
- ♋ 13 14:32
- ♌ 15 23:21
- ♍ 18 11:03
- ♎ 21 00:01
- ♏ 23 11:26
- ♐ 25 19:27

☽ Moon

Dec 1970
- ♑ 28 00:01
- ♒ 30 02:23

Jan 1971
- ♓ 1 04:07
- ♈ 3 06:26
- ♉ 5 10:00
- ♊ 7 15:08
- ♋ 9 22:08
- ♌ 12 07:23
- ♍ 14 18:57
- ♎ 17 07:52
- ♏ 19 20:03
- ♐ 22 05:15
- ♑ 24 10:32
- ♒ 26 12:36
- ♓ 28 13:02
- ♈ 30 13:36

Feb 1971
- ♉ 1 15:48
- ♊ 3 20:34
- ♋ 6 04:06
- ♌ 8 14:06
- ♍ 11 01:57
- ♎ 13 14:49
- ♏ 16 03:21
- ♐ 18 13:44
- ♑ 20 20:36
- ♒ 22 23:42
- ♓ 25 00:05
- ♈ 26 23:29
- ♉ 28 23:53

Mar 1971
- ♊ 3 03:01
- ♋ 5 09:46
- ♌ 7 19:55
- ♍ 10 08:10
- ♎ 12 21:05
- ♏ 15 09:30
- ♐ 17 20:23
- ♑ 20 04:37
- ♒ 22 09:28
- ♓ 24 11:07
- ♈ 26 10:46
- ♉ 28 10:16
- ♊ 30 11:43

Apr 1971
- ♋ 1 16:50
- ♌ 4 02:05
- ♍ 6 14:15
- ♎ 9 03:16
- ♏ 11 15:27
- ♐ 14 02:02
- ♑ 16 10:37
- ♒ 18 16:45
- ♓ 20 20:07
- ♈ 22 21:08
- ♉ 24 21:06
- ♊ 26 21:58
- ♋ 29 01:43

May 1971
- ♌ 1 09:33
- ♍ 3 21:02
- ♎ 6 09:58
- ♏ 8 22:03
- ♐ 11 08:07
- ♑ 13 16:08
- ♒ 15 22:19
- ♓ 18 02:39
- ♈ 20 05:11
- ♉ 22 06:31
- ♊ 24 08:01
- ♋ 26 11:26

☽ Moon

May 1971
- ♌ 28 18:15
- ♍ 31 04:47

Jun 1971
- ♎ 2 17:25
- ♏ 5 05:35
- ♐ 7 15:27
- ♑ 9 22:44
- ♒ 12 04:02
- ♓ 14 08:01
- ♈ 16 11:05
- ♉ 18 13:39
- ♊ 20 16:24
- ♋ 22 20:30
- ♌ 25 03:11
- ♍ 27 13:05
- ♎ 30 01:22

Jul 1971
- ♏ 2 13:45
- ♐ 4 23:58
- ♑ 7 07:03
- ♒ 9 11:26
- ♓ 11 14:14
- ♈ 13 16:32
- ♉ 15 19:10
- ♊ 17 22:46
- ♋ 20 03:56
- ♌ 22 11:16
- ♍ 24 21:09
- ♎ 27 09:11
- ♏ 29 21:49

Aug 1971
- ♐ 1 08:49
- ♑ 3 16:31
- ♒ 5 20:46
- ♓ 7 22:34
- ♈ 9 23:26
- ♉ 12 00:55
- ♊ 14 04:10
- ♋ 16 09:49
- ♌ 18 17:57
- ♍ 21 04:18
- ♎ 23 16:22
- ♏ 26 05:08
- ♐ 28 16:55
- ♑ 31 01:54

Sep 1971
- ♒ 2 07:03
- ♓ 4 08:51
- ♈ 6 08:43
- ♉ 8 08:37
- ♊ 10 10:24
- ♋ 12 15:20
- ♌ 14 23:37
- ♍ 17 10:28
- ♎ 19 22:46
- ♏ 22 11:32
- ♐ 24 23:43
- ♑ 27 09:52
- ♒ 29 16:38

Oct 1971
- ♓ 1 19:36
- ♈ 3 19:41
- ♉ 5 18:42
- ♊ 7 18:53
- ♋ 9 22:10
- ♌ 12 05:29
- ♍ 14 16:15
- ♎ 17 04:47
- ♏ 19 17:30
- ♐ 22 05:31
- ♑ 24 16:04
- ♒ 27 00:11

☽ Moon

Oct 1971
- ♓ 29 04:56
- ♈ 31 06:26

Nov 1971
- ♉ 2 05:55
- ♊ 4 05:27
- ♋ 6 07:14
- ♌ 8 12:55
- ♍ 10 22:43
- ♎ 13 11:04
- ♏ 15 23:49
- ♐ 18 11:29
- ♑ 20 21:36
- ♒ 23 05:51
- ♓ 25 11:47
- ♈ 27 15:03
- ♉ 29 16:08

Dec 1971
- ♊ 1 16:25
- ♋ 3 17:51
- ♌ 5 22:16
- ♍ 8 06:40
- ♎ 10 18:18
- ♏ 13 07:01
- ♐ 15 18:37
- ♑ 18 04:07
- ♒ 20 11:32
- ♓ 22 17:09
- ♈ 24 21:09
- ♉ 26 23:44
- ♊ 29 01:38
- ♋ 31 04:01

Jan 1972
- ♌ 2 08:21
- ♍ 4 15:49
- ♎ 7 02:32
- ♏ 9 15:02
- ♐ 12 02:57
- ♑ 14 12:25
- ♒ 16 19:03
- ♓ 18 23:27
- ♈ 21 02:35
- ♉ 23 05:17
- ♊ 25 08:13
- ♋ 27 12:01
- ♌ 29 17:21

Feb 1972
- ♍ 1 00:55
- ♎ 3 11:06
- ♏ 5 23:17
- ♐ 8 11:37
- ♑ 10 21:49
- ♒ 13 04:36
- ♓ 15 08:11
- ♈ 17 09:51
- ♉ 19 11:11
- ♊ 21 13:35
- ♋ 23 17:52
- ♌ 26 00:14
- ♍ 28 08:39

Mar 1972
- ♎ 1 18:59
- ♏ 4 06:59
- ♐ 6 19:36
- ♑ 9 06:48
- ♒ 11 14:42
- ♓ 13 18:39
- ♈ 15 19:37
- ♉ 17 19:28
- ♊ 19 20:12
- ♋ 21 23:26
- ♌ 24 05:45
- ♍ 26 14:47

☽ Moon

Mar 1972
- ♎ 29 01:41
- ♏ 31 13:48

Apr 1972
- ♐ 3 02:26
- ♑ 5 14:19
- ♒ 7 23:37
- ♓ 10 04:57
- ♈ 12 06:32
- ♉ 14 05:55
- ♊ 16 05:16
- ♋ 18 06:45
- ♌ 20 11:46
- ♍ 22 20:23
- ♎ 25 07:34
- ♏ 27 19:55
- ♐ 30 08:30

May 1972
- ♑ 2 20:28
- ♒ 5 06:34
- ♓ 7 13:27
- ♈ 9 16:35
- ♉ 11 16:48
- ♊ 13 15:58
- ♋ 15 16:16
- ♌ 17 19:37
- ♍ 20 02:55
- ♎ 22 13:35
- ♏ 25 02:00
- ♐ 27 14:32
- ♑ 30 02:12

Jun 1972
- ♒ 1 12:14
- ♓ 3 19:51
- ♈ 6 00:27
- ♉ 8 02:14
- ♊ 10 02:24
- ♋ 12 02:44
- ♌ 14 05:09
- ♍ 16 11:02
- ♎ 18 20:38
- ♏ 21 08:42
- ♐ 23 21:14
- ♑ 26 08:36
- ♒ 28 18:02

Jul 1972
- ♓ 1 01:18
- ♈ 3 06:21
- ♉ 5 09:24
- ♊ 7 11:05
- ♋ 9 12:29
- ♌ 11 15:05
- ♍ 13 20:15
- ♎ 16 04:48
- ♏ 18 16:14
- ♐ 21 04:45
- ♑ 23 16:09
- ♒ 26 01:06
- ♓ 28 07:28
- ♈ 30 11:50

Aug 1972
- ♉ 1 14:57
- ♊ 3 17:33
- ♋ 5 20:17
- ♌ 7 23:55
- ♍ 10 05:22
- ♎ 12 13:27
- ♏ 15 00:19
- ♐ 17 12:48
- ♑ 20 00:37
- ♒ 22 09:42
- ♓ 24 15:28
- ♈ 26 18:40

☽ Moon

Aug 1972
- ♉ 28 20:43
- ♊ 30 22:55

Sep 1972
- ♋ 2 02:11
- ♌ 4 06:53
- ♍ 6 13:15
- ♎ 8 21:36
- ♏ 11 08:14
- ♐ 13 20:41
- ♑ 16 09:06
- ♒ 18 19:04
- ♓ 21 01:09
- ♈ 23 03:44
- ♉ 25 04:27
- ♊ 27 05:14
- ♋ 29 07:38

Oct 1972
- ♌ 1 12:24
- ♍ 3 19:30
- ♎ 6 04:34
- ♏ 8 15:26
- ♐ 11 03:52
- ♑ 13 16:43
- ♒ 16 03:50
- ♓ 18 11:12
- ♈ 20 14:22
- ♉ 22 14:38
- ♊ 24 14:03
- ♋ 26 14:44
- ♌ 28 18:14
- ♍ 31 00:59

Nov 1972
- ♎ 2 10:26
- ♏ 4 21:46
- ♐ 7 10:16
- ♑ 9 23:10
- ♒ 12 11:01
- ♓ 14 19:55
- ♈ 17 00:44
- ♉ 19 01:53
- ♊ 21 01:05
- ♋ 23 00:30
- ♌ 25 02:11
- ♍ 27 07:24
- ♎ 29 16:14

Dec 1972
- ♏ 2 03:42
- ♐ 4 16:22
- ♑ 7 05:06
- ♒ 9 16:53
- ♓ 12 02:32
- ♈ 14 08:59
- ♉ 16 11:59
- ♊ 18 12:25
- ♋ 20 11:57
- ♌ 22 12:34
- ♍ 24 16:02
- ♎ 26 23:21
- ♏ 29 10:09
- ♐ 31 22:51

Jan 1973
- ♑ 3 11:29
- ♒ 5 22:46
- ♓ 8 08:02
- ♈ 10 14:57
- ♉ 12 19:24
- ♊ 14 21:40
- ♋ 16 22:38
- ♌ 18 23:40
- ♍ 21 02:23
- ♎ 23 08:15
- ♏ 25 17:51

☽ Moon

Jan 1973
- ♐ 28 06:09
- ♑ 30 18:53

Feb 1973
- ♒ 2 05:55
- ♓ 4 14:22
- ♈ 6 20:28
- ♉ 9 00:53
- ♊ 11 04:09
- ♋ 13 06:44
- ♌ 15 09:12
- ♍ 17 12:31
- ♎ 19 17:58
- ♏ 22 02:34
- ♐ 24 14:13
- ♑ 27 03:03

Mar 1973
- ♒ 1 14:21
- ♓ 3 22:30
- ♈ 6 03:37
- ♉ 8 06:50
- ♊ 10 09:30
- ♋ 12 12:29
- ♌ 14 16:07
- ♍ 16 20:42
- ♎ 19 02:47
- ♏ 21 11:15
- ♐ 23 22:25
- ♑ 26 11:14
- ♒ 28 23:12
- ♓ 31 07:54

Apr 1973
- ♈ 2 12:48
- ♉ 4 14:58
- ♊ 6 16:12
- ♋ 8 18:04
- ♌ 10 21:31
- ♍ 13 02:46
- ♎ 15 09:49
- ♏ 17 18:50
- ♐ 20 06:01
- ♑ 22 18:48
- ♒ 25 07:20
- ♓ 27 17:09
- ♈ 29 22:53

May 1973
- ♉ 2 01:01
- ♊ 4 01:15
- ♋ 6 01:34
- ♌ 8 03:36
- ♍ 10 08:12
- ♎ 12 15:30
- ♏ 15 01:09
- ♐ 17 12:41
- ♑ 20 01:29
- ♒ 22 14:16
- ♓ 25 01:05
- ♈ 27 08:14
- ♉ 29 11:28
- ♊ 31 11:53

Jun 1973
- ♋ 2 11:21
- ♌ 4 11:49
- ♍ 6 14:51
- ♎ 8 21:15
- ♏ 11 06:51
- ♐ 13 18:42
- ♑ 16 07:36
- ♒ 18 20:18
- ♓ 21 07:28
- ♈ 23 15:47
- ♉ 25 20:36
- ♊ 27 22:17

☽ Moon

Jun 1973
- ♋ 29 22:08

Jul 1973
- ♌ 1 21:55
- ♍ 3 23:30
- ♎ 6 04:23
- ♏ 8 13:04
- ♐ 11 00:47
- ♑ 13 13:44
- ♒ 16 02:14
- ♓ 18 13:07
- ♈ 20 21:43
- ♉ 23 03:40
- ♊ 25 06:58
- ♋ 27 08:10
- ♌ 29 08:29
- ♍ 31 09:34

Aug 1973
- ♎ 2 13:12
- ♏ 4 20:35
- ♐ 7 07:36
- ♑ 9 20:29
- ♒ 12 08:51
- ♓ 14 19:13
- ♈ 17 03:15
- ♉ 19 09:13
- ♊ 21 13:26
- ♋ 23 16:07
- ♌ 25 17:49
- ♍ 27 19:33
- ♎ 29 22:52

Sep 1973
- ♏ 1 05:17
- ♐ 3 15:23
- ♑ 6 04:00
- ♒ 8 16:29
- ♓ 11 02:40
- ♈ 13 09:56
- ♉ 15 14:59
- ♊ 17 18:47
- ♋ 19 22:00
- ♌ 22 00:56
- ♍ 24 03:58
- ♎ 26 08:00
- ♏ 28 14:17
- ♐ 30 23:47

Oct 1973
- ♑ 3 12:01
- ♒ 6 00:48
- ♓ 8 11:22
- ♈ 10 18:28
- ♉ 12 22:35
- ♊ 15 01:08
- ♋ 17 03:28
- ♌ 19 06:24
- ♍ 21 10:18
- ♎ 23 15:28
- ♏ 25 22:27
- ♐ 28 07:57
- ♑ 30 19:56

Nov 1973
- ♒ 2 08:57
- ♓ 4 20:25
- ♈ 7 04:19
- ♉ 9 08:25
- ♊ 11 10:00
- ♋ 13 10:46
- ♌ 15 12:19
- ♍ 17 15:40
- ♎ 19 21:15
- ♏ 22 05:06
- ♐ 24 15:10
- ♑ 27 03:12

☽ Moon

Nov 1973
- ♒ 29 16:16

Dec 1973
- ♓ 2 04:31
- ♈ 4 13:49
- ♉ 6 19:08
- ♊ 8 20:58
- ♋ 10 20:52
- ♌ 12 20:44
- ♍ 14 22:20
- ♎ 17 02:53
- ♏ 19 10:43
- ♐ 21 21:19
- ♑ 24 09:40
- ♒ 26 22:42
- ♓ 29 11:09
- ♈ 31 21:33

Jan 1974
- ♉ 3 04:37
- ♊ 5 07:59
- ♋ 7 08:28
- ♌ 9 07:42
- ♍ 11 07:41
- ♎ 13 10:21
- ♏ 15 16:53
- ♐ 18 03:11
- ♑ 20 15:46
- ♒ 23 04:49
- ♓ 25 17:00
- ♈ 28 03:31
- ♉ 30 11:40

Feb 1974
- ♊ 1 16:52
- ♋ 3 19:05
- ♌ 5 19:12
- ♍ 7 18:52
- ♎ 9 20:10
- ♏ 12 00:57
- ♐ 14 10:00
- ♑ 16 22:15
- ♒ 19 11:20
- ♓ 21 23:15
- ♈ 24 09:12
- ♉ 26 17:11
- ♊ 28 23:10

Mar 1974
- ♋ 3 02:59
- ♌ 5 04:48
- ♍ 7 05:33
- ♎ 9 06:52
- ♏ 11 10:39
- ♐ 13 18:19
- ♑ 16 05:40
- ♒ 18 18:37
- ♓ 21 06:33
- ♈ 23 16:02
- ♉ 25 23:09
- ♊ 28 04:32
- ♋ 30 08:39

Apr 1974
- ♌ 1 11:40
- ♍ 3 13:56
- ♎ 5 16:23
- ♏ 7 20:24
- ♐ 10 03:27
- ♑ 12 13:55
- ♒ 15 02:33
- ♓ 17 14:43
- ♈ 20 00:20
- ♉ 22 06:53
- ♊ 24 11:11
- ♋ 26 14:17
- ♌ 28 17:03

☽ Moon

Apr 1974
♍ 30 20:00

May 1974
♎ 2 23:38
♏ 5 04:42
♐ 7 12:05
♑ 9 22:14
♒ 12 10:33
♓ 14 23:02
♈ 17 09:19
♉ 19 16:10
♊ 21 19:54
♋ 23 21:45
♌ 25 23:11
♍ 28 01:25
♎ 30 05:15

Jun 1974
♏ 1 11:10
♐ 3 19:21
♑ 6 05:48
♒ 8 18:01
♓ 11 06:42
♈ 13 17:51
♉ 16 01:46
♊ 18 05:58
♋ 20 07:21
♌ 22 07:30
♍ 24 08:11
♎ 26 10:57
♏ 28 16:39

Jul 1974
♐ 1 01:20
♑ 3 12:18
♒ 6 00:41
♓ 8 13:25
♈ 11 01:10
♉ 13 10:20
♊ 15 15:53
♋ 17 17:56
♌ 19 17:43
♍ 21 17:10
♎ 23 18:18
♏ 25 22:45
♐ 28 06:59
♑ 30 18:10

Aug 1974
♒ 2 06:45
♓ 4 19:26
♈ 7 07:14
♉ 9 17:12
♊ 12 00:14
♋ 14 03:48
♌ 16 04:26
♍ 18 03:42
♎ 20 03:44
♏ 22 06:36
♐ 24 13:33
♑ 27 00:14
♒ 29 12:52

Sep 1974
♓ 1 01:28
♈ 3 12:57
♉ 5 22:50
♊ 8 06:35
♋ 10 11:39
♌ 12 13:54
♍ 14 14:12
♎ 16 14:17
♏ 18 16:13
♐ 20 21:46
♑ 23 07:21
♒ 25 19:37
♓ 28 08:14

☽ Moon

Sep 1974
♈ 30 19:25

Oct 1974
♉ 3 04:39
♊ 5 12:00
♋ 7 17:29
♌ 9 21:02
♍ 11 22:55
♎ 14 00:10
♏ 16 02:23
♐ 18 07:14
♑ 20 15:43
♒ 23 03:19
♓ 25 15:56
♈ 28 03:13
♉ 30 11:59

Nov 1974
♊ 1 18:22
♋ 3 23:00
♌ 6 02:29
♍ 8 05:18
♎ 10 07:58
♏ 12 11:23
♐ 14 16:38
♑ 17 00:41
♒ 19 11:38
♓ 22 00:11
♈ 24 11:58
♉ 26 21:04
♊ 29 02:57

Dec 1974
♋ 1 06:21
♌ 3 08:31
♍ 5 10:40
♎ 7 13:42
♏ 9 18:13
♐ 12 00:34
♑ 14 09:03
♒ 16 19:47
♓ 19 08:11
♈ 21 20:34
♉ 24 06:44
♊ 26 13:15
♋ 28 16:15
♌ 30 17:05

Jan 1975
♍ 1 17:33
♎ 3 19:21
♏ 5 23:38
♐ 8 06:38
♑ 10 15:57
♒ 13 03:02
♓ 15 15:22
♈ 18 04:03
♉ 20 15:20
♊ 22 23:22
♋ 25 03:20
♌ 27 04:00
♍ 29 03:14
♎ 31 03:13

Feb 1975
♏ 2 05:52
♐ 4 12:09
♑ 6 21:41
♒ 9 09:16
♓ 11 21:44
♈ 14 10:21
♉ 16 22:08
♊ 19 07:34
♋ 21 13:18
♌ 23 15:13
♍ 25 14:37
♎ 27 13:39

☽ Moon

Mar 1975
♏ 1 14:33
♐ 3 19:05
♑ 6 03:39
♒ 8 15:08
♓ 11 03:48
♈ 13 16:18
♉ 16 03:52
♊ 18 13:42
♋ 20 20:48
♌ 23 00:31
♍ 25 01:20
♎ 27 00:51
♏ 29 01:07
♐ 31 04:09

Apr 1975
♑ 2 11:07
♒ 4 21:44
♓ 7 10:16
♈ 9 22:43
♉ 12 09:53
♊ 14 19:14
♋ 17 02:26
♌ 19 07:14
♍ 21 09:42
♎ 23 10:42
♏ 25 11:40
♐ 27 14:19
♑ 29 20:08

May 1975
♒ 2 05:33
♓ 4 17:33
♈ 7 06:02
♉ 9 17:03
♊ 12 01:44
♋ 14 08:07
♌ 16 12:38
♍ 18 15:45
♎ 20 18:05
♏ 22 20:25
♐ 24 23:51
♑ 27 05:30
♒ 29 14:08

Jun 1975
♓ 1 01:31
♈ 3 14:00
♉ 6 01:18
♊ 8 09:49
♋ 10 15:21
♌ 12 18:45
♍ 14 21:10
♎ 16 23:40
♏ 19 02:58
♐ 21 07:34
♑ 23 13:55
♒ 25 22:32
♓ 28 09:32
♈ 30 22:01

Jul 1975
♉ 3 09:53
♊ 5 18:58
♋ 8 00:22
♌ 10 02:50
♍ 12 03:55
♎ 14 05:21
♏ 16 08:22
♐ 18 13:31
♑ 20 20:45
♒ 23 05:55
♓ 25 16:58
♈ 28 05:26
♉ 30 17:52

☽ Moon

Aug 1975
♊ 2 04:01
♋ 4 10:16
♌ 6 12:44
♍ 8 12:54
♎ 10 12:51
♏ 12 14:30
♐ 14 18:59
♑ 17 02:24
♒ 19 12:08
♓ 21 23:32
♈ 24 12:02
♉ 27 00:44
♊ 29 11:52
♋ 31 19:34

Sep 1975
♌ 2 23:07
♍ 4 23:29
♎ 6 22:37
♏ 8 22:45
♐ 11 01:40
♑ 13 08:10
♒ 15 17:50
♓ 18 05:31
♈ 20 18:06
♉ 23 06:42
♊ 25 18:12
♋ 28 03:06
♌ 30 08:20

Oct 1975
♍ 2 10:03
♎ 4 09:39
♏ 6 09:09
♐ 8 10:35
♑ 10 15:28
♒ 13 00:09
♓ 15 11:39
♈ 18 00:20
♉ 20 12:42
♊ 22 23:51
♋ 25 08:56
♌ 27 15:19
♍ 29 18:46
♎ 31 19:55

Nov 1975
♏ 2 20:07
♐ 4 21:10
♑ 7 00:45
♒ 9 07:58
♓ 11 18:41
♈ 14 07:16
♉ 16 19:37
♊ 19 06:13
♋ 21 14:36
♌ 23 20:47
♍ 26 01:04
♎ 28 03:47
♏ 30 05:36

Dec 1975
♐ 2 07:33
♑ 4 10:58
♒ 6 17:11
♓ 9 02:51
♈ 11 15:05
♉ 14 03:38
♊ 16 14:11
♋ 18 21:48
♌ 21 02:53
♍ 23 06:27
♎ 25 09:27
♏ 27 12:27
♐ 29 15:52
♑ 31 20:16

☽ Moon

Jan 1976
♒ 3 02:32
♓ 5 11:34
♈ 7 23:20
♉ 10 12:08
♊ 12 23:19
♋ 15 07:00
♌ 17 11:15
♍ 19 13:25
♎ 21 15:10
♏ 23 17:47
♐ 25 21:51
♑ 28 03:23
♒ 30 10:33

Feb 1976
♓ 1 19:46
♈ 4 07:16
♉ 6 20:12
♊ 9 08:15
♋ 11 16:58
♌ 13 21:32
♍ 15 22:58
♎ 17 23:13
♏ 20 00:13
♐ 22 03:18
♑ 24 08:53
♒ 26 16:48
♓ 29 02:41

Mar 1976
♈ 2 14:21
♉ 5 03:17
♊ 7 15:55
♋ 10 01:58
♌ 12 07:55
♍ 14 09:59
♎ 16 09:45
♏ 18 09:18
♐ 20 10:33
♑ 22 14:47
♒ 24 22:19
♓ 27 08:33
♈ 29 20:36

Apr 1976
♉ 1 09:33
♊ 3 22:15
♋ 6 09:06
♌ 8 16:36
♍ 10 20:15
♎ 12 20:54
♏ 14 20:14
♐ 16 20:15
♑ 18 22:43
♒ 21 04:47
♓ 23 14:27
♈ 26 02:36
♉ 28 15:37

May 1976
♊ 1 04:04
♋ 3 14:52
♌ 5 23:09
♍ 8 04:20
♎ 10 06:39
♏ 12 07:03
♐ 14 07:04
♑ 16 08:31
♒ 18 13:02
♓ 20 21:26
♈ 23 09:06
♉ 25 22:06
♊ 28 10:21
♋ 30 20:38

Jun 1976
♌ 2 04:37

☽ Moon

Jun 1976
♍ 4 10:20
♎ 6 13:59
♏ 8 15:58
♐ 10 17:07
♑ 12 18:45
♒ 14 22:30
♓ 17 05:43
♈ 19 16:31
♉ 22 05:21
♊ 24 17:36
♋ 27 03:28
♌ 29 10:39

Jul 1976
♍ 1 15:46
♎ 3 19:34
♏ 5 22:33
♐ 8 01:05
♑ 10 03:49
♒ 12 07:53
♓ 14 14:35
♈ 17 00:39
♉ 19 13:10
♊ 22 01:40
♋ 24 11:39
♌ 26 18:18
♍ 28 22:23
♎ 31 01:13

Aug 1976
♏ 2 03:55
♐ 4 07:03
♑ 6 10:54
♒ 8 15:57
♓ 10 23:00
♈ 13 08:48
♉ 15 21:04
♊ 18 09:53
♋ 20 20:33
♌ 23 03:30
♍ 25 07:03
♎ 27 08:42
♏ 29 10:05
♐ 31 12:28

Sep 1976
♑ 2 16:28
♒ 4 22:19
♓ 7 06:11
♈ 9 16:17
♉ 12 04:29
♊ 14 17:31
♋ 17 05:06
♌ 19 13:10
♍ 21 17:16
♎ 23 18:28
♏ 25 18:34
♐ 27 19:21
♑ 29 22:13

Oct 1976
♒ 2 03:48
♓ 4 12:09
♈ 6 22:49
♉ 9 11:10
♊ 12 00:14
♋ 14 12:23
♌ 16 21:49
♍ 19 03:24
♎ 21 05:26
♏ 23 05:17
♐ 25 04:48
♑ 27 05:55
♒ 29 10:05
♓ 31 17:52

☽ Moon

Nov 1976
♈ 3 04:45
♉ 5 17:22
♊ 8 06:20
♋ 10 18:27
♌ 13 04:35
♍ 15 11:45
♎ 17 15:33
♏ 19 16:32
♐ 21 16:04
♑ 23 16:04
♒ 25 18:29
♓ 28 00:47
♈ 30 11:00

Dec 1976
♉ 2 23:41
♊ 5 12:37
♋ 8 00:20
♌ 10 10:11
♍ 12 17:54
♎ 14 23:12
♏ 17 02:01
♐ 19 02:54
♑ 21 03:11
♒ 23 04:48
♓ 25 09:35
♈ 27 18:31
♉ 30 06:42

Jan 1977
♊ 1 19:42
♋ 4 07:12
♌ 6 16:20
♍ 8 23:23
♎ 11 04:47
♏ 13 08:44
♐ 15 11:18
♑ 17 13:02
♒ 19 15:12
♓ 21 19:30
♈ 24 03:19
♉ 26 14:40
♊ 29 03:36
♋ 31 15:19

Feb 1977
♌ 3 00:11
♍ 5 06:17
♎ 7 10:36
♏ 9 14:04
♐ 11 17:11
♑ 13 20:13
♒ 15 23:44
♓ 18 04:44
♈ 20 12:22
♉ 22 23:05
♊ 25 11:49
♋ 28 00:02

Mar 1977
♌ 2 09:24
♍ 4 15:18
♎ 6 18:34
♏ 8 20:37
♐ 10 22:41
♑ 13 01:39
♒ 15 05:59
♓ 17 12:05
♈ 19 20:22
♉ 22 07:05
♊ 24 19:38
♋ 27 08:15
♌ 29 18:40

Apr 1977
♍ 1 01:24
♎ 3 04:39

☽ Moon

Apr 1977
♏ 5 05:40
♐ 7 06:08
♑ 9 07:40
♒ 11 11:23
♓ 13 17:49
♈ 16 02:51
♉ 18 14:02
♊ 21 02:37
♋ 23 15:24
♌ 26 02:42
♍ 28 10:51
♎ 30 15:12

May 1977
♏ 2 16:24
♐ 4 15:59
♑ 6 15:54
♒ 8 17:59
♓ 10 23:28
♈ 13 08:29
♉ 15 20:03
♊ 18 08:50
♋ 20 21:35
♌ 23 09:12
♍ 25 18:30
♎ 28 00:28
♏ 30 02:56

Jun 1977
♐ 1 02:54
♑ 3 02:07
♒ 5 02:43
♓ 7 06:35
♈ 9 14:33
♉ 12 01:56
♊ 14 14:49
♋ 17 03:28
♌ 19 14:53
♍ 22 00:28
♎ 24 07:35
♏ 26 11:41
♐ 28 13:02
♑ 30 12:49

Jul 1977
♒ 2 12:56
♓ 4 15:31
♈ 6 22:02
♉ 9 08:32
♊ 11 21:14
♋ 14 09:49
♌ 16 20:51
♍ 19 05:58
♎ 21 13:09
♏ 23 18:13
♐ 25 21:04
♑ 27 22:14
♒ 29 23:04

Aug 1977
♓ 1 01:23
♈ 3 06:54
♉ 5 16:17
♊ 8 04:29
♋ 10 17:03
♌ 13 03:56
♍ 15 12:25
♎ 17 18:48
♏ 19 23:35
♐ 22 03:02
♑ 24 05:30
♒ 26 07:41
♓ 28 10:46
♈ 30 16:11

Sep 1977
♉ 2 00:51

☽ Moon

Sep 1977
♊ 4 12:26
♋ 7 01:02
♌ 9 12:13
♍ 11 20:34
♎ 14 02:07
♏ 16 05:45
♐ 18 08:28
♑ 20 11:04
♒ 22 14:12
♓ 24 18:29
♈ 27 00:40
♉ 29 09:21

Oct 1977
♊ 1 20:33
♋ 4 09:08
♌ 6 20:57
♍ 9 05:58
♎ 11 11:29
♏ 13 14:11
♐ 15 15:27
♑ 17 16:51
♒ 19 19:35
♓ 22 00:26
♈ 24 07:33
♉ 26 16:52
♊ 29 04:07
♋ 31 16:39

Nov 1977
♌ 3 05:02
♍ 5 15:16
♎ 7 21:50
♏ 10 00:41
♐ 12 01:03
♑ 14 00:50
♒ 16 01:59
♓ 18 05:58
♈ 20 13:12
♉ 22 23:09
♊ 25 10:48
♋ 27 23:19
♌ 30 11:52

Dec 1977
♍ 2 23:05
♎ 5 07:17
♏ 7 11:33
♐ 9 12:22
♑ 11 11:26
♒ 13 11:00
♓ 15 13:09
♈ 17 19:10
♉ 20 04:53
♊ 22 16:50
♋ 25 05:29
♌ 27 17:51
♍ 30 05:13

Jan 1978
♎ 1 14:30
♏ 3 20:34
♐ 5 23:03
♑ 7 22:54
♒ 9 22:05
♓ 11 22:50
♈ 14 03:04
♉ 16 11:29
♊ 18 23:06
♋ 21 11:50
♌ 24 00:02
♍ 26 10:55
♎ 28 20:07
♏ 31 03:03

Feb 1978
♐ 2 07:13

☽ Moon

Feb 1978
♑ 4 08:50
♒ 6 09:05
♓ 8 09:48
♈ 10 12:56
♉ 12 19:50
♊ 15 06:23
♋ 17 18:55
♌ 20 07:09
♍ 22 17:39
♎ 25 02:03
♏ 27 08:27

Mar 1978
♐ 1 13:01
♑ 3 15:58
♒ 5 17:51
♓ 7 19:45
♈ 9 23:08
♉ 12 05:17
♊ 14 14:47
♋ 17 02:48
♌ 19 15:11
♍ 22 01:49
♎ 24 09:41
♏ 26 15:01
♐ 28 18:37
♑ 30 21:23

Apr 1978
♒ 2 00:04
♓ 4 03:20
♈ 6 07:50
♉ 8 14:21
♊ 10 23:27
♋ 13 10:58
♌ 15 23:30
♍ 18 10:43
♎ 20 18:52
♏ 22 23:38
♐ 25 02:00
♑ 27 03:27
♒ 29 05:27

May 1978
♓ 1 08:59
♈ 3 14:26
♉ 5 21:52
♊ 8 07:18
♋ 10 18:41
♌ 13 07:16
♍ 15 19:14
♎ 18 04:24
♏ 20 09:38
♐ 22 11:31
♑ 24 11:42
♒ 26 12:10
♓ 28 14:36
♈ 30 19:51

Jun 1978
♉ 2 03:49
♊ 4 13:53
♋ 7 01:30
♌ 9 14:06
♍ 12 02:34
♎ 14 12:54
♏ 16 19:28
♐ 18 22:01
♑ 20 21:52
♒ 22 21:07
♓ 24 21:56
♈ 27 01:52
♉ 29 09:20

Jul 1978
♊ 1 19:37
♋ 4 07:33

☽ Moon

Jul 1978
♌ 6 20:12
♍ 9 08:44
♎ 11 19:47
♏ 14 03:46
♐ 16 07:49
♑ 18 08:33
♒ 20 07:42
♓ 22 07:26
♈ 24 09:45
♉ 26 15:49
♊ 29 01:30
♋ 31 13:27

Aug 1978
♌ 3 02:10
♍ 5 14:28
♎ 8 01:29
♏ 10 10:10
♐ 12 15:42
♑ 14 18:03
♒ 16 18:15
♓ 18 18:05
♈ 20 19:29
♉ 23 00:05
♊ 25 08:30
♋ 27 19:58
♌ 30 08:39

Sep 1978
♍ 1 20:46
♎ 4 07:15
♏ 6 15:37
♐ 8 21:39
♑ 11 01:19
♒ 13 03:08
♓ 15 04:09
♈ 17 05:50
♉ 19 09:42
♊ 21 16:55
♋ 24 03:30
♌ 26 16:00
♍ 29 04:10

Oct 1978
♎ 1 14:16
♏ 3 21:47
♐ 6 03:06
♑ 8 06:52
♒ 10 09:42
♓ 12 12:12
♈ 14 15:06
♉ 16 19:22
♊ 19 02:05
♋ 21 11:51
♌ 24 00:03
♍ 26 12:31
♎ 28 22:50
♏ 31 05:52

Nov 1978
♐ 2 10:03
♑ 4 12:40
♒ 6 15:03
♓ 8 18:05
♈ 10 22:11
♉ 13 03:34
♊ 15 10:44
♋ 17 20:15
♌ 20 08:08
♍ 22 20:56
♎ 25 08:06
♏ 27 15:38
♐ 29 19:23

Dec 1978
♑ 1 20:44
♒ 3 21:35

☽ Moon

Dec 1978
♓ 5 23:36
♈ 8 03:39
♉ 10 09:50
♊ 12 17:54
♋ 15 03:49
♌ 17 15:37
♍ 20 04:33
♎ 22 16:39
♏ 25 01:32
♐ 27 06:07
♑ 29 07:16
♒ 31 06:53

Jan 1979
♓ 2 07:08
♈ 4 09:41
♉ 6 15:17
♊ 8 23:42
♋ 11 10:14
♌ 13 22:16
♍ 16 11:09
♎ 18 23:40
♏ 21 09:50
♐ 23 16:07
♑ 25 18:27
♒ 27 18:12
♓ 29 17:26
♈ 31 18:11

Feb 1979
♉ 2 22:02
♊ 5 05:32
♋ 7 16:05
♌ 10 04:25
♍ 12 17:17
♎ 15 05:36
♏ 17 16:11
♐ 19 23:50
♑ 22 04:00
♒ 24 05:12
♓ 26 04:52
♈ 28 04:54

Mar 1979
♉ 2 07:09
♊ 4 12:57
♋ 6 22:33
♌ 9 10:46
♍ 11 23:42
♎ 14 11:41
♏ 16 21:49
♐ 19 05:37
♑ 21 10:56
♒ 23 13:52
♓ 25 15:05
♈ 27 15:48
♉ 29 17:36
♊ 31 22:08

Apr 1979
♋ 3 06:23
♌ 5 17:57
♍ 8 06:51
♎ 10 18:44
♏ 13 04:15
♐ 15 11:18
♑ 17 16:22
♒ 19 20:02
♓ 21 22:41
♈ 24 00:51
♉ 26 03:27
♊ 28 07:48
♋ 30 15:11

May 1979
♌ 3 01:56
♍ 5 14:40

☽ Moon

May 1979
♎ 8 02:47
♏ 10 12:09
♐ 12 18:24
♑ 14 22:25
♒ 17 01:25
♓ 19 04:18
♈ 21 07:30
♉ 23 11:20
♊ 25 16:28
♋ 27 23:50
♌ 30 10:07

Jun 1979
♍ 1 22:40
♎ 4 11:10
♏ 6 21:04
♐ 9 03:14
♑ 11 06:23
♒ 13 08:06
♓ 15 09:56
♈ 17 12:52
♉ 19 17:18
♊ 21 23:22
♋ 24 07:24
♌ 26 17:46
♍ 29 06:13

Jul 1979
♎ 1 19:07
♏ 4 05:56
♐ 6 12:55
♑ 8 16:07
♒ 10 16:59
♓ 12 17:23
♈ 14 18:57
♉ 16 22:42
♊ 19 04:59
♋ 21 13:40
♌ 24 00:29
♍ 26 13:00
♎ 29 02:05
♏ 31 13:45

Aug 1979
♐ 2 22:05
♑ 5 02:22
♒ 7 03:28
♓ 9 03:05
♈ 11 03:10
♉ 13 05:21
♊ 15 10:40
♋ 17 19:16
♌ 20 06:28
♍ 22 19:10
♎ 25 08:13
♏ 27 20:12
♐ 30 05:38

Sep 1979
♑ 1 11:33
♒ 3 13:59
♓ 5 14:03
♈ 7 13:29
♉ 9 14:12
♊ 11 17:53
♋ 14 01:26
♌ 16 12:24
♍ 19 01:15
♎ 21 14:10
♏ 24 01:53
♐ 26 11:35
♑ 28 18:39
♒ 30 22:48

Oct 1979
♓ 3 00:23
♈ 5 00:28

☽ Moon

Oct 1979
♉ 7 00:44
♊ 9 03:07
♋ 11 09:08
♌ 13 19:11
♍ 16 07:50
♎ 18 20:44
♏ 21 08:02
♐ 23 17:09
♑ 26 00:11
♒ 28 05:16
♓ 30 08:28

Nov 1979
♈ 1 10:09
♉ 3 11:16
♊ 5 13:26
♋ 7 18:23
♌ 10 03:14
♍ 12 15:19
♎ 15 04:16
♏ 17 15:29
♐ 19 23:56
♑ 22 06:01
♒ 24 10:36
♓ 26 14:17
♈ 28 17:16
♉ 30 19:54

Dec 1979
♊ 2 23:02
♋ 5 04:01
♌ 7 12:08
♍ 9 23:32
♎ 12 12:28
♏ 15 00:07
♐ 17 08:36
♑ 19 13:54
♒ 21 17:12
♓ 23 19:50
♈ 25 22:40
♉ 28 02:07
♊ 30 06:32

Jan 1980
♋ 1 12:29
♌ 3 20:47
♍ 6 07:47
♎ 8 20:37
♏ 11 08:54
♐ 13 18:16
♑ 15 23:51
♒ 18 02:24
♓ 20 03:33
♈ 22 04:51
♉ 24 07:31
♊ 26 12:10
♋ 28 19:02
♌ 31 04:08

Feb 1980
♍ 2 15:20
♎ 5 04:03
♏ 7 16:45
♐ 10 03:18
♑ 12 10:11
♒ 14 13:19
♓ 16 13:54
♈ 18 13:43
♉ 20 14:35
♊ 22 17:57
♋ 25 00:34
♌ 27 10:09
♍ 29 21:52

Mar 1980
♎ 3 10:39
♏ 5 23:22

☽ Moon

Mar 1980
♐ 8 10:37
♑ 10 19:01
♒ 12 23:45
♓ 15 01:10
♈ 17 00:40
♉ 19 00:12
♊ 21 01:47
♋ 23 06:55
♌ 25 15:57
♍ 28 03:51
♎ 30 16:48

Apr 1980
♏ 2 05:21
♐ 4 16:34
♑ 7 01:42
♒ 9 07:59
♓ 11 11:06
♈ 13 11:40
♉ 15 11:11
♊ 17 11:41
♋ 19 15:11
♌ 21 22:51
♍ 24 10:11
♎ 26 23:09
♏ 29 11:34

May 1980
♐ 1 22:21
♑ 4 07:14
♒ 6 14:03
♓ 8 18:33
♈ 10 20:44
♉ 12 21:24
♊ 14 22:07
♋ 17 00:51
♌ 19 07:13
♍ 21 17:31
♎ 24 06:10
♏ 26 18:36
♐ 29 05:04
♑ 31 13:14

Jun 1980
♒ 2 19:29
♓ 5 00:09
♈ 7 03:23
♉ 9 05:29
♊ 11 07:22
♋ 13 10:29
♌ 15 16:21
♍ 18 01:46
♎ 20 13:54
♏ 23 02:26
♐ 25 13:01
♑ 27 20:45
♒ 30 02:03

Jul 1980
♓ 2 05:48
♈ 4 08:46
♉ 6 11:30
♊ 8 14:33
♋ 10 18:44
♌ 13 01:02
♍ 15 10:10
♎ 17 21:54
♏ 20 10:32
♐ 22 21:41
♑ 25 05:44
♒ 27 10:34
♓ 29 13:11
♈ 31 14:53

Aug 1980
♉ 2 16:55
♊ 4 20:09

☽ Moon

Aug 1980
♋ 7 01:12
♌ 9 08:23
♍ 11 17:54
♎ 14 05:31
♏ 16 18:14
♐ 19 06:07
♑ 21 15:10
♒ 23 20:32
♓ 25 22:43
♈ 27 23:10
♉ 29 23:40

Sep 1980
♊ 1 01:49
♋ 3 06:39
♌ 5 14:21
♍ 8 00:30
♎ 10 12:21
♏ 13 01:05
♐ 15 13:27
♑ 17 23:44
♒ 20 06:30
♓ 22 09:27
♈ 24 09:37
♉ 26 08:53
♊ 28 09:21
♋ 30 12:46

Oct 1980
♌ 2 19:56
♍ 5 06:18
♎ 7 18:30
♏ 10 07:14
♐ 12 19:37
♑ 15 06:36
♒ 17 14:53
♓ 19 19:31
♈ 21 20:43
♉ 23 19:55
♊ 25 19:17
♋ 27 20:59
♌ 30 02:38

Nov 1980
♍ 1 12:17
♎ 4 00:31
♏ 6 13:18
♐ 9 01:25
♑ 11 12:14
♒ 13 21:09
♓ 16 03:20
♈ 18 06:21
♉ 20 06:51
♊ 22 06:27
♋ 24 07:18
♌ 26 11:22
♍ 28 19:36

Dec 1980
♎ 1 07:12
♏ 3 19:59
♐ 6 07:57
♑ 8 18:11
♒ 11 02:35
♓ 13 09:03
♈ 15 13:21
♉ 17 15:36
♊ 19 16:40
♋ 21 18:03
♌ 23 21:33
♍ 26 04:32
♎ 28 15:04
♏ 31 03:35

Jan 1981
♐ 2 15:41
♑ 5 01:41

☽ Moon

Jan 1981
♒ 7 09:12
♓ 9 14:42
♈ 11 18:43
♉ 13 21:44
♊ 16 00:17
♋ 18 03:07
♌ 20 07:20
♍ 22 14:02
♎ 24 23:45
♏ 27 11:48
♐ 30 00:11

Feb 1981
♑ 1 10:36
♒ 3 17:55
♓ 5 22:21
♈ 8 01:01
♉ 10 03:10
♊ 12 05:51
♋ 14 09:42
♌ 16 15:10
♍ 18 22:34
♎ 21 08:11
♏ 23 19:54
♐ 26 08:28
♑ 28 19:45

Mar 1981
♒ 3 03:50
♓ 5 08:12
♈ 7 09:48
♉ 9 10:23
♊ 11 11:42
♋ 13 15:05
♌ 15 21:02
♍ 18 05:19
♎ 20 15:30
♏ 23 03:13
♐ 25 15:50
♑ 28 03:51
♒ 30 13:14

Apr 1981
♓ 1 18:40
♈ 3 20:25
♉ 5 20:04
♊ 7 19:47
♋ 9 21:33
♌ 12 02:36
♍ 14 10:55
♎ 16 21:37
♏ 19 09:38
♐ 21 22:14
♑ 24 10:30
♒ 26 20:56
♓ 29 03:56

May 1981
♈ 1 06:57
♉ 3 06:59
♊ 5 06:01
♋ 7 06:17
♌ 9 09:39
♍ 11 16:54
♎ 14 03:23
♏ 16 15:37
♐ 19 04:13
♑ 21 16:19
♒ 24 03:00
♓ 26 11:04
♈ 28 15:43
♉ 30 17:10

Jun 1981
♊ 1 16:49
♋ 3 16:39
♌ 5 18:42

☽ Moon

Jun 1981
♍ 8 00:25
♎ 10 09:54
♏ 12 21:54
♐ 15 10:31
♑ 17 22:20
♒ 20 08:35
♓ 22 16:43
♈ 24 22:18
♉ 27 01:16
♊ 29 02:21

Jul 1981
♋ 1 02:57
♌ 3 04:47
♍ 5 09:25
♎ 7 17:41
♏ 10 05:01
♐ 12 17:34
♑ 15 05:19
♒ 17 15:01
♓ 19 22:25
♈ 22 03:43
♉ 24 07:18
♊ 26 09:41
♋ 28 11:41
♌ 30 14:20

Aug 1981
♍ 1 18:54
♎ 4 02:23
♏ 6 12:57
♐ 9 01:22
♑ 11 13:19
♒ 13 22:56
♓ 16 05:34
♈ 18 09:49
♉ 20 12:43
♊ 22 15:18
♋ 24 18:16
♌ 26 22:09
♍ 29 03:31
♎ 31 11:02

Sep 1981
♏ 2 21:09
♐ 5 09:23
♑ 7 21:48
♒ 10 07:58
♓ 12 14:33
♈ 14 17:55
♉ 16 19:30
♊ 18 20:59
♋ 20 23:39
♌ 23 04:08
♍ 25 10:28
♎ 27 18:40
♏ 30 04:52

Oct 1981
♐ 2 16:59
♑ 5 05:48
♒ 7 17:00
♓ 10 00:32
♈ 12 04:01
♉ 14 04:43
♊ 16 04:41
♋ 18 05:52
♌ 20 09:34
♍ 22 16:04
♎ 25 00:56
♏ 27 11:37
♐ 29 23:48

Nov 1981
♑ 1 12:45
♒ 4 00:50
♓ 6 09:51

☽ Moon

Nov 1981
♈ 8 14:38
♉ 10 15:45
♊ 12 15:00
♋ 14 14:37
♌ 16 16:32
♍ 18 21:52
♎ 21 06:32
♏ 23 17:36
♐ 26 06:00
♑ 28 18:52

Dec 1981
♒ 1 07:08
♓ 3 17:15
♈ 5 23:48
♉ 8 02:31
♊ 10 02:30
♋ 12 01:40
♌ 14 02:08
♍ 16 05:37
♎ 18 12:57
♏ 20 23:38
♐ 23 12:10
♑ 26 00:59
♒ 28 12:53
♓ 30 23:00

Jan 1982
♈ 2 06:32
♉ 4 11:02
♊ 6 12:49
♋ 8 13:01
♌ 10 13:21
♍ 12 15:37
♎ 14 21:16
♏ 17 06:45
♐ 19 18:59
♑ 22 07:50
♒ 24 19:24
♓ 27 04:49
♈ 29 11:58
♉ 31 17:03

Feb 1982
♊ 2 20:20
♋ 4 22:17
♌ 6 23:49
♍ 9 02:15
♎ 11 07:01
♏ 13 15:15
♐ 16 02:44
♑ 18 15:35
♒ 21 03:14
♓ 23 12:08
♈ 25 18:17
♉ 27 22:31

Mar 1982
♊ 2 01:49
♋ 4 04:48
♌ 6 07:50
♍ 8 11:27
♎ 10 16:33
♏ 13 00:16
♐ 15 11:02
♑ 17 23:46
♒ 20 11:52
♓ 22 21:01
♈ 25 02:37
♉ 27 05:39
♊ 29 07:44
♋ 31 10:09

Apr 1982
♌ 2 13:36
♍ 4 18:18
♎ 7 00:26

☽ Moon

Apr 1982
♏ 9 08:32
♐ 11 19:06
♑ 14 07:40
♒ 16 20:17
♓ 19 06:19
♈ 21 12:22
♉ 23 14:59
♊ 25 15:48
♋ 27 16:43
♌ 29 19:09

May 1982
♍ 1 23:44
♎ 4 06:32
♏ 6 15:23
♐ 9 02:16
♑ 11 14:49
♒ 14 03:43
♓ 16 14:45
♈ 18 22:03
♉ 21 01:21
♊ 23 01:54
♋ 25 01:38
♌ 27 02:26
♍ 29 05:43
♎ 31 12:02

Jun 1982
♏ 2 21:11
♐ 5 08:31
♑ 7 21:11
♒ 10 10:07
♓ 12 21:43
♈ 15 06:19
♉ 17 11:06
♊ 19 12:34
♋ 21 12:13
♌ 23 11:57
♍ 25 13:36
♎ 27 18:29
♏ 30 03:01

Jul 1982
♐ 2 14:24
♑ 5 03:14
♒ 7 16:02
♓ 10 03:35
♈ 12 12:48
♉ 14 18:59
♊ 16 22:03
♋ 18 22:46
♌ 20 22:35
♍ 22 23:19
♎ 25 02:44
♏ 27 09:57
♐ 29 20:47

Aug 1982
♑ 1 09:35
♒ 3 22:16
♓ 6 09:23
♈ 8 18:20
♉ 11 01:00
♊ 13 05:21
♋ 15 07:40
♌ 17 08:40
♍ 19 09:40
♎ 21 12:22
♏ 23 18:20
♐ 26 04:10
♑ 28 16:41
♒ 31 05:23

Sep 1982
♓ 2 16:10
♈ 5 00:23
♉ 7 06:26

☽ Moon

Sep 1982
♊ 9 10:57
♋ 11 14:18
♌ 13 16:46
♍ 15 18:57
♎ 17 22:02
♏ 20 03:32
♐ 22 12:29
♑ 25 00:31
♒ 27 13:20
♓ 30 00:18

Oct 1982
♈ 2 08:05
♉ 4 13:09
♊ 6 16:39
♋ 8 19:39
♌ 10 22:44
♍ 13 02:08
♎ 15 06:22
♏ 17 12:20
♐ 19 21:02
♑ 22 08:37
♒ 24 21:35
♓ 27 09:11
♈ 29 17:24
♉ 31 22:03

Nov 1982
♊ 3 00:22
♋ 5 01:58
♌ 7 04:10
♍ 9 07:39
♎ 11 12:45
♏ 13 19:42
♐ 16 04:51
♑ 18 16:20
♒ 21 05:20
♓ 23 17:41
♈ 26 03:06
♉ 28 08:31
♊ 30 10:36

Dec 1982
♋ 2 10:58
♌ 4 11:26
♍ 6 13:32
♎ 8 18:10
♏ 11 01:34
♐ 13 11:26
♑ 15 23:15
♒ 18 12:11
♓ 21 00:55
♈ 23 11:33
♉ 25 18:36
♊ 27 21:48
♋ 29 22:12
♌ 31 21:33

Jan 1983
♍ 2 21:49
♎ 5 00:44
♏ 7 07:15
♐ 9 17:13
♑ 12 05:25
♒ 14 18:26
♓ 17 07:02
♈ 19 18:07
♉ 22 02:35
♊ 24 07:39
♋ 26 09:28
♌ 28 09:10
♍ 30 08:35

Feb 1983
♎ 1 09:47
♏ 3 14:31
♐ 5 23:28

☽ Moon

Feb 1983
♑ 8 11:32
♒ 11 00:40
♓ 13 13:01
♈ 15 23:45
♉ 18 08:30
♊ 20 14:51
♋ 22 18:31
♌ 24 19:46
♍ 26 19:49
♎ 28 20:30

Mar 1983
♏ 2 23:50
♐ 5 07:14
♑ 7 18:28
♒ 10 07:29
♓ 12 19:46
♈ 15 06:00
♉ 17 14:04
♊ 19 20:19
♋ 22 00:52
♌ 24 03:43
♍ 26 05:18
♎ 28 06:48
♏ 30 09:56

Apr 1983
♐ 1 16:19
♑ 4 02:29
♒ 6 15:05
♓ 9 03:30
♈ 11 13:36
♉ 13 20:58
♊ 16 02:14
♋ 18 06:13
♌ 20 09:26
♍ 22 12:11
♎ 24 15:04
♏ 26 19:04
♐ 29 01:28

May 1983
♑ 1 11:00
♒ 3 23:08
♓ 6 11:42
♈ 8 22:16
♉ 11 05:35
♊ 13 10:03
♋ 15 12:48
♌ 17 15:01
♍ 19 17:36
♎ 21 21:11
♏ 24 02:17
♐ 26 09:27
♑ 28 19:06
♒ 31 06:59

Jun 1983
♓ 2 19:41
♈ 5 06:58
♉ 7 15:04
♊ 9 19:37
♋ 11 21:32
♌ 13 22:21
♍ 15 23:37
♎ 18 02:36
♏ 20 07:59
♐ 22 15:54
♑ 25 02:08
♒ 27 14:06
♓ 30 02:51

Jul 1983
♈ 2 14:46
♉ 5 00:05
♊ 7 05:41
♋ 9 07:50

☽ Moon

Jul 1983
♌ 11 07:54
♍ 13 07:43
♎ 15 09:10
♏ 17 13:37
♐ 19 21:31
♑ 22 08:10
♒ 24 20:26
♓ 27 09:10
♈ 29 21:20

Aug 1983
♉ 1 07:36
♊ 3 14:42
♋ 5 18:08
♌ 7 18:37
♍ 9 17:49
♎ 11 17:51
♏ 13 20:43
♐ 16 03:33
♑ 18 13:58
♒ 21 02:25
♓ 23 15:09
♈ 26 03:07
♉ 28 13:37
♊ 30 21:48

Sep 1983
♋ 2 02:52
♌ 4 04:47
♍ 6 04:36
♎ 8 04:13
♏ 10 05:49
♐ 12 11:07
♑ 14 20:33
♒ 17 08:45
♓ 19 21:29
♈ 22 09:10
♉ 24 19:12
♊ 27 03:24
♋ 29 09:24

Oct 1983
♌ 1 12:54
♍ 3 14:15
♎ 5 14:42
♏ 7 16:06
♐ 9 20:20
♑ 12 04:29
♒ 14 15:59
♓ 17 04:40
♈ 19 16:18
♉ 22 01:47
♊ 24 09:10
♋ 26 14:46
♌ 28 18:50
♍ 30 21:32

Nov 1983
♎ 1 23:30
♏ 4 01:53
♐ 6 06:08
♑ 8 13:30
♒ 11 00:10
♓ 13 12:40
♈ 16 00:36
♉ 18 10:06
♊ 20 16:45
♋ 22 21:10
♌ 25 00:19
♍ 27 03:01
♎ 29 05:56

Dec 1983
♏ 1 09:40
♐ 3 14:56
♑ 5 22:28
♒ 8 08:38

☽ Moon

Dec 1983
♓ 10 20:52
♈ 13 09:16
♉ 15 19:32
♊ 18 02:23
♋ 20 06:02
♌ 22 07:44
♍ 24 09:01
♎ 26 11:18
♏ 28 15:26
♐ 30 21:43

Jan 1984
♑ 2 06:07
♒ 4 16:30
♓ 7 04:33
♈ 9 17:14
♉ 12 04:35
♊ 14 12:39
♋ 16 16:47
♌ 18 17:50
♍ 20 17:36
♎ 22 18:07
♏ 24 21:03
♐ 27 03:12
♑ 29 12:12
♒ 31 23:10

Feb 1984
♓ 3 11:21
♈ 6 00:03
♉ 8 12:04
♊ 10 21:38
♋ 13 03:20
♌ 15 05:09
♍ 17 04:32
♎ 19 03:39
♏ 21 04:44
♐ 23 09:21
♑ 25 17:48
♒ 28 05:01

Mar 1984
♓ 1 17:29
♈ 4 06:06
♉ 6 18:08
♊ 9 04:29
♋ 11 11:47
♌ 13 15:21
♍ 15 15:47
♎ 17 14:52
♏ 19 14:49
♐ 21 17:40
♑ 24 00:36
♒ 26 11:08
♓ 28 23:37
♈ 31 12:13

Apr 1984
♉ 2 23:55
♊ 5 10:04
♋ 7 17:59
♌ 9 23:01
♍ 12 01:11
♎ 14 01:29
♏ 16 01:41
♐ 18 03:43
♑ 20 09:10
♒ 22 18:26
♓ 25 06:25
♈ 27 19:02
♉ 30 06:30

May 1984
♊ 2 16:01
♋ 4 23:25
♌ 7 04:42
♍ 9 08:02

☽ Moon

May 1984
♎ 11 09:54
♏ 13 11:22
♐ 15 13:50
♑ 17 18:43
♒ 20 02:55
♓ 22 14:08
♈ 25 02:39
♉ 27 14:13
♊ 29 23:22

Jun 1984
♋ 1 05:53
♌ 3 10:19
♍ 5 13:27
♎ 7 16:03
♏ 9 18:48
♐ 11 22:26
♑ 14 03:48
♒ 16 11:40
♓ 18 22:17
♈ 21 10:39
♉ 23 22:37
♊ 26 08:03
♋ 28 14:09
♌ 30 17:30

Jul 1984
♍ 2 19:27
♎ 4 21:26
♏ 7 00:28
♐ 9 05:02
♑ 11 11:22
♒ 13 19:41
♓ 16 06:10
♈ 18 18:25
♉ 21 06:51
♊ 23 17:09
♋ 25 23:43
♌ 28 02:41
♍ 30 03:29

Aug 1984
♎ 1 04:03
♏ 3 06:04
♐ 5 10:29
♑ 7 17:24
♒ 10 02:25
♓ 12 13:12
♈ 15 01:27
♉ 17 14:12
♊ 20 01:31
♋ 22 09:20
♌ 24 13:00
♍ 26 13:33
♎ 28 12:57
♏ 30 13:23

Sep 1984
♐ 1 16:29
♑ 3 22:54
♒ 6 08:11
♓ 8 19:24
♈ 11 07:46
♉ 13 20:32
♊ 16 08:25
♋ 18 17:35
♌ 20 22:48
♍ 23 00:19
♎ 24 23:41
♏ 26 23:04
♐ 29 00:31

Oct 1984
♑ 1 05:27
♒ 3 14:02
♓ 6 01:19
♈ 8 13:50

☽ Moon

Oct 1984
♉ 11 02:28
♊ 13 14:13
♋ 15 23:59
♌ 18 06:40
♍ 20 09:56
♎ 22 10:32
♏ 24 10:08
♐ 26 10:43
♑ 28 14:04
♒ 30 21:12

Nov 1984
♓ 2 07:49
♈ 4 20:20
♉ 7 08:53
♊ 9 20:10
♋ 12 05:30
♌ 14 12:33
♍ 16 17:07
♎ 18 19:29
♏ 20 20:30
♐ 22 21:34
♑ 25 00:17
♒ 27 06:05
♓ 29 15:32

Dec 1984
♈ 2 03:41
♉ 4 16:19
♊ 7 03:23
♋ 9 11:56
♌ 11 18:08
♍ 13 22:35
♎ 16 01:51
♏ 18 04:27
♐ 20 06:58
♑ 22 10:20
♒ 24 15:47
♓ 27 00:18
♈ 29 11:48

Jan 1985
♉ 1 00:36
♊ 3 11:59
♋ 5 20:17
♌ 8 01:28
♍ 10 04:39
♎ 12 07:13
♏ 14 10:07
♐ 16 13:48
♑ 18 18:28
♒ 21 00:38
♓ 23 09:01
♈ 25 20:04
♉ 28 08:52
♊ 30 21:00

Feb 1985
♋ 2 05:58
♌ 4 11:02
♍ 6 13:09
♎ 8 14:11
♏ 10 15:49
♐ 12 19:08
♑ 15 00:26
♒ 17 07:36
♓ 19 16:37
♈ 22 03:42
♉ 24 16:26
♊ 27 05:10

Mar 1985
♋ 1 15:22
♌ 3 21:28
♍ 5 23:42
♎ 7 23:47
♏ 9 23:47

☽ Moon

Mar 1985
♐ 12 01:28
♑ 14 05:54
♒ 16 13:10
♓ 18 22:50
♈ 21 10:19
♉ 23 23:06
♊ 26 12:01
♋ 28 23:13
♌ 31 06:51

Apr 1985
♍ 2 10:25
♎ 4 10:54
♏ 6 10:11
♐ 8 10:17
♑ 10 12:56
♒ 12 19:03
♓ 15 04:30
♈ 17 16:17
♉ 20 05:12
♊ 22 18:00
♋ 25 05:25
♌ 27 14:09
♍ 29 19:24

May 1985
♎ 1 21:22
♏ 3 21:17
♐ 5 20:56
♑ 7 22:11
♒ 10 02:37
♓ 12 10:55
♈ 14 22:25
♉ 17 11:23
♊ 20 00:00
♋ 22 11:04
♌ 24 19:53
♍ 27 02:06
♎ 29 05:40
♏ 31 07:07

Jun 1985
♐ 2 07:33
♑ 4 08:34
♒ 6 11:51
♓ 8 18:46
♈ 11 05:23
♉ 13 18:10
♊ 16 06:44
♋ 18 17:21
♌ 21 01:31
♍ 23 07:32
♎ 25 11:47
♏ 27 14:37
♐ 29 16:30

Jul 1985
♑ 1 18:22
♒ 3 21:35
♓ 6 03:40
♈ 8 13:19
♉ 11 01:43
♊ 13 14:22
♋ 16 00:54
♌ 18 08:25
♍ 20 13:29
♎ 22 17:10
♏ 24 20:16
♐ 26 23:12
♑ 29 02:21
♒ 31 06:25

Aug 1985
♓ 2 12:33
♈ 4 21:42
♉ 7 09:40
♊ 9 22:31

☽ Moon

Aug 1985
♋ 12 09:27
♌ 14 16:57
♍ 16 21:15
♎ 18 23:43
♏ 21 01:51
♐ 23 04:36
♑ 25 08:24
♒ 27 13:31
♓ 29 20:24

Sep 1985
♈ 1 05:41
♉ 3 17:27
♊ 6 06:26
♋ 8 18:09
♌ 11 02:27
♍ 13 06:52
♎ 15 08:34
♏ 17 09:17
♐ 19 10:40
♑ 21 13:49
♒ 23 19:11
♓ 26 02:50
♈ 28 12:42

Oct 1985
♉ 1 00:34
♊ 3 13:35
♋ 6 01:58
♌ 8 11:33
♍ 10 17:09
♎ 12 19:12
♏ 14 19:13
♐ 16 19:05
♑ 18 20:35
♒ 21 00:54
♓ 23 08:27
♈ 25 18:46
♉ 28 06:59
♊ 30 19:58

Nov 1985
♋ 2 08:30
♌ 4 19:03
♍ 7 02:18
♎ 9 05:51
♏ 11 06:31
♐ 13 05:52
♑ 15 05:53
♒ 17 08:25
♓ 19 14:41
♈ 22 00:42
♉ 24 13:06
♊ 27 02:07
♋ 29 14:22

Dec 1985
♌ 2 00:59
♍ 4 09:13
♎ 6 14:33
♏ 8 16:56
♐ 10 17:13
♑ 12 17:00
♒ 14 18:15
♓ 16 22:49
♈ 19 07:36
♉ 21 19:40
♊ 24 08:44
♋ 26 20:43
♌ 29 06:44
♍ 31 14:43

Jan 1986
♎ 2 20:45
♏ 5 00:44
♐ 7 02:47
♑ 9 03:42

☽ Moon

Jan 1986
♒ 11 05:01
♓ 13 08:39
♈ 15 16:02
♉ 18 03:13
♊ 20 16:11
♋ 23 04:14
♌ 25 13:47
♍ 27 20:51
♎ 30 02:09

Feb 1986
♏ 1 06:19
♐ 3 09:31
♑ 5 12:01
♒ 7 14:35
♓ 9 18:32
♈ 12 01:20
♉ 14 11:37
♊ 17 00:16
♋ 19 12:38
♌ 21 22:24
♍ 24 04:58
♎ 26 09:07
♏ 28 12:06

Mar 1986
♐ 2 14:51
♑ 4 17:55
♒ 6 21:42
♓ 9 02:48
♈ 11 10:03
♉ 13 20:03
♊ 16 08:22
♋ 18 21:04
♌ 21 07:38
♍ 23 14:39
♎ 25 18:22
♏ 27 20:05
♐ 29 21:20
♑ 31 23:25

Apr 1986
♒ 3 03:11
♓ 5 09:03
♈ 7 17:11
♉ 10 03:35
♊ 12 15:50
♋ 15 04:41
♌ 17 16:09
♍ 20 00:23
♎ 22 04:50
♏ 24 06:15
♐ 26 06:16
♑ 28 06:41
♒ 30 09:05

May 1986
♓ 2 14:29
♈ 4 23:00
♉ 7 09:58
♊ 9 22:25
♋ 12 11:17
♌ 14 23:14
♍ 17 08:44
♎ 19 14:40
♏ 21 17:02
♐ 23 16:57
♑ 25 16:15
♒ 27 17:00
♓ 29 20:54

Jun 1986
♈ 1 04:42
♉ 3 15:44
♊ 6 04:26
♋ 8 17:15
♌ 11 05:11

☽ Moon

Jun 1986
♍ 13 15:17
♎ 15 22:37
♏ 18 02:36
♐ 20 03:35
♑ 22 03:00
♒ 24 02:50
♓ 26 05:12
♈ 28 11:34
♉ 30 21:53

Jul 1986
♊ 3 10:31
♋ 5 23:19
♌ 8 10:55
♍ 10 20:49
♎ 13 04:39
♏ 15 09:58
♐ 17 12:34
♑ 19 13:10
♒ 21 13:18
♓ 23 14:59
♈ 25 20:02
♉ 28 05:10
♊ 30 17:18

Aug 1986
♋ 2 06:03
♌ 4 17:26
♍ 7 02:44
♎ 9 10:04
♏ 11 15:35
♐ 13 19:17
♑ 15 21:22
♒ 17 22:44
♓ 20 00:52
♈ 22 05:27
♉ 24 13:35
♊ 27 01:00
♋ 29 13:39

Sep 1986
♌ 1 01:08
♍ 3 10:05
♎ 5 16:33
♏ 7 21:11
♐ 10 00:40
♑ 12 03:28
♒ 14 06:07
♓ 16 09:27
♈ 18 14:33
♉ 20 22:25
♊ 23 09:13
♋ 25 21:44
♌ 28 09:38
♍ 30 18:57

Oct 1986
♎ 3 01:02
♏ 5 04:35
♐ 7 06:47
♑ 9 08:52
♒ 11 11:45
♓ 13 16:03
♈ 15 22:13
♉ 18 06:35
♊ 20 17:14
♋ 23 05:36
♌ 25 18:01
♍ 28 04:19
♎ 30 11:04

Nov 1986
♏ 1 14:19
♐ 3 15:19
♑ 5 15:49
♒ 7 17:28
♓ 9 21:29

☽ Moon

Nov 1986
♈ 12 04:14
♉ 14 13:24
♊ 17 00:26
♋ 19 12:45
♌ 22 01:24
♍ 24 12:45
♎ 26 20:58
♏ 29 01:13

Dec 1986
♐ 1 02:08
♑ 3 01:28
♒ 5 01:23
♓ 7 03:48
♈ 9 09:48
♉ 11 19:09
♊ 14 06:41
♋ 16 19:09
♌ 19 07:43
♍ 21 19:30
♎ 24 05:04
♏ 26 11:06
♐ 28 13:20
♑ 30 12:55

Jan 1987
♒ 1 11:54
♓ 3 12:36
♈ 5 16:50
♉ 8 01:12
♊ 10 12:38
♋ 13 01:18
♌ 15 13:44
♍ 18 01:14
♎ 20 11:08
♏ 22 18:29
♐ 24 22:35
♑ 26 23:42
♒ 28 23:17
♓ 30 23:24

Feb 1987
♈ 2 02:09
♉ 4 08:52
♊ 6 19:22
♋ 9 07:54
♌ 11 20:21
♍ 14 07:25
♎ 16 16:44
♏ 19 00:04
♐ 21 05:09
♑ 23 07:57
♒ 25 09:09
♓ 27 10:07

Mar 1987
♈ 1 12:37
♉ 3 18:11
♊ 6 03:26
♋ 8 15:23
♌ 11 03:54
♍ 13 14:54
♎ 15 23:34
♏ 18 05:57
♐ 20 10:32
♑ 22 13:48
♒ 24 16:18
♓ 26 18:45
♈ 28 22:12
♉ 31 03:46

Apr 1987
♊ 2 12:16
♋ 4 23:33
♌ 7 12:03
♍ 9 23:27
♎ 12 08:05

☽ Moon

Apr 1987
♏ 14 13:40
♐ 16 17:01
♑ 18 19:21
♒ 20 21:45
♓ 23 01:01
♈ 25 05:40
♉ 27 12:05
♊ 29 20:42

May 1987
♋ 2 07:38
♌ 4 20:06
♍ 7 08:06
♎ 9 17:28
♏ 11 23:09
♐ 14 01:41
♑ 16 02:36
♒ 18 03:42
♓ 20 06:24
♈ 22 11:22
♉ 24 18:38
♊ 27 03:55
♋ 29 14:59

Jun 1987
♌ 1 03:25
♍ 3 15:55
♎ 6 02:24
♏ 8 09:06
♐ 10 11:53
♑ 12 12:05
♒ 14 11:45
♓ 16 12:54
♈ 18 16:55
♉ 21 00:08
♊ 23 09:54
♋ 25 21:22
♌ 28 09:51
♍ 30 22:33

Jul 1987
♎ 3 09:54
♏ 5 18:02
♐ 7 22:05
♑ 9 22:43
♒ 11 21:49
♓ 13 21:36
♈ 16 00:00
♉ 18 06:04
♊ 20 15:32
♋ 23 03:12
♌ 25 15:49
♍ 28 04:25
♎ 30 15:59

Aug 1987
♏ 2 01:09
♐ 4 06:47
♑ 6 08:51
♒ 8 08:37
♓ 10 08:01
♈ 12 09:09
♉ 14 13:37
♊ 16 21:58
♋ 19 09:18
♌ 21 21:57
♍ 24 10:23
♎ 26 21:35
♏ 29 06:49
♐ 31 13:23

Sep 1987
♑ 2 17:04
♒ 4 18:22
♓ 6 18:37
♈ 8 19:34
♉ 10 22:57

☽ Moon

Sep 1987
♊ 13 05:54
♋ 15 16:21
♌ 18 04:49
♍ 20 17:12
♎ 23 03:58
♏ 25 12:30
♐ 27 18:48
♑ 29 23:08

Oct 1987
♒ 2 01:51
♓ 4 03:39
♈ 6 05:35
♉ 8 08:57
♊ 10 15:03
♋ 13 00:30
♌ 15 12:33
♍ 18 01:05
♎ 20 11:49
♏ 22 19:41
♐ 25 00:57
♑ 27 04:32
♒ 29 07:26
♓ 31 10:19

Nov 1987
♈ 2 13:39
♉ 4 18:02
♊ 7 00:15
♋ 9 09:09
♌ 11 20:44
♍ 14 09:28
♎ 16 20:47
♏ 19 04:46
♐ 21 09:16
♑ 23 11:32
♒ 25 13:13
♓ 27 15:40
♈ 29 19:35

Dec 1987
♉ 2 01:05
♊ 4 08:13
♋ 6 17:19
♌ 9 04:39
♍ 11 17:29
♎ 14 05:39
♏ 16 14:40
♐ 18 19:33
♑ 20 21:07
♒ 22 21:20
♓ 24 22:10
♈ 27 01:05
♉ 29 06:36
♊ 31 14:28

Jan 1988
♋ 3 00:16
♌ 5 11:47
♍ 8 00:34
♎ 10 13:16
♏ 12 23:39
♐ 15 05:58
♑ 17 08:15
♒ 19 08:02
♓ 21 07:27
♈ 23 08:31
♉ 25 12:36
♊ 27 20:01
♋ 30 06:11

Feb 1988
♌ 1 18:05
♍ 4 06:54
♎ 6 19:35
♏ 9 06:41
♐ 11 14:35

☽ Moon

Feb 1988
♑ 13 18:36
♒ 15 19:25
♓ 17 18:44
♈ 19 18:35
♉ 21 20:50
♊ 24 02:41
♋ 26 12:11
♌ 29 00:12

Mar 1988
♍ 2 13:05
♎ 5 01:31
♏ 7 12:26
♐ 9 20:58
♑ 12 02:31
♒ 14 05:07
♓ 16 05:42
♈ 18 05:45
♉ 20 07:05
♊ 22 11:20
♋ 24 19:26
♌ 27 06:53
♍ 29 19:48

Apr 1988
♎ 1 08:04
♏ 3 18:25
♐ 6 02:28
♑ 8 08:19
♒ 10 12:10
♓ 12 14:24
♈ 14 15:47
♉ 16 17:31
♊ 18 21:10
♋ 21 04:04
♌ 23 14:33
♍ 26 03:15
♎ 28 15:36

May 1988
♏ 1 01:39
♐ 3 08:52
♑ 5 13:54
♒ 7 17:36
♓ 9 20:38
♈ 11 23:23
♉ 14 02:21
♊ 16 06:31
♋ 18 13:05
♌ 20 22:51
♍ 23 11:11
♎ 25 23:49
♏ 28 10:05
♐ 30 16:57

Jun 1988
♑ 1 20:58
♒ 3 23:33
♓ 6 02:00
♈ 8 05:03
♉ 10 09:02
♊ 12 14:14
♋ 14 21:18
♌ 17 06:57
♍ 19 19:02
♎ 22 07:56
♏ 24 18:57
♐ 27 02:17
♑ 29 06:00

Jul 1988
♒ 1 07:30
♓ 3 08:33
♈ 5 10:37
♉ 7 14:26
♊ 9 20:16
♋ 12 04:08

☽ Moon

Jul 1988
♌ 14 14:11
♍ 17 02:17
♎ 19 15:21
♏ 22 03:12
♐ 24 11:41
♑ 26 16:07
♒ 28 17:25
♓ 30 17:23

Aug 1988
♈ 1 17:53
♉ 3 20:24
♊ 6 01:42
♋ 8 09:51
♌ 10 20:26
♍ 13 08:45
♎ 15 21:51
♏ 18 10:11
♐ 20 19:54
♑ 23 01:48
♒ 25 04:04
♓ 27 04:01
♈ 29 03:29
♉ 31 04:22

Sep 1988
♊ 2 08:11
♋ 4 15:36
♌ 7 02:14
♍ 9 14:47
♎ 12 03:50
♏ 14 16:06
♐ 17 02:25
♑ 19 09:44
♒ 21 13:43
♓ 23 14:51
♈ 25 14:30
♉ 27 14:29
♊ 29 16:43

Oct 1988
♋ 1 22:38
♌ 4 08:30
♍ 6 21:00
♎ 9 10:03
♏ 11 21:57
♐ 14 07:57
♑ 16 15:44
♒ 18 21:04
♓ 20 23:58
♈ 23 00:58
♉ 25 01:22
♊ 27 02:55
♋ 29 07:28
♌ 31 16:02

Nov 1988
♍ 3 04:01
♎ 5 17:03
♏ 8 04:46
♐ 10 14:05
♑ 12 21:12
♒ 15 02:36
♓ 17 06:33
♈ 19 09:12
♉ 21 11:02
♊ 23 13:12
♋ 25 17:19
♌ 28 00:51
♍ 30 11:58

Dec 1988
♎ 3 00:55
♏ 5 12:50
♐ 7 21:55
♑ 10 04:06
♒ 12 08:25

☽ Moon

Dec 1988
♓ 14 11:53
♈ 16 15:03
♉ 18 18:11
♊ 20 21:42
♋ 23 02:34
♌ 25 09:57
♍ 27 20:27
♎ 30 09:08

Jan 1989
♏ 1 21:33
♐ 4 07:11
♑ 6 13:14
♒ 8 16:31
♓ 10 18:31
♈ 12 20:35
♉ 14 23:35
♊ 17 03:56
♋ 19 09:56
♌ 21 18:02
♍ 24 04:32
♎ 26 17:00
♏ 29 05:48
♐ 31 16:29

Feb 1989
♑ 2 23:29
♒ 5 02:51
♓ 7 03:52
♈ 9 04:17
♉ 11 05:44
♊ 13 09:22
♋ 15 15:39
♌ 18 00:32
♍ 20 11:34
♎ 23 00:04
♏ 25 12:56
♐ 28 00:29

Mar 1989
♑ 2 08:57
♒ 4 13:36
♓ 6 14:59
♈ 8 14:37
♉ 10 14:25
♊ 12 16:16
♋ 14 21:27
♌ 17 06:12
♍ 19 17:39
♎ 22 06:23
♏ 24 19:10
♐ 27 06:53
♑ 29 16:25
♒ 31 22:44

Apr 1989
♓ 3 01:37
♈ 5 01:51
♉ 7 01:07
♊ 9 01:31
♋ 11 04:57
♌ 13 12:30
♍ 15 23:39
♎ 18 12:31
♏ 21 01:13
♐ 23 12:38
♑ 25 22:14
♒ 28 05:32
♓ 30 10:03

May 1989
♈ 2 11:51
♉ 4 11:55
♊ 6 12:03
♋ 8 14:19
♌ 10 20:22
♍ 13 06:29

☽ Moon

May 1989
♎ 15 19:06
♏ 18 07:47
♐ 20 18:51
♑ 23 03:53
♒ 25 11:00
♓ 27 16:12
♈ 29 19:25
♉ 31 20:59

Jun 1989
♊ 2 22:02
♋ 5 00:16
♌ 7 05:27
♍ 9 14:28
♎ 12 02:30
♏ 14 15:10
♐ 17 02:12
♑ 19 10:41
♒ 21 16:56
♓ 23 21:36
♈ 26 01:05
♉ 28 03:45
♊ 30 06:08

Jul 1989
♋ 2 09:19
♌ 4 14:37
♍ 6 23:04
♎ 9 10:29
♏ 11 23:08
♐ 14 10:30
♑ 16 19:01
♒ 19 00:35
♓ 21 04:06
♈ 23 06:40
♉ 25 09:10
♊ 27 12:14
♋ 29 16:31
♌ 31 22:41

Aug 1989
♍ 3 07:18
♎ 5 18:27
♏ 8 07:04
♐ 10 19:01
♑ 13 04:16
♒ 15 09:59
♓ 17 12:46
♈ 19 13:59
♉ 21 15:10
♊ 23 17:38
♋ 25 22:13
♌ 28 05:11
♍ 30 14:29

Sep 1989
♎ 2 01:47
♏ 4 14:22
♐ 7 02:50
♑ 9 13:12
♒ 11 20:01
♓ 13 23:07
♈ 15 23:38
♉ 17 23:22
♊ 20 00:15
♋ 22 03:50
♌ 24 10:43
♍ 26 20:32
♎ 29 08:14

Oct 1989
♏ 1 20:52
♐ 4 09:28
♑ 6 20:44
♒ 9 05:06
♓ 11 09:37
♈ 13 10:42

☽ Moon

Oct 1989
♉ 15 09:53
♊ 17 09:19
♋ 19 11:09
♌ 21 16:46
♍ 24 02:14
♎ 26 14:10
♏ 29 02:55
♐ 31 15:22

Nov 1989
♑ 3 02:46
♒ 5 12:08
♓ 7 18:24
♈ 9 21:08
♉ 11 21:09
♊ 13 20:19
♋ 15 20:51
♌ 18 00:45
♍ 20 08:53
♎ 22 20:24
♏ 25 09:12
♐ 27 21:29
♑ 30 08:26

Dec 1989
♒ 2 17:41
♓ 5 00:47
♈ 7 05:11
♉ 9 06:59
♊ 11 07:15
♋ 13 07:49
♌ 15 10:41
♍ 17 17:18
♎ 20 03:45
♏ 22 16:17
♐ 25 04:36
♑ 27 15:10
♒ 29 23:37

Jan 1990
♓ 1 06:10
♈ 3 10:56
♉ 5 14:04
♊ 7 16:02
♋ 9 17:52
♌ 11 21:02
♍ 14 02:57
♎ 16 12:16
♏ 19 00:15
♐ 21 12:43
♑ 23 23:27
♒ 26 07:25
♓ 28 12:50
♈ 30 16:34

Feb 1990
♉ 1 19:27
♊ 3 22:12
♋ 6 01:26
♌ 8 05:51
♍ 10 12:13
♎ 12 21:09
♏ 15 08:33
♐ 17 21:06
♑ 20 08:29
♒ 22 16:52
♓ 24 21:49
♈ 27 00:16

Mar 1990
♉ 1 01:42
♊ 3 03:37
♋ 5 07:02
♌ 7 12:24
♍ 9 19:46
♎ 12 05:08
♏ 14 16:24

☽ Moon

Mar 1990
♐ 17 04:55
♑ 19 17:00
♒ 22 02:30
♓ 24 08:08
♈ 26 10:16
♉ 28 10:27
♊ 30 10:42

Apr 1990
♋ 1 12:49
♌ 3 17:49
♍ 6 01:41
♎ 8 11:44
♏ 10 23:17
♐ 13 11:47
♑ 16 00:14
♒ 18 10:51
♓ 20 17:56
♈ 22 20:58
♉ 24 21:03
♊ 26 20:12
♋ 28 20:39

May 1990
♌ 1 00:08
♍ 3 07:17
♎ 5 17:27
♏ 8 05:22
♐ 10 17:55
♑ 13 06:20
♒ 15 17:29
♓ 18 01:53
♈ 20 06:31
♉ 22 07:42
♊ 24 07:00
♋ 26 06:34
♌ 28 08:29
♍ 30 14:07

Jun 1990
♎ 1 23:30
♏ 4 11:21
♐ 6 23:59
♑ 9 12:11
♒ 11 23:08
♓ 14 07:59
♈ 16 13:54
♉ 18 16:42
♊ 20 17:15
♋ 22 17:10
♌ 24 18:25
♍ 26 22:41
♎ 29 06:46

Jul 1990
♏ 1 18:00
♐ 4 06:35
♑ 6 18:39
♒ 9 05:06
♓ 11 13:29
♈ 13 19:36
♉ 15 23:28
♊ 18 01:31
♋ 20 02:43
♌ 22 04:28
♍ 24 08:17
♎ 26 15:18
♏ 29 01:38
♐ 31 13:59

Aug 1990
♑ 3 02:08
♒ 5 12:18
♓ 7 19:54
♈ 10 01:12
♉ 12 04:54
♊ 14 07:41

☽ Moon

Aug 1990
♋ 16 10:12
♌ 18 13:11
♍ 20 17:33
♎ 23 00:16
♏ 25 09:55
♐ 27 21:57
♑ 30 10:22

Sep 1990
♒ 1 20:50
♓ 4 04:05
♈ 6 08:23
♉ 8 10:55
♊ 10 13:04
♋ 12 15:52
♌ 14 19:51
♍ 17 01:18
♎ 19 08:34
♏ 21 18:05
♐ 24 05:51
♑ 26 18:35
♒ 29 05:53

Oct 1990
♓ 1 13:42
♈ 3 17:42
♉ 5 19:06
♊ 7 19:47
♋ 9 21:29
♌ 12 01:16
♍ 14 07:20
♎ 16 15:26
♏ 19 01:23
♐ 21 13:08
♑ 24 02:02
♒ 26 14:13
♓ 28 23:21
♈ 31 04:14

Nov 1990
♉ 2 05:32
♊ 4 05:06
♋ 6 05:07
♌ 8 07:23
♍ 10 12:47
♎ 12 21:08
♏ 15 07:39
♐ 17 19:39
♑ 20 08:31
♒ 22 21:06
♓ 25 07:31
♈ 27 14:06
♉ 29 16:37

Dec 1990
♊ 1 16:23
♋ 3 15:28
♌ 5 16:00
♍ 7 19:38
♎ 10 02:59
♏ 12 13:27
♐ 15 01:43
♑ 17 14:34
♒ 20 02:58
♓ 22 13:47
♈ 24 21:44
♉ 27 02:08
♊ 29 03:26
♋ 31 03:02

Jan 1991
♌ 2 02:54
♍ 4 04:56
♎ 6 10:32
♏ 8 19:58
♐ 11 08:05
♑ 13 21:00

☽ Moon

Jan 1991
♒ 16 09:04
♓ 18 19:23
♈ 21 03:27
♉ 23 09:00
♊ 25 12:06
♋ 27 13:23
♌ 29 14:04
♍ 31 15:44

Feb 1991
♎ 2 20:02
♏ 5 04:00
♐ 7 15:22
♑ 10 04:15
♒ 12 16:16
♓ 15 01:58
♈ 17 09:11
♉ 19 14:24
♊ 21 18:10
♋ 23 20:56
♌ 25 23:12
♍ 28 01:50

Mar 1991
♎ 2 06:03
♏ 4 13:08
♐ 6 23:34
♑ 9 12:12
♒ 12 00:30
♓ 14 10:10
♈ 16 16:37
♉ 18 20:40
♊ 20 23:36
♋ 23 02:27
♌ 25 05:43
♍ 27 09:40
♎ 29 14:49
♏ 31 22:01

Apr 1991
♐ 3 07:58
♑ 5 20:19
♒ 8 08:58
♓ 10 19:17
♈ 13 01:49
♉ 15 05:05
♊ 17 06:41
♋ 19 08:17
♌ 21 11:04
♍ 23 15:29
♎ 25 21:36
♏ 28 05:33
♐ 30 15:41

May 1991
♑ 3 03:54
♒ 5 16:50
♓ 8 04:03
♈ 10 11:34
♉ 12 15:07
♊ 14 16:02
♋ 16 16:14
♌ 18 17:30
♍ 20 21:00
♎ 23 03:07
♏ 25 12:41
♐ 27 22:20
♑ 30 10:40

Jun 1991
♒ 1 23:41
♓ 4 11:35
♈ 6 20:24
♉ 9 01:12
♊ 11 02:36
♋ 13 02:16
♌ 15 02:10

☽ Moon

Jun 1991
♍ 17 04:02
♎ 19 09:00
♏ 21 17:18
♐ 24 04:15
♑ 26 16:49
♒ 29 05:47

Jul 1991
♓ 1 17:50
♈ 4 03:33
♉ 6 09:51
♊ 8 12:42
♋ 10 13:03
♌ 12 12:35
♍ 14 13:12
♎ 16 16:33
♏ 18 23:40
♐ 21 10:15
♑ 23 22:55
♒ 26 11:48
♓ 28 23:34
♈ 31 09:19

Aug 1991
♉ 2 16:31
♊ 4 20:54
♋ 6 22:47
♌ 8 23:09
♍ 10 23:34
♎ 13 01:51
♏ 15 07:33
♐ 17 17:10
♑ 20 05:33
♒ 22 18:26
♓ 25 05:51
♈ 27 15:00
♉ 29 21:59

Sep 1991
♊ 1 03:02
♋ 3 06:19
♌ 5 08:13
♍ 7 09:35
♎ 9 11:51
♏ 11 16:42
♐ 14 01:14
♑ 16 13:02
♒ 19 01:57
♓ 21 13:19
♈ 23 21:55
♉ 26 03:59
♊ 28 08:25
♋ 30 11:58

Oct 1991
♌ 2 14:58
♍ 4 17:44
♎ 6 21:00
♏ 9 01:59
♐ 11 09:57
♑ 13 21:09
♒ 16 10:03
♓ 18 21:52
♈ 21 06:33
♉ 23 11:55
♊ 25 15:09
♋ 27 17:37
♌ 29 20:20
♍ 31 23:46

Nov 1991
♎ 3 04:12
♏ 5 10:08
♐ 7 18:21
♑ 10 05:15
♒ 12 18:05
♓ 15 06:32

☽ Moon

Nov 1991
♈ 17 16:07
♉ 19 21:49
♊ 22 00:22
♋ 24 01:25
♌ 26 02:37
♍ 28 05:11
♎ 30 09:46

Dec 1991
♏ 2 16:32
♐ 5 01:32
♑ 7 12:40
♒ 10 01:26
♓ 12 14:18
♈ 15 01:06
♉ 17 08:09
♊ 19 11:21
♋ 21 11:55
♌ 23 11:39
♍ 25 12:23
♎ 27 15:37
♏ 29 22:03

Jan 1992
♐ 1 07:29
♑ 3 19:08
♒ 6 07:58
♓ 8 20:51
♈ 11 08:22
♉ 13 16:59
♊ 15 21:54
♋ 17 23:26
♌ 19 22:56
♍ 21 22:22
♎ 23 23:42
♏ 26 04:31
♐ 28 13:19
♑ 31 01:07

Feb 1992
♒ 2 14:08
♓ 5 02:50
♈ 7 14:14
♉ 9 23:35
♊ 12 06:07
♋ 14 09:30
♌ 16 10:15
♍ 18 09:47
♎ 20 10:05
♏ 22 13:11
♐ 24 20:25
♑ 27 07:32
♒ 29 20:33

Mar 1992
♓ 3 09:10
♈ 5 20:06
♉ 8 05:04
♊ 10 12:03
♋ 12 16:49
♌ 14 19:20
♍ 16 20:13
♎ 18 20:55
♏ 20 23:19
♐ 23 05:12
♑ 25 15:07
♒ 28 03:44
♓ 30 16:22

Apr 1992
♈ 2 03:03
♉ 4 11:17
♊ 6 17:32
♋ 8 22:18
♌ 11 01:45
♍ 13 04:09
♎ 15 06:10

☽ Moon

Apr 1992
♏ 17 09:10
♐ 19 14:40
♑ 21 23:40
♒ 24 11:37
♓ 27 00:19
♈ 29 11:13

May 1992
♉ 1 19:09
♊ 4 00:28
♋ 6 04:09
♌ 8 07:07
♍ 10 09:56
♎ 12 13:05
♏ 14 17:15
♐ 16 23:21
♑ 19 08:12
♒ 21 19:43
♓ 24 08:24
♈ 26 19:52
♉ 29 04:16
♊ 31 09:19

Jun 1992
♋ 2 11:58
♌ 4 13:35
♍ 6 15:28
♎ 8 18:33
♏ 10 23:26
♐ 13 06:28
♑ 15 15:49
♒ 18 03:18
♓ 20 15:59
♈ 23 04:02
♉ 25 13:28
♊ 27 19:13
♋ 29 21:42

Jul 1992
♌ 1 22:15
♍ 3 22:37
♎ 6 00:27
♏ 8 04:53
♐ 10 12:16
♑ 12 22:15
♒ 15 10:02
♓ 17 22:44
♈ 20 11:06
♉ 22 21:35
♊ 25 04:44
♋ 27 08:08
♌ 29 08:39
♍ 31 08:01

Aug 1992
♎ 2 08:17
♏ 4 11:15
♐ 6 17:56
♑ 9 04:00
♒ 11 16:06
♓ 14 04:50
♈ 16 17:11
♉ 19 04:09
♊ 21 12:35
♋ 23 17:36
♌ 25 19:15
♍ 27 18:47
♎ 29 18:11
♏ 31 19:38

Sep 1992
♐ 3 00:49
♑ 5 10:05
♒ 7 22:08
♓ 10 10:55
♈ 12 23:02
♉ 15 09:46

☽ Moon

Sep 1992
♊ 17 18:39
♋ 20 00:58
♌ 22 04:18
♍ 24 05:08
♎ 26 04:55
♏ 28 05:44
♐ 30 09:33

Oct 1992
♑ 2 17:28
♒ 5 04:52
♓ 7 17:37
♈ 10 05:35
♉ 12 15:48
♊ 15 00:08
♋ 17 06:35
♌ 19 11:01
♍ 21 13:27
♎ 23 14:40
♏ 25 16:04
♐ 27 19:28
♑ 30 02:17

Nov 1992
♒ 1 12:42
♓ 4 01:12
♈ 6 13:18
♉ 8 23:18
♊ 11 06:49
♋ 13 12:19
♌ 15 16:23
♍ 17 19:28
♎ 19 22:02
♏ 22 00:51
♐ 24 05:00
♑ 26 11:37
♒ 28 21:18

Dec 1992
♓ 1 09:22
♈ 3 21:48
♉ 6 08:16
♊ 8 15:36
♋ 10 20:05
♌ 12 22:47
♍ 15 00:55
♎ 17 03:33
♏ 19 07:19
♐ 21 12:42
♑ 23 20:04
♒ 26 05:42
♓ 28 17:27
♈ 31 06:06

Jan 1993
♉ 2 17:29
♊ 5 01:41
♋ 7 06:10
♌ 9 07:49
♍ 11 08:20
♎ 13 09:30
♏ 15 12:41
♐ 17 18:30
♑ 20 02:46
♒ 22 13:00
♓ 25 00:47
♈ 27 13:27
♉ 30 01:36

Feb 1993
♊ 1 11:14
♋ 3 16:56
♌ 5 18:51
♍ 7 18:29
♎ 9 17:59
♏ 11 19:23
♐ 14 00:07

☽ Moon

Feb 1993
♑ 16 08:19
♒ 18 19:04
♓ 21 07:11
♈ 23 19:50
♉ 26 08:11
♊ 28 18:51

Mar 1993
♋ 3 02:16
♌ 5 05:40
♍ 7 05:52
♎ 9 04:46
♏ 11 04:39
♐ 13 07:33
♑ 15 14:27
♒ 18 00:52
♓ 20 13:10
♈ 23 01:51
♉ 25 13:58
♊ 28 00:47
♋ 30 09:13

Apr 1993
♌ 1 14:21
♍ 3 16:10
♎ 5 15:55
♏ 7 15:32
♐ 9 17:09
♑ 11 22:23
♒ 14 07:35
♓ 16 19:32
♈ 19 08:14
♉ 21 20:07
♊ 24 06:26
♋ 26 14:45
♌ 28 20:39
♍ 30 23:59

May 1993
♎ 3 01:20
♏ 5 01:57
♐ 7 03:34
♑ 9 07:50
♒ 11 15:43
♓ 14 02:50
♈ 16 15:23
♉ 19 03:16
♊ 21 13:07
♋ 23 20:37
♌ 26 02:03
♍ 28 05:46
♎ 30 08:18

Jun 1993
♏ 1 10:22
♐ 3 13:01
♑ 5 17:26
♒ 8 00:39
♓ 10 10:56
♈ 12 23:13
♉ 15 11:18
♊ 17 21:11
♋ 20 04:05
♌ 22 08:26
♍ 24 11:18
♎ 26 13:45
♏ 28 16:37
♐ 30 20:28

Jul 1993
♑ 3 01:48
♒ 5 09:14
♓ 7 19:09
♈ 10 07:10
♉ 12 19:36
♊ 15 06:06
♋ 17 13:07

☽ Moon

Jul 1993
♌ 19 16:47
♍ 21 18:24
♎ 23 19:39
♏ 25 22:00
♐ 28 02:12
♑ 30 08:26

Aug 1993
♒ 1 16:36
♓ 4 02:43
♈ 6 14:38
♉ 9 03:22
♊ 11 14:46
♋ 13 22:46
♌ 16 02:43
♍ 18 03:41
♎ 20 03:35
♏ 22 04:27
♐ 24 07:45
♑ 26 13:57
♒ 28 22:41
♓ 31 09:18

Sep 1993
♈ 2 21:20
♉ 5 10:08
♊ 7 22:15
♋ 10 07:36
♌ 12 12:51
♍ 14 14:20
♎ 16 13:44
♏ 18 13:15
♐ 20 14:53
♑ 22 19:53
♒ 25 04:18
♓ 27 15:12
♈ 30 03:28

Oct 1993
♉ 2 16:12
♊ 5 04:26
♋ 7 14:41
♌ 9 21:33
♍ 12 00:35
♎ 14 00:47
♏ 16 00:00
♐ 18 00:23
♑ 20 03:41
♒ 22 10:48
♓ 24 21:17
♈ 27 09:38
♉ 29 22:20

Nov 1993
♊ 1 10:12
♋ 3 20:24
♌ 6 04:06
♍ 8 08:47
♎ 10 10:42
♏ 12 11:00
♐ 14 11:21
♑ 16 13:34
♒ 18 19:07
♓ 21 04:27
♈ 23 16:29
♉ 26 05:13
♊ 28 16:47

Dec 1993
♋ 1 02:16
♌ 3 09:32
♍ 5 14:43
♎ 7 18:03
♏ 9 20:04
♐ 11 21:39
♑ 14 00:05
♒ 16 04:51

☽ Moon

Dec 1993
♓ 18 12:58
♈ 21 00:18
♉ 23 13:03
♊ 26 00:45
♋ 28 09:45
♌ 30 15:59

Jan 1994
♍ 1 20:14
♎ 3 23:30
♏ 6 02:28
♐ 8 05:34
♑ 10 09:16
♒ 12 14:25
♓ 14 22:03
♈ 17 08:41
♉ 19 21:21
♊ 22 09:34
♋ 24 18:54
♌ 27 00:38
♍ 29 03:39
♎ 31 05:33

Feb 1994
♏ 2 07:49
♐ 4 11:14
♑ 6 16:01
♒ 8 22:16
♓ 11 06:22
♈ 13 16:49
♉ 16 05:19
♊ 18 18:04
♋ 21 04:26
♌ 23 10:47
♍ 25 13:27
♎ 27 14:06

Mar 1994
♏ 1 14:43
♐ 3 16:53
♑ 5 21:23
♒ 8 04:14
♓ 10 13:09
♈ 12 23:58
♉ 15 12:27
♊ 18 01:28
♋ 20 12:53
♌ 22 20:38
♍ 25 00:13
♎ 27 00:46
♏ 29 00:14
♐ 31 00:41

Apr 1994
♑ 2 03:37
♒ 4 09:45
♓ 6 18:50
♈ 9 06:08
♉ 11 18:47
♊ 14 07:47
♋ 16 19:40
♌ 19 04:44
♍ 21 09:58
♎ 23 11:40
♏ 25 11:19
♐ 27 10:48
♑ 29 12:05

May 1994
♒ 1 16:34
♓ 4 00:46
♈ 6 12:00
♉ 9 00:50
♊ 11 13:43
♋ 14 01:26
♌ 16 10:58
♍ 18 17:30

☽ Moon

May 1994
♎ 20 20:54
♏ 22 21:51
♐ 24 21:43
♑ 26 22:17
♒ 29 01:18
♓ 31 08:02

Jun 1994
♈ 2 18:30
♉ 5 07:13
♊ 7 20:02
♋ 10 07:21
♌ 12 16:28
♍ 14 23:16
♎ 17 03:48
♏ 19 06:20
♐ 21 07:32
♑ 23 08:37
♒ 25 11:09
♓ 27 16:44
♈ 30 02:06

Jul 1994
♉ 2 14:22
♊ 5 03:12
♋ 7 14:17
♌ 9 22:43
♍ 12 04:48
♎ 14 09:14
♏ 16 12:34
♐ 18 15:09
♑ 20 17:30
♒ 22 20:38
♓ 25 01:56
♈ 27 10:30
♉ 29 22:12

Aug 1994
♊ 1 11:04
♋ 3 22:22
♌ 6 06:30
♍ 8 11:42
♎ 10 15:07
♏ 12 17:56
♐ 14 20:53
♑ 17 00:17
♒ 19 04:33
♓ 21 10:27
♈ 23 18:54
♉ 26 06:12
♊ 28 19:06
♋ 31 06:59

Sep 1994
♌ 2 15:36
♍ 4 20:33
♎ 6 22:56
♏ 9 00:25
♐ 11 02:25
♑ 13 05:44
♒ 15 10:42
♓ 17 17:31
♈ 20 02:29
♉ 22 13:47
♊ 25 02:41
♋ 27 15:11
♌ 30 00:55

Oct 1994
♍ 2 06:39
♎ 4 08:56
♏ 6 09:22
♐ 8 09:47
♑ 10 11:44
♒ 12 16:09
♓ 14 23:18
♈ 17 08:55

☽ Moon

Oct 1994
♉ 19 20:34
♊ 22 09:27
♋ 24 22:15
♌ 27 09:04
♍ 29 16:21
♎ 31 19:46

Nov 1994
♏ 2 20:19
♐ 4 19:46
♑ 6 20:02
♒ 8 22:48
♓ 11 05:03
♈ 13 14:43
♉ 16 02:43
♊ 18 15:41
♋ 21 04:20
♌ 23 15:32
♍ 26 00:08
♎ 28 05:22
♏ 30 07:21

Dec 1994
♐ 2 07:13
♑ 4 06:43
♒ 6 07:51
♓ 8 12:23
♈ 10 21:03
♉ 13 08:55
♊ 15 21:59
♋ 18 10:24
♌ 20 21:12
♍ 23 06:00
♎ 25 12:27
♏ 27 16:17
♐ 29 17:45
♑ 31 17:58

Jan 1995
♒ 2 18:39
♓ 4 21:49
♈ 7 04:56
♉ 9 15:57
♊ 12 04:57
♋ 14 17:19
♌ 17 03:36
♍ 19 11:39
♎ 21 17:53
♏ 23 22:32
♐ 26 01:36
♑ 28 03:26
♒ 30 05:03

Feb 1995
♓ 1 08:05
♈ 3 14:12
♉ 6 00:08
♊ 8 12:42
♋ 11 01:16
♌ 13 11:31
♍ 15 18:51
♎ 18 00:00
♏ 20 03:55
♐ 22 07:12
♑ 24 10:10
♒ 26 13:14
♓ 28 17:16

Mar 1995
♈ 2 23:29
♉ 5 08:50
♊ 7 20:54
♋ 10 09:39
♌ 12 20:27
♍ 15 03:54
♎ 17 08:18
♏ 19 10:52

☽ Moon

Mar 1995
♐ 21 12:57
♑ 23 15:31
♒ 25 19:09
♓ 28 00:17
♈ 30 07:25

Apr 1995
♉ 1 16:58
♊ 4 04:48
♋ 6 17:39
♌ 9 05:15
♍ 11 13:38
♎ 13 18:20
♏ 15 20:13
♐ 17 20:51
♑ 19 21:53
♒ 22 00:37
♓ 24 05:50
♈ 26 13:40
♉ 28 23:52

May 1995
♊ 1 11:52
♋ 4 00:44
♌ 6 12:54
♍ 8 22:33
♎ 11 04:30
♏ 13 06:53
♐ 15 06:59
♑ 17 06:36
♒ 19 07:39
♓ 21 11:39
♈ 23 19:12
♉ 26 05:46
♊ 28 18:06
♋ 31 06:59

Jun 1995
♌ 2 19:16
♍ 5 05:45
♎ 7 13:12
♏ 9 17:03
♐ 11 17:50
♑ 13 17:05
♒ 15 16:52
♓ 17 19:13
♈ 20 01:28
♉ 22 11:34
♊ 25 00:02
♋ 27 12:55
♌ 30 01:01

Jul 1995
♍ 2 11:35
♎ 4 19:55
♏ 7 01:18
♐ 9 03:37
♑ 11 03:43
♒ 13 03:21
♓ 15 04:37
♈ 17 09:22
♉ 19 18:19
♊ 22 06:22
♋ 24 19:15
♌ 27 07:06
♍ 29 17:11

Aug 1995
♎ 1 01:23
♏ 3 07:29
♐ 5 11:14
♑ 7 12:52
♒ 9 13:28
♓ 11 14:46
♈ 13 18:40
♉ 16 02:24
♊ 18 13:39

☽ Moon

Aug 1995
♋ 21 02:23
♌ 23 14:12
♍ 25 23:50
♎ 28 07:15
♏ 30 12:51

Sep 1995
♐ 1 16:56
♑ 3 19:45
♒ 5 21:47
♓ 8 00:07
♈ 10 04:14
♉ 12 11:21
♊ 14 21:47
♋ 17 10:15
♌ 19 22:19
♍ 22 08:01
♎ 24 14:49
♏ 26 19:20
♐ 28 22:30

Oct 1995
♑ 1 01:10
♒ 3 03:59
♓ 5 07:35
♈ 7 12:41
♉ 9 20:04
♊ 12 06:09
♋ 14 18:19
♌ 17 06:45
♍ 19 17:11
♎ 22 00:15
♏ 24 04:06
♐ 26 05:56
♑ 28 07:14
♒ 30 09:23

Nov 1995
♓ 1 13:17
♈ 3 19:20
♉ 6 03:35
♊ 8 13:54
♋ 11 01:56
♌ 13 14:36
♍ 16 02:02
♎ 18 10:17
♏ 20 14:40
♐ 22 15:57
♑ 24 15:49
♒ 26 16:15
♓ 28 18:58

Dec 1995
♈ 1 00:50
♉ 3 09:39
♊ 5 20:34
♋ 8 08:44
♌ 10 21:24
♍ 13 09:25
♎ 15 19:08
♏ 18 01:06
♐ 20 03:13
♑ 22 02:46
♒ 24 01:52
♓ 26 02:44
♈ 28 07:05
♉ 30 15:20

Jan 1996
♊ 2 02:29
♋ 4 14:55
♌ 7 03:30
♍ 9 15:29
♎ 12 01:54
♏ 14 09:29
♐ 16 13:25
♑ 18 14:07

☽ Moon

Jan 1996
♒ 20 13:15
♓ 22 13:02
♈ 24 15:36
♉ 26 22:16
♊ 29 08:41
♋ 31 21:10

Feb 1996
♌ 3 09:45
♍ 5 21:22
♎ 8 07:29
♏ 10 15:34
♐ 12 20:57
♑ 14 23:29
♒ 16 23:59
♓ 19 00:09
♈ 21 01:58
♉ 23 07:08
♊ 25 16:13
♋ 28 04:10

Mar 1996
♌ 1 16:46
♍ 4 04:12
♎ 6 13:40
♏ 8 21:05
♐ 11 02:32
♑ 13 06:07
♒ 15 08:15
♓ 17 09:50
♈ 19 12:15
♉ 21 16:58
♊ 24 00:59
♋ 26 12:05
♌ 29 00:36
♍ 31 12:14

Apr 1996
♎ 2 21:26
♏ 5 03:56
♐ 7 08:21
♑ 9 11:30
♒ 11 14:09
♓ 13 17:00
♈ 15 20:42
♉ 18 02:05
♊ 20 09:54
♋ 22 20:24
♌ 25 08:43
♍ 27 20:48
♎ 30 06:26

May 1996
♏ 2 12:42
♐ 4 16:05
♑ 6 17:54
♒ 8 19:39
♓ 10 22:28
♈ 13 03:00
♉ 15 09:24
♊ 17 17:47
♋ 20 04:15
♌ 22 16:27
♍ 25 04:58
♎ 27 15:32
♏ 29 22:30

Jun 1996
♐ 1 01:42
♑ 3 02:29
♒ 5 02:44
♓ 7 04:19
♈ 9 08:22
♉ 11 15:10
♊ 14 00:15
♋ 16 11:07
♌ 18 23:21

☽ Moon

Jun 1996
♍ 21 12:06
♎ 23 23:37
♏ 26 07:53
♐ 28 12:01
♑ 30 12:47

Jul 1996
♒ 2 12:06
♓ 4 12:07
♈ 6 14:41
♉ 8 20:43
♊ 11 05:52
♋ 13 17:07
♌ 16 05:31
♍ 18 18:16
♎ 21 06:13
♏ 23 15:42
♐ 25 21:23
♑ 27 23:17
♒ 29 22:47
♓ 31 22:00

Aug 1996
♈ 2 23:04
♉ 5 03:32
♊ 7 11:48
♋ 9 22:57
♌ 12 11:28
♍ 15 00:07
♎ 17 11:54
♏ 19 21:50
♐ 22 04:48
♑ 24 08:22
♒ 26 09:11
♓ 28 08:49
♈ 30 09:15

Sep 1996
♉ 1 12:19
♊ 3 19:07
♋ 6 05:29
♌ 8 17:53
♍ 11 06:28
♎ 13 17:50
♏ 16 03:19
♐ 18 10:30
♑ 20 15:12
♒ 22 17:39
♓ 24 18:43
♈ 26 19:46
♉ 28 22:23

Oct 1996
♊ 1 04:01
♋ 3 13:13
♌ 6 01:11
♍ 8 13:48
♎ 11 01:00
♏ 13 09:45
♐ 15 16:07
♑ 17 20:37
♒ 19 23:51
♓ 22 02:22
♈ 24 04:50
♉ 26 08:11
♊ 28 13:34
♋ 30 21:56

Nov 1996
♌ 2 09:15
♍ 4 21:56
♎ 7 09:28
♏ 9 18:01
♐ 11 23:26
♑ 14 02:43
♒ 16 05:14
♓ 18 07:59

☽ Moon

Nov 1996
♈ 20 11:3[illegible]
♉ 22 16:1[illegible]
♊ 24 22:1[illegible]
♋ 27 06:3[illegible]
♌ 29 17:2[illegible]

Dec 1996
♍ 2 06:10
♎ 4 18:22
♏ 7 03:38
♐ 9 08:58
♑ 11 11:15
♒ 13 12:14
♓ 15 13:44
♈ 17 16:55
♉ 19 22:09
♊ 22 05:17
♋ 24 14:14
♌ 27 01:08
♍ 29 13:44

Jan 1997
♎ 1 02:31
♏ 3 13:01
♐ 5 19:27
♑ 7 21:54
♒ 9 22:00
♓ 11 21:51
♈ 13 23:21
♉ 16 03:39
♊ 18 10:52
♋ 20 20:28
♌ 23 07:49
♍ 25 20:26
♎ 28 09:20
♏ 30 20:47

Feb 1997
♐ 2 04:50
♑ 4 08:44
♒ 6 09:21
♓ 8 08:34
♈ 10 08:29
♉ 12 10:56
♊ 14 16:52
♋ 17 02:12
♌ 19 13:52
♍ 22 02:38
♎ 24 15:22
♏ 27 02:56

Mar 1997
♐ 1 12:00
♑ 3 17:38
♒ 5 19:54
♓ 7 19:57
♈ 9 19:33
♉ 11 20:37
♊ 14 00:48
♋ 16 08:50
♌ 18 20:07
♍ 21 08:59
♎ 23 21:35
♏ 26 08:41
♐ 28 17:39
♑ 31 00:06

Apr 1997
♒ 2 03:58
♓ 4 05:42
♈ 6 06:19
♉ 8 07:20
♊ 10 10:28
♋ 12 17:02
♌ 15 03:21
♍ 17 15:59
♎ 20 04:36

Moon

pr 1997
♏22 15:18
♐24 23:31
♑27 05:32
♒29 09:50

lay 1997
♓ 1 12:50
♈ 3 14:59
♉ 5 17:04
♊ 7 20:20
♋10 02:12
♌12 11:32
♍14 23:43
♎17 12:26
♏19 23:11
♐22 06:50
♑24 11:51
♒26 15:20
♓28 18:18
♈30 21:17

un 1997
♉ 2 00:38
♊ 4 04:54
♋ 6 11:02
♌ 8 19:57
♍11 07:42
♎13 20:34
♏16 07:50
♐18 15:39
♑20 20:02
♒22 22:20
♓25 00:08
♈27 02:38
♉29 06:23

ul 1997
♊ 1 11:35
♋ 3 18:32
♌ 6 03:44
♍ 8 15:21
♎11 04:20
♏13 16:19
♐16 01:02
♑18 05:45
♒20 07:29
♓22 08:00
♈24 09:03
♉26 11:53
♊28 17:04
♋31 00:38

Aug 1997
♌ 2 10:26
♍ 4 22:14
♎ 7 11:16
♏ 9 23:50
♐12 09:44
♑14 15:42
♒16 17:58
♓18 18:01
♈20 17:45
♉22 18:57
♊24 22:56
♋27 06:10
♌29 16:18

Sep 1997
♍ 1 04:26
♎ 3 17:29
♏ 6 06:09
♐ 8 16:53
♑11 00:23
♒13 04:10
♓15 04:59
♈17 04:25
♉19 04:21

☽ Moon

Sep 1997
♊21 06:38
♋23 12:32
♌25 22:12
♍28 10:27
♎30 23:32

Oct 1997
♏ 3 11:57
♐ 5 22:42
♑ 8 07:03
♒10 12:28
♓12 14:59
♈14 15:25
♉16 15:16
♊18 16:26
♋20 20:45
♌23 05:09
♍25 16:58
♎28 06:04
♏30 18:15

Nov 1997
♐ 2 04:26
♑ 4 12:30
♒ 6 18:33
♓ 8 22:34
♈11 00:43
♉13 01:45
♊15 03:04
♋17 06:32
♌19 13:37
♍22 00:32
♎24 13:28
♏27 01:42
♐29 11:28

Dec 1997
♑ 1 18:38
♒ 3 23:57
♓ 6 04:07
♈ 8 07:23
♉10 10:00
♊12 12:35
♋14 16:25
♌16 22:57
♍19 08:59
♎21 21:34
♏24 10:06
♐26 20:07
♑29 02:48
♒31 06:58

Jan 1998
♓ 2 09:56
♈ 4 12:43
♉ 6 15:52
♊ 8 19:42
♋11 00:42
♌13 07:45
♍15 17:30
♎18 05:43
♏20 18:33
♐23 05:24
♑25 12:39
♒27 16:27
♓29 18:08
♈31 19:21

Feb 1998
♉ 2 21:24
♊ 5 01:09
♋ 7 06:57
♌ 9 14:56
♍12 01:09
♎14 13:16
♏17 02:12
♐19 13:55

☽ Moon

Feb 1998
♑21 22:29
♒24 03:10
♓26 04:42
♈28 04:42

Mar 1998
♉ 2 05:00
♊ 4 07:14
♋ 6 12:26
♌ 8 20:45
♍11 07:34
♎13 19:57
♏16 08:50
♐18 20:56
♑21 06:43
♒23 13:01
♓25 15:43
♈27 15:49
♉29 15:07
♊31 15:38

Apr 1998
♋ 2 19:09
♌ 5 02:35
♍ 7 13:24
♎10 02:04
♏12 14:55
♐15 02:52
♑17 13:04
♒19 20:41
♓22 01:05
♈24 02:30
♉26 02:09
♊28 01:55
♋30 03:56

May 1998
♌ 2 09:48
♍ 4 19:46
♎ 7 08:18
♏ 9 21:10
♐12 08:47
♑14 18:38
♒17 02:30
♓19 08:03
♈21 11:05
♉23 12:06
♊25 12:26
♋27 13:58
♌29 18:37

Jun 1998
♍ 1 03:20
♎ 3 15:16
♏ 6 04:05
♐ 8 15:34
♑11 00:50
♒13 08:02
♓15 13:31
♈17 17:22
♉19 19:47
♊21 21:26
♋23 23:39
♌26 04:03
♍28 11:53
♎30 23:04

Jul 1998
♏ 3 11:44
♐ 5 23:23
♑ 8 08:27
♒10 14:52
♓12 19:22
♈14 22:44
♉17 01:33
♊19 04:18
♋21 07:43

☽ Moon

Jul 1998
♌23 12:48
♍25 20:33
♎28 07:13
♏30 19:44

Aug 1998
♐ 2 07:47
♑ 4 17:17
♒ 6 23:31
♓ 9 03:04
♈11 05:10
♉13 07:04
♊15 09:46
♋17 13:55
♌19 20:00
♍22 04:21
♎24 15:01
♏27 03:25
♐29 15:54

Sep 1998
♑ 1 02:22
♒ 3 09:20
♓ 5 12:48
♈ 7 13:53
♉ 9 14:17
♊11 15:40
♋13 19:19
♌16 01:47
♍18 10:51
♎20 21:57
♏23 10:21
♐25 23:04
♑28 10:29
♒30 18:53

Oct 1998
♓ 2 23:23
♈ 5 00:32
♉ 6 23:57
♊ 8 23:43
♋11 01:48
♌13 07:24
♍15 16:31
♎18 04:02
♏20 16:36
♐23 05:15
♑25 17:04
♒28 02:44
♓30 08:58

Nov 1998
♈ 1 11:27
♉ 3 11:13
♊ 5 10:11
♋ 7 10:39
♌ 9 14:32
♍11 22:36
♎14 09:57
♏16 22:40
♐19 11:12
♑21 22:45
♒24 08:43
♓26 16:14
♈28 20:33
♉30 21:52

Dec 1998
♊ 2 21:30
♋ 4 21:28
♌ 6 23:55
♍ 9 06:21
♎11 16:42
♏14 05:16
♐16 17:47
♑19 04:54
♒21 14:16

☽ Moon

Dec 1998
♓23 21:44
♈26 03:03
♉28 06:05
♊30 07:22

Jan 1999
♋ 1 08:15
♌ 3 10:31
♍ 5 15:48
♎ 8 00:52
♏10 12:48
♐13 01:22
♑15 12:28
♒17 21:11
♓20 03:40
♈22 08:24
♉24 11:52
♊26 14:29
♋28 16:57
♌30 20:15

Feb 1999
♍ 2 01:37
♎ 4 09:55
♏ 6 21:05
♐ 9 09:37
♑11 21:09
♒14 05:56
♓16 11:40
♈18 15:06
♉20 17:29
♊22 19:53
♋24 23:08
♌27 03:44

Mar 1999
♍ 1 10:04
♎ 3 18:34
♏ 6 05:21
♐ 8 17:45
♑11 05:53
♒13 15:31
♓15 21:30
♈18 00:12
♉20 01:08
♊22 02:05
♋24 04:33
♌26 09:22
♍28 16:34
♎31 01:49

Apr 1999
♏ 2 12:48
♐ 5 01:07
♑ 7 13:38
♒10 00:24
♓12 07:34
♈14 10:46
♉16 11:08
♊18 10:39
♋20 11:27
♌22 15:05
♍24 22:03
♎27 07:46
♏29 19:12

May 1999
♐ 2 07:35
♑ 4 20:11
♒ 7 07:39
♓ 9 16:15
♈11 20:53
♉13 21:56
♊15 21:07
♋17 20:39
♌19 22:36
♍22 04:15

☽ Moon

May 1999
♎24 13:28
♏27 01:04
♐29 13:37

Jun 1999
♑ 1 02:05
♒ 3 13:36
♓ 5 23:00
♈ 8 05:07
♉10 07:43
♊12 07:49
♋14 07:14
♌16 08:07
♍18 12:11
♎20 20:10
♏23 07:17
♐25 19:50
♑28 08:11
♒30 19:19

Jul 1999
♓ 3 04:34
♈ 5 11:21
♉ 7 15:21
♊ 9 17:00
♋11 17:27
♌13 18:26
♍15 21:38
♎18 04:19
♏20 14:29
♐23 02:48
♑25 15:08
♒28 01:54
♓30 10:27

Aug 1999
♈ 1 16:46
♉ 3 21:08
♊ 5 23:57
♋ 8 01:52
♌10 03:55
♍12 07:21
♎14 13:23
♏16 22:39
♐19 10:30
♑21 22:59
♒24 09:48
♓26 17:49
♈28 23:09
♉31 02:40

Sep 1999
♊ 2 05:25
♋ 4 08:09
♌ 6 11:29
♍ 8 15:56
♎10 22:15
♏13 07:08
♐15 18:34
♑18 07:12
♒20 18:37
♓23 02:51
♈25 07:33
♉27 09:51
♊29 11:21

Oct 1999
♋ 1 13:31
♌ 3 17:13
♍ 5 22:39
♎ 8 05:51
♏10 15:01
♐13 02:18
♑15 15:02
♒18 03:16
♓20 12:32
♈22 17:41

☽ Moon

Oct 1999
♉24 19:25
♊26 19:34
♋28 20:09
♌30 22:46

Nov 1999
♍ 2 04:06
♎ 4 11:56
♏ 6 21:45
♐ 9 09:14
♑11 21:59
♒14 10:44
♓16 21:20
♈19 03:57
♉21 06:26
♊23 06:14
♋25 05:29
♌27 06:18
♍29 10:10

Dec 1999
♎ 1 17:28
♏ 4 03:35
♐ 6 15:27
♑ 9 04:13
♒11 16:58
♓14 04:17
♈16 12:29
♉18 16:45
♊20 17:39
♋22 16:53
♌24 16:32
♍26 18:34
♎29 00:14
♏31 09:35

Jan 2000
♐ 2 21:31
♑ 5 10:23
♒ 7 22:52
♓10 09:58
♈12 18:48
♉15 00:37
♊17 03:25
♋19 04:01
♌21 03:58
♍23 05:07
♎25 09:09
♏27 17:00
♐30 04:17

Feb 2000
♑ 1 17:09
♒ 4 05:30
♓ 6 16:01
♈ 9 00:17
♉11 06:20
♊13 10:22
♋15 12:45
♌17 14:11
♍19 15:53
♎21 19:21
♏24 01:57
♐26 12:09
♑29 00:45

Mar 2000
♒ 2 13:13
♓ 4 23:30
♈ 7 06:54
♉ 9 12:01
♊11 15:45
♋13 18:51
♌15 21:43
♍18 00:48
♎20 04:57
♏22 11:17

☽ Moon

Mar 2000
♐24 20:42
♑27 08:50
♒29 21:34

Apr 2000
♓ 1 08:12
♈ 3 15:22
♉ 5 19:29
♊ 7 21:58
♋10 00:15
♌12 03:15
♍14 07:18
♎16 12:35
♏18 19:35
♐21 04:57
♑23 16:46
♒26 05:41
♓28 17:05

May 2000
♈ 1 00:54
♉ 3 04:54
♊ 5 06:23
♋ 7 07:14
♌ 9 09:01
♍11 12:40
♎13 18:27
♏16 02:16
♐18 12:09
♑21 00:01
♒23 12:59
♓26 01:07
♈28 10:07
♉30 15:02

Jun 2000
♊ 1 16:35
♋ 3 16:30
♌ 5 16:46
♍ 7 18:57
♎ 9 23:58
♏12 07:54
♐14 18:17
♑17 06:26
♒19 19:25
♓22 07:51
♈24 17:55
♉27 00:18
♊29 02:59

Jul 2000
♋ 1 03:09
♌ 3 02:38
♍ 5 03:19
♎ 7 06:46
♏ 9 13:47
♐12 00:05
♑14 12:27
♒17 01:26
♓19 13:43
♈22 00:09
♉24 07:43
♊26 12:01
♋28 13:30
♌30 13:24

Aug 2000
♍ 1 13:27
♎ 3 15:31
♏ 5 21:04
♐ 8 06:29
♑10 18:43
♒13 07:42
♓15 19:41
♈18 05:43
♉20 13:30
♊22 18:54

☽ Moon

Aug 2000
♋24 21:59
♌26 23:16
♍28 23:55
♎31 01:33

Sep 2000
♏ 2 05:54
♐ 4 14:07
♑ 7 01:46
♒ 9 14:43
♓12 02:34
♈14 12:00
♉16 19:05
♊19 00:22
♋21 04:15
♌23 07:00
♍25 09:02
♎27 11:22
♏29 15:29

Oct 2000
♐ 1 22:49
♑ 4 09:41
♒ 6 22:33
♓ 9 10:35
♈11 19:51
♉14 02:06
♊16 06:19
♋18 09:37
♌20 12:42
♍22 15:52
♎24 19:30
♏27 00:23
♐29 07:40
♑31 18:01

Nov 2000
♒ 3 06:40
♓ 5 19:12
♈ 8 05:02
♉10 11:12
♊12 14:27
♋14 16:21
♌16 18:19
♍18 21:15
♎21 01:34
♏23 07:32
♐25 15:32
♑28 01:57
♒30 14:25

Dec 2000
♓ 3 03:22
♈ 5 14:16
♉ 7 21:26
♊10 00:50
♋12 01:48
♌14 02:08
♍16 03:29
♎18 07:00
♏20 13:11
♐22 21:57
♑25 08:53
♒27 21:25
♓30 10:26

Jan 2001
♈ 1 22:13
♉ 4 06:56
♊ 6 11:43
♋ 8 13:09
♌10 12:44
♍12 12:26
♎14 14:05
♏16 19:02
♐19 03:35
♑21 14:56

☽ Moon

Jan 2001
♒24 03:43
♓26 16:38
♈29 04:34
♉31 14:20

Feb 2001
♊ 2 20:55
♋ 5 00:00
♌ 7 00:20
♍ 8 23:35
♎10 23:45
♏13 02:50
♐15 10:01
♑17 20:58
♒20 09:53
♓22 22:44
♈25 10:19
♉27 20:05

Mar 2001
♊ 2 03:36
♋ 4 08:24
♌ 6 10:30
♍ 8 10:44
♎10 10:48
♏12 12:42
♐14 18:16
♑17 04:01
♒19 16:35
♓22 05:27
♈24 16:43
♉27 01:50
♊29 09:00
♋31 14:22

Apr 2001
♌ 2 17:53
♍ 4 19:46
♎ 6 20:57
♏ 8 23:01
♐11 03:46
♑13 12:20
♒16 00:10
♓18 12:59
♈21 00:17
♉23 08:56
♊25 15:11
♋27 19:49
♌29 23:24

May 2001
♍ 2 02:16
♎ 4 04:50
♏ 6 08:00
♐ 8 13:05
♑10 21:09
♒13 08:19
♓15 21:00
♈18 08:40
♉20 17:29
♊22 23:11
♋25 02:42
♌27 05:11
♍29 07:37
♎31 10:41

Jun 2001
♏ 2 14:56
♐ 4 20:57
♑ 7 05:22
♒ 9 16:19
♓12 04:53
♈14 17:02
♉17 02:38
♊19 08:42
♋21 11:41
♌23 12:55

☽ Moon

Jun 2001
♍25 13:58
♎27 16:10
♏29 20:28

Jul 2001
♐ 2 03:13
♑ 4 12:21
♒ 6 23:33
♓ 9 12:04
♈12 00:35
♉14 11:12
♊16 18:25
♋18 21:56
♌20 22:42
♍22 22:28
♎24 23:07
♏27 02:16
♐29 08:44
♑31 18:15

Aug 2001
♒ 3 05:53
♓ 5 18:29
♈ 8 07:04
♉10 18:22
♊13 02:58
♋15 07:54
♌17 09:25
♍19 08:53
♎21 08:19
♏23 09:50
♐25 14:58
♑28 00:01
♒30 11:47

Sep 2001
♓ 2 00:32
♈ 4 12:57
♉ 7 00:17
♊ 9 09:40
♋11 16:09
♌13 19:16
♍15 19:39
♎17 19:00
♏19 19:27
♐21 23:02
♑24 06:47
♒26 18:04
♓29 06:49

Oct 2001
♈ 1 19:07
♉ 4 06:00
♊ 6 15:11
♋ 8 22:19
♌11 02:54
♍13 04:58
♎15 05:26
♏17 06:02
♐19 08:46
♑21 15:10
♒24 01:26
♓26 13:55
♈29 02:14
♉31 12:47

Nov 2001
♊ 2 21:12
♋ 5 03:43
♌ 7 08:33
♍ 9 11:49
♎11 13:53
♏13 15:45
♐15 18:51
♑18 00:39
♒20 09:54
♓22 21:51

☽ Moon

Nov 2001
♈ 25 10:20
♉ 27 21:05
♊ 30 05:03

Dec 2001
♋ 2 10:30
♌ 4 14:15
♍ 6 17:11
♎ 8 19:56
♏ 10 23:09
♐ 13 03:29
♑ 15 09:47
♒ 17 18:42
♓ 20 06:09
♈ 22 18:44
♉ 25 06:12
♊ 27 14:38
♋ 29 19:40
♌ 31 22:09

Jan 2002
♍ 2 23:34
♎ 5 01:23
♏ 7 04:41
♐ 9 09:57
♑ 11 17:18
♒ 14 02:41
♓ 16 13:59
♈ 19 02:34
♉ 21 14:46
♊ 24 00:27
♋ 26 06:16
♌ 28 08:31
♍ 30 08:40

Feb 2002
♎ 1 08:44
♏ 3 10:35
♐ 5 15:21
♑ 7 23:08
♒ 10 09:14
♓ 12 20:52
♈ 15 09:25
♉ 17 21:57
♊ 20 08:49
♋ 22 16:15
♌ 24 19:36
♍ 26 19:47
♎ 28 18:47

Mar 2002
♏ 2 18:51
♐ 4 21:54
♑ 7 04:47
♒ 9 14:55
♓ 12 02:56
♈ 14 15:33
♉ 17 04:00
♊ 19 15:19
♋ 22 00:06
♌ 24 05:12
♍ 26 06:44
♎ 28 06:04
♏ 30 05:21

Apr 2002
♐ 1 06:48
♑ 3 11:57
♒ 5 21:06
♓ 8 08:57
♈ 10 21:40
♉ 13 09:55
♊ 15 20:56
♋ 18 06:00
♌ 20 12:20
♍ 22 15:34
♎ 24 16:22

☽ Moon

Apr 2002
♏ 26 16:16
♐ 28 17:13
♑ 30 21:02

May 2002
♒ 3 04:43
♓ 5 15:45
♈ 8 04:21
♉ 10 16:31
♊ 13 03:04
♋ 15 11:33
♌ 17 17:52
♍ 19 22:00
♎ 22 00:18
♏ 24 01:38
♐ 26 03:19
♑ 28 06:54
♒ 30 13:34

Jun 2002
♓ 1 23:37
♈ 4 11:50
♉ 7 00:06
♊ 9 10:28
♋ 11 18:15
♌ 13 23:39
♍ 16 03:23
♎ 18 06:10
♏ 20 08:42
♐ 22 11:42
♑ 24 16:01
♒ 26 22:35
♓ 29 08:00

Jul 2002
♈ 1 19:48
♉ 4 08:15
♊ 6 19:00
♋ 9 02:36
♌ 11 07:08
♍ 13 09:41
♎ 15 11:39
♏ 17 14:12
♐ 19 18:02
♑ 21 23:25
♒ 24 06:39
♓ 26 16:04
♈ 29 03:38
♉ 31 16:16

Aug 2002
♊ 3 03:46
♋ 5 12:01
♌ 7 16:27
♍ 9 18:03
♎ 11 18:38
♏ 13 20:00
♐ 15 23:25
♑ 18 05:15
♒ 20 13:16
♓ 22 23:10
♈ 25 10:47
♉ 27 23:31
♊ 30 11:44

Sep 2002
♋ 1 21:13
♌ 4 02:36
♍ 6 04:16
♎ 8 03:57
♏ 10 03:48
♐ 12 05:44
♑ 14 10:47
♒ 16 18:54
♓ 19 05:17
♈ 21 17:10
♉ 24 05:54

☽ Moon

Sep 2002
♊ 26 18:26
♋ 29 05:01

Oct 2002
♌ 1 11:57
♍ 3 14:52
♎ 5 14:52
♏ 7 13:58
♐ 9 14:21
♑ 11 17:44
♒ 14 00:51
♓ 16 11:06
♈ 18 23:13
♉ 21 11:56
♊ 24 00:17
♋ 26 11:09
♌ 28 19:19
♍ 30 23:59

Nov 2002
♎ 2 01:28
♏ 4 01:10
♐ 6 01:01
♑ 8 02:58
♒ 10 08:26
♓ 12 17:41
♈ 15 05:37
♉ 17 18:23
♊ 20 06:24
♋ 22 16:47
♌ 25 00:59
♍ 27 06:41
♎ 29 09:54

Dec 2002
♏ 1 11:15
♐ 3 11:58
♑ 5 13:39
♒ 7 17:54
♓ 10 01:45
♈ 12 12:57
♉ 15 01:43
♊ 17 13:42
♋ 19 23:29
♌ 22 06:48
♍ 24 12:05
♎ 26 15:53
♏ 28 18:41
♐ 30 21:01

Jan 2003
♑ 1 23:42
♒ 4 03:56
♓ 6 10:56
♈ 8 21:14
♉ 11 09:47
♊ 13 22:07
♋ 16 07:55
♌ 18 14:29
♍ 20 18:32
♎ 22 21:22
♏ 25 00:08
♐ 27 03:25
♑ 29 07:29
♒ 31 12:44

Feb 2003
♓ 2 19:54
♈ 5 05:44
♉ 7 17:58
♊ 10 06:44
♋ 12 17:18
♌ 15 00:04
♍ 17 03:22
♎ 19 04:48
♏ 21 06:09
♐ 23 08:45

☽ Moon

Feb 2003
♑ 25 13:10
♒ 27 19:24

Mar 2003
♓ 2 03:25
♈ 4 13:29
♉ 7 01:36
♊ 9 14:36
♋ 12 02:11
♌ 14 10:06
♍ 16 13:52
♎ 18 14:43
♏ 20 14:38
♐ 22 15:33
♑ 24 18:47
♒ 27 00:50
♓ 29 09:25
♈ 31 20:04

Apr 2003
♉ 3 08:19
♊ 5 21:23
♋ 8 09:35
♌ 10 18:53
♍ 13 00:06
♎ 15 01:41
♏ 17 01:16
♐ 19 00:51
♑ 21 02:20
♒ 23 06:57
♓ 25 15:01
♈ 28 01:54
♉ 30 14:26

May 2003
♊ 3 03:27
♋ 5 15:41
♌ 8 01:46
♍ 10 08:30
♎ 12 11:42
♏ 14 12:14
♐ 16 11:43
♑ 18 12:03
♒ 20 15:00
♓ 22 21:41
♈ 25 07:58
♉ 27 20:32
♊ 30 09:31

Jun 2003
♋ 1 21:27
♌ 4 07:24
♍ 6 14:50
♎ 8 19:29
♏ 10 21:39
♐ 12 22:12
♑ 14 22:38
♒ 17 00:41
♓ 19 05:56
♈ 21 15:05
♉ 24 03:14
♊ 26 16:12
♋ 29 03:51

Jul 2003
♌ 1 13:12
♍ 3 20:15
♎ 6 01:20
♏ 8 04:43
♐ 10 06:48
♑ 12 08:21
♒ 14 10:38
♓ 16 15:13
♈ 18 23:19
♉ 21 10:47
♊ 23 23:42
♋ 26 11:22

☽ Moon

Jul 2003
♌ 28 20:16
♍ 31 02:26

Aug 2003
♎ 2 06:47
♏ 4 10:12
♐ 6 13:10
♑ 8 16:02
♒ 10 19:23
♓ 13 00:18
♈ 15 07:59
♉ 17 18:51
♊ 20 07:40
♋ 22 19:44
♌ 25 04:48
♍ 27 10:27
♎ 29 13:41
♏ 31 16:00

Sep 2003
♐ 2 18:31
♑ 4 21:51
♒ 7 02:14
♓ 9 08:06
♈ 11 16:08
♉ 14 02:49
♊ 16 15:31
♋ 19 04:07
♌ 21 14:02
♍ 23 20:04
♎ 25 22:49
♏ 27 23:52
♐ 30 00:57

Oct 2003
♑ 2 03:21
♒ 4 07:45
♓ 6 14:20
♈ 8 23:07
♉ 11 10:04
♊ 13 22:44
♋ 16 11:40
♌ 18 22:41
♍ 21 06:01
♎ 23 09:27
♏ 25 10:09
♐ 27 09:55
♑ 29 10:37
♒ 31 13:41

Nov 2003
♓ 2 19:51
♈ 5 05:02
♉ 7 16:28
♊ 10 05:14
♋ 12 18:09
♌ 15 05:47
♍ 17 14:35
♎ 19 19:41
♏ 21 21:23
♐ 23 21:03
♑ 25 20:32
♒ 27 21:48
♓ 30 02:25

Dec 2003
♈ 2 10:55
♉ 4 22:29
♊ 7 11:25
♋ 10 00:10
♌ 12 11:40
♍ 14 21:06
♎ 17 03:46
♏ 19 07:19
♐ 21 08:16
♑ 23 07:55
♒ 25 08:13

☽ Moon

Dec 2003
♓ 27 11:09
♈ 29 18:08

Jan 2004
♉ 1 05:01
♊ 3 17:57
♋ 6 06:38
♌ 8 17:38
♍ 11 02:37
♎ 13 09:37
♏ 15 14:32
♐ 17 17:17
♑ 19 18:24
♒ 21 19:11
♓ 23 21:28
♈ 26 03:05
♉ 28 12:45
♊ 31 01:18

Feb 2004
♋ 2 14:02
♌ 5 00:49
♍ 7 09:02
♎ 9 15:12
♏ 11 19:57
♐ 13 23:34
♑ 16 02:13
♒ 18 04:27
♓ 20 07:26
♈ 22 12:45
♉ 24 21:29
♊ 27 09:21
♋ 29 22:11

Mar 2004
♌ 3 09:17
♍ 5 17:17
♎ 7 22:30
♏ 10 02:02
♐ 12 04:57
♑ 14 07:51
♒ 16 11:10
♓ 18 15:26
♈ 20 21:28
♉ 23 06:09
♊ 25 17:34
♋ 28 06:22
♌ 30 18:06

Apr 2004
♍ 2 02:45
♎ 4 07:52
♏ 6 10:24
♐ 8 11:50
♑ 10 13:33
♒ 12 16:32
♓ 14 21:23
♈ 17 04:24
♉ 19 13:42
♊ 22 01:09
♋ 24 13:55
♌ 27 02:13
♍ 29 11:59

May 2004
♎ 1 18:02
♏ 3 20:38
♐ 5 21:08
♑ 7 21:16
♒ 9 22:46
♓ 12 02:51
♈ 14 10:02
♉ 16 19:56
♊ 19 07:46
♋ 21 20:34
♌ 24 09:06
♍ 26 19:51

☽ Moon

May 2004
♎ 29 03:22
♏ 31 07:08

Jun 2004
♐ 2 07:52
♑ 4 07:12
♒ 6 07:10
♓ 8 09:38
♈ 10 15:48
♉ 13 01:36
♊ 15 13:43
♋ 18 02:37
♌ 20 15:04
♍ 23 02:09
♎ 25 10:49
♏ 27 16:12
♐ 29 18:15

Jul 2004
♑ 1 18:01
♒ 3 17:22
♓ 5 18:26
♈ 7 23:03
♉ 10 07:50
♊ 12 19:44
♋ 15 08:40
♌ 17 20:55
♍ 20 07:43
♎ 22 16:38
♏ 24 23:08
♐ 27 02:47
♑ 29 03:57
♒ 31 03:54

Aug 2004
♓ 2 04:34
♈ 4 07:59
♉ 6 15:25
♊ 9 02:32
♋ 11 15:19
♌ 14 03:29
♍ 16 13:49
♎ 18 22:09
♏ 21 04:36
♐ 23 09:08
♑ 25 11:46
♒ 27 13:08
♓ 29 14:33
♈ 31 17:46

Sep 2004
♉ 3 00:15
♊ 5 10:23
♋ 7 22:50
♌ 10 11:05
♍ 12 21:16
♎ 15 04:53
♏ 17 10:25
♐ 19 14:29
♑ 21 17:35
♒ 23 20:09
♓ 25 22:55
♈ 28 02:56
♉ 30 09:23

Oct 2004
♊ 2 18:54
♋ 5 06:53
♌ 7 19:22
♍ 10 06:00
♎ 12 13:31
♏ 14 18:10
♐ 16 20:58
♑ 18 23:06
♒ 21 01:37
♓ 23 05:13
♈ 25 10:24

☽ Moon

Oct 2004
♉ 27 17:37
♊ 30 03:10

Nov 2004
♋ 1 14:52
♌ 4 03:31
♍ 6 14:59
♎ 8 23:22
♏ 11 04:05
♐ 13 05:56
♑ 15 06:33
♒ 17 07:38
♓ 19 10:37
♈ 21 16:10
♉ 24 00:15
♊ 26 10:25
♋ 28 22:10

Dec 2004
♌ 1 10:49
♍ 3 23:00
♎ 6 08:45
♏ 8 14:43
♐ 10 16:54
♑ 12 16:42
♒ 14 16:10
♓ 16 17:24
♈ 18 21:51
♉ 21 05:51
♊ 23 16:31
♋ 26 04:37
♌ 28 17:13
♍ 31 05:32

Jan 2005
♎ 2 16:18
♏ 4 23:59
♐ 7 03:44
♑ 9 04:11
♒ 11 03:07
♓ 13 02:50
♈ 15 05:26
♉ 17 12:05
♊ 19 22:23
♋ 22 10:41
♌ 24 23:20
♍ 27 11:23
♎ 29 22:12

Feb 2005
♏ 1 06:50
♐ 3 12:21
♑ 5 14:32
♒ 7 14:27
♓ 9 14:00
♈ 11 15:21
♉ 13 20:17
♊ 16 05:17
♋ 18 17:12
♌ 21 05:54
♍ 23 17:44
♎ 26 03:58
♏ 28 12:20

Mar 2005
♐ 2 18:29
♑ 4 22:11
♒ 6 23:49
♓ 9 00:32
♈ 11 02:03
♉ 13 06:05
♊ 15 13:43
♋ 18 00:43
♌ 20 13:16
♍ 23 01:10
♎ 25 10:59
♏ 27 18:29

☽ Moon

Mar 2005
♐ 29 23:56

Apr 2005
♑ 1 03:47
♒ 3 06:31
♓ 5 08:45
♈ 7 11:28
♉ 9 15:49
♊ 11 22:54
♋ 14 09:02
♌ 16 21:16
♍ 19 09:26
♎ 21 19:26
♏ 24 02:25
♐ 26 06:46
♑ 28 09:32
♒ 30 11:53

May 2005
♓ 2 14:42
♈ 4 18:35
♉ 7 00:01
♊ 9 07:28
♋ 11 17:20
♌ 14 05:16
♍ 16 17:45
♎ 19 04:29
♏ 21 11:48
♐ 23 15:38
♑ 25 17:11
♒ 27 18:10
♓ 29 20:09

Jun 2005
♈ 1 00:07
♉ 3 06:19
♊ 5 14:35
♋ 8 00:46
♌ 10 12:39
♍ 13 01:21
♎ 15 12:58
♏ 17 21:23
♐ 20 01:44
♑ 22 02:52
♒ 24 02:36
♓ 26 03:02
♈ 28 05:51
♉ 30 11:44

Jul 2005
♊ 2 20:25
♋ 5 07:07
♌ 7 19:10
♍ 10 07:56
♎ 12 20:08
♏ 15 05:50
♐ 17 11:34
♑ 19 13:26
♒ 21 12:56
♓ 23 12:12
♈ 25 13:22
♉ 27 17:54
♊ 30 02:01

Aug 2005
♋ 1 12:51
♌ 4 01:09
♍ 6 13:53
♎ 9 02:08
♏ 11 12:34
♐ 13 19:47
♑ 15 23:12
♒ 17 23:38
♓ 19 22:52
♈ 21 23:01
♉ 24 01:57
♊ 26 08:42

☽ Moon

Aug 2005
♋ 28 18:56
♌ 31 07:13

Sep 2005
♍ 2 19:55
♎ 5 07:51
♏ 7 18:09
♐ 10 02:02
♑ 12 06:56
♒ 14 09:02
♓ 16 09:25
♈ 18 09:43
♉ 20 11:47
♊ 22 17:06
♋ 25 02:10
♌ 27 14:01
♍ 30 02:44

Oct 2005
♎ 2 14:23
♏ 5 00:03
♐ 7 07:27
♑ 9 12:43
♒ 11 16:05
♓ 13 18:05
♈ 15 19:39
♉ 17 22:04
♊ 20 02:44
♋ 22 10:40
♌ 24 21:48
♍ 27 10:27
♎ 29 22:14

Nov 2005
♏ 1 07:28
♐ 3 13:55
♑ 5 18:17
♒ 7 21:30
♓ 10 00:22
♈ 12 03:22
♉ 14 07:02
♊ 16 12:10
♋ 18 19:42
♌ 21 06:09
♍ 23 18:40
♎ 26 06:57
♏ 28 16:32
♐ 30 22:32

Dec 2005
♑ 3 01:42
♒ 5 03:36
♓ 7 05:44
♈ 9 09:01
♉ 11 13:45
♊ 13 19:59
♋ 16 04:01
♌ 18 14:17
♍ 21 02:38
♎ 23 15:25
♏ 26 02:03
♐ 28 08:43
♑ 30 11:35

Jan 2006
♒ 1 12:15
♓ 3 12:44
♈ 5 14:44
♉ 7 19:08
♊ 10 01:58
♋ 12 10:49
♌ 14 21:30
♍ 17 09:48
♎ 19 22:48
♏ 22 10:27
♐ 24 18:37
♑ 26 22:31

☽ Moon

Jan 2006
♒ 28 23:0
♓ 30 22:3

Feb 2006
♈ 1 22:4
♉ 4 01:3
♊ 6 07:3
♋ 8 16:3
♌ 11 03:4
♍ 13 16:1
♎ 16 05:0
♏ 18 17:1
♐ 21 02:3
♑ 23 08:1
♒ 25 10:1
♓ 27 09:5

Mar 2006
♈ 1 09:1
♉ 3 10:2
♊ 5 14:3
♋ 7 22:3
♌ 10 09:4
♍ 12 22:2
♎ 15 11:1
♏ 17 22:5
♐ 20 08:4
♑ 22 15:3
♒ 24 19:2
♓ 26 20:3
♈ 28 20:3
♉ 30 21:0

Apr 2006
♊ 1 23:4
♋ 4 06:1
♌ 6 16:2
♍ 9 04:5
♎ 11 17:4
♏ 14 05:0
♐ 16 14:1
♑ 18 21:1
♒ 21 01:5
♓ 23 04:4
♈ 25 06:1
♉ 27 07:2
♊ 29 09:5

May 2006
♋ 1 15:17
♌ 4 00:17
♍ 6 12:19
♎ 9 01:10
♏ 11 12:24
♐ 13 20:5
♑ 16 02:5
♒ 18 07:1
♓ 20 10:3
♈ 22 13:2
♉ 24 16:00
♊ 26 19:19
♋ 29 00:33
♌ 31 08:51

Jun 2006
♍ 2 20:16
♎ 5 09:07
♏ 7 20:40
♐ 10 05:04
♑ 12 10:19
♒ 14 13:32
♓ 16 16:05
♈ 18 18:53
♉ 20 22:22
♊ 23 02:49
♋ 25 08:47
♌ 27 17:08

Moon

Jun 2006
♍30 04:14

Jul 2006
♎ 2 17:04
♏ 5 05:12
♐ 7 14:13
♑ 9 19:24
♒11 21:46
♓13 22:59
♈16 00:38
♉18 03:43
♊20 08:37
♋22 15:27
♌25 00:24
♍27 11:35
♎30 00:27

Aug 2006
♏ 1 13:07
♐ 3 23:13
♑ 6 05:19
♒ 8 07:47
♓10 08:11
♈12 08:22
♉14 09:59
♊16 14:06
♋18 21:02
♌21 06:33
♍23 18:07
♎26 07:01
♏28 19:55
♐31 06:59

Sep 2006
♑ 2 14:34
♒ 4 18:14
♓ 6 18:56
♈ 8 18:23
♉10 18:30
♊12 20:59
♋15 02:53
♌17 12:14
♍20 00:06
♎22 13:06
♏25 01:54
♐27 13:15
♑29 22:00

Oct 2006
♒ 2 03:24
♓ 4 05:33
♈ 6 05:32
♉ 8 05:04
♊10 06:06
♋12 10:20
♌14 18:37
♍17 06:15
♎19 19:19
♏22 07:54
♐24 18:53
♑27 03:46
♒29 10:16
♓31 14:10

Nov 2006
♈ 2 15:46
♉ 4 16:05
♊ 6 16:46
♋ 8 19:45
♌11 02:33
♍13 13:17
♎16 02:14
♏18 14:46
♐21 01:15
♑23 09:25
♒25 15:40
♓27 20:20

☽ Moon

Nov 2006
♈29 23:29

Dec 2006
♉ 2 01:26
♊ 4 03:05
♋ 6 06:00
♌ 8 11:51
♍10 21:30
♎13 09:59
♏15 22:42
♐18 09:10
♑20 16:39
♒22 21:48
♓25 01:43
♈27 05:03
♉29 08:08
♊31 11:16

Jan 2007
♋ 2 15:14
♌ 4 21:14
♍ 7 06:17
♎ 9 18:14
♏12 07:07
♐14 18:10
♑17 01:49
♒19 06:15
♓21 08:48
♈23 10:52
♉25 13:28
♊27 17:09
♋29 22:16

Feb 2007
♌ 1 05:14
♍ 3 14:33
♎ 6 02:14
♏ 8 15:08
♐11 03:00
♑13 11:41
♒15 16:34
♓17 18:30
♈19 19:06
♉21 20:03
♊23 22:41
♋26 03:47
♌28 11:29

Mar 2007
♍ 2 21:31
♎ 5 09:24
♏ 7 22:16
♐10 10:36
♑12 20:34
♒15 02:51
♓17 05:30
♈19 05:42
♉21 05:15
♊23 06:06
♋25 09:48
♌27 17:03
♍30 03:26

Apr 2007
♎ 1 15:42
♏ 4 04:35
♐ 6 16:56
♑ 9 03:35
♒11 11:22
♓13 15:38
♈15 16:47
♉17 16:11
♊19 15:51
♋21 17:50
♌23 23:37
♍26 09:23
♎28 21:44

☽ Moon

May 2007
♏ 1 10:40
♐ 3 22:47
♑ 6 09:20
♒ 8 17:47
♓10 23:31
♈13 02:18
♉15 02:48
♊17 02:33
♋19 03:37
♌21 07:56
♍23 16:25
♎26 04:15
♏28 17:10
♐31 05:06

Jun 2007
♑ 2 15:09
♒ 4 23:15
♓ 7 05:23
♈ 9 09:26
♉11 11:29
♊13 12:24
♋15 13:45
♌17 17:24
♍20 00:45
♎22 11:42
♏25 00:26
♐27 12:23
♑29 22:04

Jul 2007
♒ 2 05:23
♓ 4 10:52
♈ 6 14:56
♉ 8 17:53
♊10 20:09
♋12 22:39
♌15 02:43
♍17 09:39
♎19 19:52
♏22 08:17
♐24 20:29
♑27 06:21
♒29 13:13
♓31 17:40

Aug 2007
♈ 2 20:42
♉ 4 23:15
♊ 7 02:01
♋ 9 05:36
♌11 10:41
♍13 18:02
♎16 04:03
♏18 16:12
♐21 04:43
♑23 15:19
♒25 22:35
♓28 02:34
♈30 04:24

Sep 2007
♉ 1 05:35
♊ 3 07:29
♋ 5 11:07
♌ 7 16:59
♍10 01:09
♎12 11:30
♏14 23:36
♐17 12:20
♑19 23:51
♒22 08:17
♓24 12:55
♈26 14:23
♉28 14:17
♊30 14:34

☽ Moon

Oct 2007
♋ 2 16:56
♌ 4 22:26
♍ 7 07:02
♎ 9 17:57
♏12 06:13
♐14 18:57
♑17 07:02
♒19 16:51
♓21 23:02
♈24 01:24
♉26 01:06
♊28 00:11
♋30 00:49

Nov 2007
♌ 1 04:47
♍ 3 12:43
♎ 5 23:47
♏ 8 12:17
♐11 00:58
♑13 13:00
♒15 23:29
♓18 07:14
♈20 11:24
♉22 12:19
♊24 11:30
♋26 11:07
♌28 13:23
♍30 19:43

Dec 2007
♎ 3 06:00
♏ 5 18:30
♐ 8 07:10
♑10 18:50
♒13 05:01
♓15 13:14
♈17 18:52
♉19 21:38
♊21 22:14
♋23 22:18
♌25 23:51
♍28 04:43
♎30 13:36

Jan 2008
♏ 2 01:31
♐ 4 14:12
♑ 7 01:42
♒ 9 11:13
♓11 18:44
♈14 00:23
♉16 04:12
♊18 06:30
♋20 08:05
♌22 10:20
♍24 14:48
♎26 22:34
♏29 09:34
♐31 22:07

Feb 2008
♑ 3 09:51
♒ 5 19:09
♓ 8 01:46
♈10 06:17
♉12 09:33
♊14 12:19
♋16 15:12
♌18 18:51
♍21 00:06
♎23 07:44
♏25 18:05
♐28 06:21

Mar 2008
♑ 1 18:32

☽ Moon

Mar 2008
♒ 4 04:24
♓ 6 10:52
♈ 8 14:23
♉10 16:14
♊12 17:54
♋14 20:37
♌17 01:03
♍19 07:25
♎21 15:44
♏24 02:06
♐26 14:10
♑29 02:42
♒31 13:33

Apr 2008
♓ 2 20:54
♈ 5 00:27
♉ 7 01:19
♊ 9 01:26
♋11 02:43
♌13 06:28
♍15 13:06
♎17 22:09
♏20 09:00
♐22 21:07
♑25 09:46
♒27 21:26
♓30 06:10

May 2008
♈ 2 10:51
♉ 4 11:58
♊ 6 11:18
♋ 8 11:02
♌10 13:09
♍12 18:47
♎15 03:46
♏17 14:58
♐20 03:18
♑22 15:55
♒25 03:51
♓27 13:37
♈29 19:52
♉31 22:18

Jun 2008
♊ 2 22:06
♋ 4 21:16
♌ 6 22:00
♍ 9 02:01
♎11 09:54
♏13 20:52
♐16 09:19
♑18 21:51
♒21 09:33
♓23 19:31
♈26 02:48
♉28 06:50
♊30 08:03

Jul 2008
♋ 2 07:53
♌ 4 08:15
♍ 6 11:03
♎ 8 17:30
♏11 03:34
♐13 15:49
♑16 04:19
♒18 15:39
♓21 01:07
♈23 08:22
♉25 13:14
♊27 15:55
♋29 17:12
♌31 18:22

☽ Moon

Aug 2008
♍ 2 20:59
♎ 5 02:27
♏ 7 11:25
♐ 9 23:10
♑12 11:41
♒14 22:55
♓17 07:46
♈19 14:09
♉21 18:37
♊23 21:48
♋26 00:18
♌28 02:50
♍30 06:18

Sep 2008
♎ 1 11:44
♏ 3 20:01
♐ 6 07:10
♑ 8 19:44
♒11 07:19
♓13 16:04
♈15 21:39
♉18 00:56
♊20 03:16
♋22 05:48
♌24 09:13
♍26 13:52
♎28 20:05

Oct 2008
♏ 1 04:25
♐ 3 15:13
♑ 6 03:48
♒ 8 16:02
♓11 01:30
♈13 07:07
♉15 09:31
♊17 10:26
♋19 11:40
♌21 14:34
♍23 19:39
♎26 02:47
♏28 11:47
♐30 22:40

Nov 2008
♑ 2 11:12
♒ 5 00:01
♓ 7 10:42
♈ 9 17:25
♉11 20:05
♊13 20:11
♋15 19:52
♌17 21:07
♍20 01:12
♎22 08:19
♏24 17:53
♐27 05:13
♑29 17:47

Dec 2008
♒ 2 06:44
♓ 4 18:22
♈ 7 02:43
♉ 9 06:52
♊11 07:34
♋13 06:40
♌15 06:22
♍17 08:35
♎19 14:22
♏21 23:36
♐24 11:12
♑26 23:55
♒29 12:42

Jan 2009
♓ 1 00:26

☽ Moon

Jan 2009
♈ 3 09:49
♉ 5 15:45
♊ 7 18:11
♋ 9 18:14
♌11 17:41
♍13 18:33
♎15 22:29
♏18 06:19
♐20 17:29
♑23 06:17
♒25 18:56
♓28 06:11
♈30 15:24

Feb 2009
♉ 1 22:08
♊ 4 02:14
♋ 6 04:05
♌ 8 04:43
♍10 05:38
♎12 08:32
♏14 14:50
♐17 00:53
♑19 13:24
♒22 02:06
♓24 12:59
♈26 21:23

Mar 2009
♉ 1 03:33
♊ 3 07:58
♋ 5 11:07
♌ 7 13:24
♍ 9 15:34
♎11 18:46
♏14 00:22
♐16 09:21
♑18 21:18
♒21 10:05
♓23 21:07
♈26 05:02
♉28 10:09
♊30 13:36

Apr 2009
♋ 1 16:30
♌ 3 19:32
♍ 5 23:01
♎ 8 03:22
♏10 09:23
♐12 18:00
♑15 05:26
♒17 18:18
♓20 05:54
♈22 14:08
♉24 18:46
♊26 21:02
♋28 22:38

May 2009
♌ 1 00:55
♍ 3 04:36
♎ 5 09:51
♏ 7 16:47
♐10 01:49
♑12 13:08
♒15 02:01
♓17 14:16
♈19 23:30
♉22 04:40
♊24 06:34
♋26 06:58
♌28 07:44
♍30 10:17

Jun 2009
♎ 1 15:16

☽ Moon

Jun 2009
♏ 3 22:43
♐ 6 08:23
♑ 8 19:59
♒11 08:52
♓13 21:31
♈16 07:51
♉18 14:20
♊20 17:00
♋22 17:12
♌24 16:50
♍26 17:46
♎28 21:24

Jul 2009
♏ 1 04:18
♐ 3 14:10
♑ 6 02:07
♒ 8 15:03
♓11 03:43
♈13 14:39
♉15 22:29
♊18 02:41
♋20 03:51
♌22 03:27
♍24 03:22
♎26 05:25
♏28 10:55
♐30 20:09

Aug 2009
♑ 2 08:07
♒ 4 21:07
♓ 7 09:34
♈ 9 20:22
♉12 04:49
♊14 10:25
♋16 13:13
♌18 13:57
♍20 14:01
♎22 15:12
♏24 19:16
♐27 03:15
♑29 14:43

Sep 2009
♒ 1 03:42
♓ 3 15:57
♈ 6 02:14
♉ 8 10:17
♊10 16:16
♋12 20:19
♌14 22:39
♍16 23:55
♎19 01:26
♏21 04:51
♐23 11:42
♑25 22:18
♒28 11:05
♓30 23:25

Oct 2009
♈ 3 09:20
♉ 5 16:33
♊ 7 21:46
♋10 01:47
♌12 05:02
♍14 07:45
♎16 10:29
♏18 14:22
♐20 20:48
♑23 06:38
♒25 19:07
♓28 07:44
♈30 17:56

Nov 2009
♉ 2 00:44

☽ Moon

Nov 2009
♊ 4 04:52
♋ 6 07:42
♌ 8 10:22
♍10 13:30
♎12 17:22
♏14 22:23
♐17 05:21
♑19 15:00
♒22 03:10
♓24 16:06
♈27 03:10
♉29 10:33

Dec 2009
♊ 1 14:23
♋ 3 16:01
♌ 5 17:07
♍ 7 19:05
♎ 9 22:46
♏12 04:31
♐14 12:24
♑16 22:31
♒19 10:38
♓21 23:41
♈24 11:38
♉26 20:25
♊29 01:13
♋31 02:45

Jan 2010
♌ 2 02:41
♍ 4 02:52
♎ 6 04:58
♏ 8 09:59
♐10 18:09
♑13 04:53
♒15 17:16
♓18 06:16
♈20 18:35
♉23 04:39
♊25 11:11
♋27 14:01
♌29 14:10
♍31 13:23

Feb 2010
♎ 2 13:42
♏ 4 16:55
♐ 7 00:03
♑ 9 10:42
♒11 23:23
♓14 12:22
♈17 00:30
♉19 10:54
♊21 18:46
♋23 23:28
♌26 01:08
♍28 00:52

Mar 2010
♎ 2 00:31
♏ 4 02:11
♐ 6 07:35
♑ 8 17:12
♒11 05:41
♓13 18:43
♈16 06:31
♉18 16:29
♊21 00:28
♋23 06:15
♌25 09:38
♍27 10:57
♎29 11:21
♏31 12:41

Apr 2010
♐ 2 16:52

☽ Moon

Apr 2010
♑ 5 01:06
♒ 7 12:49
♓10 01:47
♈12 13:30
♉14 22:54
♊17 06:07
♋19 11:38
♌21 15:41
♍23 18:24
♎25 20:16
♏27 22:28
♐30 02:35

May 2010
♑ 2 09:59
♒ 4 20:51
♓ 7 09:33
♈ 9 21:28
♉12 06:47
♊14 13:17
♋16 17:45
♌18 21:06
♍20 23:58
♎23 02:49
♏25 06:17
♐27 11:15
♑29 18:43

Jun 2010
♒ 1 05:07
♓ 3 17:32
♈ 6 05:49
♉ 8 15:40
♊10 22:10
♋13 01:50
♌15 03:54
♍17 05:40
♎19 08:13
♏21 12:13
♐23 18:09
♑26 02:21
♒28 12:51

Jul 2010
♓ 1 01:09
♈ 3 13:43
♉ 6 00:28
♊ 8 07:50
♋10 11:38
♌12 12:54
♍14 13:15
♎16 14:24
♏18 17:41
♐20 23:48
♑23 08:38
♒25 19:37
♓28 07:59
♈30 20:41

Aug 2010
♉ 2 08:12
♊ 4 16:53
♋ 6 21:49
♌ 8 23:22
♍10 23:00
♎12 22:42
♏15 00:26
♐17 05:33
♑19 14:16
♒22 01:37
♓24 14:10
♈27 02:48
♉29 14:34

Sep 2010
♊ 1 00:19
♋ 3 06:50

☽ Moon

Sep 2010
♌ 5 09:45
♍ 7 09:53
♎ 9 09:01
♏11 09:21
♐13 12:51
♑15 20:29
♒18 07:34
♓20 20:14
♈23 08:46
♉25 20:16
♊28 06:10
♋30 13:45

Oct 2010
♌ 2 18:20
♍ 4 20:00
♎ 6 19:52
♏ 8 19:52
♐10 22:08
♑13 04:16
♒15 14:22
♓18 02:51
♈20 15:22
♉23 02:29
♊25 11:47
♋27 19:14
♌30 00:38

Nov 2010
♍ 1 03:51
♎ 3 05:18
♏ 5 06:15
♐ 7 08:27
♑ 9 13:36
♒11 22:31
♓14 10:23
♈16 22:58
♉19 10:03
♊21 18:45
♋24 01:13
♌26 06:01
♍28 09:33
♎30 12:15

Dec 2010
♏ 2 14:43
♐ 4 17:59
♑ 6 23:15
♒ 9 07:30
♓11 18:39
♈14 07:13
♉16 18:48
♊19 03:37
♋21 09:22
♌23 12:50
♍25 15:14
♎27 17:37
♏29 20:49

Table of Ascendants A (Latitude 39N00 Meridian 75W00)

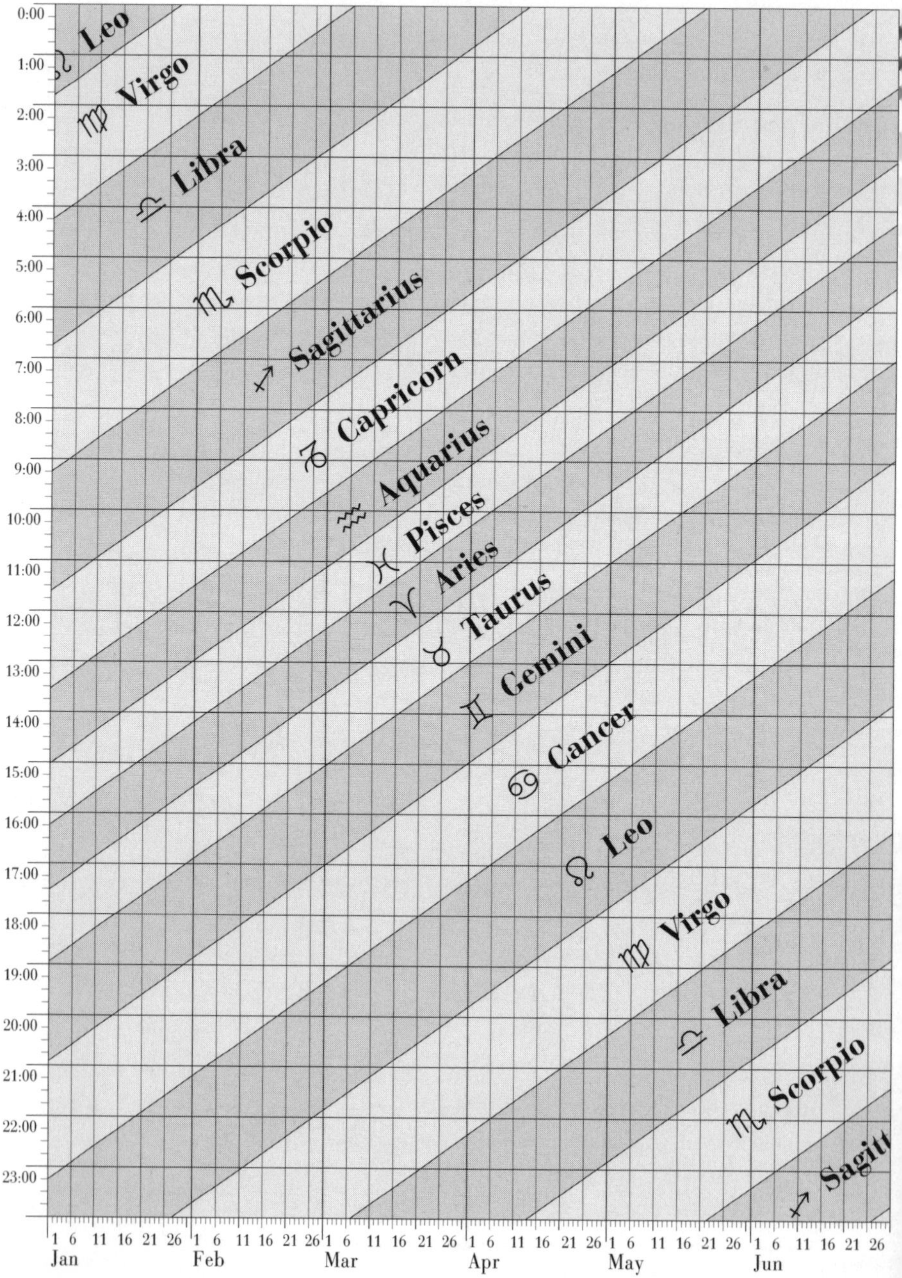

Table of Ascendants A (Latitude 39N00 Meridian 75W00)

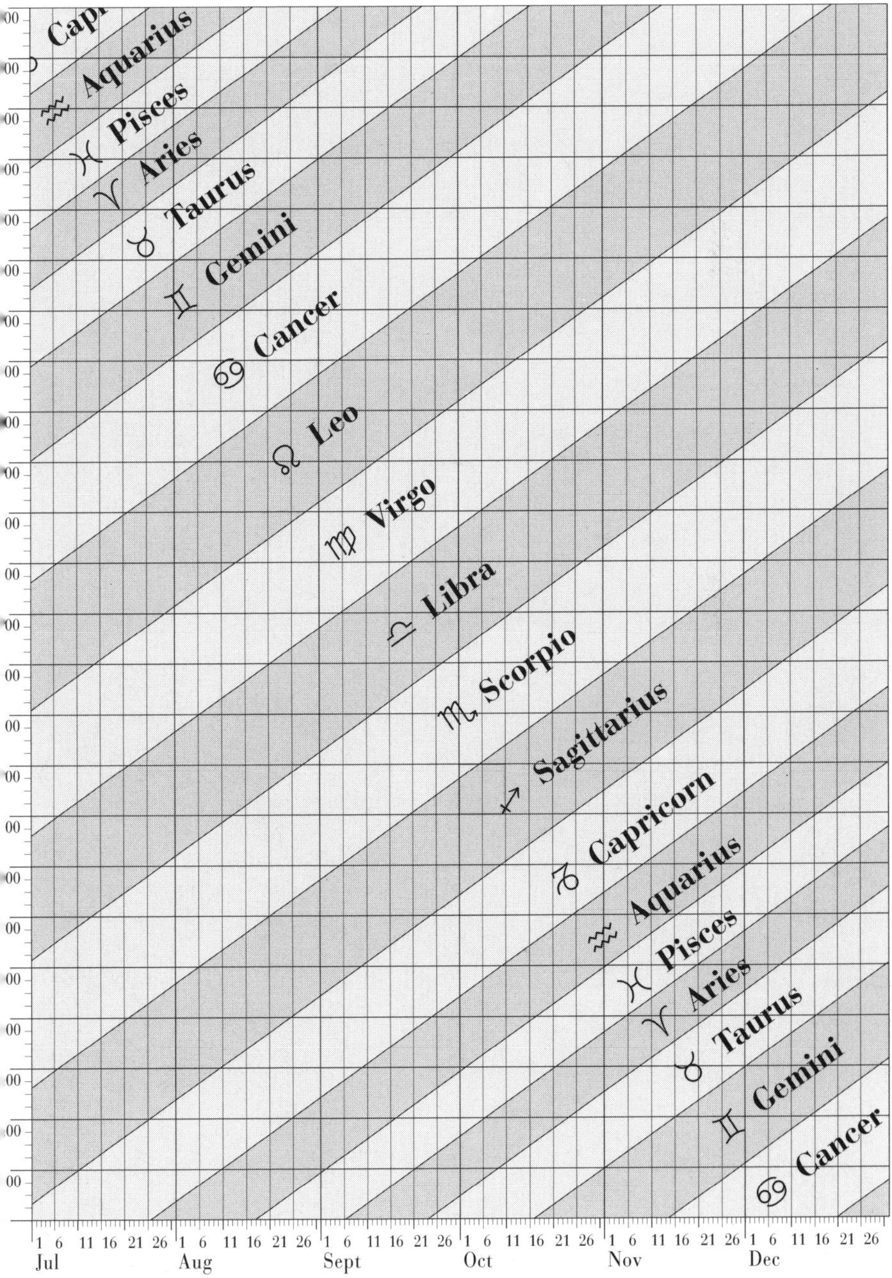

Table of Ascendants B (Latitude 45N30 Meridian 75W00)

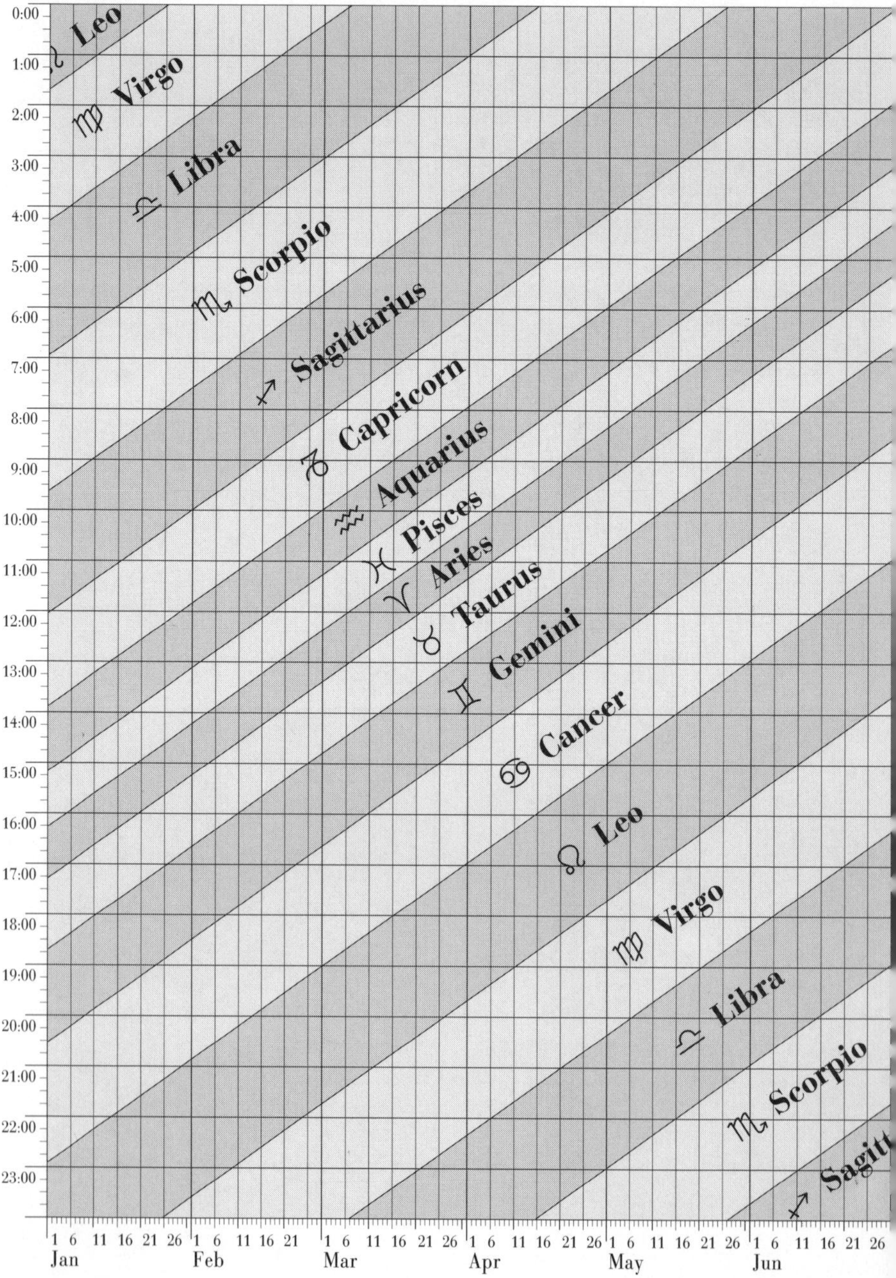

Table of Ascendants B (Latitude 45N30 Meridian 75W00)

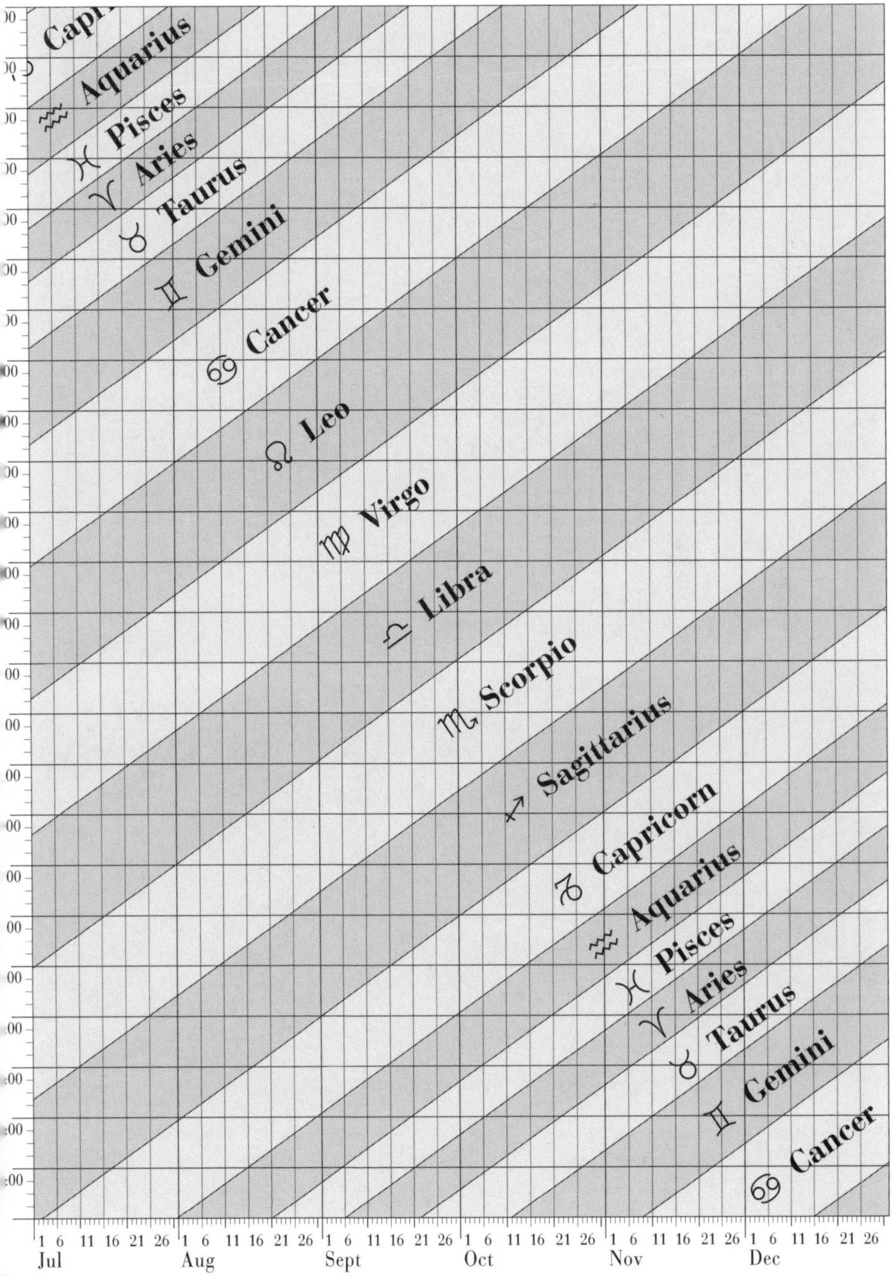

Table of Ascendants C (Latitude 51N30 Meridian 0W00)

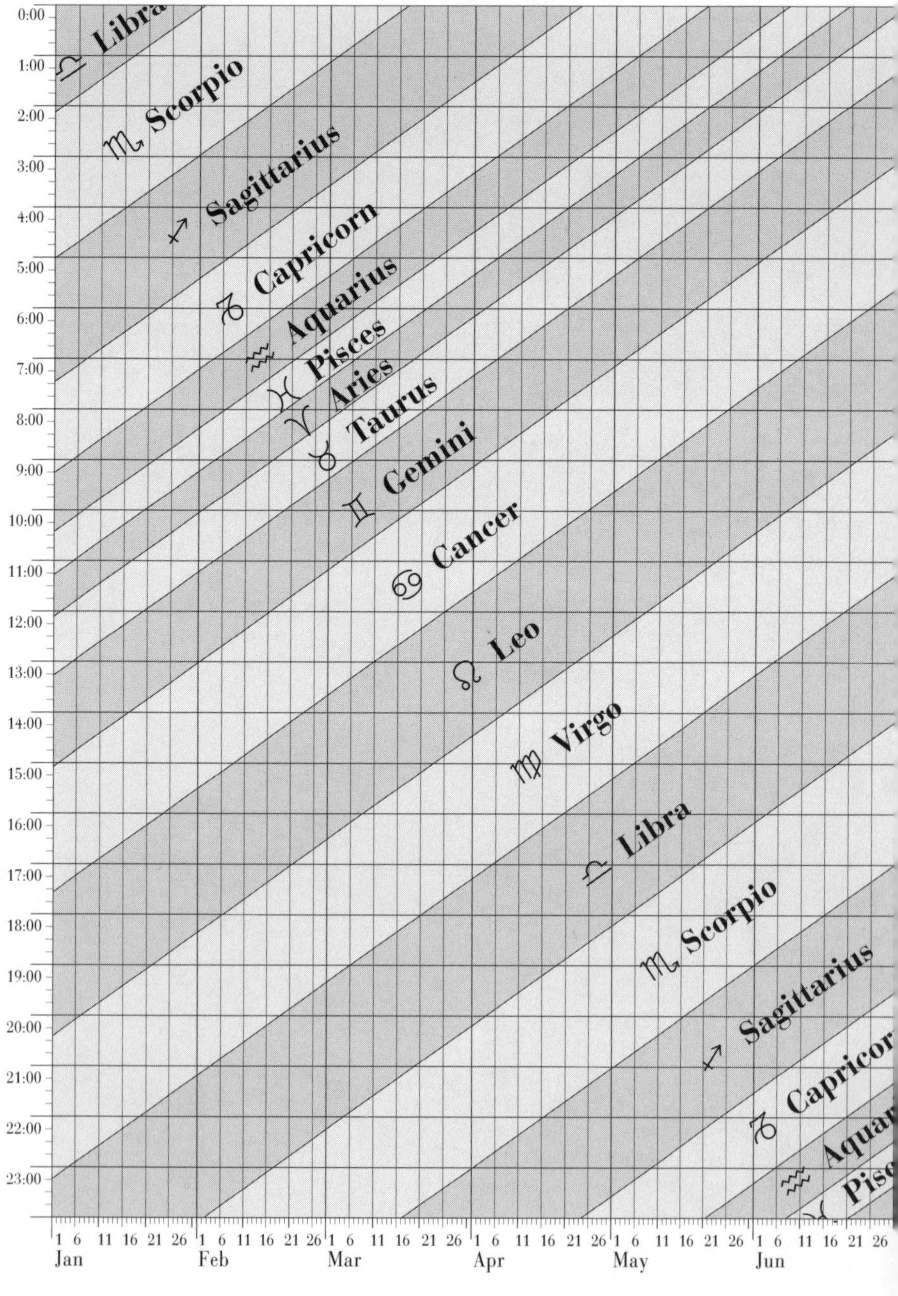

Table of Ascendants C (Latitude 51N30 Meridian 0W00)

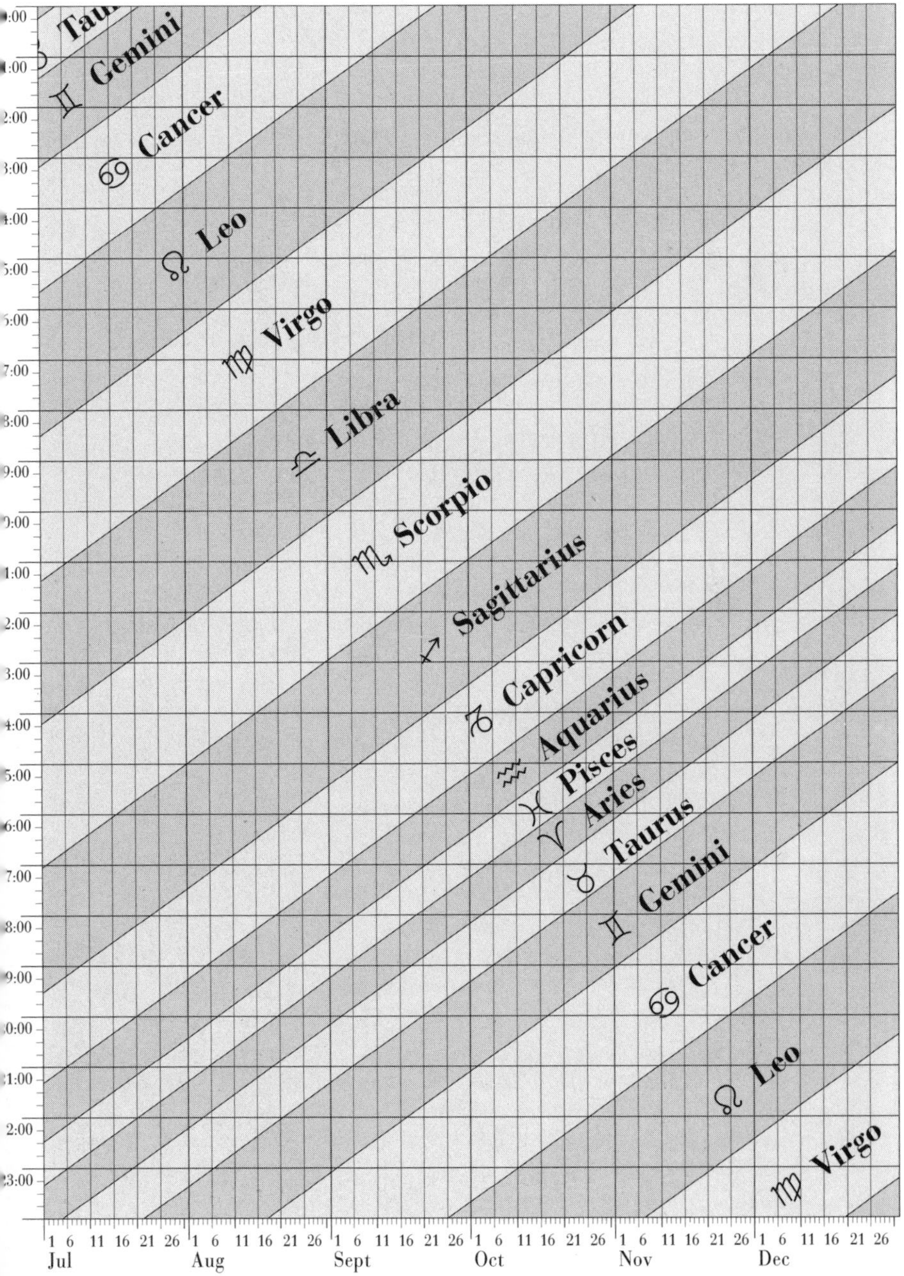

Table of Ascendants D (Latitude 34S00 Meridian 150E00)

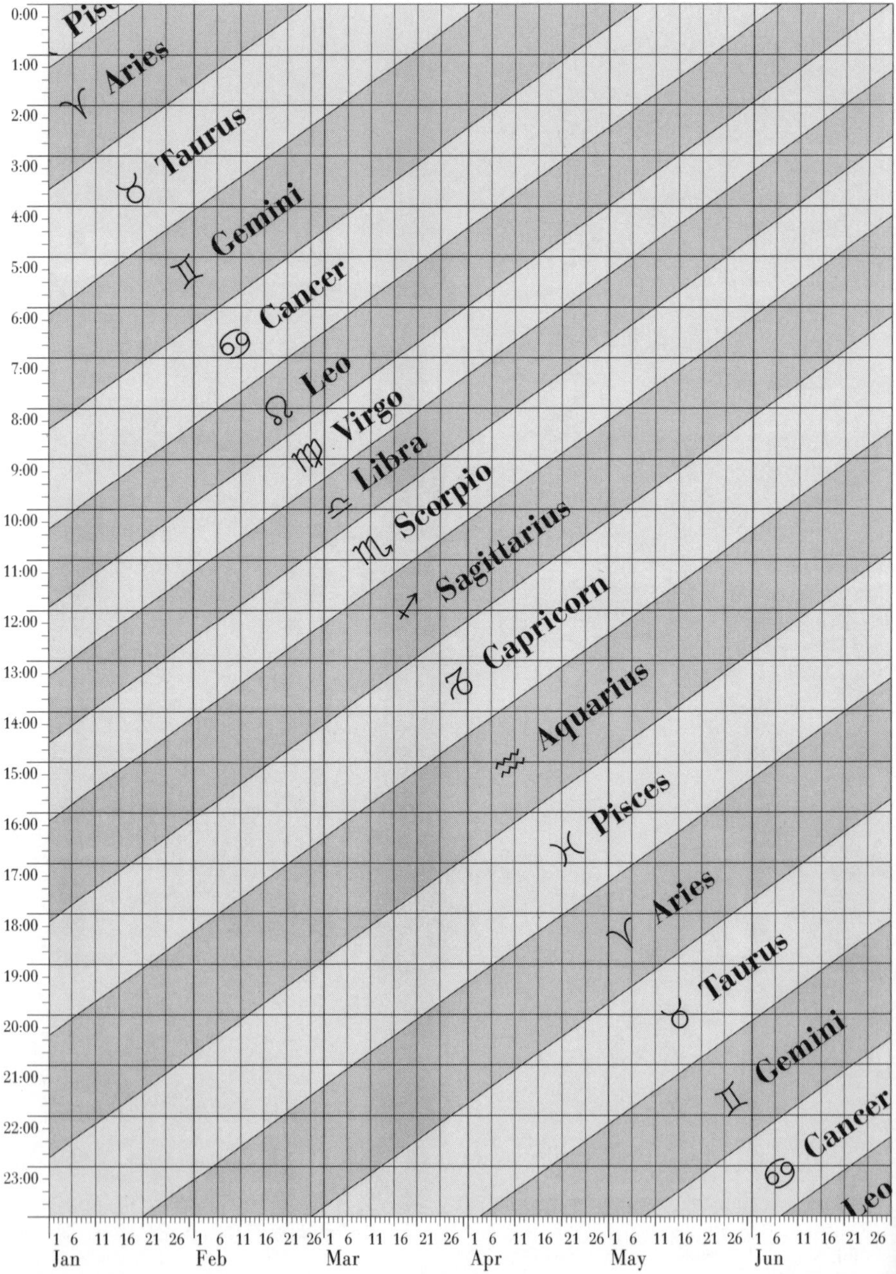

Table of Ascendants D (Latitude 34S00 Meridian 150E00)

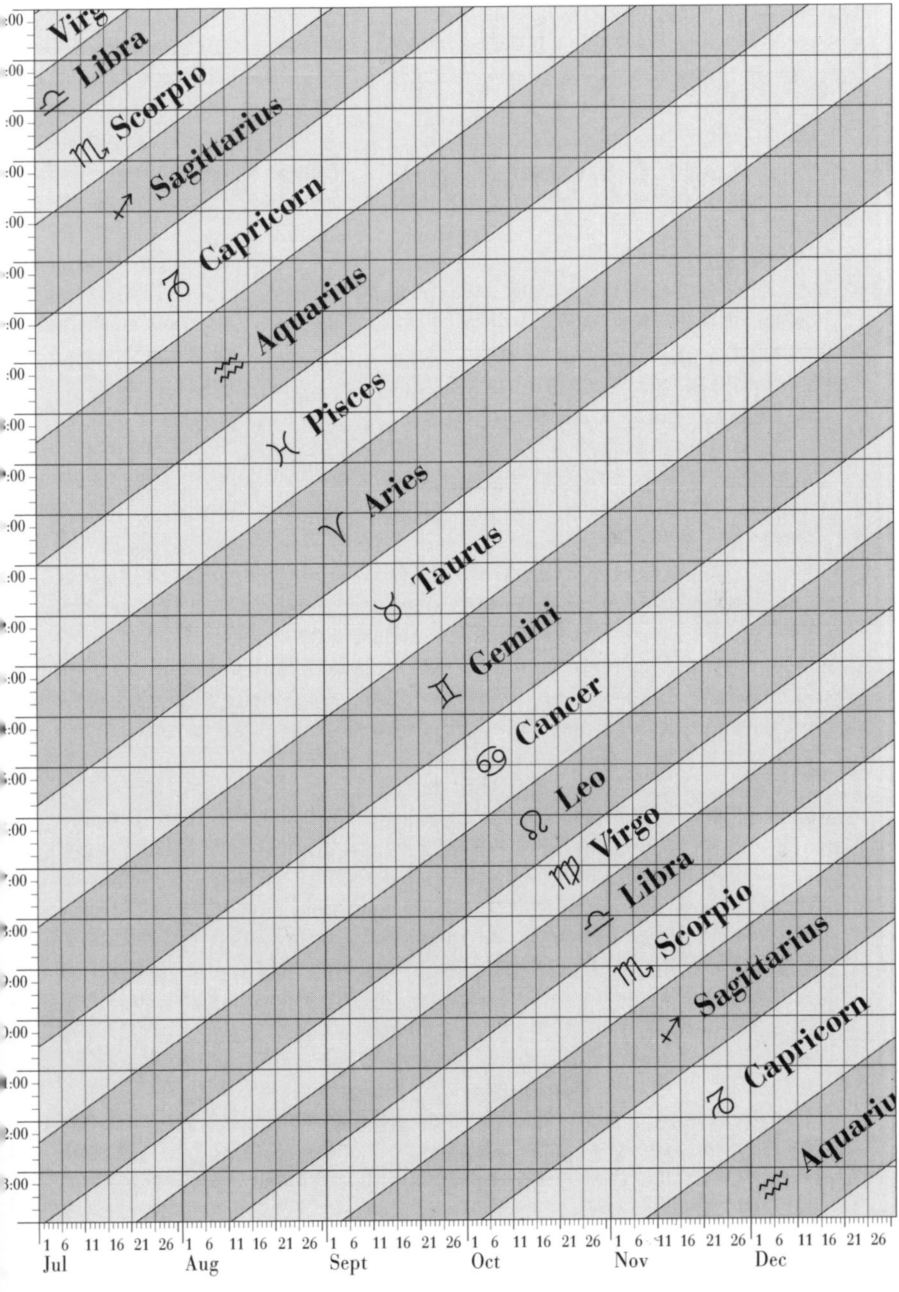

PART FOUR

INDIVIDUAL COMBINATIONS

The Sun

⊙

The Sun in the Element of Fire reflects the importance of self-expression, and describes the need to find a field of work in which the individual's creative ideas can be given shape.

The Sun in Aries ♈

Any person born with the Sun in Aries needs to discover a sense of personal potency through the exercise of initiative and the expression of original ideas. The Sun in Aries needs to find appropriate channels through which enthusiasm, vision, love of challenge and a competitive and crusading spirit can be demonstrated. Ariens are often not comfortable as committee members, and will feel most fulfilled working in a sphere where there is plenty of room for innovative thinking, independent decision-making and a minimum of hierarchical structure.

The Sun in Leo ♌

Any person born with the Sun in Leo needs to find a place in life where he or she can shine and be recognized as special. The Sun in Leo needs to discover creative outlets where originality and charismatic personal style can be expressed, and where there is an admiring audience appreciative of the person's efforts. As Leos resent hiding their light under a bushel or sharing the limelight with others, they will feel most fulfilled in a sphere of work where a sense of personal destiny can be pursued, and recognition can be achieved through personal excellence.

The Sun in Sagittarius ♐

Any person born with the Sun in Sagittarius needs to pursue knowledge through physical or intellectual journeys which expand horizons and open up a broader view of life. Restless and easily bored once a goal has been achieved, the Sun in Sagittarius needs plenty of freedom to move from one project to another, finding fresh enthusiasm through varied sources of learning and experience. Sagittarians will be happiest and most fulfilled in a sphere of work where the mind is constantly challenged and the links between different fields of knowledge can be explored.

The Sun in the Element of Earth reflects the importance of order and stability, and describes the need to make a practical and useful contribution to personal and collective life.

The Sun in Taurus ♉

Any person born with the Sun in Taurus needs to work slowly and steadily toward the acquisition of permanent values and stable material structures. Although it may take time to formulate goals and find a direction, Taureans resent being pushed and need to proceed at their own rate of speed, regardless of the expectations of others. Self-sufficiency and a sense of pride in making a solid and lasting contribution to family and society are likely to be important to the mature Taurean, who will rely increasingly on traditional values tested by time.

The Sun in Virgo ♍

Any person born with the Sun in Virgo needs to create a sense of order and harmony through the acquisition of knowledge and skills which make a practical contribution to the environment. Feeling useful is highly important to Virgoans, whose intense curiosity about a great variety of things is often combined with a desire to impart knowledge to others. Sometimes highly-strung and frightened of unpredictable change, Virgoans will be most fulfilled in a sphere of work which combines intellectual variety with a sense of being helpful to individuals or the community.

The Sun in Capricorn ♑

Any person born with the Sun in Capricorn needs to develop self-esteem and an inner sense of authority through working slowly and patiently toward a position of responsibility in the world. Capricorns need to feel that they are creating something lasting which will outlive them, and they will be most fulfilled in a sphere of work which allows them to exercise authority and make practical decisions which improve the lives of others. Often unsure of themselves in youth, Capricorns increasingly develop a sense of inner solidity through the tests of time.

The Sun in the Element of Air reflects the importance of ideas and ideals, and describes a need to formulate a personal code of ethics as a basis for individual choice and action.

The Sun in Gemini ♊

Any person born with the Sun in Gemini needs to acquire as broad a base of knowledge as possible in order to satisfy a permanent state of intellectual curiosity. Geminians are easily bored and often resistant to pursuing only one direction. They need constant mental challenge and will be most fulfilled in a sphere of work which allows them to make connections between differing spheres of knowledge. Contact with people is also important and Gemini needs the freedom to communicate with personal as well as professional contacts who represent a wide range of opinions.

The Sun in Libra ♎

Any person born with the Sun in Libra needs to express ideals of harmony and beauty through endeavors which bring greater order and balance to the environment and to society. Often gifted in the arts or in group interaction, Librans can be excellent organizers, and will be most fulfilled in a field of work which allows them to engage in cooperative ventures that initiate positive changes in the environment. Stronger and more tenacious than they appear, Librans need first to define personal goals which embody their vision of a better and happier world.

The Sun in Aquarius ♒

Any person born with the Sun in Aquarius needs to feel part of a larger human family through cooperative endeavors which create positive changes in the environment. Whether within the family or in broader and more impersonal efforts, Aquarians are natural reformers and hold an ideal vision of how human potential could best be developed. They will be most fulfilled in a sphere of work which enhances consciousness and improves the human condition, particularly through the application of psychological, scientific or political knowledge.

The Sun in the Element of Water reflects the importance of relationship, and describes a need for closeness and the sharing of emotional, imaginative and spiritual experience.

The Sun in Cancer ♋

Any person born with the Sun in Cancer needs to feel connected with the past through a sense of history and emotional interaction with others. Tougher and more tenacious than they appear, Cancerians move cautiously toward goals which they may not reveal to others until success is assured. The Sun in Cancer will be most fulfilled in a field of work providing plenty of human contact, and a sense of helping to preserve the traditional values and roots of the family, the community or the nation.

The Sun in Scorpio ♏

Any person born with the Sun in Scorpio needs to feel connected with the deeper levels of life through endeavors which penetrate the secrets of human nature. Proud and intense, Scorpio will be most fulfilled in a sphere of work providing autonomy and deep emotional commitment—material goals alone are rarely enough. Sensitive to psychic atmospheres, Scorpios need privacy and the freedom to pursue their goals without pressure or interference from employers or company hierarchies.

The Sun in Pisces ♓

Any person born with the Sun in Pisces needs to experience the unity of life through involvement in work which provides as inclusive an emotional connection with others as possible. Often highly imaginative, intuitive and even mystical, Pisceans will be happiest and most fulfilled in a sphere of work which allows them to translate their rich inner world into artistic, scientific or humanitarian contributions which reflect their deep understanding of, and empathy with, human nature, and their sense of realities that lie beyond the physical world.

The Moon

☽

The Moon in the Element of Fire reflects emotional liveliness, and describes the need to express and receive feelings in a spontaneous, enthusiastic and individualistic way.

The Moon in Aries ♈

Any person born with the Moon in Aries is inclined to express feelings impulsively, directly and without undue regard for others' needs or opinions. Intense, impatient and sometimes abrupt, the Moon in Aries loves challenge and excitement in emotional interchange, and can become restless and querulous if everyday life is too monotonous and safe. The pursuit of the difficult, even the unobtainable, can be deeply attractive for the Moon in Aries, and the need to be first in any personal situation can create a self-assertive, forceful and sometimes highly competitive manner.

The Moon in Leo ♌

Any person born with the Moon in Leo is inclined to express feelings dramatically and with great intensity. Proud and inclined to be touchy about self-image, the Moon in Leo loves to be the center of attention, and can become resentful and depressed if everyday life lacks color, inspiration and the chance to be theatrical. Generosity, constancy, devotion and a sense of honor are innate qualities, but the Moon in Leo is not inclined to silent self-sacrifice and needs plenty of loyalty, appreciation and strong emotional response from others.

The Moon in Sagittarius ♐

Any person born with the Moon in Sagittarius is inclined to express feelings in a volatile and energetic way. There is often a sense of childlike wonder and enthusiasm about life. The Moon in Sagittarius needs everyday existence to contain plenty of exciting new adventures and glorious new opportunities. Too much routine or restriction in relationships can generate intense frustration, boredom and ongoing resentment, and an interesting companion on life's great journey is invariably preferable to a safe but uninspiring personal existence.

The Moon in the Element of Earth reflects emotional self-containment and steadiness, and describes a need to express and receive feelings in physically demonstrable ways.

The Moon in Taurus ♉

Any person born with the Moon in Taurus is inclined to express feelings in concrete ways, channeling emotions into physical affection and acts of service toward loved ones. The emotional nature is peaceable, with a strong need for the comfort of sensual gratification and the reliability of a stable material environment. Although slow to anger, the Moon in Taurus can be surprisingly unforgiving if pushed too far. Unexpected change—whether it occurs in personal relationships or everyday routines—can provoke anxiety and a stubborn resistance to any new venture or idea.

The Moon in Virgo ♍

Any person born with the Moon in Virgo is inclined to express feelings in a refined and highly controlled way, showing affection through helpful acts rather than overt emotional displays. There is great delicacy of feeling, with a strong need for order and ritual in relationships and in the immediate environment. For the Moon in Virgo, the threat of disruption can provoke considerable anxiety and distress, which may be expressed only through unpleasant physical symptoms. A cool and contained surface often causes others to underestimate emotional commitment.

The Moon in Capricorn ♑

Any person born with the Moon in Capricorn is inclined to express feelings in a highly disciplined way, demonstrating love through enduring commitment and service rather than overt displays of emotion. There is a deep need for structure and stability in relationships and domestic life for the Moon in Capricorn, and a strong sense of responsibility to loved ones may be more important than the gratification of immediate personal desires. Loyal, reliable and devoted but sometimes painfully shy, those with the Moon in Capricorn rarely wear their hearts on their sleeves.

The Moon in the Element of Air reflects emotional refinement, and describes a need to express and receive feelings in a civilized, friendly and courteous way.

The Moon in Gemini ♊

Any person born with the Moon in Gemini is inclined to express feelings in a bright, witty and articulate way. Although frequently moody and erratic, the Moon in Gemini can usually offer rationalizations for any shift in feeling, and there is often a discrepancy between emotional responses and the explanations given for them. Lively, talkative and mercurial, the Moon in Gemini seeks intellectual as well as instinctual rapport in personal relationships, preferring lightness, grace and good communication to an atmosphere of emotional intensity.

The Moon in Libra ♎

Any person born with the Moon in Libra is inclined to express feelings in a refined and civilized manner. Love is demonstrated in ways which are ethical and fair, and emotions such as jealousy or anger, which might provoke conflict or appear too demanding, are often controlled or unacknowledged. The Moon in Libra needs an atmosphere of grace and harmony in personal life, and often possesses an instinctive gift for diplomacy and tact in all dealings with others. Kindness, courtesy and gentleness are innate, and the boorishness of others can cause deep and lasting distaste.

The Moon in Aquarius ♒

Any person born with the Moon in Aquarius is inclined to express feelings in ways which reflect high standards of decency and integrity. Emotions which might be deemed too selfish or demanding are usually controlled or unacknowledged. The Moon in Aquarius needs the emotional support of the group in both personal and professional life, and may sacrifice personal happiness rather than violate a collectively held ideal. Capable of great loyalty and commitment, the Moon in Aquarius may be too ethical and proud to ask others for their help and support.

The Moon in the Element of Water reflects emotional depth and intensity, and describes a need to express and receive feelings in a sensitive, fluid and subtle way.

The Moon in Cancer ♋

Any person born with the Moon in Cancer is inclined to express feelings in subtle ways which preserve an atmosphere of emotional closeness. Fearful of loneliness and inclined to place great importance on family ties, the Moon in Cancer is loyal, sympathetic and devoted but may be reluctant to allow others their emotional independence. Sensitivity and compassion are often combined with a need to look after others.

Self-sacrifice may be sincere and heartfelt, but for the Moon in Cancer it is also a means of binding loved ones so that emotional dependency is maintained.

The Moon in Scorpio ♏

Any person born with the Moon in Scorpio is inclined to express feelings in indirect ways which conceal great intensity. At times virtually psychic, the Moon in Scorpio is often gifted with deep instinctive insight into others' motives. Capable of passionate and enduring attachments, yet proud and unforgiving in the face of hurt or humiliation, a person born with the Moon in Scorpio can be frightened of the potential control loved ones may wield. There is often conflict between the longing for closeness and the fear of being at others' mercy through feelings of dependency and need.

The Moon in Pisces ♓

Any person born with the Moon in Pisces is inclined to express feelings in gentle, fluid ways which reflect a blurring of emotional boundaries between the individual and others. Highly intuitive and compassionate, but sometimes too passive, the Moon in Pisces tends to feel what others feel and is unusually receptive to collective emotional atmospheres. Frightened of too much separateness, the Moon in Pisces may prefer personal unhappiness and self-abnegation to being alone, and may be easily taken advantage of by more self-centered personalities.

Mercury

☿

Mercury in the Element of Fire describes a mind which perceives intuitively, grasping the broad picture with its underlying meaning rather than observing the practical details.

Mercury in Aries ♈

Any person born with Mercury in Aries understands life through sudden leaps of intuitive insight, which reveals potentials but often disregards objective facts or the opinions of others. There is great mental energy, but concentration is dependent on bursts of enthusiasm, and for the person born with Mercury in Aries it may be difficult to sustain interest if too many details must be considered. Mercury in Aries learns best when intellectually challenged to produce innovative ideas which do not require too much structured analyis. Learning by rote is a sure route to impatience and boredom.

Mercury in Leo ♌

Any person born with Mercury in Leo understands life through comparing it with an inner vision of reality. Self-expression is of greater importance than memorizing information for Mercury in Leo, and facts may conflict with a richly imaginative, but sometimes highly subjective, interpretation of events and people. Experience tends to be infused with mythic patterns, colors and meanings. Mercury in Leo learns best when allowed to make a creative personal contribution, rather than when restricted to a rigid and unimaginative process of intellectual development.

Mercury in Sagittarius ♐

Any person born with Mercury in Sagittarius understands life through exploring and linking a broad range of ideas, and formulating an inclusive overview. Facts are less relevant than possibilities for Mercury in Sagittarius, and an intuitive perception of meaningful connections is often finely developed. The scope of interests is varied and it may be difficult to focus the mind on one channel of study. A person with Mercury in Sagittarius learns best when allowed to freely pursue intellectual enthusiasms without imprisonment in an excessively materialistic interpretation of reality.

Mercury in the Element of Earth describes a mind which perceives realities rather than abstractions, and is well equipped to comprehend the workings of the material world.

Mercury in Taurus ♉

Any person born with Mercury in Taurus understands life through a gradual process of storing facts and forming firm conclusions based on direct experience. Patient, pragmatic and thorough, Mercury in Taurus may not display its full mental potential in youth, because the individual must accumulate sufficient experience to feel confident about opinions and judgments. Abstractions unrelated to everyday life are often uninteresting and even threatening. Mercury in Taurus learns best when allowed to proceed at an unpressured pace.

Mercury in Virgo ♍

Any person born with Mercury in Virgo understands life through a complex process of weaving detailed fragments of experience together to form a coherent and orderly whole. The analytic faculty is usually highly developed, and versatility and clarity characterize thinking and expression. Confused or ambiguous statements and events are experienced as threatening, and must be defined and fitted into the overall pattern. Mercury in Virgo learns best when provided with clear information, which can be thoroughly digested independently of others' interference.

Mercury in Capricorn ♑

Any person born with Mercury in Capricorn understands life through measuring events and experiences against a slowly developing structure of proven insights. Speculative thinking is deeply mistrusted by Mercury in Capricorn, and personal interpretation must be perpetually tested against past experience before any judgment is considered reliable and true. Mercury in Capricorn is disciplined, thorough and capable of deep concentration. But the individual may be reluctant to express original ideas if they are not supported by objective evidence and collective consensus.

Mercury in the Element of Air describes a mind which is able to formulate concepts, perceive patterns and organize ideas, using the faculty of logical analyis to clarify experience.

Mercury in Gemini ♊

Any person born with Mercury in Gemini understands life through learning a little bit about everything. Intense curiosity about diverse subjects, combined with quick perceptions, enable the individual to link disparate facts and form fast conclusions, thus acquiring great breadth of knowledge over a lifetime. Learning for its own sake can be a joy, but disciplining mental restlessness may prove a long and difficult task. Mercury in Gemini learns best when provided with constant new intellectual challenges and the stimulating input of others' ideas.

Mercury in Libra ♎

Any person born with Mercury in Libra understands life through a process of weighing and measuring personal judgments against the opinions and interpretations of others. Reflection and comparison provide the means of acquiring an increasingly objective, fair and balanced viewpoint. There may be talent in spheres such as mathematics, architecture or music, which require a deep understanding of symmetry and the relationship between ideas. Mercury in Libra learns best through the inspiration of discussion and debate.

Mercury in Aquarius ♒

Any person born with Mercury in Aquarius understands life through exploring the underlying patterns which order events and experiences. The mind is systematic and well attuned to abstract thought, and concepts have as great a reality and importance as sensory perception. Objective truth is sought for its own sake, and there is often a gift for perceiving the basic principles which underpin any sphere of knowledge. Mercury in Aquarius learns best if allowed to explore broad conceptual frameworks without too much emphasis on peripheral details.

Mercury in the Element of Water describes a mind which perceives through the lenses of instinct and feeling, and is capable of deep intuitive insight.

Mercury in Cancer ♊

Any person born with Mercury in Cancer understands life through a subtle process of testing each experience against an instinctive inner sense of truth. The memory is often highly retentive, but it may be difficult to articulate ideas because insights are felt rather than conceptualized. There is often strong artistic sensibility, for poetry, music and visual imagery convey Cancer's complex perceptions far better than logical explanations. Mercury in Cancer learns best when information is relevant to human needs, feelings and aspirations.

Mercury in Scorpio ♏

Any person born with Mercury in Scorpio understands life through an intuitive perception of intangible realities lying beneath the surface of events and situations. The mind is adept at penetrating into hidden emotional and spiritual dimensions of experience, and there is often acute sensitivity to others' unconscious feelings and motives. Mercury in Scorpio loves discovering what others have missed, and may be particularly gifted at complex research work. The individual learns best when allowed to delve deeply into a chosen field of study.

Mercury in Pisces ♓

Any person born with Mercury in Pisces understands life through instinctive receptivity to others' feelings and fund of collective experience. The imagination is a more inspiring source of knowledge than manifest reality, and there may be an intuitive grasp of scientific truths which precedes the evidence of observed facts. Music, poetry, theater and the visual arts are often preferred vehicles for Pisces' insights into the human condition. Mercury in Pisces learns best when able to link information with deeper and more inclusive levels of the psyche.

Venus

— ♀ —

Venus in the Element of Fire reflects an ideal of love which is full of romantic excitement, inspiration and the vision of future potentials for happiness.

Venus in Aries ♈

Any person born with Venus in Aries seeks relationships which offer ongoing challenge and excitement and fire the imagination, at the same time that they provide instinctual satisfaction. The pursuit of an elusive love object may seem more rewarding than the comfortable predictability of a reliable relationship, for Venus in Aries enjoys a good contest which tests inner resources. Although capable of deep loyalty, Venus in Aries can also exhibit a strongly competitive spirit, and periodic new conquests may be a means of affirming personal potency.

Venus in Leo ♌

Any person born with Venus in Leo seeks relationships which embody the high romance and drama of an Arthurian tale. Love is perceived as a spiritual force which gives life nobility and meaning, and any suffering or sacrifice is justified to achieve it. There may be a tendency to be more in love with an ideal image than with the reality of the loved one. Loyal and generous, Venus in Leo is happiest in the role of magnanimous ruler, preferring to be the protector who gives and sometimes finding it difficult to allow loved ones real emotional equality.

Venus in Sagittarius ♐

Any person born with Venus in Sagittarius seeks relationships which expand consciousness, inspire the intellect and release unlived potentials. A companion capable of sharing life's great adventure is essential to personal fulfillment, and too much cosy domesticity may provoke a strong desire to escape into more exciting pastures. Lacking in deceit and capable of great loyalty, Venus in Sagittarius nevertheless secretly longs for a permanent lover rather than a spouse, and is happiest when the partner can respond to this need in a fun-loving spirit.

Venus in the Element of Earth reflects an ideal of love which is reliable, stable, supportive in everyday life, and realistic enough to accept ordinary human failings.

Venus in Taurus ♉

Any person born with Venus in Taurus seeks relationships which can endure the tests of time and circumstance. Endlessly patient with the foibles of loved ones, Venus in Taurus can offer unswerving commitment, but may choose unhappy security rather than gambling on an emotionally rewarding but unstable future. Loyal and respectful of traditional values, Venus in Taurus is happiest giving and receiving concrete demonstrations of love, and may ignore or dismiss those more elusive expressions which do not offer tangible proofs of devotion.

Venus in Virgo ♍

Any person born with Venus in Virgo seeks relationships which are refined, ritualized and intellectually stimulating. Courtesy and mutual respect for personal boundaries are deeply important, and there is little tolerance for the more brutish aspects of human interaction. Sometimes inhibited in expressing strong emotion, the individual prefers to demonstrate loyalty and affection through small acts of service to loved ones. Innately kind and helpful, Venus in Virgo can exhibit a painful shyness often misinterpreted as aloofness.

Venus in Capricorn ♑

Any person with Venus in Capricorn seeks relationships which provide a stable structure and contribute to social or professional standing. Deeply responsible and protective of loved ones, the individual may nevertheless fail to recognize the importance of less tangible expressions of love. Respect for traditional values and a realistic acceptance of human nature provide the basis for enduring affection. But resistance to change may make it difficult for long-term bonds to develop in new directions once an acceptable status quo has been reached.

Venus in the Element of Air reflects an ideal of love in which a true meeting of minds and spirits fulfills ethical precepts as well as emotional expectations.

Venus in Gemini ♊

Any person born with Venus in Gemini seeks relationships which provide stimulating intellectual companionship. Although able to offer loyalty and commitment, Venus in Gemini enjoys flirtation and needs a wide variety of contacts in order to satisfy an intense curiosity about other people. The sharing of intellectual, artistic, spiritual or commercial interests is more satisfying than intense emotional exchanges or a daily routine devoid of inspiring conversation. Venus in Gemini is happiest when intelligence and wit are part of human interaction.

Venus in Libra ♎

Any person born with Venus in Libra seeks harmonious relationships which embody high ideals of fairness and decency. Courtesy, kindness and intelligent communication matter greatly, and Venus in Libra has little tolerance of the moods, quarrels and ordinary human selfishness which are part of most close relationships. The expression of jealousy, anger and aggression may conflict with a deeply held need for reasoned negotiation, and a strong sense of fairness may demand that loved ones adhere to highly structured codes of behavior.

Venus in Aquarius ♒

Any person born with Venus in Aquarius seeks relationships which provide friendship and shared ideals. A need for breathing space may make others' emotional intensity seem claustrophobic, and it may be difficult for Venus in Aquarius to respond to the emotional needs of loved ones unless these are communicated in a rational manner. Strong ethics give Venus in Aquarius loyalty, tolerance and a willingness to accept major differences of opinion and outlook within close relationhips, and a deep sense of integrity makes any sort of deception repugnant.

Venus in the Element of Water reflects an ideal of love in which the dissolving of individual barriers allows a deep merging of feelings and personalities.

Venus in Cancer ♋

Any person born with Venus in Cancer seeks relationships which provide a sense of emotional belonging. There is often great attachment to family and pronounced nostalgia about the past. Gentle and romantic, Venus in Cancer is also affectionate and devoted. But possessiveness toward loved ones can result in reluctance to allow them emotional independence. Extreme sensitivity to rejection and a long memory for hurts may create a defensive veneer of coolness, but Venus in Cancer feels intensely and places deep importance on close and lasting bonds.

Venus in Scorpio ♏

Any person born with Venus in Scorpio seeks relationships which provide emotional depth, intensity and the potential for personal transformation. Shallow ties are of little interest, but there is a capacity for total self-sacrifice and devotion toward a deeply loved individual. Venus in Scorpio can be extremely possessive, and the partner's loyalty must be beyond suspicion. Betrayal and humiliation are rarely forgotten or forgiven, and early painful experiences may produce a proud veneer of detachment which conceals great vulnerability and need.

Venus in Pisces ♓

Any person born with Venus in Pisces seeks relationships which provide a magical and transcendent experience of emotional fusion. There is a strong inclination to sacrifice personal needs to an ideal of selfless love, and much time may be spent searching for the perfect union. Venus in Pisces feels deep empathy toward those in trouble or pain, and compassion and even pity may influence the choice of a partner. Disillusionment may ensue when loved ones turn out to be ordinary mortals.

Mars

— ♂ —

Mars in the Element of Fire reflects abundant physical energy and a desire nature which is impulsive, willful and impatient of the limits of everyday life.

Mars in Aries ♈

Any person born with Mars in Aries expresses will and personal desire in a direct, uncomplicated and vigorous way. Initiative and courage are inspired by competition and the opportunity to win. Mars in Aries has a combative and crusading spirit, and an enthusiastic quarrel can provide release for surplus energy. There is often great impatience with situations which require slow, careful work, or provide insufficient mental or physical challenge. Mars in Aries works best if allowed to assert individual abilities without having to wait for slower folk.

Mars in Leo ♌

Any person born with Mars in Leo expresses will and personal desire in an energetic and sometimes flamboyant way which tolerates no opposition. Magnetism and vitality combine with strength of purpose to ensure the achievement of goals. There may, however, be some difficulty for Mars in Leo in recognizing the objective reality of the wishes, needs and viewpoints of other people. The individual may inadvertently be too forceful or imperious in imposing his or her will in situations which require greater flexibility and cooperation. Mars in Leo works best if allowed to run the show.

Mars in Sagittarius ♐

Any person born with Mars in Sagittarius expresses will and personal desire in an enthusiastic and impulsive way. Energy tends to flow into many different interests and projects, and may flag if creative inspiration is lacking. For Mars in Sagittarius initiative is motivated by ideals, and if the individual's imagination is fired he or she is capable of considerable achievement. Difficulties may be experienced in situations which require patience, discipline and attention to practical details. Mars in Sagittarius works best if allowed freedom of movement, mental as well as physical.

Mars in the Element of Earth reflects highly disciplined physical energy and a desire nature which is earthy, sensual and focused on achievable goals.

Mars in Taurus ♉

Any person born with Mars in Taurus expresses will and personal desire in a firm and determined way which can sometimes be inflexible. There are great reserves of physical strength and a capacity to work long and hard to achieve practical goals. Slow to initiate new activities, Mars in Taurus, once moving, can be totally dedicated regardless of hardship or opposition. Mars in Taurus may not acknowledge when it is time to quit, and stubbornness may bind the individual to personal or professional goals which would be better relinquished.

Mars in Virgo ♍

Any person born with Mars in Virgo expresses will and personal desire in careful and highly controlled ways which ensure that the individual takes as few risks as possible. Energy is sound but often subject to cyclical shifts caused by tension. Capable of considerable discipline and focused hard work, Mars in Virgo may be driven by the need for constant activity at the expense of the body's well-being. The need for security harnesses desires to practically achievable goals, but material anxieties may stifle initiative and keep the individual bound to uninspiring work.

Mars in Capricorn ♑

Any person born with Mars in Capricorn expresses will and personal desire in disciplined ways which guarantee the fulfillment of high ambitions. Capable of total commitment to long-term goals, and able to weather the vicissitudes of material life, Mars in Capricorn approaches tasks responsibly and with great determination. But the individual may forget how to relax when effort is no longer required. Gifted with tenacity, shrewdness and instinctive organizing ability, Mars in Capricorn may find it hard to do things simply for the fun of it.

Mars in the Element of Air reflects energy which is often more mental than physical. The desire nature is tempered and refined by ideals and the need to cooperate with others.

Mars in Gemini ♊

Any person born with Mars in Gemini expresses will and personal desire in ways which are civilized, clever and elusive. Energy is erratic and hard to discipline, and although versatile, Mars in Gemini tends to abandon uncompleted projects when something more interesting comes along. Often physically agile and graceful, the individual may also be gifted at debate, discussion and the energetic communication of ideas. Mercurial and sometimes physically tense and restless, Mars in Gemini works best when the mind is fully engaged and inspired.

Mars in Libra ♎

Any person born with Mars in Libra expresses will and personal desire in a refined and gracious way which accomodates others' wishes. The pursuit of goals is civilized and cooperative, but there may be difficulty in expressing anger or engaging in open competition. Ethics temper self-assertiveness to the point where a backlog of frustration may suddenly surface in extreme anger, which in turn leads to anxiety if others are offended. Initiative is inspired by approval and feedback, and Mars in Libra works best when involved in partnership or group activities.

Mars in Aquarius ♒

Any person born with Mars in Aquarius expresses will and personal desire in ways which are contained and tempered by ethical principles. There is great strength and tenacity, but energy can only be effectively focused if the individual believes in what he or she is doing. Although able to fight on behalf of others, Mars in Aquarius may find it hard to assert personal needs. Instinctively gifted at teamwork, Mars in Aquarius possesses fine organizing and planning abilities, and works best if allowed to inspire others with a vision of change and progress.

Mars in the Element of Water reflects fluctuating physical energy and a desire nature which is sensitive and strongly influenced by the emotional atmosphere of the environment.

Mars in Cancer ♋

Any person born with Mars in Cancer expresses will and personal desire in a gentle, subtle and diplomatic way. Energy levels are often cyclic and strongly influenced by moods. The need to preserve emotional closeness may make the individual indirect and reluctant to express strong feelings and needs, and resentment may build up because personal gratification is sacrificed to others' wishes. Tenacious but easily discouraged by rejection or failure, Mars in Cancer works best in an environment where others can offer support and affirmation.

Mars in Scorpio ♏

Any person born with Mars in Scorpio expresses will and personal desire in intense, determined and subtle ways. Physical energy is usually high, but there is considerable capacity for self-discipline and silent sustained effort. If the individual feels deeply about a cause or objective, he or she may exhibit great endurance, courage, self-abnegation and a willingness to overcome any obstacle—sometimes to the point where others' needs are disregarded. Mars in Scorpio works best when pursuing goals which inspire a passionate commitment.

Mars in Pisces ♓

Any person born with Mars in Pisces expresses will and personal desire in gentle, tactful and often covert ways. Energy may often seem erratic, and initiative depends upon the enthusiasm and emotional support of others. Often dreamy and indolent, Mars in Pisces works best if the imagination can be expressed through creative projects. Creative inspiration and a sense of connection with others are necessary for the formulation of goals, and without these Mars in Pisces may find it hard to define personal aspirations or assert personal needs.

Jupiter

♃

Jupiter in the Element of Fire reflects enthusiasm and confidence triggered by vision, imagination and new opportunities for creative self-expression.

Jupiter in Aries ♈

Any person born with Jupiter in Aries renews faith in life through innovative ideas and actions that validate personal potency, and make a mark on the outer world. Hope and inspiration are stirred by each new challenge successfully met. Competition and self-mythologizing are fundamental to a sense of well-being, not to achieve superiority over others but for the sheer joy of feeling vital and alive. Life is perceived as a grand heroic adventure where personal destiny is fulfilled through testing inner resources against the world's opposition.

Jupiter in Leo ♌

Any person born with Jupiter in Leo renews faith in life through developing new avenues for self-expression. Hope and inspiration are stirred by each successful statement of personal uniqueness in both private and professional life. Creative work is often a source of deep meaning and a journey of self-discovery, and the individual may experience a strong sense of personal destiny, which lifts him or her above ordinary existence and gilds the future with glowing promise. Life is perceived as a glorious drama in which Jupiter in Leo takes the leading role.

Jupiter in Sagittarius ♐

Any person born with Jupiter in Sagittarius renews faith in life through a spiritual or philosophical quest which confirms and elucidates the nature of experience. There is often a love of knowledge for its own sake, and hope and inspiration are stirred by travel and increased understanding of races, nations and cultures other than one's own. Life is perceived as a meaningful journey and a place for learning, presided over by an intelligent and benign power or deity. Material achievement is less rewarding than what is learned in the process of achieving.

Jupiter in the Element of Earth reflects enthusiasm and confidence triggered by sensual appreciation and new opportunities to achieve material or intellectual goals.

Jupiter in Taurus ♉

Any person born with Jupiter in Taurus renews faith in life through the discovery of inner strength and self-reliance. The affirmation of firm personal values increases confidence and trust in the future, while hope and inspiration are triggered by each new encounter with beauty in everyday existence. Nature, music, beautiful objects and the pleasures of the body generate strong feelings of peace and well-being. Life is perceived as a rich and rewarding place, full of satisfying and worthwhile experiences despite its imperfections and difficulties.

Jupiter in Virgo ♍

Any person born with Jupiter in Virgo renews faith in life through discovering the subtle patterns contained in manifest reality. Hope and inspiration are triggered by each new realisation of intelligent order operating in the apparent chaos of the external world. There is often a deep love of craftsmanship, an appreciation of quality in material objects, and a fine attunement to rhythm, ritual and natural cycles. Life is perceived as an integrated whole which reveals its deeper meaning through a loving and careful exploration of its parts.

Jupiter in Capricorn ♑

Any person born with Jupiter in Capricorn renews faith in life through pursuing worldly ambitions and making early dreams manifest in reality. Hope and inspiration are triggered by each new achievement and each new realization of personal competence and skill. Confidence and trust in the future grow as the individual discovers he or she can handle responsibility effectively and earn the respect of colleagues and social group. Low aims are seen as a greater crime than delay or failure, and life is perceived as whatever one makes of it.

Jupiter in the Element of Air reflects enthusiasm and confidence triggered by new opportunities for social, aesthetic and intellectual development in sympathetic company.

Jupiter in Gemini ♊

Any person born with Jupiter in Gemini renews faith in life through new intellectual challenges which keep the mind perpetually young. Hope and inspiration are triggered by each opportunity to learn something new and communicate that knowledge to others. Education and an arena in which to discuss and debate ideas are fundamental to feelings of confidence and well-being. Life is perceived as an endless and fascinating journey of mental exploration which should never be impeded by age, sex or social or material circumstances.

Jupiter in Libra ♎

Any person born with Jupiter in Libra renews faith in life through the transformative potentials of relationship. Hope and inspiration are triggered by sharing ideas and ideals with sympathetic companions, and each new experience of beauty and harmony with another individual increases confidence and trust in life. A partner who stimulates and is stimulated by the individual's creative efforts is essential for feelings of well-being. Life is perceived as a journey on which the most meaningful experiences are found in the company of others.

Jupiter in Aquarius ♒

Any person born with Jupiter in Aquarius renews faith in life through a deepening commitment to spiritual, social, scientific or philosophical ideals. Hope and inspiration are triggered by each new contribution to the increased consciousness of others, and a sense of involvement with the larger human family is essential to feelings of confidence and well-being. The fulfillment of material ambitions is rarely rewarding on its own, for life is perceived as an interrelated and evolving whole, whose future depends upon human integrity and effort.

Jupiter in the Element of Water reflects enthusiasm and confidence triggered by new dimensions of emotional interaction and exploration of the inner world.

Jupiter in Cancer ♋

Any person born with Jupiter in Cancer renews faith in life through a deepening emotional involvement with partners, family, community and nation. Hope and inspiration are triggered by each new discovery of another human being's heart. Exploration of the past—personal or historical—yields feelings of continuity and confidence, and contributing to the welfare of the community may provide a sense of connection to a deeper spiritual source. Any person born with Jupiter in Cancer perceives life as a living organism bound together through ties of compassion and mutual need.

Jupiter in Scorpio ♏

Any person born with Jupiter in Scorpio renews faith in life through discovering the hidden levels and forces underpinning external reality. Hope and inspiration are triggered by each new encounter with the depths, whether through creative work or intense emotional involvement with others. Exploration of the psychic and psychological dimensions of experience transforms ordinary existence, and deepens confidence and trust, through the revelation of secret meanings and patterns. Life is perceived as a complex organism full of mystery, depth and power.

Jupiter in Pisces ♓

Any person born with Jupiter in Pisces renews faith in life through an increasing sense of unity with others and with a higher or deeper source. Hope and inspiration are triggered by each new experience of love and compassion for fellow human beings, and religious or spiritual aspiration may impel the individual to become involved in healing work. The boundless riches of the imagination can also be a source of nourishment. Life is perceived as a mysterious unity whose meaning is revealed only through the willing relinquishment of the self.

Saturn

— ♄ —

Saturn in the Element of Fire reflects the need to find security and self-sufficiency through creative efforts that define one's specialness to the outside world.

Saturn in Aries ♈

Any person born with Saturn in Aries urgently needs to feel potent and exert influence over the environment. There may be a deep fear of being overpowered by the will of others. Defense mechanisms often include an unconscious tendency to compete with others, and an unusual sensitivity to feeling pressured or bullied. Although expressions of self-will may be controlled or even repressed, Saturn in Aries secretly longs to run the show. The individual may experience intense resentment if he or she is placed in a subordinate role in personal or professional life.

Saturn in Leo ♌

Any person born with Saturn in Leo urgently needs to feel recognized and appreciated. The individual may experience a deep fear of being unimportant if he or she does not stand out in some way. Defense mechanisms often include unconscious dependency on others' adulation in order to overcome feelings of personal insignificance. Any sign of being taken lightly by others can produce great hurt and anger. Although expressions of individualism may be controlled or even repressed, any person born with Saturn in Leo secretly longs to be a star in both public and private life.

Saturn in Sagittarius ♐

Any person born with Saturn in Sagittarius urgently needs to develop religious or philosophical views which give purpose to life. The individual may experience a deep fear of the meaninglessness of mortal existence. Defense mechanisms often include a tendency to distill everyday situations into rigid moral or spiritual generalizations which provide a sense of personal destiny. Although aspirations toward divinity may be controlled or even repressed, Saturn in Sagittarius secretly longs to be "chosen" and exempt from the lot of ordinary mortals.

Saturn in the Element of Earth reflects the need to find security and self-sufficiency through material structures which define one's strength and competence to the outside world.

Saturn in Taurus ♉

Any person born with Saturn in Taurus urgently needs to establish a solid domestic or professional base which provides a sense of protection against life's unpredictability. The individual may experience a deep fear of change. Defense mechanisms often include stubborn self-sufficiency and a tendency to cling tenaciously to outworn structures and values because they are familiar and unthreatening. Although deeply conservative attitudes may be controlled or even repressed, Saturn in Taurus secretly longs for guarantees of absolute security.

Saturn in Virgo ♍

Any person born with Saturn in Virgo urgently needs to control the external world through establishing reliable rituals in everyday life. The individual may experience a deep fear of disorder and chaos. Defense mechanisms often include an intense preoccupation with physical health, domestic details or financial matters. Knowledge as well as material security may be used as a bastion against the unknown. Although ritualistic behavior may be controlled or even repressed, any person born with Saturn in Virgo secretly longs for every hour of the day to be planned.

Saturn in Capricorn ♑

Any person born with Saturn in Capricorn urgently needs to establish rules of social conduct which preserve order and tradition. The individual may experience a deep fear of the chaotic aspects of human nature, which could erupt if conventional precepts are flouted. Defense mechanisms often include a rigid definition of social and sexual roles, and a need to wield authority through social or professional standing. Although hierarchical attitudes may be controlled or even repressed, Saturn in Capricorn secretly longs for everyone to keep to their place.

Saturn in the Element of Air reflects the need to find security and self-sufficiency through the formulation of ideas which define one's viewpoint to the outside world.

Saturn in Gemini ♊

Any person born with Saturn in Gemini urgently needs knowledge in order to make sense of life. The individual longs to discover absolute truths, and may fear being overwhelmed by irrational forces which ruin plans and destroy civilized behavior. Defence mechanisms often include rigidity of thinking and difficulty in sharing ideas. Although fear of the unknown may be controlled or even repressed, Saturn in Gemini secretly longs to have unequivocal answers to all life's questions.

Saturn in Libra ♎

Any person born with Saturn in Libra urgently needs to establish absolute definitions of right and wrong. The individual may experience a deep fear of being too selfish and thus incurring the rejection of others. Defence mechanisms often include evasiveness and a reluctance to express personal tastes and opinions. A rigid adherence to appropriate behavioral codes provides protection against social ostracism. Although the desire to please may be controlled or even repressed, Saturn in Libra secretly longs to be perfect in everyone's eyes.

Saturn in Aquarius ♒

Any person born with Saturn in Aquarius urgently needs to seek the protection of group values and ideals. The individual may fear isolation and social ostracism through being different. Defense mechanisms often include rigid moral standards and a reluctance to recognize the validity of individual needs and feelings because the collective — family, community, nation — claims prior allegiance. Although the desire to be like everyone else may be controlled or even repressed, Saturn in Aquarius secretly longs for the safe anonymity of the crowd.

Saturn in the Element of Water reflects the need to find security and self-sufficiency through relationships which define one's personal worth to the outside world.

Saturn in Cancer ♋

Any person born with Saturn in Cancer urgently needs to establish guarantees of lovability. A deep fear of abandonment may make the individual appear more passive and helpless than he or she in fact is. Defense mechanisms often include extreme sensitivity to rejection and a martyrlike stance toward unhappiness. Family ties may dominate personal life because they provide a sense of belonging. Although emotional dependency may be controlled or even suppressed, Saturn in Cancer secretly longs to bind loved ones as tightly as possible.

Saturn in Scorpio ♏

Any person born with Saturn in Scorpio urgently needs to claim the absolute loyalty of loved ones. The individual may experience a deep fear of betrayal or humiliation at the hands of those upon whom he or she depends. Defense mechanisms often include suspicion and a reluctance to forgive human frailties and mistakes. Pride may create inflexibility toward others' feelings and needs. Although the desire for absolute possession of loved ones may be controlled or even repressed, Saturn in Scorpio secretly longs for emotional dominance over others.

Saturn in Pisces ♓

Any person born with Saturn in Pisces urgently needs to feel emotional unity with others. The individual may experience a deep fear of alienation and disintegration. Defense mechanisms often include an inclination for self-sacrifice and an unconcious tendency to remain victimized, helpless or unfortunate in order to bind loved ones and ensure that they continue to provide love and support. Although the desire for complete containment may be controlled or even repressed, Saturn in Pisces secretly longs for total protection from life's cold and alien winds.

Chiron

— ⚷ —

Chiron in the Element of Fire reflects a sense of life's unfairness through frustration in creative endeavors and individual self-expression.

Chiron in Aries ♈

Chiron in Aries often involves important experiences of disappointment in the individual's efforts to assert his or her identity. For any person born with Chiron in Aries, persistent and unfair resistance from others may seem to arise whenever he or she tries to do anything original or self-expressive. The family background may reflect unfulfilled dreams and undeserved frustration in the achievement of personal goals. Profound understanding may be gained through a willingness to accept with grace what one cannot change in life, while retaining courage, initiative and a sense of self-worth.

Chiron in Leo ♌

Chiron in Leo often involves important experiences of disappointment in the individual's efforts to be recognized as special and worthwhile. The family background may reflect difficulty in allowing individual talents and abilities to be recognized, and for any person born with Chiron in Leo there may be a painful sense of one's personal insignificance in the face of a greater collective need. Profound understanding may be gained through a more objective perspective on life, where personal hurts are treated with greater objectivity yet faith in one's own uniqueness is retained.

Chiron in Sagittarius ♐

Chiron in Sagittarius often involves important experiences of disappointment in religious or spiritual matters, and in the capacity to believe in what one has been taught. The family background may reflect confused or restrictive religious and moral attitudes, and for any person born with Chiron in Sagittarius there may be painful questioning about the meaning of life and the individual right to pursue and achieve happiness. Profound understanding may be gained through a more individual approach to spiritual questions, which places less reliance on collective answers to life's great conundrums.

Chiron in the Element of Earth reflects a sense of life's unfairness through material frustration and feelings of limitation or inhibition in physical life.

Chiron in Taurus ♉

Chiron in Taurus often involves important experiences of disappointment in financial matters. Material rewards may not always match the effort put into working life. The family background may reflect material hardship, and frustrated attempts to achieve financial self-sufficiency may undermine confidence and self-worth. Profound understanding may be gained through recognizing the difference between enduring inner values and resources and those outer symbols of wealth and importance which define worth in collective eyes.

Chiron in Virgo ♍

Chiron in Virgo often involves important experiences of disappointment in the individual's efforts to feel competent and capable in everyday life. Issues of health or domestic difficulty may create a painful sense of limitation or loss of control. The family background may reflect confusion or rigidity in terms of defining personal boundaries and responsibilities. Profound understanding may be gained through accepting life's, and one's own, imperfections, and adapting with greater flexibility to the natural cycles of time, nature and personal need.

Chiron in Capricorn ♑

Chiron in Capricorn often involves important experiences of disappointment in one's reliance on authority, whether parental, social or political. The family background may reflect rigid rules of behavior or an overly simplistic interpretation of social position, and for any person born with Chiron in Capricorn there may be a painful awareness of how little real authority there is in the world. Profound understanding may be gained through recognizing the importance of self-reliance and personal authenticity, and depending less upon collective role models for a sense of worth.

Chiron in the Element of Air reflects a sense of life's unfairness through frustration in communication and a sense of isolation from the larger human family.

Chiron in Gemini ♊

Chiron in Gemini often involves important experiences of disappointment in early education and in efforts to communicate one's viewpoints to others. The family background may reflect too much or too little emphasis on intellectual development. There is often a painful sense of intellectual inferiority and a fear of being misunderstood by others. Profound understanding may be gained through a greater appreciation of one's own unique mental aptitudes, and a willingness to pursue learning regardless of the limits of age or social position.

Chiron in Libra ♎

Chiron in Libra often involves important experiences of disappointment in one's relationships with others. The reality of human nature never seems to match up to the individual's ideal of what is possible. The family background may reflect difficulty and disillusionment in partnership matters, and the individual may experience a painful sense of others' unfairness and lack of integrity. Profound understanding may be gained through a more compassionate approach toward ordinary human frailty, particularly in personal relationships.

Chiron in Aquarius ♒

Chiron in Aquarius often involves important experiences of disappointment in group and social interaction. The individual may experience a persistent and painful feeling of being an outsider, and may find a real sense of belonging extremely hard to achieve. The family background may reflect unhappy experiences of racial, religious or social prejudice—their own or that of others. Profound understanding may be gained through a greater faith in individual worth, and through objective insights into the psychological dynamics of the group.

Chiron in the Element of Water reflects a sense of life's unfairness through emotional inhibitions and feelings of hurt, limitation or isolation in important relationships.

Chiron in Cancer ♋

Chiron in Cancer often involves important experiences of disappointment in family life. The family background may reflect difficult emotional dynamics which have made it hard for the individual to trust the feelings and motives of others. Efforts to establish close and mutually supportive bonds may meet with painful frustration and disillusionment. Profound understanding may be gained through freeing oneself from unrealistic expectations of loved ones, in order to allow them their own ways of expressing affection and commitment.

Chiron in Scorpio ♏

Chiron in Scorpio often involves important experiences of disappointment in intimate life, either through sexual frustration or a sense of betrayal in personal relationships. The family background may reflect many secret power struggles and emotional inhibitions, and the individual may experience painful suspicion and fear of others' domination. Profound understanding may be gained through insight into one's deepest emotional and sexual needs, and through greater compassion toward others' fears, difficulties and defenses.

Chiron in Pisces ♓

Chiron in Pisces often involves important experiences of disappointment in one's emotional expectations of others. The individual may suffer painful feelings of disillusionment and helplessness in the face of collective human misery, and it may be hard to retain faith in life. The family background may reflect many apparently pointless sacrifices, and there may be deep spiritual questioning about the nature of human unhappiness. Profound understanding may be gained through a stronger sense of personal identity and a willingness to recognize each individual's freedom of choice.

Uranus

♅

Uranus spends approximately seven years in each sign of the zodiac. It symbolizes new collective ideals of freedom and progress, and reflects a vision of social and technological change which, although individual, is also shared with others of one's own age group.

Uranus in the Element of Fire reflects the impulse to break down or transform outworn collective restrictions on individual value and self-expression.

Uranus in Aries ♈

Uranus in Aries describes a need to break free of conventional thinking and discover personal potency through independent enterprise. Although the individual may not willingly undertake actions which are deemed selfish by partners, family or society, life will sooner or later offer the challenge of defining identity through innovative ideas and actions. There may be a reaction against the passivity of the previous generation. The expression of personal initiative, for Uranus in Aries, is the key to a sense of inner freedom.

Uranus in Leo ♌

Uranus in Leo describes a need to break free of conventional behavior and unlock creative potentials through greater self-involvement. Although the individual may not willingly undertake actions which are deemed egocentric by partners, family or society, life will sooner or later offer the challenge of remaining loyal to one's own unique vision, talents and personal destiny. There may be a reaction against the overly dutiful ethos of the previous generation. Self-expression, for Uranus in Leo, is the key to a sense of inner freedom.

Uranus in Sagittarius ♐

Uranus in Sagittarius describes a need to break free of conventional religious and moral precepts and discover a more universal understanding of life. Athough the individual may not willingly undertake actions which are deemed renegade by partners, family or society, life will sooner or later offer the challenge of developing a more inclusive worldview. There may be a reaction against the lack of tolerance of the previous generation. A broad perspective, for Uranus in Sagittarius, is the key to a sense of inner freedom.

Uranus in the Element of Earth reflects the impulse to break down or transform outworn patterns of authority, social structure and relationship to the material world.

Uranus in Taurus ♉

Uranus in Taurus describes a need to break free of conventional definitions of security and discover the strength and reliability of inner resources. Although the individual may not willingly undertake actions which are deemed risky by partners, family or society, life will sooner or later offer the challenge of defining worth by what one is rather than what one has. There may be a reaction against the naive materialism of the previous generation. The expression of individual values, for Uranus in Taurus, is the key to a sense of inner freedom.

Uranus in Virgo ♍

Uranus in Virgo describes a need to break free of conventional definitions of reality and relate to the world and the planet in a more creative way. Although the individual may not willingly undertake actions which are deemed "cranky" by partners, family or society, life will sooner or later offer the challenge of redefining one's relationship to material life. There may be a reaction against the ecological irresponsibility of the previous generation. Harmony with natural law, for Uranus in Virgo, is the key to a sense of inner freedom.

Uranus in Capricorn ♑

Uranus in Capricorn describes a need to break free of conventional social categories and define worth in terms of personal authenticity. Although the individual may not willingly undertake actions which are deemed irresponsible by partners, family or society, life will sooner or later offer the challenge of making one's way without collective affirmation. There may be a reaction against the hypocrisy of the previous generation's social values. Genuine inner authority, for Uranus in Capricorn, is the key to a sense of inner freedom.

Uranus in the Element of Air reflects the impulse to transform outworn social ideals and approaches to education and communication.

Uranus in Gemini ♊

Uranus in Gemini describes a need to break free of conventional approaches to education and knowledge, in order to discover new perceptions of life and its meaning. Although the individual may not willingly undertake actions which are deemed unsound by partners, family or society, life will sooner or later offer the challenge of developing one's own definitions of truth. There may be a reaction against the dogmatic or earthbound attitudes of the previous generation. An open mind, for Uranus in Gemini, is the key to a sense of inner freedom.

Uranus in Libra ♎

Uranus in Libra describes a need to break free of collective definitions of relationship in order to achieve greater clarity and truth in human interchange. Although the individual may not willingly undertake actions which are deemed disruptive by partners, family or society, life will sooner or later offer the challenge of balancing togetherness with individuality. There may be a reaction against the constrictive marital and family values of the previous generation. Respect for self and others, for Uranus in Libra, is the key to a sense of inner freedom.

Uranus in Aquarius ♒

Uranus in Aquarius describes a need to break free of collective prejudice and social snobbery in order to achieve more enlightened human interchange. Although the individual may not willingly undertake actions which are deemed revolutionary by partners, family or society, life will sooner or later offer the challenge of loyalty to a higher ideal. There may be a reaction against the clannishness and intolerance of the previous generation. Faith in the whole of humanity, for Uranus in Aquarius, is the key to a sense of inner freedom.

Uranus in the Element of Water reflects the impulse to break down or transform outworn modes of emotional and sexual exchange in personal relationship.

Uranus in Cancer ♋

Uranus in Cancer describes a need to redefine family ties and obligations in order to achieve a more universal sense of belonging. Although the individual may not willingly undertake actions which are deemed hurtful by partners, family or society, life will sooner or later offer the challenge of expressing love and emotional commitment in more individual ways. There may be a reaction against the tribal attitudes of the previous generation. Bonds based on empathy rather than blood, for Uranus in Cancer, are the keys to a sense of inner freedom.

Uranus in Scorpio ♏

Uranus in Scorpio describes a need to break free of emotional and sexual taboos, personal and social, in order to achieve greater honesty and depth in relating to others. Although the individual may not willingly undertake actions which are deemed "abnormal" by partners, family or society, life will sooner or later offer the challenge of exploring the deeper side of human nature. There may be a reaction against the lack of insight of the previous generation. Self-honesty, for Uranus in Scorpio, is the key to a sense of inner freedom.

Uranus in Pisces ♓

Uranus in Pisces describes a need to break free of dependency on others in order to find sustenance in the imagination and the spirit. Although the individual may not willingly undertake actions which are deemed irrational by partners, family or society, life will sooner or later offer the challenge of plumbing its deeper and higher mysteries. There may be a reaction against the rationalistic world-view of the previous generation. A connection with the inner world is, for Uranus in Pisces, the key to a sense of inner freedom.

Neptune

♆

Neptune spends approximately fourteen years in each sign of the zodiac. Consequently, between the years 1910 and 2010 included in the Planetary Ingress Tables, it will only have been in the zodiac signs between Cancer and Aquarius. The following paragraphs, therefore, cover only those signs. Neptune describes ideals and longings which, although individual, are also shared with others of one's own age group. Neptunian ideals can be glimpsed in trends in dress, music, films, art and lifestyle, as well as in new spiritual or ideological movements which—implicitly or explicitly—offer the promise of redemption.

Neptune in Cancer ♋

The generation born with Neptune in Cancer idealizes family, community and nation. This group seeks a sense of redemption through the sacrifice of individual needs and potentials, and longs for a feeling of security and belonging. Although the individual may consciously adopt more self-reliant views which reflect other factors in the birth horoscope, nevertheless Neptune in Cancer embodies a secret nostalgia for the past which is reflected in the fashion, films and music popular among those born in this age group.

Neptune in Leo ♌

The generation born with Neptune in Leo idealizes the fairy tale world with all its drama, color, and innocent simplicity. This group seeks a sense of redemption through a noble vision of life and love which is beautiful but easily bruised by ordinary human disappointments. Although the individual may consciously adopt more realistic views which reflect other factors in the birth horoscope, nevertheless Neptune in Leo embodies a secret romanticism which is reflected in the fashion, films and music popular among those born in this age group.

Neptune in Virgo ♍

The generation born with Neptune in Virgo idealizes service to family, community or nation. This group seeks a sense of redemption through self-abnegation and dedicated efforts which help to improve the lot of society. Although the individual may consciously adopt more tolerant views which reflect other factors in the birth horoscope, nevertheless Neptune in Virgo embodies a secret longing for altruism and moral purity which is reflected in the fashion, films and music popular among those born in this age group.

Neptune in Libra ♎

The generation born with Neptune in Libra idealizes love, harmony and the transcendent power of human relationship. This group seeks a sense of redemption through the pursuit of a perfect world freed of violence, greed, cruelty and conflict. Although the individual may consciously adopt more pragmatic views which reflect other factors in the birth horoscope, nevertheless Neptune in Libra embodies a secret utopian vision which is reflected in the fashion, films and music popular among those born in this age group.

Neptune in Scorpio ♏

The generation born with Neptune in Scorpio idealizes intensity, depth and emotional confrontation. This group seeks a sense of redemption through dramatic expressions of personal transformation and the revelation of powerful and often primitive feelings. Although the individual may consciously adopt more detached views which reflect other factors in the birth horoscope, nevertheless Neptune in Scorpio embodies a secret passion which is reflected in the fashion, films and music popular among those born in this age group.

Neptune in Sagittarius ♐

The generation born with Neptune in Sagittarius idealizes the future and the concept of a dawning New Age. This group seeks a sense of redemption through religious or spiritual commitment and a global vision of evolving human consciousness. Although the individual may consciously adopt more pragmatic views which reflect other factors in the birth horoscope, nevertheless Neptune in Sagittarius embodies a secret mystical hopefulness which is reflected in the fashion, films and music popular among those born in this age group.

Neptune in Capricorn ♑

The generation born with Neptune in Capricorn idealizes traditional social values. This group seeks a sense of redemption through nostalgia for an imaginary Golden Age when moral precepts were sounder and one's role in life was better defined. Although the individual may consciously adopt more liberal views which reflect other factors in the birth horoscope, nevertheless Neptune in Capricorn embodies a secret conservatism which is reflected in the fashion, films and music popular among those born in this age group.

Neptune in Aquarius ♒

The generation born with Neptune in Aquarius idealizes human potential and the possibility of a perfect society. This group seeks a sense of redemption through social and scientific progress that represents mastery over the irrational forces of life. Although the individual may consciously adopt more rounded views which reflect other factors in the birth horoscope, nevertheless Neptune in Aquarius embodies a secret reforming spirit which is reflected in the fashion, films and music popular among those born in this age group.

Pluto

♇

Pluto has an elliptical orbit and spends longer in some signs of the zodiac than others. Its shortest transit, through Scorpio, takes approximately eighteen years, while its longest transit, through Taurus, takes thirty. Between the years 1910 and 2010, it will only have moved through the signs between Gemini and Capricorn. The following paragraphs, therefore, describe the planet in those signs alone. Pluto symbolizes attitudes toward survival which, although individual, are also shared with others of one's generation.

Pluto in Gemini ♊

Any person born with Pluto in Gemini belongs to a generation whose sense of collective survival depends upon transforming the ways in which people learn, as well as redefining the nature and value of conventional education. The social issues challenging this group involve a major shift in attitudes toward schooling, language and communication, as well as a profound change in definitions of intelligence, mental health and social "normality". Although the individual may be reluctant to allow such changes, it is likely that life will require them.

Pluto in Cancer ♋

Any person born with Pluto in Cancer belongs to a generation whose sense of collective survival depends upon reevaluating the importance and priority of family bonds, and transforming unthinking emotional commitment to racial, communal or national groups. The social issues challenging this group involve a major shift in the structure of the family and of parent-child bonds, and a profound change in the instinctive tribal self-protectiveness of the past. Although the individual may be reluctant to allow such changes, it is likely that life will require them.

Pluto in Leo ♌

Any person born with Pluto in Leo belongs to a generation whose sense of collective survival depends upon individual self-expression and a reevaluation of responsibilities to family, community and nation. The social issues challenging this group involve a major shift in concepts of selflessness, duty and social obligation. Individual values, even if self-centered, may assume greater priority than collectively sanctioned self-sacrifice. Although the individual may be reluctant to allow such changes, it is likely that life will require them.

Pluto in Virgo ♍

Any person born with Pluto in Virgo belongs to a generation whose sense of collective survival depends upon transforming the material environment and healing the wounds of past abuses of the earth's resources. The social issues challenging this group involve a major shift in attitudes toward work, ecology and health. New technology and scientific knowledge may require radical changes in everyday habits, routines and relationship to the environment. Although the individual may be reluctant to allow such changes, it is likely that life will require them.

Pluto in Libra ♎

Any person born with Pluto in Libra belongs to a generation whose sense of collective survival depends upon creating new ideals of human relationship, and transforming those laws and structures which breed inequality in human interaction. The social issues challenging this group involve a major shift in attitudes toward marriage and traditional sexual roles, as well as a reevaluation of collective definitions of right and wrong, good and evil. Although the individual may be reluctant to allow such changes, it is likely that life will require them.

Pluto in Scorpio ♏

Any person born with Pluto in Scorpio belongs to a generation whose sense of collective survival depends upon a passionate commitment to the transformation of a shallow, unconscious and overly materialistic world-view. The social issues challenging this group involve a major confrontation with the darker side of human nature and an honest reassessment of personal responsibility in the more destructive dimensions of collective human interchange. Although the individual may be reluctant to allow such changes, it is likely that life will require them.

Pluto in Sagittarius ♐

Any person born with Pluto in Sagittarius belongs to a generation whose sense of collective survival depends upon more inclusive moral and spiritual values by which to live, and the transformation of a world-view which has outlived its value and truth. The social issues challenging this group involve a major shift in religious attitudes and institutions, and a broader understanding of differing national and racial customs and cultures. Although the individual may be reluctant to allow such changes, it is likely that life will require them.

Pluto in Capricorn ♑

Any person born with Pluto in Capricorn belongs to a generation whose sense of collective survival depends upon an honest reassessment of traditional social and moral values, and a transformation of laws and legislation which lack true integrity. The social issues challenging this group involve a major shift in attitudes toward authority, bureaucracy, personal responsibility and the role of government, and a deeper understanding of what leadership means. Although the individual may be reluctant to allow such changes, it is likely that life will require them.

The Ascendant

ASC

The Ascendant in the Element of Fire reflects an approach to life which is energetic, self-expressive, and inclined to infuse ordinary experiences with dramatic import.

The Ascendant in Aries ♈

Any person with the Ascendant in Aries approaches life impulsively, courageously and with enormous mental and physical vitality. There is often little regard for the details and limits of everyday reality. Those with Aries rising can become impatient and angry if people or events delay or thwart their independent action. The world is perceived as an arena in which to prove prowess and talent, and the innate desire to be first and best can sometimes transform ordinary situations into competitive events—with or without the consent of others.

The Ascendant in Leo ♌

Any person with the Ascendant in Leo approaches life with an innate sense of individual destiny, and a need to make an impact on the environment through personal style and originality. Full of energy and vitality, those with Leo rising have charisma and personal power, but they may sometimes overlook the feelings and opinions of others in the intensity of their need to fulfill an inner sense of purpose. The world is perceived as a stage on which to perform, and people, events and experiences are interpreted with great imagination and subjectivity.

The Ascendant in Sagittarius ♐

Any person with the Ascendant in Sagittarius approaches life with a keen sense of its future possibilities, and a need to expand awareness through varied experiences and contacts. Physically and mentally restless, those with Sagittarius on the Ascendant view any situation in terms of its opportunities and may become highly impatient if the limits of reality delay or deny the promised rewards. The world is perceived as a place full of potential bounty and good luck, and painful experiences are interpreted as lessons from which to learn and move on.

The Ascendant in the Element of Earth reflects an approach to life which is cautious, pragmatic, and inclined to require the support of past experience before risks are taken.

The Ascendant in Taurus ♉

Any person with the Ascendant in Taurus approaches life with patience, caution and an innate sense that anything worth having takes time to acquire. Reluctant to assert personal values and opinions until a sufficient sense of security and self-confidence has been acquired, those with Taurus rising are usually peaceable and slow to anger—unless pushed or hurried by more impulsive fellows. The world is perceived as a place of beauty and pleasure, provided an outer environment can be built which provides enough material and emotional stability.

The Ascendant in Virgo ♍

Any person with the Ascendant in Virgo approaches life with mistrust of its inherent chaos, and a strong need to bring order to the external environment. New situations are dealt with cautiously, and only when the individual has acquired sufficient information to feel knowledgeable and confident. Sensitivity and shyness may make it difficult to assert ideas and feelings without the backup of intellectual or professional skills. The world is perceived as a confusing and sometimes threatening unknown which must be approached with care and diplomacy.

The Ascendant in Capricorn ♑

Any person with the Ascendant in Capricorn approaches life with shrewdness, realism, and a reluctance to expose emotional or material vulnerability until a plan has been devised to deal with each new situation. Often both highly controlled and controlling, those with Capricorn rising are wise, strong and reliable but may lack faith in life's bounty. Innate caution can easily become suspicion of anything which appears too easy or self-indulgent. The world is perceived as a hard place where all worthwhile things must be earned through effort.

The Ascendant in the Element of Air reflects an approach to life which is inquisitive, civilized, sociable and inclined to depend on the liking and approval of others.

The Ascendant in Gemini ♊

Any person with the Ascendant in Gemini approaches life with great curiosity and a desire to learn everything about everything. Communicative, versatile and often physically and mentally restless, those with Gemini on the Ascendant need constant feedback, and as broad a range of contacts as possible with whom to share ideas and ideals. Like a child in a toy shop, Gemini rising perceives the world as an endless array of fascinating people and things to be explored—even if this means regularly leaving earlier enthusiasms behind.

The Ascendant in Libra ♎

Any person with the Ascendant in Libra approaches life with idealism, refinement and a desire to cooperate with others in harmonious interchange. Civilized and highly sensitive to the views and judgments of others, those with Libra rising, although often strong-minded, are innately courteous and reasonable—sometimes to the point where individual opinions, needs and feelings are concealed because of the fear of creating discord. Those with Libra on the Ascendant perceive the world as a place requiring constant compromise and adjustment so that peace and order can be preserved.

The Ascendant in Aquarius ♒

Any person with the Ascendant in Aquarius approaches life with strongly held ideals of how the world ought to be. Friendly and fair-minded, those with Aquarius rising are reasonable, tolerant and respectful of the views of others. But a need for collective affirmation may make the individual overly controlled, fearful of being selfish, and inhibited in the expression of personal feelings. The world is perceived as a fascinating interconnected system whose laws and patterns must be understood as rationally and objectively as possible.

The Ascendant in the Element of Water reflects an approach to life which is fluid, sensitive, and inclined to instinctively camouflage personal feelings and opinions.

The Ascendant in Cancer ♋

Any person with the Ascendant in Cancer approaches life with sensitivity, perceptiveness and a tendency to protect vulnerable feelings beneath a veneer of detachment until the environment is demonstrated to be safe and welcoming. Highly responsive to emotional atmospheres, those with Cancer rising possess instinctive gentleness and tact in dealing with others. But fear of rejection and isolation may create evasiveness and mistrust. The world is perceived as a potentially hostile place where only close, enduring human contacts can provide security.

The Ascendant in Scorpio ♏

Any person with the Ascendant in Scorpio approaches life with an instinctive sense of its complexity and depth. Pride, intensity of feeling and a serious, introverted nature create a need for privacy and a desire to fully understand others' motives before exposing personal vulnerability. Those with Scorpio rising are selective in their choice of company, and may be unforgiving and even vengeful if humiliated or betrayed. The world is perceived as a mysterious and dangerous place, to be approached with caution, knowledge and self-reliance.

The Ascendant in Pisces ♓

Any person with the Ascendant in Pisces approaches life with an instinctive sense of its unity and a compassionate response to all human emotional experience. Sometimes reluctant to define personal boundaries, those with Pisces rising are neither weak nor deliberately evasive. But they tend to mirror the feelings of others, and may appear deceptively passive and lacking in direction. Experience is infused with dramatic color, and the world is perceived as a place of beauty, mystery and suffering, alive with invisible meaning and hidden intent.

PART FIVE
RELATIONSHIP COMBINATIONS

How to use the Relationship Cards

A second set of planetary and zodiac sign cards is provided with this book, along with a second card layout marked on the cloth. This will allow the reader to discover how another person's planetary placements interact with his or her own. The other person might be a partner, parent, child, sibling, work colleague or friend—for our lives involve many kinds of relationships which satisfy different needs and affect us on different levels.

The second person's planetary and Ascendant sign placements should first be determined, using the Tables in the same way as for one's own birth horoscope. The cards should then be laid out in their appropriate places on the cloth. Once the cards are in position, it will be easy for the reader to see whether a planet in the other person's horoscope falls in the same zodiacal sign as a planet in his or her own.

The paragraphs which follow summarize some of the most important combinations between the planets in one birth horoscope and those in another. Not all possible planetary combinations are included here, although any link between two birth horoscopes will have some eventual effect, however slight, within a long-term relationship. Only those which are likely to have the maximum impact are listed below. If these links are found between two individuals in a relationship, they are likely to reflect significant dynamics which affect the ways in which both people feel and behave toward each other. It should always be remembered that no combination of planets can determine whether or not two people should, or will, remain together. Most important relationships contain a combination of harmonious and difficult astrological contacts, and much depends upon whether the individuals can deal with the energies at work between them with sufficient honesty, realism, tolerance and compassion. An example of a powerful relationship is that of Marilyn Monroe and John F. Kennedy (born 3.00 P.M., 29 May 1917, Brookline, Mass. USA).

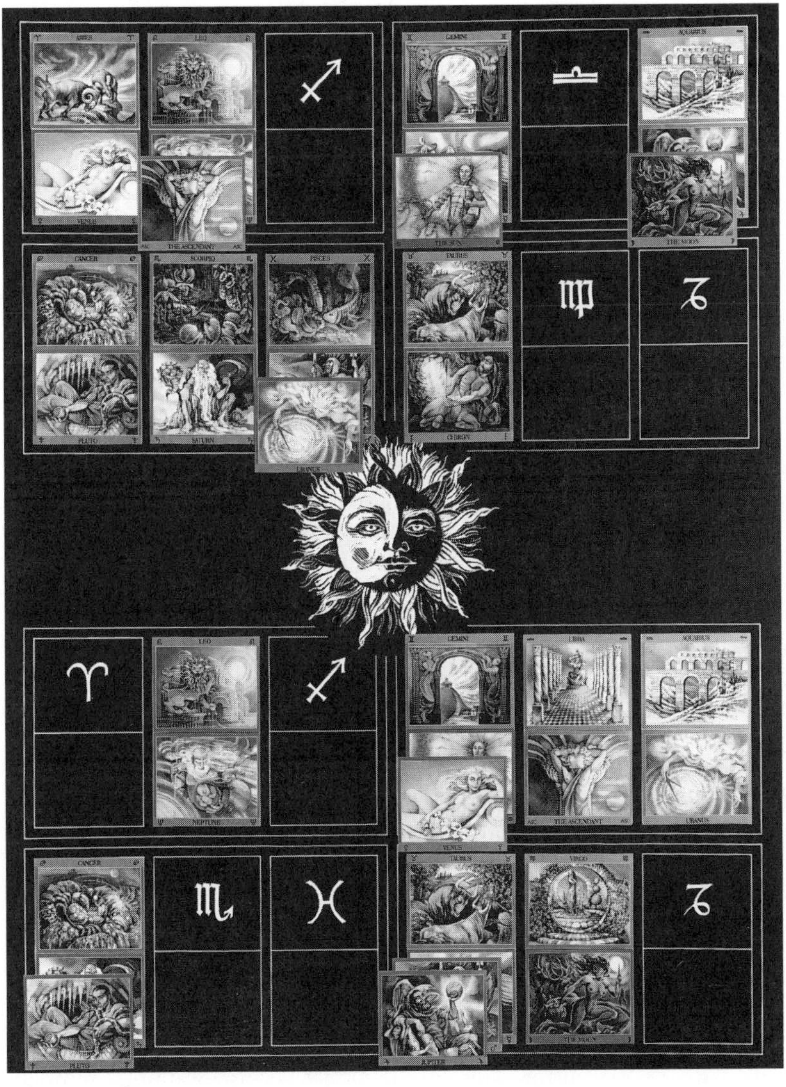

The birth placements of Marilyn (top) and JFK (bottom) are shown here. His Venus in the same sign as her Sun, and his Uranus in the same sign as her Moon, reflect both attraction and instability.

Sun with Sun in the same sign describes a similar or shared set of values and goals. This combination will not prevent occasional friction on more personal levels. Nevertheless there is an innate understanding of each other's deepest aspirations in life. A profound sense of friendship and mutual respect is possible which could help to bring feelings of continuity and stability to the relationship, even in the midst of conflict.

Sun with Moon in the same sign describes feelings of mutual empathy and emotional support. The Moon feels protective and needed, while the Sun feels magnanimous and strong in the Moon's company. The Moon's instinctive understanding helps the Sun to express individuality more confidently. Even if goals and ideals conflict, this combination contributes to a sense of comfort, security and protection against life's storms.

Sun with Venus in the same sign describes mutual admiration on the physical as well as the mental level. Although the relationship may not be sexual, there is a shared appreciation of each other's attractiveness. The Sun feels more confident because of Venus' affection, while Venus feels inspired by the Sun's unique individuality. An element of romantic idealizing brings out a mutual need to appear and behave at one's best.

Sun with Mars in the same sign describes a dynamic and inspiring, but also competitive, relationship, which may generate sudden quarrels as well as mutual excitement and enthusiasm. The Sun feels energized but sometimes angered by Mars' forceful initiative and energy, while Mars tends to adopt the self-appointed role of managing the Sun's talents and potentials. Mutual attraction can also lead to mutual rivalry.

Sun with Jupiter in the same sign describes a bond which inspires feelings of mutual generosity and idealization. The Sun is encouraged by Jupiter's optimism and magnanimity, while Jupiter feels fondness, protectiveness and faith in the Sun's potentials. Laughter, intellectual stimulation and a shared sense of adventure can also arise from this combination, with both people offering their best to each other.

Sun with Saturn in the same sign describes a sense of mutual responsibility which can be both supportive and restrictive. The Sun feels respect for Saturn's wisdom and depends on Saturn's strength, while Saturn feels protective of the Sun but may display a critical or demanding attitude, arising out of secret envy, which can sometimes cause hurt. Too much emphasis on mutual obligation may stifle spontaneity.

Sun with Chiron in the same sign describes a deep and potentially healing, but sometimes disturbingly painful, bond. The Sun feels compassionate and generous toward Chiron's fears, while Chiron needs the Sun's understanding and support. But Chiron may also experience great vulnerability because of the memory of older hurts in earlier life, and may consequently express anxiety through a defensive or critical attitude toward the Sun.

Sun with Uranus in the same sign describes a relationship full of mutual fascination, with an unpredictable quality of energy. The Sun is stimulated by Uranus' originality, while Uranus is inspired to develop greater creativity through the Sun's warmth and encouragement. But either or both people may also find it hard to meet the other's emotional needs, and may periodically seek greater independence from each other.

Sun with Neptune in the same sign describes a bond of mutual empathy and idealization, and a tendency for both people to expect too much from each other. The Sun feels enchanted by Neptune's mystery, while Neptune admires and depends upon the Sun's warmth and strength, but may try too hard to please. Honesty and the careful avoidance of manipulative behavior will bring the best out of this combination.

Sun with Pluto in the same sign describes a relationship of great fascination and intensity. The Sun is drawn by Pluto's enigmatic depth, while Pluto is compellingly attracted by, and sometimes possessive of, the Sun's vitality and specialness. Over time, unconscious power struggles may arise through each person's efforts to control the other, and deep and permanent changes are likely to occur in both people's perceptions of life.

Sun with Ascendant in the same sign describes an easy and instinctive compatibility and mutual liking. The Sun understands and offers generous support to the Ascendant's efforts at self-expression, while the Ascendant admires the Sun's strength, energy and individuality and feels more self-confident in the Sun's presence. Similarity of tastes and outlook ensure an enduring feeling of friendship and empathy.

Moon with Moon in the same sign describes instinctive empathy and a similarity in emotional needs and responses. Although the two individuals may have different goals, values and approaches to life, they are likely to draw a sense of comfort from each other, and will probably find each other easy to be with on the everyday level. Feelings are intuitively understood and responded to without the necessity for explanation.

Moon with Mercury in the same sign describes a mentally stimulating interchange which fosters lively conversation, travel and the sharing of ideas and spheres of interest. The Moon admires Mercury's cleverness, versatility and manner of expression, and offers support for Mercury's developing talents and skills. Mercury expands the Moon's intellectual outlook and helps the Moon to find new perspectives and greater objectivity.

Moon with Venus in the same sign describes feelings of mutual affection, fondness and empathy. The Moon feels deeply protective toward Venus and admires Venus' attractiveness and good taste. Venus feels confident and worthwhile because of the Moon's sympathy and concern. Both people will probably genuinely like each other, sharing tastes and values, and enjoying a relaxed and mutually courteous atmosphere.

Moon with Mars in the same sign describes feelings of mutual enthusiasm and excitement, combined with a tendency for both people to irritate each other. There is a great deal of combustible energy in this combination. The Moon is stimulated, but can also feel bullied, by Mars' assertiveness, vitality and self-centeredness, while Mars enjoys the Moon's responsiveness but may periodically indulge in provocative behavior.

Moon with Jupiter in the same sign describes feelings of mutual generosity and kindness, and also reflects a capacity for both people to laugh and enjoy new adventures together. The Moon is inspired by Jupiter's optimism and vision, and supports Jupiter's hopes and aspirations. Jupiter is warmed and encouraged by the Moon's appreciation and feels magnanimous, expansive and protective of the Moon's sensitivity.

Moon with Saturn in the same sign describes feelings of deep mutual responsibility, which may also be emotionally frustrating. The Moon admires and needs Saturn's strength and containment, and Saturn depends on the Moon's empathy, warmth and instinctive understanding. But Saturn may also experience unconscious feelings of envy, and may be overly critical or insensitive to the Moon's emotional needs.

Moon with Chiron in the same sign describes deep empathy and potential healing, but there may be emotionally hurtful elements in the relationship. The Moon is sensitive to Chiron's feelings of fear, and feels protective of Chiron's insecurities. Chiron draws comfort from the Moon's instinctive understanding, but may also react with criticism or emotional withdrawal because of pride and feelings of vulnerability.

Moon with Uranus in the same sign describes feelings of mutual fascination, but the relationship may sometimes be emotionally unpredictable. The Moon is dazzled and excited by Uranus' individualism, while Uranus is encouraged to develop creative potentials by the Moon's empathy and support. However, Uranus may make the Moon feel anxious and uncertain through moods or periodic emotional withdrawals.

Moon with Neptune in the same sign describes mutual emotional sensitivity and a virtually psychic sense of understanding. Both people are highly attuned to each other's needs and feelings, those which are unconscious as well as those which are acknowledged. Excessive idealization may accompany this almost telepathic interchange, and mutual expectations of perfect harmony may lead to hurt and disappointment.

Moon with Pluto in the same sign describes feelings of compelling intensity. The Moon is magnetically attracted—but may also feel overwhelmed—by Pluto's depth and power. Pluto feels deeply bound to, and sometimes intensely possessive of, the Moon. Over time, feelings of dependency may create unconscious power struggles at subtle levels. Honesty is extremely important to get the best from this combination.

Moon with Ascendant in the same sign describes feelings of empathy and instinctive liking. The Moon understands the Ascendant at a deep intuitive level, and approves of the Ascendant's style and manner of self-expression. The Ascendant feels stronger and more confident because of the Moon's warmth and concern. Harmony in tastes, habits and lifestyle can create an easy, comfortable emotional exchange.

Mercury with Mercury in the same sign describes a similarity in ways of thinking and articulating. Although other planetary contacts may suggest friction on other levels, both people will find it easy to communicate with each other because their minds work in similar ways. Even if ideas and opinions conflict, there is likely to be mutual tolerance and an appreciation of each other's mental abilities and talents.

Mercury with Jupiter in the same sign describes the potential for mutual creative inspiration within a relationship. Both people may share a similar sense of humor and can understand each other's hopes and aspirations. Mercury's perceptions, interests and outlook are broadened and deepened by Jupiter, while Jupiter enjoys stimulating Mercury with new ideas and the encouragement to develop new skills.

Mercury with Saturn in the same sign describes a level of communication within the relationship which can be deep and serious, but may also prove frustrating to both people. Mercury needs Saturn's realism, but may find Saturn too resistant to new ideas. Saturn, while appreciating Mercury's intelligence and versatility, may also feel envy, and may inadvertently offer a critical or noncommunicative response to Mercury's ideas.

Mercury with Chiron in the same sign describes a level of communication which is deep and mutually inspiring, but which may also involve hurtful exchanges. Mercury wants to understand Chiron's fears and insecurities, while Chiron feels healed through communicating painful issues to a sympathetic listener. However, Chiron may be overly sensitive and may react defensively or sometimes sarcastically to Mercury's ideas and opinions.

Mercury with Uranus in the same sign describes a lively and challenging mental exchange. Mercury is awakened and inspired by Uranus' originality, while Uranus is encouraged to develop new creative ideas through Mercury's interest and encouragement. Both people are likely to change and enlarge each other's outlook on life. Communication may sometimes involve heated arguments but will always prove stimulating.

Mercury with Neptune in the same sign describes an almost telepathic understanding, with a rich flow of ideas and creative inspiration.

Mercury is able to give Neptune's imaginative gifts shape and structure, while Neptune idealizes Mercury's versatility and cleverness. However, Neptune may try to avoid any conflict of opinion by agreeing with Mercury all the time, and may become inadvertently evasive or indirect.

Venus with Venus in the same sign describes a natural affinity in personal tastes and values. Both people tend to enjoy the same pleasures and find the same people and things beautiful and worthwhile. There is also likely to be a good deal of mutual liking, affection and appreciation on physical as well as intellectual levels. Artistic or aesthetic interests and preferences in friendships or social groups may also coincide.

Venus with Mars in the same sign describes an intense, magnetic and highly stimulating bond. Although not necessarily sexual, the relationship is likely to contain considerable mutual physical admiration, as well as the capacity for both people to inspire and enthuse each other. Venus is attracted by Mars' energy and initiative, while Mars feels confident and strong when offering protection and leadership to Venus.

Venus with Saturn in the same sign decribes a binding but sometimes frustrating element in the relationship. Venus feels affection and tenderness toward Saturn, while Saturn experiences a sense of protectiveness and responsibility toward Venus. However, Saturn may also feel emotionally insecure and fearful of Venus' rejection, and can sometimes display a possessive, critical or withdrawn manner toward Venus.

Venus with Chiron in the same sign describes a deep and powerful but sometimes hurtful emotional interchange. Venus feels empathy and tenderness toward Chiron's hidden fears and insecurities. Chiron feels warmed and healed by Venus' appreciation and understanding. But pride and anxiety may also make Chiron fear being seen with such clarity, and Chiron may react critically or coolly to Venus' approaches.

Venus with Uranus in the same sign describes feelings of almost electric fascination, combined with an element of instability. Venus is compellingly attracted by Uranus' originality, while Uranus is inspired by Venus' grace and charm. However, impossibly high expectations may lead to both people feeling let down and restless as the relationship becomes more familiar and anchored in everyday life.

Venus with Neptune in the same sign describes feelings of mystical harmony, as well as the potential for deep disappointment if mutual idealizations are shattered. Venus is bewitched by Neptune's mysterious elusiveness, while Neptune thrives on Venus' admiration, but may try too hard to live up to Venus' ideals. Either or both may engage in hurtful deception because they fear inflicting pain on each other.

Venus with Pluto in the same sign describes feelings of intense mutual fascination. Although not necessarily sexual, the relationship is likely to contain elements of possessiveness—which may lead to unconscious power struggles if either person denies the other sufficient emotional independence. Venus is hypnotically drawn by Pluto's depth and mystery, while Pluto is deeply moved by Venus' attractiveness and charm.

Venus with Ascendant in the same sign describes feelings of mutual affection, admiration and liking. Venus appreciates and values the Ascendant's personal style and physical appearance, and encourages the Ascendant's efforts at self-expression. The Ascendant feels greater self-confidence and self-worth because of Venus' generous validation. Courtesy, kindness and friendship are likely, whatever the nature of the relationship.

Mars with Saturn in the same sign describes a stimulating but sometimes frustrating interchange. Mars inspires Saturn but may become impatient and push too hard against Saturn's caution. Saturn may feel intimidated by Mars' confidence and may try to thwart Mars' efforts, resulting in a buildup of resentment in both people. Honesty and adaptability are important to bring the best out of this combination.

Mars with Chiron in the same sign describes a tense and sometimes hurtful combination of energies. Mars wants to help Chiron find greater confidence, but Mars' forcefulness may provoke Chiron's fears and cause defensive resistance. Chiron admires Mars' initiative and wants to offer constructive support, but unconscious feelings of vulnerability may make Chiron stubborn and inclined to thwart Mars' wishes.

Mars with Neptune in the same sign describes a mutually inspiring exchange, full of emotional and creative stimulation, but also liable to provoke feelings of anger and disappointment. Mars is fascinated by

Neptune's subtlety, while Neptune is vitalized by Mars' strength and initiative. But Neptune may become evasive through trying too hard to please, and Mars may try too aggressively to pin Neptune down.

Jupiter with Saturn in the same sign describes a potential for highly creative intellectual or spiritual exploration within a relationship. Jupiter understands Saturn's fears and offers encouragement, optimism and new perspectives on life. Saturn admires Jupiter's spirit of adventure and offers realism, reflection and sound advice. Secret envy may sometimes make Saturn dampen Jupiter's enthusiasm unnecessarily.

Saturn with Chiron in the same sign describes a similarity in the kinds of fears and anxieties which trouble both people. This could result in deep empathy and mutual understanding, but pride could create defensive behavior which makes it difficult for either person to risk being emotionally open and vulnerable with the other. Honesty and sensitivity to each other's feelings of uncertainty can help to bring the best out of this combination.

Saturn with Ascendant in the same sign describes a sense of mutual responsibility which may sometimes feel restrictive. Saturn admires but also envies the Ascendant's personal style. Loyal support may be offered, but sometimes in too critical or undemonstrative a manner. The Ascendant needs Saturn's strength and guidance, but may feel hurt by Saturn's self-control and reluctance to offer generous praise.

Chiron with Ascendant in the same sign describes a potentially strong and mutually healing bond, but feelings of vulnerability and anxiety may create defensive or hurtful behavior. The Ascendant feels drawn to Chiron's complexity and depth, while Chiron admires the Ascendant's personal style. But Chiron may also secretly feel envious or inadequate, and may offer support and advice in inadvertently critical ways.

Ascendant with Ascendant in the same sign describes a similarity of outlook, expression and personal style. If other factors are also compatible, this combination can reflect considerable mutual admiration and appreciation, as well as a feeling of being understood by the other person without having to offer explanations for personal behavior. Each individual can recognize something of himself or herself in the other.

PART SIX

THE MEANING OF THE TIME

How to use the Transit Cards

The transit cards for 1959 are shown in Marilyn Monroe's horoscope. This was the year in which she reached the peak of her career. Uranus was transiting through Leo, her Ascendant sign at birth, reflecting unpredictable change and an eventful period of life. Jupiter was transiting through Aquarius, the sign in which Jupiter was placed at birth, reflecting a time of increased opportunity and "lucky" breaks.

The three transit cards included with this book are marked with their appropriate astrological symbols of Jupiter, Saturn and Uranus. To determine in which sign these planets are moving at any particular time in life—past, present or future—use the Table of Planetary Ingresses for the required date.

The movement, or transit, of a slow-moving planet—such as Jupiter, Saturn or Uranus—through a sign in which the individual has planets or the Ascendant at birth signifies a time when important changes and realizations are likely to occur. Over the ages, philosophers and theologians as well as astrologers have questioned whether the events which coincide with such transits are "fated", or whether the individual's inner pattern of development is given concrete shape through character and choice. The interpretations given below describe certain important transits as reflections of psychological timing—the meaning of the time. Equipped with insight into inner conflicts and changes, the individual can respond with greater clarity and foresight.

When the transit cards are placed in their positions on the cloth, they will clearly indicate whether birth planets or Ascendant are being emphasized. If the transit cards are also used in conjunction with relationship combinations, periods will be highlighted which are important for both individuals, as well as for the relationship.

The meaning of the transits

Jupiter transiting through the sign in which the Sun was placed at birth reflects a period when the individual becomes aware of new potentials and possibilities for self-expression and direction in life. Increased self-confidence and hopefulness may create a greater awareness of opportunities and a willingness to take risks to make those opportunities yield rewards. This can be an exciting and energetic time when new talents are discovered, new relationships develop and new directions open up in work. However, Jupiter's promises must be firmly grounded, for this planet symbolizes intuitions and inspirations which require time and effort to yield their rewards.

Jupiter transiting through the sign in which Venus was placed at birth reflects a period of hopefulness in personal life. The individual may feel more affectionate, loving and tolerant, making new contacts or relationships which bring an enhanced feeling of worth and attractiveness. Romantic ideals of love and partnership may also be strongly activated, resulting in restlessness and a sense of restriction in long-standing relationships which do not seem to provide the hoped-for romantic excitement and sense of adventure. This is a time to be savored, but realism and awareness of the consequences of one's actions can help to avoid future regrets.

Jupiter transiting through the sign in which Jupiter was placed at birth reflects a twelve-year cycle which promises many new opportunities for professional and personal growth and expansion. This period may coincide with a peak time in working life, when everything seems to fall into place, new potentials are discovered, and "luck" appears to be on one's side. It is important to seize opportunities during this period and do whatever is possible to ground them during the next twelve-year cycle. For those who are inclined to resist change and expansion, however, Jupiter transiting over its birth position may prove difficult because frustration and need for growth may cause the individual to unconsciously create crises which bring the necessary change—apparently against the person's will.

Jupiter transiting through the sign in which the Ascendant was placed at birth reflects a period when life opens up, and new opportunities for self-expression become available. The resolution of long-standing problems or obstructions may create a sense of freedom from the past, although such resolutions are likely to come as much from the individual's own changed attitude as from any particular action or event. Transits of Jupiter activate the intuition and awareness of unlived potentials, but such glimpses of new possibilities must be acted upon to yield solid results. Increased self-confidence and trust in life help to attract support and encouragement from others.

Saturn transiting through the sign in which the Sun was placed at birth reflects a period when goals and aspirations may need to be carefully reviewed. The individual is called upon to define, clearly and honestly, what he or she truly is and wants from life. Earlier choices made from fear, dependency or the desire to please are likely to require change or relinquishment. A sense of restriction or disappointment with others may make it hard to relax and enjoy life, and external responsibilities may seem to weigh heavily. But those choices which the individual has made with loyalty to inner values are likely, during this time, to yield well-earned rewards.

Saturn transiting through the sign in which the Moon was placed at birth reflects a period when one's habitual way of relating to others is challenged. The individual is called upon to develop greater self-reliance, and to face emotional situations where fear, guilt or security needs have been obstructing personal happiness and fulfillment. A sense of depression and disillusionment may accompany this transit, and other people may seem particularly unresponsive or unsympathetic. A certain amount of resentment or self-pity is likely, before it becomes clear that frustrating personal situations are in large part the result of the individual's own past choices and actions.

Saturn transiting through the sign in which Venus was placed at birth reflects a period when the individual needs to reflect on his or her attitudes and expectations in personal relationships. Feelings of isolation and disappointment reflect a confrontation with the reality of others' separateness, rather than an indication that they have withdrawn their support. Idealisation of loved ones may be shattered at this time, and the individual may need to learn greater tolerance rather than feeling resentful because others do not meet expectations. A profound inner process is taking place which will leave the individual with greater realism and emotional maturity.

Saturn transiting through the sign in which Saturn was placed at birth occurs for everyone at roughly twenty-nine-year intervals. The Saturn cycle is extremely important, and reflects a period of redefining one's identity independently of parents, partner, spouse or collective. All that the individual has worked for bears fruit, but all that has been avoided or denied—consciously or unconsciously—must now be attended to. This time may be difficult because realizations occur about the true nature of personal relationships and life goals. Choices based on dependency or fear tend to be revealed in a truthful light, allowing the individual to build a sounder future.

Saturn transiting through the sign in which Neptune was placed at birth reflects a period when the individual is called upon to face unconscious dependency and over-idealization of others. Feelings of disappointment and disillusionment may occur, which reflect a lack of realism in one's previous dealings with the outer world. Although there may be an inclination toward self-pity and resentment, the individual would do better to work at a more objective and self-reliant approach to life. On the deepest level, this transit reflects the end of childhood expectations about other people. Some pain is likely, but the process is ultimately positive and strengthening.

Saturn transiting through the sign in which Pluto was placed at birth reflects a period when hidden emotional needs and conflicts may rise to the surface and demand recognition. "Uncivilized" feelings such as anger, aggression or intense jealousy may disturb a previously equable nature. The individual may feel harassed or thwarted by the outside world, but the enmity of others may highlight the need to be more conscious of one's own deeper motives and the consequences of one's actions. This transit calls for honest confrontation with the darker dimensions of the personality, and the individual can emerge with greater wisdom, insight and compassion toward others.

Saturn transiting through the sign in which the Ascendant was placed at birth reflects a period when the individual needs to consolidate all that he or she has been striving for. This is a potentially rewarding time, when the fruits of one's past efforts to express individuality can be seen. But the key to getting the best from this transit lies in a willingness to define oneself—values, needs, goals and expectations from others. A profound process of maturation is occurring, and the individual may be called upon to stand behind his or her convictions and endure feelings of loneliness. Realizations of past dependency and passivity can help to build a greater sense of self-sufficiency.

Uranus transiting through the sign in which the Sun was placed at birth reflects a period when all that one has defined as real and permanent in one's life is challenged. Identity, values and direction are subjected to great confusion and upheaval, and the individual may feel as if all secure landmarks have vanished. This is a time of great creative opportunity, but it is important not to panic or try to nail everything down in the hope that the anxiety will go away. The more the individual is willing to let go of old goals, attitudes, definitions of self, and even of people whom he or she has outgrown, the more productive this time of life is likely to be.

Uranus transiting through the sign in which the Moon was placed at birth reflects a period when the need for change in personal life—whether acknowledged or not—generates feelings of uncertainty and anxiety. The individual may be called upon to review those relationships where emotional dependency and security needs have blocked expression, and contributed to a sense of being thwarted or trapped. Changes in the environment are possible, as there may be a strong impulse to move to a new home, a new district or even a new country. This transit reflects a profound process of emotional awakening, and even if painful separations occur they are likely to be for the best.

Uranus transiting through the sign in which Venus was placed at birth reflects a period when old values in relationship undergo a profound process of change. Attitudes toward love, particularly those inherited from the family background, may be subject to sudden shifts, and a feeling of uncertainty may cause tension and anxiety in long-standing ties. The individual may need to allow plenty of time for reevaluation and reflection before changes are made, since feelings of being trapped could lead to impulsive actions which are regretted afterward. Changes or separations initiated by others may reflect one's own deep but unacknowledged desire for greater freedom.

Uranus transiting through the sign in which the Ascendant was placed at birth reflects a period when some upheaval in personal or domestic life is likely. This is due to a deep need for change in the environment and in the ways in which the individual expresses himself or herself, although such a need may not always be recognized. There may be a strong sense of being trapped in circumstances which previously seemed satisfactory, but which now appear limiting or stifling. The individual may be called upon to face those areas of life where real inner needs and values have been denied, and to allow greater mobility and access to new ideas and social contacts.

CONCLUSION

Every individual is a unique and complex being. Most of us, however, are prepared to recognize only a portion of what we are. We acknowledge those qualities which are pleasing to ourselves and others, and hide or suppress what we fear will make us unloved; or we identify with our own worst traits and see the rest of the world as more fortunate. We also possess, as a species, the remarkable propensity to assume that others should think, feel and want the same things as we do, and if they have the audacity to differ they must therefore be misguided, abnormal, inferior or mad. The history of human suffering is, in large part, the history of human unconsciousness, and the refusal to recognize the complicated nature of the psyche, or the degree to which we project our own unacknowledged attributes onto other individuals, social groups, races and nations. The time-honored panacea for personal and social ills has always been the successful hunting of a scapegoat—in relationships, in the family and in society. But such a remedy is becoming increasingly suspect as we are forced to face the world we ourselves have created, not just as a collective but as individuals.

Astrology at its deepest level is a profound journey of self-discovery. Every horoscope is unique—even the horoscopes of identical twins, born at least four minutes apart, show different degrees of the Ascendant rising—and every factor in a horoscope is part of the individual's nature. But not every factor is recognized or creatively lived. The brief interpretations of planet and sign combinations given in this book can offer the reader a glimpse into many facets of the personality. Some may contradict others. But if they are part of the birth horoscope they belong to the individual, and our identification with one favored quality will not make another, less favored one, go away. If the Moon is in Cancer and Venus is in Aquarius, the individual may experience deep conflict between the need for emotional closeness and the desire for freedom. We ignore such inner contradictions at our peril. Both astrological placements reflect positive, healthy qualities. But if we acknowledge the first and deny the second, we may unconsciously sabotage the very relationship we depend on most, because we dare not ask for the autonomy we need. Worse, we may be peculiarly hostile toward those who are honest enough to declare their wish for independence, and may condemn others—even those closest to us—because they express what we secretly fear within ourselves.

Using astrology to gain objective insight into the personality is a remarkably healing process. Facing internal contradictions may prove a difficult task, since many cannot be solved—they can only be worked with in an ongoing process of increasing maturity and compassion. Yet in attempting such a task we are taking full responsibility for what we are, and at the same time allowing others to be what they are—even if they are different from ourselves. Life may be hard as well as fulfilling. Astrological knowledge, rather than telling us our fate is already written in the heavens, teaches us that we have far greater inner resources than we realize. No horoscope can indicate whether an individual will turn healthy self-assertiveness into violence, or imaginative self-mythologizing into dangerous delusions of global dominion. Mozart's horoscope may look surprisingly like that of the school music teacher. Factors beyond the scope of astrology—heredity, environment, historical epoch—interact with individual character to produce unpredictable results. But we can be sure that, if we honor those living energies within ourselves which were once understood as the heavenly signature of deity, and provide them with a constructive place in our lives, we stand a far greater chance of becoming the best that we potentially are.

Further Reading

Campbell, Joseph. *The Hero with a Thousand Faces.* London: Abacus, 1975. Rev. ed. Princeton NJ: Princeton University Press, 1980.

Carter, Charles. *The Zodiac and the Soul.* 3d ed. London: Theosophical Publishing House Ltd, 1960.

Graves, Robert. *The Greek Myths.* 2d ed. 2 vols. Harmondsworth: Penguin Books Ltd, 1972.

Greene, Liz. *The Astrology of Fate.* York Beach, Me: Samuel Weiser, Inc., 1984; London: George Allen & Unwin Publishers Ltd, 1984.

———. *Relating.* York Beach, Me: Samuel Weiser, Inc., 1978; Wellingborough, UK: The Aquarian Press Ltd, 1990.

Rudhyar, Dane. *The Astrology of Personality.* New York: Doubleday, 1970.

Sasportas, Howard. *The Gods of Change.* London and New York: Arkana, 1989.

Tarnas, Richard. *Passion of the Western Mind.* New York: Harmony Books, 1991.

PICTURE SOURCES

Alinari/Mansell Collection: Museo Nuovo nel Palazzo dei Conservatori, Rome, Italy, 88; Vatican Mus., Rome, Italy, 34, 42, 68, 82. **Anderson/ Mansell Collection:** Chiesa della Minerva, Rome, Italy, 92; Mus. Capitolino, Rome, Italy, 26. **Berlin Mus.,** 38. **C.M.Dixon:** Archaeological Mus., Florence, Italy, 92; Archaeological Mus., Istanbul, Turkey, 22; Papyrus of Anhai, British Mus. London, England, 102; National Mus., Athens, Greece, 106; National Archaeological Mus., Palermo, Italy, 74; Temple of Ramses III, Medinat, Habu, Egypt, 18; Baths of Neptune, Ostia, Italy, 46; Theban Book of the Dead, British Mus., London, England, 50; Temple of Amun Ra, Karnak, Egypt, 60; Sousse Mus., Tunisia, 96; Roman Palace, Fishbourne, Sussex, England, 110. **Fitzwilliam Mus., University of Cambridge,** 10. **Larousse:** Bibliothèque Nationale, Paris, France, 54. **Mansell Collection:** Olympia, Greece, 30. **Mary Evans:** Temple of Astarte, Pompeii, Italy, 78. **Vatican Museum**, 46.